PASSION IS A FASHION

Pat Gilbert is a former editor of *MOJO*, the bestselling and internationally acclaimed music magazine. He has also contributed to *Q* magazine, the *Guardian*, *The Times* and the *Sunday Times*, and has produced radio programmes for the BBC. His new book, *Shut It!*, on the legendary TV series *The Sweeney*, is published by Aurum in 2010.

'Impressively exhaustive' *New Statesman*

'First rate, written with a vigour and verve that its subject matter would surely appreciate . . . What makes this book so special are the intimate, candid interviews – with the friends, fellow musicians, hangers-on and, of course, the four members of the group themselves' *MOJO*

'The closest you'll get to a definitive history of the band' *Sun*

'A truly great band deserves a truly great account of them to be given. And that's what the Clash have got' *Tribune*

'I thought Pat Gilbert's book about The Clash, *Passion Is A Fashion*, was genius. I thought it recreated those days when you'd get your head kicked in for wearing your dad's winkle-pickers brilliantly' *Ian Brown*

PASSION IS A FASHION

THE REAL STORY OF

CLASH

PAT GILBERT

First published in Great Britain
2004 by Aurum Press Ltd
25 Bedford Avenue, London WC1B 3AT

Paperback edition published 2005

This revised and updated edition published 2009

A catalogue record for this book is available from
the British Library.

ISBN 978 1 84513 482 2

10 9 8 7 6 5 4 3 2 1
2013 2012 2011 2010 2009

Design by Roger Hammond
Printed in the UK by CPI Bookmarque, Croydon, CR0 4TD

To my father:
Lewis Frederick Gilbert 1930—99

'Nothing great in the world has ever been accomplished without passion.'

Georg Wilhelm Friedrich Hegel

CONTENTS

ACKNOWLEDGEMENTS

THIS BOOK WOULDN'T have been written without the encouragement of John Broad, who picked me up when I was down, dusted me off and inspired me to think like a writer. I can never thank you enough. I'd also like to extend a warm double handshake to Robin, who, once I'd been picked up and dusted off, has consistently stopped me from falling down again.

Hayley and Luis – I love you, my darlings, you're allowed back into The Bunker now.

Many thanks to Graham Coster at Aurum and Celia Hayley at LAW, who believed in me, guided me, and made lots of encouraging noises which were a lifeline. Just as important were Mark Paytress and John Reed who gave me lots of practical advice and lent a sympathetic ear, managing editor Phoebe Clapham for her eagle-eyed attention to detail, and Rachel Leyshon, copy-editor extraordinaire, who deftly trimmed some rioja-fuelled excesses in the original manuscript and made many judicious nips and tucks.

Passion Is A Fashion wouldn't exist, either, without the sterling research and Clash knowledge of Steve Kirk and Graham Jones, whose info site, www.blackmarketclash.com, is peerless as an authority on gigs, set-lists and recordings.

I'm also deeply indebted to Jon Savage, the author of the acclaimed and essential Sex Pistols biography *England's Dreaming* (Faber), who gave me an unpublished interview with Joe. Thanks, Jon. Equally generous were the legendary Fred Dellar, who loaned me his comprehensive archive of Clash cuttings, and Jon Bennett, who gave me some extra Clash interview material. Cheers also to Anthony Davie, who allowed me to use a great anecdote from his excellent book on Joe Strummer and The Mescaleros, *Vision of a Homeland*.

A big thank you, too, to Tricia Ronane, who arranged access toThe Clash for *MOJO* features and other projects. Then there's the crack team of transcribers who worked under enormous pressure to do an amazing job: thank you Kathy Bacon, Sheila Gilbert and Ben Hawkes.

I've been stunned by the kindliness and generosity of all those who've helped me, however much or little, and sometimes possibly without realising it. In no particular order, a big thanks to:

Chris Knowles, Sean Anderson (ASCAP), Ian Wallace, Andy Neill, Andy Davis, Sophie Williams, Jeanette Lea, Chris Butler, Piers Gormley, Chris Reynolds, Jeff Dexter, Tami (strummernews.com), Paul Gorman, Tony

Byrne, Paolo Hewitt, Terry Rawlings, Roger Armstrong, Steve Mumford, Mat Snow, Paul Trynka, Phil Alexander, Wag, Andrew Male, Jenny Bulley, Ian Harrison, Geoff Brown, Matt Turner, Felice from Byam Shaw, Don Whistance (www.theclash.org.uk), Johnny Rogan, Planko, Manchester Kev, Stuart Williams, George Binette, Chris Salewicz, Richard Jobes, Chris Hunt, Gigi Corcoran and Phil Savill at Sony, Tom Vague, Lloyd Bradley, Nicola Joss, Matt Kent, Craig Riddington, Lois Wilson, Nardia Plumridge, Dean Rudland, Neil and Dave at Ace, Jane Titterington, Richard Jenkins, Russ Burton, Gary Pitt, Simon Griffin, Damian Steward, Alan Parker, Welsh Pete, Nickie Shield, Pockets, Paul Burgess, Peter Dogget, Jean Whelan, Roger Goodman, Bob Morris, Paul Hallam, Daryl Easlea, Tony Linkin, Paul Lewis, Nicky Demuth, Lucinda Mellor.

Then there are the interviewees and real stars of this book: thanks for your time and patience. Several were originally interviewed for the *MOJO* features and other articles that became the foundations of *Passion Is A Fashion*; most were specifically interviewed for the book itself.

Joe Strummer (God bless you), Mick Jones, Paul Simonon, Topper Headon, Bernie Rhodes, Kosmo Vinyl, Pete Townshend, Bob Gruen, Caroline Coon, Jack Hazan, Joe Ely, Johnny Green, Nick Sheppard, Pennie Smith, Peter Jenner, Sandy Pearlman, Simon Humphrey, Terry Chimes, Tony James, Robin Banks, Ray Gange, Steve Connolly aka Roadent, Glen Matlock, Glyn Johns, Micky Gallagher, Miky Campbell, Roger Armstrong, Tymon Dogg, Frank Zanhorn, Wiggy, Jock Scot, Andrew King, Ivan Julian, Rick Rubin, Susan Blond, Howie Klein, Howard Fraser, Barry Myers, Michael Bradley, Alex Michon, Sebastian Conran, Pearl Harbour, Rudi Fernandez, Jiving Alan Jones, John Brown, Richard Dudanski, Mark Perry, Jon Savage, John Tiberi, Micky Foote, Jean-Jacques Burnel, Dennis Morris, Dave Goodman, Simon Cowell, Ken Powell, Chris Reynolds, Digby Cleaver, Don Letts, Pete Howard, Bill Price, Tony Whelan, John Pearse, Jeff Dexter, Johnny Black, Kit Buckler, Vic Godard, Ray Lowry, Sylvie Simmons, Brady, John Ingham, Billy Bragg, Richard Frame, Scott Shields, Martin Slattery, Pablo LaBritain, Jane Crockford, Pablo Cook, Steve Jones.

Naturally, back issues of *MOJO*, *Q*, *Uncut*, *NME*, *Sounds*, *Melody Maker*, *Record Collector*, *The Face*, *Sniffin' Glue* and *Zig-Zag* have been invaluable. Thanks also to the staff of the British Library, plus the archivists at Camden Town Hall, Lambeth Town Hall and Westminster City Hall.

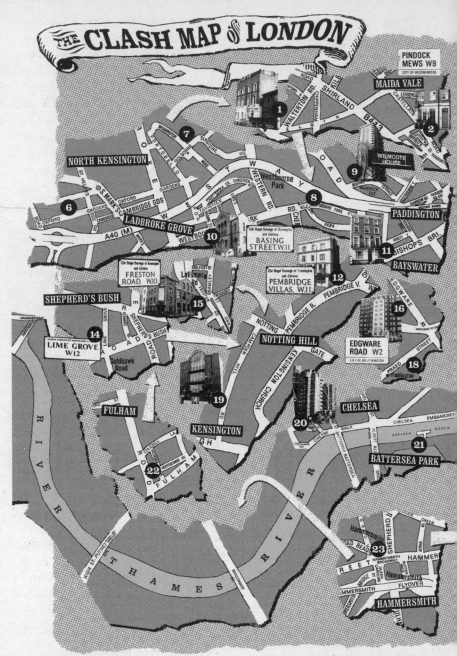

THE CLASH MAP OF LONDON

PINDOCK MEWS W9
CITY OF WESTMINSTER

MAIDA VALE

NORTH KENSINGTON

WILMCOTE HOUSE

LADBROKE GROVE

PADDINGTON

BASING STREET, W.11
The Royal Borough of Kensington and Chelsea

BISHOP'S BRI-

BAYSWATER

FRESTON ROAD, W.10.
The Royal Borough of Kensington and Chelsea

Latimer Rd

PEMBRIDGE VILLAS, W.11.
The Royal Borough of Kensington and Chelsea

SHEPHERD'S BUSH

NOTTING HILL

EDGWARE ROAD W2
CITY OF WESTMINSTER

LIME GROVE W12

Goldhawk Road

Paddington

FULHAM

CHELSEA

KENSINGTON

BATTERSEA PARK

RIVER THAMES

HAMMERSMITH

Westbourne Park

Notting Hill Gate

Map illustration by Mark Wagstaff. Many thanks to Don Whistance. Check out **www.theclash.org** for further information or visit Don's site at **http://myweb.tiscali.co.uk/donwhistance/theclash/** and then scroll all the way to the bottom of the page to start the **CLASH JOURNEY** for his comprehensive photographic Clash tour of the capital.

CAMDEN TOWN

HIGHBURY

4

5

CHALK FARM RD.

CAMDEN ROAD

COLLEGE

REGENTS PARK

ALBANY ST

PARK VILLAGE

OUTER CIRCLE

ROBERT ST

3

Camden Town

Camden High St

BAYHAM ST

PRATT ST

HIGHBURY NEW PARK N5

Grt Portland St

Regents Park

HIGHBURY PARK

GROSVENOR

ST PAUL'S

HIGHBURY GRO.

NEW PARK

PETHERTON RD

Highbury and Islington

St. Paul's

CANONBURY

100 CLUB

THE THAMES

embankment

BLACKFRIARS BRI.

CANNON STREET

LONDON BRI.

SOUTHWARK BRI.

Marble Arch

WIGMORE ST

ORCHARD ST

CENTRAL LONDON

13

OXFORD ST.

Oxford Circus

OXFORD STREET

Tottenham Court Rd

NEW

SOHO

CHARING

WESTMINSTER

VINCENT ST

BANK

MILLBANK

LAMBETH PALACE RD

LAMBETH BRI.

CAUSTON STREET SW1

City of Westminster

17

THAMES RIVER

GROSVENOR ROAD

MILLBANK

VAUXHALL

Vauxhall

THE THAMES

NINE ELMS LANE

WANDSWORTH ROAD

LANE

BRIXTON

BRIXTON RD

COLDHARBOUR

SOMERLEYTON RD

LOUGHBOROUGH RD

SHAKESPEARE RD

RAILTON ROAD

EFFRA RD

24

25 CHRISTCHURCH

TULSE HILL

26

ROAD

Tulse THURLOW PK RD.

Index

INTRODUCTION

WHEN I WAS ASKED to contribute a sleeve-note to *The Essential Clash* compilation in 2003, I wrote: 'It's a common thing to hear from Clash fans that "the group changed my life". I knew what I was talking about. They changed mine.

As a schoolboy, my two favourite groups were The Clash and The Jam. There was a distinct difference between the two. The Jam pretty much described where I was at – drab, suburban and almost exclusively white southern England, where 'Saturday Boys' drove Ford Cortinas and dated check-out girls from Woolworth's – while The Clash came from a place I desperately wanted to be: the colourful, leafy, dub-drenched streets of west London. To me, they seemed impossibly glamorous.

The Clash became an obsession: they were young, rebellious, cool, intelligent. They had that heavy, soulful punk-reggae thing happening. I always wanted to find out who they really were, and discover the reality behind the public façade.

A few Clash biographies have been published over the years, but nothing substantial until Marcus Gray's *The Last Gang in Town* in 1995. Gray's book provided the first road-map of The Clash's early lives and an excellent overview of their career, but it didn't change a basic fact: nothing I had read ever really began to explain the peculiar and unique relationships between Joe Strummer, Mick Jones, Paul Simonon and Topper Headon. It seemed that, for a group of their stature, there was also an alarming lack of factual detail about what was happening behind the scenes, especially for the second half of their ten-year career. To me, there was still an intriguing air of mystery around them. It was like Sherlock Holmes telling Watson that he sees but does not observe. I understood what happened but often I couldn't figure out why.

One reason why the truth – or something like it – remained elusive was the reluctance of many of the group's confidants to publicly reflect on the events of 1976–85. They weren't the kind of people, it seems, to give up their secrets easily. Previous biographers had failed to snag important characters like Bernie Rhodes, Kosmo Vinyl, Don Letts, Micky Foote, Robin Banks, Pennie Smith, Roadent, Caroline Coon, Bill Price, Pearl Harbour. A conspiracy of silence seemed to prevail. In the old days, The Clash camp kept its own counsel. Old habits, and loyalties, died hard. As for The Clash themselves, they had talked candidly about their experiences for the first time in Don Letts's 1999 film, *Westway to the World*, but there was a nagging feeling that some areas of discussion were still verboten or glossed over.

In 1991, I'd started writing about music full-time. When I joined the staff of *MOJO* magazine in 1998, I suddenly found myself with access to the group. Now I had the chance to ask them all the questions that had ever bugged me. Over the course of the past six years, I've interviewed each of them several times, often with the added bonus of booze (except Topper, where it was strictly tea). This gave me valuable and unexpected insights into their personalities: Paul's humour, unshakeable opinions and spirit; Joe's genuine compassion and cartoonist's worldview; Mick's wit and quicksilver thinking; Topper's confessional honesty and obvious vulnerability.

Once I'd made the decision to write this book, friends of the band who'd never spoken on record before slowly began to avail themselves. The period coincided with Joe Strummer's untimely death at Christmas 2002, which seems to have convinced many that it was time the whole story was told.

Naturally, perhaps, the more interviews I did, the more complicated the tale became. I quickly realised I was dealing with complex human beings, invariably with intelligence and insight that's rare in rock 'n' roll. A few clearly had an axe to grind; others seemed to be exploring their thoughts and feelings for the first time. A few struggled to understand their own impulses. Keith Levene arranged to be interviewed then mysteriously decided three hours before our scheduled meeting that he didn't want to talk about his past. As a writer, it's convenient when people have transparent motives: it makes the process of story-telling easier. But, more often than not, I found that people aren't that simple. Nor is life. Nor is the story of The Clash.

This book was originally going to be called *He Who Fucks Nuns*, after the line in the Clash song 'Death or Glory': 'I believe in this and it's been tested by research / He who fucks nuns will later join the church.' Joe was conceding that young rebels are ultimately doomed to become part of the establishment they once railed against. It suggested all revolutions, including his own, will ultimately end in failure.

But did The Clash ever entirely 'join the church'? Their initial, hard-line punk creed aroused so much righteous passion in their fans that any deviation from the script was bound to result in angry cries of 'sell out'. But it was the fact they tried so hard, and for so long, to keep true to their original vision, slowly bending it out of shape till it was almost unrecognisable, that makes what follows such an extraordinary story.

It's worth noting that when The Clash split up, Joe, the oldest member, was thirty-three years old, while Paul, the youngest, wasn't yet thirty. They were young men, and their ambitions, judgements and decisions occasionally reflected that. The writer and broadcaster Clive James, after seeing Hitler's architect, Albert Speer, interviewed on TV in the 1970s, said something to the effect that we should never judge people adversely unless we were absolutely sure we'd have acted differently in their shoes. Maybe we ought to bear that in mind while reading this book.

The historian Simon Schama said: 'Histories are written not to revere the dead but to inspire the living.' The Clash is history – it happened, it can't be changed and people's memories of it are already browning into sepia tones. And, like all great histories, there's much to be learned from it. Somewhere in this book I mention that the story might be construed as a revenge tragedy, but it isn't. Really, I think, it's a morality tale, the moral being that great deeds exact a heavy price.

Pat Gilbert
London
August 2004

1
THE UKULELE MAN

'First say to yourself
what you would be;
and then do what you have to do.'

Epictetus

*'Woody Guthrie was a ready-made identity
for a young man in search of a strong image.'*
ANTHONY SCADUTO, *BOB DYLAN*

It's 7 June 2001, general election day in Britain, and all the indicators say Tony Blair's going to get in again. London is warm and muggy. Joe Strummer is sitting in a private room on the first floor of the Groucho Club on Dean Street. I'm ushered in to meet him: he clasps my hand in both of his and enthuses how it's good to see a familiar face. The last time we met, or at least the last time we'd had a serious, sit-down conversation, things hadn't been quite so chummy. A piece I'd written for *MOJO* magazine had included a quote from The Clash's former manager, Bernie Rhodes, referring to Joe as 'a coward'. Naturally, Joe was upset by this; not so much, it seemed, because Rhodes had said it as because the then editor of *MOJO* had drawn it out as a headline quote. Joe described it as the equivalent of being 'slagged off by an old girlfriend' and having her point of view presented as fact in huge 24-point type. Today that episode is apparently forgotten, absorbed no doubt among the million and one other spats and hurrahs that make up the public and private life of Joe Strummer.

Joe re-lights the charred brown stub of his tiny spliff and leads me to the balcony window. He points out a bum sitting outside on the pavement on a pile of newspapers. He tells me how they've become best mates over the years. He gurgles a hurgh-hurgh laugh and his brown eyes sparkle through thick cow-lashes.

I spritz Joe – in town to promote the second Joe Strummer and The Mescaleros album, *Global A Go-Go* – with some deliberately spiky questions. The idea is to rile him up a bit, treat him as a contemporary artist rather than a cherished souvenir of the punk era whose past glories mean he can get away with saying anything. And so it starts:

Why is punk's cheer-leader sitting in the Groucho Club when there are race riots in the north of England?

He says: 'Do you think it's down to one man *for ever*? Time doesn't tick by in your world, I've taken steps to live in the real world.'

It's election day in Britain; you obviously haven't voted, have you?

'Where I live in Somerset me voting wouldn't make a blind bit of difference.'

Why did you chuck Topper Headon out of The Clash?

'It never crossed our minds to help him. Stop living in the past!'

We spar like this for a couple of hours. Joe tackles most of the stuff thrown at him head on but, rather frustratingly, even after a few drinks he greases past the thornier questions with the expertise of a seasoned politician. It's a skill that has been honed over twenty-five years of relentless interrogation; not just by journalists but by autograph hounds, Clash nutters, pub bores, the man in the cornershop who knows him off VH-1.

The question I really want to ask I leave till last. It's about Joe Strummer and his relation to his alter ego John Mellor, the son of a Foreign Office diplomat, the private-school boarder, the prospective art student whose brother took his own life at nineteen. The two, to officialdom, are but one and the same person, of course. But what of it? Is Joe still in touch with his former self? Has John Mellor been buried beneath so many years of being Joe Strummer that he now no longer exists?

'I do it because I'm half crazy,' he butts in, half answering in that slurred, mid-Atlantic grunt of his. He looks out of the window and hurgh-hurghs to himself, then continues: 'It' – and this I take to mean 'being Joe Strummer' – 'allows you to do stupid things like write ditties on the back of fag packets. If you were rational it would be a stupid thing to do. But it's about being irrational. I never stop thinking about life, asking, "Why did I do that?" Kind of blundering through life is my method.'

I tell him I want to know more about his . . . I end up describing it as his 'inner-core', the bit that deals with tragedies like his brother's death, the bit you feel you're not always getting to in interviews. He pauses. 'The core is where you write, or do your thing. It's where artists come from.' There are a few seconds of silence. He scans his mind, looking for a quick exit. 'I really think it's a sin to bore people. I'll only really share my thoughts once I've got them into a coherent bundle. I don't really like to talk about myself.'

Joe is clearly unhappy discussing who he is or isn't and why, and I'm not entirely happy asking him about it. Implicit in the questioning is the suggestion, intentional or not, that Joe Strummer isn't an entirely real person, that the cosmic ball of rock 'n' roll energy sitting opposite me, with white T-shirt and oily quiff, is a front, armour-plating picked up in his early life that's been customised and adapted down the years to protect him and to make us feel we're getting top Joe Strummer value; a convenient deceit for both parties.

But one look at Joe, lost in thought again for a moment, struggling to give you an honest answer, tells you that it's all a hell of a lot more complicated than that. He takes all this very seriously. The problem is that Joe isn't any corny show-biz reinvention like Liberace, Gary Glitter or Billy Idol. He's not even an elaborate tangle of personas like Marc Bolan, or a collection of other people's experiences like David Bowie. He's something else that hasn't yet been seen before or since in rock 'n' roll.

Later, when the interview is over, we'll end up in a Soho pub with Joe's press officer, Tony, and the entire staff of the magazine that sent me on this assignment, throwing back Tequila slammers and pints of lager. Each of us will sidle up to Joe in rotation to hear morsels of wisdom and rollicking stories of 'the old days'. Little did we know that within eighteen months he would be dead.

The raw material that evolved into Joe Strummer came into the world in Ankara, Turkey on 21 August 1952. His given name was John Graham Mellor. The exotic location of his birth was due to his father Ronald's occupation as a clerical officer in the Foreign Office. In the punk years, Joe would get endless stick about his father's job, to the point where he would fib to the music press that Ronald worked for the (rather less glamorous) Public Records Office, where he was indeed based in the mid-'70s. In the 1950s the Foreign Office was, and still is, one of the most elite and snobbish departments of the Civil Service. Its employees are expected to embody the stiffly conservative values of old Empire and their personal conduct is required to be beyond reproach. In The Clash's story, attitudes towards social class – within the group itself and from those outside observers – were to prove hugely important. Joe's parents would have been described by most people as middle-class, a detail that would have repercussions for him throughout his life.

Ronald Mellor was neither posh nor a high-flier, and his work as a cipher clerk sending coded messages (the secretive nature of the job may have been one reason Joe was never specific about it in public) meant he was regarded, in Strummer's words, as a 'junior bum'. The son of a British-born official on the railways in Lucknow, India, he was raised by relatives after his father died. The effect of his formative years under the Raj was, according to Joe, to make Ronald 'more English than any Englishman'. He worked hard and won a scholarship to university in the mid-1930s, before serving as a major in an artillery regiment for the duration of the Second World War. While still in India, he met a divorcee nurse called Anne Girvan, originally from the west Highlands in Scotland. They married, and had their first child, David, in March 1951.

Not long after the family had settled in England at 22 Sussex Gardens in Paddington, Ronald – now at the Foreign Office – was posted to Turkey. It was one of a series of assignments that put the Mellors in the frontline of the Cold War. As a child, Joe felt the tremors of dramatic world issues firsthand – a convenient explanation, perhaps, for his fascination with global politics in The Clash. In 1952, Turkey joined NATO, an event many believe prevented an all-out American–Soviet war in the Middle East. Two years later the family was sent to Cairo, Egypt, where Ronald would find himself lunching with the infamous double agent Kim Philby, and stayed until the Suez Crisis, the pivotal post-war conflict that exposed Britain's diminishing clout as an international power-player. Next, they lived in Mexico City, experiencing the devastating earthquake of 1957, then moved to Bonn in West Germany.

To the young John Mellor, born in the summer of 1952 amid fragrant date trees and political intrigue, his father's work meant little more than constant upheaval and an ever-shifting backdrop of tastes, smells, languages and climates. It was during these early years that he first began to feel like an outsider, a foreigner everywhere he went, including his father's adopted home of Britain.

'I had a life moving around different places,' he explained. 'In Mexico, I even went to a Spanish-speaking school for two years. In every situation we were freaks. I'd had an eye and earful of some very strange places. I saw some very weird things as a child.'

John Mellor was eight before he finally came to live in the UK, the country he would galvanise into punk rebellion sixteen years later. As London geared up for a decade that would make it the centre of the Swinging universe, Ronald and his wife bought a small bungalow at 15 Court Farm Road in Warlingham, a small village twenty miles out of central London and a few miles south of Croydon, Surrey. Its modest size reflected the Mellors' income and peripatetic lifestyle. When his father received another posting – this time to Iran, amid growing fears that the Shah might be deposed by a Communist revolt – John and his elder brother were packed off to a boarding school (fees paid by the Foreign Office) in nearby Ashtead. The City of London Freemen's School was housed in an elegant Palladian villa set in fifty acres of beautiful parkland. A typical private school, it modelled itself on the public school example, promoting sport, academic excellence, individual achievement and social conformity. There were around a hundred boarders, divided roughly equally between boys and girls.

The boys' first term at school was the beginning of a nine-year drought in which John and David would see their parents only once or twice a year. Karl Marx's quip 'blessed is he that hath no family' would have amused John. The experience scarred him deeply, and presumably his brother, too. The school's initiation rite, according to an interview Joe gave to *Record Mirror* in 1977, involved a choice between being beaten up and lying in a bath of used toilet paper ('I got beaten up'). Other occasions, such as birthdays, were celebrated in similar style. Joe would later describe how boarding school taught him to be independent; to cope with his deep feelings of abandonment, he 'had to pretend my parents didn't exist'. Aged nine, there was an early signal of John's unhappiness: he tried to run away one lunchtime with an older pupil called Paul Warren.

Simon Cowell (no relation to the *Pop Idol* judge) knew John during his early years at CLFS. 'We were goody-goodies then,' he explains. 'John was a great artist – he drew cartoons. He was shy and extremely nice, but somehow I felt sorry for him. He was touched with a kind of sadness. I don't know why. Maybe it was because he was a boarder and his parents weren't around.'

Gentle and dreamy, John tended to hide his finer feelings behind a brusque, diffident front. Chris Reynolds, another pupil, recalls John as 'a hard nut, a handful for the teachers'. This is possibly an exaggeration but it's clear John was no wimp. In the *Lord of the Flies* environment of the all-male dorm, where bullying was normal, his wit, sarcasm, ability to fight his corner and fondness for practical jokes made him popular. 'I shared a study room with him,' recalls Ken Powell, one of John's closest schoolfriends. 'He was a good guy to hang out with, very funny and artistic. He wrote poems and made his own Christmas cards. He always came at whatever he did from an original angle.'

Ken Powell's background parallels John's: his father was in the diplomatic service and, like Ronald, held a fairly lowly position. He is keen to impress that, in a school where there were children from extremely well-to-do families, he and John were considered to be from relatively humble stock.

Powell also described Ronald and Anna, whom he met several times, as 'reserved' rather than 'strict' and liberal enough to allow parties at their bungalow, where the male and female boarders did what teenage girls and boys do when left alone for the evening. Oddly, considering his job, Ronald had staunchly left-wing views.

It was while he was in his early years at CLFS that Johnny, as he became known, discovered rock music. It appears to have hit him with the force of a meteorite. In 1964, aged eleven, he heard The Rolling Stones' 'Not Fade Away' blasting out of the big valve radio in the school recreation room. 'I was at a really brutal boarding school where they filled you with crap,' he told the NME's Sean O'Hagan in a 1988 Clash retrospective. 'It sounded like the road to freedom. Live! Enjoy life! Fuck chartered accountancy!' His interest in school withered; he became one of the school rebels. 'Music was more important than lessons, it was all we talked about,' explains Ken Powell. 'Every new Beatles, Dylan and Stones album was crucial to us. They were the backdrop to our lives. It was a truly golden period to have been brought up in. We were in this strange, privileged bubble, creating our own world with all this great music.'

But even records had their limits when it came to alleviating the tedium of dormitory life. Holed up in his soulless surroundings, John seized upon any opportunity to kill time. One year, he signed up to perform in *The Insect Play*, a vision of a bleak, post-industrial society, written by Bohemian playwrights the Čapek brothers in 1923. John was cast as Head Ant. The play's sombre mood was perforated on the opening night when he and the rest of the cast were heckled from the audience by Goon star Harry Secombe and his son, a pupil at CLFS. Such, he learned early on, were the perils of taking the stage.

The local cinema in Epsom provided a better and more regular source of entertainment. Over the years, John queued to see scores of films from *Battleship Potemkin* to *Midnight Cowboy*. One movie in particular turned his head dramatically: David Lean's 1962 screen epic, *Lawrence of Arabia*. The story of the courageous and deeply principled ex-archaeologist, who helped lead the Arab revolt against the Turks in the First World War, stirred something within him – his own latent heroism? his memories of the desert? – and T.E. Lawrence became a role model. 'I must have been about thirteen when I first saw the film,' recalled Joe. 'It swept up my imagination. I read everything that T.E. Lawrence ever wrote after that.' This included *The Mint*, Lawrence's experience of barrack-room life in the fledgling RAF: a sensitive, poetic soul quietly and meticulously observing the men around him, part of them but apart from them. As with John Lennon, another cinematic inspiration was the 1952 Marlon Brando flick *Viva Zapata!*, which rekindled faint memories of his time in Mexico and, judging from what came later, fired a romantic passion for bandits, cowboys and revolutionary heroes.

As the 1960s went on, John became a voracious consumer of whatever popular culture he could find at school – comics, pirate radio, TV comedies like *Hancock's Half Hour*. But his chief love was music. Every detail of every groove of each new release from Bob Dylan, The Who, The Beach Boys, The Kinks, Jimi Hendrix, Them, The Stones, and many more besides, was studied and absorbed.

Significantly, his musical taste wasn't confined to white rock acts – a fact which would have a profound effect on The Clash's music a decade later. On a visit to Tehran to see his parents in 1965, he had bought 'The Best of Chuck Berry' EP on Pye International, which was to remain in his possession for many years to come and assume an almost talismanic status with him. On it was a version of 'Roll Over Beethoven', a song he knew from the *With the Beatles* LP. Realising that Chuck's was the original peeled open a whole new area for him: R&B and blues. Black US music sucked him: when the Blues Boom hit the UK in 1968, he supplemented his diet of Fleetwood Mac and Cream records with compilation albums, often bought mail-order, featuring Bo Diddley, John Lee Hooker, Bukka White, Elmore James, Sonny Terry and Brownie McGhee, Robert Johnson.

It's strange to think of the raw protestations of Mississippi share-croppers and Chicago car workers striking a chord with a middle-class white boarder in Surrey. But John instinctively connected with the music, just as Jagger and Richards and numerous other English musicians had. Steve Winwood, from The Spencer Davis Group and Traffic, observes: 'The blues had an emotion which was so different to anything else; it expressed a type of repression that was prevalent in England in the 1960s, though perhaps it was of a less obvious and more subtle type than the blues itself was about.' Bored, alone and feeling abandoned, Joe got the blues bad. In the summer of 1968, as he was sitting his O-Levels, another seismic event in the creation of Joe Strummer occurred when counter-culture erupted onto the streets. Across Europe there were riots, demonstrations, sit-ins, student protests. John watched it happen on the dormitory TV.

'The whole world was exploding!' he enthused, thirty years later. 'Paris, Vietnam, Grosvenor Square. We took it all as normal because there was no other frame of reference.' It was a wonderful summer to come of age. Jonathan Green points out in the introduction to his book on underground 1960s culture, *Days in the Life*, how the street violence of 1968 meant it was 'swiftly apostrophised as the Year of the Barricades'. The synergy between the arrival of rock and the upheavals taking place in society was apparent to everyone. It became hip to quote Plato's maxim: 'When the mode of the music changes, the walls of the city shake.'

For John Mellor, turning on the news to see anarchists, Communists and champions of the New Left throwing rocks at policemen, while Hendrix and The Doors wailed away behind him on the school Dansette, it was the most exciting thing he'd ever experienced. Revolutionary passion welled up inside him. A lot of the action was happening just up the road in central London, but since he was incarcerated in his dorm, it might as well have been happening in Timbuktu. The sense he was missing out on something momentous never left him. His instincts to go charging off into London to throw a few bricks around lay pent up inside him like a time-bomb.

Studying for A-Levels in art and history, John grew his hair long – or as long as he could get away with at boarding school – and became a hippy. He started to seek out cheap and unusual ways to get a buzz; once, having read John Lennon had tried it, he ate the filter of a Benzidrex inhaler for its supposedly narcotic effect. As he explained to Q magazine in 2002, the result was an horrific seventy-two-hour trip. 'Your veins all go completely tiny,' he winced. 'I had to swim the school relay. I don't know why I didn't die.'

An end-of-year photograph of John around this time shows a young man instantly recognisable as the future Joe Strummer, despite his school blazer and tie: handsome, surly, a faint sneer on his lips, aquiline features, a moody air of resistance. Quite what David, John's brother, made of his younger sibling's rebellious and reckless behaviour we can only guess. While John was ever more passionate, extrovert and crazy, David was quiet and had a tendency to withdraw into himself. The school joke was that David once went a whole term without uttering a word. 'He was very insular,' says Ken Powell. 'He was into an author called Lobsang Rampa, who used to write these massive books, mystical stuff about Tibet. I hardly spoke to David though I'd see him all the time. I don't know what the relationship was between the brothers; there didn't seem to be much of a connection.'

Lobsang Rampa's most famous work was *The Third Eye*, published in 1956. It was an account of his discovery of a hidden brotherhood of mystics in the Himalayas who knew all the secrets of the world and possessed superhuman powers, including the ability to fly at 400mph and appear and disappear at will. Many were enthralled by Rampa's quasi-mystical writings, although he was eventually unmasked by a private detective as Cyril Hopkins, a plumber's son from Devon. Whatever David's thoughts on

Rampa's authenticity, the books offered a mysterious and exciting world, an escape. He certainly wasn't a great mixer or talker, and it says a lot about his spectral presence that one of Joe's schoolfriends interviewed for this book didn't even remember him. This in a close-knit school of fewer than 500 pupils.

John, meanwhile, was making a racket in the recreation room. Though he showed no innate musical talent, he occasionally joined impromptu jams with fellow pupils such as Paul Buck (later to resurface in this story as 'Pablo LaBritain') and Andy Ward (future drummer with progressive rockers Camel), who performed as The Burgher Masters. The acoustic guitar John clumsily attempted to strum was a gift from a cousin. It was only in the early 1980s that he revealed it had once been played by Pete Townshend; the connection is one of several uncanny links between The Clash and The Who. The story was that the cousin had known Pete at Acton Grammar in the late 1950s, performing in a group called The Union as rivals to Townshend's band The Confederates. During its time at CLFS, however, this mighty Excalibur mostly gathered dust in the corner. 'All through my schooldays I was completely unmusical,' commented Strummer in *Westway to the World*. 'I thought only mythical beings could play music.'

Forsaking his instrument, John's last year at CLFS was instead spent absorbing the boundless complexities of his new favourite record, Captain Beefheart's *Trout Mask Replica*. He started venturing out to gigs, too: Mott the Hoople in Balham High Street and Canned Heat at Fairfield Halls in Croydon were among the earliest. His companionship was cherished. John had long gained a reputation for being the boarder most likely to make a party go with a swing, and he rarely let anyone down. 'I remember one summer's night he pitched a tent in someone's parents' garden to have a liaison with a girl,' remembers Ken Powell. 'It all seemed very wild at the time.'

In 1969, NASA put a man on the moon and Ronald – by now promoted to the slightly sinister-sounding Second Secretary of Information – returned with Anna from his latest posting in Malawi and settled down in Surrey for good. For their youngest son, not yet eighteen and now versed in sex, drugs and rock 'n' roll, it was an uncomfortable and disorientating reunion. In their absence he'd grown emotionally independent and domestically self-sufficient, and his world of rock 'n' roll records, girls and pop rebellion had little in common with their stuffy universe of embassy parties, dry Martinis and stiff upper lips. One headline-grabbing event that year seemed to say much about the chasm that had formed between father and son. For his services to Queen and country, Ronald was awarded the MBE; it may have crossed John's mind that it was, perhaps, the one John Lennon had just handed back as a protest against Britain's involvement in Biafra and its support for the war in Vietnam.

In the summer of 1970, Joe took his final exams at CLFS and, without many other choices, moved into his parents' bungalow. His plan was to pursue a place at art school in London. It was these hallowed institutions, not the universities or polytechnics, which had given birth to The Beatles, The Who and The Kinks. John was accepted by the Central School of Art in Southampton Row, housed in imposing premises off The Strand. But then something tragic happened that was to affect him deeply and cast a long shadow over his life.

When Kit Buckler, a student at Camberwell Art School, first met John Mellor in September 1970 they'd both not long taken rooms at the Ralph West Hall in Worfield Street, Battersea, south London. The hall of residence was a modern block located in a shabby, working-class district of dank bedsits and large, decaying Victorian family houses, evocatively portrayed in films like *The Lavender Hill Mob*. 'We were both first years,' Kit explains. 'We found out straight away we had a shared interest in music. Joe played a bit of guitar at the time and was really interested in the blues. That was how we became friends.'

For John, it was the first time that he'd ever really mixed with people outside his own privileged middle-class cocoon. The environment couldn't have been more different, either. Suddenly he was living amongst the crumbling brickwork, brutal architecture and vibrant street-hassle of early 1970s south London. In the capital the past is ever present, and the dentistry performed by the Luftwaffe thirty years earlier was then still clear to see – bombsites, incongruous open spaces, terraced houses left standing alone like dazed soldiers on a battlefield.

London is famous as a city of contrasts and just five minutes' walk across Battersea Bridge is fashionable Chelsea and its elegant Regency houses. These leafy, regal piles had once been owned by the likes of Oscar Wilde and George Bernard Shaw, but at this time they were inhabited by the new artistic aristocracy: Mick Jagger, Keith Richards, David Bailey. Joe loved his new home, seduced by the romance, noise, dark glamour and endless potential of this buzzing city. It was the world of all those glorious, bittersweet Kinks songs come alive in faded, waxy Victorian colours: 'Dead End Street'; 'Where Have All the Good Times Gone?'; 'Waterloo Sunset'; 'Dedicated Follower of Fashion'.

But the Swinging London that had blown John's mind had, he realised, frayed by 1970 into a darker, looser tapestry of underground happenings, progressive rock bands, heavy drugs. The signs for collective spiritual regeneration were not good. As John Dunbar, Marianne Faithfull's first husband and co-owner of the Indica Gallery, once said, 'The 1960s ended at the end of the 1960s, appropriately.' An era had clearly passed, to be replaced by something less immediately thrilling and harder to calibrate. Brian Jones was dead; The Beatles had split; Hendrix had just that month fatally overdosed; Ted Heath had unexpectedly brought the Tories back into power. The decade that could never live up to its predecessor had begun. 'By the time I reached London the whole thing was over,' rued Joe. 'Which was a bit regretful. I never did get to see The Stones, The Beatles, The Kinks, The Yardbirds . . .'

Nevertheless, London was still the cultural capital of the world, and John locked into its energy. 'It was really new and exciting to us,' remembers Kit Buckler. 'I was the Social Secretary at my college and used to put on gigs. We organised a show by the Velvet Underground at the London College of Printing. We got them really cheap.' Kit recalls John being charismatic, fun and extremely popular with the other students sharing the hall. 'He was always a lovely person, everyone congregated around him. He was a very talented painter and had a good eye for art. He was also a bit crazy, always a bit out-there.'

But the 'craziness' of this loveable young hippy may by then have had another function: masking his grief over his brother David's death. A few weeks earlier, in early August, David's body had been found in Regent's Park, not far from his digs off the Euston Road. He had taken a massive overdose of aspirin. He was studying medicine and suffering depression that few if anyone knew about. In Joe's imagination the event was elevated into a heroic deed, perhaps a way of rationalising his loss. He told the *NME*'s Chris Salewicz, 'He was such a nervous guy. I think him committing suicide was a really brave thing to do.'

'He told me about it, told me what happened,' says Kit. 'He was staying with his parents at the time. He didn't elaborate on it in any way. He felt it a lot, it was very traumatic for him.' Asked how Joe's grief affected him, Kit hesitates. 'He didn't exactly have mental problems but he had moods. They were always there. There were times when he would go into himself. If I hadn't have been close to him when it happened, I don't think he would have mentioned it to me. He didn't choose to talk about it.'

'Joe always had the ghost of his brother around him,' says Tymon Dogg, a musician who befriended John via mutual acquaintances at the Central

School of Art. 'When something really intense like that happens it stays with you. He told me this story, a really sweet thing to say, that he'd been so concerned about his brother being left out of things he once took him on a date with a girl. Joe was seventeen at the time! It was very sad, very traumatic. Joe was with his father when he heard the news [about David's death]. They found out he was into some weird stuff.'

Later, Joe revealed that the 'weird stuff' related to the occult and extreme right-wing politics. The admission, to *Melody Maker*'s Caroline Coon in 1977, was one of the few times he spoke about David to a journalist. Such was his reluctance to discuss the subject that some of his friends from The 101'ers and Clash eras were unaware he even had a brother. It's difficult to imagine how hard it must have been for John and his parents in the following months and years; certainly it did nothing to bring them closer and if anything seems to have driven them further apart.

John hadn't been in London for long when he did something significant and unexpected: he changed his name. He now called himself 'Woody', a homage to Woody Guthrie, the US hobo folk musician. Guthrie's guitar famously bore the legend 'This machine kills fascists' and his life and music, even more famously, inspired the young Bob Dylan to reinvent himself as a folk singer.

Tymon Dogg can, to this day, remember the precise moment 'Woody' was born. 'We were sitting in the hall at the Central School of Art,' he smiles. 'It couldn't have been long after his brother died. He said, "The next person who comes through that door, I'm gonna say, 'Hi, I'm Woody.'" And he did! He jumped up and greeted the person with "Hi, I'm Woody." That was it. From then on he was Woody to everyone.'

John's transformation into Woody comes so soon after David's suicide that it's almost impossible to believe the two events aren't related in some way. It's tempting to think he adopted his new name to airbrush away the painful memories of the past, to obliterate from history John Mellor the CLFS schoolboy, but it probably wasn't as straightforward as that. Perhaps the 'Woody' incident was as spontaneous and half-crazed as Tymon likes to describe it. You can certainly picture John in his new art-school environment, surrounded by exotic creatures with strange names like Tymon, suddenly thinking to himself, hang on, if you can be Tymon Dogg, itinerant musician, then, hey, I'm going to be . . . Woody Mellor!

The most intriguing aspect to all of it is the name itself – 'Woody'. Of all the appellations he could choose, it's the one, bar perhaps Dylan, that most clearly exposes his unexplored fantasies of being a folk singer, poet, or painter, or maybe just an interesting beatnik bum of no fixed talent.

Soon, Mellor began to take the Guthrie–Dylan dynamic further and created a mist around his past, as he would far more dramatically in The Clash. In 1961, Dylan, the nice middle-class kid from Hibbing, had convinced his new friends in New York that he was a troubadour waif who'd run away to join a carnival. 'Woody' was to become similarly fanciful, vague and evasive about his early years. His speech grew more Americanised and slurred, and half-craziness became his normal mien. It was as if he was constructing a character tailor-made to Sal Paradise's description of his hip beatnik friends in Jack Kerouac's *On The Road*: 'The only people for me are the mad ones, the ones who are mad to live, mad to talk, mad to be saved . . . the ones who never yawn or say a commonplace thing.'

The eighteen-year-old who left Ralph Hall in late 1970 to take up residence with some friends in a squalid shared house in north London was no longer Johnny but Woody – a long-haired, counter-articulate bum who didn't talk too much about where he'd come from, or where he was going. Though he didn't know it then, Mellor's first stage of his evolution towards being a rock 'n' roll star was almost complete. Like Dylan before him, all he needed to do now was to learn how to write songs and play guitar.

Woody's new house was in Ash Grove, Palmer's Green, a middle-class suburb of large semi-detached houses and wide, leafy avenues in north London. The house was nicknamed 'Vomit Heights'; a hand-painted sign above the door proclaimed this fact, much to the neighbours' tut-tutting. The extended list of house-dwellers included new and old chums like Simon Williams, Richard Evans (an old friend of his brother David) and Clive Timperley. But the most outlandish guest or inhabitant – no one was ever certain which – was Tymon Dogg.

Even though he was barely twenty, Tymon already had an impressive story. Born Stephen Murray, he'd landed a deal with Pye Records when he was seventeen, after sending them a demo tape. 'One day I was a screen-printer in Liverpool and the next I was in Pye's Studio 1 with an orchestra, bumping into Ray Davies,' he laughs. A few weeks later a single, 'Bitter Thoughts of Little Jane', was released under the name 'Timon'. Though it failed to chart, Paul McCartney heard it on the radio and got in contact. 'Maybe he thought it was about [Paul's ex] Jane Asher,' says Tymon. 'He wanted to re-record it. I was an incredibly big fan. I went for a meeting and there was Peter Asher, Paul Simon and McCartney . . . I walked out. I didn't think I belonged there, this spotty seventeen-year-old. Eventually, Paul came in on his own, with a dog. I said I wanted to make a record like Leonard Cohen, and Paul said, "Who's Leonard Cohen?"'

For the next year or so, Tymon worked on an album for The Beatles' Apple label, rubbing shoulders with the likes of producer George Martin, press officer Derek Taylor and American singer-songwriter legend James Taylor, who played guitar on one track. Apple wanted to market 'Timon' as a pop artist like Davy Jones; the artist wanted to be a Liverpudlian Tim Buckley. The project drifted and the material was eventually mothballed. Next, he did some recordings for The Moody Blues' label, Threshold, before turning his back on the music business and heading off to busk in Europe.

'I was eighteen,' he explains. 'I had a bit of publishing money by then, but not a lot. I felt I hadn't lived, that I'd just come down from Liverpool and it wasn't enough. I hadn't knocked around, I had nothing to say. I wanted to be a songwriter who said something.'

Back in London, Tymon holed himself up at Vomit Heights to 'escape' from his Threshold 45, 'And Now She Says She's Young', which was receiving radio play. It was there he first encountered Woody, who was playing invisible cricket at the time and possibly tripping on the household's drug du jour, LSD. Woody's first words to him were, 'I like you, you've got manners.' The vibe at the Heights was as much pissed-up student as astral hippy, and Tymon remembers he and Woody getting involved in drunken antics such as tearing down a ceiling and whacking the heads off the neighbours' flowers. Very soon, they were fast mates, forever locked in conversation about Dylan and Buckley's songwriting and the merits or otherwise of Leonard Cohen ('we loved him!'), Carole King, Tim Hardin and James Taylor.

'Joe was a sensitive guy,' recalls Tymon, himself a spiritual fellow with warm, wry sense of humour straight off the Mersey. 'He was funny and gentle, so very gentle, the only man I've ever seen lose an arm-wrestling contest to a girl! But he hid it. It was something I think he'd picked up at public school. It was defensive. He lived in this funny, Biggles world. I think he saw the world through a cartoonist's eye. He found things very odd and funny.'

The glue that bonded the Vomit Heights crowd was music: many of them, though definitely not Woody, were proficient musicians. Clive Timperley had been playing in groups since as far back as 1965. According to Marcus

Gray's Clash biography, *The Last Gang in Town*, Woody was overawed when Timperley invited him to the Marquee to watch his group support Medicine Head. The unattainable – playing onstage and getting paid for it – was there, being enjoyed by his friend. Suddenly, it no longer seemed a distant Emerald City.

Back at the Heights, parties were held late into the night where Clive, Tymon and others took it in turn to sing and play. It was around this time that Woody, under the influence of alcohol and spliff, first started making the outrageous claim: 'I'm going to be a pop star!'

'We thought it was a funny thing to say,' laughs Tymon. 'Especially in that hippy environment. Pop star? We just laughed. We didn't know where he was coming from.'

When Tymon suggested Woody accompany him busking on the London Underground, he jumped at the chance. His job was to hold the hat. 'I went bottling, as it's called,' he told Jon Savage in a hitherto unpublished interview for Savage's indispensable *England's Dreaming*. 'The idea comes from Mississippi. You're supposed to have a bottle with a fly in it in one hand and you collect money with the other. The musician knows you haven't stolen any money if the fly's still in the bottle.' In breaks between trains, Tymon taught Woody a few simple blues and rock 'n' roll tunes on the guitar: The Stones, Elvis, Chuck Berry, The Beatles, Bo Diddley, Woody Guthrie. Eventually, the musician's apprentice invested in his own instrument – a ukulele, purchased for £1.99 from a shop in Shaftesbury Avenue. His logic was, with four strings, it would be easier to play than guitar.

'He thought he didn't deserve a guitar,' says Tymon. 'There was always that kind of self-effacing side to him. He thought musicianship was something he wasn't cut out for.'

' I spent the greater part of my youth listening to music,' explained Joe in *Westway to the World*. 'It all seemed so complex at the time. It was the years of the great guitarists like Clapton and Hendrix and it seemed unobtainable, really, if you were a slow starter like I was.'

That summer, Woody dropped out of art school altogether, fed up with the emphasis on life classes and what he described as 'the lousy set-up' of lecturers chasing after the female students. There were other reasons, too. 'There was drink and drugs and by the end we were doing acid and I never went near the art school,' he told Jon Savage. 'It was an experimental time, it was great. But it was a bit much for a young guy to handle.'

That summer, via some art school friends, he got a seasonal job at Dowhouse Farm in Blandford, Dorset. In true hippy style, he was intent on getting his head together in the country. But the lure of the capital was too great and, at the beginning of 1972, Woody linked up again with Tymon and the two of them moved into a rented flat in Ridley Road in Harlesden. It was a scruffy locale with a large population of black, Irish and Greek immigrants squeezed over from nearby Ladbroke Grove and Kilburn. Kit Buckler moved his stuff in; so did Tymon's girlfriend Helen. Half a dozen others lived there as well.

The Harlesden flat was squalid and hardcore hippie: Theosophical literature, Lebanese hash, lava lamps, incense, shabby Oriental junk-shop throws, transcendental meditation. Woody was slowly slipping deeper into the upholstery of the counter-culture.

Kit Buckler hated it. 'I wasn't as adapted to squatting as Woody was,' he says. 'I came home one night and there was someone sitting on my bed doing a mantra. I thought, I'm not sure I can handle this, I'm a boy from Essex. So I moved out.'

Woody began to learn guitar in earnest; partly with a view to supplement his new day-job as a sign-writer at Allied Carpets in Harlesden, partly to advance his nebulous ambition to be a rock 'n' roller. Tymon explains how, having messed around on the instrument for a few years, his left-handed friend naturally held his guitar the wrong way around for a left-handed player. This, he thinks, explained Woody's unique, strong rhythm-guitar style – and his sausage-fingered approach to lead work – as his most dexterous hand was the one he strummed with.

Soon Woody was ready to go solo: his master unleashed him at Green Park tube station, where he performed Chuck Berry's 'Sweet Little Sixteen' (off his beloved EP) to several hundred indifferent commuters changing trains. He soon graduated to the 'loony shift', when the drunks spilled out of the pubs and their drunken generosity meant you could earn up to £5 an hour. The downside was the aggression; but Joe later explained how 'somehow the fact you were defenceless down there always protected you'. The boundaries between Woody's reality and fantasy worlds were beginning to blur: for the next few weeks, he was to eke out a living among the grimy, tiled passages of the underground, a dirty, singing, hobo mole. Going to work meant slinging a guitar over his shoulder and bunking the tube into town.

In his damp, frowzy room at Ridley Road, Woody persevered with his instrument. He learned 'Not Fade Away' and 'Heartbreak Hotel' and a dozen more old busking chestnuts. His greatest inspiration, however, came from his collection of Bo Diddley records. Bo's primitive, shuffling rhythms suited his rudimentary guitar style perfectly. Favourites included 'Mona (I Need You Baby)' and 'Don't Let It Go': both used only one chord and would survive the next few years to become popular warm-up tunes for The 101'ers and The Clash. Bo became Woody's guitar hero.

'He encouraged me to think I could play,' Joe explained. 'People can get caught thinking it's all about technique when in fact it's not really about technique at all. It's about something even more exciting and unidentifiable. Everybody else was playing twelve-bar blues at the time he kicked off, so he said to himself: "I have to do something different if I want to stand out or make it in this town." So he came up with something even more African than the blues is: the Bo Diddley style. Also, he taught Mick Jagger how to sing. Nobody knows this. I think Jagger's a great singer but when you listen to his American accent inside his songs it's actually Bo Diddley's. People like Bo gave me strength and encouragement.'

Sometime in 1972, Woody's busking career was curtailed. According to an account he gave to Jon Savage, the owner of the house they were squatting in took exception to the fact there was a black guy living there. If there was a moment in which John Mellor became politicised, it was most probably this one.

'I'd been for a drink at the Memphis Belle with this girl I knew from the local supermarket,' explained Joe. 'I arrived back at the flat and there was this police car outside, and all our stuff was being thrown out the window. Me and Tymon had found this black guy in the park who'd given us a fright, and being hippies we'd invited him back to our place to live. As soon as the landlord found out there was a black guy in the house, he starting nicking people's giros. Then we were all evicted: a gang of toughs rushed in, beat everybody up, slung 'em out. [The landlord] bunged the cops a few quid. It was then I started learning what justice was and wasn't.'

Woody had a copy of the 1965 Rent Act on him, and told the policemen what was happening was illegal. 'He said, "Don't tell fucking tell me about the law, sonny Jim." Up to that moment, I'd been doing it by the book. But from then on, if we wanted a house we just kicked the fucking door in.'

The Harlesden eviction was followed by another ugly incident. A few weeks later, while he was staying at the home of hippy activists Dave and Gail Goodall on Edgware Road, the household was again evicted illegally and all of his records smashed up. Woody took the case to the Harassment Officer at Brent Council, but he was hustled out of the tribunal for losing his temper with the law students sedately taking notes at the back, as if he were an interesting legal specimen.

Later, Joe would see his struggle in simple Marxist terms: 'I've been fucked up the arse by the capitalist system.' At the time, the brutality of the two evictions impacted on him in more personal terms. The violent destruction of his beloved old Stones, Beatles, Dylan and blues vinyl hurt him badly. To him, music was everything: like a character in Nick Hornby's *High Fidelity* he loved music so much it made him 'as close to being mad as makes no difference'.

Bruised by London life, Woody drifted back to the prim comfort and fresh country air of his parents' bungalow, where, having had little contact with him since David's death, they seemed more than happy to allow him to move back into his old bedroom and set up his latest acquisition – a second-hand drum kit – in the spare room. His wings having melted just as his dreams of being a musician were becoming real, Woody – or John, as his parents insisted on calling him – licked his wounds, bashed his tom-toms and wondered what the hell he was going to do next.

The answer lay in a romance he'd been having with a girl who'd recently taken up a place at art school in Cardiff. Electing to visit her in Wales, he turned up with a bag of clothes and his drum kit. When that didn't work out he looked up some old pals in the art school in nearby Newport. There, Woody struck up a friendship with a student called Micky Foote and his girl-friend Gillian, and moved into their flat. The college had quite a happening vibe, and Woody, glad to be back in his role of itinerant folk-bluesman, swiftly ingratiated himself with the hip set.

He was surprised to learn that one of them was Linda Keith, a former girl-friend of Keith Richards, Brian Jones and Jimi Hendrix. She'd apparently decided to move on from dating glamorous and tragic rock stars and get an art qualification. The connections to the London music scene didn't stop there: Ian Dury was going out with the daughter of one of the lecturers.

'Woody got to know everyone,' says Richard Frame, a student at Newport. 'He was a very charming and charismatic guy. Music was his thing. We used to go and see lots of local rockabilly groups like Crazy Cavan and Shakin' Stevens. It was like John Peel said – the Welsh never had a rock 'n' roll revival because it never died there. Woody loved all that stuff.'

Woody also became acquainted with a reggae club called The Silver Sands, located in a basement room down by the docks on Coronation Road. Raided by the cops on a regular basis and frequented by members of Newport's close-knit Afro-Caribbean community, it sold cans of Colt 45 lager and was one of the best places in town to score ganja. The fact Woody was permanently skint meant that he couldn't partake of much of either, but it fuelled his fondness for ska and reggae, and satiated his romantic desires to exist among those at the margins of society.

Richard Frame observes that Woody always carried a notebook with him, in which he furiously scribbled anything that excited or tickled him. One prescient entry was inspired by a conversation he had with a girl called Cathy Cooper. Asked why she always wore dresses she replied, 'Because I hate trousers.' Woody was bowled over by this comment and couldn't get it out of his mind. The phrase neatly connected fashion with attitude and had the ring of a slogan. It wasn't too long before Woody was making similar proclamations linking style and lifestyle. Micky Foote remembers a memorable early soundbite. 'He said to me, "You've gotta wear pointy shoes so you know which way you're going." I thought that was great.'

'Woody was the kind of guy who said things that you never forgot,' comments Alan Jones, who began sharing a flat with Woody in the spring of 1973. 'You'd be unlucky to meet Woody and not remember something he said. I can remember a time when I came out of my room and I was quite sleepy and he said, "Sleep's not a bankcard, you can't just bang it in and take it out whenever you want." He was like that: very direct and succinct. This is not a man who rambles, this is a man who comes out with short statements that could be said to be rude but hardly ever are. There was this amazing truthfulness coupled with humour.'

Alan was playing bass in a college band called The Rip-Off Park All Stars. They were a rock 'n' roll covers band with a corny, glammy, showbiz twist, not unlike Showaddywaddy and Mud had a couple of years later. The group all adopted zany pseudonyms: Jones was 'Jiving Al'. 'Jiver', as he was known, first clapped eyes on Woody when he wandered into one of their rehearsals.

'It was just like these shining eyes,' he beams. 'It was just like electric. What we were doing was pretty rough, to say the least, but it struck a chord with him. I just remember him walking in with those laser eyes, which he had if something was exciting him. I can remember him leaning on the wall and sinking to the floor, then just sitting there watching us.'

Woody's desire to perform with a proper band was re-ignited. He recognised that the All Stars were bad enough musicians for him to be in with a chance. When the group faded away in the summer of 1973, Alan Jones and guitarist Rob Haymer formed a new band, eventually christened The Vultures; Woody made his move. His audition saw the other members guffawing into their shirt cuffs at his croaking, tuneless singing. But Woody out-manoeuvred them. 'Well, as far as I see it, you've got no choice because you've got a drummer who's got no drums, and I've got a set of drums,' he explained. 'So you haven't really got any say in it.' He was in.

Woody and Alan's flat was at 12 Pentonville, near Newport railway station. Over the next few months, Jones got to know his flatmate very well. The Woody he describes tallies with the observations of others: an affable, loveable, often unfathomable lunatic whose moods oscillated from wild-eyed enthusiasm for some small detail – a song lyric, a funny phrase someone had used, a story he'd read in the newspaper – to long, semi-depressive periods of solitude where he'd read, paint pictures of cowboys and Indians (his favourite subject matter), write poetry and listen to music. According to Alan, the only record Woody kept at this point was his tatty Chuck Berry EP from Tehran, which had survived all his house moves and the shock eviction from Ridley Road. 'As far as I'm concerned, it's the only record worth having!' he said to Jones.

Jiver's stories of Pentonville range from the amusing to the baffling. At one point he remembers his flatmate returning from a few weeks away, bursting through the front door and declaring ecstatically, 'I've found God!' before disappearing into his bedroom for a few days never to mention the incident again. Another time, Woody gave mouth-to-mouth resuscitation to a drowned mouse, which had been lured into a trap consisting of a cheese-baited ruler and a bucket of water. He and Woody, who was signing on the dole, lived on 50p a day, enough for a pint of beer, an ounce of Old Holborn and a hot refectory meal.

Having rehearsed for several weeks, The Vultures played their first gig at the Students' Union bar in late 1973. Woody shared vocal and guitar duties with Rob Haymer on a set of rock 'n' roll oldies, country rock covers and Who and Kinks tunes. It was his first experience of playing onstage with a rock 'n' roll band. What Dylan fans in the audience made of this particular electric debut at Newport is not recorded.

Half a dozen or so gigs followed at the same venue. 'Woody got much better very quickly,' says Jiver. 'He still couldn't sing in tune, but that didn't matter because it was overridden by his incredible force of personality. We played a lot of soft stuff. Our last song was "Johnny B. Goode", which, as far as I know, he waited all night to play.'

The group's last gig was the first of two or three outside the relative cosiness of the college bar. Alan Jones ascribes it an almost mythical status, as it was here, he believes, that Woody's next incarnation – the one that became famous throughout the world – was born. The gig was at The Granary in Bristol. Woody drew a fetching cartoon-strip poster to promote the band, which profiled the members under their 'stage' names: Bobby Angelo (Rob), Woody Mellor, 'Jiving Al' Jones, Bob 'Blow' Jackson on sax and the plainly named Jeff Cooper on drums.

The Granary gig was a shambles, dogged by equipment failure and broken strings. The guitars were apparently de-tuned by saboteurs while the group took a fag break. Reacting to the farce onstage, a drunken squaddie jumped up from the audience and started a striptease. 'The song we were playing broke down,' recalls Jiver. 'Then Woody grabbed the mic and got this nihilistic sort of chant going with the audience. The guy started to take his clothes off, and Woody was shouting, "OFF, OFF, OFF!" And I've never seen this side of him before or anything like it, really, he just seemed to be solid gone, in a complete trance, you know, the eyes were steely and it was just like "OFF, OFF, OFF!" The audience were probably pissed off with us 'cos they thought we were rubbish, but they just got into it. The whole thing got a little bit scary. I mean, one minute we're playing music and the next minute we've just got this audience that are something out of Nuremberg.'

That night, Woody learned something about the way crowds could be manipulated that he'd never forget. He also realised he had a natural ability to excite and control people. The episode had unlocked something thrilling and dangerous in him: it wasn't just the crowd Jiver had found scary; it was Woody's onstage transformation into what he describes as 'a completely different person'.

But the singer would have to wait several months before he had another chance to experiment with his newly discovered gift. That winter, the group fizzled out and Woody got a job with the local council tending graves in the town cemetery. He found the work boring and depressing; he was so weak and skinny he couldn't dig graves, only pick up the dead flowers and broken jam jars. Jiver remembers him coming home and railing, 'There's gotta be more to life than this.' It was the beginning of a dark period for him when his dreams of being a pop star seemed more remote and ridiculous than ever.

His flagging spirits weren't helped by David Bowie's 1971 singer-songwriter album, *Hunky Dory*, a student favourite at the time. 'I used to hate that song ['Quicksand'],' recalled Joe. 'The one that goes, "Don't believe in yourself . . ." Times when I was really struggling in Wales, like starving to death, and some guy would put that record on in some freezing flat and I'd get so angry. There he was on the hi-fi speakers, this big rock star saying, "Don't even believe in yourself", and I was looking round thinking, "What the fuck else have we got?" I still can't stand to hear that song. Bo Diddley was much more encouraging. He said, "Get up off your ass!"'

Woody's feelings of low self-worth gnawed away at him that winter. His depression grew deeper. Then something surprising happened.

'I was sitting in my room late one night,' says Jiver, 'and Woody burst in and said, "Alan, I wanna record something! Now!" I set up my tape player and he played me a song he'd written. We recorded it there and then.'

Thirty years later, in his flat in north London, Alan plays me the tape. The song is called 'Crummy Bum Blues', and is a thrashy rocker, based around a conventional twelve-bar structure. Before they start you can hear Woody – unmistakeable even then – directing the others to 'really make it nasty and homemade . . . things are too slick these days.' If the music isn't particularly remarkable, the lyrics are fascinating, not least for the way they foreshadow the romantic cops 'n' robbers world of The Clash. The song tells the story of Woody's protestation to a girl that he isn't a crummy bum like her mamma says he is, but a hard-working man. Then he admits all in the last verse:

> An intelligent bank robber, that's what I'd like to be
> An expert in the field of cat burglary
> I'd never look down, and I'd never look back
> Shinning up the drain-pipe dressed in black . . .

It wouldn't be long before he would be hanging out with an intelligent armed robber and a real-life cat burglar. The recording of 'Crummy Bum Blues' was followed by a rough-house country-blues instrumental in which Woody plays mean slide guitar and bellows, 'Cheese!' His depression that winter appears to have unleashed his creative potential. He had written his first songs.

Woody's hobo outlaw fantasies were further stoked at the beginning of the summer when he disappeared from Newport for a month to go busking in Europe with Tymon Dogg. Their mission was to visit a pal who'd been busted for marijuana and was behind bars in a Dutch jail. The break became a crazy month-long road trip.

'I wanted to do the Woody Guthrie and Bob Dylan thing,' explains Tymon. 'We went off to Amsterdam and you weren't allowed to busk. We had a few proper gigs lined up but were penniless, so Joe said, "Let's not waste time, let's just play in the street, and then go in that restaurant over there." I was playing my violin and there was Joe, hustling this guy for money. The guy put his hand in his pocket and I thought, "Great," but he brings out a card; he's a policeman and he took my violin. We had a gig the next night. Joe scrounged around for another instrument and came up with this family heirloom – he talked someone into sneaking out a violin from their parents' house and we used that to raise money to pay the fine to get my violin back! Funny times.'

Tymon and Woody busked around Holland and France – where they were chased by police – then pressed on to Berlin where they'd arranged a handful of gigs. Woody wanted to stay on but Tymon was desperate to get back to London to start writing new material, and his argument won out. Woody hitched back to Newport. His experience of being a bona fide vagrant musician in the tradition of legendary blues figures like Charley Patton and Robert Johnson seemed to have lifted his spirits. Symbolically, he had his long hippy hair cut short in a rockabilly quiff, and asked Jiver to photograph him in his room in Pentonville, Dylan-style, with his 'attributes' – records, amps, old radios and paintings.

When the landlord came round for the first time in almost a year looking for rent, Woody decided that he and Newport had outgrown each other and high-tailed it back to London. It was July 1974. That month, he went to the first Knebworth rock festival, featuring The Allman Brothers, Van Morrison and, at the bottom of the bill, Tim Buckley. His old schoolfriend from CLFS, Ken Powell, recognised him wandering alone through the crowd. 'We stopped and had a chat,' recalls Ken. 'He was high as a kite. I could see that he'd moved on. He looked different and spoke differently. I realised that the connection we once had was gone.'

Woody stayed for a while in Tymon's flat in Chippenham Road in Maida Hill, a heavily squatted area north of Westbourne Park, before being directed to a spare room in a nearby house at 101 Walterton Road. A few hundred yards away from the squat stood a council tower block called Wilmcote House. On its eighteenth floor, a nineteen-year-old art student was holed up in his grandmother's flat, teaching himself to play guitar. Little did Woody know that Mick Jones would change the course of his life.

2

A WORKING-CLASS HERO?

'What links the greatest rock 'n' roll careers is a volcanic ambition, a lust for more than anyone has a right to expect; a refusal to know when to quit or even rest.'

Greil Marcus 'Mystery Train'

'Did you see the suits and the platform boots? Oh dear, oh boy . . .'
MOTT THE HOOPLE, 'SATURDAY GIGS'

London, 9 January 2003. Mick Jones jumps out of a black cab and hands the driver a note through the passenger window. He motions to keep the change and sashays into the foyer of the Soho bar we've arranged to meet in. Mick's taller than his slight figure suggests – he's about 5ft 11in – and his movements are neat, economical and graceful. He looks as if he's been beamed into Dean Street from the early 1960s. Jet-black pomaded hair, black overcoat, crisply laundered white shirt – he could have come straight from the set of the Francis Bacon biopic *Love is the Devil*, a Soho gangster off to the Colony Club to plan a job over a game of cards.

We find a table and place our order. Jones gets a vegetarian salad ('No cheese'), which he will barely touch, and a glass of beer. He's polite and charming, with big, expressive brown eyes and a lopsided *School For Scoundrels* grin. He speaks in a quacky, old-fashioned 1950s London accent unmolested by the modern Estuary influence. The impression he gives of starring in a period film is underlined when we're politely interrupted by a waiter: 'Mr Jones? There's a call for you. Would you like to take it at the bar?' Mick doesn't like carrying a mobile – too intrusive.

His call over, we talk for a couple of hours about The Clash's career, from the days when he used to get a lift in The Stranglers' drummer Jet Black's old ice-cream van to his last days with the group. While Joe spoke in a bizarre, scatological-but-somehow-direct way, Mick tends to veer off on tangents, which he neatly twists together just as you think he's forgotten your question. We start by chatting about his father, a south London taxi driver. Mick explains how he also used to manage a betting shop and had connections with the local boxing fraternity. 'I remember when I was young seeing my father on telly,' he says. 'It was a Billy Walker fight, and my father was in the background, in the dressing room. It was really exciting, all of us crowded round watching him on this tiny black-and-white set.'

Billy Walker was a legend in London, and went on to open his own club, the Upper Cut in Forest Gate, in 1966. The first band to play there was The Who; The Animals and Jimi Hendrix followed suit. (Hendrix famously wrote 'Purple Haze' in the dressing-room.) Mick would have been too young to go there, but the psychedelic pop groups which took its stage in 1966 and 1967 were to have a fundamental effect on his life.

'All I ever wanted to do was play in a group,' says Jones, whose first serious rock 'n' roll purchases were Hendrix's Smash Hits compilation and Cream's Disraeli Gears in 1968. 'Once I'd discovered music and realised I didn't want to be a footballer any more, that was it. It was rock 'n' roll or nothing. I never wanted a proper job. That wasn't an option.'

After a quiet couple of years, Jones returned to the public eye in 2002 to produce Up the Bracket, the debut album by The Libertines. The experience seems to have boosted his spirits, particularly as the record had topped several end-of-year polls. (The group's second album, also produced by Mick, reached number one in 2004.) I had attended one of the mixing sessions at Whitfield Street Studios off Charlotte Street – where The Clash recorded their first album – and it was fascinating to see Jones at work, intently absorbed, shimmying around the control room, softly but purposefully spelling out changes he wanted.

Our meeting today, however, is pervaded with a profound and heavy sense of sadness and shock. Joe Strummer had died suddenly just three weeks earlier. Mick had last seen him a couple of days before he passed away, when they bumped into each other in the Groucho – one of the few water-holes in London where they could drink in relative peace.

Despite his effort to put on a brave front, grief casts a shadow across Mick's face. It must be difficult for him. His relationship with Joe was the volatile chemical reaction that powered The Clash. Their friendship in the late 1970s and early 1980s came with the complication of having always to write songs even better than their last ones. It was an association ruled by deadlines, difficult creative decisions and huge expectations.

The pressures were immense, and it sometimes showed in what the group's engineer Bill Price calls 'withdrawals and silences'. There were even, very occasionally, fisticuffs. It was a classic, creative rock 'n' roll partnership – like Lennon–McCartney, Page–Plant, Jagger–Richards – an intensely public marriage with unique tensions and emotional subtleties that only the individuals themselves could ever fully appreciate. It should go without saying there was a deep bond between them, going right back to days when, as one interviewee says, 'they used to walk round Camden eating the same bag of chips'.

'Me and Joe were the greatest collaborators and partners, but we were also our greatest rivals,' explains Mick. 'It's only natural for the songwriters in a band. It needs that to push it forwards all the time.'

From an early age, Joe and Mick wanted to be rock stars. But success seems to have meant very different things to each of them. Even at the height of the group's fame, Strummer still lived the life of a hobo bum in shabby squats, surrounded by little more than the contents of a plastic carrier bag, while Mick demanded the finest hotels. To him, it didn't seem unreasonable; he was a successful musician. Joe's squatting pal Tymon Dogg tells how he bumped into Mick in New York in 1980, during the recording of *Sandinista!* 'Mick was trying to change his hotel,' he explains. 'I asked him why. He said, "The other one was really crappy. In fact, you and Joe would have liked it a lot."'

It's inviting to explain Joe and Mick's different attitudes to success in terms of their backgrounds – Joe being the middle-class hippy poet with a message for a world (like Dylan or Leonard Cohen) and Jones the working-class guitar hero looking for a glamorous alternative to a dead-end life (like Mick Ronson or Keith Richards). But, as ever with The Clash, it seems to have been more complex than that.

'If you look at Mick's background, you can see that it wasn't just about escaping, he was searching for an identity for himself,' says his schoolfriend Robin Banks. In that respect, he and Joe were remarkably similar. Joe even wrote a song about it, 'Lost in the Supermarket'. Although it was essentially a 'gift' to Mick, who sang the number, on closer examination it seems to describe both of them: 'I'm all lost in the supermarket, I can no longer shop happily / I came in for a special offer, guaranteed personality . . .'

For a man whom *Melody Maker* journalist and onetime Clash manager Caroline Coon described as 'having the feminine grace of Keith Richards', it's somehow appropriate that Michael Geoffrey Jones was born at the South London Hospital for Women in Clapham. The date was 26 June 1955. Mick was the first and only child of Renee Zegansky and Thomas Jones, and the embodiment of the vital energy of twentieth-century London: a tangle of genes imported from abroad. His mother's family were Russian Jews who'd settled in the East End of London at the turn of the century. Stella, Mick's grandmother, was born in Whitechapel in 1899; Renee, the daughter from her first marriage, was something of a live wire. At the end of the Second World War she'd fallen for a GI and stowed away in a boat heading for America. She was quickly deported. Back in London, she found work selling jewellery and married Thomas Jones, a south Londoner whose parents had settled in the capital from Wales.

Thomas was too young to have served in the armed forces during the war – as Joe's father had – but in its aftermath he was drafted into the army for National Service. In 1947, he was posted to the newly created Jewish state of Israel, where he served in the Special Investigations Branch of the military police. Like Joe's father, he was part of a generation of Englishmen who found themselves present at important events in the reorganisation of the post-war world, and brought their extraordinary stories back with them. 'He saw some pretty terrible things out there,' explains Mick. 'What they did to the locals. It changed his views about things. He came back here and married a Jewish woman!'

Mick's first home was a flat in Mitcham on the fringes of south London, but the Joneses soon found themselves back in the hub of south London in Christchurch House, a solidly built 1930s block of private apartments on a busy junction on Brixton Hill. In 1957, the area was one of the most multi-cultural parts of the capital. In the nineteenth century, Brixton had been a prosperous middle-class suburb dominated by large terraces of three or four-storey houses, but by the Great War it had fallen into decline and many of its properties were partitioned into flats. When the first wave of West Indian immigrants arrived in Britain in 1948 on the SS *Empire Windrush*, the authorities temporarily housed over two hundred of them in an old air-raid shelter underneath Clapham Common, previously used as a holding station for German prisoners of war. The following day they were directed to register at the Labour Exchange in nearby Brixton, and many settled in and around the area.

As Stephen Inwood explains in his *A History of London*, Brixton had 'a cheap market, good shops, tolerant immigrant communities and theatrical landladies with cheap rooms to rent. Property there was cheap, dilapidated, roomy and unwanted.' For young Michael Jones, Brixton was a pulsing, colourful place to grow up. But it wasn't necessarily a happy one.

When Mick was eight, his parents split up, a traumatic event for him. In *Westway to the World*, he talks about his parents' explosive rows. Stella, who by that time lived with the family, would shield him from the worst by taking him down to play in the old bomb shelter in the basement, where they'd 'wait for the raid to pass'. When the break-up came, Thomas moved out and Renee moved to America. Mick, who would inherit his mother's urge for glamour and adventure, was left in the care of his grandmother. In 1976, Mick told Caroline Coon: '[My parents] decided I weren't happening. I stayed with my gran for a long time and read a lot. Psychologically it really did me in.'

Like most boys of his generation, his chief interests were playing football – he also collected players' autographs – and Marvel and war comics. His mother supplemented his supply of the latter by sending him magazines from the US. This kindled his interest in America, which seemed a distant and magical place. 'I used to get these American comics,' recalls Mick. 'On the back you'd see 150 soldiers advertised for just a few dollars. They had adverts for G.I. Joes [the US version of the British 'Action Man' doll]. It was all unobtainable, American stuff . . . that kind of made it even more exciting.'

He also liked going to movies and exploring London on his own, drinking in the atmosphere of the city and gazing at Tower Bridge, St Paul's Cathedral, Trafalgar Square. Later, he explained that it was all part of creating a private universe, a defence against the unhappiness created by his parents' divorce.

Music had always been played in the Jones household, and when he was twelve Mick began buying his own records: Hendrix and Cream, then The Stones, The Beatles, The Kinks. Jones treated them like sacred texts, poring over the sleeves and the label information. For hours at a time, he'd sit in front of the family's old radiogram, mesmerised by the sound coming out of the speakers. The effect on him was as seismic as Joe hearing The Stones on the boarding school radio. In 1968, he attended his first gig, a free concert in Hyde Park featuring The Nice, Traffic, Junior's Eyes and The Pretty Things. It was at this point that Mick resolved to bury any vague ambitions he still had of being a footballer and concentrate on being a rock star.

In 1966, Jones had been accepted at the Strand, an all-boys grammar school a few minutes' walk from Christchurch House. In the 1960s, as in some counties to this day, grammar schools were the upper tier of state education, and catered for pupils bright enough to have passed their 11+ exams. John Brown, one of Mick's schoolfriends, describes the Strand as 'very strict, with pretensions to be a minor public school' – that is, it strove to be just the kind of place Joe was sent to. In an area where there was huge ethnic diversity, including the new, relatively large Afro-Caribbean population, it was predominantly white. Its fusty, old-fashioned teachers and inherently conservative values didn't exactly endear it to Mick and his friends.

'It had an atmosphere very much of the pre-war era,' recalls Robin Banks – a name he assumed during the punk era. 'We were the school rebels. All we were interested in was music and doing the complete opposite of what we were told. The headmaster was called Hobbler because of his wooden leg, which was his souvenir from the First World War. We thought he was grotesque, like something out of Brueghel. Me and Mick had no interest in school whatsoever.'

Robin was born in 1953 in Whitechapel and became Robin Crocker when he was adopted by a family who lived in one of the old tenement blocks behind Brixton station. In the late 1960s, the family relocated to a council house in Crystal Palace. The comedian Ronnie Corbett lived nearby in a huge gothic Victorian pile in Upper Norwood; Robin used to walk his dog for a bit of extra cash – until it ended up in a pond and Corbett advised him to seek employment elsewhere.

'Robin was put down a year at school for being a disruptive influence and was sat next to me in class,' recalls Mick. 'In one Maths lesson we had this heated discussion about who was the best, Chuck Berry or Bo Diddley. It ended in a serious fight, rolling around on the floor. After that, we became great friends.'

Robin: 'We were punching the shit out of each other; it was hilarious. But it created a bond. It showed how much we both cared about music for a start.'

It was Mick, incidentally, who defended the honour of Bo, the man who would prove such an inspiration to him and his songwriting partner in years to come.

Robin Banks was one of those well-read and extremely bright lunatics who found school intolerably dull. He showed no fear and would do anything to alleviate boredom – climb out of windows, be rude to teachers, stand up to older bullies. Corporal punishment was such an integral part of his existence he apparently took to wearing a pair of Lederhosen under his school flannels to soften the sting of the headmaster's cane. Mick thought Robin was marvellous and the two became inseparable. There was a strong sense of a shared experience of dysfunctional family relationships.

'I think what drew us together was our backgrounds,' says Robin. 'Mick had no family by a process of abandonment, and I had no family by the process of adoption. That put us on equal footing.'

The adhesive that connected all of Mick's friends was their passion for music. Living in London, with the freedom to roam that Joe never had, their social diary revolved around gigs and clubs. Most of the major London venues were easily accessible to them by bus or tube. The highlight of their week was Sunday afternoons, when they'd drop acid and check out the groups playing at the Implosion Club at the Roundhouse. The performers included the cream of the late 1960s underground, including Pink Floyd, Kevin Ayers and Tyrannosaurus Rex. 'I used to go there and idiot-dance, in the days before I'd worked out what I really liked,' Mick says in Bob Gruen's book of superlative Clash photographs (simply titled *The Clash*). 'If you look at the back of [San Francisco acid rockers] Stoneground's album there's a picture of me in the front, doing an idiot dance. I've got really long hair.'

Implosion, a successor to the famous Middle Earth Club, was run by, among others, a young hippy activist called Caroline Coon and Jeff Dexter, a former Mod mover 'n' shaker. The idea was that the bands would play for free and the profits would be distributed among worthy underground causes. Some of the box office takings went towards kitting out the Electric cinema on Portobello Road and refurbishing the Roundhouse's leaky roof. The Strand boys' appreciation of hippy altruism, however, extended no further than exploiting it; they would bunk into the gigs for free.

In the summer of 1969, Mick gave up revising for his exams in favour of attending some of the most momentous concerts of the late 1960s. In June, he and Robin witnessed Led Zeppelin's first big UK gig at the Albert Hall, and the following month they saw The Stones' free gig in Hyde Park. The latter had unexpectedly become a memorial for guitarist Brian Jones who'd drowned in his swimming pool just two days before. Mick, who is visible in some of the crowd shots, has often joked that most of the three thousand white butterflies released in Brian's memory landed on his head.

His interest in The Stones – then entering their creative zenith with the Jimmy Miller-produced LPs *Beggars Banquet, Let It Bleed, Sticky Fingers* and *Exile On Main Street* – soon bordered on the obsessive. 'Their latest album would come out on the Thursday and by the Friday night we knew it inside out,' he recalls. 'We'd played every track a hundred times and already knew all the words. Then that night we'd go to the pictures to see *Easy Rider* or something . . . That was our whole world.'

The Stones' drug-bust at Redlands in 1967 had transformed Jagger and Richards from spotty yobs into glamorous outlaw figures. Keith in particular, with his scarecrow hair, lurid velvet coats and crooked smile, looked every inch the rakish Regency libertine. This idea of the rock star as desperado was a powerful one, and Mick and his friends adopted a similarly decadent, flamboyant pose.

Robin Banks: 'My method of rebellion was to be as disruptive as possible. Mick's was to have the longest hair and the tightest trousers in the school, which was really quite shocking because it was a very conservative institution.'

In 1968, Mick and his grandmother had moved from Brixton to live with Stella's sister and sister-in-law in Park West, a huge, up-market private block off the Edgware Road, near Hyde Park. There was a swimming pool in the basement and plush, art deco lobbies. The area was a universe away from the residential streets of Brixton. Situated just a few minutes' walk from Oxford Street, London's major shopping thoroughfare, it backed on to the area around Paddington Station. It was an impermanent, buzzing, cosmopolitan environment.

Mick's coterie of smothering old ladies gave him plenty of affection, pocket money and, for a thirteen-year-old schoolboy, an incredibly free rein. He was pampered, indulged and certainly a little spoiled, perhaps to compensate for his mother's absence. In the years to come, Mick would be accused at times of being petulant, demanding and 'needing a valet'; it's inviting to think his taste for getting his own way developed here.

'Mick was in total control of his situation,' recalls Robin. 'He was allowed to do whatever he wanted. Stella was great but Mick used to shout, "Go and make the fucking tea!" I thought, this isn't the way I treat *my* gran. But it was still blatantly obvious there was a deep love there. Stella used to say to me, "Robin, please get him to have his hair cut. Can't you do something? Anything? He looks like a yeti." She used to go on and on at me. I was between a rock and a hard place.'

Mick's relocation to Park West throws up a number of interesting questions about his social class. Marcus Gray in *The Last Gang in Town* wonders why Mick never mentioned this swanky address during the early years of The Clash, the guitarist preferring instead to suggest his teenage years were spent on the eighteenth floor of the high-rise council block to which he and his gran would later move.

The Clash's manager Bernie Rhodes has this to say about Jones: 'Is he middle class? Yes, of course he is! You compare him with the immigrants that come over here. Oh, I see, you're one of those people who think [radio DJ and TV personality] Danny Baker's working class because he likes West Ham, is that it? I think you're very naive.'

Comments like these open up a whole can of worms about class definitions and attitudes in Britain. John Lennon had question marks raised over his right to sing about being a 'Working-Class Hero' because of a predicament not unlike Mick's – being raised in his teenage years by an older female relative in a comparatively posh environment. Lennon himself always regarded himself as working-class. Robin Banks and another school friend, John Brown, wouldn't hesitate to describe Mick in the same way.

Kosmo Vinyl, one of The Clash's inner-circle in their later years, comments: 'Mick's dad was a taxi driver and mine was a bricklayer. They seemed interchangeable occupations. We had a similar backgrounds, living in flats and so on. But what class that makes us, I don't know. All I know is we felt we'd had similar upbringings.'

Meanwhile, Sebastian Conran – son of Habitat-founder Terence and *Superwoman* author Shirley, and sometime clothes designer for The Clash – says: 'I get the impression that being a taxi driver was a fairly middle-class occupation back then. The fact Mick went on to art school and higher education, and was a bright guy, meant there was a certain amount of denial about his background.'

Ultimately these observations underscore an essential truth about Jones's early life: it didn't fit any convenient social patterning. It was a latch-key London existence: unsettled, transient, urban and, if anything, most markedly striped by the shadow of his absent parents.

Tellingly, it was a background that many key players in The Clash would share.

By the early 1970s, Mick's list of favourite groups had been swollen by the arrival of glam rock. Unlike Joe, who distrusted glam's artifice (and was a jeans and T-shirt man anyway), Jones embraced it whole-heartedly, revelling in the frisson of its androgynous styles and muscular rock 'n' roll. 'I'd been into The Kinks, The Stones and The Beatles,' Mick explains. 'But then I got more into the flash end of things. I followed The Faces, Mott the Hoople, Slade . . .'

Clothes became an increasingly important part of Mick and his friends' existence. Banks describes them as 'dandies', who'd wear everything from top hats to brightly patterned jackets and colourful shoes. Some of these were pilfered from trendy boutiques like Alkasura on the Kings Road, not far from the Sophistocat furniture shop where a live lion cub lived among the antique tables and chairs.

'We used to go nicking up Carnaby Street on a Saturday,' smiles Jones. 'We got caught a couple of times.'

Mick became smitten by Mott the Hoople. A heavy but poetic rock band, they were fronted by vocalist Ian Hunter and named by their loveably nutty producer, Guy Stevens, after the book by Willard Manus which he'd read while in prison on a dope offence. Guy was a legend in his own right, having helped turn The Who and The Small Faces onto R&B while DJ-ing at the Scene Club in the mid-1960s, and then producing and A&R-ing Procol Harum, as well as Spooky Tooth, Free and numerous other groups on Chris Blackwell's Island label. Mick held him in such high esteem that he had a poster on his bedroom wall of The Stones at Hyde Park with Guy, who was in the audience, ringed in felt-tip pen. The Strand posse had latched onto the group early, sometime between their 1969 self-titled debut album and 1970's *Mad Shadows*, long before the band's commercial breakthrough in 1972 with a cover of Bowie's 'All the Young Dudes'.

In his last couple of years at school, Mick started hanging out with some older pupils, who'd started their own Mott-inspired band called Schoolgirl. It was unusual for a younger kid to mix so freely with his elders, but Schoolgirl quickly took to Mick. One member of the group was John Brown. 'Mick was a couple of years younger than us but I didn't have any problems with that,' he says. 'We got to know him through Robin. He was a really cool kid. I warmed to him straight away 'cos he liked comic books and he read a lot of science fiction. We had a lot in common; more than any of the other guys that I was hanging round with, actually.'

Free to do pretty much as he pleased, Mick joined Robin and the fledgling Schoolgirl on their forays to far-flung cities to watch Mott. Robin recalls: 'We used to bunk the trains, jumping off before they pulled into the station, then run down the track and climb over a fence. That way you didn't need to waste money on a ticket. One of us got caught once, snagged on the barbed wire. We used to go all over the place, up to Liverpool, down to Plymouth.'

The Strand contingent became acquainted with Mott's road manager, Stan Tippins. He took a shine to them and would smuggle them in for free through the stage door. Mott prided themselves on the close relationship they had with their fans, and they honoured Mick and his friends with a nickname: the Mott Lot. At one gig in Dagenham, Mick was so thrilled to see the group's guitarist, Mick Ralphs, at the other end of the bar that he nervously tipped his drink down his shirt. Ian Hunter jokingly referred to one of the gang, Schoolgirl's singer Kelvin Blacklock, as 'Jagger' because of his fleshy lips. Blacklock was often pulled up on stage to sing on encores. The whole Mott experience had a profound impact on the boys. 'Having that relationship with a successful band was a real buzz,' says John Brown. 'You could see what it was like from close up. It made being famous feel like a real possibility.'

The Strand boys' other favourite was The Faces – Rod Stewart's group featuring three former Small Faces plus guitarist Ronnie Wood. Their Cockney braggadocio chimed with Mick and his friends' cocky teenage swagger. Though they were more elusive quarry, being a bigger group, they were stalked with similar tenacity to Mott the Hoople. 'We used to end up in their dressing room,' remembers Robin. 'We'd be sitting there ignoring Rod Stewart and trying to speak to Ronnie Wood.'

The boys' intense fascination with Mott and The Faces gave them something Mick would never lose: a sense of identity inextricably wrapped up with the larger appeal of being in a gang. To their mind, they were always two steps ahead of the provincial kids they met in Liverpool, Newcastle, Southampton: cooler, better dressed, more sussed. It was an arrogant supposition, which was, in many ways, given substance by their inner London backgrounds. 'Mick and I laugh about it to this day, but we thought we were smarter than everybody else in the whole world,' says Robin.

Up to his mid-teens, Mick Jones had shown no musical ability or desire to play an instrument. With the optimism of youth, he appeared to assume that getting the posing right was probably as good a tack as any to steer him towards future stardom. But some of those around were already taking steps to push their ambitions to another level. In 1971, Schoolgirl – now featuring John Brown, Kelvin Blacklock and a couple of other Strand pupils, Jim Hyatt and Bob Goffman – had begun rehearsing in earnest at a musty church hall in the shadow of Battersea Power Station. Mick used to turn up and watch, and was eventually promoted to roadie. In another example of The Clash walking in The Who's shadow, Townshend and co would soon acquire the hall and turn it into Ramport Studios, where they'd record, among other things, their 1973 Mod concept album, *Quadrophenia*.

Schoolgirl were as hopeless as they sounded and didn't get round to playing to an audience until 1972, when they secured a dozen or so pub gigs. By this time, Mick was re-sitting his O-Levels, having failed them all the year before. Inspired by his friends, Mick invested in a second-hand Hofner guitar, which he bought for £16. He asked Robin, who played guitar, to tune the instrument and show him a few chords. The first thing he taught him was the riff to Cream's 'Spoonful'.

When Schoolgirl crashed in late 1972, John Brown and Mick decided to team up and form their own band, subsequently named The Delinquents. Meanwhile, Mick enrolled at night-school to kill time until he was old enough to go to art school – where else? – the following year. In his book *Revolt Into Style*, George Melly described these institutions in the 1950s and 1960s as 'a refuge of the bright but unacademic, the talented, the non-conformist, the lazy, the inventive and indecisive: all of those who didn't know what they wanted but knew it wasn't a nine-to-five job.' He rued the change to the entry requirements in the late 1960s, when students needed five O-Levels.

Mick and Joe, though, were attracted mostly by their reputation for being what Melly calls 'the incubators' of great British pop. As it would turn out, none of The Clash would like art school much, possibly because art schools became less radical in the 1970s, though they would enjoy the accolade of being arguably the last great English rock band to emerge from this peculiar system.

During 1973 and 1974, Mick and John Brown grew close. In the outside world, the 1970s was sliding to its nadir: three-day weeks, wage freezes, strikes, political assassinations, the intensified bombing of North Vietnam, Nixon's landslide election victory in the States, IRA bombings, the threat of petrol rationing. But in Mick and John's exciting glam bubble, planning The Delinquents gave their life a hard, vibrant edge. It was a fresh opportunity to fantasise about stardom. What would they wear? Who would play drums? Who would sing the songs? Spending ever more time with Mick, John was astonished by how well-read and culturally advanced he was. The picture he paints is of a likeable, switched-on young dude taking the lead in their social life.

'He'd scope these things I had no idea about,' remembers John. 'He phoned me up once and said there's this great film on at the Collegiate Theatre. He said it's only been shown at the Edinburgh film festival and it went down a storm, but we've got to get down there now. I said OK, jumped in a cab and met him there. The film was *Dark Star* by John Carpenter . . . It was typical of Mick to find these gems. He also took me to see *Badlands* in a cinema in Oxford Street, and *The Night Porter* and *A Clockwork Orange* at the NFT [National Film Theatre]. He was plugged into the culture that was only there if you knew where to look . . . Mick was the first into everything. He was hip before the rest of us knew what hip meant.'

Mick's precocity was magnified by the monthly packages he received from his mother in the US. Aware of his passion for music, she supplied him with two cutting-edge US music magazines, which, unlike the heavily imported *Rolling Stone*, were almost impossible to find in London. 'She used to send me *Rock Scene* and *Creem*, with those great photos by Bob Gruen,' says Mick. 'That was my total inspiration. I was lucky she was living in America. When I saw that stuff, it was like, wow! There weren't many people over here who were into that sort of [underground US] music in those days. Only a handful.'

'Mick was always pulling something out of the hat,' says John Brown. 'He knew all the best places to get records in Portobello Road. He had an amazing knowledge of music, stuff I didn't have a clue about, like The Raspberries.'

In 1973, Mick and his grandmother moved out of Park West into a flat on the eighteenth floor of Wilmcote House, a council tower block overlooking the Westway, the elevated arterial route into central London that dominates Ladbroke Grove, Westbourne Grove and Paddington. High-rise tower blocks were designed as an answer to post-war housing shortages and had sprung up in the 1960s where Victorian slums had been cleared. By the mid-1970s they'd became symbols of urban despair: large modernist hutches where human beings became alienated from one another. They had captured the imagination of poets and writers: J.G. Ballard's 1975 novel *High Rise* – which Mick read – depicted a tower block in which social order completely breaks down, and *Crash* (1973) told the story of a community of stranded road-crash victims that had evolved in a triangular island under the Westway. Mick's symbolically desperate and disturbing new home would later become a cornerstone of Clash legend. In the meantime, Mick and his gran made themselves comfortable and imbibed the wonderful view across London.

Over the next couple of years, John Brown became a frequent visitor. 'Mick never talked about his family life,' he says. 'He was intensely private about it. He was an only child doted on by his gran. But he didn't seem any different to me at that time – other than he didn't have to let anyone know where he was going or when he'd be back.'

Robin celebrated Mick's house-move by dangling off Stella's balcony, a couple of hundred feet off the ground, and feigning losing his grip. His reckless streak and nose for danger was soon to result in a disturbing incident. On leaving school, he'd found a job at the *West London Weekly* newspaper selling advertising space and writing copy. When he was laid off, he started hanging out with some old mates who were robbing betting shops for their easy cash pickings. Sometime in late 1973, he was involved in a stick-up in

Streatham, south London; the gang was caught and he was convicted of armed robbery. He was sent first to Wormwood Scrubs and then to Albany, the maximum security facility on the Isle of Wight. He was the youngest prisoner in the jail.

Thirty years on, Robin and I are speaking in the Coach and Horses pub on Poland Street in Soho. He's a warm, charming individual with a wicked cackle and a splendid sense of humour. You can see why he was a welcome addendum to The Clash camp. It's also clear from his loose, sauntering gait why Tony Parsons believed he was the person who 'taught Joe Strummer to walk'. Robin has not long returned from Iraq, where he was part of the Human Shield protest against the war. On his head is a grey suede trilby, tilted at a jaunty angle, bought in an Iraqi street market. One of only a handful of Shields to have stayed in Baghdad throughout the war, he's working on an account of his adventures, while also penning political satires for various magazines. He is philosophical about what happened back then. 'It's the kind of thing you only do when you are young,' he says. 'Why did I do it? I was feeling a little bit avaricious that day. No, I really thought, why not? I didn't have a job.'

The episode was obviously deeply shocking for everyone who knew him. Today, he makes light of the subject, but it's hard to imagine what the reality of one of the toughest jails in Britain was like for a nineteen-year-old who might be seen holding R.D. Laing's *The Divided Self* in one hand and the *Racing Post* in the other.

In The Clash, Mick was criticised for glamorising Robin's story when he used it for the basis of his song 'Stay Free'. But back then, the idea that Mick would ever get to write about his and his friend's experiences in a rock song was still a distant dream. Robin went to prison for two years, and Mick got on with pursuing his goal of being a rock 'n' roll star.

In September 1973, Mick began his Foundation course at the Hammersmith College of Art and Building in Shepherds Bush. It was situated in Lime Grove, opposite the BBC's studios, and hadn't changed much since the 1950s, when Don McCullin studied there en route to photographing a fifteen-year-old Mod called Mark Feld (later Marc Bolan) for *Town* magazine and then world fame as a Vietnam War photographer. McCullin described it as 'a school for bricklayers as well as budding artists'. Mick would later recount how he got the stick from the brickies for his faggy, glam-rock attire in the song '1-2 Crush On You': 'Standing in a queue of a school canteen, guys in the corner they were laughin' at me . . .' Unlike Don McCullin, Mick wasn't a wizard with a camera. But he did have a guitar, and within a year the college refectory would be reverberating with the sound of The Delinquents.

On Wednesday, 28 November 1973, in the Student Union bar at Newport Art College, Woody Mellor and his pals tuned into the BBC's late-night rock programme, *The Old Grey Whistle Test*. There was a certain amount of both old and grey about the *Whistle Test*, but it was mandatory viewing for music fans, since it featured mainly live performances and interviews with the top rock stars du jour. That night, any cobwebs that had formed on presenter 'Whispering' Bob Harris were blown away by a little-known glam rock band from America called The New York Dolls.

Fronted by the Jagger-esque David Johansen, and with Johnny Thunders on guitar, they looked dangerous, camp, grotesque, authentic and exciting. Though they mimed to their featured song, 'Jet Boy', the racket was glorious: pure, primitive, schlocky B-movie rock 'n' roll. Topping that, they also came with a ready-rolled tragic heroin story: Billy Murcia, their original drummer, had expired in a bathtub during a trip to the UK to support Rod Stewart and The Faces the previous year. Guitarist Johnny Thunders looked as though he might join him in junkie heaven at any moment.

Woody and the rest of The Vultures were gobsmacked. They thought The Dolls were magnificent. It filled them with hope knowing something so conspicuously trashy could get on the TV. They sought out a copy of the group's self-titled debut album; Woody was amused to discover it included a cover of Bo Diddley's 'Pills'.

The New York Dolls were an invisible skein linking Joe, Mick and many of the other key players in punk. Mick and John Brown's Dolls epiphany was even more dramatic than Joe's. Though they didn't acquire the first album until the follow-up came out in July 1974 – they purchased the two together on import from a shop in Soho – the effect was instantaneous. The Dolls became their idols, eclipsing everything that had gone before. In Albany, Robin received a letter from Mick: 'Our group's going for a New York Dolls image. We're going to have our hair curled!'

'The Dolls had a massive effect on me,' Mick told *MOJO* in 1999. 'They were incredible. They blew my mind, the way they looked, their whole attitude . . . they didn't care about anything. They weren't great-sounding by anyone's standard, but that didn't matter.'

'We loved The Dolls,' adds John Brown. 'That was the main idea we were going for. We wanted to play loud and have the clothes and the lifestyle. We wanted to do something of our own and be successful and famous along those lines. We loved posing, we loved the whole package, we had this tremendous drive to make it.'

Mick had been concentrating on playing bass but, in a symbolic gesture, he sold a stash of rare sci-fi comics at a convention in Russell Square – where the film critic Dennis Gifford was speaking and Theodore Gershuny's cheapo terror-flick *Silent Night, Bloody Night* was showing – and bought his first decent guitar: a black Fender Telecaster. As a yellowing homemade press release belonging to John Brown attests, in May 1974 The Delinquents' line-up came together with 'Michael J. Jones' on guitar/vocals, John Brown on bass/vocals, ex-Strand boy Paul Wayman on lead guitar and Mike Dowling on drums. Dowling was an advert-sourced addition with a conveniently spacious Austin Cambridge estate car.

In an age when most teenage bands were covering Fleetwood Mac, Cream and Led Zeppelin or, like The Vultures, the obligatory rock 'n' roll and 1960s pop standards, The Delinquents messed around with hip US garage-punk tunes like The Flamin' Groovies' 'Second Cousin', MC5's 'Sister Anne' and The Standells' 'Good Guys Don't Always Wear White'. They also performed 'World Park Junkies' by Chris Spedding's group The Sharks (a big favourite) and Neil Young's 'Ohio', as covered live by Mott. The press release describes The Delinquents as 'loud 'n' punky' and states: 'the music played is in a Mott-Sharks vien [sic]'.

Mick, the youngest by at least two years, swiftly emerged as the group's wunderkind. His originals accounted for a couple of songs they performed at their hurried and consequently ropy debut on 19 June 1974 at the Queen Elizabeth College in Campden Hill Road, Kensington. A couple of months later, they recorded a demo at a studio in Holborn, featuring the songs 'You Know It Ain't Easy' and 'Hurry'. Surprisingly, neither were Mick's, though he contributed and sang the chorus to the former, a fairly unremarkable but accomplished soft-rock number.

Some promo photos from this time, taken on a bombsite down by the Thames, show Mick in a tight blouse, dark flares, black gloves, long, curly Burne-Jones hair and pop-star shades. Another shot from the same session is especially interesting, since it pictures the group standing in front of a wall sprayed with the word 'PUNK' – though, as John Brown explains, it actually said 'SPUNK' but he'd deliberately obscured the 'S'. The picture was taken only a few months after Joe had been photographed in Newport with his new quiff and neckerchief: one the narcissistic, wannabe rock star; the other the tumbleweed cowboy poet.

That summer, Mick took a holiday job as a clerical assistant in the Department of Health and Social Security in Praed Street, Paddington. In The Clash years, he told the *NME* he was disgusted at the appalling treatment of black and Irish workers claiming benefits. In a letter to Robin, he complained the staff were 'utter morons who treat me badly . . . they have no rock 'n' roll in their life'. In July 1974, the IRA bombed Birmingham, Manchester and London's Westminster Hall. Part of their campaign involved sending letter-bombs to government offices. As The Clash later alluded to in 'Career Opportunities', one of Mick's jobs was to open the mail.

Their promo shots signalled that The Delinquents were clearly as ahead of their time as Joe was comfortably anchored in the past, but that didn't aid their attempts to get noticed by the outside world. That autumn, the group continued to go about their business in the jejune way teenage bands do: they registered their name and placed adverts in the *Melody Maker* touting for management and gigs. In the last three months of 1974, the group organised a string of pub dates, including a couple of out-of-towners in Reading and Woking, and one at Mick's college. But by the start of 1975, Mike Dowling's commitment was starting to wane. He left and The Delinquents advertised in *Melody Maker* for a replacement. One of the respondents was a Norwegian living in London called Geir Waade. Blond and good-looking, with bags of confidence, he convinced them he was the man for the job. Little did Mick realise that recruiting Geir was the first in a series of events which would end in catastrophe.

Geir Waade had been resident in London since the early 1970s, when he moved to Britain from Oslo with his friend Casino Steel. The general idea was to join an English rock group and make it big. Casino eventually became part of a near-legendary outfit called The Hollywood Brats. The Brats are important because they were probably the first group in England to have all the attributes which people associate with The Dolls: theatrical, androgynous, nihilistic, nasty and musically basic. There's an argument, not entirely unconvincing, that they were an important bridge between glam rock and punk, though they never released a record while they were together and played only small venues. (For their full story, check out the sleeve-note for their album, eventually released in the UK on Cherry Red in 1980, five years after they split up.)

Around the same time Geir joined The Delinquents, their guitarist, John Wayman, left. Geir suggested The Brats' Eunan Brady fill the post. From Dublin, Brady – as he preferred to be called – was a small, feisty

Keith Richards lookalike who really did play guitar like ringin' a bell. Joe's old mate Jiving Al Jones performed in a band with him until recently, and he describes Brady's playing much as John Brown remembers it back then: 'When he's hot, he's brilliant, totally mind-blowing. The rest of the time you're looking at him desperately waiting for something great to happen.'

Brady was unsure about joining The Delinquents for a number of reasons, but chiefly because a) Geir, for all his enchanting Nordic gab, was a pretty so-so drummer and b) Mick and John seemed too young and inexperienced to be a bright prospect at that point. In February 1975, Brady finally capitulated and joined the group; immediately, this shift in dynamic had the effect of diminishing Mick's status. He was back to being the young kid again.

Even so, according to John Brown, Mick and Brady developed a mutual fascination with each other, and swapped clothes and scarves and jewellery, just as The Clash would in years to come. (Brady even claims that, at one point, Mick appropriated his identity and went round calling himself 'Brady'.) Yet although he was the group's songwriter, and therefore the heart of the band, there was a feeling that Mick was losing control. This was exacerbated when it was collectively decided to approach Kelvin Blacklock, the flamboyant former Schoolgirl singer, to front the group, which, now the stakes were raised, clearly needed someone who could aspire to a David Johansen role.

John Brown, who knew Kelvin well from the Schoolgirl days, and felt he was the kind of guy who was too ambitious and tended to lack judgement, was wary of their new recruit, as was Mick. Yet they saw wisdom in the choice, too. This was the point where they recognised that a great band needed strong characters who could excel in individual roles, regardless of whether you liked them or not, rather than subscribing to the all-mates-together model that The Beatles had unwittingly provided as a template for mega-stardom a decade earlier. But this pact with the devil was to exact its price – though not before the group received a small boost from an anonymous music fan in Chalk Farm.

'We ended up going to the Roundhouse to see a gig,' recalls John Brown. 'Were going upstairs and someone called out, "God, The fucking New York Dolls have arrived!" We were just so full of it as we walked through the door, we were like, "Yeah, got it in one, mate, we're what's happening!" It was the crowning moment: we looked the part and they'd never even heard us play. That's what we were aiming for.'

The new group began rehearsing in March 1975, and within a month they'd secured an audition for Tony Gordon (later manager of Sham 69 and Culture Club), who had close links with Pye Records. Gordon offered the band a management contract on the spot, with the caveat they re-name themselves Little Queenie after the Chuck Berry song. They willingly acquiesced; and they also elected to sack the hopeless but loveable Geir, whom they felt was holding them back. His replacement was occasional Schoolgirl drummer Jim Hyatt. 'Mick was against it,' remembers John Brown. 'He liked Geir and saw it as being disloyal. But we thought it was the most sensible thing to do.'

A demo session was duly arranged at the end of May at Pye's studios in Bryanston Street, Marble Arch – where Tymon Dogg had cut his single seven years earlier. The group recorded 'Little Queenie' and a version of Glasgow R&B singer Frankie Miller's 'Fool in Love'. What happened next threw everyone: disappointed with the session, the plucky Kelvin phoned Mott's former producer, Guy Stevens, and explained Little Queenie's situation. Stevens was now on the skids due to his alcoholism, but just about solvent via a £100-a-week retainer from Warners. (The joke was it was paid to keep him away from the studio, not in it.) Guy's advice was to tear up their contract and go with him. He swung around the other group members during a monumental bender in a pub in Marylebone; Mick and John Brown got to sit with Mott's heroic mentor for hours, planning their big break. It was their idea of heaven, the best day of their lives, what could possibly go wrong?

Guy attended a rehearsal in Acton, and the band powered through their set. All seemed to go well – then Guy called over Kelvin for a pow-wow. He said: 'The skinny young rhythm guitarist has gotta go.'

'He didn't have disrespect for Mick that I know of,' John Brown expands. 'He just wasn't in his plan and that was it. [Deep sigh] I remember . . . I was taken to one side by I think it was Guy and Kelvin and they told me: "Basically it's not working with Mick. We want to expand the rhythm guitarist's role into a keyboard role." And I thought they were bloody mad. First of all, it's not the sound we're looking for, really, it's two guitars, massive, up front in your face, not a keyboard.'

He adds, 'Mick was a songwriter. Kelvin writes the odd song but that's Mick's greatest strength from the word go, The Delinquents onwards, he always had ideas, he could write songs, they were good songs. And at that point, the only songs in our repertoire were a couple of punky sort of covers, and Mick's songs, as far as I can remember, made up the rest.'

John illustrates Mick's songwriting skills by referring to a slow, sophisticated number whose title is long forgotten, which had a clever arrangement featuring a neat descending guitar line and a slick, twelfth-fret bass pattern. John didn't take the ousting of his friend lightly. 'Notwithstanding the fact I'd be shitting on my friend, you know, the co-founder of the band,' he says, 'I said to the others, "You're mad, you've got it wrong." This went on for three or four days. I had people ringing me up, coming round to see me, sending cabs round to get me, "Come and see me, I've gotta talk to you." I said, "Guy, you know, we've gotta talk this out." And in the end I just caved in. They had the weight of Warners behind them. I thought, "Fuck, they must know what they're talking about." I was blinded by ambition, really, and I felt like a real bastard. But I told Mick myself . . .

'I knew it was the wrong thing,' he continues, 'just like Mick knew it was wrong having Kelvin in the band. But you do it and live to regret it. The whole band just shifted from that moment onwards, the whole direction went "whoooop" and we were like Mott the Hoople – which is not a bad thing if you wanna be Mott the Hoople but we didn't want to be a second Mott the Hoople. And that's what Guy did to us, you know, and it wasn't right and before too long we split up.'

There's one thing with which everyone agrees: Mick took his sacking with incredible dignity. To be spurned and betrayed by his friends, to be rejected from their circle, must have wounded him enormously. To be considered unworthy as a musician by his favourite group's producer must have doubly cut him to the quick. To make matters worse, he had temporarily moved out of Wilmcote House and was living with a girl in a bedsit in Gladsmuir Road in Archway, above a basement flat Kelvin had taken. The band often rehearsed in Kelvin's place.

'About a week after this all happened Mick came downstairs from his bedsit and, um, I just felt so bad,' says John Brown. 'And he was cool, you know, but he must've been really hurting inside. He sort of said, "Hello, how's things goin'?" We talked for a bit and then he went out again. I felt terrible.'

Within a few weeks Little Queenie had changed their name to Violent Luck on Guy's recommendation and recorded a session with Guy and engineer Bill Price at Air Studios on Oxford Street. Kelvin played the tape to Mick; he broke down in tears, he was so upset. He moved his stuff back to his gran's. The demo was as far as it went with Violent Luck: by the following summer the project had foundered.

Mick, meanwhile, hooked up with a friend of Kelvin's called Tony James, who shared his passion for The New York Dolls and The Stooges. Having immediately hit it off, they toyed with the idea of starting a band under a name that had been thought of – then discarded – by Little Queenie: The London SS.

Tony James points out that Mick's dismissal from Little Queenie was a defining moment for him. 'Mick was devastated, but instead of giving up he said, "Right, I'm gonna learn to play properly." And at that point he went down Denmark Street and bought himself a better guitar.' It wasn't any old guitar, either, but a vintage Les Paul Junior, similar to the one used by his hero Johnny Thunders. 'I remember him at his gran's flat spending hours picking out the guitar solo to "You Can't Always Get What You Want", continues Tony. 'Mick was determined to make it.'

'When I came out of jail, Mick was a brilliant guitarist,' says Robin. 'You know that line in "Stay Free"? "I practised daily in my room . . ." That was exactly what Mick did. You cannot overestimate the passion and drive of that man. He was single-minded about making it. That was what made him different.'

If Mick had gazed down from his eighteenth-floor eyrie towards Notting Hill, he might have spotted a converted church on Campden Street where an art student called Paul Simonon was getting some stick from his lecturers for trying to paint like Leonard da Vinci. It wouldn't be long before his and Paul's paths would fatefully cross.

3
BASS CULTURE

'A gaunt, moody and beautiful bass-player, with a taste for Gauloises and existentialism, was something you didn't get in Gerry and the Pacemakers.'

Paul Du Noyer on Stuart Sutcliffe, *Liverpool: Wondrous Place*

'*Reporter: Do you prefer a brush or palette knife?*
Tony Hancock: It depends whether I'm painting or eating an apple.'
THE REBEL

'I started painting when I was a baby,' says Paul Simonon, weaving in and out of the midday traffic off Golborne Road in west London. 'My father was a Sunday painter, and I followed on from him. He only painted on Sundays because he worked the rest of the week. That was it, I was going to be a painter and I directed all my energies into painting and drawing.'

Today, 29 March 2001, Paul is picking up some of his paintings from a framer. He is gathering material for a prestigious exhibition in the West End, which will eventually take place eighteen months later at the Hazlitt, Gooden and Fox gallery in Mayfair. Paul quit playing bass for a living in the early 1990s, and since then he's re-immersed himself in his great pre-Clash passion: art. Paul has been referred to numerous times as 'the coolest man ever to strap on a bass', a notion promoted by Pennie Smith's famous photograph of him smashing his guitar at the New York Palladium on the cover of *London Calling*. He looks pretty cool this afternoon, too, sporting a blue suit, gold-rimmed aviator shades, cropped hair and a rakish, Terry-Thomas grin.

In pictures of The Clash, Paul always looks sullen and moody, but in person he's friendly, wry and humorous. His gappy front teeth lend him a rogue-ish charm – as does the small cicatrice on his left cheek. In conversation, he shifts between the playful and the deadly serious. He comes across as a man who knows his mind and has few regrets.

Pennie's photo is symbolic because it communicates the disrespect Simonon had for his instrument, especially in his early days with The Clash. As he says, 'I'm not a musician – or at least I didn't *arrive* a musician.' Ironically, he rarely broke his basses; his preferred method of abuse was customising them. It was a creative method of destruction of which the pop artist Gustav Metzger – who demonstrated his art under the Westway, on the playground Paul used as a kid – would no doubt have approved.

First, off would come the scratch plate for a Pollock-style drizzle of coloured paint, then the real work began. 'I used to whack lumps out of the body,' Paul explains in his croaky south London brogue. 'Much to the amusement of the roadies. It was, "Here comes Paul with his new bass, better get the hammer ready." I used to chip bits out of it, just to give it some life. I hated the bloody things. I wanted to be a guitarist like Pete Townshend, not a bass-player. But playing guitar was a mystery for me at that time.'

Simonon was called 'the James Dean of punk', but he was much more its Stuart Sutcliffe. What he brought to the band, initially at least, had little to do with musicianship and everything to do with image, poise and attitude. As with the tragic Hamburg Beatle, his bass-playing skills paled against his cinematic, *nouvelle vague* good looks and an interest in evolving new visual styles for the group – the Rauschenberg paint-spattered shirts, the Hollywood cowboy gear, the punked-up US Marine fatigues. It was Paul's presence that ensured The Clash's iconic status and gave them a subcultural edge.

'It was a skinhead-Mod thing,' he says, explaining his enchantment with fashion and image. 'You dressed to intimidate or for people to leave you alone. I thought we needed that attention to detail when it came to clothes. It was like when we splashed paint on our gear, I realised you had to be careful with that: Joe and Mick went a bit over the top. I remember us walking down Golborne Road and all these West Indians were pointing at us, going, "Ha ha ha ha!" I discreetly did the shirt and maybe the shoes, but the others had the shirt, the trousers, the socks, the jackets. You have to have a bit of style, you can't go at it like a lunatic.'

The conversation returns to painting. I mention the comedian Tony Hancock's early 1960s flick, *The Rebel*, in which the saturnine Hancock trades his bowler hat for a beret and moves to Paris to establish himself as an artist. 'I love that film!' says Paul. We talk about the end-of-the-pier English melancholia of Hancock's *Punch and Judy Man*. 'Have you seen *French Dressing*?' he asks. 'I think it's Ken Russell's first film. It's about an English seaside town which tries to hold a film festival like Cannes. I like that

Englishness – that idea we're gonna have good fun on the pier despite the rain. The English weather makes me want to paint.'

After driving around the West London streets Simonon pounded as a teenager, and rioted in with The Clash, we arrive at a Spanish bar. He parks next to a meter but doesn't put in any money. I find out later this is nothing: for years he used to motor around here without even a driving licence. I ask him whether he did, indeed, teach himself to drive in fifteen minutes, as suggested by a caption to one of the photographs in Pennie Smith's *The Clash: Before and After* photo book.

'That was a bit of an exaggeration,' he says. 'But when the Clash were on tour, whenever our driver stopped, I always jumped in the driving seat and drove off, much to everyone's terror. I remember in one place the security guard came running after me round the car park. It was almost like that shot in *The Harder They Come* with the car driving across the lawns and the golf course with the windscreen wipers going. I suppose I had a reputation as the practical joker.'

Those in and around The Clash stress how important Simonon was in the power structure of the group: his opinion held the same weight as Mick and Joe's and, though he rarely lost his cool, his taciturn and playful front masked a stubborn and passionate core. Mick describes his contribution as 'immeasurable'. It's arguable that much of The Clash's hard-line posturing derived from his streetwise codes. He was also the emotional anchor of the group: unflappable in times of crisis. Two close Clash associates, Johnny Green and Kosmo Vinyl, both use the word 'solid' to describe him.

Howard Fraser, the group's driver, comments: 'I never saw Paul say much, but I did see him do a lot.'

'It was straightforward to be honest,' says Don Letts, The Clash's video-maker. 'Paul Simonon either likes this or he doesn't like this. But there is always some moral or intellectual idea behind it. He just had an idea instinctively of what The Clash were about. They are about this, and they are *not* about that. Paul was essentially The Clash's musical and cultural barometer. He's silent but deadly.'

If Mick and Joe's stories were about taunting authority, testing its boundaries to see what victories they could score, Paul's was about escaping authority altogether. His background was arty but hand-to-mouth. It combined elements of both Mick's and Joe's early lives: the latch-key, inner-city upbringing of the former, and unsettled, peripatetic world of the latter. His experiences imbued him with the richness of London street life, which would later colour the atmosphere of The Clash. Living among the first generation of black immigrants in Brixton and Notting Hill, Paul was submerged not just in the sounds of ska and reggae, but also in the culture that produced them. Unlike virtually every other white English rock band from The Stones onwards, The Clash, via Paul, got their injection of black music virtually from source.

The most influential English musician to regard his instrument as primarily an *objet d'art* was born Paul Gustave Simonon on 15 December 1955 in a rented flat in south London. His mother, Elaine, was a librarian and his father, Antony, at that stage, was, like Joe's dad, a clerk in the Civil Service. His job was considerably less romantic, though: he worked in the social security department. He didn't stay long in the position. 'It was a complete disaster; he was asked to leave,' says Paul.

The Simonons had no permanent home of their own. They lived in the Brixton area for a while, then moved to the top-floor flat at 69 Oxford Gardens in Ladbroke Grove, where Paul attended Oxford Gardens Infant School. Then in 1959 they relocated to Ramsgate, on the Kentish coast, and then to a string of other southern towns including Canterbury and Bury St Edmunds. The reason for the ever-changing scenery was his father who 'had a hundred different jobs,' according to Paul.

Antony Simonon, like Ronald Mellor, was a largely self-educated man and 'very much a disciplinarian'. He had wanted to pursue a career as a painter and go to art school but his father had strong opinions about such airy-fairy stuff, and insisted he get a job. In the early 1950s, he was drafted into the army for his National Service and posted to Kenya. The Kenyan Crisis proved to be one of the ugliest moments in British post-war colonial history, and the methods by which British soldiers suppressed the rebel Mau Mau uprising – massacres, hangings, concentration camps, chopping the hands off corpses for finger-printing – resulted in a dark stain on an already tatty colonial copy-book. Antony saw what happened with his own eyes; it had a deep effect on him.

Having tried his hand as a bookshop proprietor, Paul's father settled back in London with his family, now with the addition of another son, Nick, born in 1959. For a while the family lived in Shakespeare Road in Brixton, in the heavily black area around Railton Road, the infamous 'Front Line' where trouble regularly flared between West Indians and police. At this point, though they never knowingly met, Paul and Mick were living just twenty minutes' walk away from each other.

It appears that Paul and his brother were a mischievous pair, possibly a reaction to their father's authoritarian approach. Digby Cleaver, a Clash roadie in their later days, recounts the story of Paul and his brother accidentally setting fire to their parents' flat one night while they were out, and desperately trying to hide the evidence. Paul was by now attending Effra Primary School, where Robin Banks was two years above him. 'It was in the heart of Brixton,' Robin recalls. 'It was very multi-ethnic, a lot of the kids were from West Indian families that had just arrived here.'

In *Westway to the World* Paul remembers being surrounded by Jamaican music and hanging out with his mates in and around the Granville Arcade, off Somerleyton Road. Most of his friends were black – an oddly race-conscious observation to make today, perhaps, but in the early 1960s it would have been a highly unusual experience for a white child outside small pockets of London and other big cities that attracted Caribbean workers such as Coventry, Bristol and Liverpool. Paul would grow to love the capital's exuberant, emergent black subculture, which Colin MacInnes wrote about so vividly in *City of Spades* and *Absolute Beginners*. He liked the rhythmic music, the energy, the flashy suits and hats, the food (though it possibly didn't taste that extraordinary: Paul has little sense of smell). Though kids don't naturally discriminate against colour, they aren't insensitive to racial issues. Simonon recalls going to see *Zulu* – the Cy Endfield film of the defence of Rorke's Drift in 1879, when 145 British soldiers held at bay several thousand Zulu warriors – in a theatre full of black faces. 'Very odd,' he says.

Antony enjoyed the cinema and often took his eldest son along to the matinée shows at the Astoria – where Paul would later perform with The Clash when it was the Brixton Academy. Paul's favourites were noisy westerns, the early Bonds – *Dr No, From Russia With Love* – plus, of course, that great English schoolboy staple, war films. By the late 1950s the British war film had entered a new phase. Film-makers were now targeting adults who had grown up during the Second World War and found the whole thing a fantastic adventure – like the boy in John Boorman's *Hope and Glory* – as well as those who'd fought in it.

With the nation's illusion of post-war supremacy dashed at Suez, it also seemed British cinema-goers needed reassurance that the immense sacrifices of the Second World War had been worthwhile. Thus blossomed a rash of stirring colour films – *The Great Escape, 633 Squadron, The Heroes of Telemark, The Guns of Navarone, Operation Crossbow* – with dashing international casts, cartoonish Nazis, extravagant pyrotechnics and magnificent military hardware. They made war look impossibly, and irresponsibly, glamorous. They also made it quite clear the Allies won. Splendid guilty pleasures that they were, they made an indelible mark on audiences – and especially on kids like Joe, Mick and Paul. Central to these movies were old-fashioned values like sacrifice, heroism and victory at all costs, ideas that would seep into The Clash's collective philosophy and vocabulary.

It was Simonon, though, with his artistic eye, who seems to have responded most enthusiastically to these movies' striking martial imagery. It was he who would create The Clash's quasi-military look, and reproduce powerful images of war – German fighter-bombers, rifle targets, camouflage patterning – on the group's stage-backdrops and record sleeves. Guns fascinated him: he was toying with one during the band's first ever interview, has one tattooed on his chest, spent a night in jail for firing one at a pigeon and would even keep a replica of a German machine-pistol in his flat in Oxford Gardens.

But it wasn't until 1966, three years after his parents split up, that Paul discovered the genre that would become his enduring cinematic passion – Spaghetti Westerns, the budget European movies, often with a Mexican emphasis, which were shot in Spain and Italy and achieved international success following Clint Eastwood's iconic performance as The Man With No Name in *A Fistful of Dollars.*

His mother's new partner had won a scholarship to study Italian baroque music in Siena and Rome, and Paul and his brother went with them. Like Joe, Paul experienced the unfamiliar sights and sounds of a foreign culture at a very impressionable age. For Simonon – who, on the surface at least, seemed to have reacted stoically to his parents' divorce – it was an almost surreal trip.

'One minute we were in an inner-London ghetto and the next we were wandering the streets of Siena,' he says. 'I remember telling people at school we were going to Italy and one of my mates said, "Are you going near Cowboyland?" and I said, "I dunno, we probably are . . ." That seemed to be what was important at the time. But what I remember most was hearing all that Spaghetti Western music. My mum said she took me to see the film *Django* while we were there. You'd go to people's houses and there'd be all these bizarre Spaghetti Westerns on TV. That's where my obsession with those films and the music started.'

Being abroad had other benefits. Paul and his brother took advantage of his mother's comparatively lax discipline. 'We refused to go to school, because you had to wear these blue frocks with bows under your chin,' he laughs. 'We'd grown up in Brixton! So we said, "We ain't doing that", and instead we just walked the streets of Siena and Rome. In Siena we were taken on by these teenage Italian girls. The girls were mad about The Beatles, and because my name was Paul it made it more special. We would go round their houses and play with their brothers. We were like their pets.'

Paul was taken to see some of the finest art in the world, and feasted on the work of the Renaissance masters, but the sojourn in the sun didn't last long. In December 1966, the family returned home (Paul turned 11 on the ferry crossing from France), and the boys found themselves back in the drab, rain-soaked streets of south London. Paul was enrolled at William Penn, a typical rough and ready comprehensive school near Crystal Palace. He was at least a term behind in his schooling.

Forever being 'the new boy', as Simonon puts it, making new friends and adapting to different schools, may have attributed to what some people interviewed for this book describe as his 'shyness'. The Clash's road manager Johnny Green believes it's cautiousness. 'I've never thought of Paul as shy,' he says. 'But what I quickly noticed was he liked to weigh people up before he gave away anything of himself. It seemed like a self-preservation mechanism to me. He wanted to check you were cool before he opened up. To some people he never did.'

Without his father's firm hand, Paul became increasingly wayward. In 1969, he became a skinhead. It was a street fashion that had evolved out of Mod, and its sharp imagery – close-cropped hair, Levi's jeans or Sta-Prest, thin red braces – wagged two fingers at the woolly, unkempt, pacific codes of the hippies. Kevin Rowland, singer with 1980s soul band Dexy's Midnight Runners, was a fashion-conscious teenager in north London at the time and embraced the new trend. In *The Look*, Paul Gorman's superb book on postwar British fashion, he gives a fascinating account of the precise adjustments to attitude and wardrobe that led to the emergence of the skinhead: 'It wasn't a numbskull look, as reported in the media, but a sophisticated fashion statement only a few could understand – [based on] middle-aged, conservative and all-American [fashions], the same as astronauts and G.I.s.' Rowland also emphasises that skinheads listened 'exclusively to reggae'.

With Paul's eye for functional, military lines and his love for Jamaican music, skinhead was almost a bespoke culture for him. It held all the attractions that the hippy universe didn't: street suss, cool sounds, a tough image. There was a link, too, between skinheads and Jamaican 'rude boys', who wore suits with shortened trousers and sleeves – exposing the wrists and ankles – wraparound shades and trilby hats. According to the skinhead expert George Marshall, writing in *The Sharper Word*, it was Desmond

Dekker's visit to the UK in 1967 that had popularised the look and helped influence the transition of Mod into skinhead.

On the weekends, while Mick was up the Roundhouse swirling his long hair around, Paul and his pals attended the morning discos at Streatham Locarno, which catered for the schoolboy skins with a diet of ska, rock steady and reggae. Afterwards, there were the inevitable shoplifting sprees. Sometimes Simonon would jump the trains to seaside destinations like Whitstable and Rochester in Kent to take in the sea air and 'do a bit of robbing'.

The skinhead movement quickly became synonymous with casual violence and, somewhat ironically, racism. It should go without saying that Paul had no time for 'Paki-bashing', as it was dubbed. He did, though, find himself caught up in gang fights. 'I quickly found out that being a skinhead didn't stop you being attacked by other skinheads. If you were a Ted and saw another Ted walking down the street it was fine. With skinheads it was wanton violence among gangs. Reggae music was the backdrop to the whole thing. I didn't buy Bluebeat singles, I didn't have a record player. But my mates did. We went to the clubs that played that stuff. It made more sense going to the clubs, because that's how they were hearing the music in Jamaica, on sound systems, rather than on record players. They didn't have electricity over there.'

Having experienced the freedom of a school-free life in Italy, Simonon drifted back into 'hopping off' class. He didn't dislike going to school; like Herman Melville's Bartleby, he simply 'preferred not to'. Besides art and English, he found it a drag. One year, he didn't bother turning up at all in his final term, then enjoyed the statutory ten-week summer holiday. 'A very long break,' he grins. 'That holiday went on for ever.'

In 1970, it was agreed by Simonon's parents that he would be better off living with his father, who was renting a small flat on Faraday Road at the fag end of Portobello Road in Ladbroke Grove, west London. Faraday Road was considered the worst street in the area. As with Brixton, Ladbroke Grove was a once lower-middle-class Victorian neighbourhood whose grand four-storey houses had been subdivided into shabby flats in the years before and after the Second World War. In *Absolute Beginners*, the area is described as the 'residential doss-house of our city'.

It was an attractive prospect for the first wave of West Indian immigrants for exactly the same reasons as Brixton: cheap rooms to rent, close proximity to central London, good amenities, a history of absorbing immigrant communities. By 1953, five years after SS *Empire Windrush* docked, there was already a substantial West Indian community established there; tellingly, the tenant who first discovered the victims of mass-murderer John Christie at 10 Rillington Place, a grimy Victorian house at the back of Ladbroke Grove station, was a newly arrived West Indian immigrant. That was the tone of the place: damp, transient and dark, where grubby rooms hid tawdry, wallpapered-over secrets.

Paul's father ran a book stall on Portobello Market. The place was then, as now, a rowdy farrago of antiques, books, second-hand clothes, fruit and veg, fresh fish and bric-a-brac. It was highly popular with tourists, and the local community of actors and musicians – Julie Christie, Edward Fox, Cat Stevens – who lived in the leafy avenues and crescents of the posh locales that abutted the area: Holland Park and Notting Hill (the backdrop for the Profumo Affair).

Portobello Road was home to hip outlets like I Was Lord Kitchener's Valet, the vintage military clothing store which had sold Jimi Hendrix his famous braided jacket. Powis Square, a few minutes' walk from Faraday Road, was the setting of *Performance*, Nicolas Roeg's film about a London gangster hiding out in hippy Bohemia. It was, in the late 1960s, the most happening place in London.

Paul had gone from one colourful, heavily multi-cultural area to another – and from having a free rein to being a virtual prisoner. His father insisted his son do the household chores – cooking, cleaning and washing – and earn his own pocket money with a double paper-round, one before and one after school. Paul also manned a stall at the top of the market, selling hand-shaped candles that had been created using hot wax and a rubber glove. He relishes the tale of how he doubled the price of the goods when the owner left him in charge one day and trousered an extra £100 or so. 'I remember going back to the flat and looking at all this money,' he says. 'I'd never seen that amount of cash in my life.'

The transition to his father's rigorous, disciplinarian regime would have a profound effect on him, not just because it toughened him up, but because it refocused his mind on his gift as an artist. The room he slept in was his father's studio. 'On the walls were hundreds of postcards and pages torn out of books: Vermeers, Caravaggios, Van Goghs. Like most sons I wanted to do what my father did.' Paul's father would encourage him to copy images into a sketch-pad, refining his lines and foreshortening.

Antony had by this time forsaken Catholicism and joined the Communist Party, and press-ganged Paul into delivering Party literature to the run-down houses around Golborne Road. It was an unusual introduction to politics, which seemed to have had little impact on the fifteen-year-old, who, even in the early days of The Clash, would deadpan that he didn't even know who the prime minister was. In the evenings, Paul was set extra homework; he was only allowed out occasionally, to meet a girlfriend or go to the pictures with his father. If he bunked off school, it was solely to paint. In a perverse way, Paul enjoyed the ascetic regime: it pulled out the best in him. In later years, he'd observe how life with his mother had been 'too soft'. 'Looking back, being with my father made me self-sufficient,' he states. 'It taught me how to boil an egg. It was tough but I needed it. I learned the value of hard work.'

Occasionally, he managed to escape his father's shackles and hang out with his schoolfriends. They'd wander around Tavistock Road and Westbourne Grove, checking out the blues parties where reggae music and marijuana mingled pungently. Paul became part of the local weave, intoxicated by its energy and excitement: the late-nights crowds on the pavement, the gangs clustered around their beat-up motors, the tall, elegant houses with weeds taking root in their sooty, peeling facades, the sound of reggae and dub blaring out of their open windows. 'I'd walk past all these houses with West Indian music playing late at night,' he said in *Westway to the World*, 'and get pulled into parties when I should have been going home. Most of the kids I hung out with were black – I got to the point where I only spoke patois with my mates.'

His school was the Isaac Newton on Wornington Road, an all-boys comprehensive in the shadow of Trellick Tower, the council block that dominates Ladbroke Grove like a gigantic, concrete fortress. Today, Erno Goldfinger's modernist edifice is hailed as a masterpiece of 1960s brutalism and is Grade II listed, but for years it was generally regarded as a thirty-one-storey eyesore and a social and architectural catastrophe. In 1971, Isaac Newton felt the effect of its namesake's famous discovery when sections of Trellick, then still being constructed, were in danger of collapsing on it, leading to the school's temporary closure.

Paul has been accused of creating a romanticised caricature of his 'Dickensian' schooldays; but he was pretty much telling it straight. Anthony Whelan was a pupil at Isaac Newton around the same time as Simonon. His recollections gel with Paul's of an institution that specialised in riot control rather than teaching, and was a universe apart from the public-school pretensions of Joe's – and Mick's – alma maters. 'Isaac Newton was a school for dummies,' he explains. 'That was the general feeling. It was a shit-hole. Seriously. You felt like you were dumped there till you got a job or signed on the dole. There was no discipline. Most of the pupils were black, Irish or

Greek. Very few were [English] white. But there wasn't much racism as I can remember; everyone was in the same boat. No one had anything. I remember the standard of behaviour was appalling. Kids wanking in class, windows being broken, fights in the playground, people setting things on fire. It was something else, though it just seemed normal at the time.'

Rather than being intimidated by the orgy of bad conduct, Paul seemed to enjoy it. His art skills made him popular, and he befriended the toughest kids in his year. As the photographer Don McCullin – who went to a similarly rough school in Finsbury Park – observed, being good at English or History might get you branded as a teacher's pet, but 'drawing was all right'.

Thanks mostly to his father's extra tuition – and help from a sympathetic teacher who 'virtually wrote the answers on the blackboard' – he managed to pass two O-Levels, one of which, not surprisingly, was art. The other was English, for which one of the set texts was Graham Greene's *Brighton Rock*. Its dour English gangsters, Catholic themes (Simonon was brought up a Catholic) and shabby seaside setting enthralled him. Its appeal was enduring: when he checked into hotels in The Clash days, it was under the name of the novel's cut-throat teenage anti-hero, Pinkie Brown.

After leaving Isaac Newton, Simonon concentrated on working up a portfolio to get into art school, while taking seasonal work carrying carpets at the department store John Lewis. Still moving with street trends, he grew his skinhead out into a lank, smoothie style, then an off-the-shoulder 'Budgie' cut – a mode made fashionable by Adam Faith in the 1972 TV series of the same name, in which Faith played a small-time London crook.

In 1973, Paul's hard graft paid off and he won a scholarship to Byam Shaw art school in Campden Street in Notting Hill Gate. Entry was by portfolio rather than via formal qualifications. It was a buzzing place with many overseas students: Lebanese, Italian, Sudanese, Swedish, French, Kenyan. There was a liberal splashing of posh girls, too, including, during Paul's stay there, the future *Thornbirds* actress Rachel Ward, and Clio Goldsmith, niece of Sir James. Paul felt out of place and said later to *NME*'s Chris Salewicz: 'Everybody there is rich. You can . . . nick their paints, nick their canvasses and they don't really miss it.'

Being arty but streetwise was part of Paul's appeal in punk; but it didn't necessarily gel with life at Byam Shaw. His unusual combination of qualities – talented but unpolished, intelligent but not verbal, mischievous and unschooled – was not always appreciated, especially in a country where male creatives were preferred to fit the traditional Kingsley Amis, Bacon, Bailey or Hockney models – tweedy, drunken, cheeky or fey.

His three years there were to prove frustrating. Interviewed for this book, Pete Townshend said this about the influence of art school on the individual members of The Clash: 'What is certain is that they would have been privy to many radical ideas, extreme political and philosophical points of view and probably archly opinionated notions of what was and was not "cool".' Oddly, except for notions of what was 'cool', this didn't appear to be the case for any of them, and particularly Paul.

'Within a year I got completely disillusioned with the whole procedure,' he says. 'So I started mucking around and was told I had to do the Foundation year again. A lot of the teachers were into American abstract art. I was into figurative art. My father had taught me to paint using the traditional methods of Leonardo, with glazes and so on. It's a laborious process that takes two years to do one picture. The other students thought my pictures were great but the teachers used to take the piss out me.'

Paul's last major work before he 'took his grant and vanished' in the spring of 1976 was designed to hit back at his critics for misunderstanding his apparently old-fashioned work: it was a large canvas of a car dump. By that time, though, he'd met another art student who was studying about a mile or so down the road in Shepherds Bush. Mick Jones had little interest in being a serious artist but was determined to be a pop star.

Paul's early interest in rock music was played down in the punk years, no doubt to underline the fact he wasn't an obsessive rock fan like his bandmates. The truth was he liked a bit of early Stones, Kinks, Who and Bowie. He also knew ska and reggae inside out, of course. But as a potential musician he was a non-starter.

When he first encountered Mick, he had no experience of playing an instrument, didn't even own a record player and had just one LP in his collection, *The Eddie Cochran Memorial Album*, which he'd impulsively bought one day from Ted Carroll's influential vinyl stall, Rock On, on Golborne Road. He'd only been to a couple of gigs in his life – one of which was The Sensational Alex Harvey Band at the Hammersmith Odeon earlier in 1975. He had certainly never heard of The New York Dolls.

Nevertheless, on his image alone, Jones and his new manager Bernie Rhodes thought he would be the perfect recruit for their new project when he turned up at their rehearsal room one day in early 1976 chaperoning a mate.

In 1975, the Nashville Rooms in West Kensington was a grimy old Victorian pub. With gummy carpets, grubby upholstery and plenty of Earl's Court low-life propping up the bar, it was straight from the pages of Patrick Hamilton's *Hangover Square*, only with long hair and sideburns. Most evenings, it hosted gigs. On Saturday, 2 August 1975, Mick Jones and Tony James went there to check out a new group from Liverpool called Deaf School.

'I was a middle-class kid from Richmond,' says Tony, who was carrying a copy of Blue Öyster Cult's *Secret Treaties* LP the day he'd first met Jones. 'I'd been down to see The Delinquents rehearse, and hit it off with Mick. At that time, we thought our circle of friends were about the only people in the country who knew about The New York Dolls, The MC5 and The Stooges. It was a terrible time for music and fashion over here. You couldn't even buy Bob Dylan shades, only aviator shades. We used to go to gigs virtually every night to see what was out there.'

The Deaf School gig was to witness one of the most momentous events in British rock 'n' roll history: Mick crashing into future Clash manager Bernie Rhodes. Mick remembers seeing a character at the bar wearing a cap, and approaching him. 'I asked him if he was a piano player,' recalls Mick. 'I was thinking of Gene Vincent and The Blue Caps. He said, "No, but you're wearing one of my T-shirts."'

At the time, Rhodes was printing T-shirts for Malcolm McLaren, owner of the Sex boutique in the Kings Road. The T-shirt that Mick was wearing bore the legend: 'One day you'll wake up and know what side of the bed you've been lying on'. It had two long lists: one hip (Eddie Cochran, Jamaican rude boys, Joe Orton), the other unhip (Mick Jagger, the National Front, The Archers).

'We went to that gig hating everything,' recalls Tony James, who offers a slightly more dramatic account of the fateful evening. 'We were thinking, "We're the only two people in the world who believe there's something else happening out there." Then this little guy comes up to us, in a black cap, wearing the same T-shirt. We said, "Could you stand over there a bit? You're wearing the same T-shirt as us." He said, "Fuck off! I fucking designed this T-shirt, you cunts! What have you got going for you?" So we told him we were forming a group called The London SS. He was interested. It was obviously a suicidal name, but it had attitude. He seemed to be impressed and said, "OK, I'll be your manager."' Rhodes explained he was already working with a band called The Sex Pistols, that they were being nurtured and were going to be really big. The various scattered particles of what would become punk were suddenly drawing together.

At this time, The London SS still hadn't a settled line-up. It was merely an idea: raw garage punk dressed up in Nazi chic. The object was to be shocking musically and visually. In July 1975, Mick and Tony had placed an ad in the *Melody Maker* which read: 'Lead guitarist and drums to join bass-player and guitarist/singer, influenced by Stones, NY Dolls, Mott, etc. Must have great rock 'n' roll image.' This led to a guitarist called Brian James getting in touch: visually and musically he seemed just the ticket and was given the thumbs up, but first he had to extricate himself from an MC5-inspired band he was playing with in Belgium called Bastard.

Meanwhile, Mick and Tony shopped around for other musicians. For a short while, possibly just one rehearsal, a version of The London SS existed featuring Mick, Tony, guitarist Matt Dangerfield, former Hollywood Brats singer Andrew Matheson and keyboardist Casino Steel, plus Mick's fellow victim of the Little Queenie putsch, Geir Waade. The group grew out of jamming sessions at Dangerfield's squat at 47a Warrington Crescent, near Mick's gran's flat.

Robin Banks, who had recently been released from jail, recalls, 'There was a gang fight in a Wimpy Bar in Paddington. There was a bit of trouble because of what [the group] were wearing. I got stabbed in the neck with a plastic spoon.'

In October, Mick and Tony responded to a 'musician wanted' advert in *Melody Maker,* which had the temerity to mention their sacred 'Johnny Thunders'. They were curious to find out who'd placed it. It turned out that it was The Sex Pistols, whom they'd yet to meet. Meanwhile, Malcolm McLaren, the group's manager, was looking to manage more acts. A couple of weeks later, Matheson and Steel arranged to meet him at the Pistols' rehearsal place in Denmark Street. Mick and Tony tagged along.

'I remember a bunch of guys with hair down their backs,' says Pistols bassist Glen Matlock. 'They looked ridiculous. We were all laughing. One of them [Mick], instead of going upstairs, picked up a guitar and started jamming with us and it would have worked except for the hair. Later we tried to contact him, without Bernie knowing, but at the address we had there was just this Norwegian guy who would only speak to us through the letterbox.'

Behold one of the great, tantalising 'what ifs' of rock 'n' roll – though perhaps The Pistols were too far ahead of their time even for Mick. To him, their hacked-off hair and closely shaved faces looked as startling and offensive as 'the raw epidermis' on the face of George Carmody, the detestably square character in Malcolm Bradbury's satire of 1970s college life, *The History Man.*

Tony James: 'We went down to Denmark Street and there were these guys there with really short hair. It was quite a shock. We thought The Dolls were revolutionary because they had long hair. We didn't realise that short hair could be used as a reaction to the excesses of rock 'n' roll.'

During that autumn, Rhodes's involvement in The London SS became more intense. 'Once Bernie was on board I started getting The Phone Calls,' says Tony. 'Bernie introduced me to this whole world, and in retrospect it was a terrific education. His whole managerial stance was, "You know nothing. You haven't got one original idea. If you want to be another New York Dolls you're wasting my time. You haven't made one statement that means anything." To us, this was Chinese. He was saying that we didn't have anything to say, and we clearly didn't. It was all that "I love you, babe", regular kind of stuff.'

Little did Jones and James realise that Rhodes was on a serious mission. His relationship with McLaren had become strained since the latter had returned from the US, where he'd been nannying none other than The New York Dolls through their dead-cat bounce. (The title of The Dolls' second album, *Too Much Too Soon*, famously said it all.) In Malcolm's absence, Bernie had recruited Johnny Rotten to the fledgling Pistols, thus creating the line-up that would trail-blaze punk rock less than a year later. But now Malcolm was back, he had re-appropriated his charges. This left Bernie with an axe to grind and a barely disguised hunger to construct a rival to The Pistols.

His preferred method of management was hectoring and probing, to promote a state of perpetual self-questioning. 'Bernie would phone me up at my suburban house in Twickenham,' smiles Tony. 'He'd say, "You guys are wasting my time! Have you read any Sartre? Go down the library and get some. I tell ya what, I'll give you a list." And so I went down the library and got out all these books on modern art, Dadaism. And it taught me something really important: that we had to have a bigger idea. This was Bernie's taunt to us. He'd ring me up at home and terrorise me, and I'd want to weep afterwards . . . He'd say, "The trouble with you, James, is that you're too fucking safe. What I want you to do is to tell your parents that you're not gonna spend Christmas with them, you're gonna spend it with hookers in Praed Street. And buy a copy of *Gay News* and *Spare Rib* from your local corner shop."'

In November 1975, Mick, Tony and the recently returned Brian James badgered Bernie for an HQ where they could audition the respondents to their ads in the music press for a 'young Stooge' vocalist and 'skinny psychopath' drummer. Rhodes found them a basement under a workmen's café, the Paddington Kitchen, on Praed Street (the entrance was off Norfolk

Mews; today it's a Korean restaurant). He turned up with some speakers and microphones, which, it transpired, The Pistols' Steve Jones had stolen from a David Bowie concert. Mick put up a Holocaust film poster. The ghost of Sir Alexander Fleming, who discovered the medicinal properties of penicillin in the building opposite, looked on curiously.

'We put all our records on the jukebox in the caff upstairs,' explains Mick. 'That's where we used to meet people and sort of vet them. It was like our own little flat, you know what I mean? If they passed the vetting process we used to take them round the back to the rehearsal room. We saw all the main players.'

The auditions that took place from early November 1975 to January 1976 have become legendary; many musicians who would later make a name in punk descended to the basement, including Rat Scabies, Keith Levene, Topper Headon, Terry Chimes. They jammed tunes from Lenny Kaye's legendary *Nuggets* compilation, plus the Flamin' Groovies' 'Slow Death', MC5's 'Sister Anne', The Beatles' 'Bad Boy' and The Dolls' 'Personality Crisis'. There were also a couple of Mick originals, 'Protex Blue' and 'Ooh Baby Ooh', and a Tony and Brian composition 'Portobello Reds' (which later re-surfaced as 'Fish' on The Damned's first album.) None of the applicants fitted the bill or wanted to join.

Nick Headon, soon to become better known to the world as 'Topper', tried out on drums at the time. 'I probably looked a right state – I had really long hair and an afghan coat,' he recalls. 'My feet are so small I used to wear women's shoes, green platforms. Mick was going, "Hit the drums like [The New York Dolls'] Jerry Nolan!" I got on well with Mick straight away, we respected each other's abilities. But I wanted to earn £25 a week and play something I was familiar with, so after a couple of rehearsals I did a runner and went off to do a soul tour.' There was even an applicant from several hundred miles away. 'We got a letter from this bloke in Manchester called Morrissey,' laughs Tony. 'We thought he couldn't possibly know anything about rock 'n' roll coming from the north. So we chucked it in the bin.'

Bernie, who had a Jewish background (as did Mick), challenged the group's decision to call themselves The London SS. The name, thought up months earlier by John Brown, Geir Waade and Mick, was contrived as a terror tactic to outrage the pre-rock 'n' roll generation who'd faced Hitler and heard in real time Richard Dimbleby's harrowing radio broadcast of Belsen's liberation in 1945. In the 1970s, Nazism was the prevalent subject in music, art, film, literature. Nazis appeared on TV screens almost daily in numerous war movies, the highly popular series *The World at War* and the situation drama *Colditz*.

'The Blue Öyster Cult always had that [Nazi] imagery and that was what we liked at that time,' explains Tony. 'Films like *The Night Porter, The Damned, Cabaret* – it was all big. One night we were asked to meet Bernie at the Bull and Bush pub on Shepherds Bush Green. It was a really heavy pub and very crowded. Bernie took out this bag full of SS paraphernalia – swastikas, daggers, all this stuff. He emptied it out on the table and said, "So what do you think of it?" We kind of looked at each other and said to Bernie, "Erm, can we go somewhere else to discuss this?" And he said, "If you call yourselves The London SS this is what you'll have to deal with."'

In January 1976, a drummer called Roland Hot was auditioned at the Paddington Kitchen. With him for moral support was his friend Paul Simonon. Mick immediately saw that Paul had rock star potential: tall, blond, cool, cinematic looks. Sadly, he had no musical talent whatsoever.

Simonon: 'The first time I met Mick Jones was in the basement with The London SS. All I could see was hair. I don't think I even saw his face. He said, "Sing 'Roadrunner'." I said, "What's that?" [Jonathan Richman's calling card was only available on bootleg at that time.] It was a bit of a disaster. There was this bloke in the corner, and I said, "Are you the manager?" And his immediate retort was, "What's it to you?" And I thought, "Well, that's fair enough . . ."'

Roland Hot hung around for a few days, and played on a recording of the group rehearsing (Tony James unexpectedly unearthed the tape in Summer 2005). Meanwhile, Paul disappeared back into the fabric of Notting Hill.

At Praed Street, Bernie's educational methods were seemingly beginning to yield results. 'We started to get the idea, bit by bit,' says Tony. 'I was in the café one day and I said to Bernie, "I've got this idea for a song called 'Rockets For Sale', about selling nuclear warheads in Selfridges." He said, "Wow. That's a good idea. I like that." Then he said, "Have you ever thought about writing a song about, I dunno, anarchy?" He gave us a correspondence course in the university of rock 'n' roll. Whether he got it second-hand from Malcolm, I really don't know.'

The search for suitable candidates for the group continued. 'Every night we'd go to the Red Cow, the Golden Lion, the Windsor Castle, Imperial College, the University of London,' says Mick, wearily. One person attracted their eye, but he was already taken. 'There was this group called The 101'ers,' says Tony. 'They used to play at the Windsor Castle on Harrow Road, which was about 200 yards from Mick's tower block. We'd watch them from the back of the hall, thinking, "Damn! They look so shit." They played this dreary pub rock. But there was something that drew us to see them – this guy Joe Strummer scrubbing on his Telecaster. But they all looked like garage mechanics to us.'

In early 1976, Bernie asked Malcolm McLaren along to watch The London SS rehearse. By this time, The Pistols had played their first gig, and were starting to create a small but fiercely electric buzz. McLaren's verdict on Mick's group was: they ain't happening. After that, Brian James and Rat Scabies went off to start The Damned and The London SS fizzled out – but not before Bernie gave one last tutorial.

'Mick and I so desperately wanted to get into the world of rock 'n' roll,' says Tony. 'So one day we got into Bernie's Renault 5 and he said, "I'm gonna show you something." We drove to Hamilton Terrace [in upmarket St John's Wood] where there was obviously this fabulous society party going on. And there were loads of famous people, rock stars getting out of cars. Bernie said, "I know the bloke who's having that party, and I could get you in. But you know what? You ain't ready yet."'

A few weeks later, Mick was walking down Portobello Road and bumped into a familiar face: Paul Simonon. He mentioned the meeting to Bernie who remembered the guy with the blond hair and gap-toothed grin, who'd mauled 'Roadrunner' with his croaky south London monotone. He told him: 'Forget Tony James, start a band with that bloke.'

In September 1974, Woody Mellor's group The 101'ers played their debut gig – a support slot for south London reggae band Matumbi at the Telegraph pub in Brixton. The group had been formed that summer by Woody and his new housemates, after Woody had grown exasperated with trying to eke a living busking on the underground with Tymon Dogg. Fired by his baptism into rock 'n' roll with The Vultures in Newport, he now 'wanted to do something electric'. The group's squat at 101 Walterton Road was on a wide avenue of large houses in Maida Hill, north of Westbourne Grove: the two locales were bisected by the Westway, which Mick's tower block overlooked. 'There were rows and rows of buildings boarded up,' Joe recalled in 1999. 'The only way you could start a group was to live in one, because we were penniless. We started The 101'ers with one amplifier and one speaker.'

The area around Walterton Road was full of squatted properties; mostly they were local authority houses that had been emptied while awaiting rede-velopment. The squatters ingeniously diverted free water and power from the mains supplies. In the winter of 1973, the squatting community had protested against the London Electricity Board, which, under pressure from the Greater London Council, was threatening to shut off power to the area. A group of demonstrators occupied the LEB offices in Kensington Gardens, which ended up in a vicious punch-up with the police.

It has been argued that squatting is an intrinsically political act: it involves illegally occupying someone else's property. It's conspicuously anti-capital-ist. The whole of squatting culture chimed with the anarcho-leftist flavour of the early 1970s underground scene, promoted and supported by publications such as the *International Times* and *Oz*. But for the inhabitants of 101 Walterton, there was little if no political dimension to their occupancy, nor much hippy idealism for that matter.

'The communal living thing – the utopian view, if you like – wasn't our thing at all,' explains Richard Nother, alias Dudanski, who played drums in the group and had befriended Woody via his brother, Pat. 'Ours was a musi-cians' house. Other houses were wino places, some were junkie dens; it was a very diverse area. The only thing that brought people together was they were having hassles with the LEB or the GLC. There were a lot of musicians, Irish people, South Americans, Spanish. Any young person landing in London wanting somewhere to live for free headed there.'

Joe recalled: 'There was a bunch of junkies living one side of us and some alcoholics, like the ones who spend their days in the local park, on the other. Someone walking past tried to chop me to pieces with a hatchet once when I was opening the front door.'

John Tiberi, who'd later work with The 101'ers, remembers the unique vibe of the community. 'There was a Free Shop, where things were free!' he laughs. 'It got really fucked up. Then there was That Tea Shop [the hang-out run by Woody's old flatmates Dave and Gail Goodall] – that kind of thing worked and was good. But there was also a down side to it: lots of chaos and moving. People fucked up on drugs. But there was a great striving for soli-darity and all in all it was quite organised.'

The 101'ers' live debut at the Telegraph was in aid of the Chile Solidarity Campaign, to raise money for the victims of General Pinochet's CIA-backed coup in Santiago, which had deposed probably the world's first-ever democratically elected Marxist government. The gig was secured by the group's Chilean saxophonist Alvaro, one of two Chileans living at 101. Once again, Joe was being exposed to new cultures and learning about international issues; six years later, he would work the events in Santiago into The Clash's 'Washington Bullets'. The Telegraph gig saw The 101'ers perform ramshackle versions of R&B chestnuts like Chuck Berry's 'Roll Over Beethoven' and Larry Williams' 'Bonie Maronie', plus Them's striding rocker 'Gloria'.

'I'd never played a gig before,' recalls Dudanski. 'And Woody's playing was so primitive we thought he'd only just picked up a guitar. Matumbi were great; they'd had problems with their van and turned up late, and when they arrived, they let us use their drum kit and amps. We enjoyed ourselves. We brought down a few mates from north of the river who gave us a big cheer. It was enough to get me interested . . . something there had germinated.'

Woody was jazzed to be back on stage, and playing with like-minded souls. They, in turn, were taken with this new addition to their circle, who'd been wowing them with his gentle, endearing craziness throughout the summer. 'He was a gas!' laughs Dudanski. 'He was a lovely bloke: good fun to be with, a good laugh. Kind-hearted, open . . . There was a quiet side to him, too. There is a part of most people you can't know, I suppose, but to me he was always a very gregarious bloke, always willing to talk to anyone.'

For the next few months, the group drifted through various line-ups and gigs. Joe took work as a gardener in Hyde Park and a janitor at the English National Opera in St Martin's Lane, where he quickly got the boot. With his pay-off he bought a Vox AC30 amp. By early 1975, mostly due to Woody's enthusiasm, The 101'ers started to shape up. The line-up coalesced around Alvaro (sax, vocals), Woody Mellor (vocals, guitar), Simon Cassell (sax), former Ash Grove resident Clive Timperly (guitar), Marwood 'Mole' Chesterton (bass), Jules Yewdall (vocals, maracas) and Richard Dudanski (drums). Every Wednesday, they played a gig at their own 'club night' in the upstairs room at the Chippenham pub, a few doors away from 101. Tymon Dogg, who occasionally sat in on rehearsals, recalls they wheeled their gear there in a stolen pram.

The Charlie Pigdog club – named after the group's psychotic mongrel – had a warm, friendly, hippy vibe, where people brought their own sandwiches, rolled spliffs and danced to The 101'ers' raw rock 'n' roll. 'Having the club was great,' says Dudanski. 'For any rock 'n' roll band you need to have that regular punter reaction. It started out as a place for mates, then it soon attracted people from all over the place. Things started to get a bit heavier then. There was always the SPG [the Special Patrol Group] waiting around outside to beat people up. But playing every week for two or three months was just right for getting the thing together.'

That spring, Woody underwent another transformation. The previous summer, on his return from Europe, he and Tymon had seen Canvey Island pub rockers Dr Feelgood play at the Windsor Castle. The electrifying stage-act of their guitarist, Wilko Johnson, who strutted and jerked like a possessed rooster, Fender Telecaster in hand, had hypnotised Woody: he was deeply impressed. At Charlie Pigdog, Woody worked up his own performing style: the juddering 'electric leg'; the head looking sideways; the thrashing right hand; the Elvis sneer; the slobbering delivery; the crazed look in the eye.

He also invested in a new Telecaster – which would survive The Clash and Mescaleros, and take poignant centre stage at his funeral in 2002. The means by which he acquired the instrument trumped Mick's off-loading of his sci-fi comics: it was paid for with the £100 Woody received for marrying a South African woman who wanted British citizenship. One can assume that Ronald and Anna Mellor were not invited.

Perhaps feeling a little out of kilter with this mad Englishman vying for the spotlight, Alvaro quit. That meant Woody was one singer closer to being The 101'ers' sole frontman.

That spring, along with his new stage persona came two other important acquisitions. The first was a Spanish girlfriend, Paloma, the sister of Richard Dudanski's future wife, Esperanza. 'It was the beginning of Joe's love affair with Spain,' says Richard. 'It was then he first got in touch with the culture of Flamenco, the poetry of Lorca, the spirit of the Spanish people, if you like.' The second was the name by which most of the world would soon know him. 'I could only play six strings or none at all,' Joe explained. 'That's why I called myself Joe Strummer.' The change of identity was part of a wider re-branding of The 101'ers' members, involving Richard (now 'Snakehips Dudanski'), Clive Timperley ('Evil C' – Clive backwards) and Simon Cassell ('Big John'). Paloma became 'Palm Olive'. Dudanski stresses that the whole thing was an in-band joke, but concedes it was symbolic: 'Joe was always conscious of rock 'n' roll mythology. I think he was getting it quite clear to himself that he wanted to be a successful frontman in a successful rock 'n' roll band. And there's no question that coincided with his calling himself Joe Strummer.'

The name-change was, in that sense, like his appropriation of 'Woody'; a handle for his aspirations. This time, he was hellbent on becoming a musical

Everyman, the people's troubadour, a greasy rock 'n' roll street poet. But there was no essential change in his ideology or personality. Joe's dramatic reinvention to authenticate his punk persona would come later.

In July 1975, The 101'ers got a small significant break, courtesy of one of Joe's old mates from Newport who was now working for *Melody Maker*. Allan Jones (not to be confused with Jiving Al Jones), who'd tipped the group in his column earlier in the year, wrote a short but spirited feature on the band. In it, he recalled one of the Charlie Pigdog gigs he'd witnessed. The scene he pictured was heavily romanticised, if not completely fanciful, with gypsies and Irish battling it out, punters getting razored and bottled, and the night closing with the cops storming in. Allan was a writer and, even if it didn't happen like that, perhaps that's what it *felt* like in the later, rowdier days of the club. He also described the group's twenty-minute version of 'Gloria' as 'the perfect soundtrack for the last apocalyptic days of the Third Reich'.

Once Charlie Pigdog had shut down in April 1975, the *Melody Maker* feature enabled The 101'ers to find gigs further afield. The group were already playing regularly at the Elgin pub on Ladbroke Grove, firing up crowds with a selection of raucous 1960s pop and R&B. In the coming months they'd sharpen up a repertoire ranging from 1960s Stones and Small Faces hits, to vintage rockers from Chuck Berry, Bo Diddley, Eddie Cochran and Little Richard. The set was seasoned with a connoisseur's grab-bag of oldies culled from budget compilations, including James Wayne's version of the New Orleans standard 'Junco Partner' and bandleader Johnny Otis's 'Willie and the Hand Jive'. In the photographs Jules Yewdall took that year, collected in his book *Joe Strummer With The 101'ers and The Clash 1974–76*, Joe looks magnificent: a full-on 'greaser', with black shirt, straight jeans, long quiff and huge mutton-chop sideburns.

Joe Strummer, The Performer, was growing ever more forceful. 'Being on stage empowered him to be this different character,' recalls Dudanski. 'Pouring beer over people, confronting hecklers. At one gig someone was shouting for "Route 66" all night, which we'd dropped from our set, so Joe said, "You fucking cunt, what you saying?" and went over to sort him out. He became this powerful frontman.'

By this time, Joe, Richard and Joe's old pal from Newport, Micky Foote, had moved out of 101 Walterton into a squat in St Luke's Road off Westbourne Park Road. Practical and resourceful, Foote was now organising the group's transport and equipment, and manning the mixing desk at gigs. 'Joe was fucking good at what he did,' says Micky. 'It was in a completely different league to the group in Wales. He was developing the style he took into The Clash.'

In the summer of 1975, the music press started to identify a new trend in London's smaller venues of which The 101'ers were ostensibly a part. It involved twenty-something musicians blasting out edgy R&B in packed saloon bars. It was dubbed 'pub rock' for obvious reasons. On the face of it, it was pure nostalgia for the gritty, primitive energy of 1950s rock 'n' roll, a hard, fast, sweaty antidote to the dominant musical styles of the era: the soft Californian rock of The Eagles and America; the archness of glam pop; the complex conceptual works of Pink Floyd and The Who; the bombastic, symphonic rock of ELO and Queen. But there was something else to it, too: a feeling of desperation and a primitive desire to thrill that foreshadowed punk.

The 101'ers, however, never felt they were part of the pub rock scene (if indeed any of the groups did). 'There was no question of us wanting to be The Feelgoods,' explains Dudanski. 'They were a parallel thing, a high-energy outfit. The Count Bishops, Eddie and the Hot Rods, we were all doing a similar thing – playing fast R&B. We felt really apart from it, actually. Chilli Willi and the Red Hot Peppers and Ducks Deluxe, they were proper musicians. We felt like the poor family relations.'

Roger Armstrong, who ran the Rock On vinyl stall with Ted Carroll, saw the group perform around this time. 'They weren't really big then, just a few bits in the music press,' he explains. 'I met an old friend from college at the Elgin and they were playing in the background. I remember thinking, "Hmm, kind of an odd band." They used to have people sit in and that night they had a trumpet player, a soul trumpet player with a rock band. They weren't afraid to use – how shall I say? – non-musicians, even though the core band were very good players.

'I used to think it was terrible that pub rock took on such a negative connotation,' he continues, 'because it hides the fact that there was a lot of good bands making very, very good music during that period. It carried the flag for some real, street-level rock 'n' roll. And don't forget, in those days rock 'n' roll in many people's eyes was those faux, dressed-up poppy bands like Mud or Showaddywaddy. Pub rock's influence on punk has been vastly underrated.'

As the year progressed, The 101'ers' reputation as a thrilling live experience spread. In August, the *NME* ran a live review by Chas De Whalley, who praised their rock 'n' roll spirit while drawing attention to their lack of musical finesse. As Tony James noted, he and Mick went to see them a couple of times at the Windsor Castle pub on the Harrow Road. It's even possible Paul heard them in Elgin as he wandered down Ladbroke Grove. Who knows? By the end of the year, they were playing two or three times a week in pubs in north and west London, including the Elgin, Red Cow, Nashville Rooms and Hope and Anchor, plus various college and out-of-town gigs.

Slowly, their set was swelled with originals, mostly from Joe's pen, though the democratic nature in which the songs were worked up in rehearsals meant they were credited as group compositions. Mostly, the tunes were fairly standard rockin' fare, with an American, cars 'n' girls feel: 'Letsagetabitarockin', 'Motor Boys Motor', 'Steam-gauge '99'. Another composition, 'Sweety of the St Moritz', detailed the experience of a two-night stand at the Soho club of the same name in June.

In November, Joe went to see Bruce Springsteen at the Hammersmith Odeon: he was pleased to see another Telecaster-toting singer extolling the virtues of motoring and females. Around the same time, The 101'ers – now slimmed down to Joe, Evil C, Mole and Dudanski, plus new guitarist Dan Kelleher – recorded a demo session with The Feelgoods' producer Vic Maile in his Rickmansworth studio. Joe and Richard, excited to be in a proper recording studio for the first time, were pleased with the result; but it was generally felt that Mole was holding the group back and he was sacked in January 1976. His departure may have been hastened by The 101'ers' signing to the London booking agent, Albion (home to The Stranglers), at the end of the previous year. 'Mole was constantly having depressions and getting aggressive,' says Micky Foote. 'He had definite mental health problems; it's been well documented.' He died in 1999.

'When you start off and have only been together a week, playing Chuck Berry songs is what you do,' says Dudanski. 'But we soon started introducing our own songs and getting an agent to arrange our gigs. It went from a loose thing to a tight ship. When we got rid of Mole it radically changed us. It was the beginning of the end, actually.'

Though there was sadness concerning Mole's exit (the saddest person of all being Mole himself), the change initially seemed for the best. To signal a new beginning, Joe went out and bought a huge brown zoot suit, which, on Strummer's instruction, Micky Foote dry-cleaned between gigs. Dan Kelleher moved to bass. Ironically, it was at one of Mole's last gigs, at Dingwalls on 7 January 1976, that The 101'ers had caught the attention of Ted Carroll, who'd started the independent Chiswick label the previous year. So far it had just two releases on its books, an EP by The Count Bishops and a reissue of Vince Taylor and his Playboys' 1959 rocker 'Brand New

Cadillac' – a song that The Clash would in due course make their own. Ted was on the look out for a third.

Roger Armstrong: 'Ted said, "You've gotta see this band, the lead singer's a fucking star! He's amazing!" I said I'd seen them before. So a couple of nights later we went down to this college bar [Imperial College in South Kensington]. It was a typical student place with long-haired people standing around drinking. There was no stage, the group were just on the floor in the corner and I'll never forget it. Ted and me were just standing, like, six feet away from Joe. There was the two of us and maybe six other people, and Joe's playing like it's the biggest gig of his life. I mean it's this full-on passion going on, and he was wearing a fantastic suit. It was one of those suits like Little Richard's, with a life of its own. He just looked incredible, with that stomping foot and hammering guitar. I thought, "Fuck! That guy's astonishing. I mean, to be doing this in front of six interested people and twenty-five disinterested people in a student bar . . . If he can do this, what'll he be like if he ever gets famous?"'

Carroll and Armstrong approached Joe after the gig and sounded him out about a possible single. In a *Melody Maker* 101'ers retrospective in 1981, Joe told Paolo Hewitt: '[They] said, "Do you want to make a record?" So we said, "Yeah!"' A couple of sessions were booked for March at the tiny eight-track Pathway Studios in Archway, with Armstrong at the controls. It was here Roger witnessed an early version of Strummer's 'Spliff Bunker', to which he'd retreat to write lyrics in his later Clash days.

'Joe was very shy,' recalls Roger. 'We were overlaying the vocals in the studio, which was tiny – about 16 feet square – packed full of bits of equipment, and I lost him. Eventually, I found him huddled writing something behind the amplifier. There was the amplifier and a little bit of space and two baffles either side of him, and he was in there working on a lyric. Finally, he came out, but you knew you weren't gonna get a [practice] run-through with Joe. I mean, you might get him to sing a bit to nail some levels, but after that you knew you had to get it down fast. 'The band were very good,' he adds. 'It wasn't kind of take after take after take with them. They got the stuff down quick. And Joe was very good. He was a man of passion and that's what you got: his passionate vocal on the tape.'

The song that emerged from the sessions as a potential A-side was a Joe composition, 'Keys To Your Heart'. A brisk, bouncy rocker, it was a love song with a dark, confessional twist ('I used to be a teenage drug taker') and a middle section that breaks down into an ad-libbed rap before building up to a stomping finale. There had also been a reference to being 'drugged up' in

'Crummy Bum Blues', Joe's songwriting debut from his Newport days. It's tempting to think of Joe's ruminations on substance abuse as evidence of dark habits, but it seems much more likely he was simply toying with drug imagery, to mimic inspirations such as Dylan and John Lennon. As with his previous desire to be 'a cat burglar', his lyrics were already blurring the reality of what Joe was experiencing and the imaginary, more dangerous worlds of the character he invented to narrate his songs. Dudanski confirms that The 101'ers were strictly spliffers: 'At one gig someone came up to us and did the nudge-nudge thing,' he laughs. 'We played so fast he thought we were on speed. We couldn't afford speed, let alone all play a whole gig on it.'

After so little interest for so long, suddenly, it appears, there was a queue of people wanting to record the band. The son of a Kensington art dealer, John Tiberi saw the group in early 1976. Urbane and well connected, Tiberi put them in touch with his friend Simon Jeffes of the Penguin Café Orchestra. 'I was squatting in a house just the other side of Bayswater Road,' explains Tiberi, who was christened 'Boogie' by Joe. (Tiberi smoked Winston cigarettes; John Lennon called himself 'Dr Winston O'Boogie'.) 'I'd heard of The 101'ers, then went to see them. I loved the kind of deep instinct they had for rock 'n' roll. Woody, he had that thing he never lost, with the Telecaster chopping away. The first thing I thought was, "You ought to make a record." So I went up to Strummer and said, "What about it?" I hooked up with the band as producer. The group were based around Joe, but they were just a bit amateur. They were aware of the situation. Mole was kicked out. Dan Kelleher came in and he wrote a couple of songs, but they weren't really R&B. There was a little bit of confusion about their direction. I was intrigued by it at the time. [A less R&B direction] seemed a way to go. They had a song called 'Sweety of the St Moritz', about the guy who ran that club in Wardour Street. That kind of songwriting was quite seductive.'

Clearly keeping their options open, The 101'ers recorded a session with Simon Jeffes at the BBC radio studios in Maida Vale, which the group considered superior to the Chiswick material. This led to a heated debate over whether the Chiswick material was strong enough to issue as a single.

Meanwhile, events in the bigger world were about to set The 101'ers spinning off course. On 3 and 23 April 1976, the group were booked to play the Nashville Rooms, with an up-and-coming London group as support: The Sex Pistols. Joe knew about this group from Neil Spencer's review in the *NME* of their gig supporting Eddie and the Hot Rods at the Marquee a few weeks earlier; that night they'd trashed the headliners' gear and famously proclaimed, 'We're not into music . . . we're into chaos.' The Pistols already carried with them a threat of danger. Younger than the pub rock bands, and plugged into the extremes of subterranean boutique fashion via their connection with McLaren, they were making people feel uneasy.

Joe watched the group arrive at the soundcheck with their entourage: young kids, fashionable, outrageous, visually confrontational – a profusion of mohair sweaters, shades, sex-shop couture and smoggy, working-class London accents. Sid Vicious was wearing an Elvis-style gold lamé jacket he'd bought in Kensington Market. Joe overheard McLaren discussing stage-wear with the group. He was fascinated with the entrepreneurial manager-group dynamic; it was almost like a backstage confab of ten years earlier between Andrew Oldham and The Stones, or Chas Chandler and Hendrix.

Dudanski wasn't so impressed. 'What I really remember was that McLaren ruled the roost,' he says, and adopts a whiny north London accent. '"Do this, Do that!" I didn't like the McLaren angle. It was a very manipulative situation from the start. If you were sixteen you would think, "Yeah, great!" but I thought we had something going ourselves. I suppose it was easy to be cynical about what The Pistols were doing. The Bromley Contingent were a bit posy; John Lydon was being a nasty snot-rag.

'The first night the sound was awful but the second time it was really good and you could hear Steve Jones's guitar,' he adds. 'To an extent it was a Saul on the road to Damascus conversion for Joe. We'd be talking about this since we started – "Something has to happen, it can't carry on like this" – the idea of there being a rejuvenation. It was now obvious something *was* happening.'

The second gig was attended by Mick Jones, Tony James, Paul Simonon, Keith Levene and numerous other future punk stars. The Pistols' circle also included fabulous and exotic characters like Nils Stevenson, a dashing Kings Road miscreant who worked for Richard Buckle, the *Sunday Times* ballet critic, and Malcolm's partner Vivienne Westwood, who designed the clothes for his shop. Several songs into the set, which was thin and lacklustre, Vivienne got into a fight with the girl next to her. The girl's boyfriend thumped Vivienne in retaliation. McLaren flew across the front of the stage, fists flying, before Lydon abandoned the mic and jumped into the mêlée. This sudden explosion of violence electrified the room.

The 101'ers looked on agape. Vivienne wasn't a pub drunk throwing a few wild haymakers after one too many. This fight had got a reaction. Musically, there wasn't that much separating The 101'ers from The Pistols, but ideologically they were from different planets. The former were worthy and retro; the latter violent, nihilistic, elitist, arrogant, revelled in negativity and clearly *were* on speed. Joe's pièce de résistance was 'Keys To Your Heart', an up-tempo, bittersweet love song; Lydon whined sardonically about having no feelings for anyone except his beautiful self. The Pistols and their followers were glamorous, dangerous street-trash, the disturbing Droogs from *A Clockwork Orange* plugged into amplifiers.

The previous November, an *NME* piece on pub rock had categorised The 101'ers as the 'young-ish' bucks of a new, exciting scene. Suddenly, Joe was confronted with the realisation they were the old men of an arthritic cause. 'After I saw The Sex Pistols I realised we were yesterday's papers,' was his dramatic verdict.

'Joe told me that when he first saw The Pistols it was the opposite of what entertainment had always been about,' says Bob Gruen, the American rock photographer. 'Before, bands wanted to please their audiences, but The Pistols didn't give a shit whether anyone liked them or not. They even looked as if they'd felt they'd achieved something if you didn't like them. It was a whole different way of thinking.'

The realisation may have been instant for Joe but the decision to do something about it took longer. The 101'ers were on the verge of putting out a record, the culmination of nearly two years' hard slog. It wasn't clear either where Joe might fit into a group like The Pistols anyhow. He was older and from a radically different culture. While he computed the impact of the Nashville gigs, his group continued playing. These gigs saw Joe do exactly what so many other pub rock musicians would do after punk went overground in 1977: he Johnny Rotten-ed up his act.

'He subtly changed,' recalls Dudanski. 'He got more belligerent in a way I didn't like so much. It was more of a snarl, which wasn't his natural pose. But that was purely to do with his performances; it didn't seep into his social life with The 101-ers.'

Another sign of Joe's unrest was a hardening line towards his new name: calling him Woody was now strictly verboten. Jiving Al Jones, who hadn't seen Joe since Newport, turned up at a gig a few weeks later at the Red Cow in Hammersmith. 'I felt a little bit, sort of, uneasy with him,' he says. 'I felt he'd changed personality rather. He'd snap back at you, "Don't call me Woody, my name's Joe." I was finding that a bit weird, the fact that he'd now christened himself Joe. There was a certain amount of, not aggression, but intent about that: Do not call me Woody 'cos I'll bite your fucking head off.

'When I saw him perform I was completely blown away. This was a completely different man from the person I had known. He was much happier and much more excitable, he'd obviously found a groove. Something had changed, he'd found something, this was like a man who had found something in his life.'

In the audience at the Red Cow that night were the fledgling Clash – Mick, Paul and guitarist Keith Levene. They'd come to figure out whether or not Joe Strummer might after all be the elusive singer they'd been searching for.

4
FROM RUSSIA WITH LOVE

'What are they gonna say when he's gone? . . . That he was a *kind* man, he was a *wise* man, he had *plans*, he had *wisdom? Bullshit*, man!'

Dennis Hopper's photojournalist on Colonel Kurtz, *Apocalypse Now*

'Looking inside Rodchenko's copy of Ten Years of Uzbekistan was like opening the door onto the scene of a terrible crime.'
DAVID KING, THE COMMISSAR VANISHES

Debates about the greatest managers in rock often throw up the same three names: Colonel Tom Parker (Elvis), Brian Epstein (The Beatles) and Peter Grant (Led Zeppelin). Each represents a different phase in the development of post-war music – rock 'n' roll, pop and rock – and a particular way of doing business. The Colonel was the carnie huckster with a fat cigar who sold Elvis to the world as a good-lookin' piece of wholesome American beef. Brian Epstein was the dapper theatrical who cultivated The Beatles, then lost them millions in merchandising revenue. Peter Grant was the bearded giant who threatened to break legs.

There are other famous managers, of course, from Don Arden and Andrew Oldham and Simon Napier-Bell to Robert Stigwood, Larry Parnes, Albert Grossman and Malcolm McLaren. But one you rarely hear about is Bernard Rhodes. In Johnny Rogan's book, *Starmakers and Svengalis*, an authoritative rumination on British music-biz movers and shakers, Rhodes only gets three sentences. McLaren has a whole chapter; so does New Order manager Rob Gretton. One reason for Rhodes's poor showing is that, for all his egotistical rantings, self-promotion is not his strong point. He is a private man who has always shunned the limelight in favour of a mysterious existence. He dislikes having his photo taken and rarely gives interviews.

Even so, one paragraph is a pitiful epitaph for a man who had such a vast influence on the British music scene in the late 1970s and early 1980s. If managing The Clash wasn't enough, Rhodes was also responsible for bringing John Lydon into The Sex Pistols and nurturing the careers of three of the finest English groups to emerge in the wake of punk: Dexy's Midnight Runners, The Specials and The Subway Sect. This much is fact. Among his other claims are coming up with the idea for Public Enemy and iMac computers. These assertions are more difficult to take seriously, and his making them has further magnified his reputation as an eccentric. But maybe they do have some basis in a sort of skewed and distant truth. In the early 1980s, Rhodes certainly did associate with hip-hop visionary Russell Simmons and Apple's Steve Wozniak and Steve Jobs.

Paul Simonon has this to say about Bernie: 'You can't over-estimate Bernie's importance. He set up the whole punk scene, basically. He saw how non-musicians like myself and John [Lydon] could contribute.'

Clash road-manager Johnny Green adds: 'He had ideas and style, a very charismatic mix. He was into politics and philosophy but he would mix it all up, making connections to cars, travel, fashion, attitude of mind. His brain incorporated lateral thinking at amazing speed, and that can be deeply attractive. He made you re-examine your life in a fresh and radical way, from the socks you were wearing to where you put your cross on a voting slip. The difficulty was dealing with him on a material level.'

'Bernie used to drive me home from gigs in his Renault,' recalls Glen Matlock. 'He used to talk at you for an hour and after he finished you'd think, "What was all that about?"'

Kosmo Vinyl, Rhodes's right-hand man during the latter half of The Clash's career, thinks of him as 'a true radical, a man with a unique mind. There has never been anyone involved in music that thinks like Bernard. He's always looking at the whole culture, not just a part of it. His ideas are completely out of the box. Sometimes he comes at things at such an unexpected angle, it can completely throw you. He is a one-off.'

Bernie's relationship with The Clash was always amazingly volatile, and there was a two-year stretch, during 1979 and 1980, when he didn't work with the group at all, having been sacked for supposedly being impossible to communicate with. According to several sources, including Bernie himself, he was subsequently 'begged' by Joe to come back into the fold. Since The Clash collapsed in 1985 he has had little, if anything, positive to say about them. When I interviewed him in 1999 he was particularly rebarbative. It was during our conversation that he unleashed the quote that had riled Strummer so much when it was used as a headline: 'I didn't realise that Joe was such a coward. Mick I didn't realise was such an egomaniac. Paul was this pussy-whipped guy and the other one [Topper] I couldn't stand because he was such a provincial tosser.'

Rhodes's bitterness and bile seems to stem from a genuine belief that The Clash had failed in their objectives – that is to say, the objectives he believes he set them in 1976. At the launch in Camden Town of Bob Gruen's photo book, *The Clash*, Bernie planned to grab the mic to deliver a speech. He was prevented from doing this by the organisers, but he was walking around with a copy of the address in his hand all evening (which I saw). Its content echoed the sentiments he expressed in our interview in 1999: 'The Clash's talent was to represent the kids, but they didn't,' he said then. 'Do you know how the Americans started jazz? They found all this stuff on the floor after the Civil War – trumpets, drums – and made music with it. All I had was those four blokes and I did as much as I could. Obviously one would have wanted more.

'When Joe met me he was an arsehole,' he added. 'He saw The Sex Pistols and that was it, right? I introduced him to that scene. He doesn't know what to say, he doesn't know what to do, they're all an embarrassment. They wanted me to contribute to their live album [*From Here to Eternity*] and I told them to fuck off! I can't be seen with them.'

Of his own contribution to the band, he says this: 'Every group has a mad man. The Pink Floyd had [Syd Barrett]. That horrible band from Wales trying to be The Clash . . . Yeah, that's right, The Manic Street Preachers – the guitarist was the nutty one. The Stones had Brian Jones. The Beatles never had a nutty one, that's why they're so horrible. I'm the nutty one in The Clash, but I'm not a victim, I'm a winner.'

Virtually everyone interviewed for this book has a strong opinion about Bernie, whether it's reverence, distaste or fascination. Many wonder what drove this small, balding man with the brothel creepers and leather jacket. But they all concur on one point: he's an extraordinary person, the like of which they've never met before or since.

Information about Rhodes's early life has, until now, been sketchy. He was, as The Subway Sect's Vic Godard says, 'always a man of mystery'. One of Bernie's strategies during punk was to draw a veil over his own and the group's histories – not only to create an alluring mystique around them, as Howard Hughes did with his RKO stars in 1950s Hollywood, but also to signal that what they were doing was new, different, exciting, without precedent. Joe Strummer called The Clash 'almost Stalinist' in their approach to the new venture. It was an extremely apt phrase. Rhodes became a kind of Aleksandr Rodchenko figure, airbrushing events and people from The Clash's pasts, as if they were out-of-favour commissars being removed from an old Party photograph in the Kremlin archives. This process would put a huge strain on some of the band's friendships, but nonetheless seems to have been willingly embraced by them.

None of the group was more guarded about their formative years than Bernard himself. Perhaps he didn't think the facts of his life were important, above and beyond several salient elements such as: being from immigrant stock; claiming he was 'an ideas person' for The Who and Marc Bolan in the 1960s; and allegedly providing Malcolm McLaren with 'all his ideas'. ('I gave Malcolm [The Sex Pistols] 'cos I wanted to see how far he could run with it,' he told me.) But from the details Rhodes revealed in our interview, and the testimonies of others, it's now possible to shed more light on the man people around the group sometimes referred to as 'The Boss'.

The story begins in the immediate aftermath of the Second World War. The Soviet Union was devastated after its grim victory against the Nazis. (Even conservative estimates put the number of Russian dead at around 20 million.) The last months of the war had seen brutality on an unimaginable scale as the Soviets had pushed the Germans back to Berlin. Russian paranoia created a mentality where commanders believed any Russian villagers who'd survived the Nazis' advance and withdrawal must have been collaborators and therefore should be executed.

For many women, both Russian and German, 1945 was an indescribably horrific year. One of the most chilling lines in Antony Beevor's *Berlin* argues the worst mistake the German military authorities made was not destroying alcohol supplies in advance of the Russian onslaught. The thinking was that drunken soldiers would fight badly. Instead, they raped relentlessly and brutally.

In aftermath of this chaos, Rhodes's mother – who was Jewish – fled the country, pregnant with Bernard. Her own parents had been murdered during the purges of the 1920s. Bernard never knew who his father was. His mother eventually arrived in England, and found lodgings in the East End of London, where, according to Rhodes, she had to buy a birth certificate on the black market to establish citizenship. Bernie was born soon afterwards. His circumstances appeared to give him a vitality and drive.

'Bernie told me once he grew up in a home – or something like a home – and he had a part-time job in a butcher's shop,' explains Simonon. 'When he got back from work he was the top boy because he had all the sausages. They were eating very basic fare. That put him into his entrepreneurial ways and means, cutting a few deals.'

Joe: 'I love Bernie, though in his world I don't think love existed. He had a very hard upbringing. He was a small guy that people must have picked on. He came out with a particular personality. Those small guys either become comedians or get round it somehow.'

In 1954, Rhodes began living and hustling on the streets of the capital. His mother was by then working as a seamstress, he said, 'making suits for Cary Grant and people like that at Huntsman & Co, the tailors [based in Savile Row]. These days she'd be written about in *Vogue*. She was paid a pittance. As a little kid, I used to see her working at ten o'clock at night. I was living in a one-room tin shack in the East End. I was on the street; prostitutes used to take me in. It was there that I heard Amos Milburn and all the greats, because American servicemen used to use the prostitutes. When I was nine, I was hearing the best. I used to meet Cary Grant and all these people.'

It was while Bernard's mother was working at another Savile Row tailor, Hawes & Curtis, in the early 1960s that a young man called John Pearse was apprenticed to her. Pearse would later become famous in fashion circles as the man who started Granny Takes a Trip, the psychedelic boutique in the Kings Road, which clothed everyone from The Beatles, The Small Faces and The Stones to Jimi Hendrix, Bob Dylan and The Byrds.

'Bernard drove a Jeep,' recalls Pearse, who's still in the trade and now owns a clothing shop in Soho. 'He used to tell people we were in a band, even though we weren't. He liked that idea of gangs. Bernard never knew who his father was – I think he was looking for a family, and that's what The Clash became, in a funny way. We met through his mother. I thought he had potential. He was very much into fashion.'

Rhodes and Pearse ended up sharing a flat at 68 Hamilton Terrace in St John's Wood, a long thoroughfare of smart Victorian villas. (Hence the address of the party to which Mick Jones and Tony James weren't invited.) Pearse recalls that Rhodes was at art school at the time (Bernie has since told me he attended Goldsmiths). The year would have been 1963 or 1964. Mick Jagger had a mistress who lived in the flat above them; he would pop down for a smoke and a chat, and before long the place became a hang-out for a colourful collection of misfits who, according to Pearse, were 'preparing themselves, though they didn't know it, to go on and do important things'.

These included Donovan, Viv Prince of The Pretty Things, Marc Bolan, Micky Finn, The Small Faces, and hip guys like Jeff Dexter and Guy Stevens from legendary Mod club the Scene in Ham Yard, Piccadilly. The Who would swing by every now and then, too.

While researching this book, I've spoken to Jeff Dexter, The Small Faces' Ian McLagan and Kenney Jones, plus Pete Townshend – none of whom remembers Bernard in the 1960s. But it's quite possible the eighteen-year-old Rhodes had late-night conversations with them around the kitchen table and did generate some interesting ideas. So has Rhodes exaggerated his connections to those artists? 'Probably,' says Pearse. 'But he was always an interesting conceptualist. He would talk for hours. He would stay up all night talking, always the last to go to sleep.'

Bernie was also something of an operator even at that age. 'He was good at getting money out of people,' adds Pearse. 'I remember someone smashed my scooter, a woman, in St John's Wood. I went round her house with Bernie and he wouldn't stop talking till she gave me the money. Such tenacity, he was like a dog with a bone. She must have thought he was a very rude young man. He was a conspiracy theorist as well. But he was great fun, always. We went hitch-hiking together to Tangiers one summer, via St Tropez. It was a golden period. We stopped off at Torremolinos in Spain. It was little fishing village then and we bumped into Orson Welles and lots of *La Dolce Vita* characters, Eurotrash royalty.'

In the late 1960s, Bernie gave up driving his Humber Super Snipe coupé down Carnaby Street and settled down with his girlfriend Sheila Harrison, a librarian at the London School of Economics. They had a child and bought a flat on Camden Road, opposite the Brecknock pub. Clash soundman Micky Foote has a vague idea that Rhodes made money designing puzzles for a children's toy firm. By 1974, when he began designing and printing T-shirts for Malcolm McLaren, he was selling leather jackets in Antiquarius, the antiques market in Chelsea, and had a sideline doing repairs on Renault cars in the Railway Yard in Chalk Farm.

His story brings to mind a quote from Pete Meaden, 1960s Mod visionary, The Who's first manager and someone it's quite possible Bernie ran into at Hamilton Terrace or the Scene Club. The insight comes from an interview given to the *NME* in 1978 not long before Meaden apparently took his own life: 'I wonder where all the Mods went – they're probably all in garages, second-hand car outfits, scrap-yards. 'Cos there's something called Mod Suss – you know, sussing out a situation immediately, controlling it. So I would think they'd get into the car game – that's where most of the money is made very quickly.'

But, at thirty, Bernard Rhodes's 'Mod Suss' was soon to find a very different outlet.

In April 1976, Mick Jones and Paul Simonon started hanging out together at 22 Davis Road, a squat in Acton Vale, west London. A one-bedroom upstairs maisonette, built at the turn of the last century, it was a five-minute walk from Mick's college in Lime Grove. Mick had moved in to live with his girl-friend, Viv Albertine, a fellow student at the art school whom he'd befriended at a Roxy Music concert the previous year. Her ex-boyfriend Alan Drake also lived in the squat.

The flat attracted many visitors from the growing pre-punk fraternity. Among them was John Richie, alias Sid Vicious, loveable idiot savant and best friend of John Lydon. 'Originally Sid was put down as a thicko,' says Mick. 'But he really wasn't. He was a very imposing, intimidating figure. The first time I saw him he was wearing a full-length rubber coat down to his ankles, no socks, brothel creepers and shades, and a totally shaved head. He looked fantastic.'

Sid and Paul hit it off well. Both were good-natured, had a mischievous sense of humour and tendency to hide their intelligence by 'playing the lunkhead', as Johnny Green puts it. They were also heavily into image and clothes. Simonon seems to have been much more at home in this street-wise, subterranean environment than in the stuffy life classes at Byam Shaw. 'Sid and Paul used to go shoplifting to get us our food,' smiles Mick. 'We would be sitting there starving, so they'd go out to buy a packet of cigarettes and come back with a couple of tins of beans. They were like the hunters, scavenging for our dinner.'

Simonon – who cycled over from Notting Hill every day on his pushbike – continued to be coached by Mick. By now, though, he had abandoned any ideas to be 'a guitarist like Pete Townshend'. 'To this day I really admire Townshend,' he says. 'He's great. I think people don't realise what a great influ-ence he was on us. I didn't want to be the bass-player, I wanted to be the guitarist. They had all the flash stuff going. I didn't want to be Bill Wyman or Entwistle. But I remember Mick trying to show me an E shape on a guitar. After about an hour, I was still getting nowhere, so Mick got me a bass instead.'

'We borrowed a bass from Tony James and painted all the notes on the fretboard,' says Mick of the cheap catalogue guitar that Simonon would play on and off for the next nine months. 'Paul turned out to be a fantastic bass-player, but it was very frustrating at first.'

The nascent group were still scoping for new members. One line-up, featuring Mick, Paul, a singer called Billy Watts and guitarist Keith Levene, got as far as acquiring a name – The Young Colts – and were photographed, with Alan Drake, on the pavement outside Davis Road and posing on a stairway round the back. Also in the frame at this time was sometime *NME* writer and future Pretender Chrissie Hynde. In the booklet to *The Clash on Broadway* box set, Mick recalls playing the 1960s standard, 'Every Little Bit Hurts', with Chrissie up in his gran's flat. But that particular collaboration came to nothing.

The only members of The Young Colts to survive into The Clash were Mick, Paul and Keith Levene. A couple of years younger than Mick, Levene was a child whizz from Southgate in north London, who had taught himself to play guitar when he was twelve. He idolised Steve Howe of Yes and had even roadied for the group while still at school. Mick had met Levene at 47a Warrington Crescent, one of a number of locations where Jones's bands would rehearse, including Riverside Studios in Hammersmith and The Pistols' place in Denmark Street. Mick had been astonished by Keith's imaginative and accomplished musicianship. The elfin kid also had a sharp, sardonic edge to his personality that both Bernie and Mick liked. They agreed he was their most promising find yet after Paul.

The following week, Mick took Levene down to Hennekey's pub (now the Earl of Lonsdale) on Portobello Road, to meet Paul. 'Mick said, "This guy comes across as a bit thick but he's a really great artist," Keith told *Perfect Sound Forever* website. '"I think he could be the bass-player but he can't play." I was cool with that. We were looking for something. We didn't know what it was. We were just looking to be different.'

It was during this period that Mick, Paul and Keith started surveying Joe. On Thursday, 13 May, the day after The 101'ers played the Red Cow in Hammersmith, the future Clash had a fateful meeting – though no words were exchanged. The incident occurred at the Labour Exchange in Lisson Grove – the decrepit thoroughfare north of Marylebone with the dubious claim of being the birthplace of George Bernard Shaw's Eliza Doolittle. Jones – collecting dole money for his Easter break – was accompanied by Viv Albertine and Paul, who, like his band-mate, was surprised to see the singer of The 101'ers standing in the next queue. In the grim, edgy atmosphere of the dole office, Joe clocked them staring at him. I thought there was going to be a bit of trouble,' said Strummer in *MOJO*. 'I was weighing up which one to punch first – I decided on Mick because he looked thinner; Paul looked a bit tasty.'

There has always been confusion in The Clash's memories over the exact sequence of events that followed. But it seems possible that it was the very next Saturday that Mick and Paul, plus The Pistols' Glen Matlock, bumped into Strummer again, this time in Portobello Road. Since Glen knew Joe from supporting The Pistols, they stopped and exchanged pleasantries. Mick took the opportunity to inform Joe that he didn't like his group but thought he was 'great'. That afternoon, after a few pints at Hennekey's, Jones and the others had each bought a lurid lady's car-coat from a junk-shop in Golborne Road. Although he didn't say anything then, Strummer was impressed by their cool, gang-like image. He thought they 'looked like a group'.

The pull between the two parties was slowly getting stronger, planets on a course to collide. The following week, on 25 May, Bernie approached Strummer at a Sex Pistols gig at the 100 Club. Rhodes told Strummer there were 'some boys' he wanted him to meet, who were forming a band like The Pistols. When Bernie phoned the singer the next day at The 101'ers' squat in Orsett Terrace in Paddington, the group's guitarist Dan Kelleher answered and pretended to be Joe. He wanted to find out what the hell was going on. Bernie twigged what was happening and hung up. Rhodes decided to seek out Joe in person and, that Sunday, he and Levene collared him after The 101'ers' gig at the Golden Lion on Fulham Broadway. They took him into the street, where, in the light drizzle, Bernie offered him an ultimatum: he had forty-eight hours to decide whether he was in or out.

Having no idea who was in this new group other than Levene, Joe had little idea of what he was potentially 'in' or 'out' of. It's also quite possible – certainly Levene thinks so – that neither Mick nor Paul knew anything about Bernie's official approach to their future singer. Such obfuscation was to become typical of Rhodes's management style. Divide, control, keep everyone guessing. 'There was never a plan,' says Mick. 'Bernie might have had a plan, but we never did. Even then it was always difficult to figure out what was going on.' Yet, in a way that foreshadowed many of Rhodes's finest coups, his unilateral action set in motion a chain of turbulent and decisive events during the next few days.

After the Golden Lion gig, Joe drove home in the old hearse The 101'ers used to transport their gear. The timing of Rhodes's approach couldn't have been worse. Two weeks earlier, The 101'ers had signed their single deal with Chiswick. The significance of this to Joe and the rest of the group cannot be overestimated. It was the culmination of nearly two years' hard graft playing grubby pubs around the country – over 100 shows in total. Finally someone had recognised the group's talent and was prepared to put his money where his mouth was. If 'Keys To Your Heart' took off it might lead to a major deal and the kind of attention Dr Feelgood were getting.

And what would Joe be jacking it in for? In later interviews he would claim that as soon as he saw The Pistols he knew 'that R&B was dead, that the future was here somehow'. But what was that future? 'Punk' didn't exist then, it didn't have a name, it was just a few dozen misfits going to see a group that had yet even to record any demos, let alone sign a record deal. The 101'ers were months ahead of The Pistols in terms of a career. And what of his bandmates?

Only a few days earlier, Clive Timperley had left/been ousted from the group because he felt uncomfortable with Strummer's more aggressive tilt and the decision to forsake softer, more sophisticated tracks like 'Surf City' for the raw R&B they started out playing. Dan Kelleher and Joe had never seen eye to eye anyway. But what about Dudanski?

Joe kept returning to his instinctive feeling that something momentous was germinating, that it was a historical inevitability that something exciting had to happen, and this was it. 'There was nothing going on in music,' he said. 'We'd been trying to stir things up a bit with The 101'ers but we were fighting a losing battle.'

The evening after Strummer was delivered his forty-eight-hour ultimatum, he was in his room at Orsett Terrace deliberating on his situation when the phone rang. It was Bernie: he couldn't wait, he wanted the answer now. In or out?

The next morning, Tuesday, 1 June 1976, Bernie and Keith arrived at Orsett Terrace in Bernie's Renault 5 and drove Joe over to Acton. When he was shown into the living room he was met by the two guys he thought were going to jump him in the dole office. There's a great picture in Pennie Smith's book of Mick and Paul in 1978, which Strummer captioned: 'These two looked like this in the flat in Shepherds Bush.' Sucking on a fag cupped in his hand, eyebrows raised, Mick resembles a dodgy second-hand car salesman, while Paul leans casually on his shoulder in enigmatic splendour.

'So you got a few tunes then?'

The four of them went into the front bedroom and they ran through Mick's '1-2 Crush on You' and 'Protex Blue'. Joe recalls being impressed by Simonon's moves and Keith's look. In return, Strummer gave his most bilious, spluttering best.

That night Richard Dudanski was about to go to bed when Joe knocked on the door of his room. 'He told me that The 101ers had finished, they were over, and there was a new band with Mick, Keith and Paul. I knew the guys he meant, they'd been to see us play. He wanted me to be the drummer. I said, "Let's talk about it in the morning."'

When Dudanski woke up, Bernie was already prowling around the house. There was a sense of urgency in the air, the chill wind of change. A hostile takeover bid was in progress. Rhodes's presence was a hectoring reveille that woke up the somnolent atmosphere of the house. He ejected Micky Foote from his room, which doubled as the band's office, and called in Dudanski to tell him about the new project.

'He gave me a forty-five-minute socio-political spiel about the group,' sighs Richard. 'Bernie said it was all part of a bigger thing, all connected. I thought, "No way am I going to work with this guy." We'd already got rid of Clive, all we needed was to get rid of the bass-player to have a new band, but no way was I gonna work with this guy. When I came back to talk to Joe about it I said, "I'm not going with him." It was, "No way, Joe, no way." I felt pretty fed up about it all.'

'I went down to see Joe at Orsett Terrace,' says John Tiberi. 'There was a lot of talk about this new band. You didn't necessarily expect the same kind of ideological dimension at that time and not from a pub rock band. What The Pistols were doing was very attractive. The youth angle was there. I thought Bernard was a prat. Joe knew that, too, but I could see Joe's predicament and so could he.'

Micky Foote: 'They were round Orsett Terrace for two days and nights speeding and burning holes in my carpet – Sid and Keith Levene. I carried that carpet back from the East End – a beautiful Wilson Embassy carpet. I came back and there was wax all over it, fags stubbed out on it, candles all over the place. This was while Joe wanted to be left alone and was calling people in to his room for a chat. I said to him, "I don't give a fuck, whatever you want to do, do it." Richard was the same, but he was a bit more, "Think of the band, we've done a record, we've got an identity for ourselves, let's not throw it away." He wasn't going, he thought they were speed-freaks. We were the hottest R&B band in town, but it was never gonna get outside London, it was never gonna sell records. It was always gonna be cabaret.'

Whatever his final rationalisation of the situation, Joe quit The 101'ers for good. They played their last gig at Haywards Heath, East Sussex, the following weekend. Clive Timperley, the man who had planted the germ of ambition in Joe five years earlier by 'actually supporting Medicine Head at the Marquee', was invited on stage for a valedictory encore. Joe had already moved into The Future.

The next evening, Strummer ran into Chiswick Records' Roger Armstrong at a Jam gig at the Windsor Castle pub. In his inimitable, half-crazed and loveable Strummer style, he managed to drop the bombshell that he was splitting The 101'ers – and therefore scuppering any chance of the forthcoming 45 getting any airplay or promotion, or selling many copies – without causing too much collateral damage.

'I was at the bar getting a drink and there was a tap on the shoulder,' recalls Armstrong. 'Typically, Joe started halfway through the sentence. So the first thing he says to me was, "Have I done the right thing?" So I'm looking at him saying, "What are you talking about, Joe?" He says, "I've left the band", and he points to this skinny kid behind him and says, "And I've started a band with him." "Him" was Mick Jones. I said, "Well, what the fuck do you expect me to say, you know what I mean? You expect me to put a record out and you've broken up the band. Oh yeah, I'm absolutely fucking delighted."

'But to me, the real classic was the way Joe put it. It wasn't, "I've left the band and I'm worried about what I've done", but "Have I done the right thing?" So we weren't that pleased, obviously, but there wasn't a lot we could do so we stuck the record out anyway.'

'Keys To Your Heart' was sent out to journalists a few weeks later with a press release pointing out in the postscript that the group's frontman and chief songwriter had left The 101'ers and was now pursuing a career with his new band, The Heartdrops.

In the 1890s, gin was one of London's biggest exports to the world. A century and a half earlier when Hogarth was alive, the spirit had been the ruin of the capital's lower orders who wanted to get completely sloshed for a few pennies. But by the end of Victoria's reign, gin had reclaimed its status as a classy drink, just the thing to imbibe with a slice of lemon and a splash of Indian tonic water. The chief producer in the capital was Gilbey's, who'd built a distillery in Camden Town, a working-class district of north London, in 1879, and moved it a few years later into the abandoned Roundhouse, an architectural delight a mile to the west in Chalk Farm. This huge circular edifice, designed by Robert B. Dockray, once housed the winding gear for pulling trains and carriages up the steep gradient from Euston Station. Its interior had been illustrated in Dickens's *Dombey and Son* – a sign of the great Coming of the Railways.

By the First World War, Gilbey's had taken over most of the North-Western Railways' yard at Camden, and turned the old wagon and stabling buildings into bonded warehouses. From these depots, gin and wine were transported via 'The Gilbey's Special' locomotive to the Docks at Tilbury and then to the Empire. In the 1960s, Gilbey's was swallowed up in a merger and the railway yard, in decline since the Second World War, fell into disuse. Like many other remnants of Victorian prosperity, it lay decaying – damp, ugly, soot-stained and neglected, awaiting the gentrification that would come two decades later.

It was the most easterly building of the former bonded warehouse number two that in June 1976 received a new lease of life, as it prepared to export a completely different product from London to the world. Bernie Rhodes, who used Harry's Motors, a garage based in the yard, for his business fixing up Renault cars, purportedly persuaded the local council that the disadvantaged youth in the area needed some rehearsal space to learn to play their instruments. They subsequently granted him a lease on the property.

It was, of course, a typical Bernie move and, sometime in May 1976, his new band to rival Malcolm's Sex Pistols moved in. The line-up was: Joe Strummer, vocals and guitar; Mick Jones, guitar and vocals; Keith Levene, guitar; and Paul Simonon, bass. There was no permanent drummer, and that was the next task: auditions.

Rehearsal Rehearsals, as it was dubbed, had a grim and brutal resonance that suited the band's tough, history-less, no-frills approach. Bernie drummed into them: this is new, this is different, this is important. Rehearsals' bare walls looked like a set from a Maxim Gorky drama or *The Insect Play*. Only this time Joe's performance of Head Ant was for real. Over the next few weeks Rhodes applied his barbed, cajoling sophistry to creating an atmosphere that had an edge and promoted an electric sense of intent.

Micky Foote jumped ship with Joe. As a soundman, handyman and solid, gruff, unflappable presence, he was clearly a valuable asset to the new group. He observed how Bernie vetted the band's entourage according to criteria such as class, attitude, enthusiasm and image.

'Bernie collected together the people he wanted,' says Micky. 'He was very, very fearful of people he didn't want getting involved. He wanted people who wouldn't go against him, a control freak par excellence. He'd phone up Rehearsals and say, "Who's there? Oh yeah? Tell him to fuck off! I've told Mick not to bring him down there! Get Mick on the phone now!" Boogie wasn't allowed near it; Tony James definitely wasn't allowed anywhere near it.

'Bernie separated people. There was a process of pulling people away from where they were and from their friends. Mick's friends were shit, Joe's were shit, Paul's were shit. Tymon was a fucking hippy cunt. Bernie didn't want anything to do with him. "Fucking hippy, keep him away!" With Chrissie Hynde it was, "She's American, what does she know about anything? Tell her to fuck off!"'

On the group's part there seemed to be a willingness to surrender to Bernie's methods, based on an intuitive understanding, even a sort of fateful resignation, that this was what was required if they were to clear the decks to do something extraordinary. Mick was clearly in Bernie's thrall. Keith was young, sharp and talented, and already embedded in The Pistols' elitist culture. Paul liked Bernie's ascetic regime: perhaps it reminded him of his father's discipline, which had brought out the best in him. And, as someone who'd spent a lifetime moving from one new area to another, severing ties with his friends was no big deal. For Joe it was a pragmatic choice in his quietly relentless ambition to be a star. 'I was different from the other guys because I'd scrabbled around for years,' he said. 'I'd been banging my head against the wall with The 101'ers. I finally had found someone with vision. He knew how to make stuff interesting.'

'The 101ers had gone as far as they could go,' agrees Micky Foote. 'They'd outgrown each other. Clive Timperley was wearing Hawaiian shirts. It was a horrible hippy crowd, they were the Freston Road lot, the B-class squatters. Bernie was trying out different combinations of people. It was a totally different vibe to being in a cosy little band with all your mates.'

John Tiberi: 'Bernie was approaching it from the Mao Tse-tung angle. It was like a revolution, the cut has to be made. Take no prisoners.'

For those left behind it was a case of feeling either wounded, relieved or philosophical, or a mixture of all three.

'Bernie obviously realised that I was middle-class and Mick was . . . a bit raunchier,' says Tony James. 'And that became apparent when I teamed up with Billy Idol, who was obviously middle-class as well, to form Generation X. Street credibility wasn't an issue before punk. Rock 'n' roll was always a way out for working-class kids, but it wasn't their exclusive domain.'

Tymon: 'In a way it was OK for me. I was slightly separated from "the poxy hippies". Bernie came round my house and asked me to support the group at some gigs. I turned up in Camden Town to meet the group with half a haircut and half a moustache. I had a complete army uniform on. I said to Mick recently, "I was in a state when I met you, wasn't I." He said, "Well, half of you was."'

Tony James's comment about being excluded or unwelcome because of his class is important, because it chimes with the idea that Bernie was a hard-line Marxist who had an aversion to anyone he considered bourgeois. This is clearly untrue: for a start, his comments suggest he subscribes to the theory that everyone these days is bourgeois ('You say The Clash are working class? They say "fuck" and have a working-class stance, but compared to my background they were all middle class'). Second, in the next few years he was to become fond of several unquestionably middle-class and materialistic Clash associates such as Sebastian Conran. The point is Rhodes favoured people with edge, passion, swagger and conviction.

Yet the fact remained that there was disparity within the group. Paul, Mick and Keith were streetwise London kids, clued up, young and smart, hanging out around town since their early teens. Joe was older, wiser and educated at a posh boarding school in Surrey. Though he'd long rejected his parents' middle-class values, it was clear that out of everyone involved in the new group, he was the odd man out. He had been chosen because he was the best frontman in town – as Micky Foote points out, 'They came looking for us, we didn't go looking for them' – but there was pressure on him to meet, or exceed, Bernie and the group's expectations. He was also required to slot into the speedy, yobbish milieu that soon would become known as punk. It was obvious that vital adjustments needed to be made.

'We had no concept of what young people were doing,' says Micky Foote. 'The squatting scene wasn't full of eighteen- or nineteen-year-old kids, that's for sure. It was post-university middle-class people and a few wayward drunks in their forties smashing things up. The teenagers were at home behaving themselves and having nowhere to go. There weren't any flats to rent, they were all squatted by these middle-class student types who'd never done a day's work in their lives. The working-class youth didn't go out squatting but they were feeling a bit cramped up in their bedrooms.'

This was the beginning of a radical period of reinvention for Joe. As a student of rock 'n' roll lore, he knew all about what Marc Bolan's biographer Mark Paytress called 'tinkering with the façade to . . . transcend the reality of the conformist, standardised life patterns of those around [you]'. This is clearly what he'd done when he became 'Woody'. Strummer also recognised the conviction with which everyone from Dylan to Big Bill Broonzy – who infamously mutated back from a successful R&B pop singer into a dungareed, country-blues hobo for the benefit of 1950s white student audiences – had embraced their new personas.

'I think Joe was quite uncomfortable with the transition he had to make,' states Dudanski. 'That was the beginning of a year that was a real personality bender for him.'

Micky Foote agrees: 'It was very difficult for him. But he knew that it had to be done. He knew there needed to be a process of change if he was going to take it to another level.'

The next few weeks saw modifications in Strummer's outward bearing: his voice became a slurred Cockney grunt and his demeanour grew rougher. His characteristic gentleness was buried deep in a subcutaneous layer. Back in Newport, he had written about wanting to lead a criminal lifestyle, to be 'a cat burglar' or 'an intelligent bank robber'. Now, with The Pistols' Steve Jones, a former house-breaker, and Robin Banks, a convicted armed robber, knocking around, he was rubbing shoulders with just such fascinating miscreants. It was as if he was finally joining the outlaw gang of his teenage fantasies – and he was the enigmatic poet, like a punked-up version of Dylan's Alias character in Pekinpah's *Pat Garrett and Billy the Kid*.

Sebastian Conran, who was also educated at boarding school, tells a story about Joe later that summer. 'We went into a workmen's café, and ordered a cup of tea. When it came I said, "Thank you." Joe took me aside and said, "Look, you don't say thank you, you say ta."'

The clearest signal that Joe wanted to be viewed as a freshly minted, déclassé creation and not just a crazy old greaser from the hippy community was his blank refusal to be acknowledged as Woody – a name by which many of his friends still knew him.

'They'd known Woody, now this was someone else called Joe,' says Micky Foote. 'He had to forcibly say it to people. He said it to me: "I'm not fucking Woody, call me Joe." He had to say it to everybody. "I'm fucking sick of telling you, I'm not fucking Woody!" He really had to press it home.'

Within a couple of weeks, Joe was looking, talking and, thanks to Bernie, thinking like a member of the group who were already recognisable as The Clash.

A famous pop business personality stated imperiously in a 2004 radio interview that 'The Sex Pistols were every bit as manufactured as The Monkees or The Bay City Rollers'. He is right, of course. But his point – that some of the greatest-ever rock 'n' roll groups were pieced together by Svengali figures – would have been made even more effectively if he'd used The Clash for his example. The Pistols had grown out of a boyhood friendship between guitarist Steve Jones and drummer Paul Cook. With The Clash, not one of its members had known another before Bernie and Mick started shopping around for talent in The London SS in late 1975 and early 1976.

Rhodes's selection process was intuitive but utterly ruthless. It was like *Pop Idol* in extremis. He was as hard, if not harder, than the toughest judge on those TV talent shows (and wittier and more intelligent). He and Mick had handpicked the group from dozens of candidates over a period of nearly nine months. The band had been built to exacting specifications, and their international success in the years to come suggests his and Mick's choices were mostly good ones. (Naturally, Rhodes considered Mick as just another musician who passed his auditions; Jones more generously saw their relationship as a partnership.) All the group needed now was a drummer.

The auditions for the fifth member took place at Rehearsals throughout June. Joe was still in contact with his old schoolfriend Paul Buck, now styling himself Pablo LaBritain, who sat in on drums for a week or so. Some of the first pictures of the group feature him. They also show Joe with short hair and Mod-ish school tie – the only member with long hair is Mick. Pablo was fired by Jones after he messed up a couple of songs during a mini 'showcase' at rehearsals in front of the Pistols (minus Rotten), and by mid-June he'd been replaced by Terry Chimes. Born into a working-class family in East London, Chimes had tried out for both The London SS and the Billy Watts line-up.

'When I met the guys in The Clash, they were as obsessed with success as I was,' says Terry. 'I'd been to hundreds of auditions and all I'd got was these half-asleep musos who didn't know what they were trying to do. But this lot were hell-bent on success and very focused. I realised that was all we had in common. But it was enough.'

He moved his kit into Rehearsals. The building was cold and damp, even in summer. A couple of ancient Belmont barber's chairs lined the wall. Bernie had got the boys to give the main downstairs room where they practised a lick of emulsion. The soundtrack to their toil was Ras Michael's *Rastafari* LP and their slap-dash decorating skills were the origin of their Pollock/Rauschenberg paint-splattered clothing – a look inspired in part by Glen Matlock, who'd similarly customised his jeans a few weeks earlier.

'Keith was really into the splash-painting and the Jackson Pollock bit,' recalls Terry. 'But Paul was the artist. Keith thought Jackson Pollock was great because it was wild, whereas Paul said, "I like Jackson Pollock because of this, but I prefer so and so because of this . . ." He went into it in a lot more depth.'

The Abstract Expressionist touches mirrored the passionate, explosive music the group were playing. The drizzled clothes suggested a rejection of conventional forms, just as Pollock and Rauschenberg's paintings had swept away Modernism and redefined art in the years after the Second World War. Large Abstract canvasses were the favoured artworks in the upper tiers of Ballard's *High Rise*. 'The look of a Rauschenberg', according to screenwriter Paul Schrader, was also the desired effect for the bloody denouement of *Taxi Driver*. A mural by Paul reprising his 'car dump' theme gave Rehearsals an arty, urban, loft-ish atmosphere, and the physicality of the room was a metaphor for something new, dangerous, urban and exciting.

Terry's first impressions of the group articulate a sense of Joe being confused and unsure in his new environment. 'I was told by Bernie that Mick had passed his audition with The London SS,' explains Chimes. 'I was called back in and all of a sudden the singer had changed. There was now this guy called Joe. He had such a strange speaking voice, I thought, "What's he going to sing like?" I didn't know what the hell he was about when I first met him. He was very distant. He'd say hello but you'd never get much out of him.'

His descriptions of the others tally with those of most other observers at the time. 'Mick was friendly and really enthusiastic. He read the *NME* a lot and wanted us all to be interested in what was going on, but we weren't. Paul was pretty straightforward. He didn't say much, but he was a nice enough bloke. Keith Levene was into challenging everyone around him. I didn't mind, I thought, "If that's what's required, if that's his role, then fine." He liked to take people straight out of their comfort zone. I said to Joe, "What's this guy's problem?"'

Joe confided in Chimes that he'd been to McDonald's with Keith where they were served some tasteless milkshakes. Keith refused to drink his and 'made a big fuss'. Joe felt he ought to have made a big fuss, too. 'He thought that an anti-mediocrity stance was right for the band,' explains Terry.

In this confrontational, hard-line atmosphere, the group egged one another on to display ever greater tokens of commitment, like apparatchiks fearing a purge. Rehearsals were held every day, including Sundays.

Terry Chimes said, 'We decided early on we were gonna work hard and there'd be no slacking from anyone. It was like living in an oven with people winding each other up and heating up. There was this strange false reality where people were saying, "We can either do it the total way, the heavyweight way, or else the wimp way." So there was no choice really. In hindsight, you don't launch a project by getting sick of it seven days a week; you're more efficient working a few days a week. Bernie was very against it being a social scene. He'd say, "Are you here for a goal or are you here just eating a cucumber sandwich?" He had a way of wording things to make you feel stupid, and get you to do things his way.'

In the last two weeks of June, the pace was frenetic enough to put together a short set of songs. Mostly they were from Joe's and Mick's existing material – including 'Protex Blue', '1-2 Crush On You' and 'Keys To Your Heart' – plus 'Deny', 'I'm So Bored with You', a couple of Kinks and Who numbers, The Troggs' 'I Can't Control Myself' and covers of 'Too Much Monkey Business' and 'Junco Partner'. They performed them loudly and aggressively, and the sound had a trebly, metallic edge thanks to the three-guitar format. Having been at various points The Mirrors, The Psychotic Negatives, The Phones, The Weak Heartdrops (from the Big Youth track 'Lightning Flash (Weak Heart Drop)' – later shortened to The Heartdrops – the group settled on The Outsiders. Mick and Joe walked into Camden to break the news to Ted Carroll and Roger Armstrong at their Rock On shop, now at 3 Kentish Town Road.

'It was a beautiful summer's day and Joe and Mick came in and said, "We've got a new name, we're not The Heartdrops any more,"' recalls Armstrong. 'I said, "What are you?" And Joe said, "We're The Outsiders." And it was such a weird coincidence – there was a pile of albums on the counter that we'd just sorted out. I went over and held up The Outsiders album on Capitol [from 1966]. They were as sick as parrots.'

The band were finally named by Paul after he'd noticed the word 'clash' cropping up several times in an edition of the *Evening Standard*. It seemed to suit who they were and what they were creating: a clash of personalities, a clash against reactionary values, a clashing, dissonant sound.

On 4 July 1976, as America celebrated its bi-centennial, and Israeli commandos rescued 100 hostages from Ugandan skyjackers, the group made their live debut supporting The Sex Pistols at the Black Swan in Sheffield. It followed a tradition of new London groups road-testing themselves out of town; it was the same city where The Small Faces had played their first gig eleven years before. The Clash were so excited they were up at 5 a.m. and on their way by 7 a.m., even though Sheffield was just four hours' drive away, and the gig didn't start till 8 p.m. 'We were so desperate to go out and do it after all those rehearsals,' explains Chimes. 'Joe and I felt like The Pistols were the opposition. The others, Mick and Paul, were saying, "No, they're our comrades in arms."' Travelling up in the van, the impish Paul provided the entertainment by wrestling one of Levene's shoes off him and trailing it along the motorway at the end of a rope.

The gig – entrance 90p – had been arranged by McLaren, who'd told the promoter the support was The 101'ers. 'We filled in,' recalls Micky Foote. 'We didn't tell the geezer till the last minute that Joe Strummer was coming up with his new band. He was like, "I booked the fucking 101'ers!" But there were at least half a dozen people there who looked a bit punky. Word had got up there. There were sixty or seventy 101'ers fans who were a bit disappointed . . . I was doing the sound and we talked this guy in a music shop in Walthamstow – I think Bernie knew him – into lending us a PA. The group were rattling round with the equipment in the back of this great big van. They had all the gear on, it was pretty exciting. Joe's out of his suit and into a pair of jeans and shoes dripping with paint. There was everything to do, everything to change.'

Onstage, Joe transformed into a spluttering punk madman, his 'electric leg' in overdrive. Simonon wore a stylish two-tone suit, bought from his teenage schoolmate, Clive Teagle, and threw great shapes. The first song they ever played was the instrumental 'Listen'. Joe remembered Paul starting the bass intro to the latter and failing to stop climbing the scale at the appropriate point. This elicited guffaws of laughter from the group. The Sex Pistols were relieved that their competition didn't look too threatening.

The only 'review' at the time was an anonymous letter in the following week's *Sounds*. After trashing The Pistols it read: 'Clash were just a cacophonous barrage of noise. The bass guitarist had no idea how to play the instrument, and even had to get another member of the band to tune it for him. They tried to play 1960s R&B but failed dismally.' Micky Foote, however, remembers The Clash being 'well-received' and Bernie enthusiastically telling the promoter 'they were gonna be the next big thing'.

The Black Swan may have been an inauspicious start, but it was a necessary baptism, which, in one fell swoop, had created a scene: it may not have had a name yet, but now there were two groups doing it. The bond between The Clash and Pistols was further consolidated the following night, when they teamed up to see The Flamin' Groovies, The Ramones and The Stranglers perform at Dingwalls, a venue housed in another cluster of old Victorian industrial buildings, by Camden Lock, just a couple of minutes' walk from Rehearsals. (The groups were playing the second of two American bi-centennial gigs, the first at the Roundhouse down the road the previous evening.)

After the show, Simonon, Steve Jones and Paul Cook were talking in the crowded bar. The Stranglers' bassist, Jean-Jacques Burnel, takes up the story:

'We'd had a bite to eat and were Indian-filing out of Dingwalls and I walked past Paul Simonon. He had this nervous thing where he used to turn his head and spit. He did it just as I was walking past and I thought he was spitting at me. So I turned round and went WHACK! and punched him. [Simonon claims the fight started after Burnel kicked him.] He fell back into Jones and Cook and spilt their drinks. The next thing I know, all three of them had bundled on top of me. I was trying to fight them off. The bouncers came over and chucked us out into the courtyard. There was a face-off outside. I wanted to finish it off.'

It was a balmy summer's night. On one side of the cobbled courtyard were Simonon, Chrissie Hynde, Rotten, Cook and Jones. On the other were The Stranglers and their gang of biker followers The Finchley Boys. As Simonon and Burnel squared up to each other, The Stranglers' usually pacific keyboard player, Dave Greenfield, went beserk and threw Rotten up against the old ice-cream van in which his group carted their gear around. Rotten's immortal words were 'Nuffink to do with me . . .' Meanwhile, Joe and The Stranglers' singer Hugh Cornwell, who knew each other from the pub rock days, peered on sagely. Hugh remarked: 'Looks like your bass-player's having a punch-up with my bass-player.'

The fight came to nothing. 'The Finchley boys were heavyweights, not a bunch of art-school kids,' says Burnel. 'There was no contest.' After this incident, The Stranglers became personae non gratae so far as The Clash and Pistols were concerned. The showdown reinforced the idea of a hierarchy among the new groups. This new scene was exclusive, not inclusive, and The Pistols and Clash were the elite. The Stranglers, pub rockers from Guildford, weren't even considered part of it, even though they were young, aggressive and played mean R&B. The Simonon–Burnel face-off and the fracas at the Nashville, when Vivienne Westwood fought the girl next to her, suggested violence was now an accepted, even anticipated, part of the new group's scene. The fight was no longer merely symbolic.

Having been ejected from Davis Road, Paul and Sid moved in with Joe for a while at Orsett Terrace. They lived off food stolen or scavenged by Paul and Sid from Portobello Market. In the evenings, they sat around smoking and listening to records. In the sleevenotes to *The Story of The Clash*, Joe, writing as 'band valet Albert Transom', describes how the turntable favourites were Bo Diddley, Big Youth, Prince Jazzbo, The Who's *Sell Out*, the first two Stones LPs, Ronnie Hawkins and the Hawks, Leadbelly, Howlin' Wolf.

Paul has a different story. 'That was Joe having a joke,' he says. 'Joe had the sleeves to some of those records but not the records themselves. We couldn't afford to buy them. We literally didn't have a penny between us. Someone did have the first Ramones LP, which was a big influence.' Meanwhile, an ancient black-and-white TV in the corner flickered with Nadia Comaneci's triumphs at the Montreal Olympics.

On 24 July, The Clash received their first press, when Caroline Coon interviewed Strummer and Jones for her column in that week's *Melody Maker*. Ostensibly, she was writing a requiem for the ill-fated 'Keys To Your Heart', but it turned into a big hurrah for The Clash. 'We're challenging complacency, standing up for rock 'n' roll,' said Mick. 'We want to get rid of rock 'n' rollers like Rod Stewart who kiss royalty after gigs.'

Back at Rehearsals, The Clash were hard at it. In June, July and August, they wrote or re-worked fourteen songs. Some of them – like 'Deny', 'Janie Jones (about the notorious society vice queen), 'What's My Name', '48 Hours', '1977' and 'London's Burning' – would be recorded for the group's debut album the following spring. Others such as 'I Know What to Think of You', 'How Can I Understand the Flies?', 'Mark Me Absent', 'Deadly Serious' and 'Sitting at My Party' would be dropped over the next few months.

Rhodes organised an invite-only showcase for industry figures and journalists on Friday, 13 August. The most important guests were the three writers that were championing The Clash and Pistols in the music press – *Melody Maker*'s Caroline Coon and *Sounds*'s Jonh Ingham and Giovanni Dadomo. Roger Armstrong and Ted Carroll were also there.

'Bernie had bought a couple of bottles of really cheap, nasty German wine, so Ted went out and bought two or three bottles of drinkable stuff,' recalls Roger Armstrong. 'I remember the seating was a dentist's chair and an orange-crate. They had their little stage area and it was really great, 'cos they actually did it like they were doing a show. They were hiding behind a curtain. I think somebody got up, it might have been Caroline, and made an announcement – "The CLASH!" – and they ran on with their painted jackets, gave it everything, and there's like ten of us there.'

Micky Foote says: 'They were fucking brilliant! I'd listened to it for two months but anyone who came in there would've been blown away. The three guitars sounded phenomenal. Each of them knew exactly what they wanted – Keith Levene had a Marshall with a pre-amp, Joe had a Telecaster going through a Vox, Mick tried lots of different set-ups. It was a sound designed for maximum impact.'

The group were rewarded with a review in *Sounds*, written by Giovanni.

It was a virtual love-letter, noting 'a compelling tapestry of sound and colour' and 'plenty of that old Mod flash'. It concluded that they'd 'frighten The Sex Pistols shitless'. There was no time for the group to sit on their laurels, though. A gig with The Pistols and a new, Pistols-inspired group from Manchester called The Buzzcocks had been booked for a gig at The Screen on the Green cinema in Islington on the August Bank Holiday. This meant the punishing regime had to continue.

'Bernie would come down at some point every day,' says Micky Foote. 'He'd want a presentation of what they'd been doing. "What about that one? Are you still doing that one?" He was very hands-on about it. He had lots of input. His input was inspiring them to be better and think about what they were doing and why.'

'His input was everything,' said Joe. 'He said to us, "Write about what you feel is important." He never told us to write about this or that, he just told us to write about what was happening. Don't write love songs.'

But there were early signals that the group were buckling under their immolating rehearsal schedule. 'There were lots of excuses to leave early or go off and buy guitar strings,' recalls Terry Chimes.

Micky Foote: 'Keith was taking lots of speed and was becoming increasingly unreliable. He was there when he was there. Joe was keen. Mick, it had to be in his time. Paul was enthusiastic; you never saw him without a bass in his hand. It's always hard to get five people somewhere at the same time. There'd be a lot of "I gotta go at half past five"'.

At The Screen on the Green 'Midnight Special' all-nighter, The Clash suffered from bad sound and a wearying day helping to build the stage (McLaren's punishment for their having the support slot). They'd also had to guard the equipment throughout the day's three showings of Clint Eastwood's *The Outlaw Josey Wales*. Joe even had to warn off some would-be thieves who tried to walk off with some amps. Charles Shaar Murray, reviewing the group for the *NME*, famously quipped: 'They are the kind of garage band who should be speedily returned to their garage, preferably with the motor running.'

It was their first critical mauling. The Clash's rise to greatness was by no means a given thing.

In the time of Queen Elizabeth I, there were probably just a few thousand black people living in England, mostly slaves or ex-slaves. In 1601, the Virgin Queen, in a seventeenth-century precursor of British Fascism, ordered the expulsion of 'the great numbers of negars and Blackamoores which . . . are crept into this realm'. It didn't happen, but her edict set an example of colour prejudice that was to echo down the centuries.

In the late 1950s, in the reign of the next Queen Elizabeth, there were an estimated 125,000 blacks living in Britain, mostly arrived from the Caribbean in the years following the SS *Empire Windrush*. The first really significant sign of black–white unrest in London was the Notting Hill Riot of 1958. On the last day of August, violence had flared after a gang of white men set upon a Swedish woman with a black husband. Nightly clashes between blacks and whites followed. Ill-feeling towards the black community had been inflamed by organs as ostensibly informed as *The Times*, which demonised West Indians with stories of them enticing white females to smoke hemp to 'stimulate sexual desire'.

Two decades later, things hadn't got much better. In many ways, they'd got worse. Ultra-right-wing political parties like the National Front and the British Movement were growing in strength. West Indian – and Asian – communities were targets of prejudice and violence. The idea that the police were 'institutionally racist' was taken for granted. It was the disturbing world depicted so vividly in *Babylon*, Franco Rosso's film about a black musician in South London, which starred Aswad's Brinsley Forde. Harassment was continual and widespread. The SPG (Special Patrol Group), a mobile rapid-reaction force formed in 1965, was especially notorious for intimidating blacks and Asians.

In August 1976, at the end of a long, dry summer (the hottest that century), there was another big race riot in Notting Hill. It happened at the Carnival, a celebration of West Indian culture in Britain. Earlier in the month, the West Indies cricket team had humiliated England in the Fifth Test at The Oval in south London. The victory, cheered by thousands in the streets of Brixton and Kennington, felt like a home win. The game sparked heated debates about the status of Black Britons. This added to the crackling racial tension on the streets.

The Clash's video-maker, Don Letts, the son of West Indians who'd settled in Brixton, was enjoying Carnival's last day. 'It is interesting how people look back on it as a black and white riot,' he says. 'It wasn't. It was a wrong and right riot. It wasn't the black kids against the white police, it was youth at a black festival against the police. Don't forget this is 1976 you are talking about, a time when the country is in a bit of a state, there are no opportunities, there is a depression, recession, a lot of unemployment. Then you have all this "SUS" stuff going on. [Police stopping and searching individuals on suspicion of their being engaged in a criminal activity; it's now generally accepted that this archaic power, dating from the Napoleonic War, was much abused in the 1970s and 1980s to harass racial minorities.] This didn't affect the white guys as much as us. You'd get pulled up all the fucking time, because you looked suspicious. I used to drive quite a flash car in those days, an old Zodiac with fins. When I was going out to the movies, I used to give myself an extra half an hour so I could get pulled up by the police and asked, "Who the fuck are you?" What they wanted to know was: "Who are you and why are you driving a car like this?"'

Having got up late after the Screen on the Green gig, Paul, Joe and Bernie wandered down to the Carnival. It was to be an extraordinary day, which would become a cornerstone in Clash legend. When a black youth was arrested near Portobello Road for alleged pickpocketing, trouble flared. Riot police assembled for a charge. Their line came under fire from a barrage of cans, bricks and bottles. The riot exploded. 'It was like *Zulu*,' recalled Strummer. In the commotion, Paul and Joe lost Bernie under the Westway. Simonon recalls with glee throwing bricks at the lines of police and almost unseating a police motorcyclist in Ladbroke Grove with a traffic cone. As the riot exploded, Joe tried to set light to an upturned vehicle but the matches he lit kept blowing out in the breeze. In *Westway to the World*, he does an impression of a 'big fat [West Indian] woman screaming, "Lord, they're going to set the car alight!"'

Don Letts was photographed as the riot started: a lone Rasta figure seemingly confronting several dozen policemen preparing to charge. The shot was later used for the cover of the *Black Market Clash* compilation. 'That picture looks like I am walking towards the cops,' says Don. 'I am actually walking across the road. Behind me there are about 5,000 brothers all bricked up ready to throw; there are cops ahead of me. I am like, "OK, I'd better move to one side here." That is the moment they captured.'

At one point, Paul and Joe were cornered in an alley by a gang of black youths. They were asked to turn out their pockets. 'All they found was bricks and bottles,' says Paul. Joe had with him a second-hand transistor radio he'd bought in Golborne Road. He refused to let the gang have it and started yelling at them. Then what Simonon describes as a 'Rasta General' arrived and ordered the kids to leave them alone. It was a moment when the cultural complexities of the situation hit home. 'We realised it wasn't our story,' says Paul.

The riot left Strummer and Simonon exhilarated. For Joe, who'd had to observe the *événements* of 1968 from afar, it was the opportunity he'd been waiting for to unleash his deeply-felt anti-establishment brio. Perhaps he would have thrown a few bricks around whatever his experiences in the capital. But having spent several years busking and squatting, always being moved on, always being hassled, forever watching the police pushing racial minorities around, he relished the opportunity to get his own back. Simonon, a product of the streets of Brixton, Lewisham and Ladbroke Grove, perhaps felt the antagonism more instinctively.

Kosmo Vinyl, talking about the shared experiences of Mick, Paul, Bernie and himself, points out: 'We all hated the police. You were brought up to be wary of them – you'd never dream of speaking to a copper unless you had to. There was unspoken understanding that they were on the opposing side.'

As evening fell, and the streets of W11 got more dangerous, Joe and Paul wound their way back to the squat at Orsett Terrace. Sid was inside. They retold the events of the day with a wide-eyed mix of excitement, exhaustion and disbelief. Vicious was crestfallen that he'd missed out on all the fun. He wanted to go back and torch some cars himself. Joe, Paul and Sid walked back towards Ladbroke Grove along Tavistock Road. In front of them were around 500 black youths gathered outside the Metro Club.

'Suddenly, this black woman leaned out of her window and shouted, "Don't go up there, boys, they'll kill you", recalled Joe. 'We said, "Bollocks!", but another woman came out of a basement and grabbed us. We could see the 500 youths, the hardcore of the hardcore. We went home.'

For The Clash, the riot was a defining moment: it cemented the notion that they were street-fighters, outlaws and pro the black community. As a symbol of everything the group stood for, it was an absolute gift. The Clash and the Notting Hill Riot would remain inseparable.

That week, The Clash played two more gigs – at the 100 Club on 31 August (supporting The Pistols) and at the Roundhouse on 5 September (with The Kursaal Flyers and Crazy Cavan). The latter proved to be a disaster, not least because Joe's attempts to educate/rile/convert the audience between songs resulted in a barrage of guffaws and heckles. After the show, Bernie told the group they were 'shit' and enquired where Joe had found 'those old Johnny Rotten scripts'. It was to be Keith Levene's last gig with the group.

'It was obvious to me there was a problem,' explains Micky Foote. 'There was a problem with him and Mick, and a problem with his reliability. Reliability is very important. He was doing too much speed. You're never gonna get on with someone who wasn't there.'

Chimes disagrees: 'Keith was always around as far as I can remember, though Joe did call him Phantom the Guitar Player.'

Joe: 'Our idea of a good time was scoring a lump of dope the size of a match head. Now and then we'd get some blues or some sulphate. But Keith was more pro on speed. He took it in a very pure form.'

Strummer had taken onboard Bernie's suggestion 'to write about what's happening' and penned a song about the events at Notting Hill – 'White Riot'. According to Joe, Keith wasn't interested in rehearsing it. Levene felt that it was musically regressive and lyrically crass. But his waning commitment arguably had roots in deeper reservations about the group.

Micky Foote: 'I don't think it was dangerous enough for him. He was hanging out with Sid – it wasn't really a druggy scene at that point but it was edgy. And it was all a bit, "Are you working with Joe Strummer from The 101'ers? He's a bit old, isn't he?" It was a bit of a stigma. They found it more difficult to take him in as one of them because he was a bit older and a bit middle-class. Keith's scene dragged him out of it, as much as he didn't want to bond up with it.'

The 'problem' between Mick and Keith was mostly personal. Keith tells of Jones 'yelling' at him a lot, and chewing him out for failing to turn up to a rehearsal that a) allegedly hadn't even been arranged and b) was on a Saturday afternoon when Keith was working. Speaking to *Perfect Sound Forever* website, Levene claims Mick's antagonism stemmed from an incident in July, when Viv Albertine had announced it was Keith's birthday while they were waiting together at a bus stop.

'[Mick] found out that I was three years younger than him,' he says. 'Ever since that day, he was just this total fucking bitch cunt to me. There wasn't a thing I could do that wasn't wrong.'

It's certainly possible that Mick's attitude towards his bandmate did change when he realised Keith was his junior. Since Levene was born in 1957 and Mick in 1955, there were two (not three) years between them, still a considerable gap at that age.

One afternoon at Rehearsals when Keith was absent, Mick instigated a discussion about Keith's role in the group. 'Mick was putting forward the idea in a very roundabout way that they didn't need three guitar players in the band,' recalls Terry Chimes. 'I wasn't listening very much, but Joe said, "Shall we get rid of him, then?" I jumped then, and thought, "You can't get rid of someone just on a whim." I thought it was Joe and his crazy behaviour. But Mick said, "I think you're right." And Paul, who didn't say very much, said, "I think you're right." I was shocked. So they'd all been thinking of this but never said it. But when Keith left it seemed easier to progress and get things done. He slowed it down.'

Micky Foote said: 'It was a shock when he got the boot. It was a situation of someone who's not really on it getting chucked out and then being "I'm really hurt, man". It was a classic case of I'd rather fuck off than you tell me to fuck off.'

Levene's quick and unsentimental sacking said a lot about the atmosphere of The Clash. Bernie had instilled in Joe, Mick and Paul a collective ruthlessness that they'd used effectively and decisively. Keith was given no warning or second chance. His lack of commitment was rewarded with his instant dismissal. This wasn't a band that, like The Stones with Brian Jones or The Beatles with Pete Best, was going to let things fester or palm off harsh decisions on management.

Ironically, Rhodes was alarmed by their action. 'Bernie was quite shocked when he turned up at Rehearsals and I'd sacked Keith,' said Joe. 'He was a favourite of Bernie's. I can see now that Bernie was worried about losing control.'

Keith Levene was soon airbrushed from the picture. A rumour began to circulate that put his dismissal down to hard drug use. He was the first victim of what Foote describes as 'friendly fire' in The Clash camp. There were plenty more victims to come.

5
THE KIDS ARE ALRIGHT

'Free your passions!'   Situationist slogan, Paris 1968

*'I think it was an idea that made them, an idea and a song. You should
have seen them the day they were first mustered in – derelicts, outcasts,
criminals of every kind . . . But wait till you see them now!'*
ERROL FLYNN AS GENERAL CUSTER ON HIS 7TH CAVALRY, *THEY DIED WITH THEIR
BOOTS ON*

'The Sex Pistols – I'll give Malcolm the credit, he's a good marketing man
who stole all my ideas, right?' froths Bernie Rhodes. 'When I worked with
Malcolm and Vivienne, I had to stop him from talking in such a tossy accent.
[Adopts camp voice] "Oh, hellooo!" It was like, fuck off! I am the punk, I am
the philosopher.'

Rhodes first met Malcolm McLaren in the 1960s at a bowling alley in
Stamford Hill, north London. It was a hangout for the early Mods from that
area: teenage peacocks like Johnny Moke and Marc Bolan. After that, Bernie
and Malcolm frequented the Soho coffee-bar scene. Beak Street, Old Compton
Street and Carnaby Street were taking off as centres for young men's fashion.
The two men shared a Jewish background, and, a familiar strand in this story,
an unstable family environment. McLaren's father left his family when Malcolm
was two – he was brought up mainly by his mother and grandmother – and
his family was suburban and well-to-do. He went on the beatnik trail in the
mid-1960s, and his teenage life was spent at a succession of art schools: Harrow,
Chelsea, Chiswick, Goldsmiths. He was thrown out of most of them.

The teenage Malcolm portrayed in Craig Bomberg's insightful biography,
The Wicked Ways of Malcolm McLaren, is an insecure, over-sensitive, tortured,

explosive late-developer with a rapacious but flittering intellect. His interest darted from Egyptology to the Renaissance and German Expressionism to Surrealism. You get the impression that he was never really an aficionado of anything. For him, the ideas were always more exciting than the form, and causing a disturbance always more attractive than sitting down and creating anything of substance.

When Bernie rekindled his friendship with Malcolm in 1974, the consensus is that McLaren was the senior partner in the relationship. He was by then one of the most exotic and influential creatures on the Kings Road. In his least charitable moments, McLaren dismisses Rhodes as 'just the bloke who printed my T-shirts'. But it's clear there was an intellectual parity between the two and a sizzling rapport. This makes it almost impossible to answer the question that Tony James raised: 'Whether Bernie got [his ideas] second-hand from Malcolm, I really don't know.'

In the early 1970s, McLaren had opened Let It Rock at 430 Kings Road, Chelsea. The shop caught the wave of the growing rock 'n' roll revival, selling Ted drapes and brothel creepers and, later, zoot suits and peg trousers. The revival scene was given a boost in August 1972 by The Rock 'n' Roll Show at Wembley featuring US stars Little Richard, Billy Haley, Jerry Lee Lewis, Bo Diddley and, somewhat incongruously, The MC5, who endured a hail-storm of bottles and beer cans. Later that year, Let It Rock was commissioned to make the clothes for Ken Russell's biopic of the Austrian composer, *Mahler,* and for *That'll Be Day*, Claude Whatham's wonderful film about a fictional English rock'n'roll group in the late '50s called The Stray Cats, featuring David Essex, Ringo Starr, Keith Moon, Dave Edmunds and Billy Fury.

Let It Rock was a magnet for outsiders and people seeking something different; it attracted everyone from cool musicians like Iggy Pop, Ian Dury and The New York Dolls to Rudolf Nureyev and image-conscious London street kids like John Lydon, Steve Jones and Paul Cook. In the tradition of Granny Takes a Trip and Mr Freedom – one of 430's previous incumbents – Let It Rock became an extraordinary subterranean junction of fashion, art and music.

The shop's popularity made McLaren a minor Kings Road celebrity, but it would soon land him in trouble. In 1975, he changed its name to Sex and began stocking rubberware, handcuffs, bondage gear, leather trousers, bollock-locks and other fetishistic items. It also sold T-shirts with provocative designs, such as a pair of breasts (as worn by Steve Jones at the Nashville and on the Bill Grundy TV show), a young boy licentiously smoking a cigarette (an image culled from a paedophile mag), the hood of the Cambridge Rapist (then terrorising the university town) and the infamous Gay Cowboys (two good-looking young cowpokes stripped to the waist with their enormous dicks brushing against each other). In July 1975, one of the shop's habitués, Alan Jones (no relation to The Vultures' bassist), was arrested in Piccadilly for wearing the Gay Cowboys shirt. The incident made the front page of the *Guardian* and landed McLaren and Westwood with a fine for contravening indecency laws. (During the police investigation, Bernie arrived at Mick's gran's flat – Rhodes had not long met Mick and Tony – with a bag of the offending T-shirts, and persuaded the guitarist to hide them in his bedroom.)

Bernie is usually credited, together with Malcom and Vivienne, with the idea for the 'You're gonna wake up one morning . . .' T-shirt, which Mick Jones was wearing the day he met Rhodes. This suggests Bernie had input in Sex's creations. However, the Sex T-shirts exposed early ideological differences between Malcolm and Bernie. Glen Matlock, who worked in the shop, strongly objected to some of the designs (including the young boy) and so, according to Jon Savage's *England's Dreaming*, did Rhodes. The disagreement is interesting because it reinforces the theory that Bernie's radicalism was of a less confrontational, more tasteful and less sensationalist type than his friend's.

John Tiberi voices the opinion that, certainly to begin with, Rhodes wasn't 'the punk' or 'the philosopher'. 'You got the impression that Bernie was a chancer,' he says. 'With Malcolm, there was a sense that he was a sort of visionary. There was some of that with Bernie but he didn't have the same style. Bernie got Rehearsals for disadvantaged children. He made his money running an advert for Renault repairs in *Time Out*. Malcolm wasn't like that.'

The notion that it was actually McLaren, not Rhodes, who was the original punk philosopher is attractive because Malcolm had already proved his ability to be shocking and innovative with Let It Rock and Sex. He was also enamoured with a European philosophy that had loud echoes in his work and life: Situationism.

Mentioning the Situationists in the context of punk often elicits theatrical groans and accusations of punk being intellectualised thirty years after the event. This may be so, but the fact Malcolm was so influenced by the movement highlights important differences between himself and Rhodes, and The Pistols and The Clash.

An offshoot of Surrealism, Situationism came to prominence during the Paris riots of May 1968. It was a political art movement which called for a revolution of everyday life and was intended to expose the lies of consumerism. No art book will ever successfully explain what exactly that means, but that's part of the fun: Situationism was an esoteric concept and ripe for contradictory interpretations.

Its chief attraction for McLaren, it seems, was that it was an art of ideas and politics rather than of gouache or canvas. In fact, the leading Situationists expelled some of its exponents for producing paintings and sculptures, which they considered conventional and bourgeois. Slogans daubed on walls were big Situationist fare. Dressing up as Father Christmas, walking into Selfridges and handing out 'free' toys to children – as Malcolm had apparently done at college – was a typically incendiary Situationist statement. The movement had the added allure of being run by its leader, Guy Debord, as if it were a political party, with purges, excommunications and a creeping feeling of paranoia. (Debord would eventually take his own life in 1994, adding to the cult surrounding him.)

In Lydon's autobiography, *Rotten: No Irish, No Blacks, No Dogs*, Caroline Coon makes this point: 'Malcolm and Bernie were anti-intellectual . . . That's why they went into Situationist politics. Situationist politics is merely sloganeering – second-rate sloganeering at that – all pulled out of the 1960s dustbin.' In recent years, John Lydon has professed bewilderment that anyone should take seriously the idea that this obscure European art movement had anything to do with something as spontaneous and streetwise as punk rock.

Roadent, alias Steve Connolly, who worked as a roadie for both The Clash and The Pistols, says: 'With The Pistols, it was never a big deal with the group themselves, it was only the management that was interested in it. I only learned about the Situationists by getting pissed with [Malcolm's friend and Pistols graphics designer] Jamie Reid. With The Clash, it was never brought on board at all. Only perhaps that idea of like, "Oh don't come complaining, write a song about it", which is the famous thing Bernie said to Joe. That was quite a Situationist thing to say. The idea of Bernie rushing into Rehearsals and saying, "Let's all go out on a *dérive*!" is totally alien. No, in the Clash camp it was never really mentioned.'

It's arguable that Malcom's fascination with Situationism gave him an edge as a cultural energiser. Seven years after he travelled to Paris to visit the battlefields of the May 1968 demonstrations, where striking Renault workers had stood shoulder-to-shoulder with anarchists and radicals, McLaren was creating a stir with his Sex boutique. He was selling outrageous, provocative clothes in an anti-consumerist way. He was challenging attitudes towards taboos like paedophilia and incest.

Meanwhile, Bernie was making a living patching up the very same vehicles those Renault workers in 1968 had been bolting together. Yet while Rhodes may, in some ways, have had the mindset of a small-time operator, generating income from car repairs, T-shirts, second-hand leathers and old reggae records, he had qualities that the restless, notoriety-seeking McLaren didn't. Micky Foote argues that 'Malcolm was Mr Smooth, Mr PR, he was way ahead of Bernie on that score, he was a showman. But Bernie was in it for the long game. Malcolm was "How many T-shirts can I sell at the Wembley Country Music Festival?" Bernie was building something bigger.'

'I didn't think Bernie was a Marxist and I certainly didn't think Bernie was a Situationist either,' says Johnny Green. 'I think he was lost in no-man's land somewhere with all his conflicting ideas. That's what made him a good manager for The Clash early on, because it is the same thing. There are no colours now for the mast.'

McLaren once told a journalist that he wanted to destroy everything and lectured him on anarchy and revolution. Bernie preferred to think otherwise. 'Revolution sets a country back a hundred years,' he said in 1981. 'Revolution is very, very dangerous. I don't think [The Clash] ever were revolutionary. I think we were always interested in the politics of the situation.' In the decade after 1975, it proved to be Bernie's Realpolitik instincts, not Malcolm's nose for turmoil and headlines, that would create the more resilient, enduring and commercially successful group.

However, asked about Malcolm McLaren in the summer of 1977, Mick Jones said of his rivals' manager, a tad disloyally: 'He's the one visionary of our time.'

The 100 Club started life in the 1930s as a restaurant called Mack's. It was located in the basement of 100 Oxford Street, at the northern boundary of Soho. During the Second World War, Mack's began hosting live jazz music, and became a haunt of G.I.s on furlough in the capital. Glenn Miller and his band even played there one night, shortly before his plane went missing en route to France. During air-raids everyone stayed put, safe in the knowledge that this subterranean bunker was as safe as most basement air-raid shelters in the area. Victor Feldman, an English jazzman who ran the club, advertised it with the legend 'Forget the doodlebug – come and jitterbug!'

On 20 and 21 September 1976, the 100 Club staged the legendary Punk Special, usually referred to as the Punk Festival. The event had been organised by McLaren and Rhodes to publicise their respective groups and hopefully create a record company bidding war. The line-up underscored the elitist hierarchy of punk. The first night featured The Sex Pistols and The Clash, plus two groups formed for the occasion by The Pistols' friends and followers: Siouxsie and the Banshees and Subway Sect. The second night had the rustics, also-rans and red herrings: Buzzcocks, The Damned, Chris Spedding and the Vibrators and French group Stinky Toys.

The Punk Festival has passed into rock lore. The bands bristled with contempt for the outside world, and each other. Sid Vicious – then drummer with The Banshees – threw a glass at The Damned, which smashed on a pillar, injuring a girl's eye. The incident strengthened the association between punk and casual violence. Sid, who was convinced of his own innocence, was arrested and charged. (When his case came to court a year later, The Clash testified in his defence.) On the first night, there was a ruckus when, in an echo of Bernie's reservations about The London SS name, he refused to allow The Banshees to use The Clash's backline – now painted a delicious fluorescent pink – after Siouxsie insisted on wearing a swastika armband. Sid, whose theatrical idiocy seemingly allowed him to get away with anything, retaliated by calling Bernie 'a fucking old Jew' from the stage.

The Clash's performance – their first as a four-piece – was dogged by sound problems, but without Keith Levene, they suddenly gained a crisp visual symmetry. It was the debut of their three-man frontline, with the skinny, angular Simonon and Jones throwing shapes and leaping around either side of the beaming, pneumatic Joe. Bootlegs of the gig reveal several key transformations in their music. Most of inferior early songs – including 'Mark Me Absent', 'Sitting at My Party' and 'I Know It' – have been dropped and the remaining material is generally played harder and faster. Lyrically, there's a groping towards a more politic thrust: 'White Riot' is unveiled for the first time and the anti-hero of 'Janie Jones' has been created by changing the main rap from 'I'm in love with rock 'n' roll' to '*He's* in love with rock 'n' roll'. In a similar vein, 'I'm So Bored With the USA' began life as 'I'm So Bored With You'. As Mick explains in *Westway to the World*: 'Joe suggested we make it "I'm So Bored With the USA". It immediately became something else, a song about the Americanisation of England. Though we were brought up on American TV, we were always saying there were too many McDonald's here, too much American influence. That was what the song was about.'

Dave Goodman, The Pistols' sound engineer, remembers: 'The Clash were great. Well rehearsed. I tuned their guitars up for them at the soundcheck. They were really quite out. Simonon's bass-playing was very impassioned. He got good very quickly.'

The Subway Sect's Vic Godard says, 'They were really good that night. It was the last time they played some of their early songs like "How Can I Understand The Flies?" [This song actually survived a few more gigs.] To us, they felt like Eric Clapton in their ability.' Goodman also recalls an incident which intensified The Clash's role as social commentators – though bootlegs now confirm this actually happened at their show at the 100 Club on 3 September: 'In the middle of the set, Mick Jones broke a string, so Joe got out a small transistor radio and put it up to the mic. The announcers were discussing [IRA] terrorism. I put some delay on it and it sounded really good. It sounded like we knew what we were doing.'

The group's growing onstage power at the festival was boosted by the large 'W' speaker bins that Goodman had recently acquired, and which Bernie and Malcolm had to manhandle up the stairs at the end of the night. The speakers' previous owner had been none other than The Who.

The week of the Punk Festival was important to The Clash for another reason – they gave their first full-length interview. Three months earlier, a Williams and Glyn bank clerk called Mark Perry had started a fanzine called *Sniffin' Glue*. It had been inspired by the homemade blues and rock 'n' roll publications around at the time, and also Brian Hogg's pioneering 'zine about 1960s music, *Bam Balam*. The debut issue featured a piece on The Ramones and The Flamin' Groovies' shows in Camden, plus Blue Öyster Cult, Doctors of Madness and The Brats. Hand-written, opinionated and Xeroxed, it had by its second issue become an enthusiastic champion of the nascent punk scene. The *Sniffin' Glue* interview was conducted by Steve Walsh, an art student friend of Perry's. Mark accompanied him on his assignment. He transcribed the interview tape and edited the piece that appeared in the third issue in early October.

'When we first got there, it was just an old warehouse, pretty bleak. We wondered whether we were in the right place. Then Paul Simonon greeted us. He shouted out, "Up here!" and he was waving this gun around. It was like this sort of fake pistol. I remember thinking, "What's he doing that for?" I said, "How'd we get up there?" He goes, "Up the ramp." It was pretty derelict, and they had like two or three rooms in there; we just sat around on some old chairs.'

The discussion that followed set the tone for all of the interviews The Clash would give that year. It was polemical and combative, but not without wit and humour. It also provided just about all the ammunition their critics would ever need to machine gun them in later years. Bernie's catechisms and drilling had fused The Clash's ideas into something approaching a cohesive ideology. Even though the politicisation of their music was in its infancy, it was clear that the issues they'd address on the first album were high on their agenda.

The chief thrust was that people were being misinformed, and they saw it as The Clash's role to educate them about what was really going on. (Joe: 'I just feel like no one's telling me anything, even if I read every paper, watch TV and listen to the radio!') Mick emphasises that the group are concerned with the politics of the street. He says his inspiration is 'out there', gesturing to the window. The group, they explain, are also anti-hedonist. They stand for 'change and creativity'. People, according to Mick, have become apathetic and boring. Bands which simply enjoy themselves – The Damned are given as an example – are 'taking their audience for a ride, feeding the audience shit!' Joe considers that 'the situation is far too serious for enjoyment, man. Maybe when we're fifty-five we can play tubas in the sun, that's all right then to enjoy yourselves, but now!' If The Clash could lay their hands on some money, they add, they would 'get something together immediately' in terms of staging events and creating new venues for groups.

For all his willingness to promote the group's cause, Mark Perry maintained a healthy scepticism: 'I was cynical. You don't come from Deptford and fall for every old line. We weren't like, "Oh yeah, I believe every word" sort of nonsense, you know what I mean? It was like they were putting us on bit.' He adds, 'I was real working class. Deptford was one of the severest places in London, well known for being hard. So I had the credentials. I mean, you look at people and you know whether they're hard or not. People like Mick, they're not hard, which is OK, but when they're trying to put on this front it was like nonsense. But then, at the same time, you didn't want to blow it for them. It wasn't like you were the *Sun* or something. I was never of that mindset, "Oh, let's reveal the truth!" We were part of it, we wanted to encourage it, we didn't want to blow it out of the water. I was there to build it up. *Sniffin' Glue* was very critical but I still wanted to be a supporter of what I felt punk was all about. The Clash, they're our band, the last thing I wanted was to pull holes.'

Early in the interview, there's a debate about the trousers worn by The Hot Rods' Dave Higgs in the previous week's *NME*. Joe Strummer, a shabby greaser just a few months before but by now firmly entrenched in Clash Think, underscores the connection between image and attitude. 'You can't say, "That's clothes and this is music." It's a state of mind, a complete thing. If anything was going on in that bloke's head he would do something about it.'

Mick concluded that 'trousers reflect the mind', inspiring Joe to coin his first great Strummerism, connecting attitudes towards outlook and fashion. 'Like trousers, like brain!' he declared.

Paul Simonon didn't say anything during the exchange. Perry felt 'he wasn't eloquent enough to put over ideas. He was very quiet, he was very nice, he didn't say much at all.'

Significantly, Terry Chimes wasn't invited to participate in the *Sniffin' Glue* interview. There was a reason for this. Since the group's inception, he'd been the member least interested in The Clash's ideological cant. He was open about the fact he didn't like Bernie's modus operandi. For him, The Clash was simply a vehicle to advance his ambitions to be a pop star. Bernie ensured the flow of information from the group was carefully managed. It would have been suicidal to give the dissident Chimes a voice.

'I didn't know what Bernard was all about,' says Chimes. 'He just seemed like this really peculiar person with odd ideas. I didn't trust him. I was arguing with him from the day I met him. Bernie would have made a good politician, he had a way of turning things around. If I questioned him, he'd then question my commitment. So Bernie would turn the others against me, which I got sick of.' Chimes concedes, however, that Rhodes' approach was 'necessary' and that 'it worked'.

'Bernie was great for us,' agrees Simonon. 'Not that he could ever tell us what to do, but he would suggest things. Could you imagine a group now who sat around having political discussions? Why are you in a group? What's your aim? What do you want out of it? There aren't enough Bernies around.'

Four months after they moved into Rehearsals, the atmosphere was still brusque, paranoid, bristling and stern. Yet it was also vibrantly creative. Daily attendance was mandatory. Paul, who was by now sleeping on an old mattress in the upstairs office, could often be found refining his mural or customising his clothes with a splash of paint in the yard. He would also while away the cool, late summer evenings playing along to The Ramones' debut LP and old reggae and ska 45s, like The Ethiopians' 'Train To Skaville', Big Youth's 'Hit The Road Jack', Bob Marley's 'Dancing Shoes'/'Don't Look Back', Desmond Dekker's 'The Israelites' and The Rulers' 'Wrong 'Em Boyo'. The singles were installed on the Rehearsals jukebox, purloined from Star Entertainment, a games firm in the yard run by one of Bernie's mates.

'Paul was the youngest and arguably the best-looking,' says Micky Foote. 'He'd be sitting there working his fucking bollocks off to learn his bass parts. He had to. The others weren't about to carry any passengers. He was relentlessly and ruthlessly slaughtered if he didn't get it right.'

After the Punk Festival, The Clash emerged from under the wing of The Pistols to headline their own gigs and to support other acts. There were a few unremarkable out-of-town shows – Tiddenfoot Leisure Centre in Leighton Buzzard, Lacy Lady's in Ilford and a half-remembered gig in Guildford, which, the story goes, was attended by just one bloke while a fight between squaddies and bouncers raged downstairs.

Looking back through the flawed prism of history, it's easy to imagine that the Punk Festival radiated ripples of energy to the rest of the country, like an old Pathé News graphic of the TV transmitter at Alexandra Palace. But it didn't, really. In autumn 1976, The Clash were still a tiny, esoteric backwater of music. Probably fewer than 1,000 people had ever seen them perform. Jon Savage and Mark Perry calculate there were probably as few as one or two hundred committed punk fans. Very few people outside London experienced the buzz first hand. In the capital, though, momentum was building.

'We were starting to pull big crowds,' explains Micky Foote. 'The difference to The 101'ers' gigs was when you went into the hall, the punters were there before you went on stage. It was tense, there was a crackle in the air. With The 101'ers, you'd do one set, get some applause, do another, play back-to-back Chuck Berry and they'd go "Whoopee!" With The Clash, the people were there, they *wanted* it. It wasn't like they'd drifted in for two pints of lager and a packet of crisps.'

At their headlining gig at the ICA on 23 October, billed as 'A Night of Pure Energy', Patti Smith, whom the group had seen the previous evening at the Hammersmith Odeon, signalled her endorsement by jumping up onstage and dancing. Afterwards, she whisked Paul away to Birmingham, where The Clash were scheduled to play the next evening. A few weeks later, she sent him a gift: a brand new stereo Rickenbacker bass. At that point, Paul might have preferred some hard cash: the ICA was the gig for which Simonon, who refused to sign on the dole (another evasion of authority), stuck up some fly-posters then devoured the unused flour-and-paste glue because he was so hungry.

But while The Clash were making friends, they were also creating enemies. Punk was seen, correctly, as threatening. Two gigs in particular signified the subcultural unease that The Clash and Pistols stirred. The first was at the University of London Union (ULU) in Malet Street on 16 October. The group were booked to perform with Shakin' Stevens and the Sunsets, one of Joe's old rock 'n' roll favourites from Newport. Shakin' Stevens's audience was mostly Teddy Boys. In the mid-1970s, Teddy Boy culture was tribal, beery, violent, resolutely working-class and highly conservative. Many Teds were middle-aged men who'd grown up with rock 'n' roll in the 1950s. Often, their sons would follow them into Ted-dom, as if it were a family trade. They thrived in unfashionable London suburbs like Harrow and Croydon.

New Society photographer Chris Steele-Perkins was sent to chronicle the scene in 1969, and ended up joining it. Interviewed by journalist Ian Harrison to promote his book *The Teds* (with writer Richard Smith), he describes the culture as 'edgy. There was a lot of "What are you looking at?"' The adrenalised atmosphere seduced him. 'It got in my bloodstream,' he says.

In 1976, the tensions between Rockers (favouring leathers and Gene Vincent) and Teds (drape jackets and Elvis) erupted at an aborted Bill Haley gig in London. There was a huge thump-up and scores of casualties. Into this world walked The Clash. Though no record of the ULU set-list survives, it's almost certain they played '1977' – 'No Elvis, Beatles or The Rolling Stones!' It's doubtful any of the audience deciphered the 'Elvis' lyric but it made no odds anyway: with their painted shirts, dyed, spiky hair and cacophonous punk, The Clash were clearly from a different tribe.

Mark Perry was in the audience. 'It was extraordinary,' he recalls. 'There were no other fuckers there from the punk scene at all. This was before the big punk-Teddies war. It was still a bit tense with all these roughs about. I was in the dressing room and Mick had been head-butted by a Teddy Boy and had a cut across his nose. Suddenly all these Teddy Boys were trying to get to The Clash. It was like, "Who do you think you lot are? Weird-looking lot. You poofs or something?" They tried it on.'

'There was a lot of aggression,' remembers Sebastian Conran. 'I was backstage at the time and there were people trying to fight and rip out the plugs on the performance. I remember I had a tie made out of zips.' In the sleeve-note for *The Story of The Clash*, 'band valet Albert Transom' reports that Sebastian was throttled and that the group armed themselves with chairs and rushed the Teds. In Joe's cartoonist's imagination, this may have happened. The reality, however, was grimmer.

Mark Perry: 'What was the band's reaction? They were scared. The Clash were never really hard men, were they? They were like musos in a way. But who wouldn't have been scared? These Teds were fucking hard-nuts.'

Even so, Terry Chimes – the band member arguably least interested in romanticising The Clash's physical confrontations during this period – is adamant that The Clash stood their ground. 'None of us ever flinched in the face of aggression from outside,' he states emphatically.

Punk's intrinsically hermetic, provocative attitude was highlighted again at a headlining gig at the Royal College of Art on 5 November – Guy Fawkes Night. The show was billed as 'A Night of Treason'.

'There was a load of students who were trying it on,' says Perry. 'They were long hairs who were quite aggressive towards the group. This bloke was heckling so Sid Vicious jumped on stage and asked the bloke out for a fight. It wasn't like any of The Clash were doing it; they were quite happy to play their music. I got involved, because I was going out with Caroline Coon then. She was going, "Oh, don't get involved, Mark." I was like, "What do you mean? There are some students out there having a go at the band!"'

Also in the audience that night was Jon Savage, standing next to Sid and about to cut his teeth as a journalist for *Sounds*. He'd first seen The Clash at Fulham Town Hall the previous week. He recalls: 'I actually recorded that gig, and on this tape you hear him [Sid]. He was right next to me looking like a speed demon, looking very lairy. So I stayed out of his way. He wasn't interested in me and he got up onstage saying all this stuff: "Come on, cunt!" and "We'll do you!" I thought, "Really, this is *terribly* exciting!" As they say in [Savage's Pistols biography] *England's Dreaming*, violence was sexy then. We all know a lot better now. I hate violence, I don't want it in my life at all, but we were all children and we didn't know what was going on.'

The *Westway to the World* film revisits the story of Sid Vicious jumping into the audience to fight the hecklers, with Paul and Joe diving in to back him up. Challenged afterwards as to why he didn't join the fray, Jones quipped: 'Well, someone's got to stay in tune.' His apparent refusal to fight delineated his role as the pacifist in the group, the musician who genuinely was anti-violence. Yet this episode is actually a classic case of the group mis-remembering events and blurring several incidents into one to make a point. What really happened was that Joe sought out the offenders after the show with Sid and, embracing his new punk persona, thumped one. The other Clash members were all trapped backstage at the time.

Around this time, Terry Chimes figured that The Clash weren't the group for him. He wanted an easier life. Far from being pleased at the news of his departure, Rhodes was riled – as were the rest of the band. Paul was so annoyed that he threatened to damage Terry's car.

'When I left I thought Bernie would be happy, but he wasn't,' chuckles Chimes. 'He said, "Look, you're the foil. Whenever these guys come up with something, you say what the man in the street or the press would say, you immediately confront them with the rational argument against what they're saying. If they can get past you, they can get past the world without being shot down in the first minute." That was how he saw my role. I was just nine-teen at the time, so I wasn't aware of the wider stuff going on.'

Chimes wouldn't be swayed. He would honour the November gigs and then leave. Following his departure, in now typical style, the group denounced him, disseminating a story, re-told in the first *Clash Songbook*, that Terry wanted out after a wine bottle had shattered on one of his cymbals. The inference was he didn't have the mettle to accept The Clash's mission. The truth was he couldn't stand Bernie's politburo-esque machinations and the permanently tense atmosphere within the group.

'I was uncomfortable with the constant hardening up,' he explains. 'I found it unnecessary and wearing. I thought, "I'm not very happy. What's the point in being in this band if I'm not happy?" It was actually really hard work and severe and with all these pressures put on us. I thought, "I want to be a rock star and have a good time." Which they hated, of course.'

In 1991, Joe told Kosmo Vinyl that, during a group meeting, Terry revealed his goal in The Clash was to own a Maserati – though Paul claims it was a Lamborghini: 'He was very honest, he just didn't understand we were trying to see if something new could be forged.'

Chimes says, 'I just wanted to get paid for playing the drums. The wine bottle story? I didn't care, really, because I was out of it by then.'

Before he quit, Chimes played on the group's first proper demo session, recorded for Polydor at their Marble Arch studios in November. Since The Pistols signed to EMI on 8 October, The Clash had been the main focus of the record company A&R men, the next biggest punk group in the pecking order. Their hard work was paying off; it felt inevitable that they'd follow The Pistols to a major label. The producer of the Polydor recordings, chosen by Bernie, was none other than Guy Stevens, Mott the Hoople's mercurial mentor who, less than eighteen months before, had fired Mick from Little Queenie/Violent Luck. Bernie knew Guy from the Mod days, and had given him a namecheck among the 'likes' on the 'You're gonna wake up one morning . . .' T-shirt.

Stevens was regarded as perfect for the job. He was an outsider within the industry, a maverick, intense and uncontrollable wild man driven by passion. Formerly a clerk at Lloyds of London, he'd dropped out of the rat race in the early '60s to pursue a rock 'n' roll lifestyle, before such a thing really existed. His CV was impeccable: writing the sleeve-note on Joe's cherished Chuck Berry EP; turning The Who and The Small Faces onto R&B; recording Jerry Lee Lewis, Free and Mott; serving time for a dope rap in the late 1960s. Guy was a living connection to much of the 1960s counter-culture that The Clash held dear. He was the energy of Mod in aspic, undiluted by huge success or riches, though clearly damaged by the events of the previous decade.

'You got to remember that Guy served time in prison while his baby [Procol Harum's 1967 hit 'A Whiter Shade of Pale'] was a worldwide number one,' states his friend Jeff Dexter. 'Things like that really hurt. He got into a bad way.' The story goes that after he was released from prison, Guy even found a bill for Procol Harum's studio time on his doormat.

The Clash were invited to meet him. They went up to his flat in Swiss Cottage, above a Rolls-Royce dealership. They were surprised at what they found. The bearded, balding, ginger-haired Guy wasn't in great shape. Even since Mick had last worked with him, his alcoholism had worsened. 'It was fairly sordid in there,' remembers Roadent. 'Hundreds and hundreds of old records, and bottles of strong drink hidden away in odd places. I found bottles of gin in the bathroom cabinet. He had some strange ways. You'd ask if you could have some of his drink but he wouldn't trust you with the bottle, so he'd put it in his mouth and then offer it to you.'

'He was listening to Led Zep's *The Song Remains The Same*,' Mick recalls. 'He was so disgusted with it he took the record off the turntable and threw it across the room like a frisbee. Anyway, it hit Joe in the eye! I felt there was a kinship, we were all outsiders. He was an inspiring person to be around.'

In Guy's bathroom there were two photos pinned to the wall: one was of Hitler, the other of Bob Dylan. There was also an inflatable life-raft in its packaging. 'Just in case,' Guy explained. He was enthusiastic and entertaining. He'd never heard The Clash at that point but he already 'loved' them. If Mick held a grudge against Guy, he certainly didn't show it. If anything, he still felt he had everything to prove to his favourite group's former mentor. 'I don't think he remembered me from before,' says Jones.

The Clash recorded five songs: 'Career Opportunities', 'White Riot', 'Janie Jones', 'London's Burning' and '1977' (these versions of 'Career Opportunities' and 'Janie Jones' are included on *The Clash on Broadway* box set) in a session overseen by Polydor A&R man Chris Parry and engineer Vic Smith – the team which would later produce The Jam. But their *alla prima* method – quickly rendering the music onto tape under Guy's ebullient direction, without many overdubs, backing vocals or effects – yielded disappointing results. Mick believes that Guy didn't get the opportunity to turn the demo session into the 'major number' he wanted to. 'They didn't know how to deal with him,' he explained in the *The Clash on Broadway* booklet.

'Guy's big catchphrase was "I love it! I love it! I love it!"' says Roadent. 'He was a nutter but he didn't really capture the madness of The Clash. It was really flat, there was no dynamic in it. It was dead. The group saw that. They were listening to it afterwards and no one was excited by it. It was like, "Is that it?" None of them was happy with it. The record company agreed the session wasn't very good. Guy was Mick's hero, and he had to admit, "Well, he's lost it a bit."'

Micky Foote comments: 'The Polydor stuff sounded like A.N. Other band. The whole vibe was "It doesn't sound like this up at Rehearsals, does it?"'

Unofficial recordings of the whole session underscore Stevens's failure to translate The Clash's meaty live sound to tape. The recordings lack sonic sophistication, depth or resonance. Guy's ability to channel the magic of the 1960s into punk had spectacularly failed to materialise – at least for the time being.

There was no time for another session. In two weeks' time, The Clash were embarking on their first nationwide tour, as support to The Pistols, and they had no permanent drummer.

The Western Arms sits on the corner of Ladbroke Grove and Kensal Road, a nicotine-stained, malty souvenir from another age. Just a few yards away, the Grand Union Canal winds its course to Little Venice, then north up to Camden Town and the back of the old railway yard and Rehearsal Rehearsals. The city's ancient, watery arteries have been transformed from neglected relics of Victorian prosperity into coveted mooring sites for expensive house-boats. The London of The Clash is slowly disappearing but, for the time being at least, the Western Arms lies untouched.

The gentrification of Ladbroke Grove is a bête noire of *The Roughler*, a west London magazine that Joe Strummer used to read – feet up on the table, stetson on head – whenever he was in a pub in this part of town. At the time of our interview the publication (based in the nearby complex which once housed the legendary reggae imprint, Trojan) was being put together by Roadent – though a break-in in summer 2004 had temporarily halted its production. The issue we're looking at, in the garden of the Western, examines the recent refurbishment of the Earl of Percy's snug bar, Paul Simonon's second home when he lived at nearby Oxford Gardens. *The Roughler* prefers its pubs to be unmolested by developers and to serve a perfectly poured pint of Guinness.

Roadent appears to have survived the ravages of punk rock and its aftermath. You can catch a glimpse of him back in 1977 striding across the stage in the live Clash footage from Munich, included on the *Essential*

Clash DVD: tall, thin, his fair hair *en brosse*. He is also a star of the German-made *Punk in London* documentary, in which he's interviewed upstairs at Rehearsals.

Roadent's mind works with intimidating quicksilver precision. Talking about the early Clash, he twists up snatches of Situationism, Marxism, Nazism and Euclidean geometry into a surreal, comic-portentous monologue. He also reads aloud, mock-theatrically and hilariously, the passages relating to him in a previous Clash biography.

Roadent was one of several key Clash associates whose energy and ideas would create a sparky, challenging, edgy atmosphere around the group. Over the years, he, Johnny Green, Robin Banks, Jock Scot et al became a sort of punk equivalent of the RAND corporation, the 'malignant university' of intelligent misfits which the US Army and Navy tapped for their unconventional thinking. They were always much more than mere apostles and the term 'roadies' is ludicrously inappropriate: a bit like calling Joe Strummer a musician. 'Bernie didn't understand why we'd hang out with the road crew,' smiled Joe. 'But these were the people who threw their lot in with us when we didn't have two pennies to rub together. We developed a bond. It was great to have their enthusiasm and cutting criticism.'

Brought up in Coventry, Roadent came into The Clash's orbit after attending the ICA gig in late October – the one at which fans Jane Crockford and Shane MacGowan indulged in some ritualistic blood-letting, courtesy of a broken beer bottle. The incident prompted an angry Joe to launch into a typically scatological onstage lecture: 'All of you who think violence is tough, why don't you go home and collect stamps? That's much tougher.'

Roadent was nineteen at the time and had not long been released from prison in Birmingham, where he'd served two weeks for burglary. 'Thieving was a way of life then,' he says. He collared Joe and told him he was sleeping rough; Strummer, in an early example of The Clash's legendary generosity towards their followers, offered him a mattress at Rehearsals.

'Rehearsals was all like pastely pink, blue and white,' he recalls. 'We had this faux leather sofa, three sheets, one blanket and a one-bar electric fire. The fireplace was boarded up. No hot water. Bernie had put a pay phone on the wall, but we had the key so it didn't really count. There were huge rats around. We used to go off exploring the tunnels under the railway at night. It was a bit rank, very damp. Paul was lucky 'cos he couldn't smell it; he had no sense of smell. In fact, we used to go down to the Standard on Westbourne Grove after a gig, and he would eat the hottest curry they had. He could just about taste it then.'

Roadent was educated at a grammar school (not a boarding school, as some writers have said). He was fascinated by history and politics, and, like Robin Banks, had flirted with crime and paid for it with jail. In Tony Parsons's landmark *NME* interview with the group a few months later, he observed Roadent reading *Mein Kampf*. Freed from the liberal mindset of the squatting environment, Joe had also become captivated, though certainly not seduced, by radical political literature and extremist organisations.

'I think I gelled with Joe straight away,' says Roadent. 'We had our fascination with [European terrorist groups] the Red Army Faction, the Baader-Meinhoff Gang and Brigate Rosse. There was that interesting contradiction – they believed in their causes so much they were prepared to die for them, but then again, going out and killing people isn't really persuading them you've got a just cause. But we were just learning and fumbling our way around these things. There were other, quite contradictory things that we used to believe in as well. Unfortunately, neither of us had a university education to indoctrinate us, so there wasn't any attempt to try to be that centred. People have slagged off The Clash and Joe for taking on new identities whenever they felt like it, but that was part of them growing up. Only William fucking Hague knows his politics at fourteen or whenever. Most people really don't know, and rarely know, until they're dead; so changing is quite an honest thing to do, I think.'

Roadent was quickly accepted into The Clash fold and made Rehearsals his home. He shared the upstairs room with Paul – and sometimes Joe when he wasn't holed up at an abandoned ice-cream factory in Foscote Mews, in his old W9 stomping ground. Roadent and Simonon grew close for a while. They shared a child-like sense of mischief, larking around on Sebastian Conran's motorbike and having *Westworld*-style shoot-outs with BB guns once Rehearsals had been shut up for the night.

'Paul was a lot more hedonistic than the others,' he says. 'He was really out for a laugh and a good time. He would see the funny side of things; he would just sit back and laugh. I think that was partly because he felt he was a little bit inarticulate, so he held himself back from joining in. Of course, we all hated him 'cos the women loved him. But he laughed and watched everything. Maybe that was the artist in him, observing what was going on.'

Roadent was also exposed daily to Paul's reggae obsession. They played records continuously on an old Gerrard turntable plugged into Joe's spare AC30 amp. 'We used to listen to *The Harder They Come* over and over again. Paul would skip over 'Many Rivers To Cross', he said it sounded like a hymn.'

But Roadent's relationship with the group wasn't entirely hitch-free. He seems to have been presciently sensitive to an issue that would soon divide the group in their later years: 'The one I found hard to get on with was Mick. But then, didn't everyone?'

On 13 November 1976, *Melody Maker* published the first major music press feature on the group. The author was their early champion, Caroline Coon. Three months before, Caroline had written a landmark piece, also in *Melody Maker,* about the fresh crop of bands led by The Pistols and The Clash. It was here she appropriated the term 'punk' to describe them. She explained how the term 'punk' was 'coined about six years ago to describe the American rock bands of 1965–8 who sprung up as a result of hearing The Yardbirds, Who, Them, Stones.' Since then, she argued, the phrase had acquired 'the glamorous connotations once implied by the over-used word "rebel"'. It was, therefore, a perfect name for this new scene. Caroline played down any link between what was happening in America and the new bands emerging in the UK. She emphasised that the English groups had 'only the most tenuous connections' to the New York punk groups like The Ramones, Television and Patti Smith.

Her November feature on The Clash was to prove equally momentous. Looking back on it now, it's a sophisticated piece of journalism that served its purpose commendably. Like Mark Perry, Coon is a willing and enthusiastic conduit for the group's punk rhetoric but refuses to let any bullshit or lazy assumptions go unchallenged. (When Joe contends that his only other option for work is a factory, her brusque riposte is: 'Yes, but someone's got to work in a factory . . .')

This time, Paul gets equal billing with Joe and Mick as a Clash spokesperson. This provides Caroline with an opportunity to draw attention, for the first time, to the John–Paul–George dynamic of the band. (Alas, there is no Ringo; the departing Terry is gagged; the official reason for his non-appearance is that he had 'a serious argument with Joe' about whether he should quit the country because of its dire state.) Strummer is revealed as the angry, middle-class rebel; Jones, the hip, guitar-slinging kid from a broken home; Simonon, the unmusicianly, reggae-mad yob from London's worst schools. Each member gives his own account of his background: an exercise in self-image that most people schooled in rock 'n' roll and outlaw myths would relish.

It's easy to forget that Mick and Paul were still young; barely out of their teens. Strummer, the old, wiser one, was only twenty-four. Naturally, as punk rockers they play up the negatives in their early lives: divorce, abandonment, lack of opportunity. Yet, despite accusations of this being the start of the 'Clash Myth', most of what they say in their self-painted little swagger portraits is true. The only untruth, oddly, concerns Joe's school: assuming the mistake wasn't Caroline's, he fibs his boarding school was in Yorkshire, a playful reference to the brutal, provincial institutions of Victorian literature, like Tom Brown's Rugby or Nicholas Nickleby's Dotheby's Hall, perhaps? Maybe 'Surrey' sounded too middle-class for comfort. The views the group would express in the piece would very soon become enshrined as something approaching a Punk Constitution.

'That interview was crucial,' recalls Coon. 'They were saying, "You hippy! The hippy movement has failed!" They were anti-drugs, anti-denim, anti-*Top of the Pops*. There was this wonderful dialogue as these two generations clashed.'

Caroline was exhilarated by The Clash's idealism, however callow. In the late 1960s, she had been a star of the counter-culture, running Release, which arranged legal aid for people arrested for drug offences. Caroline had protested outside the *News of the World*'s offices after the Jagger–Richards drug-bust in 1967 and staged the events at the Roundhouse, which Mick and his friends attended. She had watched with horror as the ideals of the hippy movement slowly crumbled in the mid-1970s.

'It felt like a betrayal when rock' n' roll became the establishment,' she says. 'The richer those bands got, the less they talked about being young people and the more they talked about what it was like being in rock 'n' roll bands. About 1972, 1973, you were getting pictures of Elton John shaking hands with Princess Margaret. The rebels who were meant to be expressing your feelings about wanting to change culture and society were changing sides. They were playing huge stadiums, driving Bentleys but not putting too much back to the people. So there was a sense of disappointment and betrayal. The perception was that the hippy movement had failed.'

A lot has been said about the doldrums of the 1970s from which punk erupted. It was an era when there was seeping unease about the nation itself, a deep, indistinct feeling that Britain was ailing. Writers have talked of similar feelings in, say, 1912–13 when the country was rocked by the dual loss of the Titanic and Captain Scott's expedition to the South Pole, or in 1956 with the Suez Crisis. Musically, it's quite clear that, post-glam, all the real action was happening on the periphery: in reggae, disco, pub rock even. In wider society, there was an overwhelming sense that, despite the progress of the 1960s, nothing much had changed. Britain was still run by the Second World War generation – Ronald Mellor's generation. Smoking a joint in public would automatically get you arrested. Immigration was a growing issue and racism deep-rooted and widespread. A TV comedy like *Fawlty Towers* could still get a laugh from a hospital curtain being pulled back to reveal (cue sniggering) a *black* doctor.

Kurt Vonnegut once made the observation that artists were like canaries in a mine, warning of potential danger long before other people had seen it coming. Certainly, punk coincided with the beginning of deeper changes in society. Arthur Marwick writes simply and eloquently on the subject in his *Culture in Britain Since 1945*. He points to the early 1970s as the beginning of the end of post-war 'consensus' – a comparatively happy period when most elements of society had worked together for the benefit of the country. The end of consensus paved the way for the 'inevitable political chaos' of the Thatcher years that Strummer prophesies in Caroline's *Melody Maker* feature. Marwick believes the transformations in the 1970s were in part attributable to the worsening economic conditions in the UK: oil prices rocketing; unemployment passing 2 million in 1975; inflation running at over 20 per cent. A week after the Punk Festival at the 100 Club, the government had to go cap in hand to the International Monetary Fund for a loan of $3.9 billion to bail out the economy. This loan came with conditions: it was to be recouped via reduced spending on social welfare. This sounded the death knell for the vision of a New Jerusalem, which The Clash's parents had been promised in the 1950s.

Pete Townshend sees The Clash's concerns as coming out of the same disaffection that he'd felt. 'The Clash were an "echo" of earlier bands like The Who,' he says. 'So what they were echoing was the post-war atmosphere of discontent, frustration, disaffection and quite deep and anarchic depression and anger that grew out of the failed Labour movement reforms instituted straight after the war, like the NHS and the dole, and the shockingly high taxes of the end of that era. It is inevitable that educated young men like The Clash would feel compelled to turn their backs on both the left and right and appear to be anarchistic.'

He adds: 'The Clash were poets. As artists working with pop music they were completely free to express and reflect their unhappiness with the world around them. They also expressed annoyance that the bands that went before – like The Who – had not been militant enough.'

It's a curiously modern idea that every decade or so a youth-generated musical movement will come along and transform culture and society. But even after rock 'n' roll in the 1950s and The Beatles in the 1960s, there was no reason to expect a third great musical and social shift in the 1970s. Yet there was a largely unexpressed belief that this would occur.

Bernie Rhodes says: 'I remember around 1974 and 1975 people were bored. They had Roxy Music and David Bowie but they still got bored. When people are really bored, something will happen.'

Micky Foote concurs: 'It was really terrible then, 1973, 1974, 1975. It was Roxy Music, Queen, Led Zeppelin, it was all these mega-monster bands or little tribute bands down the pub. I don't think the kids were doing anything, they were just hanging about slagging people off. But everyone was waiting for something, even though they had no idea what it was.'

Tony Wilson, the future head of Factory Records, summed it up thus: 'Those years were unbelievably awful. First of all you watched heroes from the 1960s grow fat, limp and pointless. How many bad Van Morrison albums did you buy before you finally stopped? And the people who were happening were this pompous, sententious fucking crap. People forget how bad it all was. Two words: Rick Wakeman.'

Bernie and Malcolm had sensed that a new youth movement was brewing, a cauldron of nebulous energy without an outlet, in 1975. The number of kids who were bored and looking for something new was reaching a critical mass, though Robin Banks and others make the point that the boredom young people experienced was of a largely unconscious kind: few realised quite how dull things were until punk arrived like an electric shock to shake them from their slumber.

On 24 May, Bernie, Malcolm and Glen Matlock went to see The Sensational Alex Harvey Band at Hammersmith Odeon. Talking in Paul Gorman's *The Look*, Matlock says: 'It was absolutely packed with these kids, and that's when I think the penny dropped with Malcolm. That coincided with us getting [The Sex Pistols] together and Malcolm realising The New York Dolls had had it.' One of the 'kids' at that show happened to be Paul Simonon – attending one of the very few gigs he ever went to as a teenager.

Back at Rehearsals, Caroline Coon was being wowed not only by The Clash's spiky, political pronouncements but their new image. That autumn, following on from the Jackson Pollock look, the group had stencilled their shirts and boiler suits with slogans taken from their own lyrics and the militant reggae records on constant rotation at Rehearsals. The legends read: 'Heavy

Duty Discipline'; 'Sten Guns In Knightsbridge'; 'Heavy Manners'; 'Creative Violence'. The stencilled clothes, an idea suggested by Bernie, were a nod to 1950s Lettrism; they also acknowledged the pioneering clothes of Mr Freedom's Tommy Roberts – the first person to popularise T-shirts bearing slogans.

The stencilling didn't stop with their clothes. Paul's bass soon bore the legend 'Pressure', which had roots reggae overtones (Leroy Smart's 'Too Much Pressure'; Greyhound's 'The Pressure is Coming On'; Toots and the Maytals' 'Pressure Drop') while Joe's Telecaster proclaimed 'Noise'. Mick, meanwhile, preferred to leave his treasured Les Paul Junior *au naturel*.

'I bought along my own camera,' recalls Caroline. 'I took the photo of the group against the wall with their hands up [later used for the sleeve of 'White Riot']. And there on Joe's back, as they turned round, were the words 'Hate & War', which was exactly what punk was, the negative to peace and love. It was the antithesis of the hippy ideal, a hard, protesting, angry, anarchic full stop to all that overblown mainstream rock 'n' roll.'

(Simonon's 'White Riot' boiler suit was shown at London's Barbican Centre in 2000 as part of an exhibition of rock fashion. Most of us know it from the grainy, doctored black-and-white image on the 'White Riot' single sleeve. It's actually something of a work of art: 'White Riot' is painted in yellow with a tomato-red trim and the whole thing is delicately flecked with coloured paint.)

Another of the slogans was 'Passion is a Fashion'. Joe wore it on a zipped blouson, splashed with white paint. It's possible that it was inspired by a graffito on the wall of Malcolm's Sex boutique, 'Does passion end in fashion?', though in a 1977 interview, Joe claimed, and no one has ever contradicted him, that he'd never been into the shop. It's also, of course, a neat inversion of the maxim 'fashion is a passion'. As a slogan, it was powerful but ambiguous – does it mean being passionate is a passing fad? Or that passion is a (commendable) way of doing things? Either way, passion was a word that summed up The Clash's approach to their art better than any other.

Joe's word-play was often clever and inspired, but his punk persona sometimes led him into dangerous territory. In a December interview in the *NME*, he expounded his theories on violence in response to the 'Creative Violence' legend sprayed on Simonon's jacket. Having formally denounced violence from the stage at the ICA, only to wade enthusiastically into the ruck at the Night of Treason a week later, Joe now spent the interview toying with a flick-knife.

'Suppose I smash your face in and slit your nostrils with this, right?' he said. 'If you don't learn anything from it, then it's not worth it, right?' Joe then explained that if his adversary *had* learned something from the experience, 'Well, that's in a sense creative violence.'

The *NME* interviewer, Miles, the late 1960s counterculture hipster, is too polite or, possibly, too distracted by the positive aspects of Joe's theorising – much of the interview deals with the evils of racism – to point out that he sounds like an idiot. Joe's words also contradicted The Clash manifesto he'd outlined at the start of the piece and which would remain the group's ideological lodestone throughout their life: 'I think people ought to know that we're anti-Fascist, we're anti-violence, we're anti-racist and we're pro-creative. We're against ignorance.'

It must have been strange for the likes of Tymon Dogg and Richard Dudanski to pick up the music press that week and see their loveable, half-crazed old friend, his hair now butchered and dyed blond, ruminating on carving up his political adversaries with a switchblade. But Joe's combative rhetoric was creating a stink and forcing people to think. This was the beginning of Joe's emergence as a 'politician'. As politicians do, he was forcing himself into believing his own rhetoric.

Behind the scenes, though, the pressure of being punk's cheer-leaders and 'creating something new' was already starting to take its toll on arguably the most conscientious and sensitive member of the group. Sometime in November, Mark Perry bumped into Mick at a gig.

'He was very questioning about what they were doing,' he recalls. 'Mick was going, "We're saying all this but I just hope we can live up to it." Joe kept up that hard persona more, he wasn't so introspective. Mick always seemed to be worrying about what the kids thought, whether the group could handle the responsibility. Many times I stood at a party when he was brooding over it.'

Whatever Mick's worries, The Clash were poised to take their message to the nation. In the last week of November, The Clash began rehearsing with their new drummer, Rob Harper-Milne (then calling himself Rob Harper). A friend of Billy Idol's from Sussex University, Harper had seen the group at Ilford: he described the impact of their frontline as being like 'three Eddie Cochrans'. He had replied to the advert for a drummer the group had placed in the *Melody Maker*.

Previously considered for the post had been Rusty Egan (later of Glen Matlock's post-Pistols group The Rich Kids) and Paul's younger brother Nick. There was even talk of installing Roadent behind the kit. Joe was willing to offer the job to his simpatico pal, even if he was a complete drumming novice; but the more musically minded Mick wasn't.

Interviewed by Myles Palmer for his book *Small Talk, Big Names*, Rob Harper, aged twenty-seven at the time, recalled his impressions of the group. Clearly he took a dislike to the bass-player, who was by now seeing Caroline Coon. 'The women loved Simonon, I've never seen anything like it,' he said, perhaps exposing the root of his ill-feeling. 'I thought he was a complete berk. The other two I got on really well with, but Simonon was just thick.'

The Anarchy tour was due to start on Friday, 3 December 1976 at Norwich Polytechnic. Twenty-four dates were scheduled, the last on Boxing Day at the Roxy Theatre in Harlesden. The Clash, booked to play bottom of the bill to Johnny Thunders's new group The Heartbreakers, as well as The Damned and The Pistols, were understandably thrilled about their first major tour, if not their place in the running order.

But then fate intervened. Or, perhaps more accurately, Steve Jones's fondness for Anglo-Saxon. The Pistols' first TV interview, on Wednesday, 1 December 1976, ranks among the great television moments of all time. A filmed interview with Queen, then enjoying their twelve-week stay at number one with 'Bohemian Rhapsody', had been scheduled for inclusion on Thames Television's early evening *Thames Today* programme. When it was unexpectedly pulled because of clearance problems, EMI's promotions manager Eric Hall (now a famous footballers' agent) persuaded the show's producers to accept their new signings, The Sex Pistols, as substitute guests. They would wish they hadn't.

Watching it back today, it's still utterly hilarious. Jones is wearing his Sex boutique 'tits' T-shirt and leather keks. Rotten is pimply and withdrawn, rocking back and forth on his chair, a nervous, skulking child. The presenter, Bill Grundy, tipsy and testy after a long lunch with *Punch* magazine, provokes the group into an argument. Then the tense, three-minute exchange spirals out of control, a horribly compelling playground fight:

BILL GRUNDY: . . . Go on, you've got another ten seconds. Say something outrageous.
STEVE JONES: You dirty bastard.
BILLY GRUNDY: Go on, again.
STEVE JONES: You dirty fucker.
BILL GRUNDY: What a *clever* boy!
STEVE JONES: You fucking rotter!

The next day, The Pistols were front-page news (the *Daily Mirror*: 'The filth and the fury!') and overnight became the most famous new group in the country.

The result was that the Anarchy tour bus zig-zagged around Britain to find the gigs the groups were scheduled to play were cancelled due to pressure from worried local councils. Only seven shows out of the twenty-one eventually went ahead. All the groups *wanted* to play and were frustrated and disappointed by the often last-minute cancellations. But at least The Pistols had the consolation that their reputation as a menace to society was snowballing. The Grundy incident had brought them the kind of publicity that Malcolm could have only dreamed of. For The Clash it was largely a waste of time.

On 8 December, matters worsened when EMI pulled their funding of the tour, before eventually deciding to drop the group altogether. This left Malcolm and Bernie covering the extra expenses out of their own pocket. The previous day The Damned had been thrown off the tour for intimating they'd go ahead and play the Derby date, even though The Pistols had been banned from appearing.

Ask any of the people on that tour what they remember of it and the response is the same: long motorway journeys, hours sitting in brown-carpeted hotel rooms, waiting to hear if the gigs were on or off, and long, amphetamine-assisted drinking sessions to relieve the boredom.

Roadent comments: 'On the Anarchy tour it all went horribly wrong. You're not sure what the fuck you're doing, you're spending your time on coaches going from one place to another. Not a tour bus, but those old-fashioned coaches. It was very unreal, it wasn't like touring. Also The Clash were originally bottom of the bill – it was like The Damned were above them, for God's sake! I had a tour poster with all the dates crossed out and then the replacement gig written in, which I'd then have to cross out as well.'

None of the English groups seemed too enamoured with their old hero, Johnny Thunders, either. His ripping yarns of life in The Dolls were entertaining, but his raging heroin habit wasn't. The Gretsch White Falcon guitar Joe used throughout the tour was bought off Thunders, who needed the cash for drugs. Divisions soon appeared within the Pistols-Clash camp. Simonon hung out with Cook and Steve Jones, while Glen Matlock roomed and talked music with Mick. Later – and this underscores how volatile the atmosphere was – Bernie and Malcolm mooted a swap: Paul to join The Pistols and Matlock The Clash. In the event, it came to nothing: Paul simply didn't bother turning up to the meeting to discuss it.

Michael Wale, the comedy scriptwriter, once said, 'Performers are usually bad travellers. They get bored easily. What else is there to do but drink away the boredom in their hotel?' He was talking about Tony Hancock but he may as well have been describing the Anarchy revue. At Cleethorpes, a few days after he turned twenty-one, Simonon spent all afternoon in the bar with Steve Jones and Paul Cook. 'I got completely sloshed,' says Simonon. 'I went on stage, hit the first note then went reeling backwards into my bass cabinet. Joe was laughing his head off but Mick was really pissed off. It was terrible. It was a disaster. So I didn't repeat that situation again. I was always clear and precise after that. Just one shot of vodka in the dressing room. I jumped in the deep end once and learned my lesson.'

'The best time we had was in Bristol [it was actually Plymouth],' Joe told Jon Savage in his unpublished *England's Dreaming* interview. 'We checked into this bed and breakfast, and I was so tired I fell asleep immediately. Meanwhile, Malcolm and Bernie decided to move everyone into the Holiday Inn, but forgot about me. Eventually, someone came back and woke me up. That night they broke into the hotel swimming pool, rock 'n' roll madness! Micky Foote got completely drunk and dived into the shallow end and split his head open on the tiles.'

The coup de grâce on that night was provided by one of the roadies, who crapped in Bernie's bed.

Until recently, no recordings of The Clash from the Anarchy tour were thought to have survived. However, in 2004, a tape of their set at the Electric Circus in Manchester surfaced. It catches The Clash in their early, clattering glory. The songs are played fractionally slower than on the first album, and 'Protex Blue', a totem from their earliest days, is re-worked as a political song 'about Big Brother' (though the all-new lyrics are indecipherable). Rob Harper proves to be a tough, reliable drummer, though how enjoyable he found the experience is questionable: that evening he had been on the receiving end of a Mick tutorial on rock 'n' roll cool.

'Mick Jones said to me, "Rob! Don't waddle when you walk!"' he told Myles Palmer. 'I knew what they were doing, I wasn't a naive teenager, but I'd rather not have the fame than be ordered about.'

Harper also observed a contradiction that the group would increasingly find difficult to gloss over. 'My hazy, romantic notions of how pop music was put together were completely burst by being in The Clash. Because they were strong characters they were going for it. They were saying one thing to the media, but behind the scenes they were saying, "We want to be the next Rolling Stones."'

In the audience at the Electric Circus was the cartoonist Ray Lowry. Ray had been baptised into the world of rock 'n' roll in the early 1960s when he saw The Beatles play at a fête in Omskirk. They performed after the marrow contest. He'd also seen The Stones supporting The Everly Brothers. 'The Clash were marvellous,' he says. 'Other people said the same – the electricity! – they looked as though they were wired into the mains ... Keith Richards had a touch of it when he was younger. The Pistols came on later and they were disappointing. To be honest with you, that was the first and only time I think they absolutely burned like a torch. There was no holding back. Later on, Joe was conscious of getting nodes on his throat, but then he let his voice rip. We were probably wearing flares at the time. We were totally changed by the evening. It was terrific.'

When the Anarchy bus returned to London on the evening of 23 December, it disgorged The Clash onto Oxford Street. 'I was really destroyed,' recalled Joe. 'When I got off the coach we had no money and it was just awful. I felt twice as hungry as I'd ever felt before. Christmas was here and me and Micky Foote had our little bags in our hands and I just felt like it was the worst thing in the world that the tour had ended.'

Joe wandered up Tottenham Court Road towards Camden in the freezing December night, deliberately not wearing his woolly jumper. He later said he wanted to get as cold and as miserable as he could. He had no permanent place to live. He had no money. The Clash still had no regular drummer. Worse still, they were lagging behind the competition. It seemed only fair that The Pistols had made a splash with 'Anarchy in the UK', but The Damned had signed to Stiff and issued a single, 'New Rose', and The Buzzcocks were preparing to release an EP in a few weeks' time.

That Christmas, The Clash had a roast turkey dinner at journalist Jonh Ingham's house with some of the other punks. They watched Johnny Thunders shoot up smack in the kitchen, and wondered what the hell 1977 had in store for them.

6

TWO SEVENS CLASH

'I chased my fancied meal through prose, and found . . . only a few men who had tried honestly to be greater than mankind; and only their strainings and wrestlings really fill my stomach.'

T.E. Lawrence to Edward Garnett, quoted in Colin Wilson's *The Outsider*

'Rubbish!'
LEE PERRY, SARM EAST, 1977

According to Peter Ackroyd's momentous *London*, in Saxon times Covent Garden used to be called Ludenwic. 'Wic' means 'marketplace' and in the 1700s, Covent Garden still held a market, now on London's first ever piazza, designed by Inigo Jones. The market was the greatest in England, selling fresh garden produce destined for the tables of London's great and poor. But by the mid-1970s this ancient part of the capital was ailing and dilapidated and awaiting re-development.

In late December 1976, the Roxy club opened in Neal Street, across the road from Covent Garden tube station. It had formerly been a gay club called Chagaurama's. Started by Malcolm McLaren's accountant, Andy Czezowski, the Roxy was the first tailor-made punk venue. As there were only two English punk records – The Sex Pistols' 'Anarchy In the UK' and The Damned's 'New Rose' – and the supply of cool new US punk was limited, the resident DJ, Don Letts, played mostly dub and reggae.

'People have the misconception that I turned all punks onto reggae,' says Don, holding court in one of the private upstairs rooms at the Electric cinema on Portobello Road. 'Not the case. It was all the punks who didn't live anywhere near black people that were turned on. Which in those times was a lot of people. But punks like Paul Simonon, Joe

Strummer and John Lydon were definitely well into reggae before I came along.'

For three years in the late 1960s, Don was the only black pupil at Archbishop Tenison grammar school in Brixton, the alma mater of another character in this story, Ray Gange, a couple of years his junior. Don, whose parents came to England from the Caribbean in the late 1950s, was in his early teens one of the biggest collectors of Beatles memorabilia in the country.

Not that this made school any easier in the racially unenlightened 1960s and 1970s. 'It was character-building stuff, dude!' he says. 'Talk about making a problem your asset! No one would ever call you a "wog". It was like "Kitty-cat-eater", "Brillo-pad", "nig nog", all this shit. I am starting to read my Angela Davis and George Jackson stuff, I am getting politicised. So I'm like, "Yeah, I *am* a black bastard!" And it did make me really strong. But at that time I was also immersed in white culture. I have to say: growing up in that environment did turn me onto a lot of the better aspects of white popular culture. I was listening to a lot of music I would normally not have listened to at home because my parents played blues, ska and reggae. But the whole experience made Don the big-mouth motherfucker he is now. I knew I had to hold my ground otherwise I was going to go under.'

In the mid-1970s Don was offered a job in Acme Attractions, a rival to McLaren's Let It Rock/Sex shop. It was through the Kings Road scene that Letts befriended The Sex Pistols and Bernie Rhodes. Besides selling clothes, Don provided another essential service: selling weed under the counter to visiting pop stars like Bob Marley. He also compiled reggae tapes for his famous customers.

'I wish I could tell you what a trip that was,' he says. 'Back in those days C-90 tapes were a currency. I was swapping tapes with Deborah Harry, Lenny Kaye, Patti Smith, The Pistols. I mean anybody who was anybody, they were all in the shop at the same time. It wasn't just a shop, it was the most happening club in town. Probably the happiest period of my entire life. I would swan around in dark glasses, my pockets were the till. If somebody didn't have the money to buy something, I would fucking give them it. I didn't care!

'That is where I became friends with Paul and Mick. When punk rock all kicked off, Acme Attractions was already happening, so I am like the king of the block and I really worked it, a right flash cunt. Then all of a sudden there are these other guys on the block, mainly John [Lydon], Joe, Paul and Mick. There was a period when it was like, "Who is that cunt?" We'd be eyeing each other, you know that thing with young guys, they'd be looking at me and I'd be looking at them, they wouldn't speak to me, I wouldn't speak to them.'

The Clash performed at the Roxy on New Year's Day, playing two sets. Joe's shirt was painted with a huge '1977'. 'The vibe was a free, electric vibe,' recalls the photographer Dennis Morris. 'Everyone there was looking for something different from the way things were, whether it was fashion, music, whatever.'

The Roxy was to be The Clash's last live appearance for two months and, by mutual consent, their last gig with the disillusioned Rob Harper. He was not only denounced, as was customary – Bernie circulated a rumour he was sacked for ideological transgressions – but also airbrushed from the story altogether. His name was never mentioned in any Clash interview until several years after they split. With more demo sessions looming, The Clash persuaded Terry Chimes to return to Rehearsals to help out. It wouldn't be the last time he was called upon to solve a drumming crisis.

Around this time The Clash made a crucial decision, one which would have a profound effect on British music and culture. They decided to start playing reggae. Initially, they'd been resistant to the idea. 'We had an early song called "Dig a Hole",' says Simonon. 'It went, "Dig some reggae but don't play any."'

'We didn't take the decision lightly,' said Joe, who'd toyed around with Desmond Dekker's 'The Israelites' and a U-Roy song in The 101'ers. 'We went to the pub with The Pistols to discuss it. They didn't think it was such a great idea but we could see the potential to combine it with what we were doing to make something powerful.'

Their hesitance to add reggae to their set had its roots in their sensitivity to its status as the voice and soundtrack for London's black community. The music was born out of the violent, Third World struggles in Jamaica; it had resonance for blacks on the racially edgy streets of the capital. When artists like Eric Clapton had covered Marley's 'I Shot the Sheriff' and McCartney had added a reggae motif to Wings' 'Jet' in 1974 there seemed to have been a spectacular failure on their part to connect with, or understand, the culture that had originally produced reggae. For them, it was simply music.

With The Clash, there was a distinct, qualitative difference. It wasn't lost on them that they were a bunch of white, ex-art students. But it wasn't as if they were jumping out of a limo to put down some cod-reggae chops at a plush studio, either. Their identification with the West Indian community was passionate and genuine: Paul and Mick had lived in heavily black areas of London most of their lives. Simonon spoke in patois with his old school-friends in Ladbroke Grove. There was also, of course, the not insignificant matter of Joe and Paul's participation in the Notting Hill Riot. They'd stood shoulder-to-shoulder with blacks as they fought the police – until they'd been mugged, of course. The Clash's profound, exuberant MacInnes-esque affection for Anglo-Caribbean culture was obvious, from Joe's nights at the Silver Sands in Newport to Mick's love of dub to Paul's misspent youth at Notting Hill blues parties.

There was another reason to marry punk with reggae: both had a similar purpose. Caroline Coon points out that, before punk, 'reggae carried the torch of protest that white rock music had had in the late 1960s but then lost'. This was true: as the reggae writer David Katz argues, Jamaican music had been a vehicle for social and political commentary going back to the days of Laurel Aitken's 'Ghana Independence' and Lord Lebby's 'Ethiopia' in the late 1950s. When Lee Perry politicised Bob Marley a decade later, the stage was set for reggae protest songs to reach an international audience. As the Jamaican producer and singer Roy Cousins once said, 'If you listen to reggae music, you don't need to buy the paper. Reggae music tell you everything wha' happen in Jamaica.'

In 1976, political tension in Jamaica was at its height. Supporters of Michael Manley's socialist government and Edward Seaga's right-wing JLP party were fighting gun battles on the streets. By June 1976, over 150 lay dead and Manley, bowing to pressure from his opponents, declared a state of emergency in the country. He feared the admission that Jamaica was on the brink of political meltdown would, to the international community, legitimise a CIA-backed, right-wing coup, like Chile had suffered in 1973. In December 1976, in an attack that many believe was politically motivated, Bob Marley was wounded by gunshots at the former home of Chris Blackwell (of Island Records) on Hope Road in Kingston.

Reggae music that year reflected the turmoil: Prince Far-I's 'Heavy Manners', Joe Gibbs's 'State of Emergency', Max Romeo's 'War In Babylon', Tapper Zukie's 'MPLA' (Manley supported the Cuban soldiers fighting in Africa for the Movimento Popular de Libertacao de Angola). The group Culture celebrated the arrival of 1977 with their song 'Two Sevens Clash', in honour of Marcus Garvey, Jamaica's charismatic early twentieth-century black nationalist, who had an apocalyptic vision that, in 1977 – 'when the two sevens clash' – the chosen Jamaicans would be returned to Africa. (Garvey died in obscurity in London in June 1940. He was buried in Kensal Green cemetery, at the northern tip of Ladbroke Grove, before his body was returned to Jamaica in 1964.)

Up at Rehearsals, The Clash made their appointment with history: they began working up a version of Bob Marley's 1966 recording 'Dancing Shoes', plus a cover of a militant reggae song that had topped the reggae charts in

1976: Junior Murvin's 'Police and Thieves'. In a further display of brother-hood, Paul artfully pinned a Desmond Morris photo of The Mighty Diamonds to his shirt.

Incredible though it seems now, the group hadn't wholly shaken off the 'racists' controversy stirred by 'White Riot', to be re-ignited when the song was issued as a single in March 1977. Inspired by the violence at Notting Hill, it called for white people to take their fight to the street like the black youth had at the Carnival.

In their December *NME* interview, Miles pointed out how 'some people thought the lyrics . . . were racialist'. That prompted Joe, who wrote the words, to scream, 'They're not racist! They're not racist at all!' He recited the lyrics to make his point: 'Black people got a lot of problems, but they don't mind throwing a brick / White people go to school, where they teach you how to be thick.' Yet the inference of the song's first line was that all blacks were advocates of violent demonstration. Joe argued in the years to come that he was merely generalising, and described the song as a 'clumsy attempt' to encourage people to protest. But political correctness, as it came to be called, was never his strong point. His phrases and images were those of the beat poet reflecting the language of the street, like the 'kebab Greeks' and 'wops' of 'Hate and War' and the 'Hey, Chi man!' line several years later in 'Lightning Strikes'. He saw nothing amiss in stating 'a black sharp knife never slips' in 'The Last Gang in Town'. He referred to Japanese as 'Nips'. It was this unsentimental, unguarded street-talk which would give The Clash's material an uncomfortable truthfulness.

Johnny Green, the band's future road manager, sees Joe's method as a cal-culated provocation. Our conversation touches on this point while discussing the furore in April 2004 over TV commentator Ron Atkinson's description of footballer Marcel Desailly as a 'fucking lazy thick nigger'. Atkinson is well known in the UK as an early champion of black players. Green comments: 'Joe wasn't scared of using those kind of words. Mick was far more what you'd now call PC. He didn't like that stuff. But Joe wanted to challenge people, he wanted to force people to think. He wasn't scared of getting people to confront [racist ideas and language], however uncomfortable it would make them feel. He wanted people to work it out for themselves.'

As the winter freeze began to bite at the unheated Rehearsals, and the group's breath formed clouds in the cold air, The Clash squared up to the issue of a record contract. It had now become a matter of some urgency. Since November 1976, Polydor's Chris Parry had been courting the group. He was desperate to sign them but his boss, Jim Crook, was reluctant to give him the go-ahead. Parry had come perilously close to signing The Sex Pistols in the weeks following the Punk Festival, but had been gazumped by EMI. Typically, Malcolm hadn't even bothered to tell Parry the deal was off. This time, Parry was determined to make it work.

John Tiberi, then a fresh recruit to The Pistols camp, believes that Bernie and Malcolm were at this point working together quite closely to take the record companies for as much as they could. The Pistols had been dropped from EMI after the Grundy television interview, so both groups were now being chased by the same labels. Afraid of being left out, the huge, American-owned CBS label was now looking for a slice of punk action.

'Bernie and Malcolm were really tight,' says Tiberi. 'Malcolm was talking to Maurice Oberstein [head of CBS in the UK], who was absolutely horrific to deal with, a disgusting person. The Jonathan King stuff was endemic in the industry. Kenny Everett, the lot. Bernie wasn't really ready to go with them, so Malcolm went first, but he fucked up. But they had this deal: if Malcolm went with CBS, then Bernie would go with Polydor.' Micky Foote, however, was 'not sure the agreement between them was as strong as that'.

In mid-January, Chris Parry finally managed to finalise a deal for The Clash with a £40,000 advance. This matched the figure EMI had given The Pistols. Bernie signalled that The Clash would sign. Behind the scenes, though, Rhodes was having second thoughts.

'Parry was a shrewd man,' recalls Micky Foote of the affable New Zealander who would go on to successfully A&R The Jam and The Cure. 'Bloody hell. He was so sharp he'd cut himself. Bernie didn't trust him and nor did I. He had stitch-up written all over him. We used to call him "Crisp" Parry.'

Whether this was paranoia or whether Parry was trying to be a slick operator, is not clear. What is certain is that CBS suddenly put a deal on the table worth £100,000. The story goes, retold in *The Clash on Broadway* booklet and scores of other places, that Bernie told the group they were signing with Polydor, then, on the morning they were to ink the deal, informed them of a change of plan and whisked them away in a cab to CBS's headquarters in Soho Square. As with many of The Clash's ripping yarns, this was not the entire story. The fact was that Mick, more business-minded than the others, strongly influenced the decision.

'We're sitting in the office at Rehearsals,' remembers Roadent. 'Bernie came in and said, "Right, well, this is the deal: Polydor have put £40,000 on the table, as we know, but CBS have just come in and they're gonna give us a £100,000 advance." It was Mick Jones who said, "Right, no question, CBS." It wasn't Bernie's decision at all. I remember that very clearly.'

On the afternoon of Thursday, 27 January 1977, the group signed the contract at Soho Square. The deal was with CBS worldwide, giving the label the option to release The Clash's records in overseas territories. Naturally, Bernie, aping Malcolm, 'forgot' to inform Parry of his coup.

Micky Foote recalls: 'This guy came over from New York, 'cos The Clash were signed to CBS internationally. This feller was sent against his wishes, and he thought it was a hell of a lot of money to be giving a band like us. He actually said that to us, we were all sitting round the fucking table, and he fucking told us that!'

The confrontational tone of the meeting would prove to be prophetic.

After the signing ceremony, Bernie and the group celebrated, not by wrecking the boardroom, as was customary in rock 'n' roll, but by going to a cinema in nearby Leicester Square to watch a movie. The choice was typically Clash: they paid £1.50 to see Glenn Ford dispatch a few Japanese destroyers in the Second World War Pacific action thriller, *The Battle of Midway*.

The next week, following a bloody weekend in London when the IRA detonated seven large bombs, the group took up an offer from CBS's charming American press officer, Ellie Smith, to order their favourite albums from the label's back catalogue. According to Roadent, Mick insisted on taking away all nineteen Bob Dylan LPs. Roadent opted for his and Sid's heroes, Abba.

The experience seemed unreal. 'I remember walking around for days thinking how much money we'd got,' recalls Simonon, then still eating irregularly, like a starved artist, and existing on hand-outs from Caroline. 'It just seemed like an unthinkable sum.'

Micky Foote: 'We all got a £1,000 signing bonus. I went down to the south of France to see my girlfriend. Mick bought a guitar and paid for his nan to visit his mum in the States. I don't know what Joe and Paul did with theirs. We were all put on £25 a week. An ounce of dope was £12. Now it's £50. So it was maybe £100 a week in today's terms, which is not a lot of money.'

To administer their publishing royalties, Rhodes purchased an off-the-shelf company called Nineden. This would prove a very smart move: it effectively meant The Clash owned all their songs.

On signing with CBS, the group, and particularly Mick and Joe, were elated: this had been their dream since they were teenagers. They were signed to the same label that put out records by their respective heroes, Mott the Hoople and Bob Dylan. But, in just a few strokes of a pen, it also threw into confusion many of the idealistic claims they'd made in the previous six months. Like many others, *Sniffin' Glue*'s Mark Perry thought the group's anti-establishment stance meant they'd finance their own records, like The Buzzcocks were doing with their *Spiral Scratch* EP, or at least sign to an independent label. It seemed ludicrous to him that The Clash, so contemptuous of the music industry, should become willing cogs in its machinery.

The Pistols were different: their signing and departure from EMI seemed more like a heist. But The Clash? Quizzed on the subject a few weeks later, a bitterly disappointed Perry famously said: 'Punk died the day The Clash signed to CBS.'

'I was aware then, and I wasn't even that political, that economic control was everything,' says Perry. 'Controlling your own destiny is everything, and it's everything in rock music as well. I felt at that time the indie scene was already established by the likes of Chiswick and Stiff. The Clash could have easily done it themselves. They could have recorded what they wanted, decided which record shops it would be in, had total control. All their talk and what they built up as their concept of how a band should act – it would have meant more if they had done their own records. I still think it's relevant because it influenced what other bands did after The Clash. They were the most hardcore group, and everyone thought, "Well, if they've done it, why don't we?" It's not as though they signed to EMI or Chrysalis or Island, it was fucking CBS, for fuck's sake! It was like, "Hold on, this is the biggest fucking record company in the world." It seemed at the time that it was fucking wrong. It just seemed to me they had blown it.'

Others involved in punk felt less strongly about the issue, seeing it as an inevitable economic development rather than a betrayal. 'I was rather pragmatic about it,' explains Jon Savage. 'They were a rock band and they wanted to get on the majors. So big fucking deal. The Sex Pistols had already shown what you could do when you got on a major by all that fuss with EMI. It was all rather exciting. Later on, I loved The Buzzcocks, I loved the Do-It-Yourself stuff, but I just didn't think The Clash were like that.

'I talked to Mick Jones quite a lot at that period. It was such a small scene you could go round and meet these people. He was a very nice bloke, very sharp, very London, very informed. I thought Mick was an ambitious young man. I never thought he or The Clash wanted to be anything other than rock stars, really. I didn't have a problem with that; it didn't bother me at all. I liked Mick, he was very sweet and interesting. What did we talk about?

Books, records, gigs. He lent me Tom Wicker's book on the Attica State Prison riot [*A Time To Die*]. He can have it back if he wants. This was before everybody decided they had to be stupid.'

As would become customary, The Clash retorted with defensive aggression when challenged about their controversial move. They underlined the fact that the contract gave them 'complete artistic control'. 'With the *Sniffin' Glue* thing,' said Joe to *MOJO*, still snarling twenty-two years later, 'I thought, "Well, that's nice for you, but we were never your toy to begin with." I can see the point that we could have stayed homemade, started our own labels, the stuff people do nowadays, but it needed to break out and reach America and be global. Someone had to take the bull by the horns and shake it.'

The supreme irony was that the contract The Clash had signed would be a millstone around their necks and cause them untold grief in the next decade. It wasn't just that the label didn't understand them: hidden in the small-print was the bombshell that the deal wasn't just for five albums, as they thought, but, according to how it was interpreted, for as many as another five or eight albums after that – should CBS wish to pick up the option.

The other reality that quickly dawned upon the group was the advance would have to pay for their living and recording costs, plus the wages of all their entourage (rarely paid, it seems), until The Clash made a second album. It was also expected to underwrite touring costs, pay lawyers and accountants, and keep the group in equipment, strings and clothes. There was also Bernie's 20 per cent cut as manager and income tax liability, and Rhodes had agreed with Malcolm to make a retrospective contribution to cover losses sustained on the Anarchy tour. (Though it's possible this was never paid, either.)

CBS and the group wanted to move quickly – and they already had. A month after The Clash had inked the deal, they'd already recorded and delivered their debut album. The process had started in January, while Polydor were still chasing them. The group had cut a bunch of demos at the National Film and Television School in Beaconsfield, forty minutes' drive out of London. They had booked the school's eight-track studio facility via one of its ex-students, Julien Temple, the filmmaker friend of The Pistols who would go on to direct *The Great Rock 'n 'Roll Swindle*, *Absolute Beginners* and, in recent years, the underrated Wordsworth and Coleridge film, *Pandaemonium*.

Since a 'conventional' producer – if Guy Stevens could ever be described as such a thing – had found it difficult to create a vivid snapshot of the group's raw sound, it was decided that Micky Foote, their live soundman, should oversee the recordings. This way it was hoped the vibe at Rehearsals could be replicated.

A tape of the Beaconsfield session that has leaked out gives an extraordinary fly-on-the-wall insight into the session. The over-riding impression is of a charged, macho atmosphere: present are the group and their girlfriends, including Caroline, plus Micky Foote, Roadent, Julien Temple and Sebastian Conran. Communication is blunt and testy, though there's a subtle warmth between Joe and Mick – clearly the king bees. In the background, Simonon plunks at his bass incessantly. Mick is the musical director, spelling out to Paul a change he wants in a bass line, but there's a strong impression that Joe is 'the leader'.

The session is in chaos. The group finish 'London's Burning' then take a break. Someone enquires whether anyone wants anything to eat. This results in a couple of minutes of order-taking, then the conclusion that they ought to wait till they return to London as the engineer is only booked until 9 p.m. Mick suddenly accuses Micky Foote of saying that he looks like the guitarist out of The Derelicts. 'Who said that?' says Foote. 'You did,' says Mick, spikily.

Foote, in charge of his first recording session with the group, is at the receiving end of their frustrations about the studio sound (Joe: 'it sounds like buckets of concrete'; Mick: 'it sounds like kids playing a toy guitar') and the slow progress they're making.

MICK: Shall we just carry on?

JOE: Ask Mickie Most in there . . . (another minute of muffled studio chatter) Can't we do 'White Riot' first? We can go back to ['London's Burning'] if you wanna do it . . .

MICKY FOOTE: No.

JOE: We just specially tuned the guitar . . .

FOOTE: Joe . . . (inaudible comment about Joe's vocal)

JOE: Does it sound rough, or not?

FOOTE: No, it sounds good.

JOE: Then why do another one?

FOOTE: 'Cos we're picking the best out of two.

JOE: I don't care, it's no skin off my nose.

FOOTE: OK, look, Joe, if you don't want to do it then we'll do—

JOE: All right . . . we'll do that again. But at the end of each take we want something from you, right? We've finished 'London's

Burning', right? Then ten minutes later we're now thinking about doing 'White Riot' . . . You can't come out and say do ['London's Burning'] again. We wanna hear straight away what you want. Then we don't get side-tracked.

MICK: Is Micky supposed to be producing this?

JOE: Yeah, he is.

MICK: You must be joking!

FOOTE: Shut up . . .

MICK: Don't tell me to shut up!

Though rough, the Beaconsfield material was deemed good enough for Micky Foote to be appointed producer for the CBS recordings. The first session was booked for Friday, 28 January – the day after the deal was signed – at the label's studio at Whitfield Street, just around the corner from Goodge Street tube station. The session took place in the small studio three on the first floor. The group were thrilled to discover that Iggy and the Stooges' 1973 masterpiece, *Raw Power*, had been made in the same building (though in the larger studio one downstairs).

The plan was to record 'White Riot', together with a B-side, '1977', as a debut single for release in March. The group were then booked in for three long weekends (Thursday to Sunday), beginning 12 February 1977, to record an album. The engineer on the sessions was Simon Humphrey, who was twenty-one at the time. On their arrival, The Clash made it quite clear that they didn't care much for the studio, or the staff. They may have signed up to one of the largest record companies in the world, but that didn't mean they were going to tone down their moody, aggressive behaviour. Their rebellion, the integrity of which was called into question after the CBS deal, was now manifesting itself symbolically as a worker-management struggle.

Two cultures, the old and new, clashed. 'They wouldn't shake my hand because I was a hippy,' recalls Humphrey. 'They ribbed us mercilessly for having long hair and cowboy boots. Pre-punk the record companies had this laid-back, post-1960s attitude, very Californian – particularly CBS, which was an American company with a lot of American acts like Santana, Earth Wind and Fire, Blue Öyster Cult. They turned up in full punk battledress. There was no let-up in that respect. They were keen to record but they didn't understand too much about the process. The one thing they'd say was, "Is this how you record Abba? Is this how you record a rock band? Then don't do that, then." It was that really early let's-push-up-against-everything attitude.'

The chaotic, abrasive atmosphere within the group spilled out in the studio. A rivalry was developing between Mick and Joe. Ostensibly, it was played out over their time-keeping but it possibly belied deeper tensions about control and leadership.

'Mick would turn up and say, "Who else is here?" And I'd say, "Actually, Mick, you're the first one." He'd say, "Fuck that!" and bugger off, because it would be uncool to be the first one there. Then Joe would turn up and say, "Where's Mick?" And I'd say, "He was here earlier but left." So Joe would say, "Bloody hell!" and storm off. Then they'd reconvene later.

'Joe Strummer just wasn't interested,' continues Humphrey. 'He'd turn up late. He didn't want anyone else there when he recorded his vocals. He'd sing with his mic up against the wall and play his guitar at the same time, because he couldn't divorce the two. He tried to preserve his live performance on the record, which he probably succeeded in doing. Mick Jones picked up the studio vibe very quickly. He was the one running the show. He was the one teaching Paul to play bass. Paul was the moodiest with the most attitude. I didn't even talk to him. He was really scary. He had the notes painted on his bass. There was some dispute over whether he played on that album, but he did. [According to Micky Foote, the only thing Paul didn't play was the middle-eight of 'White Riot', which has a subtly different bass pattern.] But Mick had taught him to play the bass lines parrot fashion.' Terry, meanwhile, seemed 'an outsider. He was told what to do.'

Micky Foote's input into *The Clash*, as the album would be called, has always been hotly debated. Several people interviewed for this book have trotted out the line that Foote's 'producer' credit was a fortuitous function of the circumstances: since The Clash were unwilling to cede control of the session to CBS, someone the group trusted had *to be seen* to be directing the sessions. Robin Blanchflower, the CBS A&R man dealing with The Clash, concluded Foote was as capable as anyone of fulfilling this role.

Simon Humphrey interprets Micky's job as more of a facilitator or go-between: 'Micky Foote was the line of communication between the band and me. They wanted someone on the other side of the glass who was on their side. But he didn't get his hands on the desk. You couldn't really say he was the producer.' He adds: 'Mick sussed him out quite soon.'

Besides a short quote in an *NME* interview published when *The Clash* was released, Foote has never before given his side of the story. We are talking in the Western Arms in Ladbroke Grove. Disarmingly, he points out he was under no illusions about his role, or his lack of experience. 'I'm not an engineer, I never pretended to be one. That wasn't my job. What was my job? It was to make sure it sounded like *we* wanted it to, not how [CBS] wanted it. The pressure was to do it on time and to make sure it didn't get taken over by the engineer. I credit Simon [Humphrey] with a lot of patience. He'd never worked with a band like The Clash before. It must have seemed like anarchy to him. He sat there and did what he was supposed to do.'

Micky explains how his first preference was to record the album 'live' at Rehearsals in front of an audience. He wanted it to sound like The Velvet Underground's *Live at Max's Kansas City*. Nothing came of this but the idea coloured his approach to the Whitfield Street session. 'I made sure it wasn't over-this'd or noise-gated that,' he recalls. 'It was plug your amp in, turn it up to number three and don't mess about with anything. In the control room, you could press a button and if this thing on the screen went round in a perfect circle the sound was supposedly all right. It was like, "Fuck that shit, turn that stuff off!" Most of the guide vocals were used. Joe's voice wasn't in the greatest of condition. He had nodes, he had a lot of trouble. He was permanently with a packet of Lockets. To sing above Mick Jones's guitar, you're not fucking joking!'

Simon Humphrey says: 'The first time I met Joe was when they were setting up to record. He'd put his twin reverb [amp] right next to the drum kit. I said, "You can't put that there, it'll have to go there behind a screen, because it's gonna affect the drums. So he said, "Why's that, then?" I said, "Because it needs a bit of separation." He said, "I don't know what separation is, and I don't like it." He had a terrible guitar sound; even Mick didn't like it. So not much of it got on the record.'

Micky Foote tells me that Joe was playing 'mindgames. It wasn't supposed to sound nice. It was done to keep Simon from cleaning it up.'

Humphrey adds that CBS, who owned Fender, sent Joe 'a brand new Telecaster . . . as a present' but that Joe 'thought it was hilarious, this brand new Telecaster in a box with the tag still on it. He never played it. He had no interest in it at all. Mick, on the other hand, had about three guitars by that time, including his Les Paul Junior, which was really classy and he really loved it. Then one day it fell over and the neck snapped. He was absolutely devastated. He had a tear in his eye. He was so upset that he went home.'

Bernie, meanwhile, was making his presence felt in his inimitable fashion. He told the engineer that he'd worked with The Who and Mott the Hoople, and pitched in with a bunch of off-the-wall ideas about how the group should be recorded. This caused an argument. Mick and Joe told him to piss off. But the myriad faders, buttons and blinking lights on the recording console gave the group an opportunity for some fun at Rhodes's expense. 'We said, "Look, if you press that button it changes the sound completely, it makes it sound like Led Zeppelin", laughs Foote. 'He was like, "Does it?" There was a lot of that going on.'

After a while, the freeze between group and producer thawed a little. In this atmosphere of détente, Mick, the least inclined to treat the CBS crew as hippy lepers, began quizzing Humphrey about the equipment and techniques he was using. In a breach of punk etiquette, and in contrast to Joe's trenchant punk aggression, Mick suggested he and Humphrey should have a bite to eat at the Spaghetti House restaurant across the street. It was there they talked about subtle ways of enriching the record.

'Mick wanted to get into overdubs and double-tracking solos,' recalls Humphrey. 'He saw the possibilities there, and he was the one driving it all forward with ideas. But it was difficult to make judgements sometimes. Mick would play a solo, and shout through, "What was that like?" We didn't know what to say, because it wasn't that polished. In punk terms, we didn't know whether it was a good solo or a bad one, we didn't have any reference points.'

'Mick would come in the control room and say, "Play that back,"' remembers Micky Foote. 'And you'd get halfway through the solo and you'd say, "Look, Mick, you've obviously Keef'd it up at the end . . ." And he'd go back and redo it. But you listen to those solos on the first album and you'll hear a run, and then there'll be a note you're not expecting and he'll lose it. I'm not saying anything other than that it was difficult to keep the Keith Richards and Mott the Hoople off the guitar tracks.'

The Clash sessions were swift – 'they basically played their set and we recorded it live,' says Humphrey – but there were still the inevitable hours of hanging around between overdubs and mixing. The vibe was enlivened by the presence of Roadent, Clash friend Mark 'Frothler' Helfond, 'Mad' Jane Crockford and Sebastian Conran. 'One of them graffitied a wall and was told off by the studio manager,' says Simon. 'They used to gob all the time, which wasn't particularly nice.' During the recording of 'White Riot', there was an attempt to capture the sound of Sebastian's air pistol firing into the wall. Another time, a microphone was set up on the landing and a sheet of corrugated iron thrown down a stairwell. None of these noises was used, though a sound-effect record of glass breaking was added to the single version of 'White Riot' (the basis of which was actually the Beaconsfield version), together with the sound of a police siren and a fire alarm.

During breaks, the group would roll spliffs and decant to the Valiant Trooper pub around the corner. Humphrey saw little evidence of amphetamine use, undermining Mick's later claim that he took so much speed while making the album that he couldn't remember anything about it. (In fact, Jones himself subsequently dismissed the speed story as 'just something I said at the time'.) In the evenings, if not required, the group would troll around Soho, before returning to the studio to listen back to the day's work. One night, Joe went to the Speakeasy club on Margaret Street and was badly beaten up in the toilets by a Teddy Boy friend of John Lydon, who like the Pistols' singer believed The Clash were 'working-class fakes'. Strummer lost part of a tooth, adding to his already rotten dentistry. Joe was philosophical about the fight and revelled in recounting it.

One Thursday, 24 February, Joe, Mad Jane and Roadent went to see The Jam at the Roxy. 'We're just walking up the road,' remembers Roadent, 'and this unmarked police car comes screeching in front of us. The cops jump out, grab us and slam us over the car. Then they took us to Tottenham Court Road nick – apparently, some strip club had had a brick thrown through its door. It was quite heartbreaking, really, 'cos me and Joe decided that it was my turn to confess, I can't remember why. So when the copper came in and said, "Why did you do it?", I said, "I dunno, youthful exuberance?" And he went, "You're a bit old for youthful exuberance, aren't you?" Then he admitted that he knew it wasn't us and told us to fuck off. He said we weren't to be seen on their patch again, which was a bit hard because we were recording an album on Whitfield Street.'

During the penultimate session, it transpired that, all-in, there was less than thirty minutes of material. Usually, LPs contained at least forty minutes. The decision was made to add the group's version of 'Police and Thieves'. This would change the geography of the album drastically: it was six minutes long, twice the length of any other track. The group spent the week arranging the song at Rehearsals. Set to a straight rock beat, Junior Murvin's version received its final punk makeover. 'It must be said that Mick Jones is a brilliant arranger,' Strummer said in *Westway to the World*. 'Any other group would've played on the off-beat, trying to assimilate reggae, but we had one guitar on the on, the other the off. I mean, he really set it up. He's a genius.'

Roadent recalls arriving on the last day, Sunday, 27 February, to pack away the group's gear. The Clash were sitting in the control room, listening back to 'Police and Thieves'. Everyone agreed it was astonishing. Joe's only question to Roadent was: 'Do you think it's too long?'

The Clash was delivered to CBS on 3 March. The sleeve for the album was designed in-house, with help from Bernie and Paul, and featured a Kate Simon shot of Joe, Mick and Paul posing street-gang-style on the trolley ramp of the old Tack Room opposite the Rehearsals building. Paul has a Union flag sewn to his shirt pocket, Joe's hair is still dyed blond and Mick's hair is the shortest it would ever be during The Clash's career. 'Bernie nearly threw a party when Mick got his hair cut,' remembers Micky Foote. 'He hated it. It was a struggle. Mick, Mick, Mick . . . everyone was saying it. Get your fucking hair cut. You had to drag him along. I don't think he ever liked it.' The back of the LP featured a Rocco Macauley shot of the first baton charge at the Notting Hill Riot. The ripped edges, Xeroxed images, flashes of fluorescent 'spray-paint', distressed band logo and manual-typewriter font would, together with Jamie Reid's Situationist-inspired Sex Pistols graphics, become a blue print for punk iconography in the years to come. The sleeve impishly credits Terry Chimes as 'Tory Crimes'.

Listening to *The Clash* twenty-five years after its release is still an exquisite pleasure. Tony Parsons, then writing for *NME*, described it in his 16 April 1977 review as 'some of the most exciting rock 'n' roll in contemporary music' and concluded that The Clash 'chronicle . . . what it's like to be young in the Stinking '70s better than any other band'. Passionate and eloquent, this analysis quickly became the received take on the LP. It still rings true now: even shorn of its social context, *The Clash* buzzes and sparks with intense energy and, 'better than any other band' (except, at a squeeze, Ian Dury and the Blockheads, whose *New Boots and Panties*, described a parallel, but essentially different urban experience), provides a vivid, insistently honest Polaroid of London in the punk era.

There are many elements that shape its unique musical topography: for one, it owes very little to the 1960s garage punk which was an early inspiration for both Mick and Joe. The songs (bar 'Police and Thieves') show virtually no R&B influence: instead, they tend to rattle along ferociously, trammelling a series of neat major-minor chord changes like old Bob Dylan folk sides played at twice their ordinary velocity. The verse-chorus-middle-eight structures enhance the feeling you're hearing a protest record: 'Career Opportunities', '48 Hours', 'Hate and War', 'Remote Control', 'I'm So Bored With the USA', 'White Riot', 'London's Burning' – all rail against the status quo. Even the earliest material The Clash played together, like 'Deny', 'Protex Blue' and 'Janie Jones' are twisted, inverted love songs that in some way seem to blame society for their protagonists' negative experiences, whether drugs, ill-fitting condoms or payola.

Musically, too, there's an enormous amount of semi-disguised musical sophistication, primarily a result of Mick's (even then) prodigious arranging skills. Even something as ostensibly basic as 'White Riot' is actually teeming with intelligent detail: the ascending bass run on the first line of the verse ('Black man has got a lot of problems'), followed by a descending, harmonic lead guitar figure on the second ('but they don't mind throwing a brick'). Then there's the contrapuntal, walking bass line on the bridge, the nagging, strangulated guitar overdubs on the instrumental and the added, atmospheric, adrenaline-pumping sound effects. In fact, there are unexpected FX and overdubs all over the album, including the phasing on 'Cheat' – Bernie and Micky Foote's nod to The Small Faces' 'Itchychoo Park' – the dub echo on 'Career Opportunities' and 'Police and Thieves', the baleful harmonica on 'Garageland'. Atop all this, there are also Joe, Mick and Paul's complementary voices: Strummer's nodal, gruff bark; Jones's mellifluous Cockney ('It's so grey in London Town!'); and, chipping in on the terrace choruses, Paul's bleating south London monotone.

Joe's lyrics are poetic and clever. People don't often talk about Ray Davies of The Kinks in relation to The Clash, but his approach to lyric writing is the closest in many respects to Strummer's. Joe went one better than Bernie's dictum to write about what he knew. Instead, he wrote about what he felt, and perhaps what he imagined kids 'cramped up in their bedrooms' were feeling, as Micky Foote put it. This displacement of his personal viewpoint gave his lyrics a tremendous power. It was an extraordinary connection between experience and imagination and subtle characterisation.

The Clash deals with boredom, identity crises, the brutality of a modern, concrete environment, drugs, unemployment, deceit, frustration, rejection. Its vocabulary is rich in evocative language: 'wops', 'Greeks', 'old bag', 'skag', 'Ford Cortina', 'letter bombs', 'repression'. Many of the tangiest words and phrases are in Joe's ad libs. 'London's Burning' name-checks the Westway and echoes passages from *High Rise*, in which Ballard had written 'strong winds circulated around the open plazas . . . buffeting the lower floors'. Strummer conjures the more poetic image: 'the wind blows round the empty blocks looking for a home'. On 'What's My Name', for which Keith Levene gains his only co-credit, Joe assumes the fantasy character of a petty thief (shades of 'Crummy Bum Blues' again), who breaks into houses with 'my celluloid strip' and whose father is a rotten gambler who loses his winnings and has to negotiate re-entrance to the family abode through the letterbox. Then there's the pièce de résistance, 'Police and Thieves' – six minutes of edgy militant reggae given a crisp, 4/4 rock treatment, stuck halfway through side two. The melancholy 'Garageland', inspired by Charles Shaar Murray's damning Screen on the Green review, rounds off the album with a hint of what was to come: The Clash chronicling their own career in song.

On Friday, 11 March 1977, at the Harlesden Coliseum – a cinema specialising in trashy Bollywood and kung-fu flicks – the group showcased the album and unveiled their new look: zippered, militaristic pants and jackets in bright, clashing colours, with natty epaulettes and lapels. The new threads – dubbed by *NME*'s Nick Kent as 'pop star army fatigues' – were made upstairs at Rehearsals by two young seamstresses, Alex Michon and her friend Kristina. Abandoning the tachiste, Pollock image was symbolic: The Clash had shed their old skin and moved into the future. They hoped their audience would join them.

A week after the Harlesden gig, 'White Riot'/'1977' was released in a Sebastian-designed sleeve featuring Caroline Coon's 'up-against-the-wall' shot of the group still in their stencilled boiler suits and shirts. Despite very little radio play – only John Peel played it at the BBC – the single hit number thirty-eight. *The Clash* was released on 8 April 1977 and climbed to number twelve.

'The first album came out and went straight in the charts!' recalls Simon Humphrey. 'The people at CBS, me included, were all totally amazed. Those were the days when that didn't really happen with a new rock group. The suits had stayed away from the studio, they'd just left us to it, they weren't that interested. They didn't realise the extent and depth of what was happening.'

Not all of the reviews of *The Clash* were complimentary, however – *Melody Maker*'s Michael Oldfield got a 'headache' from the 'tuneless repetition of chords at a breakneck pace' – but many of those that were positive bordered on the rabidly ecstatic. 'It is the most important album ever released,' Mark Perry declared in *Sniffin' Glue*. 'It's as if I'm looking at my life in a film.'

Tens of thousands of other young people across Britain knew exactly what he meant. The Clash had created a looking-glass that reflected, in quite specific and detailed ways, the lives of ordinary youngsters. No British band had done that since The Kinks (and arguably Mott the Hoople in the early 1970s), and even then theirs was a melancholy yet celebratory look at London life, not an invective or angry one. To suburban kids *The Clash* offered a vision of a tough, exciting, exotic, urban world – an environment to be embraced and enjoyed vicariously, and an anger in which you could participate. To urbanities it was hard and real and true.

Coinciding with the release of the album, *NME* printed a cover story

on the group by Tony Parsons, a twenty-one-year-old journalistic wunderkind who had been working in a gin distillery a year previously. The
headline read: 'Thinking Man's Yobs'. Parsons was working-class, from
London, his father was a Royal Marine decorated in the Second World
War, and he bristled with attitude. He was locked into The Clash's wavelength, and suffused with their influences, right down to his having brewed
the same alcohol spirit that had once been stacked up for export in
Rehearsals.

His feature was ambitiously conspiratorial: he was interested in creating
a myth, and the group willingly, knowingly and enthusiastically fed him the
lines. His descriptions are impressionistic and designed to authenticate The
Clash's image as tower-block rebels fighting a war against society. Joe is portrayed as a desperate, knife-wielding tough, unwilling to use his 'blade'
against the Ted who pummelled him only because he'd 'probably have to do
a few years'; Mick is a guy who advocates violence and threatens to break
people's legs; and Paul an ex-Chelsea football hooligan (!) who's in the group
to get laid and have a good time. All the subtle nuances of their pre-punk
lives are deliberately concreted over.

The interview, conducted on a Circle Line tube train, then up at
Rehearsals, was a carefully stage-managed attempt to establish the group's
anti-establishment agenda and present an insurrectionary mission statement. It seems contrived and faintly irresponsible today – especially the
emphasis and glorification of violence (Mick: 'We ain't ashamed to fight') –
but the tacit conviction of both group and writer that this deceit is a justifiable
means to an end (to challenge racism and change the culture of apathy) is
impressive. This is also the interview in which the idea is mooted that, should
The Clash ever get rich, they'd start a radio station.

Parsons finished his piece with a vision of Mick staring down from his
tower block to the fires burning down below. It was as if London was burning again, just as it had done at many pivotal points in its history, from
Boudicca's razing of the city in the first century AD to the Blitz. Parsons' was
image-making at its most powerful.

The danger, of course, was The Clash believing they were the people
Parsons described. With Joe, the demarcation between fantasy and fact in his
life had dissolved long before he joined The Clash. On 4 May, Mark Perry
witnessed how the demands of The Clash's public image were also impacting on Mick Jones. That night both men found themselves at the aftershow
party for Mott the Hoople's former singer Ian Hunter at the Hammersmith
Odeon. It was the first time Perry had seen Mick since his 'Punk died the day

The Clash signed to CBS' comment. (The issue of *Sniffin' Glue* with the rave review of *The Clash* had not yet appeared.)

'It was funny backstage because the group Japan were there, they were still a funk-metal group then, and they were saying, "Can we have our photo taken with Mick Jones?" They were all posing and Mick was like, "Growl, growl." Then Mick said to me, "What is that you said about us?" I said, "What do you mean? It was true." He said, "You don't want to fucking say that. You should be careful, you might find yourself in the River Thames with concrete boots on." I was like, "What are you talking about, you fucking idiot?" That's what he said to me. It was like nonsense, you know what I mean? He was threatening me. Mick!'

'Later on, I went with him to a lig down the Fulham Road at this flash restaurant,' he continues. 'There was the most lavish spread I have ever seen in my life. Here was this fucking giant octopus sitting on the table with all its poor old legs chopped up, and you took a bit of its leg and, you know, "Sorry, old mate", the head and everything. Me and Mick Jones met Ian Hunter together. I was in awe of Ian Hunter, so was Mick, but there was that thing where I was the editor of *Sniffin' Glue* so I had to act a certain kind of way, and Mick was the guitarist in The Clash, so he had to act a certain way. Hunter did this thing where he said, "You younger guys, you're what rock is about. People like me are old now, we are going to make a few records but the future is about you guys."'

Mick, who less than two years previously had been chucked out of his group by Mott's mentor for being the superfluous, skinny-little-boy rhythm guitarist, was now being informed by one of his boyhood heroes that he was the future of rock 'n' roll. 'It was all very weird,' says Perry. 'But that was the strange world we were suddenly living in. It had a deep effect on you.'

In a joint promotion with the *NME* that April, the group gave away a free EP, 'Capital Radio'. The first 10,000 copies of *The Clash* came with a red sticker, which, if attached to the coupon in the *NME*, snaffled you the 45. 'Capital Radio', one of the 'hates' on Bernie's 'You're gonna wake up one morning' T-shirt, bemoaned London's independent radio station, a conservative institution that Joe felt should be promoting punk rock and reggae. The song began with a shouted reference to the Nazis' propaganda minister: 'It's time for the Dr Goebbels show!' On the night of 26 March, he and Roadent indulged in some of their own propaganda and sprayed 'White Riot' across the front of the Capital Radio building and on the wall of the BBC.

Throughout March 1977 The Clash desperately continued their search for a permanent drummer. They later claimed to have auditioned 205 candidates for the job. It probably felt like that many but the figure was closer to a few dozen. The advert put in *Melody Maker* stressed 'no jazz, no funk, no laid back'. Chris Bashford, who later drummed with the punk group Chelsea, was typical of many applicants. He plucked up the courage to bang on the door of Rehearsals and spoke with Bernie, who gave him a test-pressing of 'White Riot'/'1977' to listen to. 'Joe phoned me at work the next day and I went to Camden to play all the hits and more on a rainy afternoon,' he recalls in the sleeve-note of the various-punk-artists *The Clash Tribute* CD.

Bashford didn't get the job. Jon Moss, later of Culture Club, was offered the position but, in an accelerated re-play of Terry Chimes's experience, found Rhodes insufferable and ducked out after only a few rehearsals. Then, on 24 March, The Clash attended a Kinks show at the Rainbow. At the bar, Mick bumped into Nick Headon, who had successfully auditioned for The London SS, before leaving to join a soul group. Headon, who was twenty-one, was an incredibly talented drummer, capable of playing jazz, funk, soul, disco, anything. Jones asked him to come up to Rehearsals the following day to show him what his new group was doing.

Nicholas Bowen Headon was born 30 May 1955 in Bromley Hospital in Kent. His parents were originally from Wales, and his father was a school headmaster. Both were musical, and sang and played the piano. Nick lived in Orpington until he was twelve, then the family moved to River, a village on the outskirts of Dover, where his father was appointed head of the local grammar school.

It was around that time that Headon began misbehaving. 'When your father's the headmaster, to be accepted you have to be a lot more naughty than the other kids,' he explains. 'I got into trouble to show that I wasn't the teacher's pet.'

Nick inherited his parents' love of music and taught himself to play the piano. At school, he began playing drums. His heroes included Buddy Rich, Billy Cobham and Man's Terry Williams. 'I listened to rock, but I used to play trad jazz every Sunday at the Louis Armstrong pub. The Marines band at Deal had a band called Force 9 – there were nine of 'em – and I got the job as drummer. For two years they thought I could read music. I said to the bass-player, "Don't grass me up – just tap me when I have to stop!" I liked lots of different sorts of music – rock stuff, jazz, stuff with just piano and brushes. I just loved playing.'

When he left school with three O-Levels, Headon worked for a year as a shipping clerk at Dover docks. His boss was the father-in-law of Johnny Green, who remembered him as 'a quiet, friendly boy who was very nervous'. After playing in local Dover groups with his friend Steve Barnacle, Nick moved to London where he married his girlfriend Wendy and secured work with the Canadian rocker Pat Travers. Nick was small and slightly built; Travers sacked him for not hitting the drums hard enough. It was following this blow to his confidence that he auditioned for The London SS, but then absconded to play a tour of US airforce bases with a soul group called The G.I.s. On his return, he joined another London-based Canadian group, Fury, who were about to sign to CBS (they cut some demos with Simon Humphrey), but again he was given the boot for not pounding the drums aggressively enough.

He wasn't going to make that mistake again. 'With The Clash I knew exactly what they wanted,' says Topper. 'I thought, "Whatever happens I'm going to knock shit out of those drums." As a result, I had to re-learn my style.'

The Clash were impressed by his playing. He was immediately given the job, a punk makeover – dyed short hair, bespoke fatigues, monkey boots – and a copy of *The Clash* in order to learn the songs. He was re-christened 'Topper' by Paul, after the Micky the Monkey character in the *Topper* kids comic, whose sticky-out ears supposedly resembled Headon's, and his wages were the same as the rest of the group, £25 a week. 'It's no secret that when I joined The Clash I thought, "I'll stick with them for a year to make my name",' says Headon, who was nearly pipped at the post by Mark Laff, later of Generation X. 'Then I planned to go on and do something more interesting musically.'

After Topper was publicly unveiled at the Roundhouse on 10 April, there were another two weeks of intensive rehearsals before the group played some warm-up gigs in France for their twenty-eight-date, headlining White Riot tour of Britain. On the night of Tuesday, 26 April, as the group were waiting for the coach to arrive to take them to Dover, Topper lay on the freezing cold brick floor of Rehearsals staring at the ceiling. He had been living in The Clash's unsentimental, abrasive, factional world for just a few weeks. Already a wiry, restless knot of nervous energy, he was finding it a strain to maintain an artificial hardman front in keeping with the group's image.

'That whole Clash violence thing . . . Paul could look after himself, but me and Mick weren't fighters,' he says. 'Joe would much rather talk himself out of an argument than fight with anyone. The situation was new to me. It was really confusing. I felt quite alone. I lay there thinking, "I don't really know any of these people." I was scared. I thought, "Shall I do a runner while I've got the chance?" But I didn't, of course.'

The White Riot tour kicked off at Guildford Civic Hall on 1 May 1977. The support acts were The Buzzcocks, Subway Sect and all-girl group The

Slits, featuring singer Ari Up, Joe's ex-girlfriend Palmolive and Viv Albertine. The Jam – who'd been signed by Chris Parry after losing The Clash – were also invited along, but left following an argument with Bernie.

'The first night of the White Riot tour was unbelievable,' recalls Robin Banks. 'We couldn't believe what was happening to us. We looked out into the auditorium at all the people packed in there. Suddenly, it was like the dream of becoming rock stars had come true.'

The tour lived up to its name. Robin, Chrissie Hynde, Don Letts, Roadent, Sebastian Conran and Subway Sect's roadie, Barry Auguste – now appropriated as Topper's drum tech and dubbed 'Baker' because Paul thought he looked like one – joined the group on a nationwide orgy of incendiary rock 'n' roll, petty theft, partying and vandalism. The Clash and their entourage were viewed as threatening, spiky-haired alien life forms by many they encountered. There were many memorable moments. The tour bus was apprehended by police near St Albans after the manager of the Holiday Inn in Newcastle reported the group had stolen some pillows cases and a room key. (Joe and Topper took the rap and were later charged with theft.) Footage shot by Don Letts shows Topper, Paul and Robin enraging a woman at a motorway service station merely by playing on a child's see-saw. In Leicester, Mick repeatedly sang 'What a Norman!' instead of 'What a liar' at the end of 'Deny' in celebration of the eccentric tour-bus driver.

'The tour was amazing,' says Caroline Coon. 'When that band got out on stage there has been nothing better in rock 'n' roll. It was heart and soul, flesh and blood, total commitment to the extent that they'd come off stage absolutely soaked in their own sweat. They literally couldn't speak they were so exhausted. They had to lie on the dressing-room floor.'

The tour's London date was at the cavernous Rainbow Theatre in Finsbury Park on 9 May. It was by far the biggest crowd the group had ever played to. In 1988, Joe described it as 'the night that punk really broke out of the clubs . . . it really felt like we were in the right place doing the right thing at the right time.' During The Clash's set there were riotous scenes as around 200 seats were trashed and the debris thrown at the stage. Paul Simonon's father, interested to see what his son had been up to since quitting art school, watched this surreal theatre of violence from the back of the hall.

Not everyone enjoyed the show. Richard Dudanski, who was by now playing drums in Tymon's new group, Tymon Dogg and the Fools, managed to blag his way backstage via his connection with Palmolive (his sister-in-law).

He'd been drinking all afternoon and was by his own admission 'pissed out of my brain'. He managed to speak to Joe for a few minutes, but his trademark floppy hat and droopy moustache sent alarm bells ringing in the dressing room: Hippy! 'I heard this voice behind me shout, "Who the fuck's that prick with the hat?"' recalls Dudanski. 'It was de rigueur punk attitude at the time. It was Steve Jones, who was there in his leathers . . . I wasn't a punk, that was obvious. So we ended up rolling around on the floor, fighting. I think Steve may have got the better of me, he was probably a lot more used to that sort of stuff than me.

'The Clash went on and they were really powerful. Which made it worse. It was difficult . . . they'd nicked my singer. But I still thought I'd made the right decision. The songs Tymon and I were playing were much more musical. But of course we didn't have much success, it was difficult to get gigs. You saw Joe having all this success with The Clash . . .'

Another of Joe's old pals who felt the singer had moved on into another, more glamorous and unreal world was 'Jiving' Al Jones of The Vultures. He saw The Clash later that month at the Top Rank, Cardiff. 'I went into the dressing room and everybody looked as if they were speeding their bollocks off,' says Jiver. 'I realised then that it wasn't like before, when you could say, "Oh, hello, Joe, how's it going?" They were as high as anything. Joe had left the planet at that point. I didn't feel we had a connection.'

While the group were away on tour, CBS scheduled a new single without their knowledge or permission – one of the oldest, most cynical tricks in the record company manual. This made a mockery of the group's declarations about 'control', artistic or otherwise. On 13 May, 'Remote Control', easily the 'softest' and musically un-punk track on *The Clash*, was released in a picture sleeve that lazily reproduced the album cover in miniature. Bernie and The Clash were enraged. Only a few months into their relationship, group and label had their first major showdown.

The problem seemed to lie in the whole culture at CBS. In early 1977, Johnny Black, now an author and music journalist, was working in the CBS press office under Ellie Smith. 'There were loads of people at CBS at a junior level who really liked The Clash,' he explains. 'It was just the higher-ups who didn't really understand what they'd signed. It was standard record company practice to put out singles without consulting the group – they couldn't see why a band like The Clash would get so worked up about it.

'Maurice Oberstein was used to working with groups like Abba,' he adds. 'It was a different culture.'

The tour wound up in Dunstable at the end of May and The Clash returned to London. It was time to take stock. Almost exactly a year after they'd formed, the group had a Top 20 album and had completed a major jaunt around the UK. They were generally regarded as the most exciting new group in Britain. The first six months of 1977 had been a blur, and the frenetic pace wasn't about to slacken.

On a hot summer's day in 2004, Alex Michon is stirring a frothy coffee in the Patisserie Valerie on Old Compton Street in Soho. We're sitting at a formica table; surrounding us on the walls are reproductions of cartoons by Toulouse-Lautrec. The place has a strong whiff of art deco London about it, but this is an illusion. The original patisserie, built in 1926, was bombed by the Luftwaffe, and the present restaurant constructed after the war. The history of the building intrigues Alex. As the person who made The Clash's clothes, it's evident that she herself has been part of history. Today, she's still interested in art and rock 'n' roll, and is about to show some sketches of Billy Fury at an exhibition in east London; but for her, The Clash belong to another time. 'I call it "now-ness" and "then-ness,"' she explains, showing me an old Paul Simonon shirt she's kept. 'It's important to move on and not dwell on the past, but at the same time it was an extraordinary thing to be involved with. I don't mention it much – you're one of only two people who've ever tracked me down.'

Alex first saw The Clash at the Royal College of Art in November 1976. 'I thought, "This is it,"' she says. 'Then one day one of my flatmates, who was at St Martin's, said to me, "I've just met this funny little man. He says he is the manager of The Clash, and he is talking about making some clothes." She thought he was just this weirdo. We had a meeting. He said, "Can you make trousers?" I went, "Yes, of course I can!" I had never made anything in my life.'

Bernie introduced Alex to the band, who were initially suspicious of her presence at Rehearsals. But she soon established a close relationship with the group. Paul she found 'cool, moody, really aloof, impish and very enthusiastic about the clothes'. Mick was 'like a poodle, very chatty'. On her first day at work, he barked at her for agreeing to make Micky Foote a pair of Clash trousers before the group got theirs; he later apologised profusely. 'He was very sweet after that.' Joe was 'a very caring man' who 'showed me immense kindness'. Rhodes, meanwhile, 'was really horrible to me'.

The White Riot tour brought home to Alex, like everyone else in the Clash camp, just how big punk had become. But the momentum had to be maintained.

Once the tour was over, The Clash knuckled down to writing new material for a third single, scheduled for late summer. Sometime in June or July 1977, Tony James popped round to see Mick at his gran's flat. 'I have vivid memories of Joe turning up with a bunch of lyrics, and the pair of them going upstairs to his bedroom for an hour and writing "Complete Control" on acoustic guitar,' says Tony. 'I could see it would take them to another level. It was more sophisticated than anything they'd done before.'

By this time, the group had scattered across London. Paul often stayed at Caroline's flat in Tregunter Road in Chelsea, Topper was in Finsbury Park with wife Wendy, and Joe and Roadent were occupying a squat in Canonbury. Roadent had given it a Pop Art feel by affixing an empty Cornflakes box to the wall above the mantelpiece.

'We had this great record collection,' says Roadent. 'There was Trinity, The Abyssinians, Abba, and Middle of the Road – that was a big one. Me and Joe had a big thing for the singer of Middle of the Road [Sally Carr of 'Chirpy Chirpy Cheep Cheep' fame] 'cos we thought her voice was so fucking good. We wanted to write some songs for her. So we went out and found her, but she said no 'cos she was making too much money doing oldies tours in Sweden. And she'd never heard of us.'

On 5 June, Joe and Roadent attended a reggae all-nighter at the Hammersmith Palais, the events of which would later inspire the lyrics for what many believe to be The Clash's finest song, 'White Man in Hammersmith Palais'.

Out on the streets things were getting hairy. Wherever they went, the group seemed to encounter violence. The subcultural frisson was tangible. Their punk clothes attracted cat-calls and jeers, and hassle from the police. Joe wrote about it in another new song, 'City of the Dead': 'What we wear is dangerous gear, it'll get you picked up anywhere . . .' Following the release of 'God Save the Queen', John Lydon was razor-slashed near Wessex Studios, where The Pistols were still working on their debut album, *Never Mind the Bollocks*; in another attack, Paul Cook needed fifteen stitches after being smashed with an iron bar in Shepherds Bush.

Scuffles between Teddy Boys and punks were becoming commonplace down the Kings Road on a Saturday afternoon. The Clash were startled by the violence they'd incited. Intent on undermining these subcultural rifts, and in a display of half-crazed bravado, Joe and Sebastian Conran dressed up as Teds and ventured out to rockabilly dances.

'We were both into the music and the style, the look,' recalls Conran. 'Before punk came along I used to wear a white T-shirt, blue jeans, a black leather jacket. I used to wear the same uniform day in, day out. That was pretty much my look and I rode a motorbike and I was into rock 'n' roll. Joe and I had great fun. It was extremely exciting going out to these places. We were terrified we'd get recognised.'

The most dangerous Ted haunt they gate-crashed was the White Hart pub in Tottenham. Roger Armstrong and Ted Carroll, of Chiswick Records, were regulars. 'You either had to know someone, or be a Ted, or have the image. Otherwise, you'd get the shit kicked out of you,' Armstrong explains. 'Ted and I used to go up there and stick our sunglasses on. One of the guys would come straight over as soon as we walked through the door to make it clear we were not to be fucked with, 'cos we were the guys who sold them all the old records at the shop. Oh Jeez, it was rough. You'd be standing watching a band and all of a sudden four tables would come flying past you and some guy was getting the shit kicked out of him in the middle of about thirty of them. There was a mixture of these old Teds and these kids like [TV actor] Jesse Birdsall and his crew, who got into the scene through the movie *American Graffiti*, which had a huge influence.'

Ironically, the death of Elvis on 16 August 1977 resulted in an unexpected truce between some of the punks and Teds. 'Joe, Sebastian and I used to go down to this caff called John's on Great Titchfield Street, near Sebastian's place on Albany Street,' recalls Alex Michon. 'We went there for our breakfast. There was this big black chef called John. When Elvis died it was very, very touchy because a lot of rockabillies went there. That day we wore black armbands, and we got the thumbs-up from the Teds. It was a bit touchy down at Big John's.'

After the 'Remote Control' debacle, Bernie negotiated with CBS to release a third single in October – a non-album track, which would be promoted with another UK tour. Charles Shaar Murray once pointed out that just as Mott the Hoople wrote songs about what it was like being in Mott the Hoople, so The Clash wrote songs about life in The Clash. 'Complete Control', which carried on where 'Garageland' left off, recounted the group's escapades on the White Riot tour and the problems with CBS over 'Remote Control'. The title came from an impassioned Bernie speech one evening in the Ship pub in Wardour Street demanding 'complete control', which had Paul and Joe in stitches.

The group came up with an inspired choice of producer for their next batch of material: Lee Perry. It transpired that Perry was in London that summer with Bob Marley, who, after the attempt on his life in Jamaica, was working in the capital. Perry was aware of The Clash's cover of 'Police and Thieves', which he'd co-written, having been alerted to it by the reggae correspondent of *Sounds*, Vivien Goldman. The group were invited to meet the producer at Island's studios in Basing Street, off Portobello Road.

'Lee Perry was amazing,' remembers Micky Foote. 'We went down to the studio and ended up smoking Christ knows what. The Clash were brilliant. They were genuinely excited. Lee Perry couldn't believe that these white guys were singing about reggae and writing songs on the same kind of topics, the political stuff. That crossover, he couldn't believe it, he thought it was amazing. He said he'd talked to Bob Marley about it, and Bob was writing a song with our name in it. Bob Marley was writing a song about The Clash! ['Punky Reggae Party' was released as the B-side of 'Jammin' in December 1977.] We asked Lee Perry to work with us on a couple of tracks and he said, "Yeah, great."'

The group booked into Sarm East studio in Whitechapel. The studio was in a shabby old Victorian house in Osborn Street – the site of the first Whitechapel murder in 1888, and a recurring address in the Jack the Ripper story that followed. The area was steeped in the foggy, vibrant thrill of the East End's colourful history. In the sticky summer heat, versions of 'The Prisoner', 'White Man in Hammersmith Palais', 'Complete Control' and a cover of 'Pressure Drop' by Toots and the Maytals were recorded. ('White Man' was never completed because Joe hadn't finished the lyrics.) According to Micky Foote, Perry was paid £2,000 to work on two sessions. Much to his annoyance, Paul, who idolised Lee Perry, had to be driven home with summer flu soon after he recorded his bass parts, and therefore didn't get to hang out with his hero.

Roadent recalls: 'It was quite odd for us 'cos it was quite a small studio with a staircase at the back. And Lee Perry had never worked on a console that big. The one word he'd learnt from The Clash was "rubbish". He thought it was great. He kept dancing around doing all these kung-fu moves shouting, "Rubbish!" It was quite novel.'

Perry did a dub mix of 'Complete Control'. The group were impressed but realised it would be commercial suicide to release it as the single. 'His mix was fucking brilliant,' says Roadent. 'It was like *The Upsetter* album [a collection of Perry productions released in 1969], you know the LP where it's misty and it's foggy and it's layer upon layer upon layer? It's like you get tangled up in the sound, but it would have been completely inaccessible to most people. So Micky Foote re-touched it. But I thought the first mix was brilliant.'

Micky Foote says, 'The mix he did was amazing. But it was too deep, too much emphasis on the deep notes. Too severe, too echoey. So we re-mixed it and brought up the guitars. It wasn't re-recorded.'

To promote the single, the group set out on the Get Out of Control tour. It began with a series of dates in Europe. The mood of the group is caught in the interview footage shot in Munich for Wolfgang Büld's *Punk in London* film. They are in high spirits, adrenalised and comradely. But they look tired and pasty, a product of fitful eating, and their measly £25 wages, which bought them few comforts. (Strummer claimed that the group weren't paid for several weeks after the White Riot tour to cushion the blow of the tour's £28,000 loss.) Mick complains that they'd been in Germany three days before he 'had a thing to eat'. Simonon voices his excitement at seeing the Berlin Wall and recounts how they've been ejected from their hotel by police and have nowhere to stay: 'A lot of people have been really horrible to us. We *want* to like to Germany but . . .'

Back in Britain, The Clash took a short breather before heading out on the UK leg of the tour. On Sunday, October 16, after a rehearsal, Joe and Mick wandered over to the Roundhouse to check out an evening of punk acts, featuring The Vibrators, 999 and The Radiators From Space. At the bar they got chatting to two young, working-class musicians from Barking, Essex – Billy Bragg and Philip 'Wiggy' Wiggs – who had their own group, Riff Raff. The pair had seen The Clash at the Rainbow and, seemingly like the rest of Britain, were still busy learning all the words and chords to the first album. Wiggy, a Stones fan who styled himself on Keith Richards, and recognised more than a little of 'Keef' in Mick Jones, was interested to know why one of their numbers declared 'No Elvis, Beatles or The Rolling Stones!'

Mick grinned. 'Well, you gotta say all that stuff, ain't ya?'

Meanwhile, CBS were talking to Bernie about The Clash's next album. This time, the label wanted the group to use a name producer. They had a reason for this. Earlier in the year, Rhodes and Micky Foote had flown to New York with tapes of *The Clash* to play to the company's American executives. They didn't understand what they were hearing: they thought the album was 'too rough' and passed on their option to release it.

For The Clash, exhausted after their first burst of success, a new album was the last thing on their mind. 'Our response was, "What do you mean a second album?"' said Joe. 'It took so much out of us making the first one.' The producer issue was a thorny one: the band's experience with Guy Stevens and Lee Perry, both of whom on paper looked ideal candidates, suggested The Clash's sound wasn't easy for any outsider, however cool or crazy, to nail on tape. Late one night at their Canonbury squat, Joe and Roadent brain-stormed the problem and came up with a name: John Lennon.

'I think we had a bit of an inferiority complex at the time,' recalls Roadent. 'I finally got John Lennon's phone number in New York and said to Joe, "Right, come on, we can do this!" And he was like, "Nah, he wouldn't be interested in us." And then I lost my phone book, so we never did ring him. I think he would have been absolutely great.'

The next part of the Get Out of Control tour was due to start in Belfast on 20 October, but the gig was cancelled at the last minute because the insurers withdrew their cover. The Clash took advantage of being in a virtual war zone and were photographed by Adrian Boot posing next to armoured cars and being frisked at an army checkpoint: the group in their quasi-military punk gear and hair-trigger squaddies with berets and taches wearing the real thing. Many regarded it as a cheap and tasteless publicity stunt. It would, as Michael Bradley, the bassist in Derry band The Undertones, said, 'come back and bite them in the arse'.

Mick wasn't unaware they were dabbling with something of which they knew nothing. 'I just felt like a dick,' he told *Melody Maker*'s Ian Birch. 'I should imagine they'll lap it up in London, though. The soldiers crouching in cubby holes thought we were dicks. The kids thought we were dicks.' Mick also thought that it was unwise to use the group's stage backdrop in Ireland, showing as it did a violent Belfast street scene. 'I feel we might be rubbing their faces in it. It's great in Bournemouth because everyone is fucking asleep . . . But in Belfast you don't need to be reminded.'

The tour resumed in Dublin. By late 1977, punk mania had taken off in provinces. Punk rock had long since ceased to be a small underground/art-school movement and was now a huge, nationwide phenomenon. Following the Bill Grundy incident, the riot at the Rainbow, The Pistols' 'God Save the Queen' controversy and Johnny Rotten's razor injuries, punk was discussed almost daily in the tabloid newspapers. A new punk orthodoxy, a distorted, over-simplified version of the original ideas promoted by The Clash and The Pistols, had independently established itself, like a uncontrollable mutant. Violence was now expected at punk gigs. And so was spitting. 'Violence was the backdrop to the whole movement,' says Paul. 'You didn't even think about it. It was the currency. It was just there every night.'

Richard Hell and The Voidoids, booked as support on the tour, had been briefed about what to expect. Quoted in Bob Gruen's photo-book, Hell describes how his guitarist Bob Quine was 'hating the moronic English "punk" scene'. Hell adds: 'It was kind of humiliating to be in a position of playing for an audience that was there to cheer for a band that was basically built out of what we'd created (we being The Ramones and me and the Dolls) but at the same time I could see what got people in England excited.'

Ivan Julian, playing bass, remembers: 'There was a lot of violence. It was a terrifying scene sometimes. Richard was hit so hard with a missile one night it knocked his head right back. But The Clash were great. I didn't really see Paul Simonon at all. He'd turn up for the gig and that was it. Mick was really friendly; we discovered we were born at almost exactly the same minute. Joe was a bit aloof but a very sweet guy, a really genuine person. Topper I recognised from when I was rehearsing in the Kings Road in 1975 with [soul group] The Foundations. He was always hanging out down the studio there. I remember one night a kid came in the dressing room with punk-style pants on. Bernie Rhodes was livid. He kinda lost his mind. He was screaming, "I invented those trousers five years ago! Where did you get them, you little fuck?"'

The tour was chronicled for *NME* by Mick's hero from the American underground music press, Lester Bangs. (His Clash pieces are anthologised in the collection of his writing, *Psychotic Reactions and Carburetor Dung*, and IPC's *NME Originals: The Clash* magazine.) Bangs paints an intimate portrait of The Clash on the road: kids invited back to the group's hotels to sleep on the floor of their rooms, casual violence, Paul Simonon being the joker in the pack, forever winding up Bangs and calling him 'Mo-lester'. Bangs notes that Joe reads Sven Hassel novels, while Mick borrows Lester's copy of Charles Bukowski's *Love is a Dog from Hell*. The writer is occasionally disturbed by what he witnesses. He sees a food fight get out of control in a hotel foyer, resulting in the group's driver, Mickey, duffing up a male fan, before Robin Banks, covering the tour with Kris Needs for *Zig Zag* magazine, steps in and grinds a sandwich into the boy's face.

Bob Gruen was also there covering the tour for *Creem*. He'd first met the group the previous year. (Paul had warned him, 'We're a bunch of cunts', to which Bob had replied, 'You look like a bunch of cunts!') 'I was drawn to their conversation,' he explains. 'The band would stay up every night and talk to anyone who wanted to talk. They weren't just out to meet cute girls. They were available to all their fans. It was the roadies' job to get their fans into the dressing room and the hotel, which was the opposite to other bands. They wanted to know what the fans were thinking. That helped inspire them.'

After one gig, Paul held a conversation with Kris Needs while pissing in a sink. In Plymouth, Topper shot up his room with an air-pistol. Another show saw Joe sustain a direct hit in the mouth from a gobbing fan. (He growled at the audience, 'When I spit, I spit on the floor!') Joe then complained of toothache but a trip to the dentist revealed he had glandular fever. He refused, however, to cancel any dates. By December, Joe's hair had grown back from a crop into its pre-punk quiff. According to Paul, Strummer went out to remonstrate with the audience one night for throwing bottles at all-girl French support act The Lous and was bottled off himself because the crowd didn't recognise him. And finally, there's a story from the tour that one of Bernie's customers is supposed to have complained of putting their Renault in for a service via Rhodes's small ad, only to pick it up a few days later with 1,000 extra miles on the clock. This happened the week The Clash played in Scotland.

Jon Savage saw the group at the Manchester Apollo. 'It was one of the best rock 'n' roll shows I have ever seen,' he says. 'The kids were going mental like they do in Manchester and ripping this theatre up. It was just wild and I was in the press pit dodging all the chairs. It was just fantastic . . . Mick Jones caught my eye and went, "What's going on? This is madness. Have we done this?" Which I thought was really rather sweet.'

Behind the scenes, though, all was not well. The tour saw the departure of Roadent after just six days. The friction between him and Jones was, he felt, taking all the fun out of being around the group. Bob Gruen noticed that some days the pressure seemed to get to Mick and he sank into 'dark moods'. It was the road crew that usually bore the brunt of this. 'Mick was becoming quite demanding,' Roadent explains. 'That was why I stopped working for them.'

'We did a gig at Edinburgh Clouds,' he expands. 'In the afternoon I'd gone out to buy picks and strings for Mick and stuff for Joe and skins for Topper. I asked Richard Hell's people if they needed anything, and when I got back I hadn't actually been able to get any of Richard Hell's stuff, but I'd got Joe's strings and everything. Mick walked in and said, "Have you got my stuff? Oh no, but I suppose you've got Richard Hell's stuff, haven't you?" I was like, "Fuck off, Mick, you need a valet not a roadie." I went to Bernie and said, "I'm fed up with all this, give me the train fare back to London." In London, I went to Malcolm McLaren and said, "Give us a job", and he gave me a wage. Which Bernie never did. Looking back, I can see that Mick was difficult to deal with. He was demanding but, when I think about it, he was also quite considerate at times. But I'd had enough by then.'

Perhaps instinctively, Roadent sensed that the chaos, raw excitement and unpredictability of The Clash's early days had been replaced by a more ordered and professional environment. There was something else, too.

Inevitably, a hierarchy was evolving, which detached the group, now punk stars, from their old friends and crew. 'Up to signing the record deal,' he says, 'you know you're not in the band, you're not on stage with them, but you feel part of them, like a fifth member or something. You have input. But as soon as the band signs a contract, you're not part of that contract and alienation starts setting in. You don't see it at the time. You feel this is something more than just a band; you feel like you're breaking a mould. But it turns out you aren't.'

Meanwhile, CBS was keen to focus the group's attention on their next album. At the Manchester show at the Elizabethan Ballroom, filmed for the Granada TV show *So It Goes*, an important character was in the audience. Blue Öyster Cult's producer, Sandy Pearlman, had been selected from a shortlist prepared by CBS as a possible producer for The Clash's next album. A New Yorker, Pearlman had been contacted by CBS A&R man Dan Loggins (brother of Kenny) and flown to the UK on Concorde to spend a week watching CBS's British 'punk' roster, including The Only Ones, The Tourists, The Vibrators and The Clash.

The group were expecting him. Outside the gig, there had been a near riot and, since there was a firemen's strike, Army Green Goddess tenders lined the street. Pearlman picked his way through the broken glass in the foyer, where fans had burst through the glass doors of the venue, and joined Micky Foote at the mixing desk. Foote discreetly signalled to Joe onstage.

'We'd like to dedicate this next song to Ted Nugent . . . Aerosmith . . . Journey . . .' spat Strummer to boos and jeers. 'And – most of all – to Blue Öyster Cult!' The Clash then ripped into 'I'm So Bored With the USA'.

'After seeing that, I was ready to do the project,' recalls Pearlman. 'I thought such venom deserved my personal touch on it. I went backstage right then and said, "I'm up for it. Let's start right away!" Three days later, I met the group at CBS's headquarters in Soho Square. They told me they wanted to record with me and the reason was they loved the sound of [Blue Öyster Cult's] 'Godzilla' and 'Don't Fear The Reaper'. I thought it would have been because of [New York punks] The Dictators, but it wasn't. It wasn't CBS that hired me, it was The Clash. It wasn't to create an American sound, it was to create an *extreme* sound. And I did.'

That evening, The Dictators were playing at the Roundhouse and The Clash decided to check them out. 'We went down to the tube station and they never paid,' recalls Sandy. 'They snuck in, and there was this really fat Jamaican lady who was taking tokens, and she looked at them and they looked at her. She looked at them again, and she didn't even bother to try and stop them from sneaking in – they looked *nasty*. So we got over to the Roundhouse, saw The Dictators. After the show, The Clash went to talk to the band privately, to make sure they were, you know, "certified revolutionaries". And then we went back to CBS again the next day and agreed to do the record.'

This may have been the impression that Pearlman was given, but, in the chaotic, volatile world of The Clash, the choice of producer was in no way a done deal. Behind the scenes, there was a continuous dialogue about what the record should sound like. Getting Mick, Joe and Paul to agree on anything was difficult at the best of times. Mick contends that 'we weren't concerned about who did it, because it was going to be great whatever. It wasn't number one on our list of things to think about.'

What was number one on the list was the fact The Clash only had a handful of new songs. For the B-side of their forthcoming single, 'Clash City Rockers', they'd had to re-work an old 101'ers song, 'Jail Guitar Doors'. Mick penned some new verses about his pop heroes, including MC5's Wayne Kramer (the group's singer, Rob Tyner, had been present at the 'Clash City Rockers' session that autumn at Whitfield Street), Fleetwood Mac's Peter Green and good ol' 'Keef'. To get Mick and Joe's creative juices flowing, Bernie suggested they go on a writing trip to Jamaica. This way they could learn what reggae and poverty were really about. It might also give them some perspective on their own lives in London. He managed to wheedle some cash out of CBS for the purpose. Paul and Topper weren't invited.

'I was really pissed off about the whole situation,' Simonon says. 'Actually, now you mention it, I'm still pissed off. They knew about my reggae addiction.'

'We just sat around, waiting for them to come back with some songs,' recalls Topper. 'I did nothing. Seriously. Nothing.'

Mick and Joe flew out in late November 1977. The political tension in Jamaica had eased off since 1976, but not much. In December 1977, just a few weeks after the ten-day trip, twelve JLP gunmen would be shot dead by government special forces in a sting operation. This incident became known as the Green Bay Massacre, and inspired Tapper Zukie's 'Murder'. On their arrival, Strummer and Jones checked into the Pegasus hotel in Kingston. They didn't know anyone on the island and didn't have a guide. The next day they ventured down the docks to try to buy some grass. A local took their money and disappeared. Joe berated Mick for giving them all their cash, but, to their amazement, the guy returned a few minutes later with the goods. But the streets were edgy and they soon realised they were in a bad part of town. The people were experiencing Third World levels of poverty, with no jobs and no food, and shouted out 'White pigs!' to the pair wearing their tailor-made Clash punk regimentals. 'I don't know how we didn't get killed,' said Joe. 'I think they thought we were sailors or something.'

A taxi ride around the city to find Lee Perry's famous Black Ark studio, where The Clash were the only white faces pinned on the wall, proved unsuccessful. It turned out Lee Perry was out of town. After dark, it was obviously too dangerous to venture out. From their hotel, Mick and Joe could hear gunshots. After they managed to snaffle a TV, they didn't bother leaving the hotel, except for trips to the cinema. They saw *Zeppelin* on a huge open-air screen. It was only at the end of their trip they realised all the action for tourists was happening at the Sheraton down the road. Robin Banks received a postcard detailing their experience signed 'Yours, scared shitless, Mick'.

Simonon says: 'When I found out that Joe and Mick had spent most of the time in their hotel, I felt a lot better. Culturally, they weren't quite there. I asked them, "Why didn't you look up all these people whose records we owned?" I think they felt cut off from the rest of the world. I know Joe wished that I'd gone.'

To retaliate for being left behind, Simonon went with Caroline on a week-long cultural tour of Russia. They soon realised why they'd got such a cheap deal: it was −40°C. 'They had amazing museums in Moscow,' he recalls. 'But the city was dilapidated. There was the Russian Museum of Achievement. Things hadn't been tended to, it was all quite grim and falling apart. It was quite like America in terms of its size and expanse. I also went to Leningrad. I brought back some posters and the red stars, which became an important element in The Clash image.'

When Simonon returned, Joe and Mick were already working on the new material they'd written in Jamaica. Hanging around Rehearsals was a tall, gangly guy from Gillingham, who'd helped out on the Get Out of Control tour following Roadent's departure. His name was Johnny Green, and more than any of their other close associates, he was about to contribute great things to The Clash legend.

7
THE ENEMY WITHIN

'Have you heard of the Red Brigade?'
'No, but if they come, we'll kill them.'

Juvenile street-gang, *City of God*

*'What makes you think it's for anything? Why can't it just be a filthy
mess of meaningless shit?'*
'I suppose it could. But I'm pretty certain it isn't.'
CHRISTOPHER ISHERWOOD, *DOWN THERE ON A VISIT*

On 20 November 2003 Johnny Green is striding down Chalk Farm Road
towards the gates that lead into the cobbled yard where the Rehearsal
Rehearsals building stands like an ugly-beautiful reminder of a gas-lit, horse-
drawn London. Green doesn't look vastly different from the beleaguered
roadie-savant of The Clash's *Rude Boy* film. He's 6ft 4in, his sandy hair is
teased into a quiff, and he's wearing a long camel-coloured Crombie. There
is still something menacing and gangster-like about him: a cross between
Robert Mitchum in *Night of the Hunter* and Michael Caine's Jack Carter. A
silver cap glints on a crooked front tooth and, behind purple-tinted glasses,
his blue eyes narrow theatrically whenever he tells a story. His loud, nicotine-
stained chuckle adds to the impression of an ageing Teddy Boy hood.

But Johnny Green is no cartoon baddie – though he can wear that hat if
required, and did so whenever the occasion demanded during his two-and-
a-half years as The Clash's road manager. His extraordinary on-the-road
tales are collected in his rambunctious and much-praised *A Riot of Our
Own: Night and Day with The Clash*. Green is a philosopher and a man
whose rapacious appetite for living has taken him through many great
adventures, from sharing John Peel's doorstep with Marc Bolan in the late
1960s, to punk in the 1970s and a stint in the early 1990s as Kent county education adviser on sex and drugs. He's now enjoying a ninth life as an author
and family man on the Kent coast.

These days Johnny describes his life-method as 'networking with menace'. An example? A few months after our Camden meeting, we are checking out Mick and Tony James's new group, Carbon-Silicon, in Colchester. Before the show, he spots Tony James across the bar.

GREEN: 'Tony James!'
JAMES (clearly not pleased to see him): 'Johnny Green. Yes, I read your book, and you were extremely rude about me.'
GREEN: (beaming) 'Fuck off, Tony! I was rude about *everybody*, including myself!'

Green has written a book about his latest passion, the Tour de France, called *Push Yourself Just a Little Bit More*. Cycling, he'll tell you, is the new rock 'n' roll, where beautiful men like Marco Pantani die young in the pursuit of immortality.

Crossing Chalk Farm Road, we pass the corner where George's café once stood. This was where, in 1977 and 1978, The Clash wolfed down egg and chips and discreetly eyed up the Italian proprietor's beautiful daughter. The café, I discover later, was the one Tony Hancock used to frequent in the early 1960s, just for the pleasure of asking for 'plum duff' and 'raspberry jam'. Across the road is the Caernarvon Castle, The Clash's old local. 'Every Sunday, they used to have strippers. All the local gangsters' wives would be there, dressed up in their finery,' Green explains. 'We had a table at the back where no one ever bothered us. The boys drank lager. Always lager.'

We walk into the railway yard and nose around inside the former Rehearsals building, now a second-hand clothes store. Johnny points out where Simonon's mural was and the exact position of the old Belmont barber's chairs in which Bernie and Micky Foote used to park themselves. He looks bemused-melancholy about the fact that one of the great energy centres of punk is now a boutique selling old leathers and reproduction Clash T-shirts. The soot-blackened building has an atmosphere: for Johnny, it's full of ghosts and distant memories. There's an eerie, personal resonance for me, too. My great-grandfather, Ben, used to work in this very building – Gilbey's number two bonded warehouse – in the years directly before the German machine-guns in Flanders decimated the workforce.

About a mile or so south of Rehearsals is 31 Albany Street. By the autumn of 1977, it had become The Clash's answer to The Pistols' Sex shop – a thriving nexus where the group intersected with the worlds of art, design, textiles, fashion and politics. The house – with a 'posh' entrance on St Anne's Gate – belonged to Sebastian Conran. In 1975, Sebastian Conran's father, Terence, suggested his son take out a lease on the house, and rent it out to his fellow students at the Central School of Art. 'That was my slightly miserly, Rachmanist venture,' Conran chuckles. The four-storey property, backing on to Regent's Park, is a fine stucco Victorian townhouse. A bust is recessed into the white-stone frontage and, at ground level, there are heavy, cast-iron railings, topped with tasselled, spear-headed finials.

In 1977 and '78, Sebastian Conran worked with Paul and Bernie at Albany Street to produce Clash clothes, posters, flyers, record sleeves, backdrops and T-shirts. A special company called Upstarts was formed to keep this arm of the operation separate from the group's other finances. In late 1977, Rhodes relocated The Clash's office from Rehearsals to the large first-floor room overlooking Regent's Park; Joe had already moved into the small upstairs attic room, with a pile of books, a tape recorder and a record player. He joined Micky Foote, who lived at Albany Street with his girlfriend. Sebastian's younger brother, Jasper, had a workshop in the basement.

Joe made himself at home. He enjoyed adorning the million-pound property with slogans. When Elvis died in August 1977, he had graffitied the mirror in Sebastian's room with the words 'Elvis was a tidal wave'. He later scrawled another Strummerism on the wall of his own room: 'To live outside the law you must read comics'. It was a little in-joke for Dylan fans. ('To live outside the law you must be honest' from 'Absolutely Sweet Marie'.)

Elsewhere in the building, Alex Michon was sewing The Clash's 'pop star army fatigues'. Showcased at Harlesden in March 1977, they had been Paul's idea. He recalls having a conversation with Joe about what sort of trousers The Clash should wear. It was part of a wider discussion about fashion and attitude. 'If you got chased down the road with bondage trousers on you'd never get away,' explains Simonon. 'With Clash trousers or army fatigues you were ready for anything. Ready to leap over a wall or escape.'

Alex Michon says, 'Bernie did me a drawing of the trousers and then he hit me with a load of politics. He said, "It's going to be really rough out there, there is going to be fighting on the streets, you've got to know where you are coming from."'

The agreed trouser design had rock 'n' roll pedigree: it was based on a pair Antony Price made in the 1960s for Mick Jagger. Conran had come across some of Jagger's cast-offs and unpicked them. They had parallel legs joined to a boxer-short design. Sebastian added an extra 'basket' to the crotch, so the trousers would be tight but not constricting if vaulting obstacles. Zips, D-rings and military-style map-pockets were then sewn on. Everything was double- or triple-stitched, including the innovative breast-pocket images, like Paul's Mighty Diamonds picture on his jacket and the Notting Hill Riot image on Mick's shirt.

'Those clothes got knackered really quickly,' says Alex. 'The Clash wore them out because they had them on all the time, onstage and off. They got soaked in sweat every time they played. Joe came in one day and we asked him if he wanted a new shirt. He said, "No, I want a new body."'

The central location of Albany Street – twenty minutes' walk from Oxford Street – made it an ideal crash-pad after a night on the town. On one occasion Paul Weller arrived unannounced and stayed up all night smoking dope with Joe. Some guests were less welcome. Robin Banks and Johnny Green, who quickly fell in with each other as partners-in-mischief, used to get horrendously drunk and kick in the door at night. There wasn't much Sebastian could do about it. Robin even ended up living there for a while. He and Johnny would bully Jasper for beer money.

Alex Michon's diary entry for January 1978 gives a unique window into The Clash camp. Althia and Donna's 'Up Town Top Ranking' was the record of the moment. 'Paul is back from Russia to be taught Mick's new bass lines and gives away Lenin badges,' she writes. 'Clash rehearsing fifteen new numbers. Chrissie Hynde talks of bikers and will occasionally break into song. More stories from The Boss [Bernie] concerning being arrested in Spain after hitching back from Africa, the best fish 'n' chip shop in London, the IRA shop in Kilburn, the East Enders who used to shop at Let It Rock.' She lists fragments of Bernie's conversations: 'Events move much faster than people'; 'I like to be driven around London so I can notice where walls have been pulled down or who has had their house painted'; 'You've got to remember, Sebastian, that every art movement – any revolutionary art movement – was at the beginning political'; 'I like to have people around me who know the situation and are cool.'

'Why does he do it?' Alex writes. 'Why does The Boss cause so many problems for himself? All the work and worry for what?'

When Johnny Green arrived back in London after Christmas 1977, he made a bee-line for Rehearsals. Several months before, he'd seen a picture of the building in the *NME* and was intrigued by its sinister architecture. Johnny had blagged his way on to the Get Out of Control tour by tagging along with a friend who'd been hired to ferry the group's gear around in his lorry. By the end of the tour, Green had been promoted to the band's personal driver, taking Joe, Mick, Paul and Topper from gig to gig in a rented mini-bus. He thought they were extraordinary people, who inspired unquestioning loyalty. They loved his 'fuck off' attitude and fearlessness.

Johnny was twenty-seven when he met the group. He was two years older than Joe and five years older than Mick, Paul and Topper. He'd done some living in his time: 1960s Gillingham Mod, Carnaby Street dandy, teenage husband, the Notting Hill hippy scene, Gandalf's Garden, acid, forestry, organic food production, hard drugs, a degree in Arabic studies as a mature student. Along the way he'd learned a few lessons about self-image, reinvention, connection; he was, and is, a fan of Rimbaud. You can imagine him trying anything, just to 'find out what it was like'. Even at twenty-seven, he was a thrill-junkie, raconteur, closet intellectual, bar-room brawler – a combination of traits that left him, like The Clash themselves, without a neat pigeonhole in the book of English archetypes.

In Jamaica, Joe and Mick had worked on a handful of new tunes, including 'Last Gang in Town', 'Tommy Gun' and, about their experience in Kingston, the courageous and direct 'Safe European Home' ('I went to the place where every white face is an invitation to robbery / Sitting here in my safe European home, I don't wanna go back there again'). While they were waiting for Paul to come back from Russia, they began rehearsing, with Mick playing bass. There was no room for sentimentality or latitude: on his return, Paul was handed a set of headphones and rough tape that Mick had made of the new material.

'He was only gone a week,' recalls Johnny Green. 'He came back and he was a bit slow to learn the parts. Meanwhile, Topper is fast at learning, he's only been here eight or nine months, and he's picking things up and contributing to the process. They're all downstairs and Paul's upstairs. He's like a Special Needs kid – he's sitting there and he has to learn the songs. He's saying, "I'll just go and get a cup of tea", and it's like, "No, Paul, you sit there and have another go at it; I'll make the tea." The others are two or three weeks ahead, they don't want to slow down to his level. They're moving with such purpose, they're on a songwriting roll.'

Johnny began sleeping on the old mattress upstairs at Rehearsals and replaced Roadent as the group's confidant, outboard energy-source and quality-control adviser. 'I don't think Bernie had a way of fitting that into the way things were supposed to be,' said Joe. 'We knew those people kept our feet on the ground. The relationship with the road crew where they could say, "That's fucking poxy!" They attended rehearsals and said things like, "What the fuck was that?" Or, "That's not good enough, you're The Clash." They carried that flag for us. It's like the Roman emperor who has the slave standing behind him saying he's a wanker as he leads his Triumph into Rome, to keep his head from expanding.'

Dossing down upstairs, Johnny would often find himself talking late into the night with Joe after the others had left for the evening. Strummer's mother would sometimes phone to check if Joe was OK; Green became their intermediary, passing on messages and information. Joe and Johnny began to engage on an emotional and intellectual level.

'I was reading a book about Elvis,' says Green. 'Joe had a quality that he had – he'd zero in on you and make you the centre of attention. He made you feel very special. I'd pass on messages from his mum. I think Joe was reinvented as a person, but he never denied his past. He'd talk about his home life. It wasn't a no-go area, it wasn't as if he didn't acknowledge it. He'd sit and ask me about my life when I lived up north for a few years, and his life in Newport. We'd talk about the difference between provincial life and London, and what it was like to be in a band that wanted to be somewhere. He wasn't about creating this figure, which was the Billy Idol approach; he was happy to share his self-reflections.'

Johnny talked to Joe about the death of his brother, David. 'He did wonder whether he was insensitive to its causes,' says Green. 'He hadn't seen it coming. He thought: was there something I could have done? Something that would have changed the progression of the moods? Why was he not alert to it? He also talked about whether he should just let go of that guilt. But then: how did you let it go? It was something that obviously troubled him.'

Another of Johnny's jobs was fielding Patti Smith's late-night, transatlantic calls to Paul, who was still friends with the singer-poet. Johnny describes Simonon as 'lovely. He takes the piss out of himself. He could be serious and I think he's an immensely cool human being without having to try. I've rarely met someone who's cool but can still laugh at themselves. I found him good company, lively and energetic. He wasn't stupid, he was a sharp bloke, and what I really learned quite quickly was how much he hid behind it, he'd put up this "fuck you, cunt", thicko front to stop people getting at him, a protection. He did that within the framework of the band, too, so he didn't have to be at the forefront of the decision-making process, yet he never allowed himself to be removed from it. He would get quite cross if Joe and Mick were sorting out things that didn't involve him. But then he'd go back to playing the lunkhead when it suited him.'

And then there was Mick Jones. 'Mick had his own little rituals that had to be observed,' explains Johnny. 'But the moment he walked into Rehearsals it was serious business. What strength, what purpose, what vision! Mick never dreamed of a holiday, just rehearsing day in, day out, an absolutely driven man. And yet he was still very pleasant to be around. If you got to know his routine – tea and biscuits at 4 p.m. – it was fine. He was the driving force behind that band. Everything good about them musically was down to Mick Jones and Topper.'

In December 1977, Mick made it clear to Bernie that he wanted to move out of his gran's flat into his own place. Rhodes didn't understand why he would wish to forsake a poky room in a council tower-block for a flash pad in Notting Hill. Jones, now twenty-two, signed to the same label as Barbra Streisand, and with a top twenty album under his belt, conversely wondered why he was meant to live like an impoverished student. Through Caroline Coon's influence, he managed to get funds to rent a two-bedroom flat in Pembridge Villas off the southern end of Portobello Road. The rent, according to Tony James, who moved in as his flatmate, was £50 a week, split between them.

The flat quickly became an after-hours hang-out for the partying punk fraternity: friends like Glen Matlock, Danny Kustow from The Tom Robinson Band, Generation X's Billy Idol and Derwood. Tony James says, 'My most vivid memory of Pembridge Villas was Mick buying a video machine with his advance. He had a tape of his favourite film of all time, *Zulu*. People were taking lots of drugs and hanging out all the time. It went on all night, every night, with *Zulu* playing till three in the morning. I used to go to bed. I'd be lying there listening to the Rorke's Drift bit and Stanley Baker giving the great speech. Then it would start again.'

There were other destructive forces, besides the relentless volleys from the Warwickshires' Martini-Henry rifles. 'Robin Banks used to come round regularly, which I'd dread,' says Tony. 'Downstairs was a posh lawyer and Robin used to jump up and down on the floor and shout, "Wake up you bastard!"'

It was Johnny Green's job to collect Mick for rehearsals and he could see that the guitarist was gleefully embracing a decadent rock 'n' roll lifestyle. By this time, cocaine was on the scene. While speed and dope had become acceptable punk drugs because they were cheap, coke was considered extravagant and degenerative. Rod Stewart and Elton John took coke. Minor royalty took coke. A gram of coke in 1978 was around £40 to £60; a similar wrap of speed was £6.

'I'd go to his place around midday and make him his drink,' recalls Green. 'It was a bit like the Court of Louis XIV. He might have a girl there, he had a few regulars. I'd chop him out a line. It was a slow process to get him going. It was all done very carefully, the idea being to keep him in a good mood. If he was not pleased with the way things were going he'd let you know. His temper was not a nice thing to be around. My technique was to get him up in a soft, customer-friendly way.'

Johnny Green also contends that Mick was 'very calculatedly using Tony's money'. He also recalls that Jones was forever asking why Generation X, who had signed to Chrysalis, were driven around in black limos and had plenty of cash, while The Clash existed hand-to-mouth. This notion that Tony's group lived comparatively lavishly pervaded the Clash camp. One afternoon Topper and Robin thought it only fair to 'borrow' some money they found in Tony's room. Tony suspected who was behind the theft, and Mick was put in the awkward position of having to retrieve the roll of notes.

Tony, however, is adamant that it was The Clash who were the better-off group. 'The Clash always had much more money than us,' he says emphatically. 'We were ripped off much worse than they were. They had video players! Theirs were some of the first machines to come out, no one had a video then. They didn't own houses and cars but they had their rent paid and plenty of pocket money.'

During the last week of January 1978, Pembridge Villas became the location of a discovery that would have dramatic implications for the Clash camp. John Brown, Mick's old schoolfriend and Delinquents band-mate, happened to be there when it happened. He had received an unexpected call from Mick asking if he wanted to come round to the flat. The last time he'd seen Mick was several months earlier at the Ian Hunter gig at Hammersmith Odeon; Mick and Tony had guffawed loudly when he'd told them the name of his new punk group: The Tools. 'I thought, "You pair of fucking wankers!"' laughs Brown.

The night at Mick's flat began smoothly enough. 'He had this whole wall of albums,' recalls Brown. 'He started pulling them out and playing them really loudly. He'd just come back from Jamaica and he started banging on loads of reggae and dub. He was having a great time. He was like a kid with a new toy, but sharing it with me, which is cool. It was like, "Look what I've got now! You know that dream of being pop stars we had at school? Well, it's come true! Come and share it!" He loved playing the reggae records. He said, "Listen, they've even got it for kids!" and he put on a single that had kind of Pinky and Perky voices on it.

'We started reminiscing about [The Delinquents],' he continues. 'There was a mirror with a load of coke on it and Mick was bending down to have a snort and I said, "Do you remember when Paul Wayman went in to buy a Sharks single and he ended up coming out with a Sparks single?" Mick went, "Pfffffffff!" and blew all the coke everywhere. It was a really nice, friendly vibe.'

Then the mood darkened. A promo copy had arrived of The Clash's new single, 'Clash City Rockers', due to be released in mid-February. Jones eagerly put it on the record deck and cranked up the volume, keen to let everyone hear the group's latest creation. His look of puzzlement turned to anger. He turned to John and asked him if he could hear what was wrong with it. John said, no, he couldn't, it sounded great. Mick then shouted, 'They've fucking speeded it up! The fuckers have speeded it up!' 'He was . . . flipping mad isn't the word for it', says John. 'He was really, really upset by it.'

Behind Jones's back, someone had varispeeded the master of the song – a trick popular with producers to give a record an extra bit of zip at the cutting stage. To Mick's mind it was a traitorous act. Eventually, he calmed down and the party got back into a groove. John Brown was humorously berated for wasting good tobacco in a normal cigarette, instead of rolling a spliff. At one o'clock in the morning, the resident in the flat below began his nightly tattoo on his ceiling with a broom handle, yelling, 'Turn that bloody noise down!'

Mick opened the living-room window and shouted down to him, 'If you don't shut up, I'll buy the whole building and have you evicted!'

The next day, an inquiry was set up to find out what the hell had happened with 'Clash City Rockers'. There had been several attempts to record the track between September and December 1977, all at the larger downstairs studio at Whitfield Street, with Micky Foote producing. The tempo of the song had been difficult to nail. It became clear that it was Micky Foote who had varispeeded the final cut. 'It was a step too far and I knew that,' he says. 'I was chiselling my own tombstone. It was the wrong thing to do. In terms of professional integrity, for someone who's supposed to be working with the band, it was a bad move.'

Accounts of Foote's subsequent dismissal invariably finger him as a baddie. Ostensibly, it all seems simple enough: he went behind the group's back and was rewarded with the boot. Most books and articles say Mick sacked him, though an article in *Q* magazine in 2004 claims it was Joe. But what really happened is more complex and sheds fascinating light onto the web of complex relationships within The Clash camp. Quizzing Foote reveals the importance of his role as Bernie and the group's go-between. Rhodes, he points out, was the figure dealing directly with Maurice Oberstein at CBS. Despite his off-the-wall ideas, and for all his obfuscatory spiel, it seems Bernie liked to do business efficiently and wanted to appear to Oberstein to have complete control over his charges.

'Bernie wanted it to seem to CBS that he could say, "Guys, I want a single, two B-sides; Micky, you record that; CBS, here you are,"' explains Foote. 'He wanted to be seen to be able to deliver the product. I was the delivery man. I think Bernie thought that all you had to do was press the red button, the light goes on, and hey presto it comes out the other end. It doesn't work like that.'

Micky had told Bernie that he believed the tempo wasn't right and they needed to record the single again. This wasn't impossible but there was a danger of losing momentum and alienating CBS. It was already nearly four months since 'Complete Control' was released. 'If you're a new band signed to a big label,' says Foote, 'you've got to come in on the deadlines and there's a lot of pressure on you to do that. But at the same time, the band had enough weight to say, "We want to do the session again, we want more time." But Bernie wasn't interested. He said we had to meet the deadline.'

There was another reason why Micky varispeeded the record without the group's knowledge: it involved his role as producer. Foote wanted to create a working relationship where there was some objective distance between him and the group. 'Mick thought we should have this relationship where I confided in him,' he says. 'I didn't allow that, or else where's my own identity in it? I needed to have an independence where I can say, "Can we do that again, Mick, and forget the Keith Richards ending?"'

It was Joe who took it upon himself to chew out his old friend. He confronted him at Rehearsals. 'He went, "What's this? It sounds like Pinky and fuckin' Perky,"' says Micky. '"We know you've done something to it. You and Bernie."' Foote told Joe and Mick that he would persuade Rhodes to postpone the release date and allow them to re-record the track. But the damage was already done. Jones saw it as conclusive evidence that Foote was Bernie's stooge and couldn't be trusted. 'Mick made it clear what he thought,' says Micky. Strummer was 'more philosophical' and believed that it was a lesson everyone could learn from.

Micky concludes: 'To be in between The Clash and Bernie was a difficult position to be in. But it was a fair cop. It was a management decision and it's easy to understand why they didn't like it. Fuck it, I didn't even like the song that much anyway. "Clash City Rockers"? Sounds good, dunnit, therefore it must be good, right?'

Jones bit his lip and, in March 1978, the speeded-up version of 'Clash City Rockers' was released. It reached number thirty-five, seven places lower than 'Complete Control'. (All subsequent Clash compilations have the corrected version.) It might have performed better if the group had promoted it on *Top of the Pops*, BBC 1's peak-time, Thursday night chart programme. But The Clash still deemed this bastion of the music establishment phoney (artists mimed to a re-recorded version of their track) and it was therefore strictly verboten.

Instead, the song was performed live on the BBC-2 youth programme, *Something Else*, together with 'Tommy Gun'. Joe Strummer and Paul Simonon were interviewed. In terms of a TV audience it was by far their biggest yet and a rare grandstand to communicate their views. Robin Banks remembers Joe being jumpy beforehand and disappearing to find something to calm his nerves. Discussing the issue of 'why young people feel disillusioned', they were pitched against Joan Lestor MP, the chairman of the Labour Party.

The backdrop to some pre-recorded vox pop interviews preceding the piece is a multi-racial, high-rise estate in London. In previous filmed interviews – such as the London Weekend Television slot with Janet Street-Porter and the *Punk in London* backstage footage from Munich – it had been Simonon, widely regarded as the least verbally forthcoming Clash member, who had been the most vocal.

This time it's no different. Joe seems unsure how to come across – wise old owl or disaffected punk rocker? He states: 'Most young people feel remote from the mechanics of government, they don't feel a part of it.' Joan Lestor asks how Joe might change that. He says, 'You learn at school how it works, right, or at least I did, I've forgotten now (laughs) . . . it's just so boring, it doesn't interest anyone. All the parties look the same and it looks a big mess.' His solution to the political quagmire is a sort of dumbed-down version of Bolshevism with a liberal dash of gulag: 'All the people who own the factories, who drive a Rolls-Royce, you get rid of them somehow and put them in a camp. You'd save a lot of money, because the workers do all the work.'

Simonon, meanwhile, looking young and a little self-conscious, manages to hold a sustained argument with Lestor. His argument benefits from sticking to The Clash's broad 1976 mission statement: 'We're anti-Fascist, we're anti-violence, we're anti-racist and we're pro-creative.' He argues that The

Clash are challenging the status quo by playing reggae music to display their solidarity with blacks. Lestor thinks that is commendable and steers the discussion towards the National Front, saying that they're being beaten and people shouldn't be gloomy about the future. Paul notes that there's a danger in even drawing attention to the NF: 'By putting something down it always increases an interest in it and makes it stronger.' Lestor tells him that the NF didn't perform well in the recent Ilford North by-election; Paul whips back, 'Yes they did, they got almost exactly the same as the Liberals!' (The National Front candidate, John Hughes, received 2,216 votes and John Freeman from the Liberal Party 2,248.) When he's drawn back into the conversation, Joe quips, 'Maybe I'll grow up to be prime minister.'

It's easy to be cynical about The Clash's clumsy attempts to discuss politics, but they should be put in context. It shouldn't be forgotten that it was unusual for a rock group to be debating social issues on television at all. Even with the inevitable playing dumb that attended punk, Joe and Paul are far more articulate than, say, Mick Jagger is during the infamous TV interview with David Frost on his release from Brixton jail in 1967.

But what's perhaps most significant about the *Something Else* debate is it once again saw The Clash dismissing party politics, right and left, and marshalling their energies towards a simple, unequivocal objective: defeating racism. This, more so than any other issue, would dominate their agenda in Britain in the next few years.

Strummer's appearance on *Something Else* was his first major engagement since being discharged from hospital at the end of February. A few weeks earlier, he had been diagnosed with hepatitis. This, he claimed, was contracted from the spitting on the Get Out of Control tour. Hepatitis is often associated with intravenous drug use but no one interviewed for this book believes Joe was experimenting with heroin, though it's undeniable heroin was around, and the singer was clued up enough about its effects to talk to the press about being 'smacked out' as a means of escaping reality. Strummer himself was always adamant that he never tried the drug, though in his Joe biography, *Redemption Song*, Chris Salewicz says Mick admitted at the time that Strummer did indeed catch the disease from a dirty needle, though injecting what no one is sure.

The Clash were scheduled to demo their new material with Sandy Pearlman, who'd flown over to the UK to catch them on a series of low-key dates at the end of January. Demo sessions were held at Whitfield Street but were cancelled after a couple of days because Joe was too ill to continue. 'He'd gone an orange-yellow colour,' recalls Pearlman. In mid-February, he was admitted to Western Hospital in Fulham. In his room he had a poster for *Grutzi Elvis*, a film by Diego Cortez, the soundtrack of which featured Strummer singing 'Heartbreak Hotel'. Joe was surrounded with literature: Dashiell Hammett, Jean Genet, a three-volume set of Trotsky's *History of the Russian Revolution*.

While in hospital, he was interviewed for the *NME* by Howie Klein (who wrote as 'Jack Basher'). Klein was a music journalist and San Francisco radio DJ who'd begun championing The Clash on his show. Later he would become president of Reprise Records. He was a good friend of Sandy Pearlman's and was accompanying the producer on his UK visit to write a Clash story for *Creem*. Strummer told him: 'We always go on the defensive when confronted with this political stuff. We see it as a trap, a hole to get stuck in. We wanna move in any direction we want, including a political direction.'

The Clash were put on hold for most of the rest of February, much to the irritation of Bernie, who was keen to proceed with the second album and bank the advance that came with it. The Clash's coffers had been further drained by the £10,000 loss incurred on the Get Out of Control tour. 'I first realised how ill Joe was when I was in the kitchen where Jasper Conran had his workshop,' remembers Alex Michon. 'Joe had pissed in all these milk bottles, and the piss was bright red. Very shortly after that it got serious and he was in bed. Micky Foote was really upset about it. We were all very worried. Bernie phoned up and was screaming at me, going, "He's going out drinking, isn't he? I work so hard while he's out drinking!" I said, "Yes, he is drinking – I've just made him a cup of tea." But Bernie was livid, he was shouting, "My son wants a bicycle and I can't buy him a bicycle because of that cunt going out drinking." . . . It was the first time he had mentioned his son.'

Not long after Joe had made a full recovery, he moved out of 31 Albany Street, though not before he and Paul had thrown some flowerpots at Bernie as he'd arrived in the building. His change of address was not entirely of his own choice. The Clash's association with Sebastian Conran had become an issue in the music press. The previous summer, Joe, who'd long styled himself as déclassé, had remarked in an interview in the *Sunday Times* magazine that Sebastian had 'a very high-class voice but he means well'. Since then, Tony Parsons had been making barbed comments about Sebastian in the *NME* and, in recent weeks, *Sounds* journalist Garry Bushell, a champion of the new wave of unsophisticated prole punk bands led by Sham 69, was complaining that Joe Strummer was 'singing about a white riot while living in a white mansion'.

In Britain, you're prejudged by how you speak and the school you went to. For a singer-songwriter like Nick Drake, this wasn't a problem. But Joe's private-school education was becoming a hot potato: it suggested he was a fraud. His link with Sebastian was further putting The Clash's street-credibility – there's no other phrase for it – in jeopardy.

Johnny Green comments: 'You may ask, "Why was someone like Sebastian tolerated in The Clash camp anyway?" But Sebastian is quite an ebullient character, slightly fey, in a well-heeled public-school way, but a likeable man who has learned to take a bit of flack. I would say that that was a very important criteria around the camp at that time. If you can take it, or even give a bit back, you are all right. It didn't really matter how you spoke or your background, it was about your attitude. Can you stand on your own two feet, can you take this stuff? And Sebastian could. He was full of energy. I would say that Sebastian Conran was fine, he was a dynamic sort of guy.'

'I liked Joe and Paul,' says Sebastian. 'Paul was obviously interested in what I was doing, the clothes and stuff. He didn't get involved in the politics – he just stood there looking handsome and playing bass and being nice. He had this lovely, toothy grin. Joe and I had the same background; he was very intelligent and was prepared to talk to me. It was Mick who I didn't get on with. It was mutual dislike. He just scowled a lot.'

Strummer succumbed to pressure to leave Albany Street. Very soon, Sebastian was greeted with sour asides from Mick whenever he turned up at Rehearsals. 'There was suddenly a lot of "What's he doing here?" going on,' recalls Sebastian. 'That wasn't particularly nice, because I'd been hanging out with them for at least eighteen months by then.' The rejection hurt. 'I felt fairly betrayed, that sort of denial of my existence. One minute I was everyone's mate, and then the next minute I was an untouchable just because of what Tony Parsons said. I felt that they all knew where I had come from – there was a lot of pretending going on with them anyway – and all of a sudden it was like a Stalinesque retouching of photographs.'

When I first interviewed Johnny Green in 1999 he set me a teaser: just how loyal is Joe to his friends? The truth is that Sebastian never blamed Joe for what happened. He says, 'Despite everything, Joe was always very loyal.' Sebastian recognised Strummer was under pressure to move on. Number 31 Albany Street invited a skewed interpretation of The Clash's financial situation, though it accurately reflected their happiness to gatecrash someone else's flash premises.

Tragically, Conran's inevitable denouncement was followed later in the

Joe and Mick in action, America, September 1979. 'They were fucking brilliant live,' says one-time manager Peter Jenner. 'All you needed was a decent PA and some lights, and then you just let them get on with it. It's a miracle it happened sometimes with all the chaos.'

Neal Preston, Corbis

Ain't been to no music school: a surly John Mellor (top row, ninth from left) at City of London Freemen's, circa 1966. 'He was a good guy to hang out with, very funny and artistic,' explained friend Ken Powell. 'He always came at what he did from an original angle.'

Courtesy of Chris Reynolds and Ken Powell

The Delinquents' wunderkind, 'Michael J. Jones', with band-mate Paul Wayman, September 1974. The shot — taken outside bassist John Brown's house off the Old Kent Road — sees Jones wearing a Johnson's shirt with a pop-art/cartoon pattern. 'He was a real cool kid,' says John Brown.

Courtesy of John Brown

Pat Garrett and Billy the Kid: 'Woody' with new, gun-slinging friend, photographed by Jivin' Al Jones outside a newsagent's in Bristol. The two had travelled from Newport to see Captain Beefheart at the Colston Hall on 21 April 1973.

Alan Jones

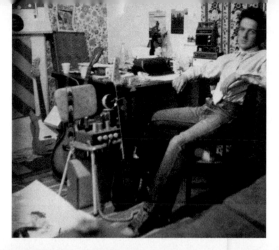

Bringing it all back home to Wales: 'Woody' Mellor in his room at 12 Pentonville, Newport, early summer 1974. He had recently had his hair cut into a quiff, and written his first song, 'Crummy Bum Blues'. Note the cowboy artwork on the floor.
Alan Jones

'Young-ish' pub rock stragglers The 101'ers in winter 1975. From left: Joe Strummer, Clive Timperly, Richard Dudanski and Dan Kelleher. 'Being on stage empowered Joe to be this different character,' recalled Dudanski. 'Pouring beer over people, confronting hecklers.'
Julian Yewdall

Wilmcote House, Mick and his gran's home on the Warwick Estate, Royal Oak. They lived on the eighteenth floor — Mick's friend Robin Banks used to hang off the balcony for kicks. In the foreground is another famous Clash totem, the Westway flyover.
Craig Biddington

London's burning with sushi now: The Clash's HQ in Camden Town, Rehearsal Rehearsals, in summer 2004. The building in which the group began life is now part of the Stables Market. A new frontage houses a Japanese food stall, while inside you can buy secondhand leathers — and Clash T-shirts.

Craig Riddington

The former Tack House opposite Rehearsal Rehearsals, where Joe, Mick and Paul posed for the cover of The Clash. Six years later, in July 1983, the building was turned into a rehearsal studio by manager Bernie Rhodes, and became the group's last HQ. Clash 'ideas person' Kosmo Vinyl opened a private drinking den upstairs.

Craig Riddington

Erno Goldfinger's infamous Trellick Tower, located off Golborne Road in Ladbroke Grove. During the latter stages of its construction in the late '60s, a section was in danger of collapsing — Paul Simonon's secondary school, Isaac Newton, in nearby Wornington Road was briefly closed as a result.

All the young punks: Keith Levene (in black) and Paul Simonon on stage at the Screen on the Green cinema, Islington, 29 August 1976. The gig inspired Charles Shaar Murray to suggest they should be returned to a garage with the motor running. Levene would only last another two shows before being sacked.
Joe Stevens

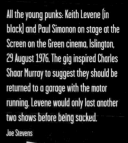

Independence day: poster for The Clash's debut gig, supporting The Pistols at the Black Swan, Sheffield on 4 July 1976. A letter to 'Sounds' the following week concluded they were 'a cacophonous barrage of noise – they tried to play '60s R&B but failed dismally'.
Courtesy Graham Jones, blackmarketclash.com

Resident DJ Don Letts and club manager Andy Czezowski outside The Roxy in Covent Garden. The picture was taken on the day the club closed down, 28 May 1977. 'People have the misconception I turned all punks onto reggae,' says Don. 'But people like Paul Simonon, Joe Strummer and John Lydon were definitely into it before I came along.'
Erica Echenberg

The Clash at the ICA on 23 October 1976, with Terry Chimes on drums. 'It was much easier after Keith Levene left,' he explains. The evening ended in bloodshed when fans Jane Crockford and Shane MacGowan carved each other up. Strummer quipped: 'Why don't you go home and collect stamps? That's much tougher.'
Bob Gruen, Starfile

No room at the Holiday Inn: Joe bandages the hand of confidant and roadie Steve 'Roadent' Connolly on the Anarchy tour bus. The Clash and Sex Pistols managed to play only seven gigs of the tour. Roadent was to quit a year later, complaining that Mick needed 'a valet', not a roadie.
Caroline Coon, Camera Press London

Three's a crowd: Mick revs up for an encore with Sham 69's Jimmy Pursey and The Pistols' Steve Jones at the Music Machine, July 1978. The gig was part of the On Parole tour, during which The Clash delighted audiences with a version of 'Pretty Vacant'.
Justin Thomas

Pass the guacamole: Joe's turn to serve, backstage at The Rainbow in December 1977. Riders were always a bugbear for The Clash. Paul rails, 'Who wants mushrooms with a bit of bacon wrapped around its head when you've just got off stage? It's ridiculous.'

Caroline Coon, Camera Press London

At Heathrow, en route to the first North American tour, 30 January 1979. Topper's drum roadie, Baker, is third from left beside perplexed businessman. Their first stop was Vancouver; next they journeyed to Seattle, where they learned Sid Vicious had died.

Johnny Green

A previously unseen picture of The Clash recording 'Give 'Em Enough Rope' in Basing Street studios, off Portobello Road, in June 1978. It was Topper's first album with the group. 'He was an unbelievable musician,' recalls producer Sandy Pearlman.

Joe Stevens

The final mixing of 'Give 'Em Enough Rope' at the Record Plant on West 44th Street, New York. Sandy Pearlman is seated in the centre, wearing a baseball cap. Paul and Topper had been flown in from London for a playback.

Bob Gruen, Starfile

Joe lying down on the job at Heathrow, attended by Topper, on 20 October 1977. The group were flying out to Belfast for a gig at the Ulster Hall, which was eventually cancelled. Instead, The Clash posed at an army checkpoint — 'We looked like dicks,' Mick later commented.

Caroline Coon, Camera Press London

Strummer with US country rock'n'roller and Clash adoptee, Joe Ely, backstage at the Tribal Stomp festival in Monterey, 8 September 1979. Later, the group would play an unscheduled show at Ely's hometown, Lubbock. 'At some [places in Texas], the audience looked at them like a pig looks at a wristwatch.'

Roger Ressmeyer, Corbis

Outside is America: Mick with essential kit on the first US tour, February 1979. The Clash were supported by their hero Bo Diddley, who donated his bunk on the tour bus to his $20,000 custom-made guitar.

Bob Gruen, Starfile

Legendary road manager Johnny Green during the Pearl Harbour tour, February 1979. The T-shirt is a Fifth Column design, showing a kamikaze pilot. 'A lot of the madness was to do with Johnny,' says their driver Howard Fraser. 'He was a powerful mover.'

Johnny Green

'Who's in charge of seat allocation?' The Clash take a flight on their first US tour, with mysterious fifth member. All the shows on that tour sold out instantly. 'They were ready to be defensive,' says DJ Howie Klein. 'But what they found in America was worship.'

Bob Gruen, Starfile

The Clash on stage with Jamaican dub maestro Mikey Dread, with whom they recorded 'Sandinista!' and toured in 1980 and '81. 'If you see what a hurricane does to an island in the Caribbean, then that's what the theatres looked like after The Clash played,' he says.
Bob Gruen, Starfile

Mick with one of his teenage heroes, Guy Stevens, who produced 'London Calling' in his inimitable 'lunatic-genius' style. Ironically, in 1975, Stevens had ousted Jones from Little Queenie, a group Mick had formed with schoolfriend John Brown.
Bob Gruen, Starfile

A previously unseen shot of The Clash playing football in Regent's Park during summer 1979. Simonon and Jones are poised to tackle unknown player, while Robin Banks (far left) watches on.
Johnny Green

Joe and his girlfriend Gaby Salter, standing in the car park outside Wessex Studios during the recording of 'London Calling'. At the time they were living with Gaby's mum in a council flat on the World's End Estate in Chelsea. The Thameside location inspired the line 'And I live by the River!' on the album's title track.
Johnny Green

Paul Simonon, nursing a bottle of Southern Comfort, with Clash caretaker manager Caroline Coon. 'The Clash had a complex relationship with people they saw as being authoritative,' she says. 'They could be mean to the people who worked for them.'
Bob Gruen, Starfile

Topper on the tour bus with girlfriend and Barry 'Scratchy' Myers, Clash tour DJ. 'The Clash were very stylish, the look was important,' says Scratchy. 'Image played a big part in it.'
Johnny Green

Some things are worth waiting for: fans queue overnight for tickets to see The Clash at Bond's in New York. To appease the Fire and Building Departments, The Clash had to halve the capacity of their shows — and double the length of their residency. 'It got us huge coverage in America,' says Kosmo Vinyl.
Bob Gruen, Starfile

'Can I borrow some gloop?' Joe and Paul backstage at Bond's. 'They were the first band to really embrace the cross-cultural revolution,' explains New York producer Rick Rubin. 'They brought reggae to rock fans... and it was the same with hip-hop.'
Joe Stevens

The Quest-meister: Kosmo Vinyl at Bond's. 'He was a PR man but he was also a facilitator,' says one-time manager Andrew King. 'Kosmo was good at moving things along. He was a tremendous asset.'
Joe Stevens

Lead singer of The Explosions and Bond's aftershow DJ, Pearl Harbour, with Fee Waybill of The Tubes. 'Being English guys, I didn't think they liked American stuff,' she says. 'But I was wholly wrong. Joe especially liked country music.' Pearl was later married to Paul.
Paul Slattery

Roadie Digby Cleaver (in cap) and Kosmo Vinyl find new roles as Strummer body-artists. Digby was recruited in September 1981 when Mick's previous guitar tech left. 'Mick wanted a girl [for the job],' laughs Cleaver. 'But they were frightened off by his reputation.'
Pennie Smith

Mick and Joe visiting a temple while touring Japan, January 1982. 'They loved us,' says Mick. 'Some bands had disgraced themselves there, so we had made an unconscious decision to treat them gently. They gave us presents.'
Pennie Smith

Kosmo, Joe and manager Bernie Rhodes at La Guardia airport en route to Buffalo, October 1982. 'Every group has a madman,' says Rhodes. 'I'm the nutty one in The Clash, but I'm not a victim, I'm a winner.'
Bob Gruen, Starfile

The good's gone: The Clash support The Who in Philadelphia, as part of the latter's autumn 1982 'Farewell Tour'. 'They managed the stadium crowds far better than The Pretenders, who did the tour before,' concludes Pete Townshend.
Bob Gruen, Starfile

The post-Mick line-up of The Clash: from left, Joe, Vince White, Pete Howard, Nick Sheppard, Paul. 'I said to Joe, "You've got to stop lighting them from the back,"' says Clash friend Jock Scot. '"It looks like three copies of the FA Cup up there. Their ears do not take the light well."'
Mike Laye, Corbis

Mick rehearsing with his new outfit, Carbon Silicon, in May 2004. He formed the group the previous year with original London SS member (later of Generation X and Sigue Sigue Sputnik), Tony James. The guitar Tony (out of picture) is playing is the Les Paul Junior used on 'The Clash'.
George Binette

Friends reunited: Mick joins Joe Strummer and The Mescaleros at a benefit gig for the Fire Brigades Union, Acton Town Hall, 15 November 2002. It was the first time they'd performed in public together for 19 years. 'It was just like when The Clash started out,' says Tyman Dogg (centre), 'playing through the same amp.'
George Binette

Los Amigos — fronted by Mick Jones and Tymon Dogg — perform at a 'concierto homenaje Joe Strummer' in Granada, Spain, on 21 August 2003. The show, in a mountain gypsy encampment, celebrated Joe on what would have been his 51st birthday.

Craig Riddington, Retna

Gouache on the roof: Paul Simonon on the parapet of the Shell Building, Charing Cross, March 1999. The painting he's working on was later shown as part of his celebrated 'From Hammersmith to Greenwich' exhibition of riverside views. "I just want to catch the emotion of the scenery and the weather," he says.

year by the death of his close friend Henry Bowles at the hand of bouncers at a Subway Sect gig. Conran became reclusive and, for years, never talked about his time with The Clash or punk.

Micky Foote's departure was more gradual. He continued to work with Bernie, but it was obvious to him that Mick no longer wanted him involved in the record-making process. Jones's frostiness towards him meant that manning the sound-board at gigs was an uncomfortable experience. The three low-key Clash concerts at the end of January were the last he worked. The Clash were becoming like The Stones: they could freeze you out overnight.

I ask Micky if he felt betrayed by Joe. 'No,' he says forcefully. 'He felt that I could and should stand up for myself. I had to prove myself, like everyone else. He could only help me so far. He told me that he never said I should stop producing the records. I never turned round to him and said, "Yes, Joe, but you never backed me up." It was up to him: people do what they do. He had to retain his relationship with Mick, and that's more important than his relationship with me, surely? I'm not writing the fucking songs. I have to deal with Mick, he had to deal with Mick. But I never felt betrayed by him at all.'

The Conran and Foote expulsions have been construed by some as Mick attempting to tip the balance of power within the group in his favour. After all, two of Joe's closest friends were removed from The Clash's inner-circle within a matter of months (three, if you include Roadent). But several of those close to the group feel the events of the spring of 1978 were simply indicative of the way the group did business, and would continue to do so until Mick's departure. If Mick, Joe or, indeed, Paul felt strongly enough about something to dig in their boot-heels, the others usually capitulated. In this sense, the group was always democratic in its commitment to a sort of Clash Darwinism, in which the most passionately held view won out.

Mick felt passionately about the sonic detail of the records they were making, Joe less so: his favourite records were scratchy old blues and folk sides, recorded at the back of furniture shops in Memphis and New Orleans. It would seem only natural that Jones interpreted Micky Foote's action as an unforgivable betrayal, which might have set a precedent for Bernie/CBS, not Mick, to dictate the quality of The Clash's music. What's more, by that time Jones was technically just as capable of producing a Clash record as Micky Foote, and it was highly unlikely, anyway, that CBS would agree to Foote overseeing The Clash's second album in favour of Pearlman. So the future of The 101'ers soundman was never rosy. Perhaps he saw the inevitable coming, and 'chiselled his tombstone' before someone else did. But although he allowed his old friend to drift away, Joe never forgot Micky's personal loyalty to him. Talking to Jon Savage in 1988, he reflected with considerable humility: 'There are very few honourable men in [The Clash] story, but Micky Foote is one of them.'

With Sebastian Conran, it was a fairly straightforward case of The Clash's obsession with their public image distorting their personal values. Joe bowed to tacit pressure from the others to drop Sebastian because to continue associating with him would've meant forever having to fend off uncomfortable questions about his living in the posh house of a Habitat heir. Again, it was a case of weighing Strummer's working relationship with Bernie, Mick and Paul – and consequently the future of the group – against his friendship with Sebastian. It was tough on Joe, and even tougher on Sebastian, but The Clash, as everyone involved would eventually find out, was much bigger than any person's feelings – including Mick's.

Johnny Green himself had this to say about Strummer: 'I think Joe frequently didn't have his hands on the reins. I think it's a complete misconception of The Clash that Joe was the leader. I would say that often he wasn't in the driving seat, nor did he want to be. He was interested in peripheral surges of energy not constant streams of energy. And I would say that Mick had a huge influence on it all, running the band, and Paul had more than people like to give him credit for in noticing detail – and I don't just mean in the cut of people's jackets. Paul took far more of an interest in it, while Joe's interest would dot in and out.'

Around Easter 1978, Conran ejected the remaining stragglers of The Clash entourage from Albany Street: the carpets Bernie had ordered for his office overlooking Regent's Park were still in their plastic wrappings and the new chairs still stacked in the corner. Meanwhile, Rhodes rented Joe a flat in a residential block off Marylebone Road.

'It was really anonymous, you know, stark,' recalls Johnny. 'I dunno who lived there. Colombian drug barons? Shoe salesmen? Some director of W.H. Smith whose wife kicked him out? It had little push-buttons, where every door down the corridor looked the same. An anonymous-looking, furnished flat. Strange. If you took him back there and he invited you in, you never really felt comfortable. It was like someone in transit.'

Strummer, lonely and dejected, decided to move his books and records into a shabby squat in Daventry Street with Boogie Tiberi and Jane Crockford. There were rusty push-bikes chained to the railings, sour milk in the fridge and a revolving door of mates to stay up with late into the night, smoking joints. After two years of monumental mindfuck, Joe was back in his own environment and on the road to finding himself again.

Leafing through the British Library's archives, the newspaper headlines in March 1978 don't appear radically different from those today. The issue which dominates the news is terrorism. There is a sense that world order is under attack: the two superpowers, the US and USSR, are locked into the Cold War, while Europe, the Middle East and Africa are, not un-coincidentally, blighted with violence and bloodshed. The same words are repeated: 'guerrilla', 'car bomb', 'hijacking', 'kidnapping', 'military advisers', 'assassination'. It's the vocabulary of a world where, rightly or wrongly, people feel alienated, excluded from the bigger political process, desperate.

On 11 March, Arab terrorists killed thirty-seven Israelis in a machine-gun attack on a bus; on 13 March, Indonesian gunmen took seventy-two hostages in a government building in Holland; in Rome on 16 March, Aldo Moro, the former Italian prime minister, was kidnapped by the Red Brigade. Closer to home, in February, fourteen were killed in a bomb explosion at Le Mons restaurant near Belfast. The prevalence of terrorism hadn't escaped Hollywood. Clint Eastwood had given up chasing criminals and was targeting a cell of political gunmen in *The Enforcer*.

It was against this hard, edgy canvas of paranoia and instability that one of the most notorious incidents in the Clash story took place. Throughout March, the group had been furiously writing and rehearsing. They'd also recorded their first session with Mick as de facto producer, while awaiting Pearlman's return from the States. For one of the tracks, '1-2 Crush On You', someone suggested a saxophone solo. Topper volunteered his old school-friend from Dover and sax session-player, Gary Barnacle. A few days later, two more of the Barnacle clan, Steve and Pete, arrived at Rehearsals with an air rifle that Topper was interested in purchasing.

Around seven o'clock on the evening of Thursday, 30 March, the Barnacles, Topper, Paul Simonon and Robin Banks climbed out onto the parapet (now knocked down) overlooking the railway line. Flying around them were some pigeons. Little did they know they were expensive racing birds, bred by one of the mechanics in the yard. Pigeon-shooting is a tradition associated with bad karma: it was an ill-fated pigeon-shooting expedition by British officers on the Nile in 1906 that first uncorked Egypt's anti-colonial sentiment. Taking aim, Topper blithely blasted away at three of the feathered flyers.

It all happened quickly. 'A couple of mechanics appeared from nowhere and hit me with a spanner,' recalls Topper. 'Then the next thing I knew someone said, "Freeze!" and there were armed police everywhere.'

A British Rail guard had spotted Topper and the others on the roof and alerted the police, believing they were a terrorist gang shooting at trains. A helicopter, three squad cars and a number of officers, some armed, were dispatched to the scene. 'The press made light of it at the time,' says Johnny Green. 'But it was really quite serious. These guys who broke into Rehearsals with guns meant business. There was a helicopter circling overhead, policemen shouting down with loud-hailers. They cordoned off the area with tape. It was fucking heavy.'

Paul recalls: 'They'd called out the whole fucking police force. There's a helicopter above us, eight police vans and the Sweeney [Flying Squad] with guns. All we had was two poxy air rifles and a pistol.'

Headon, Simonon, Banks and the Barnacles were bundled into a Black Maria and taken to Kentish Town police station where they were charged with criminal damage and held overnight. 'As soon as the coppers found out we were a punk group they turned nasty,' recalls Robin. 'They realised they'd been made fools of and they weren't happy about it.' In the morning the five men were taken to Clerkenwell Magistrates Court, where the judge demanded bail of £1,500 for each person. The group were then driven to Brixton prison, an old Victorian jail used for prisoners on remand and notorious for its racism and overcrowding.

Paul says: 'We were being booked in and the copper said to me, "Where are you from?" I said, "Brixton." He goes, "Oh, I see, a local!" We were given grey prison uniforms, which we put on 'cos we all had our punk gear on.'

Meanwhile, Mick had sprung into action. Bernie was either unavailable or wasn't in a hurry to get his charges out of jail. Mick phoned Caroline Coon, who, as well as being Paul's close friend, was, with her experience with Release, a seasoned pro at dealing with the police, lawyers and judiciary. 'Your band has been arrested,' says Caroline, 'and Bernie decides it will do you good to be in prison for a couple of days. I've been in prison; Bernie hasn't. You don't do that to people, so that's why I went and bailed them out. There was no educative reason for that. If that fitted in with some idea Bernie had, that was *wrong*.'

Caroline organised the bail with CBS and, later that day, Topper, Paul and Robin were picked up from the gates of Brixton by Johnny Green, just as Tom Keylock, the driver of The Stones, had arrived to whisk away Mick Jagger in 1967. Apparently, Simonon wore a large grin. In an echo of the fate that befell The Stones' drug-bust compadre Robert Fraser, the Barnacles were left in jail. Headon, Simonon and Pete Barnacle eventually took the rap and were fined £30 each, with a further £700 to be paid in compensation to the pigeons' owner, George Dole.

The guns on the roof incident – which would provide Joe with the title of a new song, worked up during the next month – raised questions about the group's relationship with Bernie. But it was also seized on by some of the band's critics – and even champions – as indicative of an unsavoury macho vibe which now seemed to be enveloping the group. The casual violence that had been a peripheral part of punk now seemed to be accepted Clash protocol. Many individuals around the group who weren't part of the inner circle began to feel uncomfortable.

A few months earlier at Lanchester Polytechnic (one of the low-key January dates to road-test some of the group's new material), Sandy Pearlman had turned up to see them. The group were preparing to go onstage and had given instructions not to let anyone in the dressing room. Robin was standing behind the door and was piqued that a loud, baseball-capped American guy was trying to thrust his way in.

'Someone had the bright idea of putting Robin on the door,' recalls Johnny Green. 'Pearlman was trying to get backstage but Robin wouldn't open the door to anyone. So Pearlman pushes the door open and Robin whacks him, and he goes down . . . blood everywhere . . .'

Simonon: 'Then, to make it more even dramatic Mick shouts, "Oh no! You've hit the producer!"'

Mick: 'Bernie was very much the one mopping him up, with a big hand-kerchief. It was really just par for the course. There was nothing malicious in it . . . I think [Pearlman] understood that.'

'He took a swing at me, and I took a swing at him,' says Pearlman, keen to give his side of the story. 'He cut my cheek. Jones and Strummer were appalled, really appalled. Bernard Rhodes was aghast; he thought they'd really fucked up. He thought CBS would think they were all a bunch of idiots, and that would be the end of the relationship. But, alas, my nose was not broken and I was not beaten up by The Clash, as some people have said. They were incredibly apologetic about the whole thing. I couldn't care less.'

Others found such incidents galling. 'They thought it was fantastically funny when Sandy Pearlman was punched,' says Caroline Coon, who wit-nessed the sniggers once the producer had left the room. 'Rock 'n' roll is essentially this feminine thing because you're onstage, dressing up. It works best when there's a gender blur, when men are looking both soft and hard –

definitively Keith Richards, Jimi Hendrix; Mick Jones had it, too. The minute that men slip over that line and start being worried about being seen as cissies, and go too hard or macho, it's dangerous stuff. It gets into fascist areas. The Clash wanted to get this gang of hard men around them. They were quite happy to be very violent towards people who can't fight back, like producers. The band would go on stage and preach this message of anti-violence, but nobody challenged them about what was going on backstage. If they were that tough, why did they never punch above their weight? . . . If you got close to that band it was quite heartbreaking to see the way they behaved towards the people that worked for them.'

Jon Savage: 'I just hated that whole thing. To me one of the things I liked about punk was that it wasn't like the old machismo and, obviously, being a gay bloke, I was not interested in that. I liked punk's sexuality, I liked the hopeless boys and dominating women, I thought that was a neat twist. I thought that was exciting, like Siouxsie and The Slits. The early Clash were quite vulnerable – I always thought Joe had a vulnerability to him and I really liked that. You wouldn't have thought so, but Johnny Rotten was quite an androgynous figure in a funny kind of way; he used to hang out with girls a lot. He wasn't standard-issue sexuality. But then nor were The Clash in the early days. They were like hurt, scared boys and I find that a very attractive idea in rock 'n' roll. When they started hanging around with the boys and the machismo men I just loathed it.'

The macho atmosphere had claimed Topper as a supplicant. He had even taken to wearing a yellow Bruce Lee jump-suit and working out with pseudo kung-fu and kick-boxing moves. He can be seen playfully duffing up Clash roadie Ray Gange in *Rude Boy*. 'I was never into it as much as I pretended to be,' he now admits. 'I used to run a lot and do martial arts, but I never studied it, it was too much like hard work. I just liked watching Bruce Lee films. I used to go down the garage with the punch bag in Finsbury Park.'

But while the gang mentality around the group was hardening, The Clash's music was becoming ever more sophisticated and, behind the scenes, their abrasive punk armour was softening. In March, they'd recorded some sessions at Marquee Studios in Richmond Mews, off Dean Street. CBS's Simon Humphrey, who'd worked on the first album, was selected as engineer and Mick was producer. The material they recorded showed a heavy reggae and R&B influence. The songs included the hybridised rock-reggae tune, 'White Man in Hammersmith Palais', a cover of Booker T and the MGs' 'Time Is Tight', a new version of 'Pressure Drop', Mick's 'The Prisoner', which dated from the previous summer, and also the guitarist's pre-Clash rock 'n' roller '1-2 Crush On You'. It was essentially a mopping-up operation before Pearlman came in: the idea was to release 'White Man in Hammersmith Palais' as a single and store the other cuts for B-sides.

The spirit and quality of the recordings, and their relative complexity, suggested that Mick's skills as a producer and arranger were rapidly developing. 'By the time of "White Man in Hammersmith Palais" we were getting into acoustic guitar, piano, percussion, harmonica, double-tracking, triple-tracking, backing-vocal harmonies,' recalls Simon Humphrey. 'We were trying lots of ideas. They'd got a lot more professional by then, they'd calmed down a bit. Mick had more of a producer's role, he seemed the one with the vision. Joe was the poet and the performer with those great lyrics, but he had no interest in what was happening in the studio.'

Joe's lyrics were, indeed, incredible, as tributes in magazines such as *Uncut* and *MOJO* have attested. 'White Man' was Strummer's most complex lyric yet and shows how far he'd come since the blunt sloganeering of 'White Riot'. It described the reggae all-nighter he and Roadent had attended the previous summer. Other punk writers might have written about how cool it was to witness such an event, buzzing off the heavy black vibe, but not Joe. He expresses disappointment that the music on offer wasn't as roots as he'd hoped; his expectations of black militant roots music clashed with the reality of an audience enjoying smoothed-off pop-reggae.

Subsequent verses ruminate on the futility of armed revolution ('the British army is waiting out there, and it weighs fifteen hundred tons'), the need for blacks and whites to work 'together' to find a solution (though all he himself can suggest is 'why not phone up Robin Hood, and ask him for some wealth distribution?'), new wave groups like The Jam ('they got Burton suits, ha, you think it's funny? Turning rebellion into money?') and the rise of the extreme right ('if Adolf Hitler flew in today, they'd send a limousine anyway').

'White Man in Hammersmith Palais' was a tour de force, the first evidence that, musically, The Clash could steer a course beyond punk while retaining their credibility. The group awaited Pearlman's return from the States, safe in the knowledge that they'd already banked arguably their finest recording yet.

After the unsettling start to the year – Joe's illness, the cancelled album sessions, Conran and Foote's departure, Topper and Paul's arrest – the group let off some steam with their first public appearance in three months. They'd been approached a few weeks earlier to play at an Anti-Nazi League rally in

Victoria Park, Hackney on 30 April. The park was in the heart of the East End, where the National Front was highly visible. There was a tradition here of anti-fascist activity. Cable Street, down by the East End docks, had been the site of the famous fight between locals and Oswald Mosley's Blackshirts in 1936. After a lengthy discussion, the group agreed to appear. The Anti-Nazi League had been formed in 1977 to combat the ascendance of the National Front, who'd won over 100,000 votes in London by-elections that year. The ANL was supported by another relatively new pressure group, Rock Against Racism. The afternoon line-up was Patrik Fitzgerald, X-Ray Spex, The Clash, Steel Pulse and The Tom Robinson Band.

In early 1978, Bernie had agreed to filmmaker Dave Mingay making a movie centred around The Clash. (Though, somewhat typically, Bernie had also led Nick Broomfield to believe he was engaged on a similar project.) In 1974, Mingay and his cameraman Jack Hazan had made a low-budget but highly praised film about David Hockney, called *A Bigger Splash*. Their plan this time was to document The Clash's experiences, as seen through the eyes of a casual roadie and fan. Ray Gange, a nineteen-year-old from Brixton who'd befriended Joe in early 1977, was chosen for the part. He, Mingay and Hazan were at the Victoria Park free concert.

The footage Hazan shot that day is some of the most exciting rock 'n' roll ever committed to celluloid. It's broad daylight and the huge crowd of around 70,000 surges and pitches as The Clash power into a coruscating 'London's Burning'. It's thrilling: the lighting rig blaring out bright colours in the dull afternoon light, the immensity of the crowd, bigger even than the audience they'd play to four years later at Shea Stadium. Joe sports a quiff, tight white strides, red T-shirt and white brothel creepers. Paul wears a royal-blue blouson and black trousers; he has hacked off his Bowie feathercut into a dyed-orange crop. Mick is dressed identically to Jimmy Page on Led Zep's 1976 tour – long, black curly hair, black shirt and strides, a black peaked cap (stolen from the BBC when filming *Something Else*). It's as if they've reverted to their pre-punk subcultural identities: the rockabilly, the skinhead, the glam rock star. The backdrop is the underbelly of a soaring Messerschmitt, with black Luftwaffe crosses. In the distance are council tower blocks. Topper attacks his drums, biting his lip, like a jazz octopus. The energy coming off the stage is phenomenal.

At the end of The Clash's short set, peaking with Sham 69's Jimmy Pursey helping out on 'White Riot', The Tom Robinson Band roadies attempt to pull the plugs on the group so they can't play an encore. There is a scuffle. All hell breaks loose with Johnny Green and Ray Gange in the middle of it. 'That was a really intense day,' remembers Ray Gange. 'When all the pandemonium was going on, David [Mingay] said to me, "Right, go and stir something up." I wasn't supposed to be doing any filming that day, otherwise my haircut would have been different – I had it in a quiff, which caused loads of problems later with continuity. So I went over and grabbed the mic and just started shouting at the crowd. It had been so exciting that I thought whatever was going to follow was going to be drab in comparison. I couldn't conceive that the crowd weren't prepared to storm the stage to make sure it continued, you know what I mean? Why would you want that energy ever to stop? At that moment, I just wanted it to continue for the rest of my life.'

'Gange was drinking Carlsberg from early on in the day,' says Jack Hazan. 'That began to take over. He was incensed that The Clash were only on for a short while.'

The Anti-Nazi League gig nailed The Clash's anti-Fascist colours to the mast. It was a simple, effective, unambiguous statement to a huge audience. Billy Bragg, among others, saw it as an enormously significant event in politicising young Londoners, even if it only meant their recognising the National Front as the enemy. Billy also points out that several future trades union leaders were in the crowd that day, including the Fire Brigades Union's Andy Gilchrist.

But The Clash being who they were, everything wasn't quite so straightforward. Tom Robinson was a leading champion of gay rights, and was himself bisexual. Johnny Green remembers that, backstage, members of The Clash's entourage 'took the piss out of his groundbreaking homosexual stance with shouts of "Backs to the walls, boys."' It was characteristic of the group's pre-PC, schoolyard humour, but Johnny felt sensitive enough about the relevant passage in his book to skip over it during a public reading at the NFT in 2001.

There were other confusing signals to decipher. One of the stars of that day was Joe's homemade 'Brigade Rosse' T-shirt ('Red Brigade'; Joe misspelled 'Brigate'), which also carried the initials RAF – the Red Army Faction. A facsimile of this T-shirt can now be bought as a fashion item in London boutiques. In 1978, however, it had an electric resonance. The former Italian prime minister Aldo Moro was still missing after being abducted by the Red Brigade in Rome the previous month. On 20 April, the organisation released a picture of the statesman holding up a newspaper to prove he was still alive. They would murder him unless imprisoned Red Brigade members were released. It's difficult to draw a parallel with 2004, but a possibility might be a T-shirt showing the Iraqi extremists who beheaded the American Nick Berg.

So what was Joe doing wearing the T-shirt? Did he approve of the Red Brigade's methods? Joe always claimed it was worn in the name of provocation and education. 'I didn't think they were getting the press coverage they deserve,' he told *Record Mirror*. 'It's vicious and they're murdering people – you know, they go around killing businessman and the people they see as screwing Italy up – well, I think what they're doing is good because it's a brutal system anyway, and people get murdered by the system every day and no one complains about that.'

Joe was born into the world of volatile international politics; it was only natural for him, perhaps, to feel he had to confront and publicise such issues. But there was more: as a writer, Strummer was fascinated not just with the concept of terrorism but also the personal realities of the terrorists themselves. One of the new songs played at Victoria Park was 'Tommy Gun'. It wasn't lost on him that extremists like the Baader-Meinhofs displayed Che-like terrorist chic. They were young, tragic, good-looking, wore cool shades. Joe's lyric explores the idea of such people having egos ('kings and queens and generals are learning your name') and groupies ('I'm cutting out your picture from page one, I'm gonna get a jacket just like yours'). But he makes no value judgements about whether what they're doing is good or evil: on the recorded version of the track he ad-libs about the equations in hostage negotiations – 'one jet air-liner for ten prisoners' – before concluding nothing more than 'I see all the innocents, the human sacrifice, if death comes so cheap, then the same goes for life.'

Strummer's stance was ambiguous, which left it wide open for misinterpretation. Caroline Coon argues such songs and their attendant imagery were necessary. 'The Clash were like a billboard,' she says. 'If something happened in the world they would go out and show their support for these minority groups who'd protest with guns. That's quite difficult to handle. It's the theatre of protest and violence, and you have to be careful that that doesn't spill into what you're doing. So the music was hard, on the line. Those tough, militaristic songs were what was needed as we went into Thatcherism.'

Others, such as Jon Savage, weren't convinced: 'I was really off The Clash politically after Joe had worn the RAF T-shirt at the Anti-Nazi League gig. I thought, "Oh dear." I hated that whole day anyway. I absolutely loathed it, getting hectored by Socialist Worker Party morons. It was all going horribly wrong for me; punk was all going horribly wrong. The Clash were going horribly wrong. I just see it as silly. They had this real romantic vision. A lot of people did then, it's not just The Clash. They reflected what was going on for a lot of people but I was always very wary, even in those days, of promoting violence. And I was twitchy about terrorism. I could see the fascination of it but I was always very doubtful about it. They were killing people. Did you want to kill people? No. The Clash weren't killing people, they were just a bunch of musos.'

The problem was that, for many people, what The Clash had created felt so 'real' it was difficult to see their actions in symbolic terms any more. And that often went for The Clash themselves.

In April 1978, Sandy Pearlman had arrived back in London to start work on The Clash's second album, eventually to be titled *Give 'Em Enough Rope*. The album had been demo'd twice: once with Mick sketching out the songs in two back-to-back all-night sessions with Damien Korner – British blues pioneer Alexis's son and gifted engineer – and once with Pearlman himself. Sandy was accompanied on the trip by his right-hand man, Corky Stasiak.

The Pearlman demos were recorded at Utopia Studios at Spencer Court, Primrose Hill, just the other side of the railway lines to Rehearsals. One of the reasons for choosing the studio was Paul and Topper's daily appointment with their bail officer at nearby Kentish Town police station. After just one day's recording, The Clash were forced to vacate the premises.

'On the night of the first day I heard some noise from outside the studio,' recalls Sandy. 'Corky had introduced the group to American-grade ganja, which they weren't used to. I walk out of the studio, and I notice Simonon and Headon in the lobby of the studio. An old plant had been turned over, and they'd created a dirt track for their motorbike. I realised that we wouldn't be welcome after that, so we recorded the whole set that night and left.'

Pearlman had been impressed with the drum sound at Utopia, and had wanted to record the 'proper' version of the album there, after the demos were completed. Instead, the group did a midnight flit to Notting Hill where they were booked into Island Records' Basing Street Studios, off Westbourne Grove. It was a large, swish place with a wide, stone spiral staircase connecting the floors. Basing Street had been the location of their first meeting with Lee Perry and was where Bob Marley's *Natty Dread* and *Led Zeppelin IV* had been recorded. It had also been a haunt of Guy Stevens and Mott the Hoople.

Meanwhile, Utopia refused to release The Clash mastertapes until they'd been paid/compensated. Johnny Green remembers Bernie having a flaming row with the studio managers. Eventually, the tapes were stacked in a cardboard box, which Green retrieved in the group's old Transit van. 'Did Abba have these problems?' he asks.

The sessions began in earnest in May. The cultural clash between band and producer has been well documented. Sandy Pearlman was a sophisticated New Yorker, a rock theorist with a roving intellect, and relaxed, authoritative manner. He wore a big grin and a baseball cap. As a rock critic, he'd minted the term 'heavy metal'. The Clash viewed him with a mix of curiosity and amusement, but found him amiable and entertaining. Johnny Green recalls Bernie explaining to the group that Pearlman was an important man and should be treated accordingly. 'I was given a three-line whip myself,' says Green. 'Bernie didn't say, "Look, this bloke's a tosser, but do what he says." He said, "This guy's doing an important job for us; make sure you and the group understand that."'

The group were friendly and accommodating towards their new producer but their near-the-knuckle, piss-taking humour was difficult to suppress. There was a lot of sniggering and playing at being numbskulls.

Johnny Green: 'Pearlman would say things like, "The lamb tikka from the Standard has the best texture but it's best served with a nan bread from the Star of Bengal." The band would go, "Yeah, right." They'd come out of the control room and say, "What the *fuck* is he going on about?"'

'Paul treated Pearlman like he was some wimpy American tourist,' Green adds. 'Like someone who was really thick in rock 'n' roll terms, because on a musical level what he said had no relevance under Paul's value system. If he didn't know anything about ska music, what did he know about rock 'n' roll? But I don't think they ever over-stepped the mark, and I think there was a certain caution and awareness that they could blow it. They didn't want to rock the boat too far.'

Ask any of the group about the recording of *Give 'Em Enough Rope*, and they recall long, boring hours doing numerous re-takes. After the fast, gritty, spontaneous rush of the first LP sessions at Whitfield Street, the Basing Street regime seemed dull, meticulous, interminable. Pearlman was used to making sonically pristine records and was a self-confessed technology freak. The Clash were used to leaping around onstage and playing their instruments with an overload of energy and passion. Playing with clinical precision was not their forte. An out-take from *Rude Boy*, included as an extra on the DVD version, shows the group rather sullenly and wearily performing 'Stay Free' surrounded by Blue Öyster Cult's flight cases.

The Clash member who suffered most was Paul, the least technically proficient musician. 'Sandy was a nice feller but he might as well have been wearing a white overcoat,' says Simonon. 'It was a bit laboured. We'd do each song about fifty times. That was when they got me to try out this new bass called a WAL. It's supposed to be this really fancy instrument that top musicians use and has these switches all over it. Somehow, when it was all over, I still had the bass and sold it immediately. Really boring.'

Sandy Pearlman: 'They kept on telling me, "You know, we could replace Paul's part later, so don't work too hard on it." But I have a commitment to having the band members themselves play their part. His bass playing was fine.' In fact, Simonon's bass line to 'The Last Gang in Town' was deemed so rockin' that Pearlman insisted they overdub the other instruments on top of it.

To enliven proceedings, Paul asked David Mingay, who was shooting material in the studio for the *Rude Boy* movie, to procure 8mm copies of *The Battle of the Bulge* and *The Battle of Stalingrad* from the Imperial War Museum. These were then projected onto the wall, and played backwards and forwards. Pearlman put a stop to this when he noticed the clicking noise from the film sprockets was being picked up by the microphones.

Rituals were invented to break the routine. As intimated by Johnny Green, Sandy and Corky developed a fondness for the Indian restaurants on Westbourne Grove. Paul went to McDonald's in Notting Hill the day it opened and rewarded himself with a chocolate milkshake. Topper, Paul and Robin would play pool in the recreation room and generally lark about. When the group checked out Blue Öyster Cult's show at the Hammersmith Odeon, Topper splatted a cream-cake on guitarist Buck Dharma's head at the aftershow lig.

'The other guys played Sandy up quite a lot,' says Mick. 'Personally, I can remember him sitting there all day eating cashew nuts. He said the oil in them guarded against cancer.'

'One night Paul Simonon was playing table football and he got so over-excited he started spitting on the table,' recalls Jack Hazan. 'Then he climbed up and started jumping on it, and no one said a word. Inexplicable! The group would even laugh at Maurice Oberstein when he came down. He loved them, but they treated him appallingly. They thought they were rock 'n' roll commandoes but sometimes I don't think they could differentiate between who was good and who was bad. They offended a lot of people.'

'Paul and I didn't have to do as much as Mick and Joe,' says Topper, 'so we had loads of time on our hands. We played pool, messed around. We were kids of twenty-two, we were having a laugh. If you put two twenty-two-year-olds together with a few bob in their pockets and nothing to do, they'll do silly things.'

'Paul wasn't welcome after a while,' says Johnny Green. 'Pearlman pretended to have a sense of humour, because all producers want to get on with their subjects and be one of the boys, don't they? But he wasn't one of the boys. The more Paul twigged on to this, the more relentlessly he directed his humour at him.'

Topper, meanwhile, was proving himself to be something of a drumming prodigy. Excited to be on an album for the first time, he gave a number of superb performances. Several of the new songs, including 'Julie's Been Working for the Drug Squad' and 'Tommy Gun', had incorporated his ideas – in those cases, the syncopated drum pattern on the intro and before the chorus on the former and the inaugural, machine-gun-burst motif of the latter. His one-take precision prompted Sandy to dub him the Human Drum Machine.

'Topper was an unbelievable drummer,' says Pearlman. 'After we'd finished "Tommy Gun", I said, "Let's try and play the snare drum part backwards." I knew we were getting this sucking sound from the leading edge. There was a lot of space in the arrangement and I thought this would make it amazing. So he did it in two takes. It was inconceivable! Nobody else has ever been able to do that since. It's something that I could only do now with technology.'

While the rest of the group were finding excuses to nip round to the Warwick Castle pub on Portobello Road, Mick exploited the opportunity to watch Sandy and Corky at work. If it took thirty-two takes to nail a track, then why? Why use different mics and compressors? How did you get the best drum sound? 'For Mick that was a great environment to be in as he loves the process of recording,' observes Simonon. 'He was hanging over Sandy's shoulder the whole time. He saw it as a chance to learn how to make records. Me and Joe preferred to bash out the song then leave.'

In early May, Sandy and Corky were waiting as usual for the group to turn up at the customary time-slot. They didn't appear. They imagined they were held up in traffic, though Mick only lived five minutes away. But they didn't turn up that day, or the next. Sandy tried contacting Bernie but couldn't get through. It transpired The Clash had travelled to France to play a concert at the Paris Hippodrome. Organised by the Ligue Communiste

Revolutionnaire, the event celebrated the tenth anniversary of the May 1968 uprising. All the group had taken with them were their guitars.

Johnny Green tells the story: 'It was bearded folkies. Giant pictures of Marx and Lenin. Then Bernie gives me a red spray-can and says, "Go and spray The Clash across their faces." Great big screen prints. This is not respectful at all. Bernie was never a straightforward Marxist, I never had a Marxist line from him, and I knew all that stuff. It is completely antagonistic, so where is he coming from? Anyway, he turns it into a riot – or does he? Maybe it's the band's performance. I never knew the answer, all I knew was it was one hell of a fucking great night. You should have been there. It was something else. There were police charges from the back of the hall, tear gas and the band played on. All the gear is falling apart because it's all crap and borrowed. The drum kit is falling to pieces. Wonderful, they were great, and Bernie was loving it. What is Bernie getting out of this? Is it just the dough, Bernie just a shyster on the make? I don't think so. It's the chaos, the upsetting of the political apple cart.

'After the gig Bernie heavied them over to get the money. I went up there with him. A little guy, a little man who doesn't like getting raindrops on his hair, and he is fucking heavying these French boys over, very impressive. I liked him a lot that night. Coming out of there, the group were going, "How much did we get for that?" And Bernie is going, "It is important that we understand the political structure of the French struggle." Mick's like, "How much have we fucking got in there? What was the fucking deal?" and Bernie is saying, "They will be talking about this in car factories."'

The reality was that, since the guns on the roof incident, the relationship between group and manager had deteriorated. The Ligue Communiste gig was a rare flash of Bernie magic. Caroline Coon's view that it was wrong for Bernie to procrastinate over springing Paul and Topper from jail was shared by the rest of the group. Simonon had exacted his revenge on Rhodes by painting a mural above the fireplace upstairs at Rehearsals, showing a naked Rhodes being shat upon by a flock of giant pigeons. (No photo of this has yet to come to light, but Paul reprised the theme of a naked Bernie to illustrate 'Groovy Times' in the *2nd Clash Songbook*.)

Bernie sent Micky Foote – now Rhodes's right-hand man and involved in looking after Dexy's Midnight Runners, The Coventry Automatics (later The Specials) and The Subway Sect, all of whom practised at Rehearsals – to see Johnny Green, with instructions that he should emulsion over the offending lampoon. Green phoned Paul, who said, 'Don't do it, Johnny.'

The mural stayed.

After that, Bernie's visits to Rehearsals became less frequent. Until then, his green Renault 5 with its personalised CLA5H number plate and Ferrari engine (Johnny: 'or so he said . . .') could be seen parked outside in the yard at some point every day. Now communication with the manager was almost exclusively via Micky Foote.

A growing concern among the group was money. To raise more cash, Rhodes had sold the publishing rights for the *Give 'Em Enough Rope* material to Riva Music, famous for owning Rod Stewart's catalogue. It's almost impossible to gauge the state of The Clash's finances, since even the band were unsure about them, but it seems this deal did little to alleviate their straightened circumstances. Bernie, ever the shrewd operator, knew record label advances were essentially loans, and was insistent that their debt was kept to a minimum. Johnny Green describes a day-to-day existence where he was forever going cap in hand to Rhodes for cash for basic provisions: petrol, guitar strings, tea and biscuits.

Every Friday afternoon, Rhodes turned up at Rehearsals with the group's £25 wages and £15 each for Johnny and Baker. On one occasion he didn't materialise. Green managed to get him on the phone. 'He said I had to go and see him,' recalls Johnny. 'He told me I had to learn the lesson that it never comes to you in life, you have to go looking for it. I thought, "You cunt!"' Green caught the bus up to Bernie's flat in Camden Road. It gave him a rare glimpse into Bernie's world. The living room was piled high with Marxist literature, boxes of badges and records, including the giveaway 'Capital Radio' EP, and stacks of T-shirts. According to Micky Foote, Bernie also had a piano belonging to the English folk musician John Renbourn.

Topper recalls: 'He never talked any sense. I went to him one day and said, "Bernie, I'm skint. I haven't been paid for three weeks." He said, "If I was your bank manager, would you expect me to live in your wardrobe?" And I would go away totally bemused with what he'd said. I never got on with him. To me and Paul he was just a figure of fun.'

During the recording of *Give 'Em Enough Rope,* Bernie became even more remote. He may have been losing interest. The Paris gig seemed to be indicative of the strong anarchic patterns he liked in life. Yet there were fewer and fewer opportunities for such spontaneous acts of provocation and madness. By the early summer of 1978, his relationship with Mick in particular was at breaking point. He didn't approve of his cocaine habit. He rued that 'he'd seen it all before'.

'His band management abilities were brilliant,' says Micky Foote, but as for his inter-personal skills: 'He didn't realise there was a difference between falling out with someone and doing irreparable damage to a relationship. He never knew where the boundary was in terms of fucking someone off so much they never came back. He was always pushing it to the edge.'

In July 1978, Rhodes really did push it to the edge. That month, he tried to destabilise The Clash's already fragile intra-group friendships and seemingly manoeuvred to bring The Sex Pistols' guitarist, Steve Jones, into the band. It was a power struggle that would almost split The Clash.

8
HOW THE WEST WAS WON

'Gentlemen! You can't fight in here. This is the War Room!'

Peter Sellers as President Merkin J. Muffley, *Dr Strangelove*

'I'm just a song and dance man, everyone knows that.'
JAMES CAGNEY AS GEORGE M. COHAN, *YANKEE DOODLE DANDY*

On 16 January 1978, the American photographer Bob Gruen arrived home in New York after shadowing The Sex Pistols on their twelve-day tour of the US. He spent the next forty-eight hours holed up in his darkroom in Greenwich Village. The Pistols' visit to the States was headline news and the American press was desperate for lurid tales and dramatic pictures of these exotic English punks who supposedly pissed, crapped and beat each other up onstage.

After he'd processed his film, Gruen trudged through the snow to the famous New York punk club, CBGB's, to get a well-earned beer. At the bar he was surprised to see John Lydon and *NME* photographer Joe Stevens.

'Have you heard the news?' asked Lydon. Gruen hadn't. The singer opened his overcoat to reveal a cheesy T-shirt that Warner Brothers had given away after the group's last show, in San Francisco. The legend ran: 'I survived The Sex Pistols tour'. Beneath it Rotten had scrawled 'but the band didn't'.

'We broke up.'

The Clash heard the news when it filtered back to London later that day. The mood at Rehearsals was subdued. The group had always had a close but wary relationship with The Pistols: they looked up to them, but they were also rivals. The Pistols had fulfilled their self-destructive philosophy – 'Destroy!' Their demise signalled the death of the first blast of punk rock.

This pitched The Clash in the vanguard of whatever punk was to become, if, indeed, it had a future. The sudden, unexpected and spectacular end of The Pistols seemed to lay bare The Clash's inherent conventionality. Was their fate to be another boring rock band? Johnny Green noticed an edginess in the Clash camp. 'For a while, everyone seemed to be keeping their options open,' he says.

Following the split, Malcolm McLaren and Bernie Rhodes grew close again. What happened in the spring and early summer of 1978 suggested they were conspiring to resuscitate the anarchic energies of 1976. Paranoia was endemic. On his return from Jamaica in April 1978, Lydon began inviting Paul Simonon to his house on Gunter Grove in Chelsea. Johnny Green kept Paul company. Lydon would gesture to the stack of Guinness crates in the corner and say, 'That's success, Paul!' Simonon was asked to bring his bass. This aroused suspicions. At the time Lydon was recruiting musicians for his new group, PiL.

'I did have a stint of going round to see John and taking my bass,' explains Simonon. 'We used to play reggae records. It was not to try and form a band, it was just to see how John was.'

In July, CBS released 'White Man in Hammersmith Palais'/'The Prisoner' and the band set out on the On Parole tour. The dates were promoted by a *Sounds* cover story, featuring a Chalkie Davies shot of the group in fancy dress: Joe wore a stocking over his head, bank-robber style; Paul was a Wehrmacht officer replete with Iron Cross (though an MPLA button badge obscures his Nazi insignia); Mick had a Jimi Hendrix military tunic; and Topper donned his Bruce Lee jumpsuit. The group's critics had a field day. 'The Clash used to look great,' says Jon Savage. 'Now they looked shit.'

The tour was to prove the most violent outing yet. In the provinces, punk was a powerful, positive force for change, but it had also become synonymous with moronic behaviour and people wearing safety pins through their nostrils. 'New Wave' became a catch-all term for the groups formed in punk's wake. Sham 69, The Lurkers, Stiff Little Fingers, The Undertones and 999 all released their debuts in late 1977 or 1978. Even Mick Jagger had his hair cut short. Punk's emphasis on youth had a *Logan's Run* effect: if you were over thirty you might as well have been dead.

At Glasgow Apollo on 4 July, the bouncers beat up kids in the audience. The gig is well documented in *Rude Boy*: Joe climbing off the stage to remonstrate with security; an enraged Mick screaming, 'They're dancing, not fighting!'; Paul valiantly attempting to hold together 'Janie Jones' on his own. After the show, Joe was arrested for smashing a lemonade bottle. Paul went to his aid. 'He was like a kid in a schoolyard helping out his mate; he ran over and got stuck into the cops,' recalls Johnny Green. 'I was physically carrying Topper away to safety, while Mick darts back to the hotel to establish an emergency HQ to deal with the situation.'

Paul and Joe spent the night in the cells, buzzing from a wrap of speed secreted in one of their many zippered pockets. The following morning they were charged. When they returned to the hotel to check out, TV trouper and light-entertainment doyen Lionel Blair breezed into the lobby. 'Well, that's showbiz!' he told the boys, cheerily.

Later the same day, in Aberdeen, Johnny Green was nearly killed. The beige Ford Granada estate the group was travelling in had stopped at the entrance to the Aberdeen Music Hall's car park. Green, who was behind the wheel, had opened the driver's door and was standing up, leaning out to see what the hold-up was ahead. Then the car slipped out of gear. 'The car is veering into a concrete wall, and the door is gradually closing, crushing me alive,' recalls Green. 'Joe is in the passenger seat and starts crying. He's going, "Oh God! Johnny's going to be killed!" Meanwhile, Paul and Topper leap out of the back seat and are trying with all their strength, without any effect, to stop it rolling forward. I think I'm a goner at this point, this is serious stuff. Then Mick leans over and calmly pulls the handbrake on. Thank God for Mick Jones! I thought that little crisis neatly summed them all up.' Chris Salewicz argues it was he who actually pulled on the handbrake.

The gig at Crawley on Saturday, 8 July was another bloodbath. A large skinhead contingent from London had taken the train from Victoria Station. They prowled around the crowd, standing right up to people's faces, randomly beating up anyone they took a dislike to. The support act was New York synth duo Suicide. During their set, a skinhead leapt onstage and punched singer Alan Vega in the face, smashing his nose. Blood was everywhere. The rest of the show was marred by rucking. Mark Hagen, now a BBC producer, was there. He describes it as 'the most frightening gig I've ever been to'. Afterwards he remembers returning to Crawley station to find around a hundred Teds waiting on the platform for the punks, most of whom were just schoolkids or in their late teens. After the line 'They're all too busy fighting for a good place under the lighting' in 'White Man', Joe used to adlib 'Good for you!' According to Johnny Green, after Crawley Mick persuaded Joe to stick to the script.

As with previous Clash tours, there was an open-door policy at the end of each night. The group reciprocated the unswerving, intense loyalty of their fans by making themselves available for chats and signing records and posters.

Joe, as anyone who ever met him will testify, was genuinely interested in the experiences of fans from Blackburn, Cardiff, Southampton, Aberdeen, Leicester, Portsmouth. He'd talk for hours, zoning in on people and making them feel as if they were the most important person in the room. It was an astonishing gift. Mick was happy to talk music or politics; so were Paul and Topper. They'd give fans cigarettes and swigs of their beer.

'There has never been a band in the history of rock 'n' roll that treated their fans as well as The Clash did,' says Johnny Green, proudly. 'I never once heard them complain about having to hang around to talk to the kids after the show. They actually looked forward to meeting them.'

Halfway through the tour, The Pistols' guitarist Steve Jones began turning up unannounced to join the group for encores. The Clash began rehearsing The Pistols' 'Pretty Vacant' as a special finale. The three-guitarist format sounded awesome. Mick started to wonder whether Bernie and Malcolm were planning a coup. 'There was stuff going around about individuals swapping between groups, which Joe always disliked,' recalls Simonon. 'Mick felt uneasy because Steve Jones used to turn up all the time. He may have felt that Steve was going to oust him.'

Bernie's tactic had always been divide and rule. To this day, no one is quite sure what Jones's unscheduled appearances were all about, other than vague mutterings about McLaren and Rhodes trying to stir things up. (Steve himself is adamant he was never part of any secret plot.) Certainly, they'd picked the right time to unsettle Mick. He was going through what the others called his 'poodle' stage. To say he was unpopular within the group at this time is to misunderstand the whole dynamic of The Clash. The others have all admitted that he was becoming 'a bit difficult', but now he found himself in the role of a punk Cesare Borgia, fearing a plot to depose him.

One of the biggest challenges was Mick's unashamed rock star aspirations. He was happy to admit to taking cocaine. He liked staying in good hotels and being driven around. 'He is living a very different lifestyle to the others,' explains Johnny Green. 'Joe is living quietly with his books, while Paul is off enjoying a very private, culturally rich lifestyle with Coony.'

On the Get Out of Control tour, Roadent had observed that Mick had started to become 'inward'. This is significant, because it marks a point where Jones first seems to be deeply affected by the artistic pressures heaped on him. This preoccupation with his craft, expressing itself in spells of quiet, moody introversion, was to be a characteristic of his personality until his departure from the group. It's a common trait in artists, from

Charlie Chaplin to Ted Hughes to John Lennon and Tony Hancock – all of whom, like Jones, suffered profound anxiety about their work.

Mick was, after all, now writing music to other people's deadlines. The material he was creating was ever more complex: the interweaving guitar overdubs, backing vocals, bass lines, bridges and harmonies were all his domain. These took time and brain-power to work out. His behaviour seemed to suggest a bid for space. Strummer was another classic creative-depressive, but he seemed to cope better with the stress of the artistic process. Often his words weren't finalised, or even written, until he was preparing for the final takes in the studio. A lot of Mick's work had to be done before the songs made it even to rehearsals. Expectation weighed heavily on his shoulders.

Johnny Green: 'I think 1978 is the pivotal year. The Clash have made it in terms of being on the cover of the *NME* and reaching a wide audience, but what does that mean? Paul seems to enjoy it – he was the most hedonistic in terms of finding pleasure in a situation. Joe struggles with it, but rises to the occasion. But with Mick, I think he finds it more of a responsibility than he ever imagined. He took that responsibility very seriously.'

Caroline Coon noticed Mick's personality shift, allied to a naked ambition: 'Jonesy wanted to be on *Top of the Pops* because it was the stage of getting to the masses,' she says. 'Bernie's thinking was old-fashioned, he didn't understand the medium of television. The whole thing is false, whether you play live or not. But I liked it that Jonesy was a diva. Divas are great. Part of the band had the conceit that it was wrong to embrace fame with open arms. But Mick Jones didn't. It was more his insecurities that were the problem. It was difficult getting him on the stage sometimes; he was so overcome with nerves he'd do anything to put it off. The stage isn't right, the dope's not right, can't do the gig.'

'I tend to go down the George Best school of thought,' says Johnny Green. 'Whatever Mick's foibles were as a young man – and remember he was a young man, twenty-two or twenty-three – were part of the bigger picture. The point is that nicely rounded, well-balanced human beings don't have the hunger and drive that someone like Mick Jones had. He was a consummate prima donna at times. He always wanted to sit in the front seat of the car. Joe and Paul would say, "Oh, you sat there yesterday", but he'd never budge. But with that stubbornness came a single-minded purpose and an energy.'

Joe and Paul frequently challenged Mick about his comparatively decadent, unpunk behaviour. 'His reply was "So what?"' says Green. 'They never took it further than that, which is interesting. They accepted, perhaps, that it was all part of the package. People on the outside saw Mick as this stroppy, selfish person, but we saw him as this incredibly focused and hard-working bloke.'

Mick's hair had become a badge of his rock 'n' roll lifestyle. 'I noticed that while mine and Joe's hair got shorter, Mick's was getting longer,' grins Paul. His unwillingness to conform to the punk orthodoxy of short hair seemed to reflect his attitude towards The Clash's ascetic stance.

Jones's growing separateness and lack of punctuality resulted in flare-ups. During the recording of 'Clash City Rockers' late the previous year Paul and Mick had come to blows. Early in 1978, Sandy Pearlman went to see the group rehearsing at the 100 Club, only to find that Mick and his equipment were nowhere to be seen. It was explained to the producer that the others were 'mad at him' and had thrown him out of the group. In Mick's place was another guitarist: Steve Jones. Asked why he thought Mick had been dismissed, Sandy suggests: 'Maybe it's because he wanted to be Mott the Hoople and the others didn't.'

Johnny Green believes reports of Mick's temporary sacking, if indeed that's what it was, are exaggerated. Since their earliest days, relationships within The Clash had been unstable. Now it seemed the tension that threatened to divide the group was the very thing that held them together. 'The group was still pretty solid at that time,' Johnny states. Mick, meanwhile, who won't be drawn on Pearlman other than to say 'he was a nice guy', puts another spin on it. 'He tried to get to us,' he explains mysteriously. 'But we were impenetrable.'

'It was bad at that time,' says Robin, whose humour, enthusiasm and entertaining antics helped to keep up the group's spirits. 'There would be days when Mick wasn't talking to Bernie, Joe wasn't talking to Mick, Paul wasn't talking to Joe. It wasn't a happy time for them.'

Possibly on Bernie and Malcolm's instructions, or as he himself maintains purely of his own volition, Steve Jones was present again on the final dates of the On Parole tour, at the Music Machine in Camden. So was Jimmy Pursey. The gigs were a triumphant homecoming. Fans were let in through the upstairs dressing-room windows, and the support bands' guitars ended up in the pawn-brokers. The electric atmosphere in the venue was amplified by the inevitable random violence. As with Glasgow, the bouncers had it in for the punk crowd.

'Me and [music journalist] Pete Silverton were standing talking to each other when two bouncers came over and hit us, literally knocked us to the floor, just out of the blue,' recalls Roger Armstrong. 'It wasn't even that crowded, it was early in the evening, It was like, bang! "Fuck, what was that?" Topper came over straight away and said, "Let me have a go at them, I know karate, I'll sort them out." We were like, "No, don't, they are big guys." He was a plucky little character.'

On the decks that night was a club DJ who was to become a fixture on future Clash tours: Barry Myers. Barry – a reggae, garage-rock, rockabilly, punk and soul aficionado – was reviewing all four dates for *Sounds*, but managed to persuade Bernie to let him DJ. 'What encouraged me to pursue it further was when I first spoke to Johnny Green,' recalls Myers. 'He said, "Joe wants you to know that you're playing great music. And by the way, so do I."'

The On Parole tour saw other distractions. David Mingay and Jack Hazan had been filming more footage for *Rude Boy*. The process was appropriately chaotic. There was no shooting schedule, and matters were made worse by the tensions within the group and with Bernie. Ray Gange found himself in an increasingly uncomfortable role. He was a Clash fan and hanger-on who was now the principal actor in a film to which the group were, at best, indifferent.

'When David Mingay approached me I thought there would be, like, about three days' work involved,' recalls Gange. 'Joe told me that it would be a fun thing to do, so I just went along with that. I wouldn't have done it unless Joe had encouraged me. But there was no concept of like, "Well, we want you to be this guy and this is going to happen." Every two or three days they'd have another idea and it would be "Let's film you doing this, let's film you doing that, let's film you living in a block of flats that you don't live in, let's film you signing on, let's film you hitching a ride to go to a Clash gig." There was no sequence to any of it, there was no kind of plot line, so it just didn't make any sense.

'There were a lot of problems between The Clash management and the filmmakers,' he adds. 'Because the film people were paying me, I was being drawn into their side of things, which contradicted what I wanted to be doing. I'd rather have been hanging around with The Clash. Not particularly working for them, but just hanging out with them. It started to drive a wedge between me and the group.'

Johnny Green: 'You'd say to Bernie, "The film crew . . . what's all that about?" And he would say, "Well, do you think advertisements carry a political message? Do you watch them, Johnny? Do you need a television? Should people have them, Johnny, or are they a curse?" Bernie never gave you the information you needed. We never knew what was going on.'

The Clash expressed their feelings towards the film crew's presence in various ways. At Glasgow Apollo, Mick bellowed at Jack Hazan, 'Get off the fucking stage!' This was cut into the film to look as if he was shouting at Ray Gange, fumbling to reconnect some leads. Paul had a literally more phlegmatic approach. 'Simonon beckoned me to wind down my window and then he spat in my mouth,' remembers Hazan. 'Unbelievable! They did step over the line. Johnny Green used to get totally wiped out. But Mick – when he turned up – was very disciplined. You always knew where you were with Mick. Joe was very powerful, but you never knew where you were with him. I'd say our relationship with the group was robust but not particularly friendly. Looking back, we were witnessing their break-up. They were getting very fidgety with each other. It was just a feeling. Mick's attitude was different to Joe's. Joe had short hair and a broken tooth. Mick wanted to be more glamorous. He'd wear a Bruce Springsteen T-shirt to the studio.'

When The Clash finally came off the road it was the beginning of August. They had planned to release the second album in September but it was far from finished. The *NME*, like the rest of Britain, was becoming impatient. The paper sniped that the group had been in the studio for 'six or seven years making their new LP with Dr Sandy Pearlman'.

The truth was all was not going well. Pearlman denies it, and the group's memories are hazy, but according to an interview Mick gave to Nick Kent later that year, it seems that CBS weren't overly impressed with the new recordings. He said the label's Muff Winwood and Jeremy Ensall believed the material 'lacked substance' and were working on their own mixes. There were also issues about Joe's voice: it was decided that most Americans wouldn't have a clue what he was singing about. One of the primary objectives, from CBS's point of view, was to make the album palatable for the US market.

The record company's attitude inevitably dented Pearlman's confidence. In a move that was almost certainly political, the producer used his influence to move production to his favourite studio, the Automatt in San Francisco. This took control away from the UK arm of CBS. If the album was made acceptable for Pearlman's friends at CBS/Epic in New York, then it would be his mixes that made the record. Relocating the operation to the States would also remove Joe and Mick from the constant friction and mind-games with Bernie and the distractions of the *Rude Boy* filming. (The crew's lighting, for one thing, was putting the guitars out of tune in the studio.) Mick describes it as being 'kidnapped'.

England's best-loved punk band were going to complete their second album in the home of flower-power, on the sunny West Coast of America.

Once again, Paul and Topper, whose bass and drum parts were completed, were left behind in London. 'What were they going to do in San Francisco?' says Johnny Green. 'Go shopping?'

Paul: 'Unfortunately, I think that the reality of the situation is the record company held the financial strings at this point. I suppose as Joe and Mick were the chief songwriters, CBS saw me and Topper as surplus and not necessary.' Simonon enjoyed the summer, however, frequenting his favourite haunt, the Tate Gallery, and, in early September, he went to see Frank Sinatra perform at the Royal Albert Hall. He wore Dr Marten's with his tux. Meanwhile, Topper was left to pursue his favourite pastimes, playing pool and drinking in the pub.

On 6 September, Topper and Johnny attended the premiere of *The Buddy Holly Story* at the Odeon, Leicester Square. One of the other guests was Keith Moon. The following morning, Moon died of an overdose in a flat at Curzon Place in Mayfair. Around the same time, Topper moved out of his flat in Queens Road, Finsbury Park and into 8 Pindock Mews in Maida Vale. The previous inhabitants had been Sid Vicious and Nancy Spungen, who had left London for a new life in New York. The bathroom resembled a gruesome, crimson Rauschenberg, where Sid and Nancy had squirted the ceiling and walls with syringes full of their blood. Baker, who neither drank nor took drugs, refused to clean it up. Johnny Green was roped in to do the job. The house at Pindock Mews was filled with bad junkie ju-ju. It wouldn't be long before some of it was rubbing off on Topper Headon. He was also experimenting with coke and, when the opportunity arose, heroin.

In early August, Joe and Mick flew into San Francisco. 'We'd always dreamed of going to America,' says Mick. 'We never wanted to be a parochial, little band.' The Automatt studio was on Folsom Street, not far from the docks. It was an area of old warehouses and industrial buildings, populated by struggling artists and Bohemians. There were clusters of shops, sleazy nightclubs, heavy leather bars. 'Back then, it was a little bit on the rough side, a little bit non-residential,' says journalist Howie Klein. Mick and Joe booked into a hotel in Chinatown. Away from the intense pressures of London, they relaxed and enjoyed each other's company. It was warm and sunny. The Automatt had a great jukebox filled with vintage soul, R&B and rock 'n' roll. Mick and Joe's favourites included Otis Redding's '(Sittin On) The Dock of the Bay' and The Bobby Fuller Four's 'I Fought The Law', written by Buddy Holly and the Crickets' guitarist, Sonny Curtis.

Pearlman had spent a few days in New York, preparing for the sessions, and arrived in San Francisco to discover Joe and Mick had already been to the cinema five times – to see the same film. 'I returned to find they'd discovered *National Lampoon's Animal House*,' laughs Pearlman. 'They claimed to believe it was a documentary, and that John Belushi, alias Bluto Blutarki, was the greatest living American.'

Mick and Joe found America intensely exciting. They'd seen San Francisco in *Bullitt* and scores of other movies and now they were there. The city had a vibrant music scene. They discovered artists whose records they'd bought as schoolkids performing in bars and small venues all across town. 'We were there having a party,' says Mick. 'It was like a hangover from the sixties, Country Joe and the Fish were playing. From very early on we made lots of friends, like Mo Armstrong, who is the singer of Daddy Long Legs. He was a Vietnam vet – he came back an activist. He had a Cuban wife, and there was a lot of talk, not only then but years later, about trying to play in Cuba.'

Sandy Pearlman recalls that 'they wanted to meet Mike Bloomfield, who was playing at a club in the Haight area. They were introduced, but he had no idea who they were. They became visiting dignitaries, visiting ambassadors to the San Francisco new wave and punk scene, which, of course, was, along with England in general, the most thriving punk and new wave scene in the entire known universe. They had certainly come to the right place.'

The Clash's songwriting partners became a magnet for like-minded souls, outsiders, outcasts and punk rockers. Pearl Gates was one of the latter. She was an eighteen-year-old half-Filipino singer who'd been brought up on American airforce bases in Europe. When Ian Dury and the Blockheads toured the US in March 1978, Pearl befriended Kosmo Vinyl, the group's press-man. She was also one of the 100,000 or so Americans who had bought *The Clash* on import. Gates had adopted the name 'Pearl Harbour' and formed her own punk band.

'They were sitting on the floor of the studio smoking dope and drinking brandy, they were dirty and scruffy looking,' recalls Pearl. 'They were really funny and animated and really excited because we were going to see Emmylou Harris together. I didn't think they would like her because she was pure Americano and, being English guys, I didn't think they liked American stuff. But I was wholly wrong. Joe, especially, loved American country music. I think Mick went because of Joe, really, but they got very drunk and they were really happy and made a lot of noise, it was great.'

Meanwhile, there was work to do. According to Sandy, 'The Clash had a lot of money to buy equipment in 1978.' He and Mick went shopping for a vintage 1954 Les Paul. The producer acquired two bespoke amps from Rockwood Music in California. Pearlman also had his favourite graphic EQs and an instrument 'for producing heavy guitar sounds'. The idea was to strip away the existing guitar tracks and rebuild a new layer of music. There was also complex editing of the Basing Street material. ('Tommy Gun' was pieced together from three different takes, for example.)

For three weeks, Mick and Joe knuckled down to an intense period of guitar overdubs and vocals. Sandy would later boast that there are 'more guitars per square inch on this record than in anything in the rest of Western civilisation'. The critic Greil Marcus, writing a piece for *New West*, interviewed Mick and Joe at the studio and heard a version of 'Safe European Home' with a guitar riff borrowed from the live version of Sammy Hagar's 'I've Done Everything For You', all over West Coast radio at the time. Strummer told him: 'Sandy Pearlman has being trying to turn us into Fleetwood Mac for the past six months. I think he gave up last night.'

Howie Klein remembers: 'I was in there one night and they were doing the final mix for "Safe European Home", my favourite song at the time. I left there around two in the morning. When I came back around eight in the morning they were still working on it. Everybody was like death warmed over. I don't know who, but one of them said to me, "Listen to these two." I listened to the two versions and they said, "Which one do you think?" I said, "Well, that one." So they gave me the other one and said, "Here, keep that."'

At the end of August, CBS/Epic were played the work in progress. Once again, it seems they weren't exactly knocked out by what they heard. By this time, Joe and Mick were fed up. 'We couldn't stand it any more,' says Mick. 'We missed the other two so much, and we wanted them to come over. So we went on strike.'

It was decided to move the operation to the Record Plant in New York, where Sandy had always planned to do the final mixing. 'Joe and me had a week off,' recalls Mick, 'and said we'd meet in New York. I went off to LA, and Joe and Peter Opinga – a very religious guy, read his Bible – they went across the States, just the two of them.'

Mick flew down to Los Angeles with Sandy to catch the Blue Öyster Cult's show at the Hollywood Palladium. Pearlman booked them into a hotel near the airport. 'I'd only been there for twenty minutes, I got my bag and checked into the Tropicana!' smiles Mick. 'I wasn't going to LA to stay in the airport hotel. So that was that. I went to the gig that night and had a fantastic time.'

Mick befriended a bunch of people on the flourishing LA punk scene, including The Go-Go's, who lived in a shabby block of flats in Hollywood called The Canterbury, where, according to Jones, 'every apartment had different punks in it'. On 25 August, he took a trip out into the Valley to a club called the Azteca to watch a night of Californian punk groups: The Middle Class, Negative Trend, The Dils, The Weirdos. The gig ended in a full-scale riot. Also in attendance was Jon Savage.

'The whole thing was totally trippy,' he says. 'I walked into this club and there was fucking Mick Jones. We hadn't talked because we hadn't been friendly for quite a long time. I do remember we both looked rather nervous when the cops entered holding their mace guns. I couldn't believe it. I think the crowd was actually chanting "White riot!" It was a case of being hoisted with one's petard really. Not just for him, but also for me. It was a very odd situation indeed.

'It was a harsh world in 1978. Everyone was bickering like fuck and nobody was being nice to each other. Everybody had to struggle, the initial enthusiasm was over and everybody had to get out there and actually fight to, not have a career, but to get their point of view across. Suddenly there are all these factions and everyone hating each other so it was very hard. I didn't take Mick's attitude personally, I wasn't that miffed about it. That was just the way it was: groups didn't get on with journalists.'

Strummer, meanwhile, was wending his way across America in a flat-bed Ford pick-up truck. He was absorbing the *Badlands* diners, endless scrub and romance of small-town US life. He stopped in Memphis and hung out with ancient, no-name blues guys in Beale Street. When he finally arrived in New York, several days late, Sandy's right-hand man Corky Stasiak, looked him up and down and said, 'Dude, you've turned into Hud!' (The 1963 film about the contemporary American West with Paul Newman in the eponymous role.)

New York was a whole new, thrilling, disorientating experience. 'I flew in on the Saturday night and saw it in all its glory at night-time,' says Mick. 'It was fantastically exciting, especially for someone like me who'd grown up watching American TV.' Susan Blond, Epic's chief press officer assigned to The Clash, took Joe and Mick under her wing and introduced them to the eye-opening madness of New York's street hassle. At the Record Plant, on West 44th Street, near the neon buzz of Times Square, Pearlman decided that the room they'd booked on the tenth floor had the best ambient sound for recording guitars out of the three studios they'd tried so far. It was here that Lennon had mixed *Sometime in New York City*. Mick laid down the final, intricate weave of guitar overdubs that would characterise *Give 'Em Enough Rope* in a tiny glass sound booth with stunning views across Manhattan.

The group joked that the album should be called *Give 'Em Enough Dope*. 'Most of [the pot] was deriving from a particular underground source,' says Pearlman. 'The technical term to describe this stuff was "polio-pot". It's kind of an overarching term that describes ganja of a particular potency. I think the actual stuff was Mowie Zowie and there was some Colombian stuff, too. People don't understand this but there's a big surf scene in New York. So this was all stuff that came out of the New York-transplanted California surfer underground ganja scene. They were introduced to an entirely new cultural vector.'

A brief respite from the overdub-grind came from an unexpected quarter. One day at the Warwick hotel, Mick got a call from Nancy Spungen asking him if he'd back Sid at a welcome-to-New York gig at Max's Kansas City on 7 September. The other band members for the shows included various New York Dolls and Heartbreakers. Mick was reticent but eventually Joe persuaded him to perform. The guy Jones had once shared a squat with in Acton Vale was now a smacked-out caricature of his former self. Mick was understandably nervous about his US stage debut.

'We just about managed about five songs,' he says. 'Five songs for five bucks. It was a nightmare between shows, it was full on. Sid was sort of semi there. It was a serious drug thing. Me and Joe kept looking at each other, because we couldn't believe it. The people there were as out of it as you can be without actually being dead. We weren't heavyweight drug guys, we had a lot more than that to share.'

'They barely got through a verse,' remembers Bob Gruen. 'Sid was stoned and pathetic. They played for about twenty minutes and Mick looked a bit lost – the band were so lame. There weren't that many people there. They were bored shitless and didn't know what was going on.'

On the days following that show, the final overdubs were put on The Clash's second album. The honky-tonk piano on 'Julie's Been Working for the Drug Squad' was initially laid down by a 'wild' black NY lounge pianist called Al Field, whom Mick and Joe had stumbled across in a bar. Later, to Joe and Mick's disappointment, it was re-recorded by Blue Öyster Cult's Al Lanier. Saxophone on 'Drug Stabbing Time' was provided by Elephant's Memory and Lennon session veteran Stan Bronstein. Jones would later deadpan, 'We had a lot of fun watching our album being recorded by session musicians.' The last sessions were ill-tempered and fraught.

In late September, Paul and Topper were flown over to New York to hear the final mixes of *Give 'Em Enough Rope*. Mick and Joe, having been separated from their bandmates for nearly two months, excitedly picked them up at the airport, like enthusiastic but estranged partners. US Customs had initially refused to let Paul through: all he had with him was the cardboard case in which he kept his records.

The Clash's rhythm section also found America as electric and unreal as it looked on the big screen. 'It was amazing!' says Topper. 'I couldn't believe that you could get anything to eat, day or night. Just seeing yellow cabs and people driving on the other side of the road. The subways with steam coming out. It was a brand-new experience. Submarine sandwiches and coffee machines. It was so far advanced compared to Britain. You could phone out to a deli and order some food. Over here there was no such thing as twenty-four-hour room service.'

'It seemed like a different world and planet,' recalls Paul. 'Not as glamorous as I thought it would be. I remember us walking down the street and these black guys ran up to us and went, "You guys look fantastic, where you from?" Generally we were treated with indifference.'

Bob Gruen photographed the group in Little Italy and invited them to his apartment to watch his film of The New York Dolls – one of the few documents of the group in its louche, kinetic glory. The four quarters of the group had slotted back together, creating the group's unique, bristling voltage. There was a bit of customary Simonon–Headon horseplay that night: Bob Gruen broke his thumb.

With The Clash back together again, listening to the thick, riveting power chords and meticulously interwoven overdubs of *Give 'Em Enough Rope*, it reinforced their belief in themselves. The ad-libbed coda of 'All the Young Punks', inspired by Dillinger's rap in 'Cokane in my Brain', sent shivers down spines. 'A spliff, a pound, half a pint of brown, this is the way we spell Camden Town!'

The irony of The Clash singing about their life in grotty north London while ensconced in a mixing room high above Manhattan wasn't lost on anyone. But Sandy Pearlman has this to say: 'Whether people really live all of this stuff or not, it really doesn't matter. All that matters is that the vector is put out into the culture-pool, the stream. That's the important thing. I don't care if people do, or do not, live the line that they are putting out. At the time, The Clash certainly *were* living the line they were putting out. So I didn't think that they were manipulating the data to create an impression of who and what they were that was not true, because at the time it *was* true.'

The trip to the US had re-bonded Joe and Mick. This had serious implications for another powerful force in The Clash camp: Bernie Rhodes. His influence over the group while they were in America had been negligible. The prolonged recording of the album had held little interest for him. Where were the anarchic patterns and weird angles? Just like McLaren had with The Pistols, Bernie had lost the one thing he valued most: control. CBS/Epic was talking to the group about a US tour early the next year to promote the new album and scheduling the release of *The Clash* with an updated tracklisting for the American market.

There was an attempt by Bernie at a last, anarchic hurrah, but his methods suddenly seemed forced and outdated. He'd scheduled a two-night stand at Harlesden New Roxy in late September apparently without the group's consent. The Clash were unable to honour the gigs because of Joe and Mick's recording commitments in New York. Rhodes didn't approve of what he called 'their silly indulgences, like recording in big New York studios and staying in top New York hotels'. That was what he told the press. He knew it was costing the group money they didn't have. Headon claimed the Harlesden dates were an attempt to coerce Strummer and Jones to cut short their American trip.

Rhodes tried more of his old tricks, to some effect. Caroline Coon comments: 'The Clash are arguing amongst themselves, just before the first American tour. They are so unhappy, bickering because the manager has said one thing to one member and another to someone else, and the band are ringing each other saying, "You said this about me . . ." Paul Simonon came to me and said that the US tour would have to be cancelled because the band were gonna break up. This was an absolute tragedy, it wasn't necessary. It was better to change their management than split up. So I said to Paul, "If Bernie is having a nervous breakdown and can't cope, and would rather split the band than admit that" – that was my interpretation of it – "then he would have to retire for a bit."'

There were frantic communications between the two parties throughout September and October. The group played a short European tour, then on 28 October, a couple of days after the re-scheduled Harlesden dates, news broke that The Clash had sacked their manager. Bernard Rhodes, the visionary, agent provocateur, wheeler-dealer, Renault car fixer and unpredictable thinker, was now himself left out in the chill and denounced. Rumours circulated that he'd ripped off The Clash – an obvious barb after all the arguments about money that year. But considering later developments in The Clash story, this seems highly unlikely.

Bernie himself is adamant: 'All those stories that I took from them – I took nothing, they took from me. I've made my own money.' On his dismissal, he petitioned the High Court to freeze the group's assets. The group counter-claimed that he'd breached his duties as manager.

During our interview, I ask him why he thinks The Clash sacked him. 'Because of the censorship that exists in this country, you're telling me something you don't even know!' he shouts. 'The Clash were offered money by the record company to get rid of me. They were bribed. Because I was too dangerous. They're wimps. You're in the spirit of it.'

After considering the journalist Miles for the post, the group handed the responsibility for the day-to-day running of the group to Caroline Coon.

'Bernie's a complex character, who'd built this great band, but he couldn't go forward with it,' says Caroline. 'He goes off and is incoherent and angry. You can be an ideas person, but the band still need X number of tons of electronic equipment, it needs dates organised. In 1978, The Clash wanted to play music, so if they haven't anyone to get them to the gig, put them on the aeroplane, do the carnets and customs bullshit, the band are going to sit at home in Ladbroke Grove and talk about what? Situationism?

'I was not allowed to call myself the manager,' Caroline adds. 'I had to phone up people and say, "Hello, I'm Caroline Coon, I'm not the manager of The Clash." It was a holding position.'

The Clash had come back from America with not just a new album, but with an unspoken new vision. Britain hadn't changed in their absence but they had. 'We went to America, we saw America, and we figured it out,' says Mick. 'We didn't just want to make it in England, we wanted to make it everywhere. We thought we had it, we wanted to be heard. We never thought about any of it, we never thought about what we were doing, we never knew what we were doing, we didn't have a plan, we instinctively just did it. We talked a lot about things but there wasn't a plan. We just wanted The Clash to reach everybody.'

In New York, Paul – the chairman of The Clash's visual department – checked out the store on Canal Street where Johnny Thunders used to buy his Hudson motorbike boots. They reached halfway to the knees and had a chunky metal buckle. Paul bought a pair and so did the rest of The Clash. 'I've got no hairs on the bottom of my legs because of those bloody things!' says Simonon. The footwear soon became known in Britain simply as Clash Boots.

Miraculously, on his return to London, Mick had his hair cut. Paul, meanwhile, began growing his hair longer, into a quiff. Pennie Smith's pictures taken in Caroline's flat, against a poster she and Paul had bought in Moscow, show Simonon sporting a *Thirty Seconds Over Tokyo* US airman look, and Joe and Mick with brushed-back Teddy Boy hair. The visual homogeneity and Americanised rock 'n' roll cool signalled The Clash were, for the time being at least, a solid entity again.

On 24 October, the group played the Paradiso in Amsterdam. Ferocious, focused, heavy, passionate, it was, in Johnny Green's opinion, one of the greatest shows The Clash ever played.

The Clash's Sort It Out tour zig-zagged across Britain in November and December. It had been heralded by the launch party for *Give 'Em Enough Rope* at a bar in Wardour Street. 'My mates came to the play-back,' recalls Mick. 'They stole a box full of albums and took them to Cheapo Cheapos in Brewer Street before the record was released in the shops. It was the first place you could get it in London.' Robin and Johnny – for they were the culprits – celebrated in the Ship. That night Joe hooked up with Gaby Salter, a teenage Londoner whose parents had run hip boutiques in Carnaby Street and the Kings Road, who would become his long-term partner.

Robin Banks covered the tour for *Zig-zag*. Punk in the provinces was now bigger than ever: it was rough, basic, factional. A widespread skinhead revival was also happening, centred around the dual beacons of football and Sham 69. The Clash tapped into a visible desperation and violence but their backdrop, designed by Paul, communicated their grander intentions. It was a collage of the flags of all nations.

A week into the tour, in Bournemouth, Topper and his girlfriend (he'd split with his wife Wendy) went skinny dipping. Robin pinched their clothes and the couple had to run naked back to the hotel. Johnny Green and Kris Needs rounded off the evening by scaling some cliffs. Barry Myers, who'd made such an impression on Joe at the Music Machine, was brought along as tour DJ. He soon became an integral part of the entourage. 'Johnny and the Baker were a formidable duo,' says Myers. 'Very different as people. I became a third party to them. There was constant chaos. The biggest trouble-maker in the pack was Johnny. He could be menace. He would get us in fights and trash hotel rooms and the like. He liked the chaos.'

Howard Fraser, a former writer and *NME* contributor, became the group's driver, as by that time Johnny Green had lost his licence for drink-driving. 'A lot of the madness was to do with Johnny,' says Howard. 'He was a very powerful mover. He was not just a roadie or even a personal manager, he was a lot more than that. It was the fifth Beatle syndrome.' According to

Fraser, Robin was 'mad as a hatter, mostly drunk. But he was also quite debonair. Very intelligent. A great sense of humour. A boulevardier of sorts. He was the wild card element.' Howard suffered the obligatory Simonon pranks, the worst being Paul's habit of cupping his hands over Howard's eyes every time he was engaged in a dangerous driving manoeuvre. Mick, meanwhile, is described by Howard as 'a bit of a prima donna. He had a nice, wry sense of humour and was tortuously aware of where The Clash were in the pecking order. He was aware even more than Joe of their potential cultural importance. Remember this is pre-media studies and pop culture analysis.'

Howard soon learned that working with the group involved certain responsibilities. It was no secret that there was casual heroin use around the group, but it was understood that it should stay that way: around the group, not in it. 'It was a code of honour that no one was to give Topper or, indeed, anybody else in the group, anything Class A and dangerous,' says Fraser. 'It was hard at times to deny Topper, but he was denied. It was an agreement, no personal abuse, that sort of thing. Who wants to see a non-user being initiated? I wasn't that happy about Topper's consumption of cocaine, he would get it anywhere anyway. People are always avid to turn band members on to the silliness – groupies and drugs and so on. The band were very good at allowing access to the fans, but they were also fairly acute at keeping the freeloaders and parasites away.'

On 10 November *Give 'Em Enough Rope* was released. The cover showed a picture of a dead cowboy being picked at by a couple of vultures. The image was taken from a state-sponsored Chinese postcard. The back of the sleeve employed similar Chinese Communist iconography: party members on horseback holding huge red flags. The music inside reflects 1978: heavy, powerful and a little ugly. It carries little of the tatty art-school punk spirit of the 100 Club. There is a lot of self-examination and a significant degree of self-doubt. There are references to hard drugs, terrorism and international disorder. It shows a group that has left behind the amphetamine-guzzling, grubby world of London for something altogether more elevated and global. The music owes more to The Kinks, Bruce Springsteen, Mott and *Ziggy*-era Bowie than Bob Dylan, The Ramones and Chuck Berry.

A lot of the material is directly autobiographical: there is less of the subtle characterisation of *The Clash*. The self-reflexive quality lends the material an intimacy – a diary of a rock 'n' roll group. There's a seemingly unstoppable impulse for The Clash to explain themselves. The opener, 'Safe European Home', a powerful rock anthem breaking down into a bleeping, rock-reggae coda, is about the ill-starred writing trip to Jamaica. 'Stay Free' is Mick's tender reminiscence about growing up in south London, based around his and Robin's friendship. It's nostalgic, wistful and deeply personal (references to the Albany letters; 'I practised daily in my room, you were down the Crown planning your next move') and injects an incongruous, almost feminine sensitivity into an album laden with muscular political and social comment.

'All the Young Punks (New Boots and Contracts)' mythologises the group's history, from Joe's meeting with Mick and Paul in Portobello Road ('I saw some passing yobbos and we did chance to speak') to a disillusionment with success ('face front you got the future shining like a piece of gold, I swear as we get closer it looks more like a lump of coal'). 'Guns on the Roof', 'Tommy Gun' and 'English Civil War' (the tune of 'Johnny Comes Marching Home' grafted to Joe's vision of an imminent fascist Britain) reflect extremist politics at home and abroad.

'Drug-Stabbing Time' and 'Cheapskates' are weighty and lumpen, big production numbers in search of catchy tunes. 'Julie's Been Working for the Drug Squad' is better: an offbeat, New Orleans punk-jive about a raid on an LSD factory in Wales, complete with corny backing vocals and bar-room piano. Overlong and swathed with Mott-like guitars, the rock 'n' rolling 'Last Gang in Town' romanticises The Clash as another rogueish street posse in a London full of warring subcultures – 'the Zydeco kids from the high-rise', 'rockabilly rebels', 'skinhead gangs', 'old soul rebels' – but rues that 'it's all young blood going down the drain'. Strummer's ad-libs create another texture, snatches and echoes of the language of London's streets: 'Come on, come on, Kentucky Fried Chicken!'; 'Feeling hazy for forty-five minutes, feeling crazy for forty-five more!').

What *Give 'Em Enough Rope* possesses is power and scope; what it lacks is spontaneity, plus the very thing that elevated *The Clash* into a masterpiece and for which Sandy Pearlman had no passion: reggae. For a record whose foundations were laid on Basing Street there's little of Ladbroke Grove in it. The Clash's disconnection from black culture robbed them of a magic ingredient: soul.

In *Melody Maker*, Jon Savage concluded his review thus: 'Signing to CBS then bitching non-stop, going to the USA to finish an album, which, in its allusions to drugs, four-letter words and determinedly English patois, would seem to have very little hope of American airplay. So do they squander their greatness.' Nick Kent liked the sound of the record but wrote, 'What it all adds up to, I fear, is Strummer's totally facile concept of shock-politics.'

Looking back, Joe said: 'We'd got so involved in the lifestyle of the group we no longer had lives to write about. I think Bob Dylan feels that. [His life] is far too removed from people's ordinary experience.'

It's worth noting The Clash could have made a very different LP that year, which would have created a more natural bridge between *The Clash* and *London Calling*: 'Safe European Home'; 'White Man'; 'Groovy Times'; 'Gates of the West'; the Basing Street out-take 'One Emotion'; 'Tommy Gun'; 'Stay Free'; 'Julie's Been Working for the Drug Squad'; 'The Last Gang In Town'; 'All The Young Punks'; plus, say, their cover of 'Pressure Drop' or soundcheck faves 'The Israelites' or Alton Ellis's 'Dance Crasher'.

Give 'Em Enough Rope climbed to number two in the UK but failed to reach the US Billboard Top 100, despite unfettered praise from Greil Marcus in *Rolling Stone* and Lester Bangs in *Village Voice*. The chart success in Britain was exhilarating, but the chequered notices stung. Danny Baker's *NME* review of 'Tommy Gun' – 'it's a sad report on the state of things' – angered Mick in particular.

Over the next few weeks, one adjective more than any other came to describe the album: 'overproduced'. 'If we'd have thought it was overproduced, we wouldn't have done it,' says Topper. 'There are a lot of effects on it. Even on the drums there's phasing. Being told it was over-produced made us realise that, yeah, perhaps it was.'

As Caroline Coon said: 'Here was this group that said, "Fuck the world!" but they never thought, "Fuck the media!" They were always very conscious of what people thought. They never learned that trick of ignoring them.'

The Clash – the biggest and most important new rock 'n' roll group in Britain – spent Christmas at home in London totally skint. Bernie had been granted a court order paying all the group's income to him.

In January 1979, the group went into Wessex Studios, in Highbury New Park, north London to record a Clashed-up version of 'I Fought The Law'. Their interest in the song, which both Mick and Joe had known for years, had been rekindled after hearing it at the Automatt the previous summer. They premiered their version on the Sort It Out tour. Joe had adapted a line to reflect Sid's situation in New York, where he was awaiting trial for Nancy Spungen's murder: 'I *killed* my baby and it felt so bad.'

The set-up at Wessex reverted to the successful formula of 'White Man in Hammersmith Palais' – Mick calling the shots while an experienced engineer manned the desk. This time the latter was Bill Price, helped by tape operator Jeremy Green. Price, who began studio work in 1962 with the Applejacks, was a veteran of Mott and The Sex Pistols's *Never Mind the Bollocks*. He had a reputation as a calm, urbane, unflappable presence and a master at the sound desk.

The Clash and Bill immediately hit it off. 'They were a joy to work with,' says Price. 'For a start, their material was so incredibly good and they were just very talented in different directions. Working for any band with Topper Headon in it made the process an absolute pleasure from square one. You normally start with the rhythm section, then build up, and it was fantastic with Topper. In terms of being a producer and having production ideas, Mick Jones was very good, an accomplished guitar player and also his head's brimming full of musical ideas – he can play most of them as well. Mick was very amenable to other people's suggestions. Joe was never a difficult singer to get a good performance out of, if he was in the right frame of mind.'

As well as The Bobby Fuller Four cover, the group also recorded a powerful metallic revamp of 'Capital Radio', with funky disco coda, plus two Basing Street rejects, 'Groovy Times' and 'Gates of the West' (a reworking of Mick's pre-Clash 'Ooh Baby Ooh, It's All Over'). 'Groovy Times', with prominent acoustic guitars and a light, Spanish-guitar solo, has one of Joe's best lyrics so far, moving from gritty, elegiac reportage of an England where 'high street shops are boarded up' to a snipe at Elvis Costello and the dilution of punk: 'I can remember his first appearance, now look what's happened to him.'

'That line, "They put him in a dog suit like from 1964", was a reference to the dog-tooth suits Elvis Costello was wearing,' said Joe. 'It was like The Stones on *Thank Your Lucky Stars* or something.'

One of the lines in 'Gates of the West' referred to a longing for New York: 'The city cast a shadow . . . will I see you again?' The Clash would be back there soon enough, playing their first gigs in the States to audiences that would include Bob Dylan and Andy Warhol.

It's a beautiful summer's day in Whitstable, Kent. Robin Banks and I are sitting in the front room of Johnny Green's terraced house, watching a film made about the Human Shields in Baghdad in March 2003. There is footage of several shields at the Al Daura water and oil refinery. The Americans are bombing a target nearby. Outside, Iraqi men, women and children are being blown to pieces. The explosions are getting louder. A woman, fearing her imminent death, curls up in a ball, her hands covering her face. The camera pans around to Robin Banks. He's as cool as a proverbial cucumber, drawing on a cigarette and reading a message pinned to a notice board. He's staring death in the face, too, but he looks as if he's strolling around the Tate Modern.

The film over, Johnny Green idly flicks through some old photo albums. There's a snap of him, Paul and Robin Banks having a kick about in Regent's Park in 1979. The goal posts are jackets and jumpers. Another shows the group in Johnny's old flat in West Hampstead eating a Christmas turkey dinner.

One yellowing Polaroid, taken at Heathrow, shows the group sitting in a British Airways departure lounge, awaiting their flight to the States on 30 January 1979. There's a palpable sense of excitement and anxiety. The group look their most gang-like. They wear leather jackets, hats, studded belts and wrist-bands. Stencilled Alex Michon shirts are still in evidence. Everyone bar Topper and Baker has a quiff.

The Clash set off for America as outsiders and underdogs. Somewhere among a population of 250 million there were 100,000 music fans who owned their debut album. But *Give 'Em Enough Rope* was hardly flying off the shelves. The Clash were not exactly arriving as conquerors.

As young Englishmen steeped in the romance of war movies and the Great British spirit of sacrifice and heroism, it was natural for the group to see their trip to America in militaristic terms – not so much an invasion as a 'raid', a daring attack with the odds stacked against them. They all loved Richard Fleischer's *Tora! Tora! Tora!* It was therefore decided that the outing should be called the Pearl Harbour tour. What else? Chris Townsend's Fifth Column T-shirt firm ran up a special design featuring a rising sun and a kamikaze pilot. Understandably, perhaps, the suits at Epic in New York preferred simply to call it the Give 'Em Enough Rope tour.

Tension between CBS in Soho Square and Epic in America had put the tour in jeopardy. Epic couldn't see the point of it, since *Give 'Em Enough Rope* was selling so poorly. Meanwhile, CBS in London weren't about to bankroll a tour of America. Epic finally agreed to underwrite the tour to the relatively modest tune of $30,000.

'I won't even go into the shit that was running CBS in Britain at that time,' says Caroline Coon, who spent £3,000 of her own money setting up the dates. 'The group's "fuck the record company" attitude was deserved. CBS didn't understand rock 'n' roll and were incredibly obstructive. You sign a band like The Clash with the best ideas, the best songs, the best music, hugely popular, at the right moment in time. And the record company say, "No, don't do it your way, do it this way." The Clash wouldn't have been so antagonistic towards the record company if CBS had been more interested, and intellectually understanding, of what they were about.'

The group arrived at Vancouver, Canada. Aware of the problems The Sex Pistols had encountered with hired American minders and roadies on their ill-fated US tour a year earlier, The Clash brought with them Johnny Green, Baker, Barry Myers and a full British crew. It was also cheaper: American roadies earned proper money, not Clash-level handouts.

'There was real excitement,' remembers Myers. 'We were in America for the first time, we felt like pioneers. It was like "Fuck the Americans, what do they know!" Which is sometimes true but, as we soon found out, not always. British punk – The Clash in particular – was very stylish, the look was very important. Image played a big part in it. We looked so different. We flew into Vancouver with our studded wristbands and bracelets and Customs took them off us. We were a bunch of spiky-haired, leather-clad no-goods arriving in their country. I don't believe anybody at the time would of thought of us as ambassadors.'

Mick Jones says: 'We always knew some people would despise us for [going to America]. You always felt when you followed a group around – like Mott and The Faces – that when they went big, when they had a hit, we lost them because they went to everybody. But that's the way it has to be, unfortunately. But it was worth it, to see it work. We always wanted to be international. We always said the world doesn't finish at the end of the street.'

The Clash played a warm-up gig in Vancouver, where the crowd pelted them with missiles when, after three encores, they tried to leave the stage. Topper suffered facial injuries. They then crossed the border into the US. Bob Gruen was there with his camera. He snapped the group in the snow, standing by a 'Welcome to the United States' sign. Johnny and Baker are in the picture wearing cowboy hats. The group booked into a motel in Seattle. Topper went off in search of Bruce Lee's grave.

The next morning they awoke to news that Sid Vicious had died from an overdose in his room in the Chelsea Hotel. It hadn't taken long for America to destroy Sid. 'It was really disheartening,' recalls Simonon. 'I'd shared a bed in a squat with Sid a number of times. I thought, "Who's to blame?" But Sid is probably to blame. It was shocking that a friend was not around any more. The Pistols weren't a group any more. We felt we were in this position by default. We felt we were the survivors.'

The Clash arrived in San Francisco, and Joe and Mick looked up their old friends: Pearl, Mo, Howie. The group then went shopping for leathers in a flea-market on the edge of town. A couple of days later they played a great show at the Berkeley Community Centre, where Sandy Pearlman showed up and the group acquired some baseball caps with whirring plastic helicopter blades on them. Their set opened – of course – with 'I'm So Bored With the USA'. The following day they played an unscheduled show at the old Fillmore

West for a group of radicals who resented legendary America promoter Bill Graham's monopoly on live music in the city. It was a riot. The Clash were dubbed 'the only band that matters'. Their croaky, Swinging London accents and 'w's for 'r's inspired some bright spark to rename them 'the only band that mutters'.

'The Clash came over here not really knowing what to expect,' says Howie Klein, who interviewed them for his radio show. 'They were ready to be defensive. But what they found was *worship*. Maybe they were thinking they were going to be victims of what they hated about America ideologically. Instead, everywhere they went they were being worshipped with incredible intensity. They were also being engaged by people on an intellectual basis. People whom they could respect. I think they were surprised they found so much positive energy being directed towards them, and that made them relax a little bit.'

The main support act on the tour was a treat for Joe, Mick, Paul and Topper. It was none other than Bo Diddley. Caroline Coon had tracked him down to Australia. Joe and Mick had insisted the promoter sign him up for the tour on whatever terms he wanted. He was paid more than The Clash. The idea was to highlight the link between The Clash's R&B-reggae punk and its black American heritage. The group loved Bo and he loved them back.

Howard Fraser had flown over to San Francisco with Johnny Green's partner Lindy to see the group. 'I was in the wings with Bo Diddley,' recalls Howard. 'Bo and I both watched Topper, because he was such an excellent drummer. Bo turned to me after the first number and said, "You know, that is the only white boy who's ever played my rhythm without having to be shown how to do it."'

In *Living Legend*, George R. White's biography of Bo, the great man says: 'They requested that I be on the show with 'em. Our music is entirely different, but it was a *gas*! When they first met me, I think they were scared to death, you know, but they finally came round an' we began talkin' an' laughin' an' jokin' an' stuff. When they found out that I was a cool dude, then everything was really beautiful. We rode up an' down the highway in the snow, you know, in the bus. It was *great*!'

Bo stayed up all night drinking rock 'n' rye whiskey and regaling the group with stories. His trademark rectangular guitar rode on his bunk. This particular model was hand-built in Australia and reportedly cost him £28,000.

The next gig was at the Santa Monica Civic in LA. Epic's West Coast top brass were there en masse. The group lined up to have their picture taken with them in the dressing room, but then, just as Bob Gruen was about to take the shot, The Clash got up and walked off. They thought this amazingly funny. But it also made a serious point: The Clash didn't like those corporate games. Caroline Coon, who'd organised the photo opportunity, was less amused. The incident reflected the tensions between the group and their caretaker manager, whom they thought too eager to please the Epic hierarchy.

The friction intensified after Caroline allegedly directed security to keep Howard Fraser and Lindy away from the backstage area. Later at the Tropicana, Joe and Mick held an inquest into the incident. 'I go into the room,' remembers Fraser, 'big double bed, Mick and Joe are smoking huge spliffs. "So what exactly happened?" A bit official, a bit formal. It wasn't because they were loyal to Lindy and myself, it was just the last straw. For her to do that to friends of the band who had paid their own way to come six or seven thousand miles . . . The Clash considered that to be not on, and totally against their ethos. This is what she hadn't grasped.' Caroline is quick to stress that she was under strict instructions from the group to keep everyone, however close they were to The Clash, out of the dressing room directly after the gigs. 'Obviously the group would then act "enraged",' she laughs.

Whether the incident *was* 'the last straw' is difficult to gauge, but it was clear that, after the chaos and unpredictability of Bernie, Caroline's conventional, level-headed approach to business was beginning to rankle with Mick and Joe. Her friendliness with Epic seemed like a betrayal.

'Coony was crisp and efficient,' says Johnny Green, who undoubtedly stirred matters up. 'The group weren't used to that. Maybe they thought it was getting too easy.'

Caroline was appalled by another incident, this time involving Baker. Susan Blond, the group's American press officer, was one of the Epic execs The Clash had left standing at the photo opportunity. Blond had politely asked Baker to move out of her way. He wasn't having a good day and ill-temperedly thrashed back, 'Fuck off, you cunt!' The group laughed. Blond was horrified. She turned to Caroline: 'He called me a cunt! He called me a cunt!' This became the catch-phrase for the rest of the tour.

Johnny Green asks the question: 'Did Sting's roadies get away with that sort of thing? Or would they have been sacked?'

After the Santa Monica Civic show, *Sounds* journalist Sylvie Simmons interviewed the group on their bus. 'Joe was very unfriendly,' she says. 'There was no warmth from Joe. Paul was so young and shy that it seemed he'd rather die than talk to anyone. I think they thought it was "us and them" and

I was a "them". But Mick was a sweetheart, really friendly, and very enthusiastic about being in America. I got the impression the others were pissed off with him. I think Topper was with some blonde.'

After the thrill of their West Coast reception, The Clash ventured east. The group went on a three-day tour of the Midwest on a bus hired from Waylon Jennings. But the mood soon darkened. 'We started to feel very alien and aware we were on our own,' says Johnny. 'After the novelty of the truck stops, seven-elevens and happy hours had worn off, it felt a bit bleak and desperate. In England, everyone was a punk rocker. Suddenly it seemed like no one knew who we were and no one liked us. We got stranded at St Louis airport. It stopped being pleasant and novel and fun.'

In Cleveland, they played a benefit for Larry McIntyre, a Vietnam veteran who'd lost his legs in the war. McIntyre had been banned from the swimming pool in his apartment block because his neighbours found his leg stumps offensive. In Washington DC, according to Allan Jones's gritty on-the-road piece for *Melody Maker*, Joe had a bust-up with Caroline over what he considered a pointless interview with a local college radio station, to which he'd been driven in a limo.

The tour rolled on to New York. Mick complained the hotel was a hole and demanded to be moved elsewhere. Susan Blond, whom the group liked, showed them around town. She and Joe went to Studio 54 together. She also introduced the group to her friend Andy Warhol, who attended the gig at the Palladium.

In his book *Exposures* Warhol describes the evening – and reiterates the then popularly held belief in America that the group were sort of Dickensian punk waifs. 'The most exciting night I've ever spent with Susan [Blond] yet was going to see The Clash at the Palladium. The Clash are the hottest punk band since The Sex Pistols . . . They're really young kids from very poor English families. On the way there, Susan said, "They hate the rich. They're worse than working class."'

The Palladium show was a triumph and the glitterati turned up in their hordes. For Howard Fraser, the evening once again illustrated their anti-celebrity values and loyalty to their friends and fans: 'The Palladium was an immense, very old-style traditional theatre like the Theatre Royal on Drury Lane. The stairs leading to the dressing rooms were a social register, everyone in New York was there, including Bob Dylan and Andy Warhol. The group are filing past these people. I am lingering behind, being polite, it's the band's day, I don't want to intrude. Strummer is the last one in the dressing room and he shouts, "Come on, Howard, you can come in, you're one of the band!" That disarmed me, it was lovely, it made it all worthwhile. That just showed that Joe really did care about fans who made an effort.

'The Clash had this tremendous collective sense of humour,' Fraser continues. 'It crossed my mind it could've been a wind-up. You could be hung out to dry if you moved wrongly. When there was a wind-up going on, if you didn't get the joke it could be horrible. The Clash would rib each other mercilessly, but in a really affectionate way. Paul knew he wasn't there as a brilliant musician, so Topper would dig him out endlessly. He would double the tempo just to confuse him, things like that. Topper would smile at me in the wings as if to say, "Watch now, I'm going to pull a stunt on Paul." Paul took it well. He was aloof and cool and the others respected that, but everybody was a target and had to accept it.'

The tour tested Caroline's reserves of goodwill. Paul was also put in a difficult position, caught between Joe and Mick on one hand and Caroline on the other, but, typically, seemed unruffled by the chaos and tensions around him. After New York, The Clash flew home. Soon afterwards, Caroline stopped working for the group.

'The Clash loved their fans,' she says. 'But with anyone else in the industry, the more that person liked them, the worse the group treated them. My role as manager was a holding position. I had my own career. I was in there to make sure they didn't break up. The fact was they didn't really want to be managed. They had this complex relationship with people they saw as being authoritative. They were very mean to people who worked for them. But they could be sweethearts individually when they weren't playing that gang game.'

Jack Hazan states that Caroline Coon was the first rock 'n' roll manager ever to be dismissed for being too efficient. Caroline had seen it all before. In the late 1960s, she had experienced an attempt by what she calls 'a macho gang' to seize control of Release, which she was famous for helping to run in a similarly precise, well-oiled and rigorous regime. The apparent crime of her and her allies was to have 'removed Release from the people'. After a stand-off, Caroline had regained control, having exposed the coup as 'empty posturing'. This time, the issues could not be resolved. Back in London, she demanded a meeting with The Clash. Joe told her simply: 'You're sacked.'

The sell-out tour of the States was deemed a success, even, reluctantly, by CBS and Epic. American audiences seemed to adore The Clash as much as British and European ones. The Stateside crowds instinctively seemed to understand what The Clash were selling.

The group engaged with their American audiences as they did with European ones: on a less complicated, more direct level. In the States, even their anti-racist message, so crucial in Britain where a relatively new immigrant black community was still establishing its identity, was barked out to a country where race had been an issue for over 150 years and the radicalism of Malcolm X and the Black Panthers had already scored a deep mark on US society. The Clash's message was distilled into a basic creed: question authority, involve yourself in the political process, think for yourself. The Clash were what America, schooled in Cagney, Dean and Brando, loved most: good-looking, cool, moody rebels.

The Clash excelled at this role. Maybe the hours they'd spent watching movies like *Viva Zapata!* and *A Bullet for the General* were paying off. In his celebrated book *Bandits*, the cultural historian Eric Hobsbawm identifies the notion of 'social banditry'. The idea is that there is a certain kind of bandit, beloved of the people, who has a partly selfless agenda. They are robbing the rich to serve the poor, or they are fighting and stealing to advance the cause of the downtrodden masses. Often, they are gentleman-outlaws who've chosen a path of resistance.

This was exactly the image The Clash had. It was the opposite of The Pistols' 'cash from chaos' ethos. John Lydon once likened his group to the gang in *Brighton Rock*. It was a good parallel: Pinkie's friends weren't social bandits, they were mean-spirited thugs, common criminals. With The Clash, their enemies were any figures of authority – governments, record companies, managers – and the people who worshipped them were the fans whose pay-back was low ticket prices, value-for-money records (non-album singles and, later on, low-budget double and triple LPs) and thrilling, no-gimmick rock 'n' roll shows in intimate venues. 'America really loved The Clash,' says Bob Gruen. 'The group really had that attitude of "do unto others as you would others do to you". They kind of gave out goodness to try and get it back. They went out of their way to help people. Other rock groups didn't do that.'

Johnny Green comments: 'The Clash were like badly behaved schoolboys but they were also gentleman. They don't want or need any of the excesses that other rock 'n' roll bands have. They were the opposite of groups like Led Zeppelin. There are never girls crying in the hotel foyer the morning after the gig. At the end of it all, they were a strangely honourable outfit.'

The Clash's banditry wasn't going unnoticed in high places. In 1978, Anthony Davie, author of the Mescaleros biography *Vision of a Homeland*, was a rookie police officer. While serving at New Scotland Yard he saw a very interesting document: a Special Branch file on Joe Strummer. The

Clash, it seems, were deemed a potential threat to public security.

In February and March 1979, filming of *Rude Boy* resumed. Continuity in the finished movie suffered from the group's transition into rockabilly punks: note the haircuts in the scenes where The Clash run down a flight of stairs and Paul steals money from Caroline's handbag. But this was the least of the filmmakers' worries. When the film reached the editing stage, David Mingay dropped the bombshell that the sound for all the live appearances was nowhere near broadcast quality. This meant that The Clash would have to overdub every song, taking cues from footage projected onto a screen. They booked into Air Studios on Oxford Street, with Bill Price as engineer.

The group weren't happy about the audio fuck-up, and made sure everyone knew it. The recreation of live performances smacked of phoniness. It was also very hard work. 'It was a bit of a chore,' recalls Price. 'They wanted a good result but they were pretty arsed off with Mingay.'

Simonon was particularly irritated and frustrated. Reproducing his live bass lines was difficult and uninspiring. It didn't help that there was still no clear vision of what the film was about. Simonon snapped. 'I don't quite know why,' says Price, 'but Paul actually ended up having a fight with David. It was a physical confrontation.'

'There was as much money spent on the overdubbing as on the filming,' reveals Jack Hazan. 'Plus the fact that the band didn't turn up till five o'clock in the afternoon when they were booked in for the morning. It was a costly exercise.'

'We got very good performances in the end,' says Price. 'It was a bit hard getting vocals at two in the afternoon while stuck in front of a TV screen. We were trying to get Joe Strummer to sound the same as he would have done in Victoria Park. It was difficult for Joe to psych himself up. It was tough getting the roughness and the animation of the performance.'

Amid the work on *Rude Boy*, CBS informed the group that their contract was up for renewal. Relations between band and label were so strained that Joe wasn't sure that CBS was going to take up the option to continue. The Clash had no manager. Strummer was now communicating with the record company directly. Howard Fraser had a lengthy conversation with Joe about the contract in the tea room at Air. This was directly after Kate Bush, who was working in one of the other studios, had kindly offered to make them a cuppa.

'Joe was very worried,' recalls Howard. 'He was saying, "Is Oberstein going to renew it?" I said, "Of course he is." Joe was like, "Oh, I don't know, we've heard conflicting messages." He was being a bit despondent. Maybe he was trying something out on me. "What if I underplay it? How does someone who knows us react to that?" I just said, "Look, Joe, you can write your own contract. You can go to anybody and tell them what your terms are. Don't you realise The Pistols have imploded? It's up to you guys now."

'But at that time, if you walked into Oberstein's office, he will have Abba playing and be going, "They are going to conquer the world!" Of course they were and everybody could hear it and nobody denied it. Abba were so antithetical to punk you can see why Joe felt that maybe there was a danger of being passed over for something much more bankable. But, at the same time, I don't think that Joe realised quite how powerful The Clash were. He didn't seem to have that confidence.'

The spectre of uncertainty around The Clash was made worse by the fact that, for the first time in their three years together, they no longer had a base. All their gear had been moved out of Rehearsals the previous autumn. With the action against Bernie still to come to court, they also had no ready cash. Caroline had brought in the accounting firm Quinnell's, based at 100 Baker Street, to manage the group's finances. Meanwhile, Johnny Green and the Baker were dispatched on a mission to find a suitable rehearsal space. They tried Nomis in Shepherds Bush, the Black Hole in Tower Bridge and The Who's place at Shepperton. None had the right vibe. They were established music biz haunts. The Clash were used to having their own building, secluded, twenty-four/seven and private. As Johnny Green points out, they didn't want to be sharing a Coke machine with 999 and The Lurkers.

'That was a strange period,' says Johnny. 'They'd just got back from America and, after being elated, they became a little depressed. We were going from pillar to post to find a base. You go to somewhere like America and you suddenly realise how vast a place it is. After it sank in how much they'd achieved it dawned on them how much was left to do. Which was a lot. It had only been a mini-tour. I think they were quite dispirited for a while.'

The news from the outside world didn't help. Following a general election prompted by a parliamentary 'no confidence' vote in James Callaghan's Labour government, on 4 May Britain woke up to a new prime minister. She was a fifty-three-year-old, right-wing Tory gorgon called Margaret Thatcher. On election day, The Clash unleashed 'The Cost of Living' EP headed by 'I Fought the Law' and containing the three other tracks they'd recorded at Wessex in January. Joe wanted the sleeve to feature a photo of Thatcher superimposed on a swastika. Mick told him: 'I'm not having a picture of a politician on one of my records.' Instead, Paul and Joe came up with a garish, reggae-cum-soap-packet design.

'The Cost of Living' reached number twenty-two. The *NME*'s letters page was inundated with missives suggesting that a large portion of The Clash's original fan base would no longer be buying their records.

In April 1979, Johnny Green and Baker finally found a new home for The Clash. It was called Vanilla and its walls would soon be echoing to the songs many know from their masterpiece, *London Calling*.

WORLD SERVICE

'It involved an intoxicating mix of danger, adrenaline, passion, excitement and an incomparable esprit de corps.'

Narration for the BBC's *SAS: Are You Tough Enough?*, 2004

'Jeremy Wolfenden was not conceited about his abilities, but he was realistically arrogant.'
SEBASTIAN FAULKS, *THE FATAL ENGLISHMAN*

In the early 1800s, prisoners awaiting transportation to Britain's colonies were kept in squalid hulks moored in the Thames and, in 1812, work began on a huge jail to house them on the north bank of the river. Millbank Penitentiary was a modern design with six pentagonal wings radiating from a hexagonal central hub. The jail was built on the western outskirts of Regency London, but by the end of the Victorian era, when the building was demolished, it was surrounded by a grid of roads which would become known as Pimlico. One of these was Causton Street.

Causton Street is one of those anonymous thoroughfares that was never residential or industrial. Though the site of the penitentiary became home to the splendid Tate Gallery (now Tate Britain), some of the prison's dark, sinister atmosphere was never erased from the surrounding area. In the early 1900s Causton Street was home to bootmakers, carvers, dairymen and confectioners. Number thirty-six was first home to Haley's Industrial Motors, then the Midland Rubber Company. After the Second World War, it became a taxicab garage, Vauxhall Motors.

When Johnny Green and Baker visited the building in April 1979, it was still in use as a car-repairs garage, but the owner, an Iranian businessman, rented out the upstairs room as a rehearsal space. Johnny and Baker liked the fact there were heavy, gangster-like men around, wearing camel-hair coats and smoking big cigars. It reminded them of the yard in Camden.

'There were loads of Bentleys and Rollers being sprayed out the back,' recalls Johnny. 'It all smelled a bit dodgy to me but we never asked questions. The big room was long and narrow, with skylight windows and a tiny stage. It was blank, empty and slightly seedy.'

Mick: 'We had to walk in through the cars. It was like one of those factories where you go up the stairs and there's a room where the foreman sits. It was great because no one knew we were there. No one came unless they were invited.'

They secured the room on a short let, with the proviso that they alone held the key. Johnny Green had to phone The Clash's accountants to get the money. The group moved their gear in. The rehearsal space went under the name Vanilla (later New Sounds), possibly because of its bare, magnolia-painted walls.

The Clash were thrilled to have a proper base again. The indifferent, secluded location suited their mood. They were beginning to feel like outcasts and punk pariahs. 'After being fawned over in America, there is a sense of being a fish out of water,' says Johnny. 'There is alienation and disorientation. Suddenly it seems like no one wants to know. All the people who used to like The Clash have turned on us. There's no Bernard. Coon's gone, no big bust-up, just not required.'

Incredible though it might seem, the months after returning from America were some of the darkest The Clash had yet to endure. Surviving the wearisome antics of 1978 had sapped their strength. Johnny Green and Robin Banks, two of the closest people to the group at that time, describe a distinct feeling of not so much an impending split as the group half-consciously allowing the whole thing to fall apart. It was like a marriage that had been incredible fun but immensely hard work: letting it go was in many ways the easiest, possibly even the more exciting, option.

Robin remembers the group not talking. This, he argues, wasn't because they weren't friends ('they loved each other, really loved each other, that's the funny thing,' he says) but a function of a more general malaise. 'Johnny and I were go-betweens at this point,' he explains. 'You'd be passing messages between them, placating Joe or Mick, and emphasising the positive. It was like being on a roundabout.'

The reactionary spirit of the English punk scene didn't help. The sense of The Clash's being out of sync with the mood of their fans can be gleaned from a rare TV appearance from this time. In March, they were invited to play on the regional music show *Alright Now*. They performed live versions of 'English Civil War' (released as a single in late February, it would reach number twenty-five), 'Hate and War' and, cut from the final transmission, 'The Israelites'. Den Hegarty from rock 'n' roll revivalists The Darts was the compère. Surviving footage sees the group in good spirits, but it's obvious they've moved on from punk, while their audience hasn't. Most of the crowd – with short, spiky hair, button badges and leathers – could have been beamed straight from *Something Else* a year before. So could their questions.

'Do you think you're the number one punk band in England since The Sex Pistols folded?' asks a peroxided schoolboy punk.

'Yeah, I always thought we were number one,' grins Mick. 'Except when I was depressed.'

'What made you depressed?'

'Not being number one . . .'

Den Hegarty picks up the vibe. 'Would you rather be called a rock 'n' roll band than a punk band or New Wave band?'

'That's it,' says Mick.

While they perform, a sidebar of teen-mag questions is flashed up. Paul lists his 'inspiration' as 'Joan of Arc'. Joe's 'confession' is 'an aluminium leg'. Mick 'greatest influence' is 'third-rate rock bands 68–73', Topper's is 'The Grateful Dead' and 'Barry Auguste' (i.e. Baker). It was an unusual public airing of the group's private humour.

Back at Vanilla, The Clash slowly re-orientated themselves towards the next mission: writing new material. The group initially opted for the old Rehearsals routine – turn up at about 1 p.m., finish around 9 or 10 p.m. Rehearsals took place every day, including weekends. There was a pub on the corner, the White Swan, but the group rarely went there. Towards the end of 1978, Mick had stopped using cocaine. Now the regime was herbal not chemical – cups of sweet tea and endless spliffs, which it was Johnny's job to roll. Rather than stupefying them, the dope, he says, fired them up.

As Mick was invariably late, Paul, Joe and Topper would congregate in the workmen's café around the corner on Vauxhall Bridge Road. They were all vegetarians: egg on toast was the meal of choice. Joe was living a short bus ride away. He and Gaby had moved into Gaby's mum's council flat on Whistler's Walk on the World's End Estate in Chelsea. Paul and Caroline had found a new gaff under the Westway, built on the site of Rillington Place. The dark, noisome Victorian houses had been bulldozed and the street renamed to erase the memory of Christie's killings. Paul relished his new postcode. Topper, meanwhile, was staying with a new girlfriend in Pimlico.

The vibe was almost immediately energetic and productive. The absence of Bernie allowed the group a new freedom: there was none of the hectoring, plotting, obfuscation or dealing from the bottom of the pack to which they were accustomed. The atmosphere was less abrasive and more inclusive. 'There was a high level of communication,' says Green. 'People were talking about their own lives and circumstances. They were sharing – ideas, records, experiences.'

'I think we all came into our own at that time,' adds Mick. 'We'd experienced a lot, had our up and downs, and that colours your music. All those experiences go into the record you make. We were boys before, now we were men. [Laughs.] I think America had a lot to do with that. We realised it was a bigger world – and a more serious world than our little world.'

Johnny Green: 'There was an openness about everything. I can remember Mick playing country songs. Mick loved to warm up by playing Topper's drums. They'd mess around for a bit and swap instruments, which they'd never really done before. I remember Topper playing a disco beat, then Mick joining in and then Paul coming in on bass. Paul was contributing as an equal member at that point.'

Paul: 'I had learned to play by then, so I could actually contribute stuff. That was when everyone starting throwing stuff into the pot. It was a team effort. Mick's sleeping habits meant he was an hour late or whatever, so we'd be playing something I heard on the radio, or off a record I knew. It was doubles at ping-pong but with music as the ball. We were there months and months.'

Joe and Mick would come in with song ideas and lyrics. Paul remembers the music to 'Rudie Can't Fail', 'Lost in the Supermarket', 'Four Horsemen', 'Spanish Bombs' and 'I'm Not Down' coming in structurally ready-made. Stylistically, there were no boundaries. The group experimented with jazz, soul, funk, reggae, rock and R&B. It's inconceivable that they could have achieved this progression without Topper. His extraordinary abilities allowed them to veer off in any direction they chose; sometimes, as with 'Lover's Rock', 'I'm Not Down' and 'Clampdown', a single song could incorporate rock, funk and disco. 'Musically, Topper was the glue that held it all together,' says Paul.

Topper himself comments: 'I liked the fact there were no restraints. I was an OK drummer when I joined The Clash. I was a lightweight, run-of-the-mill drummer. Then I learned how to hit the drums hard, then Mick and Joe discovered they could write lots of different types of music.' Topper, who'd been the group's final recruit, at last felt he was being appreciated, on a personal and musical level. 'Bernie didn't respect me as a musician. He thought drummers were ten a penny. Before *London Calling*, I thought we hardly knew each other as a group. That was the first time we'd all contributed to the songs. We actually got to know each other for the first time.'

Johnny Green says: 'People on the outside thought they were very serious people, because of the political angle, but they weren't. The over-riding mood was frivolity and slightly stoned silliness. They were excited and inspired by what they were doing in that room.'

The camaraderie was intensified by a new ritual: football. Directly across the road was a children's playground belonging to the blocks of tenement flats separating Causton Street from the Tate. There was a small, tarmac football pitch, surrounded with a battered wire fence. Every day the group would work for a couple of hours then cross the road for a kick around. They were joined by their mates: Robin, Kris Needs, Terry McQuade, Barry Myers, Ray Gange.

Unlikely as it may seem, it may have been something as simple as kicking a ball around every day that raised The Clash into a creative, positive mind-frame. There were echoes of Bob Marley and the Wailers knocking a ball about on Hope Road: a cool, JA thing to do. It also soaked up their aggression: nothing that came out of Vanilla would be angry in the manner of their earlier punk material.

Johnny Green saw the group's skills on the pitch as reflections of their personalities, as he interpreted them. Paul was hard and enthusiastic and had a reputation for 'going in with no fear for his own safety'. Joe was 'well meaning and tried hard but wasn't very good'. Mick was 'a fine player' but they used to laugh at his flashy style. Topper was nimble and skilled, as was Baker. And Johnny? 'I was never very good,' he admits. 'I was like Paul only more malicious. I was a dirty player.'

'My job was to kick people in the shins,' says Paul. 'Johnny just got in the way.'

Throughout May and June the new material came together. Topper can vividly remember Mick excitedly turning up one afternoon with the distinctive, strident Em/Fmaj9 riff for 'London Calling'. Many songs grew organically. Johnny recalls Mick and Joe constantly to and fro-ing across the room, showing each other chord shapes on their guitars and guiding Paul and Topper. There was a lot of ad-libbing on Joe's part and the words were continuously revised. It wasn't an overly verbal process. As Johnny says, 'With those boys, it was all in the eyes.'

The group wanted to tape the new material, and, according to Johnny Green, asked The Who's soundman, Bob Pridden, whom they knew from Shepperton, to help them out, lending them a couple of mics and a Teac tape machine (Pridden, interviewed in 2005, has no recollection of this). Joe talked about recording the whole album at Vanilla. He believed they could do it all themselves, without the record company's help. 'He was desperate to capture the contagion and excitement of that room,' reveals Johnny Green.

'We've got some crazy ideas,' Joe told *NME*'s Charles Shaar Murray. 'Suppose a group come along and decided to make a sixteen-track LP on two Teacs, which dramatically diminishes the cost factor called "studio costs". [That way] you can get a fucking LP for two or three quid. [In 1979, full-price LPs retailed for £5 or £6.] The majors don't like doing that sort of thing because it sets unhealthy precedents.' Mick and Paul, however, now contend that there was never any real plan to make *London Calling* at Causton Street. 'That was all bluff for the record company,' says Mick.

In early summer, CBS confirmed they were picking up the option on the contract. Some guys flew over from Epic to listen to the new material. They were challenged to a game of soccer in the kids' playground across the road. 'They left the pitch rather creased,' recalls Paul. 'And I don't mean their clothes.' The plan was to release the album for the UK pre-Christmas market. Meanwhile, Epic in America wanted a substantial US tour in September and October to capitalise on the success of the February trip. (A proposed June tour of the States was abandoned because of their continuing legal dispute with Bernie.)

The most pressing question was: who would produce the album? CBS wanted another established name. The Clash didn't but were in a weak bargaining position when it came to making demands. They were still at least £50,000 in debt to the label. The losses incurred from touring and the cost of making *Give 'Em Enough Rope* had yet to be recouped. Initially, it had been assumed that Sandy Pearlman would produce the next album. Mick had told *Zig-zag* as much in November 1978 but discussions were put on ice when Sandy's father died. Since then, events had moved rapidly. The new material was loose, fluid and rootsy – lots of R&B, ska and funk. This made the rock-orientated Pearlman an entirely inappropriate choice.

While Bernie was still around, he'd suggested Guy Stevens as a possible producer for their next record. Guy's last encounter with the group, cutting the Polydor demos, hadn't been a success, of course. But at that time, The Clash had little studio experience. Now they believed they could harness Guy's antic, unpredictable voltage for their own ends. 'It seemed to us like Guy's last big chance,' explains Mick. 'We thought he was brilliant. I always think there was an unconscious bond between Guy and our band.'

Joe went off in search of Stevens and found him in a pub off Oxford Street. He wasn't a pretty sight. The three years since he'd last worked with The Clash had seen him sink further into dereliction. He was dishevelled and had huge flakes of dandruff in his receding ginger hair. Yet he still burned with a manic intensity, regaling anyone who'd listen with tales about The Who, Free, his stretch in Wormwood Scrubs, Mott, Steve Winwood, Jerry Lee Lewis.

'I found a row of blokes sitting slumped over the bar staring in their beer,' Joe told Charles Shaar Murray in 1979 (the interview is reproduced in *Shots From The Hip*, Murray's superlative collection of seventies and eighties music writing). 'I spotted him because of his woolly hat. I went up to him and tapped him on the shoulder, he looked round and it was like son-finding-father in one of those corny films.'

Charlie's interview with Stevens was the last serious piece about the producer before he died two years later. On working with The Clash, Guy spluttered, 'That electricity, that manic intensity . . . It's not just "another session": I hate people with that attitude. It's electricity. It's *got to be*. It may be hard for a company like CBS to accept a concept like this, but I could quite well *die* while making a record. *It's that important.* That's why, if it came to it, I could produce anybody.'

CBS strongly resisted the idea of Guy – 'They hate his guts!' screamed Joe – but the group triumphed. Johnny Green was dispatched to deliver him a cassette of the new material. He was also told to buy a small tape recorder as Guy didn't own one. Purchase made, Johnny ended up getting drunk and leaving both tape player and cassette on the tube. He made his stop at Hampstead, they didn't.

'That was the last I saw of them,' he recalls. 'I was in a panic. I'd left the demos for The Clash's new album travelling up and down the Northern Line. I thought, "What are they gonna say?" I got really bollocked, but that was all. It was only a cassette copy. What amateurish behaviour. From the record producer to the road manager, what a fucking shambles!'

(After twenty-five years gathering dust, 'The Vanilla Tapes' were finally discovered by Mick Jones during a house-move in early 2004. They include several unreleased songs, including 'Heart and Mind', 'Where You Gonna Go (Soweto)', a bastardised version of Don Gibson's 'Oh Lonesome Me' and the instrumental 'Walking the Slidewalk'. Mick and Paul edited the thirty-six surviving tracks down to twenty-one for a bonus disc on the twenty-fifth anniversary reissue of *London Calling*.)

To try out the new stuff, the band played two 'secret' shows at the Notre Dame Hall off Leicester Square on 5 and 6 July. The gigs saw the first live airings of 'I'm Not Down', 'Death or Glory', 'London Calling', 'Rudie Can't Fail' and 'Hateful'. Joe's father, Ronald, was in attendance, the beginning of a renewed, delicately reconstructed relationship between dad and son. It was something altogether more difficult than Joe's mythic, pseudo-paternal trip with Guy. 'My father became really proud of me when The Clash started coming through,' Joe told Jon Savage. 'But it's hard to make up for years and years of feeling estranged from your parents. That wasn't necessarily his fault. When you're young, the last thing you do is see the world from your father's point of view.'

Also in the audience that night was Jock Scot, a pal from The Blockheads camp. An affable Scottish raconteur, Jock was partial to dapper pinstripe suits and magnificent quiffs. He'd moved down to London from Edinburgh the previous year to seek out Kosmo Vinyl, whom he'd met on a Blockheads tour. 'When I heard that set I went, "Well, that's it, the Americans are going to go fucking beserk for this!" It was like The Beatles or something. Not that it *sounded* like The Beatles but their effect, it was just incredible. The songs were so good.'

After The Clash played a Rock Against Racism benefit at the Rainbow – it was to raise money for reggae band Misty in Roots who were attacked and had their gear smashed up by racists in Southall – Johnny and Baker moved The Clash's equipment into Wessex Studios. It was a hot summer's day. The group were courting new management. Ian Dury and the Blockheads' mentors, Blackhill Enterprises, were in the frame. Things were looking good.

It's August 2003 and The Clash's former tour DJ Barry 'Scratchy' Myers and I are wandering around Wessex Studios. The facility is in the process of being broken up and moved to another location. The building is destined to house some fancy flats. It's an odd feeling being in this historic place. Little has changed here since 1979, and certainly not the threadbare carpets. Barry is telling me how one day he saw Guy Stevens build a huge tower of plastic chairs in the middle of the room and then kick them over. This was while the group were recording a song. The plastic chairs are still here.

The studio is in the former church hall of St Augustine's on Highbury New Park, a wide, tree-lined thoroughfare five minutes' walk from Arsenal's ground in north London. The main room is large, with a high, vaulted ceiling and overlooked by a glass-fronted control room. A flight of steps takes you up to a balcony floor where there is an office, kitchen and chill-out space. From there, a spiral staircase leads to an attic room.

Johnny Green remembers the first day of recording. 'Guy came in with a carrier bag, clinking bottles. He sat down and I asked him what was in the bag. He said, "Tequila." I took a look in the bag and he launched at me. "Don't ever touch my stuff!" He had the viciousness of an addict. He was frothing with energy. The band talked about his legend, what he'd done in the past, and here he was doing it! The group were a bit wary of him to begin with. Guy didn't know when to stop and they encouraged that loss of control.'

The group warmed up with a few covers. One was a piece from Dylan's *Pat Garrett and Billy the Kid*, another was Vince Taylor and his Playboys' 'Brand New Cadillac', one of Paul's favourite play-along-tos. Though he'd spent his youth in the States, Taylor was London-born and had moved back to Britain in 1958 to launch his pop career. He was one of the first outrageous creations of that era. 'Vince Taylor was the beginning of British rock 'n' roll', declared Joe of the man who helped to inspire Bowie's Ziggy Stardust character. 'Before him there was nothing. He was a miracle.' It seemed somehow appropriate that The Clash were short-circuiting to the birth of Britain's post-war youth explosion.

After they'd run through the song, Guy screamed from the control booth, 'That's it! It's a take!' The group explained that the song was just a rehearsal. Guy was insistent. 'Take!' Topper pointed out that the tempo sped up. Guy hit back, 'All rock 'n' roll speeds up!'

'That was the start of it,' recalls Topper. 'From then on the atmosphere was just electric.'

In 2004, Kosmo Vinyl discovered eighty-four minutes of hand-held footage the group had filmed of Guy during the sessions. The highlights are included on the *London Calling* anniversary package. Nothing you've read about Guy will quite prepare you for actually seeing Stevens in action. At one point, he bunny-hops madly across the studio floor and barks into Mick's face while he's playing a solo: a startled Jones reels back. He places a ladder on top of the piano and proceeds to scale the wall. He repeatedly smashes a plastic chair.

'*London Calling* was a joy to do because Guy Stevens was a lunatic,' says Simonon. 'I had more control over my instrument by then, and he was less concerned about everything being technically perfect. It didn't matter if I made a mistake.'

Johnny Green: 'They began zooming through stuff at an alarming rate. I remember one time Guy got hold of an aluminium ladder and he was swinging it around while the group were playing. Mick had to duck out of the way. Normally, Paul would have said, "Fuck off, you cunt!" but he didn't.'

Paul: 'You'd be thinking, "Should we stop playing?" Or there'd be a lot of laughing going on, especially when a load of chairs fell on his head. He'd be throwing himself around the room, or even throwing Bill around, which was quite an anarchic approach. The contrast to Sandy Pearlman was unbelievable. Instead of a scientist in a white coat you had a complete genius-maniac.'

'Guy Stevens was an old pal of mine,' says Bill Price. 'I was a little aghast when I realised he was going to be involved in the record. He was a very special type of producer, certainly not like you'd know today. He represented a style of production where you'd leave the music up to the band and the sound up to the engineer. His idea was to create the right atmosphere and emotion in the studio when the performances took place. The idea was that the highly excited atmosphere would produce highly excitable music.'

Bill describes the way the record was made. First, the group would play a song live together, with Guy in the room yelling encouragement and smashing furniture. This provided the takes from which they'd choose the basic drum and rhythm guitar tracks. These would then be 'repaired' if there were any mistakes. Joe 'wasn't very good at mending his parts', which meant Mick would often put down extra rhythm guitar. Then Paul dubbed on the bass, and Mick added the web of guitar overdubs. Percussion, acoustic guitar, piano, horns, sax and vocals were put on last.

The complexity of the twenty-four-track recordings is underlined by the tape box Bill shows me for 'London Calling'. There are two bass tracks (one Paul's, the other for any repairs); two backwards guitars; a lead guitar solo; two tracks of backing vocals each for Joe, Mick and Paul; several tracks for Topper's drums; a couple of rhythm guitars tracks; percussion; and Joe's lead vocal. There's also a track with a sound effect of a seagull's cry, which was mingled with the backwards guitars in the instrumental. 'Mick liked to add subtle ideas, little rude things,' laughs Price. 'On one song there's the sound of someone having sex.'

'We used to do mad stuff like tearing the velcro slowly off the studio chairs and recording it,' recalls Mick. 'We'd always pop in the toilets to do an overdub, because of the echoes. We used to bang on the pipes.'

Guy's eccentric behaviour has passed into rock lore. Every day, on the way to the studio, he insisted his cabbie drop him off at Arsenal's ground. He was as passionate about Arsenal as he was about music and he'd struck a deal with the club where he was allowed to walk around the pitch. He would gaze up at the stands from the centre circle with tears in his eyes. One day, Guy arrived at Wessex with a bloke everyone assumed was a friend. Stevens begged him to stay for the whole session. Only later, when he left demanding £67 in cash, did the group twig he was a taxi driver. (The figure comes from Johnny Green; it should be translated as 'a lot'.) Then there were the hour-long, late-night transatlantic calls to Ian Hunter in the States, pleading for reassurance.

'It was the complete opposite of *Give 'Em Enough Rope*,' recalls Johnny. 'It was all about energy levels. What enthusiasm is coming off here! You get the feeling Guy is racing through the whole thing. The group seems quite content to do that, which I remember being surprised about.'

Guy's passion had the desired effect. He created an electric, unpredictable, exciting atmosphere that resulted in edgy, spirited performances. Joe and Mick were inspired to write more material. Guy had lent Strummer Patricia Bosworth's biography of troubled Hollywood rebel Montgomery Clift, which provided the inspiration for 'The Right Profile'. 'Spanish Bombs' had a complex lyric relating to the Basque Separatists' bombing campaign of Spanish holiday resorts and the Spanish Civil War. It made reference to Federico Garcia Lorca's murder by Fascists in 1936, IRA bombings at home and the recent grounding of all DC-10 jet airliners. (The lyric has strong shades of Lorca's death-poem, 'Farewell': 'Please leave the window open'.)

Echoing their cover of 'Police and Thieves' in 1977, the group jammed a Clashed-up version of Danny Ray's contemporary reggae hit, 'Revolution Rock'. They also sped up The Rulers' 'Wrong 'Em Boyo' into a boisterous ska-punk sprint, with a corny horn line pinched from Frankie Ford's late 1950s hit, 'Sea Cruise'.

Mick and Joe weren't the only ones who were fired up by Guy. Paul had been toying with a tough, reggae bass groove at Vanilla. One day he arrived at Wessex with a lyric transposing the story of Ivan, the anti-hero of *The Harder They Come*, to his native south London. The words had been written at his new flat in Oxford Gardens in Ladbroke Grove – just doors away from where he'd lived as a kid. Joe and Mick persuaded him to sing the song himself. It was called 'Guns of Brixton'. 'The mystery of writing songs had become a bit clearer,' says Paul. 'I penned my first tune, so that was a big moment for me. The other thing I realised was songwriters got all the money. You didn't get paid for designing record sleeves and clothes.'

Simonon was immensely proud of his first Clash composition. 'Paul was so keen to get the bass line of "Guns of Brixton" right he actually marked the notes on the frets of his bass,' recalls Bill Price. 'While we were working on other songs, he spent the entire time in the studio miming the bass line until it was perfect. Paul was a very easy-going, agreeable chap. Both Mick and Joe were very fond of him, and were always keen to consider his feelings and views. He wasn't instrumental in causing any problems, that's for sure. Only if Mick decided to pick at one of the bass parts or something.'

The massive energy rush of the first two or three weeks' recording couldn't possibly be sustained. After the majority of the backing tracks were laid down, Guy's attendance became more sporadic. He would sometimes go missing for days at a time. When he did turn up, his Tequila-powered, blow-torch energy would peter out after a few hours, then he'd pass out. 'Nobody said he'd become a liability but that was what happened,' states Johnny Green. 'That's not to denigrate his contribution to the record, because Guy set up the whole atmosphere. But suddenly he was showing all the signs of someone who cannot take that much alcohol persistently.'

One incident came to symbolise Stevens's condition. One quiet afternoon while Joe was trying to figure out a piano part, Guy stumbled over and poured a bottle of red wine all over the keyboard. He thought it would improve the sound. Bill Price's blood drained from his face. The piano was a brand-new Bossendorf. In less than ten seconds, Stevens had ruined it. The only way to repair the elegant grand would be to strip it down to its 10,000 component parts and then lovingly rebuild it. (According to Bill, this work took over a year to complete at a cost of £6,500.) CBS were aghast when they heard what happened.

Mick, absorbed in perfecting the finer detail of the record, was, according to some reports, becoming less amused by Guy's antics. The Damned were also working at Wessex that summer. They were using the small overdubbing suite to add the final touches to their *Machine Gun Etiquette* LP. Roger Armstrong, who'd worked on The 101'ers' 'Keys To Your Heart', was the producer. 'Guy used to come into my studio to say hello,' recalls Armstrong. 'He was basically drunk all the time at that point. I never saw him sober. I was there one evening when Mick and Joe had a shouting match about him. Mick was saying, "If Guy keeps on like this, I'm fucking leaving."'

Mick remembers it differently. 'We weren't that bothered about Guy's [destructive] behaviour,' he says. 'That sounds terrible now. But it was just another thing. We didn't mind when, say, Guy used to chuck himself down the stairs. We were like, "Yeah? OK!" He sorted himself out, then we just carried on working.'

Bill Price: 'Once the recording became a bit more technical, Guy lost interest. He couldn't really add anything to it. Mick would be trying to follow a complicated plot where he'd double-track three layers of guitar weaving in and out of each other. Guy running around the studio waving things wasn't going to help.'

Johnny Green: 'There was a natural shift towards Mick being in control. He kind of eased into the role of producer when it came to the more technical stuff. He had a relationship with Bill that worked really well.'

Green adds that, towards the end, the band used to ring Guy and fib that they were all taking a few days off. It was more hassle than it was worth to have him around. No one liked doing it. This was, after all, the man whose picture Mick had on his bedroom wall as a teenager. Roger Armstrong got the impression that it was particularly hard for Joe. His interpretation of Joe's relationship with Guy inverts the singer's cameo of son-finding-father. He sees Stevens's vulnerability and hopelessness, his overwrought passion and sentimentality, as bringing out Joe's own paternal instincts. The child became father to the madman.

'I think Joe saw Guy as someone to look after,' Armstrong says. 'Joe was a very caring man, *morally* very caring, and I know he had a lot of sympathy for Guy. Perhaps the fact Joe was helping Guy out got *Joe* through those sessions. Guy would have been someone to focus on in the middle of all that.'

Joe himself was retreating into his own world, spending candle-lit nights in the corner of the studio in a 'bunker' built from flight cases. Inside were his essentials: a tape recorder, pens, paper, books, spliffs and beer. The studio bunker would become a trademark until the end of his life.

The overdubbing continued. Graham Parker and the Rumours' horn section were drafted in. Baker whistled the intro to 'Jimmy Jazz'. Through the group's connection to Ian Dury, The Clash recruited The Blockheads' organist, Micky Gallagher, who'd cut his teeth with The Animals, Skip Bifferty and Frampton's Camel. During his stint with Skip Bifferty he'd worked with Guy Stevens, whom he hadn't seen in over a decade. What he saw shocked him.

'They'd sent me *Give 'Em Enough Rope* to listen to and I thought, "Fuck me, what's that?"' Micky explains. 'I couldn't see where I'd fit in. The LP had a lot of energy but the recording was awful. Anyway Kosmo Vinyl came in and said The Clash were doing an album and they needed someone to play keyboards. So I went up to Wessex and sat down with Joe and Mick. It was all sounding really good and they wanted to make it more sophisticated, so I was up for that.'

Micky brought over his Hammond B-3 and added keyboards to the tracks. Joe and Mick left him to his own devices. Gallagher could adapt himself to reggae, soul, funk and even found space for subtle, chirping organ on rock tracks like 'Clampdown'. His musicianship was a delight.

When the record was nearing completion, CBS head Maurice Oberstein was invited to the studio to hear the work-in-progress. Roger Armstrong remembers it vividly. 'I came in about lunchtime and there's a fucking big Rolls-Royce the size of a small council house sitting in the car park,' he recalls. 'The car had a female chauffeur with a sort of almost military peaked cap down over her nose. She was kind of staring, spooky stuff, weird shit, it's one o'clock on a Thursday afternoon. So I kind of wandered in and there's Guy Stevens. You know those chairs with the metal legs and plastic seats that are completely indestructible? Well, there's Guy smashing one on the ground and every time he smashes it on the ground it bounces back at him. He's pissed out of his mind, going, "Fuck CBS! Fuck Maurice Oberstein! Fuck The Clash!"

'I sneaked up the stairs and hovered by the door and there are The Clash sitting around the control room. Oberstein is impeccable in his fedora hat, overcoat over the shoulder, arms folded, standing there listening to *London Calling*, and Guy's elsewhere in the building going mental. Absolutely priceless.'

Oberstein loved The Clash but found himself in a difficult position. He was head of a large corporation and enjoyed the power and kudos the position conferred. The group were like troublesome employees. They weren't easy to deal with. He was used to meetings with Abba or The Tourists. Much of what The Clash wrote about questioned the corporate culture that Oberstein embodied. Theirs was a relationship redolent of the MC5's relationship with Warner Brothers or director Haskell Wexler (who made *Medium Cool*) and Paramount. So far as CBS were concerned, they were bottling revolution and selling it for a profit. The Clash were tolerated for the same reason all their seditious antecedents were: they turned rebellion into money. Recognising this made The Clash's behaviour worse. 'They would play [1970s TV revolutionary] Citizen Smith to Oberstein's corporate fat cat,' says Bill Price. 'It was quite humorous on the surface but there was obviously lots of darker to-ing and fro-ing in the background.'

Price witnessed the episode which directly followed the playback for Oberstein – in primitive surround-sound – in the control room. At the time, The Clash were petitioning CBS to release *London Calling* as a double. They had eighteen tracks in the bag. As ever, money was an issue.

'I remember Guy Stevens wouldn't let Oberstein leave the building,' recalls Price. 'He was hanging onto Maurice's coat-tails – literally – and Maurice was trying to escape. Here was Oberstein dragging a grown man out through the studio door. When he thought he'd finally got rid of him, Oberstein realised Guy was lying in front of the limo. He was shouting, "If we don't get this, you're gonna have to kill me!" I think Maurice actually found it quite entertaining.'

In late August the group wrapped up the operation at Wessex. Bill Price was left with Jeremy Green to work on the final mixes. 'That record was Guy's – and Mick's,' says Johnny Green. 'Mick showed real humility not taking half of the credit.' The Clash had to prepare for their second tour of the US. They were going to be away from home for over seven weeks. The itinerary listed twenty-three dates, taking them from California to the East Coast, and from the deepest South up to Canada.

Meanwhile, a serious incident had severely shaken Joe. The facts weren't made public until fifteen years later, when Johnny Green's book was published. A planned gig in Derry with The Undertones was abandoned after Joe was sent a death threat from a small Loyalist paramilitary outfit calling themselves the Red Hand Commando. They'd been active since the mid-1960s and had links to the Ulster Volunteer Force. They said they'd murder Strummer if he stepped on Irish soil. The violent world of Ulster, which The Clash had used as a photo opportunity two years earlier, was suddenly very real. The relevant branch of the police was alerted to the death threat and The Clash were strongly advised to pull the show.

'The gig was in a very Nationalist area,' recalls Undertones bass-player Michael Bradley. 'It was very unlikely that anyone was ever gonna try and do something. But I'm sure if I'd got that letter, I'd prefer not to play. We had to concoct a story that we couldn't get insurance for it. It was ironic that they'd had those photos taken in Belfast.'

There is one last detail about the *London Calling* sessions that ought to be mentioned. One afternoon, Roger Armstrong arrived at Wessex and noticed a green Renault 5 parked outside with the number plate CLA5H. Bernie had dropped by to see his old charges. In the chaotic, mysterious world of The Clash, it's quite possible Rhodes was very briefly reinstated. A couple of interviewees for this book have suggested this is the case. But no one in the Clash seems to remember whether it actually happened or not.

Kosmo Vinyl had first encountered The Clash in spring 1977. He had a makeshift record stall on Portobello Road. Mick and Joe were passing and asked him not to sell 'Remote Control'. 'We ain't into it,' they told him. Kosmo removed it from his pile of 45s.

Vinyl was from the East End. He had an overload of energy and a loud, rasping, cockney voice. His gift of the gab secured him a job in legendary PR man Keith Altham's office. Soon he was working at Stiff Records and representing Ian Dury and the Blockheads. Kosmo was more than a PR: he was an ideas person, music aficionado and weather vane of taste. He fell for The Clash and, by 1979, found himself increasingly in their orbit. A regular visitor at Wessex, he enjoyed the impish wind-ups and rough 'n' tumble. 'The group could get a bit out of hand when Kosmo turned up,' recalls Bill Price. 'I might go upstairs to the lounge to have a ten-minute break only to find someone gaffer-taped to the pool table or something of that nature. I never minded that too much, because it wasn't me who was gaffer-taped to the pool table.'

Through Kosmo, The Clash were put in touch with Blackhill Enterprises, which was run by Peter Jenner and Andrew King, key figures in the late 1960s counter-culture. They'd put on the free gig in Hyde Park that Mick attended in 1968, and managed Pink Floyd in the Syd Barrett years. Once again, The Clash found themselves looking towards the survivors of the 1960s underground to steer them. Andrew King remembers first being approached for his help in 1978, while Bernie was still at the helm: 'I had a meeting with Bernie Rhodes which just left me speechless with horror. I thought, "I'm never going to be able to do business with this guy", and I'm sure Bernie thought exactly the same about me.'

The Clash needed Blackhill's help to organise the American tour in September and October. With their involvement, Kosmo came onboard, too. It was the beginning of a new phase in the group's life cycle. Blackhill were the closest The Clash ever came to having conventional management.

'If you see the relationship of The Clash as based on the to-ing and fro-ing between Joe and Mick, then it was Mick's turn to choose a manager,' comments King. 'We were seen as being a safe pair of hands. They saw us as being typical music biz types, not like Bernie or Caroline. Perhaps they thought we were able to take care of the business end a bit better. Ironically, people generally came to us because we were unconventional in our approach. But I think they thought we were straight ahead.'

Blackhill's first meetings with The Clash gave them an immediate sense of the enormous, thankless, possibly suicidal mission they were signing up for. 'It's hard to explain how difficult it is to organise a tour like that with any band, let alone The Clash who changed their minds five times every ten minutes,' groans King. 'Getting The Clash on the road was like wrestling with elephants. I could imagine that we would annoy Johnny Green because compared with what they had before we were quite professional. We had checklists and maps and itineraries. We were very concerned about the money, too. The business side. There was a hell of a lot to do.'

Peter Jenner says: 'The Clash were this strange mix of personalities. Mick was always an enthusiastic smoker, but prone to be moody. Paul was very quiet. Topper I found a delight. Strummer . . . I never got hold of what made Joe tick. He had a dialectic, a Zeitgeist, a worldview which I could never work out. As time went on, I don't think he could either. Joe looked confident, as if he knew all the answers, when I don't know if he actually did. He had very strong views that might change the next day, which I found hard to cope with. He was the commissar who, with Kosmo, would lay down the political line. So it was, "Why can't we do *Top of the Pops*?" "Because we never did." Their line was: "We won't do stadiums, we won't do arenas, we'll only do small gigs."'

The Clash's impoverished state wasn't imagined or for effect. The lawsuit with Bernie had been resolved but this hadn't helped matters. According to Andrew King, in the late summer of 1979 the group were still £50,000 in debt. He and Peter Jenner were horrified when they examined the CBS record contract. King says the deal was for thirteen albums, not five, as the group believed. That wasn't all. 'The points were unbelievable – in continental Europe they were getting a 4 per cent royalty,' he explains. 'Back then 12 per cent would have been good.'

'Columbia had this clause that they could call for an extra album at any time during any year,' explains Peter Jenner. 'They'd signed for five years so they thought, "We've done three albums, only another two to go!" But there were all these "extra" albums. The contract was stretching on for ever and ever.'

The Clash's financial problems didn't seem to overly concern the group members. This was possibly because they'd always been in debt and considered it quite normal. Existing hand-to-mouth also avoided the moral complications of being a moneyed punk act. There was always just enough cash around to live off. Joe and Paul seemed, if not content, then philosophical about existing on £100 a week. So, actually, did Mick. Despite his penchant for a flashy rock 'n' roll lifestyle, Jones was never a breadhead. Tony James explains: 'All the groups we used to admire, like The New York Dolls, were cult-ish bands which never made any money. The last reason we got into rock 'n' roll was to get rich.'

Andrew King: 'The Clash would always be asking, "Where's all the money going?" But then they'd make decisions which would lose them thousands in potential income.'

Peter Jenner: 'The one thing that really confused me was the Great Cost of Gigs Phenomenon. We were only allowed to charge £3 a ticket or something, but we had to have two support acts. We also had to stay in posh hotels. In America, they had to have suites. On the road we had to take all sorts of unnecessary crap in the way of lighting. All of which meant they lost loads of money. So we had to go to Columbia to get tour support, which meant they were always in hock to Columbia. I said, "Hey, can't we do something about this?" There was always a conflict between them being a rock band and being a revolutionary outfit.'

On Tuesday, 4 September, The Clash, their girlfriends and crew flew out to California where the tour would begin. The entourage included Johnny, Kosmo, Baker, Barry Myers, Jenner and King, lighting ace Warren Steadman, Gaby, Paul's new girlfriend Debbie (he'd split from Caroline earlier in the summer) and Topper's latest squeeze. Paul had purchased a couple of old-fashioned gentlemen's travelling trunks from Camden market. They had special drawers for socks and booze. Also along for the ride was *NME* cartoonist Ray Lowry. Johnny had petitioned to get him onboard. He sold the idea to Joe as The Clash having their own 'war artist', a punk rock R. Caton Woodville. Ray, who died in October 2008, was initially asked to pay his own way, but eventually Blackhill managed to include him in the budget.

The Clash were buzzing. They landed to glorious sunshine in San Francisco, where their West Coast buddies met them at the airport. One of them was a Mexican guy called Rudi Fernandez. He was working for the organisers of the Monterey Tribal Stomp, the first date of the tour. 'I always loved English music, The Beatles and The Stones,' says Rudi. 'I met The Clash and they were guys just like us. I used to drive them around. They smoked pot, went to the movies, gave a taxi-driver a tip. They had the music, great politics, everything. They loved America. Every place they played was like a surprise to them. They got to visit all the places they'd heard about.'

Greil Marcus once talked about The Band, Sly Stone, Randy Newman and Elvis as artists 'who tend to see themselves as symbolic Americans'. The Clash arrived in the US as symbolic Englishmen. They were polite and gentlemanly, but with an unforgiving sense of humour and wonderful sense of the ridiculous. Like all true Englishmen abroad, they dressed for the part. Their homburg hats, white shirts and dark suits were straight out of *The Godfather* but they were also totems of the England that had spawned them. There were echoes of *The Lavender Hill Mob*, *Brighton Rock* and *Performance* in their gangster chic. It was as if wartime Hollywood's influence had been absorbed, filtered through the London post-war experience, given a punk-rock/rude boy twist, and blasted back to the US.

This binding together of mythic America and down-home Ladbroke Grove solved many of their contradictions. 'I think they felt a lot more at ease in America,' says Johnny Green. 'They were a band on the loose, not just these English punk rockers. There was no identity crisis out there. People liked them for what they were. They were a cool-looking rock 'n' roll band who loved black music, refusing to play the game.'

The Monterey Tribal Stomp festival on 8 September was an attempt to revive the famous outdoor gathering of twelve years earlier. They'd been invited to play there by their San Francisco comrade Mo Armstrong. Each band member had his own log cabin at the Mission Ranch hotel. Johnny recalls visiting Mick. The others were ensconced with their girls and he was alone in a darkened room, listening to music and playing a guitar. 'We had a nice long chat, he was very pleasant company,' recalls Johnny. 'But he was someone who needed space to compose himself. Often, we'd all book into a hotel and it was like, "Where's Mick?" Usually he was up in his room, with music playing or he'd be working on a song. You know Pennie's picture where Mick's sitting alone at a table? He was like that sometimes. You kept your distance.'

Mick had employed Rory Johnson, who'd looked after The Sex Pistols on their US tour in January 1978, as his 'own official tour manager'. This appointment was apparently made without the agreement of the rest of the group.

The Monterey show was electric, with Jamaican star Earl Zero and Paul's old reggae idols The Mighty Diamonds supporting. The Clash played in broad daylight, something to which they weren't accustomed. As they launched into the opening 'I'm So Bored With the USA', Strummer grabbed his arm and wheeled back into Topper's drum kit as if he'd been machine-gunned. 'Sometimes Joe lost it on stage like a true performer,' says Green. 'I'm not saying he was out of control, he knew what he was doing, but he would go to another level. It was one of those adrenalising moments. The hairs on your neck stood up. The hippy audience was jolted into life. Joe had those pictures of him doing that hung in his house.'

The tour re-started four days later in Saint Paul, Minneapolis. The dates went under the banner of The Clash Take the Fifth. The promotional material bristled with anti-American sentiment. The image on the Fifth Column-designed tour T-shirt was Uncle Sam as a skull and crossbones: death masquerading in a stars-and-bars top hat. 'I'm So Bored With the

USA' inaugurated every show. Mick's mum, Renee, was in Minneapolis. Johnny remembers her looking very glamorous and a little like Elizabeth Taylor. Saint Paul was the start of a punishing twenty-three-date trek that would trellis across the US over the next five weeks. The odyssey is covered extensively in Pennie Smith's peerless *The Clash: Before and After*. She was covering the tour for the *NME* and captures in intimate, moody black-and-white photographs the group's elation, fatigue, excitement, desperation, loneliness, schoolboy antics and camaraderie as they journey through North America. She legendarily described the experience as 'going on a commando raid with the Bash Street Kids'.

'In the rock world, there are romanticists and classicists, and The Clash were romanticists,' she explains. 'The way they dressed, the way they talked. That whole mythology they built up around them. I remember one place where Joe was telling the bus driver to pull away because Kosmo was being pursued by every redneck under the sun. A lot of it was very funny, they enjoyed stitching themselves up to make things difficult.'

Ray Lowry: 'Mick had this red suit on that tour and he went into a diner and this girl said "Hey, it's Elvis!" Most of the Americans were gobstruck. I was touched by the way they just loved them. You might think they'd be hostile to this strange band. I was expecting the worst but it was marvellous. Everyone was dead friendly. Maybe it was their touch, how they could get on with everybody. In diners it would be guys or girls serving them, and they'd think The Clash were great.'

Pennie Smith: 'The Clash loved to find themselves in the wrong end of town. I remember Mick and I going to a radio show in the middle of America, and Mick had broken his window-winder. We stopped at this petrol station and there were these blokes, we knew it was trouble. The cab driver had vanished and Mick was pretending we had a window by resting his arm on thin air. These blokes were getting nearer and nearer and I thought, "We're dead, no doubt about it." They got to the cab door, then the driver suddenly re-appeared, reached into the car and pulled out a gun. He said to these guys, "I'm armed!" We were just these two honkies from West London and we didn't really need this. It was full-on all the time.'

Mick: 'The tour bus had previously belonged to Dolly Parton. We were pulled over by the police one day, and the driver told them Dolly was asleep in the back. They waved us on.'

As with the previous tour, The Clash had spent an enormous amount of time and effort digging out some original R&B heritage to open their shows for them. On the bill was their old friend Bo Diddley. Other dates had Stax legends Sam & Dave and voodoo blues man Screamin' Jay Hawkins. The latter would emerge from a coffin to perform 'You Put a Spell on Me'. Johnny says: 'I never saw a support act go down so badly.'

'That tour was politically charged because of Bo Diddley,' explains Pennie Smith. 'The local promoters, despite the belief they were politically correct, really weren't keen on The Clash having him around. "You're an important band, why do you need Bo Diddley?" . . . The crowds were knowledgeable, they knew why the group were putting those guys on. That whole political side of The Clash – people looked to them as an encyclopaedia. They did a lot of swotting up on everyone's behalf. America had the sense to realise that. Someone obviously did a hell of a lot of work to hire these guys and get them out on the road.'

At Boston, Micky Gallagher joined the tour. The budget was stretched to accommodate his wife and two kids. The bus was becoming like a huge, travelling family. Yet already, just a week into the tour, Gallagher, who saw himself in the Bill Preston role, felt things were falling apart.

'I was talking to the crew before the band arrived,' he says. 'Then The Clash came in and sat down in different parts of the room with their girl-friends. I didn't find out until years later that at that point they weren't talking, and one of the reasons for me being on the road was as a catalyst, as a fifth member. They had to be on their best behaviour otherwise they may not have survived. I found it very strange at the time . . . I couldn't sit down and talk with these guys because they were all in their own little worlds.'

Johnny thought Micky 'was cool. He wasn't phased by anything. The only thing was his clothes – the Ted jackets and shiny collars. It was like, "Paul, will you tell him?" "No, fuck off, *you* tell him."' Some interviewees have described the second US tour as 'The Girlfriends Tour'. Clearly, the presence of the group's womenfolk changed the dynamic within the group. ('I loved Gaby, she was brilliant,' says Ray Lowry. 'Gaby knew about old rock 'n' roll records. Topper's girlfriend was a pain in the arse.') But Johnny Green disputes Micky's reading of the overall situation. He points out that Gallagher was accustomed to The Blockheads' musical matey-ness. They liked jamming. The Clash, he argues, never had that: they were cool, difficult, unpredictable and inhabited their own spaces. They were four individuals whom Bernie had forced together to create a bigger idea. Those fraught, combative early days at Rehearsals had defined their fractious but affectionate relationships.

Andrew King comments: 'My impression of The Clash is that they were quiet, private individuals but when they were onstage everything blew up, it really did. The Clash seemed to exist quite independently of them as four individuals.'

Micky concedes as much. 'It was completely different from The Blockheads. We used to have rehearsals to get things right and be happy with that night's gig. The Clash didn't have a fucking clue what they were doing. I did great gigs with The Clash and terrible gigs with The Clash. I remember Santa Monica Boulevard in particular, great-sounding hall, and we played fucking great, spot on, great show. We came off and I said, "Congratulations, lads, that was fantastic", and they were like, "Was it?" They didn't know the difference between a musically great show and a musically terrible show. They did both, but they had no concept of the difference.'

After the show, the group threw a party for The Undertones, who were support on the first dates. 'We were a bit awestruck by The Clash,' says Michael Bradley. 'None of us even drank then, let alone took drugs. They looked impossibly glamorous. Joe was very sweet to us, but we didn't really say much to them.' The group were offered more dates on the tour but instead flew back home to Derry to see their girlfriends. Such were those crazy rock 'n' rollers The Undertones.

The tour hit New York. Susan Blond and the rest of Epic were there to greet them. Paul seized it as an opportunity to go shopping for new clobber. 'The exchange rate was good at the time, about two dollars to the pound,' he says. 'We went to a second-hand store in Greenwich Village and felt like millionaires. We had £100 wages and it was suddenly like £200. You could buy these 1950s American shirts and hack the sleeves off, because they got in the way when you were leaping around on stage. We used to slap our shirts on the floor after the show. They made a huge noise because they were so wet.'

The first night, the band deliberately left Epic's people waiting in the rain outside the stage door. 'Joe was having a bad day,' says Lowry. 'I remember he got really uptight and hurled an ashtray across the dressing room for some reason.'

The second of their two shows at the New York Palladium was famous for Paul smashing his bass. A bootleg reveals him frantically thrashing at the strings during the final encore, 'White Riot'. Pennie Smith caught the moment he demolished his instrument. It has since been voted the Greatest Rock 'n' Roll Photograph of All Time.

'He looked totally pissed off that night,' says Pennie. 'I was cutting down on the amount of onstage stuff I was shooting. When you're in tune with someone, you know their every move. I had every Joe run and Mick jump possible. I was watching Paul and realised his guitar was the wrong way up.

He started coming towards me. I had a wide-angled lens that made him look further away and when I looked up he was right on top of me. I took three shots and ducked.'

The image has shades of a narrative painting. The lighting man evidently gleaned something was happening: Paul is a leggy, angular shape starkly lit by a white, theatrical spotlight. Behind him is chaos: a girl runs onstage, chased by security. Toppled mic stands and disconnected leads litter the stage. The shot echoes The Who's auto-destruction. It's violence at its most unexpectedly elegant. Only The Clash could batter hell out of a Fender Precision and make it look beautiful. Ironically, Paul very rarely trashed his gear. This led Johnny Green to surmise in *A Riot of Our Own* that he was showing off to his girlfriend, a native of New York City.

'When you're on stage you don't think about your girlfriend, you're on the spot,' says Paul. 'He misunderstood that. It was complete frustration. Listen, we were used to playing with the audience right there in front of you. In Eric's or God knows where. At the New York Palladium the audience might just as well have been a mile away. You end up feeling as if you're going through the motions. That sparked me up and really annoyed me; it was out of frustration I did it.'

Paul's actions were so fierce he broke his watch. He gave it to Pennie Smith as a memento. The hands are frozen at the moment his bass hit the deck, 9.50 p.m., like a time-piece recovered from the wreckage of a cataclysmic event.

The tour moved inland and crossed into Canada. The group were filmed for a TV show called *The New Music*. The footage was shot after the gig at the O'Keefe Center, Toronto. It begins with Kosmo, tall and dressed in a white suit, surveying the auditorium and counting the number of wrecked seats. 'Fourteen, fifteen, sixteen . . . great!' he bellows. 'Somewhere in North America there are sixteen rock 'n' roll fans!' He keeps nervously running a comb through his bleached hair, Teddy Boy style. Mick is interviewed in the dressing room. There is no rock 'n' roll excess visible. He is politely sipping beer from a paper cup, and wearing a bright red suit and straw boater. Jones takes his natural stance of seeing punk primarily in terms of a musical revolution. 'All the fifty-two different countries ['states': he's being ironic] we've been to – I'm talking about America and Canada – the one thing they all have in common is they listen to shit music. We're here to alleviate that.'

Joe, in greasy quiff, cornflower-blue cowboy shirt and bootlace tie, is acidic and sneering. Gaby is next to him. He talks at length about the record company ('they don't know we're signed to them'), money ('all of it goes on running the group . . . after that, there's only about five bucks left'), boot-leggers ('good luck to them!'), *Rude Boy* ('it's in the garbage can, we had an argument with the people making it') and the cancelled gig in Derry with The Undertones (he toes the official line: 'we couldn't get the insurance'). At that point, The Undertones burst into the dressing room firing toy machine guns. Joe rants about the apathy among the Canadian middle-class and how people accept the musical status quo. 'Over here, people are used to paying $8, getting half measures and going home satisfied,' Joe spits. 'In England they gave up being satisfied three years ago.'

The following morning an incident occurred which summed up Mick's vacillating moods. Jones came out of the hotel and refused to board the tour bus unless someone brought him some weed. It was explained that they were only a short drive from the US border, where they could score some dope. Mick stood his ground: there was no way he was getting on the bus without a smoke. Everyone else wanted to get moving. Mick sat down in the open cargo bay of the vehicle, dapper in dark Johnson's suit and straw boater, and wouldn't budge. Pennie snapped a picture of him. He didn't move until some fans had set off in a cab, scored some weed, and returned to the hotel an hour or so later.

'Mick was stubborn,' says Johnny Green. 'He wouldn't move. What were the others doing? Rolling their eyes. We're not talking drug addiction or serious withdrawal, so this was pretty extreme behaviour. But the group respected it. No one confronted him. Mick had the same look of determina-tion on his face that had carried The Clash through problem after problem.'

Micky Gallagher thought it 'fucking ridiculous. I used to think, "I would-n't put up with that." But I was a temp, so what could I do? In The Blockheads we would have left him on the side of the road. You're either on or off the bus. It was a bit puerile, childish. But Mick was into things like that, or not moving until he'd had his fried egg sandwich in the morning.'

A few hours later, Pennie photographed The Clash at Niagra Falls, joking around as if nothing had happened.

The group headed south. The cinematic scenery changed to vast expanses of dry nothingness. Mythic America was passing outside the window. Tri-forked cacti, isolated diners, dusty Charlie Starkweather highways. Johnny and Ray Lowry remember Paul and Joe being fascinated with the cowboy artwork on truck-stop walls and menus.

In Atlanta, Epic's tour support had dried up. There was no money to pay the crew. The American roadies went on strike. Peter Jenner and Andrew

King begged the American record company for more funds. Epic were reluctant to provide the cash, though eventually they did. 'Epic had Michael Jackson and some other big acts,' says King. 'They were their priority, we weren't. Their office in New York was a horrible place. Executives used to commit suicide by jumping down the air shaft when their ratings went down. A black man would come in and shine your shoes during meetings.'

Barry Myers recalls: 'There seemed to be several tour managers. Mick had his own one. Maybe he was drifting away a bit at that point. There was a guy called Mark Wissing who didn't last very long. He got worn down very quickly. Eventually we ended up with Bruce Wayne. Cue lots of Batman jokes. When we were stuck in Atlanta, he turned up with the money for us. We were queuing up outside his hotel room waiting for the cash.'

Exhaustion robbed people of their humour. The endless travelling, passionate, ninety-minute shows and lengthy, post-gig meeting-the-fans sessions were taking their toll. Joe was volatile: he found the interrogations from US journalists wearing. He smashed *Creem* writer Dave DiMartino's tape-recorder. 'My abiding memory of that tour was the band members cuddling their girlfriends and Mick being out on a limb,' recalls Johnny. 'People were retreating into their own worlds. The distances we were travelling were immense.' In Atlanta, the group were given vitamin B-12 shots to boost their immune systems. Paul had a box of compilation tapes he'd lovingly created – reggae, dub, rockabilly, ska. These were played constantly to ease the grind of the long drives. Where possible, the group elected to fly.

Touring is dislocating and disorientating. It also throws people together in stressful circumstances. There were growing tensions within the entourage. Johnny didn't think much of Kosmo's barrow-boy approach. For all his lunatic rock 'n' roll antics, Green was a man with a passion for, and deep knowledge of, popular culture. He felt Kosmo didn't have the same reference points. Johnny refers to an incident at the start of the tour when the group rehearsed near Cannery Row: 'Lowry was in the back of the car with Andrew King and Kosmo. He thought the place didn't seem to have any cultural significance for them. It was as though they'd never heard of Steinbeck.'

Lowry: 'We loved that stuff. So did Joe. He was terrific. In Chicago, he actually put his fingers in the bullet-holes where Dillinger was shot. Joe was a marvellous man. But I don't think The Blockheads people were simpatico with that side to The Clash.'

It's possible that King and Vinyl had things on their minds other than sight-seeing. King was highly educated and urbane. Kosmo, however, freely admits his passions at that time were primarily rock 'n' roll, PR and keeping the show on the road. 'I saw my role as representing the viewpoint of the kids on the street,' he says. 'I was there to say, "Look, what would a punk fan in Barnsley think of that?" I was never interested in job titles and never pretended to be doing anything different than that.'

Andrew King agrees. 'Kosmo was where the public and private faces of The Clash met. He was the spokesman. He was very good at building up the band's enthusiasm, and the audience's. He was a PR man but he was also a facilitator. Kosmo was good at moving things along. He was a tremendous asset.'

The Clash Take the Fifth tour reached Texas, where The Sex Pistols' 1978 tour had witnessed the greatest violence. Cowboys and Mexicans had slugged it out in front of the stage. Sid's lips were exploded by a missile from the crowd. Opening for The Clash was their favourite young American country-rocker, Joe Ely. He came from Lubbock, Buddy Holly's birthplace.

'They didn't want to play the normal places,' explains Ely. 'They wanted to play the places they'd heard about on old Marty Robbins records, like Laredo, El Paso or San Antonio. At some of those joints the audience looked at them like a pig looks at a wristwatch. They didn't understand what was going on.'

After the show at Dallas on 6 October, the group had a few days off. Joe Ely invited them to play a gig at his local club, the Rox, in Lubbock. 'Any kind of serious outfit would have said "Fuck off!"' laughs Johnny Green. 'But not The Clash. Around them are American tour managers, William Morris booking agency figures and Blackhill saying, "Not a good idea." But they won't be talked out of it. We play the club, a shady place with a tiny stage, with no promotion and the minimum of equipment and they turn in a fantastic, dynamic performance.'

Afterwards, the group jumped into a Winnebago and paid a midnight call to Buddy Holly's grave in the town's municipal cemetery. The Clash set up a camp with lighted candles, ghetto blasters, beer bottles and acoustic guitars. The visit ended in a drunken jig in honour of Lubbock's unassuming prince of rock 'n' roll. They each placed a plectrum on Holly's gravestone and started back to Joe Ely's ranch out in the cottonfields.

During the drive back to Ely's, Topper began to turn blue. He was overdosing. Someone had given him some heroin. They stopped and walked him up and down a dirt track in the middle of nowhere, trying to keep him awake, trying to keep him alive. It was a surreal, shocking experience.

Johnny Green recalls: 'I thought, "We're this punk rock band from London, how do we choose to be in this position? How do we come to be in the middle of a field in Texas with the possibility of having no drummer?"'

At the time, according to Green, Topper was using heroin 'as and when', and didn't have a habit. But his predilection for other hard drugs, particularly cocaine, was becoming an issue. With a group as big as The Clash, who were constantly crossing international borders and were a target for police stop-and-checks, carrying drugs presented a problem. So did the hassle of constantly having to score. Andrew King explains that, in these sorts of circumstances, the task is usually outsourced to a third party. The cost is then lost among 'expenses' in the tour accounts.

Topper was the one most prone to conventional on-the-road excess. It was, however, as King points out, 'hardly on the scale of your legendary rock 'n' roll behaviour. He'd occasionally smash up a hotel room, which he paid for out of his T-shirt money.' Even so, there were signs that the drummer was losing control. On several occasions on that tour he transgressed some extremely worrying boundaries. For 'a joke', he defaced Barry Myers's record box with swastikas. Barry was upset: Topper was his mate. 'It wasn't in the spirit of The Clash,' says Myers. 'It was a prank that got out of hand.' During a live post-show interview on Boston's WBCN radio station – an angry Mick tells one caller, 'Fuck off, you cunt!' – Headon drunkenly hollers, 'Why are you gay?' over the chorus of The Village People's 'YMCA'.

If it was Sid Vicious, no one would have batted an eyelid, but this was The Clash. Joe and Mick dressed down Topper over his behaviour, but it was getting harder to get through to him. When he was sober, he was apologetic, loveable and remorseful.

There were a few days off, then The Clash returned to the West Coast. The surf-punk scene there was nihilistic and violent. In LA, The Clash had a flaming row with promoter Bill Graham when the latter refused to let a local punk group open for them. 'You should have seen Mick, he was magnificent,' says King. 'Joe was far less vocal in those situations.'

While the band flew, Johnny Green, Ray Lowry and a few others had taken the bus west from Lubbock to San Diego. Ray worked on his infamously acerbic, Elvis-obsessed cartoons. Some nights, he'd even got his oils out. The results amount to possibly the finest collection of art relating to a rock 'n' roll tour.

Meanwhile, Johnny was pushing himself to his physical and mental limits. 'Johnny was good for the band,' says Ray. 'He was like the nuclear warhead. I may be mythologising it, but he was dangerous in those days, crashing into hotel doors, smashing glass. That was the persona he had: dangerous.'

In San Francisco, the travelling Clash carnival met up with Mo Armstrong, Howie Klein, Rudi Fernandez and their other friends. Rudi took the group to the Rondaya, a Mexican restaurant which stayed open till the early hours. Mariachi guitarists swung by and The Clash got sloshed on Tequila and Corona beer. Joe and Mick borrowed a guitar and joined in; the others banged out a rhythm on anything they could find. 'We would go there for breakfast, lunch, dinner, then come back in the evening,' recalls Fernandez. The partying would finish up at dawn and the group would go down and watch the rising sun light up the Bay.

Rudi loved showing the group a good time. One time, mid-week, he took them to a tiny jazz club to see Wilson Pickett. The place was virtually empty. The Clash loved it: Sly Stone and Martha Reeves were sitting at tables out the back. It was the group's private appointment with America's black musical heritage. The group had an amazing night, getting drunk, dancing and singing.

By the close of the tour, the group had been away from London for nearly seven weeks. Everyone was exhausted, malnourished, homesick and dissociated from reality. 'When you get off the bus you still feel like you're moving,' Mick told Pennie. Topper had nearly died. There was at least one consolation: Bill Price's mixes of the *London Calling* material were being sent over from England. The tracks sounded amazing. Ray Lowry was dispatched to work on the album sleeve in Epic's San Francisco office. Despite Pennie's initial objections ('It was out of focus!'), the group elected to use the pic of Paul smashing his bass for the front cover. Lowry did the inner-sleeve calligraphy and came up with pink and green cover lettering, mimicking Elvis's first LP. Lowry and Johnny had picked up a tattered copy of *Elvis Rock 'n' Roll* during the tour. They slept with it at the foot of their beds. Barry Myers, 'Britain's No. 1 Deejay!', was credited as 'Birry Myers' after his taste for biriyani.

Johnny and Ray enjoyed each other's company and spent most days heroically pissed out of their minds. Johnny was a cocaine and casual heroin user; Ray wasn't. After nearly two months of unremitting excess, however, Green was wired and losing control. Matters reached a head on the last date of the tour in Vancouver. The extra chunk of money for the tour had now completely run out and, knowing they weren't going to get paid, the American road crew refused to plug in the gear. There was a showdown. It had an unpleasant conclusion. Johnny ended up gaffer-taping the chief roadie to a chair and threatening to stove his brains in with a cymbal stand unless he gave the order to fire up the PA. The man acquiesced. The Clash were blithely unaware of what was going down.

Johnny Green recalls: 'Mick said to me later, "Why didn't you tell me?" I told him it was because I knew he didn't like violence. Mick didn't condone that kind of stuff. The others accepted violence. It came with the territory, it was just there. Mick didn't.'

I suggest to Green he revelled in that kind of malevolence. 'I don't know if I did,' he says. 'You have to understand my commitment to the band was such that I was prepared to do something that could have got me a stretch or seriously hurt. I loved that band so much I was prepared to do *anything* for them; it wasn't about enjoyment, it was about doing a job. That tour was completed despite the fact there wasn't full support from the record company.'

The group's flight home was booked for 18 October. It had been a long seven weeks. Following the end-of-tour party in Vancouver, the group – exhausted, ill and hungover – stayed in bed. Their flight was leaving shortly. Johnny claims to have tried to rouse each of them, only to be told to fuck off. All of them claimed to be leaving the group. Johnny left them to it. He took a cab to the airport and assumed, ecstatically, that his association with The Clash was over.

Two weeks later, The Clash were back in Wessex with Micky Gallagher. It was 5 November, Guy Fawkes Night. The extraordinary events of tour had been forgotten. Johnny was back at work as if nothing had happened. The group were working on a track to be given away on a free flexidisc with *NME*. Written by Mick, it was a funky, soul-pop song – inspired by Viv Albertine – called 'Train in Vain'. When the deal with *NME* fell through, it was added to the album.

The Clash also cut a version of reggae artist Willie Williams's 'Armagideon Times', which they'd been messing around with in America. According to Joe, the American audiences 'didn't have a clue what they were playing'. They found The Clash's reggae dimension confusing. 'Armagideon Times' was the closest the group had come to recording a reggae song in an authentic Jamaican, rather than punk, style. Kosmo was in the control room. You can hear him calling to the group to wrap things up, two minutes and fifty-eight seconds into the track. Kosmo had a Spector-ish fixation with short pop songs. Joe's riposte is 'OK, OK, don't push us when we're hot!'

Don Letts was approached to shoot a promo video for 'London Calling', to be released as a single in December. Don found a location: the Festival Pier in Battersea Park. The Clash dressed in Crombies, hats and dark suits. They looked like 1950s south London gangsters. Like everything the group did, the shoot was low-budget and chaotic.

'Everyone says, "Great video", says Don. 'It was only my second video, the first was PiL's "Public Image", which is in a studio and very safe. This time,

I'm out on the Thames, I don't know what the fuck I'm doing, I'm making this up as I go along. Now me, I am a land-lover, I can't swim. Don Letts does not know that the Thames has a tide. So we put the cameras in a boat, low tide, the cameras are 15 feet too low. I didn't realise that rivers flow, so I thought the camera would be bouncing up and down nicely in front of the pier. But, no, the camera keeps drifting away from the bank. It took so long to prepare everything that it started to get to night. It wasn't supposed to be night. Then it starts to rain. I am a bit out of my depth here, but I'm going with it and The Clash are doing their thing. The group doing their thing was all it needed to be a great video. That is a good example of us turning adversity to our advantage.'

The video *was* great: rods of rain lashing down on the group on a winter's night, intercut with images of Big Ben and the Thames.

While the group had been away in America, a new kind of music had rampaged across Britain: 2-Tone. The Specials, who'd supported The Clash on the On Parole tour, and whom Bernie had briefly managed, were spearheading a multi-racial, ska-punk movement with Madness, The Beat and The Selecter. Teenagers adopted a rude boy/skinhead look: three-button tonic suits, red quarter-inch braces, pork-pie hats, suedehead crops, brogues. It had suddenly become fashionable for Britain's youth to dress like 1960s Jamaicans – or The Clash. Meanwhile, The Jam, who were now as big in Britain as The Clash, became the focus for a Mod revival. The year's other big New Wave successes were The Boomtown Rats and The Police. Both made The Clash puke.

It was within this climate that *London Calling* was unleashed on 14 December 1979. The Clash's protestations to Oberstein and Muff Winwood at CBS had been successful. The record would be a double that retailed at a special budget price of £5. Initially, CBS had agreed to the inclusion of a free twelve-inch with the album, but somewhere along the line the bonus disc acquired nine tracks. The deal was that the double album would only count as a single so far as the contract was concerned. Joe believed it was the group's 'first real victory over CBS'. There wouldn't be many more.

Most commentators regard *London Calling* as The Clash's mature masterpiece, the album that established them as a truly great band. There are inevitable comparisons to other doubles like *Blonde on Blonde* and *Exile on Mainstreet*. In some ways *London Calling* is even grander and more ambitious: it's a long, fluid, sprawling record, with a torrent of words and a flurry of different styles to match: rockabilly, funk, reggae, soul, rock, ska, jazz, plus off-beat, uncategorisable stuff like 'Koka-kola' and 'The Right Profile'.

Kosmo says the album was going to be called *The New Testament*, but *London Calling* prevailed. There's romance and myth in the title. *London Calling* evokes a cool, progressive, multicultural place redolent of The Clash's favoured purlieus: Notting Hill, Harlesden, Brixton – areas where 1960s Bohemian hippy collided with displaced Caribbean and gangster-ish low-life. It was the call of a romanticised, groovy London that was yet to really exist on a wider scale: a town where you could hang out on the street till late, neck Red Stripe and toke on a joint with impunity, while listening to dub wafting out of nearby blues parties and drunken revellers spilling out of noisy she-beens.

Stan Laurel's advice to Tony Hancock when making *The Rebel* was 'keep out the slang' for the benefit of American audiences. The Clash did the opposite: the grooves resonate with the sound of London's streets, from the inaugural cry of 'On the route of the 19 bus!' in 'Rudie Can't Fail' to the 'Black Maria' of 'Guns of Brixton' and 'truncheon thing' of the title track. But the album also acknowledges a group who've breathed in America and been intoxicated: there are name checks for 'skyscrapers', 'the fifty-first floor', 'skyjuice', 'snub nose .44', 'Manhattan', '42nd Street'.

The transition from *Give 'Em Enough Rope* is dramatic. The Clash have grown up from angry, uptight militant types to loose, funky guys. These are men who wear hats at a rakish angle and have lived a little: rude boys grown up. On 'Lover's Rock', Joe and Mick sing, not entirely comfortably, about love, sex and the pill. 'Death or Glory' sees Strummer cast pearls of wisdom about grown-up ex-rebels, like an old bandolero looking back on his life. It's not so much a repudiation of rebellion as a concession to the complications and responsibilities of adulthood. Joe was only twenty-seven when he wrote most of the lyrics, but like his heroes Dylan and Tim Buckley, he had the gift to write convincingly like a world-weary old man when he wanted to.

Guy's enthusiasm saturates *London Calling*. It is a joyous record, a rock 'n' roll album: spirited, human, flawed. The fat, lively horns transform 'Rudie Can't Fail' and 'Revolution Rock' into whooping, summer-street-party songs. 'Brand New Cadillac' and the Bo Diddley-like 'Hateful' siphon off some of the magic of the rock 'n' roll greats. There's melancholy, too: 'Lost in the Supermarket' is Joe's wistful 'gift' to Mick, about Jones's life, as Strummer imagined it, growing up in Christchurch House. 'The Card Cheat' is a bombastic, double-tracked-everything Wild West piano ballad, with sad, martial trumpets, Spector-ish drums and a story that ends up with the card sharp shot dead. The musical detail gives satisfying depth, as in the nagging one-hand rock 'n' roll piano riff in 'Four Horsemen', or the bass tracking Mick's vocal on the funky, Jackson Five-ish middle-eight of 'I'm Not Down'.

In the booklet to the twenty-fifth anniversary CD, writer Tom Vague draws parallels between the apocalyptic chorus of 'London Calling' and the 'dark riverside laments' of Joseph Conrad and William Blake. But the album also has echoes of a more recent ode to the Thames: The Kinks's 'Waterloo Sunset', from which 'I'm Not Down' borrows its riff and a lot of its bitter-sweet atmosphere. (Mick plays the guitar riff with a violin bow – 'a homage to the guy in The Creation,' he explains.)

'Clampdown' and 'Four Horsemen' are the muscular rockers, but there's none of the blunt, power-chord assault of 'Tommy Gun' or 'English Civil War'. Topper's brisk, jazzy snare adds a lightness-of-touch to everything. Paul's 'Guns of Brixton' is terse and edgy, and another song where the anti-hero cops a bullet.

The influence of black music is overwhelming and hugely important to the album's success. Faithfully kick-starting The Rulers' 'Wrong 'Em Boyo' with a barrel-house version of 'Stagger Lee' connects The Clash directly with one of the great myths of black America. As Cecil Brown's book *Stagolee Shot Billy* explains, the Stagolee legend was based on the murder of Billy Lyons by 'Stack' Lee Shelton on Christmas Day 1895. Shelton was a black St Louis pimp; he and his friends dared to have white girlfriends and were regarded as heroes for protecting black women from whites. 'Stagolee' became one of the great symbols of black swagger, and fascinated, among others, the Black Panthers' leader Bobby Searle. The Clash had a good deal of brass neck to sing about Stagger Lee, but somehow they pull it off in a way perhaps only the Stones and Them could have. Maybe it was because their passion for black American culture was so strong. *London Calling*, for all the resonance of its title, was a record that brought The Clash's adoration for England and America together in an inspiring way.

On its release, Garry Bushell of *Sounds* slated the album. Elsewhere it was widely regarded as an astonishing achievement. In *Rolling Stone*, Tom Carson called The Clash 'the greatest rock 'n' roll band in the world'. Charles Shaar Murray's *NME* review was equally effervescent. He did, however, identify three niggling Clash traits: Mick and Joe's inability to write credible songs about male-female relationships ('Lover's Rock'); a tendency for self-mythol-ogising machismo ('Four Horsemen'); and an unhealthy attraction to the idea of martyrdom ('Guns of Brixton'). These were pertinent criticisms at the time, but not necessarily ones that have weathered the past three decades.

However, Murray's piece concluded: 'This is the one.' The man who had consigned The Clash to a garage of car fumes three years before had written the review that secured the group's status as the most important group of their generation.

London Calling reached number nine and the title-track single number eleven. The Clash had achieved this with very little radio airplay, virtually no industry support, the indifference of CBS and without ever playing *Top of the Pops*. The group celebrated Christmas with two shows at the Acklam Hall under the Westway: the first night was sparsely attended as no one believed The Clash would appear at such a tiny venue on Christmas Day. Bob Gruen came on stage and blew a bugle. The second night was rammed.

The group had enjoyed a fantastic year. The next one would end in near disaster.

10
THE LAST OF ENGLAND

'The only performance that counts is the one which ends in madness.'

Mick Jagger's Turner, *Performance*

Butch: *'You know, when I was a kid, I always thought I was gonna grow up to be a hero.'*
Sundance: *'Well, it's too late now.'*
BUTCH CASSIDY AND THE SUNDANCE KID

On 27 December 1979, the Soviet attack on Afghanistan officially became an invasion. The US telegraphed its horror to the rest of the world. The hawks in the Whitehouse rattled their sabres. The mood across the world was suddenly dark and apocalyptic. The 1980s was to start under the shadow of the Bomb.

The same day that tanks rolled into Kabul, The Clash played one of a series of benefit concerts at Hammersmith Odeon to highlight another global disaster. Refugees were pouring into Thailand following the fall of Pol Pot in Kampuchea (Cambodia). A humanitarian crisis was looming. The Clash shared the bill with Ian Dury and The Blockheads. Mick joined them on guitar for 'Sweet Gene Vincent', and looked great in black leathers and fag dangling from his lip. Joe and Paul looked on disapprovingly. 'Mick wouldn't mind going off and jamming with Ian Dury,' says Paul. 'But me and Joe didn't go in for that. We were incapable of jamming anyway, but we also wanted to create a bit of mystery. It all came from Bernie – you keep your cards close to your chest.'

The gig doubled as a warm-up for The Clash's thirty-five-date assault on the UK, scheduled for January and February 1980. It was their first tour of Britain for over a year, and surviving tour itineraries show the group booked into hotels under their aliases: Joe was 'A. Puss', Mick 'Michael Blair', Paul 'Pinkie Brown' (the anti-hero of *Brighton Rock*) and Topper 'Algernon Sattakhi'. Many younger Clash fans, sensitive to issues of loyalty, and devoted to them in a way Mick would understand from his teenage obsession with Mott, felt The Clash had forsaken them to crack America. The tour seemed planned to assuage any such fears: it visited virtually every major town and city in the country. The title of the tour was taken from the old Tennessee Ernie Ford song, 'Sixteen Tons'. It was a comment on the group's unremittingly dire financial situation: 'Sixteen tons and what do we get? Another day older and deeper in debt.'

At Blackhill Enterprises, Peter Jenner and Andrew King were adamant that the tour should show a profit, or at least break even. This was difficult because the group still insisted on low ticket prices: £3 at most venues. Blackhill tried to reason with the group but found them reluctant to address their financial predicament. A number of meetings were scheduled, including one mid-tour at Crawley Leisure Centre on Saturday, 12 January.

'It was very hard to talk sensible business with them,' says Peter Jenner. 'Which is why I never got a contract. They were hard to get together – then, when they were all in one place, everyone would start rolling joints and cracking jokes. Their attention spans were so short because they'd start smoking dope. We'd all laugh, but it lost the chance of trying to resolve these problems.

'The Clash was a big business which was turning over hundreds of thousands, if not millions, at the box office,' he continues. 'The group wouldn't come to grips with this. They wanted the money, they wanted to live the life, but they didn't want to relate to the business issues. You'd try to have a serious conversation about the production – the crews, hotels, support bands – and you'd just get pooh-poohed for being an old fart.'

Andrew King adds: 'Band meetings with management are funny things. We're interested in the money and the band want to raise a hundred other issues. I used to wear a badge which said, "It's the money I'm after." They used to wind us up terribly. They probably thought we were boring and square. But it wasn't our job to be groovy, it was their job to be groovy. What they needed was some boringness to balance out the chaos.'

It was around this time that Paul told Jenner he'd only turn up to meetings if they provided him with a rabbit suit. They called his bluff and bought one. Paul put it on, then bounced into the room and playfully bashed everyone. The meeting descended into farce. The Clash refused to play the game. The only problem was there was no alternative plan.

The fourth date of the tour in Brighton saw Pete Townshend join the group for an encore of 'Bankrobber', 'Louie Louie' and 'Garageland'. It was a thrill for The Clash to be performing with their hero – though Pete virtually mimed his way through the Clash originals, since he didn't know the chords. Townshend had met the group for the first time earlier that day. He had warmed to them – and punk – after initially being sceptical. 'It was a joy to talk to them,' he says. 'They were friendly, positive, challenging and combative in a way that felt familiar to me – probably many of our fans were like them. I just loved their style, look and songs. They were a great rock band. Joe had a conscience. He shared his worries. I always listened to him because he researched the political background of his passions before spouting off. He could be trusted as a source.'

The 16 Tons tour showed how much The Clash had evolved since they'd last trolled around Britain on the Sort It Out tour in late 1978. They were loud, heavy and well drilled. On the September US tour, Mick had augmented his guitar sound with echo and chorus units. This gave the group a fuller, richer tone. Songs now featured extended codas and Paul was adding subtle licks on the bass.

The group were filmed for *Nationwide*. Fans can be seen climbing through the windows of the dressing room. Joe is relaxed and avuncular, and wearing a dark suit and homburg hat. 'We've spent four years together playing, so we must be four times better than before,' he asserts. 'Otherwise we'd be idiots, huh?'

'They were fucking brilliant live,' says Jenner. 'All you needed was a decent PA and some lights so you could see them, and then you just let them get on with it. It's a miracle it happened sometimes with all the chaos. They weren't an easy group to get a soundcheck from – God knows how the road crew coped.'

The excitement and energy began to fray the group's nerves. By this time Mick was already weary of touring. Jock Scot recalls, early on in that tour, the guitarist being withdrawn and fragile and unable to face the task ahead. 'We'd just checked into the hotel and Kosmo said to me, "Go up and see that Mick's all right,"' explains Jock. 'So I went up to Jonesy's room and he's sitting on his bed with his coat on, his hat on, the room's cold, it's dark. I said, "Look, you turn that on, that's the heater, that heats the room up! Is there anything you want?" He says, "If you want to help me, you can take my suitcase down to reception. I'm leaving the tour." I go downstairs and I'm saying to Kosmo, "He's lost his marbles. He's lying there on the bed with his coat on and the room's freezing and he hasn't got the heating on and he's saying he's leaving the tour!"'

Mick was pacified, but the itinerary proved to be gruelling. The group was performing in a different town every night. Simmering tension between Joe and Mick culminated in an ugly confrontation in Sheffield, on 27 January. For their final encore, The Clash were scheduled to play 'White Riot'. In the dressing room, they prepared to return to the stage. Mick suddenly turned around and told the others he wasn't going to play it. There was a heated exchange. Joe exploded and thumped Mick in the mouth.

'That was a fucking good punch,' recalls Johnny Green. 'You wouldn't take Joe as a particularly good fighter, would you? But he put everything into it. Bang! Right against the wall, splatted him. Mick was in great shock, and I think Joe was in shock as well at what he'd done. There was a kind of disbelief there: "Where did that come from?" I think it was pent-up rage against Mick for calling the shots all the time. Joe couldn't compete with him on a directorial level, he didn't have that constant drive. So Mick ain't going to play "White Riot", so the band ain't going to play "White Riot". Joe can't out-argue him, all he can do is hit him. It's a pivotal moment. He whacked him, there was blood everywhere. Cut lip. Bloody teeth. We bandaged him up, you know, bandana'd him to cover it up. Mick was in a state of shock, just doing what he was told. "Come on, out you go." He went out and he didn't finish the song. He put his guitar on its stand halfway through, so he made his point as well. They both made their point and the matter was settled. But it's interesting: the only way that Joe can respond is in a physical manner. Joe, Mr Articulate who can say anything about the world's problems, can't tell his songwriting partner, "I think you are fucking up by doing this, you are not on the right wavelength." This is really what he's saying and what he'd been saying for days.'

Mick didn't like 'White Riot' for several reasons. For a start, it wound crowds up to a dangerous pitch that often resulted in violent stage invasions. Secondly, more than any other first-album track, it musically and ideologically belonged back in 1977. Johnny Green believes Jones 'simply wanted to move on'. Tellingly, 'White Riot' wasn't played again until the last night of the tour, almost two weeks later.

There's no doubt Joe and Mick's first proper punch-up created a corrosive stain on their relationship. It certainly left a deep impression on Strummer. When asked in 2001 who the last person he punched was, Joe responded, not entirely truthfully, 'Mick Jones.' After the gig, the matter was dropped. 'It was never mentioned again, as far as I know,' recalls Johnny. 'They weren't a niggly band. On the road there was always a new crisis to deal with.'

The chief 16 Tons support act was a Jamaican artist called Mikey Dread.

In 1979, Dread – born Michael Campbell – had been in London promoting his *Dread at the Controls* album. In Jamaica, Mikey was a legend for radically challenging the way radio was programmed. His graveyard-shift show played exclusively Jamaican music, not foreign pop hits, and featured innovative, pre-recorded links and a female narrator. Mikey was also an early champion of Althia and Donna's 'Uptown Top Ranking' and was instrumental in turning it into a hit. On his return to Jamaica from London, Dread was approached by Kosmo to work with The Clash.

'I didn't know what they were, or who they were,' says Mikey Dread, speaking to me from his home in Miami. His voice is instantly recognisable from The Clash's 'Rockers Galore . . . UK Tour' and 'One More Dub'. 'But then they kept calling me so I came to England. It was cold and raining all the time. I preferred Jamaica.'

Mikey joined the tour in Scotland. It was snowing. The Clash's audiences were often hostile to his lengthy dub support sets, performed to a backing track. To defuse tension, the group would emerge from the wings as 'the Mystery Skankers', dressed in long overcoats and homburgs, and with handkerchiefs masking their faces, bandit-style. For Dread, the tour was a culture shock. 'It was scary, man,' he chuckles. 'The audience wanted to destroy all the theatres we were playing in. If you see what a hurricane does to an island in the Caribbean, then that's what the theatres looked like after The Clash played. People used to get on the stage, then jump back into the audience. I never saw that happen in Jamaica! I thought, "Are these people crazy or what?" The one thing I hated about punk rock was that you couldn't stand at the front of the stage. You had to stand way the hell back. If I was at the front the audiences were doing stuff that would create a problem. I didn't like the environment. It was not conducive to my upbringing or heritage.'

Mikey appreciated what The Clash were trying to achieve, however. 'I really liked the guys and there was never a problem with me and them working together,' he says. 'It was a fusion of two different cultures, in a way that was trying to benefit everyone. I respected them. There were times when I was shopping or walking around, and they would say, "Don't go down there, 'cos there are skinheads here." They would guide me.'

Dread took a keen interest in their attempts at reggae. In December 1979, Joe had written a ska tune called 'Bankrobber'. It echoed the sentiments of 'Crummy Bum Blues', his first ever composition written in Newport – 'an intelligent bank robber, that's what I'd like to be.' This time the song's basic conceit was informed by first-hand information: he'd spoken many times to

Robin about his extraordinary flirtation with armed robbery and his subsequent stretch in Albany.

'Bankrobber' revived Strummer's Ray Davies-style character studies: it was a classic, romanticised outlaw song, with shades of Bob Dylan's 'Pat Garrett and Billy the Kid' and *Butch Cassidy and the Sundance Kid*. Its moral was it's better to live outside the system than endure a life of servitude. Inevitably, cynics took the lyrics at face value and pointed out that Strummer's father was actually a clerk in the diplomatic service. Joe must have rolled his eyes in despair.

On 2 February, a rare rest day, the group booked into Manchester's Pluto Studios to tape the track. Mikey Dread took charge. 'Bankrobber' developed into an authentic-sounding roots-reggae track, with low, portentous harmonies and a complex rhythm track. 'When I found a white group who wanted to play reggae, I wanted to get 100 per cent behind it,' Dread explains. 'But they needed someone to show them how we do it. It's like if you get a new recipe, it's better to go to someone who's been cooking it for a while, and they can show you how to measure it out properly rather than just throw the ingredients in the pot. I showed them what our approach was.'

'London Calling'/'Armagideon Time' was The Clash's biggest chart success yet at number eleven. The group hatched a radical plan: they would fire off a string of great singles in 1980. CBS were sceptical about such an intense campaign. Worse, they were played the mixes of 'Bankrobber' and were perplexed by what they heard. 'They didn't understand it. They said it sounded like David Bowie backwards,' says Paul.

CBS refused to release it; The Clash insisted they'd deliver no substitute 45. This resulted in another breakdown in the ever-brittle relationship between label and group. CBS's promise of 'artistic control' had been exposed as a charade with the release of 'Remote Control' way back in 1977. This time, The Clash were in a position to stand their ground. Both parties seemed willing to sacrifice a potential top ten follow-up to 'London Calling' on a point of principle. The year-long singles campaign evaporated.

There was more grief to contend with. In March 1980, *Rude Boy* was given a limited theatrical release. The group had long disowned it, though they allegedly accepted a £4,000 advance on box office takings and retained a 10 per cent kick-back on the film's profit. *Rude Boy* charts The Clash's rite of passage from the zippered punk yobs of 1978 to the rock 'n' roll outfit ready to take America in 1979. The action is seen through the eyes of Ray Gange: his eponymous character's journey from enthusiastic, drunken fan-roadie to unwanted, drunken embarrassment is saddening.

The part he plays is symbolic of the punk movement's unwillingness to accept change. He is the archetypal rock fan whose group moves on to bigger and better things: he wants the chaos of 1977 and 1978 to last for ever. It can't. Meanwhile, a ham-fisted subplot follows the experience of a black kid arrested for pickpocketing in Brixton. The judicial system is revealed as institutionally racist and brutal. The film is framed within documentary footage, shot by David Mingay, of an NF demonstration in the Midlands that ended in a riot.

For all its faults – it's overlong, simplistic, clumsy, occasionally boring – *Rude Boy* gives an extraordinary flavour of the political ambience of that time. It depicts a nation in decline. Only *Scum* and portions of *DOA* match it for nailing the edginess, pessimism and moral-political confusion as Britain entered the Thatcher age. Its chief appeal for many, though, is the brilliantly shot live footage of The Clash – albeit with a reconstituted sound-track. (The DVD version graciously acknowledges the best part of the film is The Clash themselves: an option allows you just to play all the live footage.)

The group's chief objection to *Rude Boy* was the subplot: they felt it rein-forced the stereotype of the black street robber. Ray Gange had his own reservations. He was portrayed as a loutish drunk prone to racist outbursts. He may have liked a drink but he was no racist. 'I was given political view-points that I never had,' Gange says. 'I was never interested in politics. It would have been better if the character had been given a different name. I was up there supposedly playing me, so everyone else watching the film decided that's what I was like. It was a very surreal situation. *Rude Boy* took away the magic of films for me. It exposed it as being fraudulent and I'd never really thought about films as being fake. I'd gone into this thing expect-ing it to be some magical moment, but it was just put together like a patchwork quilt.'

The film was premiered at the Berlin Film Festival. The Clash boycotted the event, though Johnny Green and Baker broke ranks and attended. There was another gala showing in Leicester Square. Robin Banks found himself seated next to Bernie Rhodes, who of course had instigated the project and was there at the invitation of the filmmakers. As the credits rolled, Robin turned to him and said, 'Hmm, I didn't think much of that.' Bernie looked him in the eye and gave the immortal reply: 'Maybe that's what you were meant to think.'

In March, The Clash returned to the States for an eight-date trip. *London Calling* had reached number twenty-seven while 'Train in Vain', lifted as a single, hit number twenty-three. Support was provided by Mikey Dread and, in keeping with the policy of opening with a black R&B legend, Lee Dorsey. The tour was to be Johnny Green's last. 'I think the rot had set in,' he says. 'I thought there was a relaxation of values, an ability to come to terms with their success in America on a corporate level. That tour was sweet and effortless. It felt bland to me. I started knocking round with Lee Dorsey. He was wonderful. I'm down in the bar drinking with him, a living soul legend, and The Clash are upstairs in their suites watching television. My boys are getting a bit boring!'

Johnny cites the last straw as Paul sitting by the pool, sipping a Brandy Alexander, instructing him to wash his socks for him. It might well have happened. It's unlikely The Clash would remember it like that. The truth was that Johnny was getting restless. 'There were numerous reasons why I left,' he says. 'But, if I had to choose one, it was the fact it was becoming safe.'

Rude Boy may ostensibly be about Ray Gange, but it's also in some ways the story of Johnny Green. Here was a man who thrived on chaos. Once The Clash touring machine became better oiled, his anarchic energy ceased to have a valuable function. Roadent's acrimonious exit had coincided with a period when the group's original entourage suddenly found themselves in the role of 'valets'. Johnny was happy to tend the group. He was like a masseur in his beloved Tour de France – the guy hired to look after the physical and mental well-being of his riders. Now it seemed his personal touch was no longer required.

There was another factor, too. Kosmo Vinyl was devoted to The Clash, as Johnny was. He had increasingly come to occupy Green's position as fifth member. Kosmo seemed better equipped for the new challenge they faced: advancing the group as an international act. He was an enthusiastic communicator, facilitator and organiser. He also took a tough line on hard drugs, specifically cocaine and heroin, which had drifted in and out of The Clash camp in the last two years. As an unashamed drug-lover and chaos freak, Johnny Green found himself in a leprous position. He handed in his cards at the conclusion of the US tour. He divorced one love and married another: his girlfriend Lindy. He then headed out for Texas, where he got a job working with Joe Ely. It wouldn't be long, however, before his and The Clash's paths crossed again.

The luxuries of America may have softened the group, but that didn't mean the group embraced them. The Clash often found themselves the recipients of unwanted, extravagant gifts. Their riders were a source of particular exasperation. 'The local promoters used their imagination, for sure,' recalls Simonon. 'All very nice, but highly impractical and a waste of time.

Who wants mushrooms with a cosy bit of bacon wrapped around its head when you've just got off stage? It was ridiculous.'

The most extravagant backstage folly was at the end-of-tour party at the Motor City Roller Rink in Detroit on 10 March. The gig was a benefit for Jackie Wilson, lying in a coma since an onstage accident in 1975. 'There were all these massive dressing rooms that the sports teams used,' says Andrew King. 'There was an incredible meal laid out for us, with a whole boar's head and some suckling pigs and whole sides of beef, an absolutely terrifying spread. We went up to this massive bit of meat and stuck a fork in. It was frozen solid! The whole thing looked fantastic and gleaming and it was a fucking lump of ice. Only in America.'

The Clash stuck to their customary post-show jellybean cocktails – all the white spirits plus blackcurrant cordial and lemonade. In any case, they were all vegetarians.

The next day, Joe and Mick visited the Motown museum and nosed around the old race-riot sites of Detroit. After 'Bankrobber', The Clash were keen to record some more reggae. It was decided to travel with Dread to Kingston, Jamaica and cut a few tracks at the legendary Channel One studio. In mid-March, the group flew to JA and checked into the Sheraton hotel. There was, as usual, a cash-flow problem. Kosmo and Blackhill had to go cap in hand to Oberstein and Epic for money to cover the studio bills. Negotiations were difficult: CBS and The Clash were still in a war of attrition over 'Bankrobber'. The group were reduced to living off the credit card of Paul's girlfriend.

In 1980, the economic situation in Jamaica was even worse than in 1978, when Mick and Joe had visited the island. Michael Manley's Democratic Socialist policies and political links with Cuba had isolated the country from the US. The lack of American investment was pinching hard. Inflation was spiralling and unemployment rising. Shops lacked basic supplies. An election later that year would see Manley deposed by his rival Edward Seaga. The violence before and after the voting claimed over 1,000 lives.

The Clash hired a couple of beaten-up cars and drove downtown to Channel One. Opened in 1972, the studio had been used by scores of reggae greats, from Gregory Isaacs and Alton Ellis to Big Youth and The Mighty Diamonds. It was located on Maxfield Avenue in the notorious Maxfield Park ghetto. Paul, who had been excluded from the 1978 Jamaica trip, was thrilled to be in the home of his beloved reggae. He was, however, under no illusions about the everyday realities of Kingston life.

'It was fucking frightening,' he recalls. 'It was like Dodge City. Especially Kingston. More extreme than *The Harder They Come*. We were lucky, because we had Mikey Dread. I got on really well with him. My musical upbringing meant we could cross-reference on records. He took me on a tour of Kingston and introduced me to a guy who'd been shot seventeen times, and a guy with revolvers strapped to his ankles. He'd caught someone robbing a bank and made them crawl all the way back to the police station – he was famous all over the Island. Mikey Dread was my passport – if I didn't have him I'd be at the mercy of the locals, because if you're a white person it doesn't matter if you're rich or poor, they think you've got money.'

Micky Gallagher, Topper, Mick Jones and Mikey Dread will all agree that, while never the flashiest bass-player in town, Simonon had a natural feel and aptitude for reggae. 'Paul was a good reggae bass-player,' says Dread. 'He was deep into reggae music and understood reggae music.'

Paul and Mikey became good friends. 'I liked him as a person,' says Dread. 'We have a very special relationship. He was very friendly and tried to make me feel comfortable. They came over to my house. Topper was a good drummer. Strummer was on top of things, being a politician – he was interested in the issues facing black people and white people. Mick I couldn't figure out in all the time I was there. He was the one who was picking on everyone else. I'm not being negative. He was a very chilled guy. But he was more like a superstar, you know?'

The group set up their gear and got to work on a reggaefied version of 'Junco Partner'. Word got around that a white, foreign group were working in Maxfield Park. Crowds began gathering in and around the studio. 'The studio was full of people every day, Rasta!' Dread remembers. 'I didn't even recognise The Clash in there because it was like a big house party. There were a lot of beers. Everyone was partying, there was no control. They came to look at what was going on, not to be disrespectful, but to see for themselves. Then other elements took place. We had some rental cars. Everyone knew Mikey Dread, so when I came outside to leave, there'd be people who'd say, "Mikey, we washed the cars." But I didn't leave anyone outside to wash the cars. They wanted me to get some money from The Clash. All right, so we paid the guys to wash the cars. Then there are guys who are *watching* the cars, like security, so they want some money, too. So we're paying them and every day it's worse. I had to explain it wasn't in the budget. Then guys are asking if The Clash need people to work with them, and I'm saying, "No, The Clash don't need nobody." They're arguing that The Rolling Stones get guys in when they come to Jamaica. I'm saying, "The Clash are musicians." It was going crazy. People are threatening me. I don't think anyone in Jamaica was gonna harm them, but I didn't want to risk anybody's life in the ghetto. It was money, money, money.'

Mikey Dread advised The Clash to pack their things into the hire cars and get out of town quick. They did. They piled their amps on the roof. The group did a runner from the Sheraton and took a few days off with Mikey in Montego Bay. After the Jamaica trip, Paul disappeared to Vancouver for a month to work on a film called *All Washed Up*. Produced by Lou Adler – former Mamas and the Papas manager and the man who brought us *The Rocky Horror Show* – it follows the tale of an idealistic, teenage American girl who fronts a punk group called The Stains. Paul has a speaking part as 'Johnny', the bass-player in an English punk band called The Looters, with The Pistols' Steve Jones and Paul Cook, plus *Scum* star Ray Winstone.

The film was shelved for years, but has now been shown on cable channels on both sides of the Atlantic, re-titled *Ladies and Gentlemen, the Fabulous Stains*. Watching it today, it's easy to see why it was canned. The film is a curious period piece, like an American *Breaking Glass* without the wit or pathos. It is, however, entertaining to get a glimpse of the Pistols–Clash amalgam Bernie and Malcolm envisaged in 1976. It also shows how pervasive The Clash's 1977 creed had become in defining an international punk agenda: if she makes it, Corinne Burns wants to do something useful with her money, like 'open a radio station'. Presumably, Paul explained to the scriptwriters that Burns ought to look at the small print on her record contract first.

Simonon enjoyed his sojourn, larking around with Cook and Jones in posh Canadian hotels. They ordered booze on room service under the name of 1960s Spurs hero Danny Blancheflower and other impish misdeeds. Meanwhile, Joe, Mick and Topper checked into James Dean's old haunt in New York, the Iroquois Hotel. The idea was to get some new material down on tape.

Blackhill adhered to the prevailing management strategy of that time – record an album every year and tour as much as possible. Everyone was keen for a follow-up to *London Calling* for the 1980 pre-Christmas market. Joe and Mick found a free slot at the Power Station on 53rd Street in midtown Manhattan. Mikey Dread was in tow. According to Dread, the idea at that time was still to make a reggae/dub record. It was accepted that Mick and Joe could oversee the sessions, with Bill Price operating the desk. Mikey initially assumed he was producing. However, as Price states, 'He was never introduced to me or anyone else as "the producer".' This confusing arrangement would later result in a degree of ill-feeling between Dread and The Clash's management.

The Power Station worked on twelve-hour shifts, starting at ten o'clock. The Clash, who were sharing the studio with Chic and Diana Ross, had the day shift. 'It wouldn't normally have suited The Clash,' recalls Bill Price, 'but they were so tour-lagged that it really didn't matter which time of day you were working. Then after a week, everybody was so wiped out from being in New York it was actually easier to get people in the studio at ten in the morning because they were still up from the night before. We knew when it was time to stop work because [Chic's] Nile Rodgers would float in three or four feet above the ground in a blurred haze. He'd tell everyone how much he loved them, then fall into a chair in the back of the control room. Normally he was wearing a yellow tracksuit and huge pair of orange headphones with a radio aerial sticking out of them. He was a very nice chap. And quite brilliant, of course.'

The main room was a huge, wooden tetrahedron, which supposedly produced a 'New Age sound'. A microphone was placed at the point on the ceiling where all the surfaces met to capture the magical vibrations. Mick, Joe and Topper started by recording a few covers: 'Police on My Back' by The Equals, Eddy Grant's late 1960s group, Prince Buster's 'Madness' and 'Louie Louie'.

After a few days, the money ran out. The Clash wanted to continue working in New York. There were frantic calls to Soho Square and negotiations with Oberstein and Epic to acquire more funds. Eventually, Kosmo secured the group a cut-price, three-week block-booking at Electric Lady, the studio Jimi Hendrix built in the late 1960s at 52, West 8th Street. The psychedelic starship murals still adorned the walls. Upstairs, The Stones were working on *Emotional Rescue*.

The covers recorded at the Power Station exposed the fact that The Clash had written nothing new since 'Bankrobber'. This seemingly didn't present a problem: with a cavalier flourish, Joe and Mick decided they'd write the album there and then. They would need help.

'They put the word out that they were looking for me, and I thought it was just to hang out and say hello,' says Ivan Julian, Richard Hell's guitarist. 'We were sitting around talking and they were playing back the basic track of "The Call Up". I thought, "I gotta play on that!" So I jammed some chord changes over the main riff for about an hour and a half. Mick was the one pushing things discipline-wise. Creatively, Joe was kind of the anchor. It was very strange – a lot of the things were coming from Joe but Mick would be the one who'd say, "Let's go and record this."'

Ivan felt the Joe–Mick dynamic was sparking. 'They worked very well together,' he says. 'There was a little tension but only the kind any two people who spent hours together would have. Mick would push people when it was sometimes uncalled for. There'd be a time when the guys would feel like breaking out, and Mick would be insisting we carry on. It was like, "Come on, what's your problem?" But there weren't rows as such.'

On Easter Monday, 7 April 1980, Micky Gallagher and Blockheads bass-player Norman Watt-Roy arrived from London. Norman was to deputise for the absent Simonon. According to Gallagher, Watt-Roy had only agreed to the trip 'under great duress'.

'We got out there and went to the studios,' recalls Micky. 'The engineer and Mick were there. We said, "Right, let's hear your songs", and Mick said, "We've only got one" and they played some cover. I said, "It's not even your fucking song!" The next day I said, "Right, what've we got?" The engineer said, "Fuck all, they haven't arrived yet."

'It had been tossing it down with rain and we were soaking. So Norman and I sat down and started jamming and played what became "The Magnificent Seven". Then the guys started rolling up and said, "Oh yeah, that's good." Topper came in and put some drums on and Joe disappeared and started writing lyrics. We did a few more like that, just jamming off the cuff, Joe singing, Norman playing. We did an enormous amount of work there.'

Over the next week, they recorded half-a-dozen tracks, including 'The Magnificent Seven', 'Lightning Strikes' and the cover of 'Every Little Bit Hurts'.

The downtown setting infected Joe and Mick. New York was buzzing with a new form of music: rap. Joe and Sylvia Robinson's Sugarhill label was revolutionising dance music. Kool Herc's experiments with break-beats a couple of years earlier had created a whole new musical vocabulary. Funk and dance music was everywhere. Joe and Mick locked into the vibe, encouraged no doubt by their meeting with Chic. 'Magnificent Seven' and 'Lightning Strikes' were arguably the first rap tracks cut by a white British group.

Meanwhile, The Clash were roping in more old friends to help out. Tymon Dogg happened to be in town, scratching a living from playing gigs at Folk City on Bleecker Street. He'd bumped into Mick in Greenwich Village. Mick was with his new girlfriend, Meat Loaf's backing singer Ellen Foley. Times had changed since Tymon had been warned off The Clash camp during Bernie's first wave of purges.

'Mick said, "Do you fancy going for a drink?"' remembers Tymon. 'So we went into a bar. He was like, "Poncing around with that violin under your arm, who do you think you are? Are you sure you can play it?" He played me some of the new material they'd recorded at Electric Lady, and he said, "What d'ya reckon?" He had just changed his hotel to this really plush one [the Gramercy Park]. I said, "It sounds like your hotel room looks.""

Tymon played Mick a song called 'Lose This Skin': the next day, Tymon got a call from Joe asking him down to the studio to record it properly. Joe and Tymon's meeting was symbolic: it was as if the mind-fuck of punk hadn't happened. The two instantly renewed their friendship. 'Had Joe changed? No,' says Tymon. 'Joe was always somewhere between Woody Guthrie and Elvis. He liked the fame end of things, but he always had this incredible integrity. We had a lot of fun in New York.'

Tymon interpreted Joe and Mick's appropriation of his song as a gesture of largesse. 'The Clash worked on that track for days of their own recording time,' he says. "There was a real openness and generosity of spirit at that time. Not just me, but Mikey Dread was in there . . . It felt like they'd got this facility now and they really wanted to share it. They didn't have to do that.'

New York's twenty-four-hour madness meant there were plenty of distractions. Joe claimed to have spent the whole three weeks holed up in the 'spliff bunker' he'd built in the main studio. Topper became a man about town. Bill Price remembers him simply not showing up on a number of days. If he didn't feel well enough to drum, he would refuse to leave his room. Several times he had to be bailed out of police custody. 'I had the misfortune of being in the hotel room next to his,' says Price. 'You'd be banging on his door for hours. It would be like, "Where's Topper?" "Oh, unfortunately he's in the police holding cell – the tank.""

The sessions became chaotic and dissipated. Often, Bill would be sitting around on his own waiting for the group to arrive. When he got bored he popped upstairs to see his old mate Chris Kimsey, experiencing an even more lonely and fragmented stint, recording The Stones. 'To be honest,' Bill recalls, 'there weren't many occasions when you had the whole band in the studio at the same time. The only person there the whole time was me. A lot of the songs were started as ideas by one or two people on bizarre instruments, quite a lot by Topper, actually. He'd wander over and find a marimba in the corner and play a little something which eventually became a song. That sort of thing. These ideas would then grow. Topper would be raised into getting a drum track together, then every so often, miraculously, Joe would breeze in with a bit of paper and say, "I've got a few words to that", and before you knew it there was a song. Sometimes it would be re-recorded as a complete song with the whole band, and sometimes we'd carry on working with the original fragments. The whole process was made possible because Topper was such a fabulous musician.'

The songs kept coming. Joe and Mick were drinking in the atmosphere. At a time when England had only three TV stations, they were wowed by New York's seemingly endless number of channels. They absorbed American issues, culture and politics. The Clash attracted radicals and crazies, Vietnam vets and college intellectuals. They talked to them all night in bars and dingy drinking clubs on the Lower East Side. The new information and *Mean Streets* imagery seeped into the songs. 'The Call Up' was written about the draft, still an issue in the States. 'Stop the World' described the aftermath of a nuclear holocaust. 'Washington Bullets' listed trouble spots around the world destabilised by CIA black ops. 'Sandinista!' was an ad-lib thrown in by Strummer during the verse about Nicaragua. (The Sandinistas were a Nicaraguan people's army who'd overthrown General Samoza's right-wing government in 1979 and established a socialist regime.) There was an endless mass of vibrant humanity to inspire them. Baker explained in *The Clash on Broadway* booklet that he believed it was the street derelicts around the Iroquois which prompted Joe to write 'Broadway'. This was a wonderfully melancholy, jazz-reggae tune pitched somewhere between Lee Perry's 'City Too Hot' and Tom Waits's *Closing Time*.

The sessions wrapped up on 20 April. Paul returned to the fold in time for a live appearance on the ABC show *Fridays* on 25 April and a one-off gig at the Roxy Theater, Hollywood two days later. Then the Clash returned to London for a couple of weeks – the first time they'd been home in two months – before heading out for the European leg of the 16 Tons tour.

In Britain, in the wake of 2-Tone, it seemed as if everyone in the country had shaved his head and purloined a Fred Perry T-shirt and Levi jeans. Joe and Paul followed suit and had skinhead cuts. Over on the Continent, the style had also taken off, especially in Germany. As with the UK, many young supporters of far-right neo-fascist parties (somewhat unfortunately) adopted the skinhead fashion.

The German dates proved a little hairy. Britain had embraced *London Calling* willingly. Reggae, disco and R&B had long been prevalent in British youth culture. In Berlin, Munich and Dusseldorf there was bewilderment among some sections of the crowd. This reached a climax at the Markethalle in Hamburg, where a gang of local punks proposed to disrupt the gig as a protest against the group's supposed 'selling out'. Backstage, there was an atmosphere of foreboding.

'I remember Mick was freaking out,' says Paul. 'On the dressing room wall it said, "Don't play here it's hell." All these cryptic messages. You think, "God, what's gonna happen?" When we got on stage there was all these guys in the front row going, "You must not play zese songs." They thought we weren't punks any more or some bollocks. God knows what. So it turned into a punch-up. But me and Joe, not considering ourselves as musicians, we thought we could take those liberties. That's what made The Clash interesting because there were no rules.'

Among the 'liberties' Joe took that night was whacking one of the Germans over the head with his Telecaster. His victim apparently had been 'using the guy in front of him as a punch-bag'. British musicians had a history of going mad in Hamburg, since the night John Lennon and Pete Best rolled a German sailor and stole his wallet, only for him to shoot at them with a starting pistol. Joe's actions seemed extreme, particularly for a group who famously declared they were anti-violence. But that dimension of The Clash's message had long lost its clarity; their symbolic fight would continue to blur into real violence right until their split. A year later, Joe told the *NME*'s Paul Du Noyer: 'I began to think I'd overstepped my mark. It was a watershed – violence had really controlled me for once. So since then I've decided the only way you can fight aggro in the audience is to play a really boring song.'

Joe was arrested after the gig but charges were dropped when an alcohol test proved negative. The group made a dash for Sweden, where the audiences were almost as volatile. It was there that The Clash story took another unexpected twist. Andrew King claims he walked into Joe's hotel room – either in Stockholm or Gothenburg – and was surprised to find Bernie Rhodes sitting on the bed. 'He was giving another one of his lectures on Marxism, I couldn't bloody believe it!' says King.

Chances are this was a serendipitous meeting between Joe and Bernie; no one else recalls him being there. Or it's possible Andrew King is mistaken. The Scandinavian dates were, it's worth pointing out, when Jenner and King somehow managed to pay Paul Simonon his wages twice (he split the extra cash with security man Ray Jordan, who clocked what had happened). But the idea that a Joe–Bernie summit took place is entirely possible considering what was soon to come.

The tour finished with a couple of dates with Mikey Dread at the Hammersmith Palais. They would be the last Clash shows for over ten months. That summer, the group resumed work at Wessex on the new album. Around the same time, Ronald Reagan was chosen as the Republican presidential candidate. Ex-CIA chief George Bush (Snr) got the job of his vice-presidential running mate.

The Clash should have taken a break, but their creative juices were flowing. At the end of July, they helped out on *Spirit of St Louis*, a solo album by Mick's girlfriend Ellen Foley. The record, released the following year by CBS, is a Clash album in all but name and singer. Supplemented by various Blockheads and Tymon Dogg, The Clash play on all the backing tracks. Seven of the thirteen songs are Strummer-Jones originals, including the superlative 'The Shuttered Palace' and 'The Death of the Psychoanalyst of Salvador Dali'. In retrospect, both of these arguably would have been far better used on *Sandinista!*

Sessions for the album restarted in mid-August and continued until the end of September. CBS had finally capitulated to the group's demand to release 'Bankrobber' – it was selling heavily on import from the Netherlands – and it reached number twelve. The group's refusal to appear on *Top of the Pops* resulted in the amusing sight of the programme's resident dancers, Legs & Co, skanking to it. If the imported Dutch copies had been added to UK sales, 'Bank Robber' would probably have given The Clash their first top ten hit. The news boosted the spirits of the group – and Mikey Dread.

At Wessex, there was more puzzlement than ever about who was in charge. Mikey felt he was gradually being marginalised. 'I think it was a management decision,' he says. 'I wanted to take it to a higher level. Nobody said anything, but I got the feeling the management wanted to take them away from the reggae. After the project in Jamaica didn't work they didn't have the right opportunity. They didn't have the right ammunition. So it was like, "You do it our way now." When I went to New York everything changed. They wanted to bring in all these different producers and take away the project from Mikey Dread. This was another hurdle because we had a project to do. They selected me, I never selected them.'

Bill Price explains: 'Mikey Dread got involved in specific songs and was very instrumental in certain things. But maybe he didn't realise there were another forty songs. Nobody ever explained to me what Mikey's official role was.'

Naturally, Paul was interested in pursuing the reggae/dub tack. He wrote and sang 'Crooked Beat', about a blues party south of the river. A Jamaican vibe permeated 'Living in Fame', 'One More Time', 'Shepherd's Delight', 'If

Music Could Talk', 'The Equaliser', 'Corner Soul'. Dread produced dub mixes of 'One More Time' and 'Junco Partner'.

Topper was pleased to have Simonon back in the studio. 'Paul was brilliant,' he says. 'When I played with Norman Watt-Roy, he'd go off somewhere on the bass, I'd go off on the drums, and you sometimes didn't know where you were. With Paul, he played so solidly you could just lock back in with him. I loved his bass playing.'

The sessions produced a mountain of material. The Clash had been approached by Jack Nitzsche – the producer-arranger famous for his work with Phil Spector – to provide a song for the Al Pacino movie *Cruising*. Joe put some lyrics to a rock arrangement by Mick and the result was 'Somebody Got Murdered'. This joined other sprightly rockers like 'Up in Heaven (Not Only Here)' and 'Kingston Advice'. The small army of friends and musicians invited to pitch in included The Darts' Den Hegarty, the Barnacles, The Blockheads, Ellen Foley and Topper's dog Battersea. Tracks were fleshed out with piano, sax, Hammond, harmonica, bells, vibes, melodica.

Getting a handle on the mood of the sessions is difficult. It's indicative of The Clash's unique internal physics that some recall it as a swinging party, others as a moody, volatile marathon. Pearl Harbour, the group's friend from San Francisco, had moved to London in January 1980 and was now romantically involved with Paul. It was a halcyon time for Simonon, who would ride his motorbike over to Wessex from his flat in Oxford Gardens – a rude boy Steve McQueen.

'I was sitting in there while they were creating [the album] and they were having so much fun,' Pearl says. 'Paul was becoming a much better bassplayer and his influence on their music was growing. Topper was one of the greatest musicians ever, really, so I think he was enjoying the experimentation. Joe definitely was.'

But Bill Price witnessed some far darker moments. These largely concerned the songwriting partnership at the heart of The Clash. The situation he describes is one of a creative marriage already showing signs of burn-out. 'Mick and Joe were up and down about lots of things,' Bill explains. 'Their fights used to get really bad, and if they could maintain a musical relationship that was pretty much all that could be expected. Occasionally, it got so bad they couldn't even really do that. If the musical relationship was intact, as far as the studio was concerned, we could work with that. Musical differences would escalate into political differences. The sound of a guitar note would grow until it represented capitalism for one of them and socialism for the other. It was never shouting matches. More like silences and withdrawals.'

Price stresses, however, that on other days Joe and Mick were the best of mates. It was an unstable chemistry, he says, that 'was best not poked at if you were working with them'.

Peter Jenner adds: 'There was magic between Joe and Mick, a Lennon–McCartney thing. They complemented each other: the toughness Joe had and the musicality that Mick had. It was the friction between them that made everything interesting.'

The long, muggy summer provided the group with plenty of opportunities to soak up the atmosphere of London. They attended the Carnival together and hung out at the Durham Castle next to Stiff's offices on Alexander Street. The inevitable downtime also gave Topper every chance he needed to get into trouble. He'd moved into a flat down by the river on the corner of Hestercombe Avenue and Fulham Road. His intake of cocaine and heroin increased. Peter Jenner was concerned enough with his condition to bring it to the attention of the group: 'It was all getting a bit weird because the drugs were flying around. I said, "Let's go easy on the drugs front." There were white powders of some sort. I didn't know what, and I didn't want to know . . . I was told to fuck off and mind my own business.'

At this stage, the drugs were affecting Topper's reliability – George from support act Whirlwind had to sit in for Headon in Bologna that June – but not his performances. If anything, he was rising to the challenge of The Clash's stylistic freedom. 'When we started covering Mose Allison I knew we weren't a punk band any more,' he laughs. 'I enjoyed playing all that stuff and it brought out the best in me.'

On 10 September, The Blockheads taped their performance of 'I Want to be Straight' for *Top of the Pops*. Dressed for the part in policemen's uniforms, they hatched a plot for a late-night 'raid' on The Clash. 'We burst into Wessex and everybody froze!' squeals Micky Gallagher. 'No one could see beyond the uniforms, they genuinely thought it was a bust! I can distinctly recall Mick trying to snuff out this huge spliff he was hiding behind his back. I said, "Where's Joe?" and I realised that Joe builds these bunkers in the studio. That was where the dope was kept. From the outside it looked like a pile of flight cases. Joe's hiding in the bunker and he doesn't know what's going on, he's been in there for twenty minutes. So eventually we charge in and arrest him . . .'

The *Sandinista!* sessions segued into the recording of Pearl Harbour and the Explosions' debut for Warners, *Don't Follow Me*. The backing group featured Paul, his brother Nick and Whirlwind's Nigel Dixon. Around this time, Joe also produced The Little Roosters. By the end of September, it was clear there was enough material for at least a double album. In an act of bravado, The Clash decided they wanted to release *Sandinista!* as a triple. To many, the idea was ludicrous. Double albums were cool – triple albums weren't; they stank of the worst excesses of long-haired extravagance: *Glastonbury Fayre Revelations* or Yes's *Yessongs (Live)*. The joke wasn't lost on The Clash. 'I remember thinking, "Is this some kind of bloated arrogance?"' Strummer told Paul Du Noyer early in 1981. 'I could imagine some US group doing it, Styx or Foreigner, all them overblown outfits. But then I figured that if we could get it for the same price as one, then more power to us.'

Jenner and King strongly advised the group against a three-LP set. They believed a low-priced triple would be financial suicide. They also thought the album was 'full of padding' and would make a much better single or double. Their protests fell on deaf ears (Jenner: 'They told me to fuck off'). Kosmo was dispatched to negotiate a deal with Muff Winwood and Maurice Oberstein. An agreement was struck whereby The Clash could have a triple that retailed at £5.99 if they waived their performance royalties on the first 200,000 copies. Since *London Calling* had sold around 180,000 in the UK, this amounted to writing off all their UK sales.

The deal marked the beginning of the end of The Clash–Blackhill relationship. Jenner and King felt there was little point in carrying on if their advice was being ignored. They also believe to this day that the group were unsuspecting pawns in a secret plot by CBS to remove Blackhill as The Clash's management. As conspiracy theories go it's highly plausible. There were allegedly two reasons CBS wanted them out of the picture. First, King had incensed Oberstein by complaining to Epic in America about his conduct over the tardy release of 'Bankrobber' and CBS's seemingly overwhelming indifference to the group. (King made the mistake of making his complaint to one of Maurice's old pals.) Secondly, King maintains that Oberstein was worried that Blackhill, having rumbled that the CBS contract was for thirteen albums, not five, would use their contractual expertise to spring The Clash from the deal.

'Oberstein was brilliant with them and went behind our backs after we realised we could shorten their contract,' Jenner opines. 'The speed with which we got blown out was remarkable. The key was that Christmas when everyone was skint and Obie personally gave them £1,000 each. He suddenly became Uncle Obie, a person whom they could go to and sort out their problems. They didn't realise *he* was the problem.'

On 1 November there was a joint playback at Wessex for Pearl's and Ellen's albums, plus all of *Sandinista!* Johnny Green happened to be in town and invited himself along. He was appalled. 'It was awful,' he recalls. 'This huge hall and this record sort of meandering in the background. There was no energy. Everyone was drinking bottled beer and looking bored. I thought, "Is this what they're doing now? Is this what the boys think is good?"'

'The Call Up' was scheduled as the first single, and Don Letts arranged to film a video in a cemetery in north London. On the day of the shoot the council refused to grant the licence. The Clash ended up being filmed in 1960s singer Chris Farlowe's warehouse of militaria in Kings Cross. They dressed appropriately in Lawrence Korner combat garb. When Don was finished, the group were whisked away by Pennie Smith to a nearby railway bridge for the *Sandinista!* cover shoot. (Hence Mick's tin helmet and Topper's goggles.) Meanwhile, political cartoonist Steve Bell worked on the lavish lyric booklet.

The title of the album had been decided back in the summer, but it now had even greater resonance. When Samoza was assassinated in exile in October 1980 there was dancing in the streets of his homeland. But the rebel junta's luck was about to change. In November 1980, Ronald Reagan took office in the White House. One of his first major appointments was William Casey as CIA director. Casey vowed to take out the Sandinistas and created 'The Contras' to destabilise the country with covert terrorist acts.

It was typical of Joe's political philosophy that he saw Nicaragua as a straight fight between good and evil. The title pitched the album into a resolutely international space. This was a record that from its name onwards seemed to shoulder the burdens of the whole world.

Sandinista! was released in the UK on 12 December. It wasn't an easy album to get your head around back then, and still isn't now. Over three discs, there are some 145 minutes of music. That's an hour-and-a-half more than on *The Clash*. Taken individually, most of the tracks pass muster, and some rank among the group's very best, but the range of styles is disorientating: calypso, waltzes, jazzy laments, gospel, be-bop, dub and rap. These join the existing palette of funk, reggae, rockabilly and rock.

In Britain, 1980 saw unemployment rise above 2 million and Margaret Thatcher continue to pursue a radical right-wing agenda, but The Clash appear to have their political radar directed elsewhere – mostly towards America. 'The Call Up', 'Washington Bullets', 'Ivan Meets G.I. Joe', 'Broadway', the *Apocalypse Now*-inspired 'Charlie Don't Surf' – all seem to come straight out of the *New York Post* (perhaps they did). Other songs – the melancholic 'Rebel Waltz' and Tymon's 'Lose This Skin' – simply *feel* American, suffused as they are with a sepia, Smithsonian tinge and Dixy-fried flavour.

The sound of West London is inevitably present: 'Corner Soul', 'Let's Go Crazy' and 'The Sound of Sinners' bottle the ebullience of Carnival weekend in Notting Hill and lazy summer days on Talbot Road. 'Up in Heaven (Not Only Here)' reprises the theme of Mick's lonely tower-block life. But these tracks say little about the monochrome reality of the rest of Britain. That load is carried – alone, poetically and heroically – by 'Something About England'. Here, an old tramp reflects wistfully on his life and the changes he's seen since the First World War. The period music is lovely – asthmatic, Salvation Army brass and tinkling piano.

The sheer volume of material means that it is almost impossible to generalise about *Sandinista!* Lyrically, Joe veers from trite political sloganeering ('we don't need no gang-boss, we want to equalise') to touching, poetic epiphanies ('There is a rose that I want to live for / Although God knows I may not have met her'). There's bags of humour ('Ivan Meets G.I. Joe') and deep melancholia ('Broadway'), jazzy fun (the sprightly cover of Mose Allison's 'Look Here') and self-indulgent nonsense ('Mensforth Hill', the tape of 'Something About England' played backwards). There's lots of great reggae ('One More Time/Dub' and 'Junco Partner') and indifferent reggae ('Shepherd's Delight'), neat pop songs ('Hitsville UK') and nonsense like Micky Gallagher's kids singing 'Career Opportunities' and 'Guns of Brixton'.

Sandinista! is clearly ahead of its time – spoken-word fragments, dub mixes and soundtrack-like interludes – but it is also deeply confusing. It proves that, contrary to received wisdom, Strummer wrote better songs about rheumy-eyed down-and-outs than he did about global politics. Perhaps there should have been more songs like 'Something About England' and fewer like 'The Equaliser'. Maybe there should have been fewer songs, full stop. As Peter Jenner argues, 'It would have made a great double or a killer single.' Few could deny there's some great music on its six sides; but the overriding feeling was less would have been more.

Deadlines were so tight for the 12 December release date that Kosmo hand-delivered the three discs to *NME*'s Nick Kent, so he could write his review over the weekend of 7–8 December for inclusion in the following week's paper. He probably wished he hadn't bothered. Kent gave it a royal kicking. Words that stung included 'tepid' and 'demoralised'; 'the record simply perplexes and ultimately depresses,' he wrote. Savagely he wondered why The Clash bothered carrying on.

The Clash camp were so stunned by the review they took the unprecedented step of approaching *NME* editor Neil Spencer and asking him to have the record re-reviewed. Naturally, he refused. None of the other reviews in the music press, bar Robbi Millar's in *Sounds*, thought much of the record, either. *The Face* magazine mercilessly took the piss out of it.

As Christmas approached, it dawned on The Clash camp that they'd blown it. Their crazy, magnanimous, three-LP gesture had backfired. 'The Call Up', released as a single in November, stiffed at number forty and the album itself peaked at a disappointing number nineteen. 'Hitsville UK', Mick and Ellen's duet celebrating the blossoming independent label scene, also stiffed at number fifty-six (the group's worst UK chart placing). The adulation heaped on *London Calling* a year earlier now seemed to count for little in a business that judges you by your last record.

The group weren't the only people who were bewildered and a little hurt. The collective 'Clash' writing credit that appeared for the first time on *Sandinista!* showed that the publishing royalties were now being split among the respective co-authors of each song. Though most of the tracks were Joe and Mick's, the new system recognised, for example, that Paul and Joe were the chief creators of 'Rebel Waltz' and 'Crooked Beat', and that 'Lightning Strikes' was a Strummer-Jones-Headon collaboration.

Micky Gallagher and Norman Watt-Roy were startled to discover that they hadn't been credited with anything. They believed their contributions to the material they'd recorded in New York deserved official acknowledgement/renumeration. This ultimately resulted in a protracted legal wrangle.

Mikey Dread, who was co-credited on 'If Music Could Talk', 'Living in Fame' and 'Shepherd's Delight', was equally perturbed. Today, he strongly feels that he hasn't been sufficiently rewarded for his artistic contribution, though he makes it clear that he doesn't think The Clash themselves are at fault. It's an area that, for legal reasons, is unwise to touch upon: deals may, or may not, have been struck long ago. There's a familiar ring, however, to Dread's assertion that 'the white people benefited and the black guy didn't. The record company treat me with complete disrespect. I never got any presentation discs. I never got one for 'Bankrobber' or *Sandinista!* But the group showed me nothing but respect.'

Micky Gallagher feels equally riled, especially since Joe had proposed that The Clash and The Blockheads form their own publishing company. 'I was going to persuade Ian [Dury] to do it,' says Gallagher. 'Joe was saying, "We can call it The Hole in the Wall where musicians can come and get a fair deal." We went to see a lawyer and it was like, "Fucking no way!" It needed a strong voice to stand up and do it, and none of them did.'

Asked what went wrong with *Sandinista!* Micky has this to say: 'The relationship which really mattered was Joe and Mick as the [chief] writers.

Even though they wanted to include me, it was the fans and the press and the road crew who were all dictating how it should be. They were not strong enough to go, "No, this is how it is." They were cowed into taking this path, which they didn't have any control over. Mick was too occupied with himself, Topper was too occupied with himself, Joe didn't really have the backbone to do it. Paul? With Paul, it was the silences. I never knew what Paul thought.'

The final victims of *Sandinista!* were Blackhill management. Even if you accept Jenner and King's conspiracy theory that CBS wanted them out, it was apparent that The Clash were wearying of Blackhill's comparatively straight approach to business. 'It was really boring,' says Paul. 'It was album-tour-album-tour. There was none of the chaos we were used to.'

Bizarrely, Blackhill agreed with the group's sentiments. 'With a band like The Clash there was more to it than just having a rational career development,' says Andrew King. 'It doesn't work like that. The energy, the spirit, that doesn't come from following a sensible business plan. That has nothing to do with the spirit of rock 'n' roll. They don't fit. Name me a band that has a sensible business plan and career and I might respect it. Elton John has had a sensible career but he's not The Clash, is he?'

Having had no contract, Blackhill found it difficult to earn any money from The Clash. Both Jenner and King claim they were never paid for their services. 'They were still in debt when we left them,' says Jenner. 'We didn't take any commission, I didn't have a proper contract and took them at their word. I was very upset by the way I was treated because it was never sorted out. A lot of people got laid off at Blackhill and we eventually went downhill, because we couldn't sustain the loss in income.'

There was, however, one area in which Andrew King feels they turned around The Clash's fortunes: their publishing. According to King, The Clash all had a stake in Nineden, their publishing company. 'Very few artists own their own copyrights,' he explains. 'Pink Floyd is another example, but there are very few. I was able to go around the world and cut publishing deals and that gave them a lot of cash, which they hopefully spent. I think Mick bought his first flat with his money.'

These financial benefits, extremely modest though they were for a group signed to a major label for four years, wouldn't bear fruit until later. Meanwhile, in the first weeks of 1981, The Clash found themselves skint, ridiculed, unwanted, growing apart from each other, at odds with their management, but also Britain's greatest hope as a credible international rock act. At home, they'd been usurped by The Jam as the favourite group of the nation's youth. New Pop was taking over – Orange Juice, Aztec Camera, Scritti Politti – while Liverpool was the hub of psychedelic revival led by Echo and the Bunnymen and The Teardrop Explodes.

It was while pacing the streets of Notting Hill in January 1981 that Joe bumped into a familiar figure in blue brothel creepers outside a Wimpy bar. Since he'd split from the group, Bernie Rhodes had been managing Vic Godard and running a club-night, Club Left. He spritzed Strummer with a torrent of Bernie spiel, telling him in a highly entertaining and gloriously rude way where The Clash were going wrong. One thing he hated was the trilby hats they were wearing. He thought they made them look like a bunch of wankers.

Joe took Bernie's number and said he'd give him a ring.

The re-appointment of Bernie Rhodes as The Clash's manager in February 1981 is arguably the most significant event in the latter half of the group's career. It was far from a unanimous decision to bring him back.

There is no mistaking that Mick Jones was vehemently against Bernie's reinstatement. He hadn't forgotten that two years earlier Rhodes had tried to turn the others against him and possibly remove him from the group. Bernie's unique way of doing business was also fresh in his mind. Joe and Paul, on the other hand, craved some more of his anarchic energy. Some sources have suggested that Joe felt so strongly about the issue he threatened to leave unless Rhodes was re-employed.

'I was really on Mick's side as far as that went,' says Pearl Harbour, recalling a band meeting at Paul's flat in Oxford Gardens some time in late January. 'But I could also understand Joe and Paul, who were really passionate about trying to get something done, saying he's the guy for us because he's the only one who's doing things in a cool, progressive way instead of the traditional rock star way. The pace had become comfortable for everybody – probably too comfortable for Joe and Paul.'

Kit Buckler, Joe's old art-school mate, was now working at CBS. 'The way Joe explained it to me was that The Clash needed somebody who could deal with the record company. I don't think Joe or Mick found it easy to deal directly with Obie. I think Joe thought, after the criticisms of *Sandinista!*, that it was better to have a manager, even if it was Bernie. And I think, yes, Joe felt strongly enough about it to leave. Bernie was the only man who could keep all their egos in check.'

Kosmo Vinyl is adamant, however, that there was never a *High Noon* showdown. He is keen to impress that Joe, Paul and Mick's relationship was often played out in nuances, assumptions and sangfroid. 'People on the outside of the situation think there are lots of ultimatums,' he explains. 'But people don't always say, "If you're doing this, I'm doing that." There's a lot of that with The Clash. They knew each other so well they didn't have to say anything a lot of the time. People from big families will understand what I'm saying. Sometimes the mood was heavy, very heavy. You would walk in the room and feel it immediately. And this was a heavy issue. That whole wanting a shot in the arm thing. That was controversial.'

At the time, Mick was spending a lot of time in New York with Ellen Foley. Kosmo suggests this may have influenced Mick's perspective on the success of *Sandinista!* In America, the album had generally met with favourable notices, including a five-star review in *Rolling Stone*. Though it retailed at a premium price of $15 (there was no special low-price for overseas copies), the record reached number twenty-four in the US chart – three places higher than *London Calling*. This was without any high-profile marketing by Epic.

It seems unlikely there was anything so formal as a show of hands, but democracy prevailed. Mick bowed to pressure from Joe and Paul to allow the rapprochement with Bernie. Maybe it felt like the acceptance of an immovable eventuality. Blackhill were aghast. 'Inviting Bernie back was utter folly,' states Jenner.

It is, indeed, perplexing why Joe and Paul elected to reinstate Rhodes after the strained relations and financial obfuscation of 1977 and 1978. But Paul is emphatic that the money was never the issue. 'Listen, Bernie didn't rip us off,' he says. 'You just weren't informed where the money went. To be honest, I didn't give a shit and neither did Joe. We would just go, "Yes, Bernie", and sign the paper. Mick was more guarded. Me and Joe trusted Bernie. You need managers who aren't accountants. Sod the fucking bills. At the end of day it was like, fuck the money, it's *the idea*. We were a bit too romantic for our own good.'

This time, it was agreed that Bernie would be paid from net profits, not advances. 'They got him back on worse terms than originally!' howls Vic Godard, whose career would now take a back seat.

Mick's reaction to Bernie's return may be gauged from a story told by his old Delinquents band-mate, John Brown. Around that time, Mick was asked by Ian Hunter to produce his next session at Wessex. Mick asked John to play bass – a touching gesture, recognising their shared schoolboy passion for Mott the Hoople. But when John arrived at the studio, Mick was withdrawn and distant. 'I saw a difference in Mick that I attributed to him being, "Well, I've made it as a pop star." I sensed a bit of condescension. He was chain-smoking dope and not offering it around. And that just didn't seem like Mick to me at all, and I got really pissed off with him. It was like he wasn't the friend I knew.

'He blanked my daughter,' he adds. 'He just walked in and said, "Right, let's go." I said, "That's my daughter there. I've got a daughter, Mick, she's only two months old." But now I realise stuff was going wrong with his life and the band and his own direction, and I feel a bit humbled now by it. I presumed the worse but it wasn't the case at all. I didn't know the bigger picture.'

It's tempting to see Mick's estrangement within the group starting with Bernie's return. Certainly, Mick seemed increasingly to need a buffer between himself and the others. This isn't so strange in rock 'n' roll: in a band as intense as The Clash it's only natural that mutual friends help oil the relationships between band-members. Largely, this role went to Kosmo: he appeared to have a gift of maintaining the equilibrium in the group, of defusing internal tensions and focusing them on the next important event. He mock-heroically called their mission 'The Quest'.

Previous histories have portrayed Mick as drifting into a separate space at this time. Kosmo argues this wasn't strictly true. He believes this stems from a wider misconception about how the group interacted. 'To say Mick was off in his own quarter is to suggest the others were down the pub together every night,' he says. 'What you have to bear in mind is Joe's in Ladbroke Grove, Mick's in New York, Paul's in Oxford Gardens. Mick's with his woman in America, Joe and Paul are with their women in London. Their personal situations had changed. There was a physical distance between them. It changed the structure of the band. That was the way it was: it's called growing up. You don't get the same intensity as the beginning. They're no longer these guys at rehearsal with nothing to do. They had lives.'

The one person who was drifting away was Topper. His chosen lifestyle was making an imprint: he was becoming increasingly insular and difficult to communicate with. He is the first to admit that he didn't concern himself with questions concerning management or finance. Pearl Harbour confirms he rarely attended band meetings at Oxford Gardens. 'Mick had his entourage and I had my *fucked-up* entourage,' he says. 'I just played the drums. I wish I'd said it more at the time: "Don't ask me questions, I'm just the drummer."' With The Clash off the road, and out of the studio, Topper was bored. His casual acquaintance with junk was now becoming a habit. In January, he had bought a pair of timpani off some shady drug buddies for £500. It was obvious they were stolen. He set them up in the front room of his flat in Fulham. 'I'd been playing them all week with the windows wide open,' he explains. 'Then I read in the local paper that a woman from the New Symphony Orchestra had had her timpani nicked. I was waiting for the Old Bill to come bursting through the door. The Clash were big then and everyone knew who I was. So I ran round to this woman's house and gave them back to her.' As a reward, Topper was invited to join the NSO at a Sunday Night at the Proms performance. The skinny drummer from The Clash played his heart out on a set of tubular bells.

The rejuvenated Bernie had lost none of his anarchic electricity and anger during his sojourn from The Clash. In our interview in 1999, he was characteristically vituperative about the group's conduct during his absence and the circumstances of his reinstatement. 'They were £500,000 in debt at that time,' he barks. 'I had to dig them out of a hole. Then they had that bloody Kosmo come in with his stupidness. He was Mick's window cleaner or something, so I had to give him a purpose and make him into a decent press officer. Let's go back to the classic car analogy – it was a rusty wreck and I had to do it up and put my updated engine back in there. They didn't know what hip-hop was! I even had to get them Guy Stevens!'

For reasons that aren't clear, Epic pulled the plug on a projected sixty date US tour to ram home *Sandinista!* It's possible the change of management had something to do with it. Kosmo thinks the American label still construed the group as a cult act. Bernie was unfazed: his first Big Idea on his return was for The Clash to forsake any more long tours and instead secure prestigious week-long residencies in three major cities. The locations would be New York, Paris and London. The philosophy was to create a stir and 'to bring the mountain to Muhammad'.

Kosmo's first meeting with Rhodes was on Tuesday, 10 February, when they flew to America together to set up the New York shows. Kosmo recalls the exact date because 'it was the day after Bill Haley died'. The two didn't exactly hit it off. 'I think we were trying to size each other up,' recalls Kosmo. 'It was a stormy start, but I grew to really respect him. He is a unique individual. People say good things, and bad things. He's a radical, his perspective, his questioning of things. I quickly discovered there's no sentiment with Bernard. That's not to say he's not kind, he can be incredibly kind. He's a gentleman. It was that "this is what it takes to win the campaign" attitude. He was about winning and competing.'

With Bernie back on board, there was an attempt to resurrect some of their magical totems from the *London Calling* era. The group moved back into Vanilla. Baker was dispatched to dig out Johnny Green, who had returned from Texas: they wanted some of his chaos again.

'I survived one day with them,' recalls Green. 'We were sitting in the White Swan – Bernie, Kosmo, the whole band, and I said, "I'm going home and I ain't coming back again." They were going, "What? What?" and I went, "It's fucked, it's absolutely fucked." Bernie was going, "What's he fucking going on about, Joe? What's he going on about?" and I said, "It's fucked, you cunt, you're fucked. You are fucking coasting." And he was going, "What's he fucking saying? What's he saying, Kosmo?" It just smelt bad. I sat around in the rehearsal room. I knew what bad days were, when not a lot is going on, and it was like that. It just seemed they'd drifted even further apart than when I'd gone to Texas . . . Bernie looked like a small, shrivelled figure compared to before.'

The group's friend Jock Scot has happier memories of this second stint at Vanilla. He recalls the footie games were revived to much pleasure. During one game Micky Gallagher broke his arm, putting paid to his career for a few months. 'Jonesy was good, he could trap the ball and run with it,' says Jock. 'He could play football. Big Ray [Jordan] wasn't so hot. One day all these Japanese guys with orange mohicans turned up. It was hilarious. Jonesy's saying, "Come into the studio and see what these guys can play." They could play all these Clash numbers perfectly. But Joe wouldn't go over. He said, "I'm not going over to hear some Japanese play Clash numbers. Why don't they play their own music?" I said, "Joe, they're just starting out. When you started out you were playing Chuck Berry songs." But he couldn't get his head round it.'

Paul Du Noyer's interview with him in January presented the singer as an older, wiser, paternal presence. Joe was in the process of healing the wounds punk had inflicted on his friendships. He and Dudanski were working on an official release of 101'ers material, titled *Elgin Avenue Breakdown*. In the photos accompanying the *NME* piece, Joe could pass for a well-preserved 38-year-old rather than a man a decade younger than that. Pennie Smith's shots showed him as a kind of punk Hemingway, hunched over a typewriter, sharp pin-stripe suit, ciggie in hand. His white shirt-sleeves are unbuttoned and he is wearing half-inch braces. In one shot he actually looks the dead spit of Bogart. Strummer comes across as hard-boiled but human – and still endearingly half-crazed and passionate. He talks about religion ('I don't believe that we just get born and die and that's it'), the passing of time ('When I was younger I thought time was eternal'), *Top of the Pops* ('a farce'), the club The Clash once vowed to open ('We did have a place sussed out, the Lucky Seven, but the landlord wanted to turn it into a snooker hall'), politics ('I believe in socialism because it seems more humanitarian . . . Kick

Thatcher out . . . Disarm . . . What about Northern Ireland? How can you feel patriotic with all that going on?').

Some, however, felt that Joe was still a hopeless romantic living in a cartoonish, cops 'n' robbers world. On the first Friday in April 1981, the streets of Brixton had become a battleground between youths (white and black) and police. The riot was sparked by the arrest of a black youth in Wiltshire Road, as part of a heavy-handed crackdown on street crime dubbed 'Operation Swamp '81'. That same weekend, several hundred skinheads and Asians clashed in Southall.

Soon afterwards, Micky Gallagher visited Strummer at his flat. 'Joe was very animated,' he remembers. 'He was like, "Right on! This is it! Let the people rise up!" It was all very heavy and I was saying, "So Joe, what're gonna do – sing about it?" It was all right for him being in a nice studio, there were no consequences. But the guys on the streets of Brixton, there were lots of consequences for them. Joe was exactly the same as Ian [Dury]. He was from a posh background. All the punks pretended they were working class, and cheered the working class on, but they weren't working class themselves. The Clash were making money out of all this stuff but still saw themselves as right-on people.'

The riots in Southall and Brixton fulfilled Joe's prophecies of 1976. The 'political chaos' he predicted was now tearing Britain apart. Thatcher's bellicose stance towards the unions, immigrants and the unemployed was gaining momentum. Those at the margins of society were feeling victimised and isolated. There was a perception among fans that, at a time when Britain really needed The Clash, they seemed always to be in America. The Clash, meanwhile, holed up in dingy flats in Fulham and Ladbroke Grove (Joe had been refused a mortgage in 1980, and was renting a flat in W10), were tiring of the relentless criticism they faced on the home front. They were forever being measured against the claims they'd made in those early interviews with Mark Perry, Caroline Coon and Tony Parsons. They also seemed now to be pilloried on every street corner for their trans-cultural musical direction.

'It was really hard for us,' says Kosmo. 'We had to put up with all these blokes in leather jackets moaning about The Clash playing disco. But the band was thinking ahead of the audience. That's inevitable when you're really into music. You get into stuff before other people. Then they might get it a bit later on.'

Mick was buzzing with more musical ideas after his break in New York. He'd become even more enamoured with the city's hip-hop scene. In April, the group recorded a dance track called 'Radio Clash', based on the conceit of a pirate radio broadcast.

Then, on 27 April, The Clash set out on a month-long European tour to warm up for their June residency at Bonds Casino in New York. Their former roadie and confidant Steve Connolly, alias Roadent, was now working for an equipment hire company and found himself in charge of the PA. It was the first time he'd spent any time with the group since he'd walked out on the Get Out of Control tour in 1977. The first date was in Barcelona. 'Joe and me were in the Hotel Colon,' he recalls. 'He was going, "This is the headquarters of the CNT [the Spanish anarcho-syndicalist party in the Civil War], this is fucking great!" Then the manager said, "I'm sorry, but when Franco won the war he made the hotel move and the original hotel is now a bank." And Joe was going, "Fucking typical Franco, a fucking bank!"'

After the gig, however, the mood turned ugly. Joe and Roadent were both drunk. The latter voiced an opinion Strummer was now accustomed to hearing. 'I said to Joe, "I don't really like your band much these days,"' recalls Roadent. 'He swung at me. It was real handbags stuff. Topper and Paul had to pull us apart. The next day he came up and said, "I must have really caught you one 'cos my hand's so swollen I can hardly hold my guitar pick." But at least he was smiling when he said it.'

For all the stories of a factionalised group, The Clash still appeared to be in their 'commando raid by the Bash Street Kids' mode. The group were focused on the job in hand. Except for Topper, a strong anti-hard drugs vibe prevailed.

'Red Stripe and spliff were what The Clash ran on,' says Jock Scot. 'If Mick Jones, or Paul or Joe were taking cocaine, I never saw them, and I was there all the time. Topper was occasionally away with the fairies. Cocaine and heroin were never mooted as good ideas in that camp at all. We could not smoke enough spliff, we could not drink enough Red Stripe. Mick might have had his line here and there, and Topper obviously had his preference, but it was very much behind closed doors in their hotel rooms after the gig. I thought this was great, a very healthy attitude. Kosmo was adamant about it. He will not have cocaine in this band! He used to shout about it from dawn to dusk.'

Jock confirms that Mick was still prone to bursts of eccentric behaviour and bloody-mindedness. 'Just occasionally he would take my breath away with his carry on,' he says. 'We'd be in Spain or somewhere, lovely hot weather, we're playing at Real Madrid basketball stadium or somewhere, a huge gig, loads of punters, and Jonesy would turn up wearing a white suit with a big Nikon camera and a pair of shades. "Jonesy, look at the fucking state of you!" But he was very stylish, already a few steps ahead. Next time I was abroad I was wearing exactly the same thing! . . . Then he'd go, "I want egg and chips." Everyone would be saying, "Look, we're in Spain, they don't have egg and chips." But Mick would be determined: "I want egg and chips or I'm not doing the gig." We'd have to drive him away from the Real Madrid basketball stadium, try and find a café, somewhere where you'd go, "Hullo, we're here from Ladbroke Grove, what we want is chips and fried eggs for the guy with the camera and the white suit, the one in the hat."'

And what of the others? 'Paul would be looking cool, sitting back and watching it all, a real deep thinker,' explains Jock. 'Then you'd find Joe in his room learning introductions to the songs in Spanish. Topper would be walking around in a pair of spurs with a mad bird in tow. You could hear him coming down the corridor because of these bloody great spurs. That's how disparate the characters were just in one day. It was funny, I couldn't stop laughing the whole time I was there! They were a fantastic bunch of guys.'

At the end of the tour, The Clash flew straight from Italy to New York for what many regard as the most significant shows of their career. For a moment, they put their troubles to one side.

'When everything got on top of us we used to have a saying,' says Kosmo. 'We used to say: "It could be worse, we could be The Jam."'

11
HELL SUCKS

'War is *good* for you, you can't take the glamour out of that. It's like trying to take the glamour out of sex, trying to take the glamour out of The Rolling Stones.'

Vietnam photographer Tim Page, quoted in *Dispatches* by Michael Herr

'I am not much interested to inquire why the homesickness which so touchingly affects Chaplin at this juncture did not manifest itself during the black years when the homes of Great Britain were in danger through the menace of the Hun.'

COMPLAINT IN THE BRITISH PRESS ABOUT CHARLIE CHAPLIN'S ABSENCE FROM ENGLAND DURING THE FIRST WORLD WAR

It still irks many British Clash fans that perhaps the group's finest hour after escaping punk rock happened 'Over There'. Their residency at Bond's International Casino over the first two weeks of June 1981 is still remembered as one of the most exciting and influential events in New York during the early 1980s. It was also the key to transforming The Clash from a cool, alternative group in the States into a million-selling, top ten act.

New Yorkers got a front-row seat for the whole unpredictable, unforgettable Clash carnival. 'Bond's was great, because of the chaotic, insane energy of the whole thing,' says Rick Rubin, the producer who, with Russell Simmons, would later form the pioneering New York hip hop/metal label Def Jam. 'They were the first band to really embrace that cross-cultural revolution. They brought reggae to rock fans. In America everyone loves reggae because of The Clash. It was the same with hip-hop – I don't think the Beastie Boys would have been as into hip-hop if it wasn't for The Clash. The Beasties were really influenced by those Bond's shows.'

'Bond's got us huge coverage in America – it gave us that opportunity, that window,' explains Kosmo Vinyl. 'People who didn't have straight trousers and short hair suddenly knew who we were. It got out – it was big.'

Bond's International Casino had been picked to host eight performances by The Clash from 28 May to 3 June. The venue was scouted by Bernie and Kosmo during their February trip to the States. It was a cavernous sometime disco on the neon sleaze-fringe of Times Square. With a capacity of around 4,000, it seemed a perfect Clash venue: comparatively intimate but with character. Local promoters, however, didn't understand why The Clash didn't just play a couple of nights at Madison Square Garden like everyone else.

The Clash flew into JFK and checked into Mick's favourite hotel, the Gramercy Park. The building is steeped in history – John Kennedy lived there as a boy and Humphrey Bogart once got married on its roof. The group loved those connections. The next day they took a trip to the vintage clothes store Trash and Vaudeville on St Mark's Place to stock up on clobber: Italianate tops, bowling shirts, retro strides. These were piled up backstage at Bond's.

The atmosphere in New York was crackling. There were no tickets left for the eight shows – one a night plus a Saturday matinée for under-eighteens. On the day before the first show, the group held a press conference in Bond's foyer. An American journalist brought up The Jam's recent accusation that The Clash had sold out. Asked what constituted a sell-out, Mick Jones hit back, 'What happens is all the tickets go on sale for a concert, right, and people go and buy them, and if as many go and buy them as there are tickets, that constitutes a sell-out.' The slightly over-generous laughter from the assembled scribes signalled that New York was waiting to be taken.

The footage Don Letts shot for his abandoned *Clash on Broadway* film depicts New York as a vibrant, seedy metropolis of garbage-strewn alleys, black kids rapping on street corners, squat yellow cabs, NYC cops in blue shirts and black riding boots, pretty Hispanic girls seemingly dancing to the beat of an invisible samba. Graffiti is everywhere: trains, walls, bridges. Manhattan is scribbled with colour – a concrete canvass foreshadowing London's transformation into an urban-art zone a couple of years later. (Much of *Clash on Broadway* was destroyed in the mid-1980s after it was left in storage at a processing laboratory. On leaving the band Topper Headon had injuncted the footage. A rough cutting copy Don discovered years later provided the basis of the thirty-minute film that was included as an extra on the *Westway to the World* DVD.)

Even before The Clash hit New York, 'The Magnificent Dance', Mick's remix of 'The Magnificent Seven', was a hit on the black station WBLS. This was at a time when 'dance remix' was relatively new to the vocabulary of record-making. The Clash regarded this as a huge compliment. It also took them to a whole new audience. Don films a black guy in the street in a red guardsman's tunic singing the opening lines, 'Ring, ring, 7 a.m.'

The support for the first show was Sugarhill's flagship act Grandmaster Flash and the Furious Five. The Clash's policy of unearthing old soul rebels to open their US shows had been replaced with a new tactic: celebrating the new rap scene. Bernie was insistent that the Bond's shows should be 'culturally interesting and progressive'. Flash was joined over the next two weeks by The Treacherous Three and The Sugarhill Gang. Dub was represented by Mikey Dread and Lee Perry. Also scheduled to appear were several US and UK punk groups, including The Dead Kennedys, The Bloods and, intriguingly, The Fall.

The first night the mood was electric. Grandmaster Flash was subject to a barrage of missiles and abuse. The Clash would later blame the crowd's narrow-mindedness, perhaps with wishful thinking, on the fact that many were 'from out of town'. 'Bringing Grandmaster Flash to Bond's introduced a lot of white America to something they would not have been hearing,' says Don Letts. 'The only way you would have heard that stuff back then was when some annoying git played it on his ghetto-blaster. It was all happening in The Bronx and Harlem, in the black areas where white people wouldn't go. So The Clash in a small way, I know it would have happened anyway, but in a small way they did their bit. Tracks like "The Magnificent Seven" and "Lightning Strikes" made white rock audiences more receptive to this new thing that was happening.'

The Clash took the stage at 10 p.m. Don's film shows the group filing down the stairs towards the stage to their rousing Spaghetti Western fanfare: Ennio Morricone's '60 Seconds to Watch' from *For a Few Dollars More*. They look angular and perfectly sculpted – Joe's and Paul's hair had grown back into quiffs – and played a spectacular gig: well drilled and drawing heavily on the funk and reggae from *London Calling* and *Sandinista!* The set featured twenty-six songs and lasted over two hours. It ended with 'I'm So Bored With the USA'. According to *NME*'s Chris Salewicz, the crowd was as wild and enthusiastic as any he'd witnessed in the UK.

It was after the gig the trouble started. Fire inspectors had entered the building, and declared that the venue was unsafe to hold so many people. The following night, Bond's turned away over 1,500 ticket-holders, having had its capacity reduced to 1,750. The next day, Saturday, NYC's Building Department officially declared the venue a fire hazard and closed the club. The Clash's lawyers fought all day for a court ruling to overturn the ban, while fans who'd turned up for the cancelled matinée show tussled with police in Times Square. Mounted officers hit protesters with night-sticks and a girl was handcuffed and bundled into a police van. The Clash revelled in the fact that it was the biggest incidence of public disorder in Times Square since Frank Sinatra's bobbysoxers had overheated there in the 1940s.

Local radio ran bulletins all day about the fractious crowds and the fate of ticket-holders. Reporters interviewed Clash fans from Indiana who'd spent $200 on petrol, food, dope and hotels only to be turned away at the venue. Eventually, Bernie, Kosmo and the promoter struck a deal with Bond's and the Fire and Building Departments. The Clash would play fourteen shows to a reduced-capacity audience. A system was worked out whereby fans who'd bought tickets from the Ticketron telephone booking service would gain entrance to the already-scheduled gigs (the idea being they were more likely to be travelling from out of town), while those who'd bought their tickets from Bond's (presumably native New Yorkers) would attend a run of additional shows the following week.

The Clash soon twigged that their misfortune wasn't a quirk of fate: they'd been the victims of inter-club rivalry and shady municipal politics. But the group turned the situation to their advantage. By promising all the papers exclusives, Kosmo whipped up a frenzy of press interest. The Bond's ticket fiasco made them household names across the state. They were headline news on virtually every radio station and TV channel.

The extra dates meant more support acts: local bands like The Waitresses were invited to play – for free. The two-week stay took on the grand proportions of a royal visit. The Clash were filmed giving their support to a school in Brooklyn, and spoke passionately on the radio about education, punk rock and politics. The Gramercy Park, with its late-night bar, became a hang-out for New York's hip elite. Though representatives from Epic were banned from attending the gigs, the guest-list each night read like a who's who of the NY scene. 'It was incredible,' recalls Pennie Smith. '[The graffiti artist] Futura 2000 would be spraying a backdrop while the group were playing, Scorsese would be popping in, De Niro would be using the loo . . .'

Don Letts, meanwhile, was trying to make his film. This proved difficult. For a start, he had competition from a rather more famous Martin Scorsese, who invited The Clash to appear as extras in *The King of Comedy*. Gaby, Kosmo and Ray Jordan are the most visible 'street scum' in the scene where Sandra Bernhard flounces across Times Square. Meanwhile, Joe and Kosmo had been shown the bar across the street from Bond's where Scorsese had shot the scenes in *Raging Bull* where the washed-up Jake LaMotta bombs as a night-club entertainer. They drank there till dawn. The Clash camp also became regulars at the vibey AM/PM club and Club Negril, a downtown reggae joint.

'There was a great after-hours scene,' recalls Letts. 'Most days people weren't up till the middle of the afternoon. I would try and drag them out to do something for the film, but they were often in bed just recovering. They were playing for two and a half hours every night, sometimes doing a matinée as well, they were knackered. I was shooting whenever I could get hold of them.

'Thinking back on it, fucking hell, it was such a trip!' he smiles. 'There was a punky hip-hop party going on and The Clash were at the centre of it. We met people like The Beastie Boys – I don't think they were even The Beastie Boys then – and [Afrika] Bambata. Bambata was really intrigued by all these punks getting into hip-hop. Futura was there, Zephyr, Dondi, all these graffiti artists. PiL were in town; John Lydon, Keith Levene and Jeanette Lee would all be hanging around.'

Don Letts is unequivocal about the driving force behind The Clash's hip-hop fascination. 'Mick was deeply into the whole connection,' he says. 'If Paul brought reggae into the group, then the New York beats and the hip-hop was totally down to Mick.'

'I was so gone with the hip-hop thing the others used to call me "Wak Attack",' said Mick in 1999. 'I'd walk around with a beat box all the time and my hat on backwards. They used to take the mickey out of me. I was like that about whatever came along – I'd sort of get excited for a while.'

The Clash opened up the Bond's stage to poets and politicos with whom they were simpatico. Joe invited a spokesman for the Committee in Solidarity with the People of El Salvador (the latest Central American flashpoint) to rap out his message during 'Washington Bullets'. On 10 June, Allen Ginsberg joined The Clash onstage to recite a music-poem called 'Capital Air'.

The cultural clash continued after the group finished their set. Bond's stayed open till late and the venue encouraged fans to stick around and buy drinks. The after-show DJ was Pearl Harbour. 'I was the most hated person around because, first, I stole the regular DJs' jobs and, secondly, I played a lot of reggae and rockabilly records,' she recalls. 'The other DJs said the crowd were bored with my records. They blamed me for people leaving after The Clash played. They said the crowd wanted to hear Elvis Costello, The Ramones, Blondie and all this kind of stuff. I said, "That isn't what The Clash like, so I'm playing the records they want." There was a fight every night and, I swear to God, if I wasn't a girl they would have kicked my ass!'

They didn't kick Pearl's ass: instead, she says, they spiked her brandy. 'I suddenly felt awful, and I told Paul I thought the DJ guys had tried to poison me,' she explains. 'I was rushed to Bellvue Hospital. They put me in a wheel-chair and took me to the Emergency Ward where there were all these people with gunshot and stab wounds. Then I really started tripping. The doctor said, "You're on LSD. Would you like some Valium?" I said, "Yes, please."'

Topper's drug intake was by contrast voluntary and worrying. Filmed by Letts in the back of taxi, a stoned and unshaven Headon complains about allegedly not being paid by Bernie. He also admits to some junkie mischief: pretending the seventeen gigs were a relentless slog to justify a pick-me-up. 'It's like [theatrically feigning tiredness], "I'll manage . . . give me some more of that."'

'After the gig when the adrenaline was pumping or when you had a day off and you were looking for something to do, that's when I needed drugs,' says Topper today. 'I was gradually losing any sense of reality. Just taking drugs and messing around and throwing things out of windows. It was just live fast and smash everything up. The others did try to help me, but I could-n't help myself.'

Bond's shows had been a phenomenal success. It had taken The Clash to a new level in the States. 'In those days, there were bands that all the hipsters in town knew,' says Kosmo, 'that maybe two thousand people liked, plus they'd bring along their friends as well. Then there's another level – there're guys working in car-shops and factories and they know who you are. It's no longer this . . . I won't say "elite", but you know what I mean. It breaks out, and that's what Bond's did for The Clash.'

The group hung around in New York for a while then reconvened in London in June. They returned home triumphant conquistadors, laden with booty – clothes, records, gifts, body art (Paul had a yellow cab and sky-scraper tattooed on his arm) – and the knowledge that they'd scorched Manhattan. After the uncertainty surrounding Bernie's reappearance, Bond's fired them up again. Joe and Mick began writing a batch of new material, heavily striped by their New York experience. The Clash moved into a new rehearsal place and started work on what would become their first and last top ten US album.

By the time it was released, however, Topper would be no longer be their drummer.

Freston Road, W11, was the name given to Latimer Road when the area was redeveloped in the post-war years. It was always regarded as a shabby place, even by Notting Dale's notoriously mephitic standards. Large Victorian houses, fallen into ruin, lined the street. The story goes that when the BBC were filming the exterior sequences of *Steptoe and Son*, it was Freston Road they used for the fictional 'Oil Drum Lane'. It was just the kind of place Galton and Simpson imagined two squalid rag-and-bone men holing up.

These days, the area has changed once again. Pale-brick houses with brightly coloured plastic trim and enclosed communal gardens have replaced the crumbling townhouses. It was local resistance to plans to completely bulldoze the area in October 1977 which led to one of the strangest incidents in London's recent history. A total of 120 residents – described by one of their number as 'squatters, hobos and drug addicts' – declared themselves to be the Free and Independent Republic of Frestonia. They applied to the United Nations for membership. Their self-appointed Minister of State for Foreign Affairs was the dwarf actor David Rappaport. Meetings were held in the People's Hall on Freston Road, which doubled as Frestonia's National Film Theatre. The first film they showed was the old Ealing comedy, *Passport to Pimlico* (with a similar plot, of course). Sportingly, the Greater London Council eventually agreed to negotiate with the Frestonians, and hence what was earmarked to be a large factory estate became modern Trust housing.

Four years after that revolution, The Clash moved their gear into the People's Hall. Built in 1901 as a venue for meetings, the building had been transformed in 1980 into a rehearsals space called Ear Studios. There were parallels with Rehearsal Rehearsals and Vanilla: off-the-beaten-track, seedy, cheap, Victorian (just), located in a semi-industrial area. Inside were storage areas with half-broken jukeboxes, pinball machines and pool tables. There was also a patch of scrubby grass out the back – handy for a kick-around. Its proximity to Mick's and Paul's flats – it was just half a mile west of Notting Hill – meant it was conveniently located. Its extraordinary history sealed the deal.

That summer, Mick's guitar technician quit. Bernie was entrusted with finding a replacement. Mick Jones was adamant he wanted a girl to do the job. The idea was to challenge the tradition of having a seething mass of testosterone tuning the guitars for them. Instead, Mick ended up with a long-haired, ex-Wishbone Ash roadie called Digby Cleaver. 'Bernie tried very hard,' explains Digby, 'but all the girls in the music business were frightened off by Mick's reputation for being bloody awkward and not very together.'

Cleaver was recommended by mutual acquaintances. Bernie arranged to meet him in a café in Covent Garden. 'Bernie was forty-five minutes late then turned up with Futura 2000. They were going to have these huge white back-drops at their Paris gigs, which he would graffiti up while they were playing. Bernie spoke to Futura for ages, then turned to me and said, "What's new with you?" I went, "I like The Cramps, if that's what you mean." That's all I said, and then I was kind of dismissed. I was walking out the door thinking, "What the hell was all that about?", when The Clash's tour manager Bob Adcock grabbed me and drove me straight over to Freston Road to meet the band.'

Mick was none too pleased with Bernie's selection and made his feel-ings very clear to Digby. 'He didn't want a bloke-roadie,' Digby says. 'And he certainly didn't want one with long hair. I immediately became friendly with Topper. He was generally outgoing, happy, a nice guy. He took me aside and said, "Look, Digs, do yourself a favour and get your hair cut. Jones really don't like long hair." So I did.'

The day Digby was appointed, he got a lift home with Baker and Mick. Baker was showing him where Jones now lived in Colville Gardens, off Portobello Road. (Simon Cadell – Jeffrey Fairbrother from Hi-De-Hi – had the flat downstairs.) It would be Digby's job to pick up Mick every day for rehearsals. 'We were driving to Portobello,' recalls Digby, 'and Baker said to Mick, "Why did Bernie have to be there today?" Mick just snorted and said, "Fucking Rhodes puts me right off my music." He made it quite clear to everyone he wasn't happy about having Bernie back in.'

That summer, Britain's cities burned in a string of riots and The Specials' eerie 'Ghost Town' topped the chart. Tory back-benchers were convinced the disturbances were the fault of young blacks. They pressurised the Home Secretary, Willie Whitelaw, to dramatically curb immigration. Meanwhile, The Clash worked on new songs: 'Ghetto Defendant', 'Overpowered by Funk', 'Innoculated City', 'Know Your Rights', 'Straight to Hell'. Mick had also penned a scratchy, Stones-like rocker called 'Should I Stay or Should I Go?'

As ever, eye-witness accounts vary as to the atmosphere. Robin Banks recalls a fairly pleasant summer kicking a ball around behind the People's Hall and watching the group piece together what many regard as their strongest post-punk material. Predictably, perhaps, considering his love of the Chaos Years, Johnny Green remembers a downbeat, enervated mood when he happened to drop by one day. 'It was like I'd caught them with their trousers down,' he says. 'They were all standing in a different corner of the room looking scared something might actually happen. They didn't seem particularly excited by what they were doing. There wasn't any energy. It looked like everyone was waiting for an excuse to go home.'

Kit Buckler, Joe's pal from CBS, tells a similar story. 'I went down there a few times and they weren't talking to each other,' he says. 'It was a horrible atmosphere. The only time they seemed to be enjoying themselves was when they were playing football out the back. It wasn't organised chaos, it was just . . . no one knew what was happening.'

Kit lays the blame on Rhodes: 'With Bernie back it was so volatile. I think Joe thought Bernie had talents, and if they could hone those talents then it would be beneficial for the band. It was all the other baggage that Mick couldn't handle, I think. It got to the point where it nearly all fell apart, but it was falling apart all the time. Arguments, surliness. It swung from one extreme to another: sometimes they seemed to be having a laugh, then suddenly there'd be a really tense atmosphere.'

Digby Cleaver, the new boy, didn't sense anything was terribly amiss. He accepted the volatile chemistry, moods and growling as the norm. It's exactly how he'd imagined life in The Clash would be. What really impressed him was the group's work ethic and genuine lack of rock-star excess. He paints a charming picture of Paul and Joe turning up to Freston Road each day on their bicycles: very unassuming, very English.

'Joe used to borrow Gabriella's bike, actually, that was his favourite mode of transport,' he explains. 'Paul, he always tooled around West London on a gentleman's bicycle with cow-horn handlebars. He used to ride everywhere with his hands in his pockets, hair greased back in a quiff. He was the coolest white guy in Ladbroke Grove!' Initially, Digby found Paul quite shy, but explains, 'Once he realised that you didn't have any particular designs on him – you were you, and you wanted him to be him – he was the most humorous person, very witty. He was also a practical joker. I'd be having an intense conversation with Joe in the dressing room, then turn around and fall over because Paul had tied my shoelaces together. Basic childhood humour, but it diffused a lot of the tension.'

On 24 September, The Clash began their seven-night stand at the Théâtre Mogador in Paris. The gigs met with an uproarious reception. Then they flew to Vienna. During the night, the truck containing their equipment was detained at the German border. No-one told the roadies until later the next day, losing the crew valuable time to purloin equipment in the Austrian capital.

There were other problems. Headon's drug intake was now costing him £100 a day. He had a sizeable habit and was getting ill. The band were filmed arriving at Vienna Airport for a German rock programme, *Ohne Maulkorbe*. Dressed in cinematic black-and-white, they look great, like a 1950s Southern rockabilly act. Joe has a kiss-curl. They are sat together on a sofa. Topper, it appears, has just vomited on the arrivals-lounge carpet. The way the extant footage is cut makes it hard to tell, but the TV interviewer makes a comment about his puke being either drug-related or a 'punk' publicity stunt. Strummer is incensed:

> JOE (hoarse with rage): Fucking shut up! You fucking *cunt*.
> INTERVIEWER (embarrassed): Thank you very much.
> JOE: Well, that's what you deserve with comments like that. Let me ask you, do you think this is 1976 and you're talking to The Sex Pistols? Piss off, or I'll fucking piss all over you! If he [points to Topper] feels like throwing up it's because his stomach hurts. I don't need your jokes to fucking contend with. If you haven't got anything interesting to say, piss off!
> INTERVIEWER (acting concerned): Is it serious?
> JOE: Well, you tell me. It's life or death, never mind about being sick on stinking carpets.

The camera follows the group's coach-drive to their hotel. The mood is silly and ironic. Joe is dancing in his seat. Paul cracks a gap-toothed grin. Mick is sitting behind Paul with his back turned, hidden by popstar shades. The camera pans around to capture a smiling Kosmo shimmying in the aisle, while a ghost-white Topper, looking as if he's about to vomit again, laughs sheepishly. This five minutes of footage – interview and coach-ride – provides a unique fly-on-the-wall picture of the unstable world of The Clash. It's impossible to see where the desperation and friction finishes and the camaraderie and hilarity begins – it all appears to be part of the same thing. Tellingly, the group's performance that night, using borrowed equipment, is magnificent.

On their return to Britain, for the short Radio Clash tour that would end with seven nights at London's Lyceum, Mick caught really bad 'flu. His surly mood wasn't improved by the fact Ellen Foley was 3,000 miles away in New York. The Clash played two shows at the Glasgow Apollo.

'Mick had a silver bullet on a pendant chain that Ellen had given him,' recalls Digby. 'The first night, he danced to the front of the stage and off it flew into the crowd. Beneath him is a sea of swirling Scotsmen and it was like, bye-bye, that's gone for ever. He comes off stage and he's furious. He starts a fight with Joe in the corridor – they're coming back on for an encore, he doesn't want to go, so they have to force him back onstage.

'Topper loved winding Mick up and is being really rude about his pendant. So Mick's standing on the drum-riser screaming, "You don't care! You don't fucking care!" right in Topper's face. So Topper's there with a big bag of drumsticks, pulling them out one by one, and throwing them at Mick's head: "Will-You-Fuck-Off-My-Riser!" That's what they were like when they were annoyed with each other! Anyway, the others go into 'Armagideon Time' while Jones is going through this almost pantomimic act on his hands and knees searching for his pendant. Then he gives up looking, joins in with the group, and they're brilliant. Two fucking brilliant encores! In the end, it turns out by some absolute freak chance that a kid in the audience caught the pendant and gave it to Ray Jordan to return to Mick. So it all came right in the end.'

Before the tour, the group had begun recording new material at Ear on The Rolling Stones' mobile studio. One of the tracks was called 'Midnight to Stevens' – a eulogy to Guy who'd died on 29 August from an overdose of a drug prescribed to treat his alcoholism. The group had been devastated.

Jeremy Green, Bill Price's assistant, was in charge of the sessions. He'd partitioned the studio with baffles to achieve separation on the sound, but the vibe wasn't working out. Once the Lyceum gigs were done, Mick, missing Ellen, suggested they relocate to Electric Lady in New York. Some histories report a major Mick–Joe flare up over this issue. This story stems from a music press feature in 1984, in which Joe recounted Mick throwing a tantrum and saying, as he stormed off, 'If you record in New York, I'll turn up.' Pearl Harbour, however, vaguely recalls Mick's strop but points out 'no one objected to doing it in America. Everybody loved New York.'

It's possible that there were other factors influencing The Clash's decision to up sticks. Barney Hoskyns's review in the *NME* of one of the Lyceum gigs picked up where Nick Kent's *Sandinista*! review left off: he made no attempt to disguise his dissatisfaction with virtually every aspect of the show, from the group's stage presence ('The Clash aren't terribly exciting onstage – have you ever noticed?') to the music ('They're so darned cross-cultural . . . like lugging around some encyclopaedia of ethnic musical forms'). Prophets without honour in their own land, indeed.

The Lyceum shows were memorable for Digby. One night, Joe came off stage and starting bawling at him for messing up the guitars/tuning/set-lists. Joe was still warming up when Mick came flying in between the two of them. 'He screamed at Joe, "Leave my fucking roadie alone! You can't treat him like that!"' laughs Digby. 'I thought, "Blimey . . . that's a bit of a turn up. Maybe he likes me after all."'

The group arrived in New York in mid-November. Mick stayed with Ellen. Meanwhile, Joe, Paul and Topper checked into the Iroquois Hotel on West 44th Street, where James Dean lived in the early '50s. Joe and Paul got their hair cut by the barber in the foyer, who remembered trimming Dean's quiff. No one was quite sure where on the top two floors the actor had stayed, so every couple of days Joe moved room so he could be sure he'd slept in James Dean's bed.

The intense buzz in the city was still there from the Bond's shows. 'They were the absolute lions of New York,' states Digby. 'I didn't realise what ridiculous, common-man popular regard we were held in. You could say the word "Clash" to guys who worked in fruit shops – they'd heard of us. There wasn't a door in the city that was closed to us. Anywhere, anytime you could do whatever you wanted – what a great place to be rather than London! New York was freezing cold, but it was a really fun place where you didn't have to put your hand in your pocket.'

The set-up at Electric Lady was the same as for *Sandinista!*: Mick was de facto producer, this time with Jeremy Green as engineer. Tymon Dogg was in town playing some gigs at the Peppermint Lounge and The Clash went down to see him. Earlier in the year, he and Joe had opened up a squat together opposite the British Museum, but moved out after they 'had a bit of trouble with some guys'. Tymon was now living in New York on 102nd Street in Spanish Harlem. He was invited back into the studio, and hung around throughout the sessions, accompanied by another old friend – Micky Foote. 'They were like, "Why's he there? What's Micky Foote doing in the studio? Does he want a cheque? What's he want?"' laughs Micky. 'I was there for the last album and the first. How ironic. It seemed to me to be all enclaves. Joe had his tepee in the middle of the studio – speaker boxes and sheets. It was work, we have to do an album. That's why it was *Combat Rock*, it was like a battle. Mick wanted to write it, star in it, produce it, fucking PR it, manage it. You can't do it all.'

It was while Tymon was messing around with Mick's brand-new guitar-synth that Joe came up with the title 'Rock the Casbah'. 'I plugged my violin into this thing and started playing all these Eastern scales,' recalls Tymon. 'Joe started shouting, "Rock the casbah!" only I couldn't hear him properly. I thought he was saying, "Stop, you cadger."'

The Clash's inclination for playing ever longer, more rhythmic songs sparked Bernie to moan that 'everything was now a raga'. Joe went back to the Iroquois that night and wrote, 'The King told the Boogie-men, you have to let that raga drop.' This he later worked up into a lyric about the suppression of pop music under extreme religious regimes – sadly and ludicrously it's been misinterpreted in recent years as a broader anti-Arab statement.

Meanwhile, Topper was honing a gem. 'I just remember him sitting at the piano and playing that riff,' recalls Digby. 'He said, "What do you think of this, Digs?" I said, "You are a clever lad." It became his tune, completely by accident. He put bass and drums on it, and it sounded brilliant. He did the whole thing himself. He presented it to Joe with this soppy set of lyrics about how much he missed his girlfriend . . . Joe just took one look at these words and said, "How incredibly interesting!", screwed the piece of paper into a ball and chucked it backwards over his head. Topper's face! Joe said, "Look, I write the bloody words – I've got a set of lyrics that will fit this already." And that was what became "Rock the Casbah".'

The sessions were intense. Tymon remembers leaving Mick and Paul at 2 a.m. to work on a mix of 'Know Your Rights', only to find them still arguing about it, 'looking like death warmed up', at 10 a.m. the next day. Paul comments: 'The amount of time we spent in expensive studios arguing about the level of the bass . . . I wanted that to be more of a reggae thing, with loud bass and a lot of depth. I thought the bass should be doing a different job to what Mick said.'

The regime allowed some R&R. Hanging out in after-hours clubs, The Clash rubbed shoulders with the NY glitterati – Grace Jones, Warhol, De Niro, John Belushi. The AM/PM was still a popular watering hole, so was the University Plaza bar. Topper drank at Dylan Thomas's old haunt, the White Horse Tavern in Greenwich Village on West 11th Street. He was falling prey to the city's heroin scene. It was easier to come by and purer than the stuff in London. He never used it intravenously, just smoking or snorting. He was also using large amounts of cocaine. 'I knew Topper had a problem when I lent him a fiver at Electric Lady and it came back rolled up,' recalls Tymon.

Headon's drug-taking still took place away from the group. It was understood among the road crew that hard drugs were unacceptable within the Clash organisation. To be caught using powders by Bernie or Kosmo meant instant dismissal. However, there was an inevitable degree of clandestine snorting – it was ingrained in the culture. Headon was therefore warned off hanging out with the crew. He took no notice.

It's quite possible that the band and management were unaware of how serious Topper's addiction had become. 'I came with a reputation for being anti-drugs,' explains Kosmo. 'So I'm not the person you're gonna mention cocaine and heroin to. Some people might have been aware that Topper's situation was worse than before, but not tell me. It would be like, "Oh no, Kosmo's going to bang on for twenty minutes about how cocaine fucked up The Faces.'"

At Joe's behest, Allen Ginsberg dropped into the session with his old chum Peter Orlofsky and added a spoken-word section to 'Ghetto Defendant' – the Beat Daddy trading lines with the punk poet. The song was about heroin in the ghetto sapping the will to organise politically. Ginsberg had researched the punk scene and included phrases like 'do the worm' and 'slam dance'.

The music on *Sandinista!* had elements of pastiche: a rap song, a dub experiment, a jazz track, the funk tune, the rockabilly one – what Charles Shaar Murray once described as 'musical tourism'. In contrast, the material which emerged from the *Combat Rock* sessions was fully hybridised and highly original: a function of much of it being collectively pieced together. The prevailing musical mood is humid funk-reggae. There are echoes of Gil Scott Heron, Tom Waits, Lee Perry, Van Morrison, Perez Prado. The leitmotif of the album soon established itself as Vietnam – and America in moral decline. *Apocalyse Now* had made a huge impact on The Clash. Its influence went way beyond the title of 'Charlie Don't Surf' – the famous observation by Robert Duvall's gung-ho cavalry major in the film.

Francis Ford Coppola's psychedelic jungle odyssey came as part of a raft of movies trying to make sense of the US defeat in south-east Asia, and the trauma jungle warfare had wreaked on young conscripts: *Coming Home, The Boys in Company C, The Deer Hunter*, Rambo's inaugural *First Blood*, even *Taxi Driver*. These inverted the jingoistic nonsense of John Wayne's *The Green Berets* from a decade before. The idea of the Vietnam veteran as a patriot made outlaw by his own society was passing into popular culture. Sylvester Stallone's Rambo character became symbolic of a new subculture of dispossessed, noble warriors unable to re-integrate themselves into their post war homeland. The new songs made numerous references to the war and its veterans. Michael Herr's Vietnam memoir *Dispatches* was a favourite with all The Clash. Herr had written the screenplay for *Apocalyse Now* and would later do the same for Stanley Kubrick's *Full Metal Jacket*. His book's extraordinary stories of atrocities, trophy-mutilations, compassion, exhaustion and madness in the jungle clearly left a profound impression on Joe.

A trippy near-instrumental, 'Sean Flynn' was named for Errol Flynn's son, who was in Vietnam at the same time as Herr. Flynn, escaping his father's shadow in Hollywood, pursued a career as a war photographer and famously rode into battle on a Honda motorbike. He later went MIA. Joe understood the call to make something of one's own life: 'You know he heard the drums of war,' he wails. 'Each man knows what he's looking for.' Joe also provides a compassionate picture of young men whose lives have been ended or ruined in battle. The first verse of 'Car Jamming' tells the story of a 'shy boy from Missouri, boots blown off in a sixties war' who back home becomes a murderer. 'Inoculated City' solemnly observes 'at every stroke of the bell in the tower, there goes another boy from another side'.

Concerning himself with US foreign policy, past and present, allowed Joe to harden his leftist political stance. In a *Sounds* interview earlier in the year, he talked about the tumult in El Salvador, and how he backed the Communists rebels because he'd 'rather it was one for all and all for one, rather than fuckin' Fatso up there while we grovel around being shat on'. He was also frank about his role as a commercially successful Western protest singer, rather than frontline revolutionary soldier. 'I know I'm here to sing,' he says with candour. 'I'm not here to die in the El Salvador jungle.'

Joe's anti-war vision achieved its artistic epiphany on 'Straight to Hell', a powerful, damning vision of Vietnam's legacy, with the chilling line directed to an American-Asian war-child: 'Lemme tell ya 'bout your blood, bamboo kid, it ain't Coca-Cola, it's rice.' Digby witnessed the song's genesis. 'Most of it was recorded on one day,' he says. 'It was on the day before New Year's Eve 1981, when we were all due to fly out. It was like a mad, creative rush. They were putting hand cymbals on it – Mick was playing congas with sticks, which was an uncommon thing to do, but it sounded brilliant. Topper was playing the hand-percussion and stuff. It was extremely complex, lots of innovation.'

'[The next day] it was New Year's Eve,' Joe says in *The Clash on Broadway* booklet. 'I'd written the lyric staying up all night at the Iroquois. I went down to Electric Lady and I just put the vocal down on tape, we finished about twenty to midnight. We took the E train from the Village up to Times Square. I'll never forget coming out of the subway exit, just before midnight, into a hundred billion people, and I knew we had just done something really great.'

Topper and Mick were taking the group's music into new realms. Mick, especially, was embracing all kinds of new technology. He brought in a mate of Ellen's, Poly Mandell, to put synth keyboards on some of the tracks, and, as Digby relates, 'supervised him completely. He just went through the whole lot in an evening. Mick knew exactly what he wanted from the guys – "No, I don't like that sound, stretch that." He made very, very fast decisions. It was a bit like the film *Amadeus*, that brilliant scene where Salieri's standing there flicking through Mozart's music, and here was the stuff that was actually finished in his head. Mick already had all the stuff planned out.'

Meanwhile, a crisis was brewing which would have serious repercussions for the rest of the group. The Clash had flown back to London for Christmas. At Heathrow, Topper was stopped and searched. The customs officials found heroin on him. He was arrested and charged with smuggling a Class-A drug into Britain. When he appeared at Uxbridge Magistrates court on 17 December, The Clash feared he would be given a custodial sentence. This would have been catastrophic: *Combat Rock* was still unfinished and a tour of the Far East was booked for late January, with a UK and US tour to follow. The Clash's lawyers pleaded it was imperative he didn't go to jail. The judge imposed a £500 fine on the understanding Topper would receive help for his addiction.

When the group returned to London in the New Year, this was indeed what happened. Headon was booked into the Priory in Roehampton, which had been treating rock-star addicts since Brian Jones had been admitted there in the late 1960s. It was an enormous embarrassment for The Clash, who supposedly didn't take hard drugs. The Far East tour was also put in jeopardy. It was believed the promoter, the highly respected Mr Udo, had to pull out every stop to prevent the Japanese authorities rescinding the group's visas.

'You have to remember this was twenty years ago,' said Joe. 'Now there's a whole industry built up around heroin addiction, what with rehabilitation clinics and so on. Back then, heroin was like, "Wooah!" It was like a Russian bear or something. The big bogey-man. The Shah of Iran had fallen and the Persians had been bringing it into London. The whole city seemed to have been addicted in the twinkling of an eye. Topper fell victim to it. The rest of us were just weed-takers.'

Kosmo: 'Looking back, I don't think we were in the right frame of mind to have dealt with it properly. We had a work ethic. We didn't want to lose momentum. But it's important that people know we tried to help him – he went in for several cures. We had him in this place and a girlfriend was smuggling stuff into him. It was a hard trouble to get around.'

With Topper claiming he was match-fit again, The Clash set out on a six-week tour of Japan, Australia, New Zealand, Hong Kong and Thailand. Joe and Mick were still mixing *Combat Rock* (then tentatively called *Rat Patrol from Fort Bragg*) and had to dash for their plane. Tremors of excitement rippled through The Clash camp. None of the group had visited these countries before. Meanwhile, fans in the Far East had been patiently waiting for the group to tour there since 1977.

The Clash arrived in Tokyo on 23 January 1982. There were riotous, *Hard Day's Night* scenes at the airport and later at the train station at Osaka. The Japanese punks went wild. Joe felt uncomfortable about being part of the increasing Westernisation of Japanese culture but the group were touched by their hosts' enthusiasm and kindness.

'They loved us in Japan,' recalls Mick, 'especially because we didn't take advantage of them and we treated them with love. It was fantastic our relationship with the Japanese fans. I always remember when we were leaving the airport they threw presents down to us. They chased us to the railway stations. Some [Western] bands had disgraced themselves there, and we had made an unconscious decision to treat them gently. We got invited to their houses – Japanese people generally don't invite you to their house, to see where they actually live. There was a really good side to that place and it was a beautiful experience. One of the most wonderful times we had together was touring the Far East.'

Pearl Harbour: 'That was the best tour ever because none of us had ever been to Japan or the Far East and it was a big culture shock. It was like Beatlemania with screaming, crying girls. It was insane! They treated you like royalty and took you shopping and gave you everything for free. It was really great, the bullet trains and the temples. That really meant a lot to us. We took it all really seriously.'

The demand for extra shows was so overwhelming that Mr Udo negotiated two further dates in Osaka and Tokyo. Topper, meanwhile, was careering off the rails again. 'In Japan I was hanging out with The Crusaders' bass-player,' he says. 'We were on the thirty-sixth floor of our hotel and the window was like a big shop window. I thought it would be a great game to see who could run as fast as they could at the window to try and break it. That's what I was doing. It was reinforced glass – but what a mental game!'

The Clash flew to Sydney for a press conference to ramp up ticket sales for their impending seven-night stint at the city's Capitol Theatre. Then it was off to New Zealand, where their gear was impounded and searched for dope – Topper's reputation preceded him. Joe went off on his own, hitch-hiking around Auckland. He also took to impromptu busking sessions. Possibly as an example to Headon, Joe had declared 1982 'The Year of the Body'. He was now eschewing all drugs, including spliff, and pursuing a fitness regime based around lifting hotel furniture and early-morning runs.

Often, he was up at 6 a.m., roaming the streets, scribbling notes about the previous night's performance and planning The Clash's itinerary for the day. There is a definite sense of Joe taking charge at this point. Topper, however, was immune to the call for sobriety. At the party after the Auckland show, he got completely wrecked and had to be taken home.

On 10 February, the group arrived in Sydney. 'I watched them checking into the Sebel Town House, a very smart hotel,' recalls Digby. 'Mick was at the reception leaning over looking at the big list of rooms, trying to work out who was staying where. He said, "No, I do not want to be on the same floor as 'im." He was talking about Topper. "Sorry, mate." And Topper is saying, "No, I wouldn't want to be on the same floor as me, either, you boring old bastard."'

As with LA, Sydney had a hardcore punk scene. The gigs were chaotic and violent. The group were thrilled by the reception. They invited Gary Roley, the Aboriginal land-rights campaigner, to make a speech during 'Armagideon Time'. *Combat Rock* had yet to be mixed to the group's satisfaction, so the tapes were flown to Sydney. Work was attempted after the gigs, but proved difficult, since everyone's hearing was shot to pieces. In an *NME* interview with Roz Reines in Sydney, Mick admitted having had a row in the studio with Joe at 4 a.m. that morning. At a gig in Perth on 21 February, Strummer collapsed with heat exhaustion.

'Joe put so much into his performance,' says Digby. 'If you ever see film of Joe onstage, watch the hand holding the plectrum – rivulets of sweat run off his little finger. This is possibly a reason why he died at the age of fifty, because he put about three or four hard months' living into every show I ever saw. It was absolutely heart and soul. And on the two or three occasions when it was heart and soul plus being drunk that was kind of amusing.'

The group flew to Hong Kong, then to Thailand. In Bangkok, the group absorbed the *Deer Hunter* vibes and general craziness. They began dressing in combat gear and bandanas. Mick recalls Joe and Kosmo dancing on the bar with Thai go-go girls. The pictures of their endeavours accompanied an *NME* interview. The gig they played at Thammasat University, where the bloody student revolt of 1973 had helped to overthrow the military regime, was riotous.

Pennie Smith, who'd been with the group in Japan, was flown to Thailand to shoot the *Combat Rock* cover. 'We went over the bridge on the River Kwai,' Pennie says. 'It was sad. Then Bernie went Thai boxing. He had all the money, marooning us in this hotel, this luxury palace. The manager wouldn't let us all out at once in case we did a runner.' But Pennie sensed something was wrong. The energy that usually sparked off the group when they were together was gone. 'We went out on a railroad track to take the pictures,' she says. 'It just felt a little bit emptier than it had. It had reached the point when . . . if you're with people for long periods of time you can sense they're fed up without anyone having to say anything. There weren't the interchanges between them, and it just didn't feel quite right. Suddenly, they weren't there as a unit any more.'

The Thailand trip had a grim conclusion. Paul suddenly fell ill and was in terrific pain. He doubled up and was rushed to hospital. 'It looked like something out of Somerset Maugham, with bath-chairs on the veranda falling to pieces,' recalls Pennie. Paul was diagnosed as having a twisted colon, which would require the removal of a piece of intestine. Meanwhile, Joe had struck up a friendship with some Buddhist monks. 'They went to see Paul in hospital,' Pennie says. 'It was an incredible atmosphere with the monks in orange robes, all these dim lights, the cane bath-chairs and crickets chirping. There's Paul looking immaculate while dying – as we all thought – on the bed. The monks kept using his room to shower in. Then all of a sudden he recovered.' The tour manager had got a second opinion: a Swiss doctor said it was, in fact, a bug of some sort.

Back in London, thoughts turned to *Combat Rock*. There were sixteen or seventeen tracks, enough for a double. Neither the record company nor Bernie and Kosmo believed it was wise to release another low-price two-LP set. There were also debates about the mixes and track-lengths. Two tracks – 'Overpowered by Funk' and 'Rock the Casbah' – had percussion intros. 'Walk Evil Talk' was an eleven-minute avant-garde jazz piece, featuring just piano and drums.

The mood in the Clash camp was, once again, 'heavy'. It's widely understood that Mick favoured the longer, dancier mixes, while the others didn't. Joe disliked Jones's mix of the album so much he would later compare his declaration to 'telling your friend his breath stinks'. Once again, it seems, Mick was over-ruled.

'Eventually it became apparent that there was no one in our camp [whose mix] could please all the parties,' Kosmo explains, somewhat diplomatically. 'But I think it was an honest, creative debate. I don't think it was any kind of power play. It left a bad taste in the mouth, and I don't know what Mick says about it now. We've never discussed it since.'

Bernie suggested they recruit Gus Dudgeon to sort out the record. Kosmo wondered what the hell Elton John's producer could bring to the party. Then it transpired that Bernie had meant Glyn Johns, the seasoned engineer who'd recorded The Who, The Stones, The Small Faces, The Faces, plus numerous other groups The Clash held in high esteem. Johns had a reputation as a troubleshooter, and an unsentimental, no-nonsense guy. He had been invited to piece together The Beatles' unreleased *Get Back* album in 1969 (which later formed the basis of *Let It Be*) and was brought in by The Who two years later to transform Townshend's sprawling, over-ambitious *Lifehouse* project into the steely *Who's Next*.

According to Glyn Johns, Muff Winwood sent him a tape of 'Mick's' version of the album, which he found 'enormously impressive, really, really clever stuff with an overriding sense of humour'. But he also agreed it was 'incredibly self-indulgent and long and drawn-out'. He agreed to take the job, which he understood was to chop down the material into a single LP.

Tellingly, it wasn't Mick but Bernie, Kosmo and Joe who turned up to a preliminary meeting with Johns in London. By this time, the Thai combat rock look had been fully adopted by the group. 'Kosmo got out of the car and I thought, "Jesus Christ!",' Johns exclaims in his schoolmasterly voice. 'He looked like Rambo! Lovely bloke, though, turned out to be a sweetheart.'

Previous Clash biographies have stated that Glyn remixed *Combat Rock* at Wessex. This isn't so. The album that began life in Frestonia and was fashioned in Greenwich Village received its final edit in Glyn's garden studio at his home in Warnford in West Sussex.

Johns was a stickler for time-keeping and hated sessions to drift. During The Small Faces years, he used to knock off at midnight on the dot and bomb off home in his Jag, which had huge Marshall speakers in the back seat. He neither took drugs nor drank. He told The Clash camp that the first remixing session would begin at 11 a.m. sharp.

Joe arrived full of energy and enthusiasm. 'Extraordinary bloke!' Johns recalls. 'I immediately became very fond of him. He was fantastic to work with – a polite man, apart from anything else. Here we were in a situation where he didn't know me from Adam. He didn't interfere with what I wanted to do at all. Obviously, I ran every idea by him – he was my client – but he was very enthusiastic and very open to changes. Fairly drastic in some cases.'

Glyn and Joe re-mixed three tracks that day. Mick finally appeared at around 7.30 p.m.

'We were having a great time when the door opened and in walked Mick – clearly not a happy bunny,' recalls Glyn. 'I said, "Good evening, how do you do? Do sit down, I've got some stuff to play you." And I played through the three things that I had done and asked him if he had any comments about them.

'He said, "I don't like this. I don't like that. I don't like these changes." So I said, "Well, that's a shame because I've done them. I started at eleven o'clock this morning and you chose to come now – that's your fucking problem. If you'd been here when I was mixing them I'd have taken your ideas into account, but you chose to turn up this evening. I've finished those tracks and I'm now on the fourth one, and if you don't like it that's too bloody bad."'

Mick, as you might imagine, was extremely upset. The evening session was consequently tense and unpleasant. Glyn found it so uncomfortable he phoned Joe early the next morning and told him he wasn't prepared to continue in that sort of fractious atmosphere. Joe apparently 'flipped' and said he'd sort it out. Frantic phone calls were made between Joe, Bernie, Kosmo and Mick. The Mick Jones who arrived at the studio later that day bit his lip and knuckled down to work.

'After all that, we got on great,' says Johns. 'I mean, the poor bastard, he was pissed off – he didn't know who I was [Kosmo: 'Mick probably owned every record Glyn Johns ever made'], as far as he was concerned he had finished the work, and there is nothing more annoying than having it taken away from you like that. Some strange fucker coming along. In the end we had a great time and I was terribly pleased with the result.'

Under Joe and Mick's guidance, and in just three days, Glyn Johns excised the funky intros and codas, consigned 'The Beautiful People Are Ugly Too (The Fulham Connection)' and 'Kill Time' to bootleg's-ville, set aside 'First Night Back In London' and 'Cool Confusion' for future B-sides, and completely ditched 'Walk Evil Talk'. The running time had been dramatically reduced from 77 to 46 minutes. Joe and Mick also re-recorded the vocals for, and remixed, 'Should I Stay or Should I Go?' and 'Know Your Rights', both earmarked as singles. Their work done, the trimmed back *Combat Rock* was hastily scheduled for 14 May release, preceded by a single, 'Know Your Rights'/'First Night Back In London', on 23 April.

Then something astonishing happened, even by Clash standards. On 1 May news broke that Joe Strummer had gone missing. Today, it's widely known that Joe had been told secretly by Bernie to go AWOL as a ruse to drum up ticket sales for The Clash's UK tour, scheduled to begin at Aberdeen on 26 April. Bernie had suggested he visit Joe Ely in Texas, but Joe had another idea. On Wednesday, 21 April he took the boat-train to Paris and vanished into the city. This was not part of the plan.

Joe's now genuine disappearance was announced by Bernie with an ill-considered press statement. After some rubbish about Joe's 'personal conflict' being about 'where the socially concerned rock artist [should] stand in the bubblegum environment of today', it concluded that the singer had 'probably gone away for a serious re-think'.

Joe had gone away for a serious re-think. The irony was that it was so serious he'd decided to double-cross Bernie and Kosmo (the only people in on the original plan) and *really* go into hiding. So what was on his mind? Joe's friends in The Clash camp that I interviewed for this book seem to concur that Topper's drug problem was probably fairly high on his list, as was the fall-out with Mick over *Combat Rock*. There also seems to have been a wider disillusionment with the relentless turbulence of life in The Clash.

A few days before he vanished, Joe had visited Alex Michon, The Clash's clothes designer, who was back working for the group after a two-year break. 'He was really depressed,' she says. 'He said to me, "I don't know if I can go on, Alex." I was about to go to New York, so I was going, "Yes you can, don't be so silly." He said, "No, it's all too much." He seemed really down about the group.'

Bernie and Kosmo had taken a risk in not informing Paul or Mick about the true circumstances of Joe's disappearance. This made it even more difficult to broach the subject of Joe's turning renegade and genuinely disappearing. 'The thing between me, Joe and Bernard was definitely a crossing of the line,' Kosmo now admits. 'I didn't know what the line was, but I knew I'd crossed it and I did it in the best interests of the group. It made sense to me – we were going to keep this tight and it would be terrible if it didn't work. It wasn't a matter for debate: this is it, you're in, it's your job and this is what you have to do. Mick and Paul had every right to be aggrieved when they found out what had happened. Things are presented to you but you're thinking of a bigger picture – you have to consider that rather than the immediate situation.'

Bernie and Kosmo went through the charade of turning up in Aberdeen for the first date of the tour, but when Joe didn't show for the performance it became clear that the whole UK tour would have to be cancelled. Jock Scot, who, like everyone else, was completely in the dark about what was really going on, was hitchhiking to the gig from Fife. He was surprised to see Baker driving the group's van back towards London on the opposite carriageway.

Worse still, there was a twenty-three-date US tour scheduled for June, just a few weeks away. If this was to be postponed, the cancellation penalties would mean The Clash organisation being plunged into such crippling debt it would be unlikely to survive. 'The business situation was very, very serious,' explains Kosmo. 'If we didn't find Joe, we were screwed, basically. It would have cost us a phenomenal amount of money.'

Holed up at a friend's house in Paris, Joe was keen to let a few select friends, and his mother, know he was safe. Kit Buckler at CBS received a postcard 'saying, "Don't worry, I'm all right", reveals Kit. 'He was much better at writing notes than using the phone.'

In the first week of May, Kosmo and Bernie had their first lead as to Joe's whereabouts. The group were scheduled to headline the Lochem Festival in Holland on 20 May. The promoter, Frank Zanhorn, was assured by Kosmo that Joe would be back by then and The Clash would honour the gig. Zanhorn wasn't convinced. No one was buying tickets to his festival because no one believed The Clash would show up. A few days later, the Dutch music journalist Jip Golsteijn, unaware of Joe's vanishing act, casually mentioned to Zanhorn that he'd seen Joe in a bar in Paris the previous week. Zanhorn immediately phoned Kosmo with the news and Kosmo went into overdrive. He told everyone he knew with connections in France that Strummer had to be found, otherwise, in his words, 'everything The Clash had worked for would be gone'.

On Monday, 17 May, via Gaby's brother Mark Salter, The Stray Cats' tour manager, Kosmo procured the phone number of a girl who allegedly knew where Joe was. When he called her, she was 'freaked out' and reluctant to reveal Joe's whereabouts. Kosmo got straight off the phone and contacted a promoter he knew in Paris, who, through a detective friend with a reverse telephone directory, discovered the girl's address. Vinyl rushed to Heathrow. Within three hours he was standing in the office where she worked: 'I said, "I've got to see Joe – you know where he is." The girl cracked. She said to meet her in a café later that evening. Then in he walked.'

Joe's sense of fantasy, and desire to remain undetected, had inspired him to grow a bushy beard. He'd even run the Paris Marathon on 16 May without anyone recognising him. Kosmo's coup de théâtre as Strummer walked through the door that night was to cry, 'Fidel!'

'I remember that evening, some bar somewhere, and Joe sitting at the piano playing Dylan's "Just Like Tom Thumb's Blues" and between us trying to remember all the lyrics,' says Kosmo. 'And he agreed to come back. I didn't force his hand. We got drunk. In my memory I don't remember ever having to persuade him – but then, to be honest, I can't remember. Maybe I did.'

Joe returned to London on Tuesday, 18 May. Mick, Paul and Topper were pleased to see him fit and well. But they were none too pleased when they discovered that the whole episode had started out as Bernie's idea. The group elected to play the Lochem gig. They desperately needed the money to pay cancellation fees for the UK tour. According to Frank Zanhorn, their fee was $75,000 plus expenses.

The Lochem show has gone down in history for a simple reason: it was to be Topper's last gig with The Clash. The group were topping a bill which included Saxon, Tenpole Tudor, Bow Wow Wow and The Stray Cats. Digby recalls that Saxon had a huge aluminium eagle at the back of the stage, which Baker insisted on referring to as 'the metal budgie'. Ominously, the show took place during a terrific electrical storm. Frank Zanhorn's account of what happened that afternoon is so vivid it's worth printing in its entirety:

They came to my show by bus. And, of course, they were late and they'd picked up all kinds of hitchhikers and they were absolutely out of their heads. I still hadn't sold many tickets because it was only about three or four days earlier it was publicly announced that they would do the show. The weather was abysmal.

We immediately got into a huge argument with their agent because they insisted on having their full fee. I said, 'Well, I didn't sell any tickets because of this bad publicity.' Anyway they went onstage and after about half an hour Strummer stopped the show. I could hear the PA system, 'Where's the fucking promoter?' And I went on the stage and there were all kinds of skirmishes going on between my security and The Clash fans. Strummer said to me, 'Your security are attacking my fans' – the fans were real mean motherfuckers, they had knives, they had anything, it was a really messy situation.

Then Strummer started the show again and invited all of his fans onstage. So the crowd started pushing and knocked the fences down. About 500 of them went onstage but, even more dangerously, 500 went under the stage because it was raining so much. I could see the stage starting slowly to collapse, and in the far corner the Dutch police wanted to invade the terrain, so I had to fight off the police and get all these people out. There was thunder, lightning, rain, broken fences – it was a nightmare!

I noticed Topper was quite intoxicated before and after – he looked completely on another planet. He was really stoned whereas the others were quite lively and being their horrible selves. There was no interaction between them and Topper. God they were so . . . I was completely flabbergasted because here was this punk band that preached anarchy and fulminated against these rich rock artists and they really screwed me by insisting on having their whole fee. I was in complete shock about it.

It was just a lunatic band! Kosmo was there, he was wearing an army suit and speaking in a kind of crossword puzzle. They wanted me to pay for the roadies' hotel rooms in Amsterdam. I told them to fuck off! I aged ten years that night.

The coup de grâce was provided by the lead singer of one of the support acts, who shall remain nameless. Apparently, this person was well known within the music industry as a coprophiliac. When Zanhorn went to clear the dressing rooms, he was surprised to find a huge, freshly minted human turd in the middle of the floor. It summed up his day.

The following day, there was a band meeting at Paul's flat in Oxford Gardens. Topper's behaviour at Lochem convinced the group that he was in no condition to perform on the forthcoming US tour.

'We knew there was a problem in Holland when Topper said he needed a mirror to go on stage with,' says Mick. 'So we gave him a big wardrobe mirror and he laid it down flat.'

Digby: 'Joe told me the final straw came when he was standing in front of a full-length mirror in the dressing-room, checking out his stage attire, putting grease into his hair to go onstage, and Topper rushed in and said, "You don't mind, do you?" Then he flattened the mirror and dumped a load of charlie on it. That really pissed Joe off. It was the straw that broke the camel's back.'

There has been talk of Lochem being 'Topper's last chance', but both Kosmo and Topper are adamant that neither party ever construed the show in those terms. It appears that directly after the gig there was simply a collective realisation, possibly brought into focus by Joe's Parisian walkabout, that The Clash couldn't continue with a smacked-out drummer.

'It was difficult,' explains Kosmo. 'But what could we do? Be a group that didn't tour? Or just use Topper in the studio? We thought about all those options but it all becomes, not absurd exactly, but . . . you have to understand The Clash were a *band*.'

'We considered everything,' says Mick. 'I didn't want Topper out of the group but we had to do something.'

'I was in such a state,' Topper admits. 'They could have sent me a letter by recorded delivery telling me I was a liability and I wouldn't have known about it. When you're on heroin you have no respect for yourself and no respect for other people. I'd lost touch with the band, reality and the planet.

The first time I knew I was getting sloppy was when they had the meeting and Joe said, "You're sacked." My exact words were, "You're joking!" That's how much I knew. But they had every right because I'd lost the plot and it took me a long time to regain it.'

The meeting was emotional and tears were shed. The fact they were sitting in Paul's dingy flat on a rainy Friday evening made it all the more depressing, stark and human. According to Topper, the band explained that, far from being dismissed, he was reluctantly being 'suspended'. If he was well enough once they'd finished touring the States and the UK he was back in.

This may have been the personal line but the group's public position was characteristically blunt. According to the drummer, it also resulted in his descent into intravenous drug use. 'The next thing I read in the paper was Joe saying I'd been sacked for being a heroin addict,' states Headon. 'That's when I started putting needles in my arm. Joe knew what he'd done was wrong, we all make mistakes. We made it up later. I fucked up, Joe fucked up, we all fucked up. That was the price we paid for making those great records.'

One question remains: Was Joe's disappearance a half-conscious ploy to bring the Topper question to a head? Joe himself never suggested it was: he preferred to think of his sojourn as 'bunking off work' or a break to 'prove to myself I was alive'.

But maybe that's to misjudge Joe, or to forget about the many complex levels on which most of us operate. Don Letts has this to say: 'Paris definitely seems to me to have been an orchestrated way of getting Topper out of the band. Joe had this weird way of getting what he wanted. Sometimes he was right to the point, but he also had a way of manoeuvring situations to his advantage. That would have been a classic example of him being manipulative, but not in an obvious way. In a subtle way. That's not a negative comment, that's an observation.'

Topper Headon, arguably the finest drummer of his era, was now no longer in The Clash. His departure saw the end of the classic Strummer-Jones-Simonon-Headon line-up, which had weathered five years and fourteen sides of vinyl. Topper tried to put a group together with Rob Stoner, Robert Gordon's bassplayer, and the black singer Buster Cherry Jones, but it came to nothing. In the next few years, Topper's heroin addiction would worsen, before being beaten back in recent years. He would never play with The Clash again.

Naturally, on his dismissal, The Clash denounced him in the press in much the same way they'd done to his predecessor, Terry Chimes, back in 1976. The press statement identified the cause of the split as 'a difference of opinion over the political direction the band will be taking'. The implication was that Topper wasn't radical enough for The Clash. Perhaps that was kinder than the truth, which quickly emerged, and made sense of his sudden departure to a perplexed but not altogether unsuspecting public.

Back at Clash HQ, it was panic stations. The group had just a week to find and rehearse a new drummer for the US leg of the tour, scheduled to kick off on 29 May at the Convention Hall, Asbury Park, New Jersey. Paul had already flown to America. It was decided that the only drummer who could fill the gap would be . . . Terry Chimes.

In the five years since his original on-off relationship with The Clash, Terry had performed with several punk groups, including Generation X, and worked as a session player. He was, in many ways, the obvious choice to replace Topper. He knew everyone, was liked, and could in theory at least already play everything off the first album.

'The Clash never worked in a methodical, calm way,' says Terry. 'It appealed to me, that kind of chaos. I liked the challenge. I remember Mick saying, "We could always have Cozy Powell, couldn't we?" You know when you meet someone you knew at school and after five minutes it's just like old times? It was a bit like that. They had a lot more money, a bigger road crew. But we got into the studio, started bashing out the tracks, we had a job to do. We didn't have time to think about what we were doing.'

Combat Rock had been released on 14 May. Rather unexpectedly, it received a rapturous ticker-tape reception in the UK. This was surely a testament to the strengths of the record, rather than the popularity of the group, given that the prevailing mood in the music press after *Sandinista!* and the Lyceum gigs was obdurately anti-Clash.

The decision to trim it back to a single LP seemed to have been a judicious one. The *NME*'s X. Moore called the album 'a sharp statement, powerful propaganda'. To him, it was their best since *Give 'Em Enough Rope*. Dave McCullough, writing in *Sounds*, disagreed: he believed it was their best since *The Clash* and drew a comparison to *Apocalypse Now*: 'The Clash . . . aren't static any more, but sailing into their own *Heart of Darkness*.' There is, indeed, a trippy, foreboding feel to some of the tracks, a sticky jungle intensity that might suggest the album was recorded after they went to Thailand, not before. A post-colonial melancholia and sadness saturates 'Sean Flynn', 'Straight to Hell' and the closing 'Death as a Star'.

Elsewhere – on 'Red Angel Dragnet' (Paul and Joe's song about the killing of subway Guardian Angel Frankie Melvin), 'Overpowered by Funk' (rap from Futura), 'Ghetto Defendant' (poetry interludes from Allen Ginsberg) – the spirit of Electric Lady makes its presence felt. The New York The Clash portray is apocalyptic, sleazy but exciting: law and order is crumbling. As with *Taxi Driver*'s Travis Bickle, who has a 'cameo' in 'Red Angel Dragnet', the people are taking justice into their own hands..

Combat Rock's angular funk-reggae hybrid is given a warmth by the profusion of words: Joe's human graffiti is as abundant on record as it appears written out on the inner sleeve. He reaches new poetic heights on 'Straight to Hell', singing with bug-eyed, histrionic compassion of 'railhead towns' that 'feel the steel mills rust' and 'junkiedom USA' where 'procaine proves the purest rock man groove'.

Then there are the singles: the jerky, Spaghetti Western hectoring of 'Know Your Rights', the rollicking 'Should I Stay or Should I Go?', and 'Rock the Casbah' – a track that sounds as if it was produced and arranged by some hot-shot US dance guru, rather than a bunch of punk rockers from London.

Combat Rock is The Clash's last great statement, and maybe their most important: it translates the guilty pleasure they found in war into something touchingly and genuinely anti-war. It is also honest, confused, unashamedly un-punk and musically innovative. Like *London Calling* and *Sandinista!*, it's also flawed, tantalising and infuriating. Its two fixations, New York and Vietnam, conjoin to produce a damning indictment of American foreign policy and an exuberant celebration of American street culture: *Combat Rock* was the urbanised mirror-image of Bruce Springsteen's *Nebraska* and Tom Waits's *Swordfishtrombone* (both released within broadly the same time-frame). The Clash, it seemed, had acquired the knack of writing ugly truths about America with a directness white American songwriters didn't then dare, and wouldn't manage to do as boldly until Springsteen's *Born in the USA* two years later. Their music had much more in common with the political invective of rap songs like Grandmaster Flash's 'The Message'.

Though 'Know Your Rights' stalled in the UK at number forty-three, *Combat Rock* climbed to number two. It was kept off the top spot by Paul McCartney's *Tug of War*. The album's title proved to be apt. That week the Falklands War, the first major conflict involving British servicemen in a generation, reached its crescendo. Paratroopers took their first land objective, Goose Green, with the loss of seventeen men. Margaret Thatcher appeared on the news basking in the sordid glory of it all.

The Clash's anti-war message wasn't getting through to the British sailors in Falkland Sound. The Royal Navy discouraged its men from listening to them (and several other punk artists) onboard Her Majesty's ships. Despite their increasingly glamorous sheen, in some quarters The Clash were still perceived as a threat to the moral and political integrity of the nation's youth.

The US tour began with the three dates at Asbury Park. Before the group left for America, the road crew had a meeting with Bernie at his favourite haunt, Marine Ices, the famous Sicilian ice-cream parlour in Chalk Farm.

'Whenever the crew met for a discussion with Bernie he'd always be late,' says Digby. 'We would say, "Yes, we must discuss these items with Bernie." We'd have them written down on bits of paper and he'd come in and start talking about something completely different. When we tried to question him about what we thought we needed to know he'd accuse us of "not being with the programme".'

Bernie was in the process of opening an office for The Clash in New York. This underlined the strength of his international vision for the group. The office was in a loft space on West 26th Street and Broadway. Rhodes, betraying his latent rag-trade passion, was keen to devise a range of Clash clothing to sell in America. There were obvious echoes of the failed Upstarts project in 1977. He recruited Alex Michon to start work on some designs in the New York loft. The clothes she made, with input from Paul, used camouflage designs, and Vietnam-era military styling. The fabrics were natural with Aertex webbing for ventilation. Paul, meanwhile, petitioned Bernie to turn the property next door into a Clash-sponsored art gallery, though this didn't happen.

Alex observed a change in Bernie since the last time they worked together, in 1978. 'I had this feeling that this time he wanted to make it all work,' she says. 'He wanted to make some money out of it. We weren't messing about any more. Before it was all much less business-like.'

'Bernard wanted everything on the business side to be done well,' explains Kosmo. 'He wanted to be seen to have all that under control. You have to take care of business. Bernie probably thinks he could run any corporation in Britain. It would sure be different! Maybe it's because he thinks so out of the box he wants people to see he can still deliver.'

The Asbury Park gigs went without a hitch. For the tour, Joe had his hair cut into a mohawk. The style had been adopted by the 101st Airborne division in the Second World War: it signalled that they wished to fight and die with the suicidal courage and passion of Native Indian warriors. Travis Bickle had worn a mohawk at the denouement of *Taxi Driver*.

With Terry still raw, the set was weighted towards the first album. 'We were winging it, seriously winging it,' Digby emphasises. 'The fact that the others were so good covered up for the fact that Terry wasn't particularly . . . let's say anyone who'd seen us with Topper would notice the difference.'

The last Asbury Park show doubled as a launch party for *Combat Rock* in the US. Epic hired the funfair and a few hundred journos, PR people and record company execs rode the attractions for free. 'Rock the Casbah' was due to be released as a single in the UK in early June. Possibly as a concession to Mick after the *Combat Rock* fiasco, it was decided that Jones should do a special remix. The work was done between the Asbury Park gigs in the Power Station in New York, with Chic's engineer Bob Clearmountain.

The tour rolled on. A video for 'Casbah' was shot by Don Letts on 8 and 9 June in Austin, Texas. Letts had assembled some props and an impromptu cast of extras. 'Can you imagine? I'm in the middle of Texas, a Dread, filming an armadillo, a Jewish guy, an Arab and a limo with cow-horns on the front,' he laughs. 'It really was the most talked about thing in Texas for that whole week. A total trip! I thought it was quite a brave thing, it was done with a lot of comedy, of course – the whole thing about Jews and Arabs trying to get on. I thought it was a brave move for the band within the format of MTV videos.'

The mood on set, however, was tense. Mick wasn't happy. This explains why he's wearing a veiled camouflage hat. 'Mick was beefing about something,' explains Letts. 'He comes out onto the set wearing red long-johns and black Dr Marten's. I was like, "Mick, you look like a match stick." Everyone else was killing themselves laughing. If he had performed like that, he'd have never lived it down. The thing about film is that it's for ever. You will look like a cunt for ever. So I went and had a quick word in his ear and got him to put that combat stuff on. But he was still a bit miffed and put that mask on, it was some army thing, an anti-gas mask or something. As the video is coming to an end, Joe went over and ripped it off. That was all because he was having a moody.'

A certain major TV channel in America thought Don's video was great. They arranged to interview him for a profile. When he arrived at their offices there was some embarrassed shuffling around. The interview was off, he was told: everyone was extremely apologetic, but they hadn't realised he was black.

In July, The Clash returned to Britain to play the dates rescheduled because of Joe's disappearance. It was then back to America for another tour that stretched into September. It was so hot Paul defaulted to teenage rude boy mode and once again razored his Hollywood quiff into a skinhead.

It was around this time the group were approached by The Who to play with them on their 'farewell' 1982 tour of American stadiums. The Clash had a discussion and concluded it would be a good thing to do. It would be their last tour with Mick Jones as guitarist.

12
CLASHDÄMMERUNG

'It smells like slow death in there. This was the end of the river all right.'

Martin Sheen as Captain Willard, *Apocalypse Now*

'His rash fierce blaze of riot cannot last,
For rash fires soon burn out themselves;
Small showers are long, but sudden storms are short.'

WILLIAM SHAKESPEARE, *RICHARD II*

The approach to The Clash to support The Who came through the American agent the groups shared. The call was at Pete Townshend's behest. 'I was a huge fan, which is why they were on the tour,' he says. 'Incidentally, I hated that tour.'

There was vague talk of Topper replacing Who drummer Kenney Jones for the dates. Friends of Headon, including Johnny Green and Robin Banks, insist Townshend did make an approach. Townshend admits 'it is possible'. But Topper's condition – he'd recently been fined for stealing a bus stop sign – meant the ironic prospect of The Clash supporting their recently sacked drummer didn't become reality.

The Who weren't the first 1960s giants to ask The Clash to support them. The previous year, there had been a discussion about the group playing with The Rolling Stones in LA. This idea fizzled out after The Clash wanted equal billing. Kosmo's idea was to promote it like a boxing match, a fight between the young pretenders and reigning champions. 'Contests' were a common way of advertising gigs in Jamaica. The Stones' management said they didn't like the idea and the plans were dropped.

A tour with The Who was an attractive proposition. There was a symbolic resonance about one great West London group handing over power to another: Kosmo describes the idea as 'a passing on of the baton'. The bill would also bring closure to the strange parallels between the two bands:

Joe's first guitar, Schoolgirl's practice room, Paul's Townshend fixation, Bob Pridden's alleged input into the Vanilla demos . . .

The prospect of playing at large American stadiums presented huge ideological difficulties for The Clash, however. The group had always preferred the relative intimacy of medium-size venues. It was this philosophy of being able to see and communicate with their audience that lay behind their week-long residencies at comparatively modest venues like Bond's and the Lyceum. The Clash had in the past also publicly expressed a distaste for stadium rock shows because they represented the business at its most cynical and capitalistic: over-priced tickets, terrible views of the stage, crap sound, expensive burgers and refreshments. Wasn't that what punk had set out to destroy? But there was something else, too: The Clash to play at Shea Stadium? Like The Beatles?

The decision to sign up wasn't taken lightly. Indeed, it involved a whole shift in the band's way of thinking. It was the beginning of a realisation that if the group was to become any bigger – which in Clash terms (and I believe they still genuinely felt this) meant 'reaching even more people' rather than 'selling even more records' – they would have to jettison some of their punk-based ideas.

'One thing Bernard instilled in me,' explains Kosmo, 'and this is a key thing, is that if you're really going to compete, then compete. And that means you have to get out of these . . . not silly notions, but *unrealistic* notions. At some point we went international. The American thing was the American thing – and we had learned that what applied there did not apply back home. The Who support was an opportunity to move forward and we decided to take it. Maybe we were just thinking, "Great, half a million Who fans going cheap."'

The new mode of thinking involved some specious justifications. The 'unrealistic notions' The Clash would have to abandon clearly included playing where they could be properly seen and heard. This flew in the face of one of their most dearly held tenets: treating the audience as intimates.

The Clash's ideology was being bent out of shape again. I ask Kosmo what he believed The Clash's values amounted to at that time. 'Truth and rights, I guess,' he answers. 'Don't waste your time with Van Halen, there's a world out there. Right at the beginning we said we were anti-racist, pro-creative, against ignorance. We thought our songs and entertainment should have content and be informed. They should have integrity. I don't think any of that had changed. Bernard was interested in changing the whole culture. You don't have to have crappy clothes, bands, music. It should all be great, fantastic, exciting – and we believed in that. With our derring-do we really thought we could do it. Personally, I didn't like those stadium shows and I didn't like festivals. But it wasn't about personal preferences, it was bigger than that.'

And the money? 'The money for The Who shows was good,' he says. 'But that was never the issue.'

The tour began on 25 September at the JFK Stadium, Philadelphia. Between The Who dates, The Clash scheduled a number of smaller shows at university campuses, including Kent State in Ohio, the scene of the infamous murder of four anti-war protestors by National Guardsmen in 1970.

The flagship dates at Shea Stadium in New York, on 12 and 13 October, coincided with the release of 'Rock the Casbah' as a US single. Don Letts was asked to shoot some footage around the Shea gigs (worked into a belated promo video for 'Should I Stay or Should I Go?'). According to Kosmo, The Clash had been bemused by the way The Who operated offstage as four discrete individuals, each with his own transport, trailer and personnel, as if they couldn't bear to be together. It left a profound mark on them. It was, says Kosmo, 'a kind of horrible vision of where The Clash might end up'.

The Clash therefore decided to drive to the stadium together. The original idea was for Joe, Mick, Paul and Terry to turn up in a chequered yellow cab, but Don was keen to film the group's reaction as they travelled en route to the venue. He consequently persuaded Kosmo to hire an open-top white Cadillac. What some critics seized upon as a symbol of The Clash's degeneracy was, it seems, actually an attempt to communicate their solidarity as a band.

The sheer size of Shea Stadium was something to behold. A baseball ground, it had been built in 1964 and famously staged concerts by The Beatles in 1965 and 1966. It was located near La Guardia airport, directly underneath a noisy flight path. Its capacity was around 60,000.

The Clash were due onstage at 8 p.m., after David Johansen. They settled into their dressing room. The security around the headliners was tight. 'I remember we all had to keep at least 30 feet away from The Who,' recalls Don Letts. 'You didn't catch their eye. I remember they wouldn't let The Clash have as much volume as them, either.'

Digby Cleaver: 'Barry [Baker] and I loaded our gear on to the back corner of the stage. We were told to stand there with it and not move. They were beginning to let people in. There were thousands of them, little dots in the distance. I said, "Barry, did you ever start this box-pushing business to do this?" It was very stressful – it was October and I worked stripped to the waist, it was that hot. It was a heightened state of frenzy. We only had twenty minutes. The terrible thing about those huge great shows in America is that there are so many unions to be paid, penalties and stuff to be incurred, that if you run over by five minutes it's going to cost you in the region of $75,000. So we had to work to the limit and we did.'

The Clash went through their backstage rituals. Joe banned smoking in the dressing room for twenty minutes prior to the group's performance. Ray Jordan applied Joe's towel-and-gaffer-tape 'strum guard' to protect his wrist from getting slashed on his strings. The pre-gig drink was a quick shot of vodka.

Kit Buckler from CBS had flown over to see the shows. 'I was there for a couple days beforehand,' he says. 'It was really exciting, but the day itself seemed quite dark. I remember they weren't talking to each other in the dressing room – obviously they were nervous, it was a *huge* gig – but there was an atmosphere there. Something must have happened. The mood was so unpleasant I left and went for a beer somewhere.'

The shows themselves were fantastic. The 'Should I Stay or Should I Go?' footage shows Joe in a Daniel Boone coon-skin cap and Ray-ban shades giving it the electric leg, while Paul and Mick bound around the stage in their military head-gear, looking on the gigantic stage like gangly Action Man figures. The fifty-minute sets had an enormous impact. 'They were good,' says Pete Townshend. 'They managed the stadium crowds far better than The Pretenders, who did the tour before.'

For The Clash it was a strange experience. Paul told Bob Gruen that 'It felt a bit like miming because there were so many people there. The audience wasn't allowed to be very close, so you didn't really get the same reaction from them.'

At the aftershow party, Andy Warhol hung out with the group. Don Letts pretended he'd spiked the celebratory cake with acid. This freaked Andy out. That day, Clash production chief Roger Goodman had helped to smuggle some 500 fans the group had collected en route into the venue – a bit of old punk attitude amid the tightly orchestrated stadium security.

The Clash still had another two weeks of touring to go. They had been on the road now for four and a half months. They hadn't had a break since before Topper was sacked in May, and that was the enforced month-long lay-off caused by Joe's vanishing act. Since then, they'd played around seventy shows with Terry back on board.

Throughout the summer, Paul and Joe's relationship with Mick had further deteriorated. Jones had become increasingly isolated. He found touring difficult at the best of times. There was also the question of his waning influence over the group following Bernie's return. Though Mick concedes there was no other option, Topper's dismissal had been, in Jones's words, 'another band decision that I had gone along with'. This meant that the last three major arguments among the group – about Bernie's reinstatement, Glyn Johns's *Combat Rock* edit and Topper's sacking – had been democratically settled in Paul and Joe's favour. Mick had also been riled that he was kept in the dark about Joe's vanishing stunt. It's entirely probable that the guitarist now felt the power in the group now resided with a newly emerging and invincible Bernie-Joe-Paul-Kosmo axis. Since Bernie's return, his and Mick's distrust of each other was only ever cosmetically disguised. Now, it seemed, Mick's relationship with Joe and Paul was the worst it had even been. Kit Buckler describes it as 'almost open warfare' at this point.

Terry Chimes had a ring-side view of the developing fissure in the Clash camp. 'By then Joe and Mick obviously had a difference of opinions on a range of things,' he says. 'They had devised a system where they didn't have to confront each other all the time – there was an avoidance going on, which covered up the fact there were deeper issues there. Being on tour is a whole different world, it's a fourth reality anyway. It's easy not to be around each other, except for the show.'

So was Mick insufferable? 'There were times when people could have accused Mick of being a bit unreasonable,' Terry answers. 'But nothing that was a big deal. I remember him asking for a banana at some place and this bloke came back and said, "I can't get one, there are no bananas in the building." To get one would have meant hiring a car. Mick got very angry and said, "All I want is a banana." So the bloke said, "Look, I'll get you a case of scotch." But Mick said, "I don't want a case of scotch, I want a fucking banana!" He got very stroppy, and I was thinking, "There aren't any bananas, have a melon instead." But at the end of the day all he did was shout at the guy.'

Terry was concerned enough about the growing cleft between Mick and the rest of the Clash camp to confront Paul and Joe about it. 'I was saying, "Surely Mick is just the same as he always was,"' explains Chimes. 'But they were going, "You don't understand, you haven't had all these years with him that we've had." They felt they couldn't work with him any more. And I thought, "If they can't work with Mick, they haven't got a band." You can change a drummer and no one will notice, but you can't change a key person like that without anything happening.'

At the end of November, The Clash flew to the Caribbean to play the Jamaica World Music Festival in Montego Bay. Joe had followed Paul and cropped his hair into a skinhead: rude boys in their spiritual homeland. The set they performed leaned heavily on their reggae numbers. It was broadcast live on local radio. The DJ complimented Paul's bass-playing. Mick's effects-laden guitar wasn't, according to Paul, quite so enthusiastically received.

The group hung around for a while then drifted back to London. There had been talk of playing a gig in Cuba – Mo Armstrong, their radical friend from San Francisco, had contacts there – but eventually it proved impossible to organise. Instead, The Clash took their first proper break for six years. As 1983 approached there was nothing at all in The Clash's diary.

Though *Creem* had described it as 'a piece of shit', *Combat Rock* had scaled to number seven in the US charts, selling well over a million copies. Mick's remix of 'Rock the Casbah' had reached number eight. The Clash were now a truly international act – top ten on both sides of the Atlantic. The cumulative effect of these healthy worldwide sales was to generate some much-needed cash. The group were at last able to break free from debt.

Their newfound solvency enabled them to put the business end of their operation in order. The mess surrounding the writing credits for *Sandinista!* (which itself had reportedly notched up sales of around 800,000 copies) was partly resolved with a number of cash settlements. The office in New York was closed. The group sat down together and worked out who exactly had written what on *Combat Rock*. Topper was awarded the biggest cut of 'Rock the Casbah'.

Symbolically, 'the king of the squatters', as Kosmo and Bernie called Joe, finally put a down payment on bricks and mortar. He bought a house in Lancaster Road, Ladbroke Grove, five minutes' walk from Paul's gaff and ten from Mick's. Joe had turned thirty the previous summer: he at last seemed ready to relinquish his outsider credentials for something approaching a settled home-life. That spring, he ran the London Marathon in aid of Leukaemia Research (the sponsor was, unfortunately, the right-wing *Sun*).

Around this time, Mick split from Ellen and began dating a new girl-friend, Daisy. In May, Paul and Pearl Harbour married in New York so that Pearl could legally stay with Simonon in London. The Clash, in their different ways, were all moving on.

Despite officially being off-duty, the group remained active. In December

1982, Joe wrote and produced a single for Janie Jones, ex-vice queen and Clash-song-inspiration. 'House of the Ju-Ju Queen', featuring backing from The Clash and The Blockheads, is one of the group's buried jewels.

Unused to being inactive, Strummer seemed restless. In January and February 1983, he produced and directed a fifty-minute silent black-and-white film, *Hell W10*. It seemed only natural for a group who revelled in a cinematic self-image to make their own movie. The film starred Paul and Mick as rival underworld characters in Notting Hill, warring over a consignment of heroin. The cast featured The Clash's mates and colleagues: Kosmo, Ray Jordan, Digby, Gaby, Micky Gallagher, Pearl, Tony James, Neal Whitmore, Martin Degville, Daisy, Pennie Smith, Tymon, Sean Carasov, Mark Salter.

The chief memory of those involved is the weather: blooming freezing. 'If you look at it we're all walking round in suits,' recalls Digby. 'But underneath our shirts we all had two long-sleeved T-shirts and under our trousers we were wearing tights because it was so bloody cold. The scene at the end where we all get shot on the bit of waste-ground next to Westbourne Park bus garage . . . that was two absolutely freezing-cold nights. How Tymon managed to play the fiddle while walking by the canal I don't know. I think he had four pairs of gloves on and took them off quickly every time Joe said, "Action!"'

Don Letts: 'I think the brilliant thing about *Hell W10* is how it shows a side of Joe he'd always had, from The 101'ers straight through to The Mescaleros. He had this way of making people do things they didn't want to do. Everybody in that film did it for nothing. Joe just had to say, "Come on!" and we'd all be there for him. If Joe wanted to make a film, everyone would have helped him even if it meant freezing to death. Those people would have jumped off a cliff for that guy. I have got to say, he had that effect on me, too.'

Joe evidently had fun casting the film. Paul's character Earl is a loveable rogue with a tasty right jab. Mick, meanwhile, is the ostentatious and volatile imigrant gangster Mr Socrates. He was caricaturing his band-mates' personalities and reflecting off-screen tensions. In recent years, Paul has admitted that, at this time, the greatest discord in the group was between him and Mick, not Mick and Joe. The two survivors from The London SS were now barely speaking.

For years, *Hell W10* was believed lost. Then in 2002 the film turned up on a London market stall, and the following year it was included as an extra on the *Essential Clash* DVD.

The four-month break gave the group time to ruminate on the events of the previous year. After Topper's departure they'd launched straight into five months of fairly solid touring. They were painfully aware that it was Topper's 'Rock the Casbah' that had boosted sales of *Combat Rock*, propelling it into the US top ten. 'With Topper we had no time to assess the situation,' says Mick. 'We just had to go forward and do whatever we had to do. He was in such a state he couldn't have done that tour. But I don't think there was ever a real plan about what to do next.'

The group's new level of success in America created all kinds of difficulties, especially for Joe, caught as he was between being 'Woody Guthrie and Elvis Presley'. 'When "Rock the Casbah" was a hit in America, I saw I was becoming a professional rebel,' he admitted. 'We were becoming a joke. We'd been sincere when we were struggling, but when we hit that new plateau I thought, "This has gotta stop." If we'd carried on with a few more hit singles like that we could have had the houses in Tuscany and Lear jets. But it would've been dishonest.'

Terry Chimes had told The Clash he wasn't prepared to wait around for them. He sensed the contradictions and conflicts pulling at the group wouldn't be quickly or easily resolved. He went off to work with Billy Idol, then Hanoi Rocks.

During March and April, a familiar about-to-fall-apartness reigned. There were echoes of the moody, uncertain hiatus that occurred before they'd begun work on *London Calling*. Then the insurmountable task appeared to be cracking America and turning The Clash into an international act. Now the challenge was: where did they go now that they'd become a successful international act? Play more stadiums? Make pots of money? Become more remote? Turn into The Who? Rumours abounded at this time of a Clash split. Communication between the various factions within the group was poor. No one seemed to know how to take the band forward in a way that was acceptable to everyone. Pearl Harbour recalls that 'Mick wanted to go on holiday and the others were like, "We don't go on holidays."'

The impetus to re-start The Clash came from outside. In April 1983, they were approached by the organisers of the three-day Us Festival in Glen Helen Regional Park, Los Angeles. (The festival's title was an abbreviation of the banner 'Unite Us In Song'.) The offer was to headline the opening New Music Day on 28 May, which would also feature A Flock of Seagulls, The Stray Cats and Men at Work. They'd be playing to a crowd of around 150,000. The fee was a cool $500,000, a phenomenal amount of money.

Bernie and Kosmo believed they should do it. One reason was to get the group working again. Agreeing to the gig meant finding a new drummer. Topper had been required to sign various legal documents relating to royalty payments, and the state they'd found him in confirmed he would be unable to re-join the group. Bernie placed an advert in *Melody Maker* on 23 April. Baker and Digby were charged with whittling down the two hundred or so applicants to the best ten.

The auditions took place at Ear Studios in Freston Road. Each candidate was asked to play along to backing tapes of 'Safe European Home', 'Armagideon Time' and 'Radio Clash'. This would test their ability to play rock, reggae and funk. The successful contestants were then photographed by Baker: Joe, Mick and Paul were presented with dossiers to select the final four, who were invited to play a half-hour set with The Clash. It was a process of gruelling musical Darwinism reminiscent of the way Bernie had constructed the group back in 1976. The job went to Pete Howard, a twenty-three-year-old from Bath. 'It was so obvious that Peter fitted in the best,' recalls Digby. 'That's how he got in. What totally amazed us was how many of the bloody songs he knew perfectly already.'

In 2004, Pete Howard is playing with a group, formerly signed to Rough Trade, called Queen Adrena. Initially, he'd seemed reluctant to talk about his experiences in The Clash, but we arranged to meet up for a drink in a pub near Finsbury Park station. Disarmingly, Pete still looks young enough to be in a 'new' group. He turns out to be extremely affable and a fund of rollicking anecdotes, but says, 'You have to understand, it wasn't a particularly happy period in my life.'

Pete began drumming at school, before serving an apprenticeship in his late teens with 1960s Larry Parnes creation – and Kim's dad – Marty Wilde, then playing the nostalgia circuit. He reveals that he already knew Digby before he joined The Clash. 'When I went to the audition, Digby made me feel really comfortable about it all,' he says. 'As always, he was the total fucking gentleman and a saint. We did three or four auditions and then it got down to me and this other guy. Part of the audition was playing football – it was The Clash and their entourage versus The Damned and their entourage. Obviously you've got to imagine I was from Bath and it was like, "Oh my fucking God." It was a kind of team-bonding exercise to see what happened. It was pretty fucking exhilarating. We all went to a bar afterwards.'

Pete was hired by Bernie on a basic wage of £100 a week. This was, of course, insulting pay for a job in an internationally successful group. His elation was further dampened by the heavy, aggressive atmosphere in which he suddenly found himself. The first indication that he had not joined any ordinary rock 'n' roll band came straight after the audition.

'Kosmo and Bernie took me aside and said, "You realise you'll find yourself in a position where there's ample opportunity for you to take drugs if you want to." To be honest, I'd never taken coke in my life and I didn't know what they were talking about. I thought they meant pot. I knew that they had troubles with Topper but I didn't know they were specific about coke, so I just said, "I don't know anything about it!" The funny thing was that as soon as I got out of there someone offered me some coke. I fucking did it, it wasn't bad at all. But I had to be careful about it.'

Pete Howard gives an extraordinary glimpse into the confrontational, controlling, explosive, often unpleasant day-to-day reality of being in The Clash, long taken for granted by the people in and around the band. He soon found himself in trouble when he told a reporter that he'd previously been in a Bath-based group called Cold Fish. When Bernie saw the story in the *NME* he went ballistic, according to Kosmo: 'Bernard said, "What the fuck is all this?" And Pete said, "Well I know this guy—" We said, "No, it doesn't work this way with us, pal. We are all or nothing – we are a gang. You don't go around talking to press. We keep things tight, it's just between us."'

Since his return to The Clash fold in early 1981, Bernie seemed to have enjoyed a far less volatile relationship with Joe, Mick and Paul. One possible reason was the presence of Kosmo, who managed to act as a buffer between Rhodes and the group. Kosmo's ability to work with Bernie, and unite band and management in a common purpose (his quasi-mythical 'Quest'), was the grease that allowed The Clash to function. Bernie's ideas – Joe's disappearance, for example – were now mediated and refined by Vinyl. In the time-frame of Pete Howard's recruitment, however, Bernie seems to have regained some of his former anarchic energy. It's possible that Mick's increasingly strained relations with Joe and Paul was allowing Rhodes the opportunity to re-assert himself.

Digby recalls Rhodes reviving the 'getting paid lesson' that Johnny Green and Baker had suffered five years before: 'Baker and I were retained on a three-way sliding scale,' explains Digby. 'If the band were doing nothing we got a hundred pounds a week, in the studio we had two hundred, if the band were touring we got three hundred. So when we weren't doing much we still had a hundred-pound retainer. Bernie's idea of fun would be to be completely un-findable on the telephone all day Friday until about half past four. He would then phone one of us and say that he'd left our cheques at Stiff's offices in Alexander Street, or at the pub next door with Kosmo. So I'd arrive hot-foot at five on a Friday to find I couldn't put the cheque in until Monday, which meant I couldn't draw any money out till Thursday.'

There were a handful of rehearsals before the group's warm-up gigs for the Us Festival. This mini-tour began in Michigan, then moved on to Amarillo in Texas. There, a dwarf decked out in an armadillo costume made the evening especially memorable by back-flipping across the stage during 'Rock the Casbah'. Joe had met the Amarillo Armadillo, as he called himself, in a bar the previous night. The Clash's on-the-road craziness immediately lifted everyone's spirits. It was a reminder of the group's gift for invoking chaos and fun wherever they went. But Pete was becoming aware of a group hierarchy – with him at the bottom – and he once again incurred the wrath of Kosmo.

'Peter was a very, very good drummer,' says Vinyl. 'But we were on the bus in Texas and he was playing "Walking on the Moon" by The Police, and I just tore into him. I couldn't find anything more offensive than hearing that music on a Clash tour bus. He was probably just thinking, "Well, the drumming part is good." So I think it was a bit of a shock to him. The Police were the enemy as far as I was concerned and I would have said what I said to anyone. I guess Topper was smarter and he'd listen to the stuff we hated at home.'

Pete's wages were also an issue. 'It was at a big auditorium in Texas,' remembers Digby. 'Pete was standing at the side of the stage, face as red as a brick. I said, "What's up with you?" He says, "Does three hundred dollars a gig sound fair to you?" "Who for?" "For the drummer in The Clash." I told Pete, "Tell Bernie to stuff it up his arse!"'

The Us Festival has gone down in history as an ill-tempered and unpleasant affair, marred by violence. It seemed obvious from the start that The Clash felt uncomfortable about doing the show. It was as if Bernie had decided that, if they were going to operate at this level – playing huge outdoor gigs for hundreds of thousands of dollars – they'd make sure they were a nuisance. It was the social banditry philosophy again: The Clash burst in like a bunch of crazy outlaws, shoot the place up, take the cash and then redistribute among the needy (in this case, they talked of using it to open the club they'd been promising since 1976; in fact, some of the money was given to London pirate radio stations, and another chunk spent on trying to finish the ill-fated *Clash on Broadway* film).

On the day of the show, Rhodes decided to pick a very public fight with the festival's organiser, the Apple computers guru Steve Wozniak. During Men at Work's set, Rhodes called an emergency press conference at which The Clash suddenly declared that they wouldn't perform unless Wozniak donated $100,000 to a summer camp for disadvantaged children in California. They also tried to pressure Van Halen, headlining the following day, and some other acts into giving a portion of their fees to a worthy cause.

Pete Howard: 'We did this press conference where Joe was going, "We're not fucking puppets, we're not going to be fucked around by this spoilt brat [Wozniak], we're suing him for $12 million." But it was just Bernie playing games. I still ponder about that now . . .'

Joe later said that he (or more likely Bernie) was riled that Wozniak was 're-staging Woodstock for his own ego gratification and tax loss in his back-yard'.

Bernie: 'I put that festival together, not The bloody Clash. Apple wanted to promote their computers. I said 10 per cent of the money should go to a given cause. That's where Jerry Dammers [of The Specials] got the idea to do all the things that Geldof got the knighthood for. It started with that festival in San Bernadino. I had the manager of one act saying, "I ain't gonna give 10 per cent to no fucking poor people!" Now they're saying all these artists are wonderful people.'

Frantic negotiations took place backstage. The festival organisers finally agreed to pay around a third of the ransom, as long as The Clash took the stage immediately. The strained backstage atmosphere intensified.

'Joe wasn't happy and neither was Kosmo,' explains Digby. 'I think Bernie had been working on the two of them all day. He'd walk around just before they went into press conferences telling Joe what a bunch of bastards the journalists were and reminding him what they'd written about the group. He'd want Joe to be in the Joe Strummer mood you expected to see when he was behind a microphone with his Telecaster.'

Kosmo: 'They [the organisers] made it clear to Bernard that we were invited there as "the groovy new thing" and that the "big night" would be the one headlined by Van Halen. They said they didn't expect that much from us. Bernard said, "Fuck you! We're not going to be patronised like a bunch of idiots – we've had enough." There was someone winding up Wozniak – weird connotations and a whole bullshit philosophy. Bernard spotted the spuriousness of all this: he saw it as a capitalist's game. The discussions about whether we should play were going on throughout the previous night. In the end, I went down there [from LA] on my own . . . not one of my best days. I was at the site all day and didn't know whether they would be playing or not, there weren't the cell phones there are now. But we didn't want to be marginalised and that was Bernard at his most militant.'

The Clash eventually went on two hours late. Joe was in a filthy mood. Faced with an audience of 150,000, the biggest the group would ever perform to, Strummer could only manage a mangled and defeatist address above the voluminous hubbub: 'I s'pose you don't wanna hear me going on about this and that and what's up my arse, huh?' he growled. 'Try this one for size [adopts phoney West Coast accent]: "Well, hi, everybody! Ain't it groovy!" Ain't you sick of hearing that for the last hundred and fifty years?'

Directly after the last song of the set, the DJ at the side of the stage began addressing the crowd over the PA. Kosmo interpreted this as an attempt to 'rob the group of an encore' and ran over and punched him in the face. 'It was a fraught day,' he says. 'I just went after him and the next thing I knew everyone was there. I certainly remember Mick getting a few punches in. Oh yeah, you'd be surprised! He ain't scared.'

The American security piled in. Joe and Paul dived in to save Mick and Kosmo. 'They were all rolling around on the left side of the stage,' recalls Digby. 'Almost as soon as it started, it ended, people being separated, lots of shouting, everyone being dragged off in different directions. Me and Barry were putting the gear away. It left a really nasty taste in our mouths. We'd just earned all this money – well, we hadn't, but the band had – and it didn't feel at all good. No, it wasn't like a good Clash gig.'

'After the punch-up I remember we were all in terrific spirits,' says Kosmo. 'It felt like we were back once again, that sense of camaraderie.'

The esprit de corps wouldn't last long.

The group took a couple of weeks off, before reconvening in London in June. They began practising again in Freston Road. Thanks in part to Britain's victory over Argentina in the Falklands War, Margaret Thatcher's popularity had soared. She was returned to power that summer with a land-slide win. A £500 million cut in public spending was announced within weeks. The privatisation of support jobs within the NHS swiftly followed: tens of thousands feared for their livelihoods. The Tories' programme of right-wing economic reforms was soon to result in the most prolonged and violent industrial unrest for decades.

Meanwhile, life in West London carried on as usual. That summer, Pete Howard witnessed how the group lived outside Clash hours. He observed the social distance that had developed between Mick and the others. Joe, Paul and Kosmo, with respective girlfriends and wives, often spent their evenings drinking in the Earl of Percy at the end of Paul's road. Mick, meanwhile, hung around with his own crowd, whom the others referred to as 'the Creatures of the Night': Tony James, Martin Degville, Neal Whitmore (all later of Sigue Sigue Sputnik). Mick and Daisy were also pretty much inseparable at this time. Pete Howard believes that Joe and Paul may have resented this: he felt they wanted to revive the gang vibe. Mick didn't.

'Mick was quite an aloof kind of guy,' recalls Pete. 'I don't think it was in a contrived way, I think he was aloof because he was a big pot smoker. It was a different lifestyle. He'd stay indoors, smoke dope, watch TV and listen to music. He didn't come out much. He wasn't really a drinker at all. Joe, on the other hand, was a very sociable person. He was able to talk to anyone. He had so much fucking energy! Even if he hadn't been Joe Strummer he would have gone over and talked to the guys propping up the bar. He was able to do that in that sort of upper-class, classless way. Paul was always the gentleman. He was friendly and a really decent guy, but first and foremost he was a fucking icon. He had that street thing, an eye for style and detail. I mean, Joe couldn't dress to save his fucking life. Paul always looked just right.'

Digby: 'If I needed to find Paul on a Saturday afternoon I used to go straight to the Dub Vendor [reggae shop then under Ladbroke Grove station]. After he'd had his lunch he'd spend the afternoon in the shop just listening to tunes – and if he liked one they'd put it aside for him. Long before they were fashionable, he had two decks and a mixer. He'd make the best reggae compilations ever imaginable, with sound effects linking the songs.'

About a week or so into the rehearsals at Ear, it became evident that none of the bad feeling within The Clash which had stewed throughout the previous year had gone away. There appeared to be a conflict about where to take the group musically. Mick had become enamoured with technology: he was using a state-of-the-art Roland guitar synthesizer, which he'd bought in America. Paul referred to it as 'a dalek's handbag'. He believes Mick had got 'bored with playing guitar', but didn't know how to use the new equipment.

'Mick was turning up about two hours late every day,' recalls Pete Howard. 'Then some days he just didn't bother turning up at all. It got to the point where it was like, "If he comes, he comes, if he doesn't, he doesn't." We ended up rehearsing without him. By then Mick and Joe were finding it really hard to talk. They were poles apart. It got to the point where Joe was posting lyrics through Mick's door. He thought the music Mick was putting to them was a pile of shit. He was citing that as why the relationship between him and Mick had broken down.'

Meanwhile, Bernie had presented a management contract to each member of the group. Mick apparently declined to sign his without getting his lawyer to read it. (This may be the provenance of Joe's later comment that Mick had said: 'I don't mind what The Clash does as long as you check it with my lawyer first.') According to Digby, Bernie was incensed by this. 'Bernie twisted Joe up about it,' recalls Digby. 'Bernie was saying, "Do you really want to be in the same band as *him*? Paul's signed it, you've signed it, what makes him think he's so bloody special?"'

'In my opinion Bernie definitely put pressure on Paul and Joe to get rid of Mick,' says Pearl Harbour.

Musical atrophy set in. The rehearsals fizzled out.

In the early summer of 1983, Bernie had spent some of The Clash's funds on refurbishing the building opposite the former Rehearsal Rehearsals. (The one with the ramp up the side, where Joe, Mick and Paul had posed for the first album cover.) The building now had the look and feel of a proper rehearsal studio. Kosmo opened his own version of a private-members club upstairs with a fridge full of Red Stripe. He wanted to get a social vibe going again.

The Clash arranged to meet there in August to try to figure a way forward. CBS were, after all, expecting a follow-up to *Combat Rock* at some point. Pete Howard doesn't recall being around. Perhaps he wasn't even invited. Everyone's memories of the exact sequence of events is hazy.

Mick has never really spoken before in any detail about what went on in his last days with the group. It has always been difficult territory, for obvious reasons. He remained graciously tip-lipped about his dismissal throughout the 1980s. Even in the *Westway to the World* documentary he doesn't cast much light on what he believed really happened. But times have moved on: you get the impression that now, after Joe's death and his re-emergence as a successful producer, Jones now sees the story of The Clash as history.

During a conversation in early summer 2004, he tells me: 'We had a bunch of new songs, some of which ended up on the first BAD [Big Audio Dynamite] album. Originally, "The Bottom Line" was called "Trans Cash Free Pay One". It was a song about a cash machine or the future of finance. I gave that to Joe with that tune, but nothing came of it. By then, our relationship was . . . *bad*. We weren't really communicating. The group was dissipating.'

It was then that Bernie came up with an outside-the-box solution to the group's musical malaise – or else a cunning plan to precipitate Mick's sacking. 'He took me to the pub,' explains Mick. 'He said, "What sort of records do you want to make?" I said, "Rock 'n' roll records, Bernie." So the next thing was he told us we've got to play like New Orleans guys. That's when it got *really* bad. It quickly started to fall apart then. We were in rehearsals trying to be like New Orleans guys for Bernie. We were all looking at the floor, thinking, "What the fuck?" New Orleans music! We loved New Orleans music but it was like, "Aaargh!" It was a constriction or something. We were in a rehearsal room in Camden, not New Orleans. What with everything else going on, I think that was actually designed to make me go mad. I left pretty soon after that.'

The end came on Monday 29 August, the week of Carnival. It is somehow ironic that the break-up happened just yards away from where The Clash had started out seven years earlier – two twenty-year-old art-school drop-outs and a twenty-three-year-old pub-rock singer going nowhere. It must have felt like a lifetime ago.

Digby Cleaver was there when the showdown occurred. 'They've only rehearsed for a week and Jones is getting thoroughly disgruntled, he's the last one to arrive and the first one to go. They're not really producing huge amounts of new stuff and then it happened. One Monday I went out to make a pot of tea and came back in to see Mick putting one of his guitars into its case. Now this is unheard of. I said to him, "Are you all right, Mick?" He's got this rictus grin on his face. I went, "What are you doing? Do you want me to take the guitar home to you after rehearsals?"

'He said, "You'd better come with me", and we walked out of the room. "What is it?" "They've asked me to leave the group." My immediate reaction was, "They can't do that, it's your group, isn't it?" And his answer was, "That's what I thought until about midday today. Strummer and Simonon have just told me they don't want me in the band." I said, "What do you think of that?" He went, "I don't want to be in the fucking band with them anyway. I'll start my own fucking band."'

The story goes that Bernie ran into the cobbled yard after Mick, waving a cheque by way of apology. Mick took it. By weird coincidence, Topper arrived at that moment to see what his old group was up to.

Quoted in *MOJO* in 1999, Paul explained the incident from his angle. It seems it was he who brought the situation to a head. 'Me and Joe had been talking about it, and we got to the point where I said, "We're grown men, I can't take any more of this" and Joe agreed. We were both in agreement that we were fed up, we wanted to get on with the job, rather than waiting around for Mick. We were in the rehearsal room and Joe said, "We want you to leave." Mick said to me, "What do you say?" and I said, "Well, yeah . . ." I think he felt let down by that.'

Being asked to leave a group is a unique and particularly hurtful form of rejection. It had happened to Mick before, of course, when Guy Stevens had ejected him from Violent Luck in 1975. Then Mick had written to Robin Banks in prison and told him, 'I've been stabbed in the back for my belief in rock 'n' roll.' This time, matters were more complicated. It wasn't a boy robbed of his teenage dream. It was more like a bitter divorce. Asked what he felt that day he left The Clash, Mick famously said, 'I didn't feel anything.' One suspects he was in shock. He even dyed his hair blond for Carnival because he didn't want to be recognised.

The events that afternoon unleashed in him a new energy. After only a couple of hours' deliberation, Digby decided his loyalties lay with Mick ('I liked Mick, I didn't like Bernie') and drove over to Jones's flat in Colville Gardens. Tony James was already there. Mick was on the phone to his mate Leo Williams (former Roxy barman and Slits roadie) who played bass. Jones was talking about using drum-machines for a new project. An early incarnation of Big Audio Dynamite, initially called TRAC, was already in place by the end of the afternoon.

The reaction to the news of Mick's departure seemed generally to be dismay and disbelief. 'It seemed inconceivable,' says Tony James. 'You don't sack Keith Richards from The Rolling Stones. OK, Joe had the lyrics and was the great performer, but it was Mick's passion for rock 'n' roll that drove it all along. Mick lived for music, still does.'

Jock Scot: 'Everybody was in panic, and in a way Mick was made a scapegoat. There was no vision. But Mick was the man who did have a vision; look what he's done since. Look what everybody else has done since. When I went to see BAD performing I was gobsmacked. They should have made it up and sorted it out. It was never resolved. Jonesy just went, "Oh well, I'll do my own thing then."'

Robin Banks: 'I was stunned. I don't think Mick had an inkling it was going to happen. Getting rid of Mick was taking away the whole musical aspect of it. Carrying on without Topper was bad enough.'

So what did happen? Paul is unequivocal: he has always maintained it was simply impossible to carry on while Mick was skipping rehearsals and being remote and difficult. Paul wanted to play in a group, not stand about all day on the off-chance the guitarist might deign to appear. He stood by this position in a *GQ* interview in September 2003 – when Mick was there with him.

Joe emphasised a different dimension to the split. He always argued that it was a power struggle between the two founding fathers of the group. 'Bernie and Mick were always at loggerheads and trying to outdo each other,' he said. 'Whether in influence or control. Imagine it like a crazy car ride and sometimes no one is grabbing the steering wheel. Anything could happen! Sometimes Mick would grab the steering wheel to get me to get rid of Bernie. Eventually, the whole thing fucked up when Bernie decided he was going to "have" Mick. The worst thing about it is I let Bernie rub out Mick.'

Bernie's motive to 'rub out Mick' may have had its roots in Rhodes's dismissal in 1978, itself largely the result of his flirting with marginalising Mick. It would be to grossly oversimplify matters to suggest Bernie was driven by something as clear-cut, or petty (or grand) as revenge. The Clash story is many things, but a revenge tragedy is probably not one of them. It seems more likely it was the coup de grâce in an ongoing battle between the two strongest elements in The Clash camp.

Like many great adversaries, scratch the surface and Bernie and Mick were remarkably similar. They were both driven, stubborn, fiery, had an unswerving confidence in what they believed to be right. They were also, as Joe has pointed out, both working-class Londoners of Russo-Jewish descent.

Where they differed was in their attitude: Bernie was sharp, Mod-ish, unostentatious. He was addicted to a kind of warped Marxist dialectic, which required him forever to create new conflicts to resolve. He thrived on manipulating situations and creating chaos: Johnny Green once said Bernie did awful things to people but never with malice. It was only ever to inspire them to examine themselves and their relationship to the culture they existed in.

Mick, meanwhile, wanted to pursue what he referred to in a music awards ceremony in 2004 as 'the life' – by which he meant 'a rock 'n' roll life', one with the freedom to be creative and liberated and to live outside of the nine-to-five grind. The very thing, indeed, he and Robin had aspired to since their schooldays worshiping Mott the Hoople and The Faces.

The key battleground in the Mick–Bernie struggle was for the support of Joe and Paul. Howard Fraser, the group's driver in 1978–9, believes that Joe allowed Bernie to have too great an influence over him. He feels strongly that 'Joe's insecurity was what fundamentally destroyed The Clash. Dismissing Topper was the end of the band. Inviting Bernie back was just a footnote for that. Throwing Mick out was ludicrous.'

Others also agree that Joe was easily susceptible to manipulation when it came to adopting an anti-Mick stance. 'Joe in a sense was the weakest link,' says Robin. 'Bernie knew if he could play to Joe's weakness he could control the band as he wanted. It was a highly calculated method of undermining Mick.'

Control over Joe was important because he had the fealty of Kosmo. 'Kosmo did say to me once, "Joe is my man",' recalls Jock Scot. 'So I think there was a definite preference there. Mick in a way was an intellectual compared to Kosmo. Joe could deal with Kosmo in a straight-talking sense but Mick was an enigma. He was like this mad, camp guitarist who Kosmo thought they could replace. It was a bad summing up of the situation, but that's what happened.'

Pete Howard: 'I believe Joe stuck with Bernie because he was the only person he thought was capable of taking them to the next stage. It was as simple as that.'

If pressed, virtually everyone interviewed for this book concedes that the break with Mick was probably inevitable and that there was no other viable option, other than perhaps for the group to take a year out to try to mend broken friendships and to develop a new vision. But that begs the question: What would the next Clash record sound like? BAD? Sigue Sigue Sputnik? Professor Longhair? It seems as if all the time they were making great music – whether it was 'Janie Jones' or 'Straight To Hell' – they could forgive each other anything. The end had justified the means. But once that had gone, all they were left with was each other.

Pennie Smith argues that 'in the back of their minds, I think the group knew they had to split up once they'd broken America'. This chimes with what Joe said: where could they go after 'Rock the Casbah' except into the realms of being rich rock stars? They'd taken their outsider values as far as they could possibly go – into the US top ten and to over a million-and-a-half record-buyers. The Sex Pistols, their early rivals, never even dented the American charts.

Don Letts is characteristically blunt and amusing about the end of The Clash. 'Mick, my brethren . . . Mick is a difficult bastard,' he smiles. 'I say that with the utmost love. Mick could drive you up the wall and still can. It's like Joe says, biting his lip, in *Westway to the World*: "Some things are worth waiting for and talent is one of them." And, kid yourself not, Mick was amazingly talented. I have worked with the dude, I have seen him throw tunes in the bin people would kill themselves for! As a tune-smith, he intrinsically knows what is a good pop song. Mick takes a lot of stick for being the bad guy. But let's not kid ourselves, Joe could be a right cunt, too. The only thing was, he was a bit more manipulative about it – and again I say that with the utmost respect. We had altercations over girls and things like that, he was a loveable rogue, we had our bust-ups when we didn't speak for a while. People talk about The Clash's demise as a bad thing and I am seeing it as an inevitability. The parting was exactly the way it was supposed to be. If Mick and Joe and Paul had patted each other on the back and wished each other well then there would have been nothing happening in the first place. It was all because they had this immense amount of passion.'

On 10 September, *NME* reported Mick's departure from The Clash. The statement, released by Bernie and Kosmo, coolly denounced him in familiar terms. The Party, it seemed, was now shooting its leaders. It read: 'Joe Strummer and Paul Simonon have decided that Mick Jones should leave the group. It is felt that Jones had drifted away from the original idea of The Clash. In future, it will allow Joe and Paul to get on with the job The Clash set out to do from the beginning.'

Mick managed to issue a retort in the same edition: 'I would like to make it clear that there was no discussion with Strummer and Simonon prior to my being sacked. I certainly do not feel that I have drifted apart from the original idea of The Clash, and in the future I'll be carrying on in the same way as in the beginning.'

The reaction from many fans was horror. There had been virtually no Clash activity in Britain for a whole year. Most people thought they'd probably moved to America. But Topper and now Mick? Surely this was the end of the group. It wasn't.

The week before the press statement appeared, Pete Howard got a call from Joe. 'He was really aggressive. He was saying, "Meet us in this bar in Camden." I got there, and there was Paul and Joe and Bernie. Joe said, "I've just fucking sacked Mick Jones, he's a fucking cunt. You have to make a decision: are you with us or him?"'

This last phase of The Clash had begun in pretty much the style it would continue.

During our series of interviews, Kosmo is extremely careful when discussing the events surrounding Mick's exit. He says he won't be drawn on any specifics or pick at old wounds. But I push him to answer the question: what was going to be different second time around? He stresses that his answer applies to 'the idea of The Clash as a whole', not to any particular individual.

He says: 'This time we were going to do it without any of the excess or the bullshit.'

The last two years of The Clash do not seem to be remembered fondly by any of those involved. Until recently, the period wasn't acknowledged in any official record of The Clash. There is no reference to it in the *The Clash on Broadway* or *Westway to the World*. It was only when the 1985 single 'This Is England' was included on the *Essential Clash* compilation in 2003 that The Clash camp appeared to concede a post-Mick line-up existed. Kosmo half-jokes that he has almost deliberately wiped some of this period from his memory, and when Pete Howard recently found himself sitting at the same table in a pub as post-Mick guitarist Vince White, neither chose to recognise the other. It had been that bad.

Pete Howard had chosen to stay on with The Clash in September 1983. He admits he might not have done so if he'd known that Mick had apparently expressed an interest in his joining his new group. ('Bernie was not an easy guy to like,' he explains. 'I never really knew Mick but he was always OK with me.') Now Joe and Paul were trawling for other musicians to join the group.

On 1 October 1983, an advert for a guitarist appeared in *Melody Maker*. It was followed by two similar ads over the next six weeks. In customary Clash style the group auditioned scores of candidates, this time at the Electric Ballroom in Camden. They were required to play along with backing tapes. It wasn't revealed until later who they were auditioning for. The two guitarists chosen were Greg White, a former science student at University College London, and Nick Sheppard, previously of The Cortinas. Greg was originally from Southampton and Nick from Bristol. At the time Nick was playing in a covers band called The Spics and was living with the guys who went on to become Massive Attack. There was, however, a problem. Paul said there was no way he was going to play in a band with someone called Greg. This was, after all, The Clash. He insisted the new guy should be called 'Vince'. The name stuck.

Before any music was made, a number of group meetings were held in which Kosmo and Bernie outlined the nature of the new, post-Mick regime. 'In the new set-up there was a re-alignment and a stressing of certain things that we felt were needed,' Kosmo explains. 'The question was: we can talk the talk, but can we walk the walk? So with the new firm we had to be more focused and aware. There was a feeling that there was something in punk rock that was precious but had been lost and neglected. I specifically mean in a cultural sense – something that one had come to realise was important. Why were The Clash different? Why did we claim to be different? We'd ask all these things.'

Under the new system there would be no room for sentimentality and zero tolerance of conventional rock-star behaviour. A tough, boot-camp atmosphere would prevail. It's as if Bernie and Kosmo were trying to recreate the harsh conditions of 1976 that had fomented The Clash. Bernie found them a crummy house to rehearse in off Tavistock Road in Ladbroke Grove. 'It was cheap and horrible there,' says Pete Howard. 'The Clash clearly didn't have to go the cheap and horrible route.'

Presumably as a reaction to Mick's supposedly degenerative conduct – being late, aloof, openly appreciative of nice hotel suites and expensive guitars – the group would now be expected to endure basic facilities and modest wages. In the outside world, Paul Weller was launching his new project – the Gauloise-flavoured, coffee-bar jazz combo, The Style Council. In Camden, The Clash were returning to square one. Bernie and Kosmo – now, by all accounts a tight, conspiratorial unit – felt everyone needed shaking up. Each individual was targeted and 'beasted'. No one was exempt from their cajoling.

Pete Howard: 'With Joe, they'd say to us, "You think he's an icon? No, he's a fucking wanker!" They were trying to get us to lose that hero worship thing. Then Joe and Bernie would try to get to Paul. They'd say, "You're too fucking comfortable, you like your home and your telly, your record collection, your happy family life, you've lost your edge, you're content with looking good but you're just not there any more." I got the relentless mantra from Bernie, "You're a middle-class boy from Bath, what the fuck do you know about anything?"'

Early on, Pete Howard asked what exactly happened with Mick. Kosmo wasn't pleased. 'I'm like, "But surely I'm allowed to ask this question?"' recalls Pete. 'But Kosmo has this really weird thing – if you're getting angry and shouting at him he echoes back what you're saying. I don't know what it means, I don't know what it is, it's like being in the fucking movies . . . Fuck! I remember writing on the rehearsal room wall one day "the essence of art is doubt" or something like that, because I was trying to question this attitude. I remember Joe writing "doobie doobie doo" underneath it in a kind of "shut up, you fucking arsehole" way.'

Nick Sheppard, meanwhile, was also finding life in The Clash not quite what he expected. 'Bernie started talking to us about his ideas,' he recalls. 'It was my introduction to his methods. As we went along, those methods became more involved and complex, more insulting. Pete said being in The Clash was like a cross between being in the Boy Scouts and on an Existentialist course. It got very difficult and very stupid.'

The group's first gigs were a six-date tour of California in January 1984. Initially, they were fired up by their new challenge. The dates were the first Clash shows since the Us Festival. Bernie insisted the group travel on a tour bus with no air-conditioning or toilets. The hired hands in the group – Pete, Nick and Vince – were paid £100 a week. Seeing as they were promoting an album that had gone top ten in the States little more than a year earlier, the wages seemed meagre.

The group discovered that, generally speaking, America didn't seem unduly bothered by Mick's absence. 'People would say, "I've been with you all the way, man, ever since *Combat Rock!*"' laughs Nick. 'They didn't know about *Sandinista!*, let alone the other albums. But there were some incredible gigs.'

Rudi Fernandez, their old pal from San Francisco, caught up with them on the West Coast. 'Every time the group came over it seemed to have different people in it,' he says. 'They never talked about it. They were just excited to be back in America.'

The Clash mark two made their London debut in March 1984 at the Brixton Academy, where Paul used to go as a kid to watch war films with his dad twenty years earlier. The stage-set involved a bank of TV screens, showing evocative news-footage (riots, picket-lines, war), which kept going on the blink. A roadie with a large pole wrapped in a blanket stalked the stage whacking the ailing appliances to jolt them back into life. The dates went under the name of the Out of Control tour – suspiciously like the 1977 Get Out of Control tour.

Many people have commented how musically tight the five-man Clash were. Joe played very little rhythm guitar: it was odd to see him without his trademark Telecaster. The band showcased a few new tunes, mostly of a stripped-down rock 'n' roll hue. They had titles like 'Are You Red . . . y', 'Dictator' and 'This Is England'. Despite a new anthem proclaiming 'We Are The Clash', it didn't seem much like The Clash at all. The overriding impression was of something stylised and false.

A few old faces were on the guest-list. Johnny Green elbowed his way backstage. Joe asked him, 'What do you think?' Johnny replied, 'It's shit.' Joe said, 'I know.' Howard Fraser was there, too. Worried Joe would quiz him about the performance, he waved politely and left.

Jock Scot was equally perturbed. 'They lit the group from the back at one point,' he explains. 'Nick Sheppard and Joe and the other guitar player, they all had quite big ears. I said to Joe afterwards, "You've got to stop that lighting from the back, because it looks like three copies of the FA cup up there, their ears do not take the light well." By that time, as much as I loved Nick Sheppard, he was a wonderful guy, I knew that it was finito, over, finished.'

A scathing review of one of the Brixton gigs resulted in another roasting for Pete Howard. 'Topper would never have Paul in his monitor,' he explains. 'The musical relationship was with Joe's rhythm guitar. But my brief was to play with Paul. But if you concentrated on what Paul was doing you were fucked. But I was told that I had to have Paul in my monitor. I clearly remember a review which mentioned "the grossly club-footed rhythm section – how long has Paul been playing bass, for God's sake?" Kosmo and Bernie came in and blamed me. They said, "Club-footed? That means you're not playing with Paul." That was how it was. There was no logic there. It was Bernie's logic.'

Behind the scenes other, sadder events were impacting on the group. In March 1984, Joe's father Ronald died. Four years later, Joe talked to Jon Savage about their difficult relationship. Though they'd grown closer in the years following The Clash's success, there was still 'a lot unsaid' when he died. Joe felt the reason he and his dad never get on was down to him, not his father. 'I never really got off my high horse,' he said. 'I didn't know I was sitting on it, but I realise it now.'

Pete remembers Joe returning from the funeral mid-tour. There was obvious concern for the singer among the band, but the harsh atmosphere allowed little scope for any public acknowledgement of grief or for any sentimentality. 'He hardly reacted to it,' says Pete. 'To be honest, I think he was trying to make it not matter, not to himself . . . Maybe it was an opportunity for him to show his steel. If you're going to criticise people for worrying about home, girlfriend and money, you can't display those feelings. But whatever your relationship with your father, it's a big fucking deal when he dies. He didn't discuss it with us, maybe he did with Kosmo. They were much more on that level. '

I put it to Kosmo that it was insane for such an unsympathetic, macho atmosphere to prevail. 'Yes, it's crazy, I know that,' he says. 'I'm not saying that . . . it was tremendously uphill. You have to understand it felt like . . . *war* or something. That's how intense it was. It was heavy going: we took something on and it was hard going. We didn't successfully recreate a new camaraderie.'

The Out of Control tour took in some eighty shows that year, across the

UK, Europe and America. There were flashes of the old Clash madness. Aware of the new recruits' measly wages, Paul and Joe made a habit of dipping their hands into their pockets whenever required. In Paris, it was one of the crew's birthday and Joe decided to buy him a prostitute for the night.

Pete Howard: 'Joe got a taxi to take us to Harry's New York Bar and we got talking to this woman who was fluent in six different languages. She was a lot of money and Joe was like, "I haven't got that much money on me." He gave her what he had. The guy was actually on the job when he saw this envelope come under the door with the rest of the cash in it. Joe was great for that. He wanted us to have a good time and so did Paul – Paul was a really generous guy.'

Kosmo: 'There were times when it was great fun. You shouldn't get the impression that Bernard is all work and no play, because he's not. He's funny and enjoyable and all these things. But Bernard is the sort of person who'd go out and have a laugh, but you know next morning the job is on and there's a lot of work to do.'

A suggestion of what many felt The Clash should be doing occurred at the end of the year when they returned to Brixton Academy to play two gigs in support of the Miners' Strike Fund. In May 1984, riot police and striking miners had violently clashed outside the Orgreave coking plant in South Yorkshire. Mine-workers were protesting against pit closures and poor pay. It marked the beginning of a bleak period in the mid-1980s when Britain's traditional heavy industries were run down and the trade unions smashed. The country hadn't been so politically polarised since the 1930s.

The Clash responded to the political disquiet with rabble-rousing swagger, redolent of their protests against racism and oppressive policing in the late 1970s. But the sense of a group trying vainly to recreate the anger, aggression and even iconography of punk was overwhelming and dispiriting. The diverse threads of art, fashion, politics and culture that had once been central to the group's weave seemed to be swiftly unravelling. In 1977, The Clash *were* the culture, the two things seemed inextricable: punk suffused every aspect of the creative arts and even politics. Now the group looked dangerously like being just another band.

Bernie and Kosmo appeared to have overlooked something crucial. The Clash's cultural voltage had derived not just from the politics of anger and protest, but from their pioneering cross-cultural agenda. Playing Rasta music and hip-hop had given them a sharp political edge and immense cultural freight. Their music had been infused with soulful rumblings of Jamaica and downtown New York. They used to have a drummer who brought a touch of jazz to the party. But musical and cultural cross-pollination no longer seemed to be part of the agenda. The Clash were coming across like lily-white rockers: chunky punk power-chords, terrace chants and leather motorbike jackets.

Other aspects of The Clash mark two jangled. With Mick gone, the psycho-geographical charge The Clash once had evaporated. The Clash no longer felt a west London band; now, with members from Bath, Southampton and Bristol, it was more like a west country band. It brought home just how essential and all-pervasive the undercurrents of the capital had been in defining the character of the classic Joe-Mick-Paul-Topper line-up.

All this was probably not lost on Joe. But how much emotional energy he had to deal with it is debateable. Privately reeling from his father's death, he now had to deal with the news his mother had cancer (which would claim her life in December 1986). Meanwhile, Joe's girlfriend Gaby gave birth to their first daughter Jazz. Real life, in its unpredictable and powerful forms, seemed suddenly to be taking over Joe's world.

We discussed this subject in our interview in 2001. 'Your parents die, then you have kids,' he mused. 'That's what happens in life. Then you try to grow up.' Joe defined part of growing up as 'trying to act with honour and not being something you're not'.

At the beginning of 1985, CBS got on the group's case. A new album was due: they still owed the label another eight. There were advances to negotiate. Naturally, the label was concerned about what sort of record The Clash might deliver after Mick's dismissal. It appeared Bernie now wanted to have more input into the music. Sessions for an album took place in Munich. Rhodes was keen to make a contemporary-sounding record with programmed beats. The Blockheads' Norman Watt-Roy was recruited to help Paul with the bass. Various other session musicians were hired, including percussionist Michael Fayne.

'Dictator', 'Dirty Punk', 'Finger Poppin' and 'Movers and Shakers' took shape. They mixed anthemic football-terrace chants with awkward punk-funk. The sound was characterised by mechanised drums and stabs of squelchy synth keyboards. Lyrically, Joe was still capable of rich, onomatopoeic street-poetry ('Bring back crucifixion cry the moral death-heads legion, using steel nails manufactured by the slaves in Asia') and was clearly splendid on the two impressive Anglo-centric political commentaries, 'This Is England' ('I've got my motorcycle jacket but I'm walking all the time') and 'North and South' ('Now I know words are only tools'). But most of the time he was either dumbing down ('Dictator') or you simply couldn't hear what he was singing about ('Dirty Punk').

During the sessions, Pete Howard found himself surplus to requirements. 'I spent the whole week sitting in my hotel room,' he explains. 'I think they decided one of the ways to make it contemporary was to have a beat box there – either that or they just didn't want me on it.'

'I think it's irrelevant who played on that record,' argues Nick Sheppard. '*Sandinista!* was made by all kinds of people. You get into stupid arguments about what's "real" music. What's important is whether a record is good or bad. Records are an art-form designed to sell. But everyone [pictured] on the back cover of the album played on it – some more than others.'

The new material had been written using a variety of methods. In some cases, Nick and Vince were given chord sequences by Joe for which they were required to devise a group arrangement. This they often did without either Joe or Paul present. Other songs, like Joe's 'This Is England', were structurally complete before they were presented to the rest of the group. Others were pieced together under the musical direction of Bernie. All the tracks were credited to Strummer-Rhodes, and produced by Bernie under the pseudonym 'Joe Unidos'.

Many around The Clash found Bernie's new role extraordinary. Previously, he'd made a point of never interfering with the group's music, other than expressing an opinion about what he believed was good or bad. Now he was co-writing the songs. A clue to this dramatic development may lie in the success his old friend Malcolm was now enjoying as a pop star. In 1982, McLaren had created his own brand of novelty dance music. He'd even supported The Clash in America. His two albums had spawned three top twenty hits: 'Buffalo Girls'; 'Double Dutch'; and 'Madame Butterfly (Un Bel Di Vedremo)'.

If you subscribe to the view that where Malcolm went, Rhodes tended to follow, it would explain Bernie's sudden desire to get his hands dirty in the studio. It also throws up a highly troubling hypothesis. Could it be possible – incredible though it may seem – that Bernie may have welcomed Mick Jones's sacking not to control The Clash but to *be in* The Clash?

If this is true it would put a whole different spin on the circumstances of Mick's dismissal. It would be the equivalent of Brian Epstein ousting Paul McCartney so he could collaborate with John Lennon, or Andrew Oldham taking over Keith Richards's role in The Stones. Typically, Bernie wouldn't discuss this subject during our interview.

There is at least one important character in the story, however, whose comments appear to support the theory: Joe Strummer. In 2001, Joe told me, 'There was a lot of tension between Mick and Bernie . . . I think Bernie wanted to know what it was like to be Mick. The manager wanted to be the artist. Malcolm too, in a crazy way. Really they were like puppeteers, they wanted to be the artist.'

In the unpublished Jon Savage interview with Joe for *England's Dreaming*, the singer is even more specific: 'Bernie's trip was he wanted to know what it was like to be Mick Jones. Mick used to sit in that seat where you arrange the songs and produce them. He was fed up with organising tours and stuff, he wanted to get right in on the music. He hated songwriting because it was the one mysterious area where he couldn't go. He wanted to reduce songs to slabs of bacon off the roast, he didn't see why it should be so strange. He hated the tortured artist thing that Mick would lay on him. It was slightly out of his grasp. He used to say to me, "I've analysed life so completely that it's boring." I used to look at him and think, "That's insane." Songwriting was one of the things where he didn't understand how it was done and he resented that.'

It also appears that Bernie Rhodes' ambitions to be a pop star didn't end with The Clash. Glen Matlock tells a story about an incident that occurred in the late 1980s, by which time Rhodes would have been in his early forties. Apparently, he summoned Rat Scabies and Glen to a meeting in west London. Bernie told them that he planned to launch a punk supergroup featuring one of The Damned (Rat), one of The Pistols (Glen) and one of The Clash . . .

Glen asked, 'Who's going to join from The Clash?'

Bernie replied, 'I am.'

After the Munich sessions, Bernie was smart enough to realise the group were feeling stifled and restricted. In May 1985, he, Kosmo and Joe devised The Clash's last hurrah – a busking tour of Britain. The idea was that the group would assemble at Vince's flat, leave their wallets on the table and hitch to Nottingham with a few acoustic guitars. They'd then see where the wind would take them. Over the next two-and-a-half weeks, Britain's provincial towns and cities were thus treated to the extraordinary sight of The Clash popping up under railway bridges and in subways to entertain them with Monkees, Chuck Berry, Eddie Cochran and Cramps songs.

The group kipped on fans' floors and in cheap B&Bs. They survived on the money thrown into their hats. It was a genuinely exciting and unpredictable experience. Joe described it as 'the best tour we ever did'.

Paul agrees. 'It was like starting out fresh again,' he says. 'It was great. "We'll meet you in Glasgow in a week's time," and the idea was to leave everything behind other than the guitars. You couldn't take any money with you. We survived by our wits. It was as exciting as the Anarchy tour, you never knew where you were going next. I remember we were in Leeds, it was 2 a.m., and it was outside this black club, and people were coming out and really digging us. There were these two white guys and they were shocked it was us. They said, "Where you staying?" And we said, "We're not staying anywhere," so they invited us to stay at their mum's. The money we made from busking meant we could go further, we didn't have a plan of where to go next. There was no rules. You didn't have to be on the so-and-so plane at twelve o'clock.'

Joe: 'When we came back to London after that busking tour, we felt we had something good going inside the group. But as soon as we met Bernie and Kosmo in Holland Park . . . later, I understood that Bernie felt it was slipping out of his control, he didn't know where we were. We only came back because I lost my voice. Bernie didn't like that [loss of control].'

That summer, Joe's relationship with Bernie hit the skids. *Cut the Crap*, as it was inelegantly called, was mixed in Mayfair studios in London. It was around this time that Strummer realised it had been a mistake to let Rhodes loose on the music. It was a preposterous notion anyway: Bernie was a cultural agitator not a musician.

'I know Joe was very, very disappointed with the album,' Nick Sheppard says. 'I think he felt betrayed by Bernie's production. A lot of the musical ideas on that record were Bernie's. If you take them as production ideas they were incredibly ahead of their time, and he should be given credit for that. Unfortunately, because Bernie isn't musical, those ideas weren't successful.'

It was a difficult time for Joe. His father's death was still a recent memory, his mother was terminally ill, and he himself was now a proud father with the responsibilities and readjustments parenthood brings. Now it was dawning on him that The Clash had fucked it up big time.

It seems that Joe now had to confront the fact that his and Bernie's partnership had run its course. This could not have been easy. People have observed that Joe's insecurities allowed Bernie to exert too much control over him. But it's important to remember the original circumstances in which their relationship had been forged. Bernie had been the guy who'd given Joe his ticket to stardom. He was the man who'd plucked him out of the soft, middle-class, dead-end grind of The 101'ers and guided him to punk fame. He was the ideas engine and compass Joe needed. Under any value system, Joe ultimately owed him. And Joe was more honourable than most.

Some interviewees have argued that Bernie used Joe's middle-class background as a weapon against him, but Kosmo insists this wasn't so. 'I never saw that happen at all,' he says. 'I felt there was always an understanding that Joe had earned his right to be in The Clash through the squatting scene.'

Joe's greatest insecurity, perhaps, was that he wasn't pushing himself hard enough, that he was letting down The Quest.

I know from a personal point of view how Bernie has the ability to get under your skin. During an hour-long conversation in 1999 he cleverly, though in no way, I think, maliciously, used information I let slip about the recent death of my own father to rouse me into challenging my notions of what I was doing and where I should be going professionally. After what I'd imagined was going to merely be an entertaining conversation, I got off the phone genuinely shaken and wondering whether, as Bernie suggested, I was being cowardly in my lack (at that time, maybe still) of a grand purpose.

That is Bernie's gift and curse: to demoralise you in order to force you to challenge your comfortable assumptions about the world around you. To judge Joe adversely is to overlook the fact he'd undergone almost a decade of this peculiar hectoring, winding up and psychotropic manipulation on virtually a daily basis. That intense programme of self-examination was no different for Paul and Mick, either, but they seemed far better equipped, in their own different ways, to withstand it. Joe's propensity for deep self-reflection and relentless self-questioning made him particularly prone to Bernie's methods. He was also intellectually advanced enough to realise that Bernie's visionary thinking needed to be taken seriously: Joe, better perhaps than anyone, understood the cultural importance of what Bernie was trying to achieve. He knew that The Clash needed Bernie, but also that Bernie needed The Clash.

In June 1985, The Clash appeared at the Roskilde Festival in Denmark. The following month they played Rockscene in France and then, on 27 August, the Greek Music Festival in Athens. It would be The Clash's last gig.

The Athens show was huge – 40,000 people. There was a riot. Fences were torn down. The Style Council and The Cure were on the same bill. The Clash went on really late. 'I knew the whole thing was going down the tubes because of the atmosphere between Joe and Bernie,' recalls Nick Sheppard. 'Just before we went on stage Joe gave Bernie a look of pure contempt. I think Joe had realised by then it was a mistake to have got rid of Mick. He felt, "Oh fuck, I've dropped the plate." We did the gig, went to a night club, had a great time and the next thing I knew Joe had buggered off for a month to Spain. Bernie was tearing his hair out. He was phoning me every morning. He was incensed Joe had disappeared. It was never the best way to wake up, having a lecture from Bernie.'

In September, 'This Is England' was released and reached number twenty-four. Its melancholy observations about life in Thatcher's Britain were appreciated and critically well received, but its parent album wasn't. *Cut the Crap* was issued six weeks later. *NME*'s cherubic Mat Snow gave it an eloquent and honest panning, while *Melody Maker*'s Adam Sweeting simply stated, 'It's crap!' Jack Barron in *Sounds* unexpectedly lavished it with praise, though his bouquets seemed to have had little effect on the record-buying public. It reached number sixteen, then quickly fell off the chart.

With its synth keyboards and clumsy electronic beats, *Cut the Crap* wasn't particularly pleasurable listening. But perhaps even more off-putting were its clichéd, ironic punk graphics. In a world where indie culture had taken over and The Smiths, New Order and The Cure ruled, The Clash looked tired, uninspired and ill advised. The writing was on the wall.

The poor reviews of the album gave Joe the ammunition he needed to put The Clash out of its misery. 'It was Bernie who insisted it was called *Cut the Crap*,' recalls Pete Howard. 'When it was released and got really bad reviews we were all sitting there going, "Whose idea was it to call it *Cut the fucking Crap* in the first place? Bernie's!" Joe was kind of like, "You're right – Bernie's a fucking idiot!" Joe went off and wrote this sort of memo apologising for the record and explaining why everything had gone wrong. He was going to take out a page in *NME* and *Melody Maker* but it never happened.'

The Clash was swiftly falling apart. According to Pete, Joe arranged to meet him, Vince and Nick in a Soho pub where Strummer handed them each a 'grubby envelope' containing £1,000 and told them the group had split up. He wished them all luck, then disappeared into the night.

This was not, however, the end of The Clash. Incredibly, after Joe's departure, Paul and Bernie began auditioning singers for a new line-up. Paul, it seems, was the group member most resilient to, and inspired by, Rhodes's methods. After a decade, he was still hanging in there. Eventually, they would go on together to instigate what would become Havana 3AM.

Joe was by this time past caring what happened. 'I was feeling really guilty for [heavy sigh] a) allowing Topper to be sacked and b) sacking Mick Jones,' he explained. 'I'd already felt that we'd besmirched what honour there was by tampering with the original four. Not once, but two times . . . So when I heard they were doing singer auditions, I felt, "Oh well," rather than having a righteous freak out. You live by the sword, you die by the sword. They could have swagged some money out of Sony and cut another record. But I didn't have a leg to stand on the moral indignation front.'

Kosmo recalls that by this time Rhodes was toying with a whole new radical way of perceiving rock bands. His vision of changing pop culture clearly hadn't ended with The Clash. 'Bernard was thinking in terms of Manchester United,' says Kosmo. 'His ideas are completely outside the box. Manchester United didn't die after George Best left. So I think that is the direction he would like to have gone in – running The Clash like a football team, with different players coming in once the old ones had run out of energy. There was this Portuguese group called Menudos. They fired people when they got to a certain age. It was huge, a pop phenomenon, the first boy band maybe. Bernard felt at some point that the guys in The Clash wouldn't be able to go on for ever. You know, ego is a big thing in this world. And Bernard didn't think [a long-term proposition like The Clash] could be easily implemented or supported. This is where he's into the culture, into the politics. He's into changing things – not just doing it for the kids. It's to change culture and make it better. Maybe at some time it becomes time to kick someone out, substitute them as they do in football. It's radical – could you believe it?'

So what has Bernie Rhodes to say about the doomed last phase of The Clash?

'It was hilarious!' he says. 'What was good about it? I'll tell you: Matt Dillon saying to me, "I spent nights having all these girls wanting to fuck me, but I can't think of anything else except which was the better, the four-man Clash or five-man Clash." That's funny. What I tried to do was say, "I've got a bunch of arseholes, and I'm gonna see it as a bunch of arseholes." The funny thing was that Madonna and some hip-hop people used *Cut the Crap* as the basis of what they were doing. America and England have a very different way of operating. If I was an American, I'd be seen in the very best light. But as I'm English and don't go down the Groucho, I'm seen as either a figure of fun, or a mad man.'

By the end of 1985, Kosmo had quit and moved to America. On 23 November, the *NME* reported that Pete, Nick and Vince had left the band. The Clash had ground to a halt amid a mess of bitterness, ignoble bickering and unworkable ideas.

The last thing people heard was a rumour circulating in London that Joe had sought out Mick and begged him to re-join the group. Apparently Mick had politely said, 'Thanks, but no thanks.'

The Clash was over.

Joe later admitted: 'It had been limping to its death from the day we got rid of Topper.'

13
AFTERMATH

'And I rose up and knew that I was tired and continued my journey.'

Inscription on Edward Thomas's memorial stone, Steep, Hampshire

'Opiate, n. An unlocked door in the prison of Identity. It leads into the jail yard.'

AMBROSE BIERCE, *THE DEVIL'S DICTIONARY*

It is 22 December 2002. The car journey from Whitstable to Dover normally takes around forty minutes. Today, it's a little quicker. Johnny Green is tucked behind the wheel of his family saloon; I'm in the passenger seat. Johnny spent two years driving The Clash in the late 1970s and the experience shows. It strikes me he handles the car a little like Keith Richards's old driver from the 1960s, Tom Keylock, whom I once met: steady, economical, smooth, purposeful. These guys were used to carrying a precious cargo and getting it to its destination on time.

Our objective this afternoon is Topper Headon's house on the outskirts of Dover. Topper lives alone in a modest new-build terrace. It's the kind of place you'd imagine a young professional couple living. He answers the door while man-handling his dog, Yowsah, back into the hallway, then ushers us into his lounge: clean, airy, rows of kung-fu videos in the bookcase by the TV.

Headon looks much healthier than he did in *Westway to the World*, shot three years earlier. He's wearing jeans and a T-shirt and his hair is skinhead-short. He's friendly and funny but also nervy: a microwaved ready-meal lies untouched in front of him throughout our interview, and he smokes continually. It takes him a while to relax into the rhythm of questions and answers.

Later tonight, Topper's due to play with a local pub band. It's the first time he's drummed for twelve months; before that he hadn't touched a drum kit in years. 'I get very nervous,' he admits. 'I played last Christmas and I'm playing this Christmas. There's a big sign outside the pub, saying "Nicky

'Topper' Headon of The Clash". They're expecting the best. I think, "Do they know I'm forty-seven now, and I'm not in my twenties?" My arms ache and I haven't got the stamina. After five or six numbers I'm fucked.'

Surviving The Clash has ostensibly been harder for Topper than the others. After he was dismissed from the group in May 1982, his drug habit became totally debilitating. Mick had to endure the painful experience of ejecting him from an early version of Big Audio Dynamite because his condition was so bad. Several of Topper's attempts to launch new bands and solo records, including 1985's *Waking Up*, ended in tales of wasted studio time and blown advances. But by far the biggest thing Topper squandered was his talent.

Topper's health gravely worried his old friends. The Clash camp paid for rehab on several occasions, but with little success. For years, Headon led the squalid life of a junkie. In 1987, he was detained for eighteen months at Her Majesty's Pleasure for supplying heroin. On his release, Topper was reduced to driving a mini-cab for drug money.

'My biggest regret isn't all the cash I spent,' he says. 'It's me not touching the drums for twenty years. That's what really upsets me. I could have been one of the best. I was one of the best and I blew it.'

In recent years, Topper has been winning his battle against drugs. He's in good shape these days – he even opened a local fête early in 2004. Occasionally, you read a reference in the press to his driving a taxi for a living, but since The Clash renegotiated the deal on their back catalogue in the 1990s money hasn't been the problem. Topper would have also done well out of Will Smith's 'Will 2K' single, which heavily sampled 'Rock the Casbah' and became a chart-topper around the world on the eve of the Millennium celebrations. (Topper, of course, is credited as that tune's principal writer.)

The day of our interview, The Clash were still debating whether to perform at their Rock and Roll Hall of Fame induction in New York in March 2003. The previous night Paul had received a fax from Joe mock-threatening to use The Mescaleros' bassist Scott Shields if he continued to refuse to play. It would have been the reunion that the group had always shied away from. Rumours of an impending Clash tour had been doing the rounds on a regular basis since the early 1990s, and, indeed, some insiders say it actually came close to happening in 1996, around the same time The Sex Pistols reformed for the Filthy Lucre tour.

Depending on who you talk to, the sticking point was usually either Paul or Joe (or both). Paul seems to have been particularly resistant to the idea. His reservations were ideological and practical. After The Clash, he had cut a self-titled album with a new group, Havana 3AM, initially managed by

Bernie. But after the band's singer, Nigel Dixon (formerly of Whirlwind), died of cancer in 1993, Paul turned to painting full-time. He worked hard for years to carve himself a reputation as a serious artist, and not just another rock star turned painter. The last thing he probably wanted was to be in The Clash again. 'I think the fact that The Clash never reformed reinforced what the group was about,' he says. 'At the end of day it was like, fuck the money, it's the idea. We're a bit too romantic for our own good. I'd have loved a million pounds, but I also like to keep my dignity, too.'

Today, Paul's exhibitions in London have been hugely successful, and there's demand for his work from all over the world. In 2005, to the pleasant suprise of many, he re-engaged with the world of rock 'n' roll, teaming up with Blur and Gorillaz's Damon Albarn to play bass in The Good, The Bad and The Queen, a melancholic reggae-world music project centred on the concept of life in twenty-first century London. The last time I saw him he'd just come back from painting a series of pictures in Spain. He lives in west London with his wife, Tricia (who manages The Clash; he split with Pearl in the late '80s), and their two boys.

Mick is regarded as the member who was most amenable to a Clash reunion. Virtually since the day he left The Clash he has been making or producing records. Big Audio Dynamite, the group he formed with Don Letts, had a career almost as long and as fruitful as The Clash's – eight years and six albums – and in the early summer of 2004 he launched a new outfit, Carbon-Silicon, with his old pal Tony James.

All Mick's music since 1984 has been made in the long shadow cast by The Clash, of course. The spectre of his former group has always had the added complication of the manner in which he was dismissed. There is no doubt it felt like a betrayal: two of his friends turning on him. Publicly, however, the wounds appeared to heal fairly quickly. In May 1986, just six months after The Clash mark two crashed, Joe and Paul were invited to appear as extras in BAD's 'Medicine Show' video. (Mick had finally appeared on *Top of the Pops* a few months before, promoting that single's predecessor 'E=MC2'.) Subsequently, Joe and Mick collaborated on BAD's *No. 10 Upping Street* and were writing together again as recently as 1998, when Joe was in the early stages of putting together The Mescaleros.

Yet, as you might expect, privately there seems to have been a degree of residual bitterness on both sides about how The Clash ended. A few different stories circulate about Joe, Mick and Paul getting together over a few drinks and reviewing the events of 1983. One version has Joe effusively and drunkenly apologising to Mick, before Paul interjects to explain that, no, they were absolutely right to get rid of him, he was acting like an idiot. Another has Joe similarly pissed and remorseful, but Mick saying, 'Yeah, you were wrong to get rid of me, so piss off!'

These tales may be apocryphal. But we can gain some comfort from the fact that Joe and Mick did finally make their peace just before Joe's death. The impetus was Mick's impromptu leaping up onstage at The Mescaleros' Fire Brigades Union Benefit gig at Acton Town Hall on 15 November 2002. It was the first time Strummer and Jones had shared a stage together since the Us Festival in 1983. They performed 'Bank Robber', 'White Riot' and 'London's Burning'. Five weeks later Joe was dead.

It seems Mick has now come to terms with The Clash's turbulent story. 'What happened, happened,' he tells me. 'It was good. We achieved something amazing. I've got good memories.'

The chance of a Clash reunion was finally dashed by Joe's death.

After Topper and I had finished our interview on 22 December 2002, he went off to prepare for that night's gig and I went back to London to sleep. Then the phone rang at 2 a.m. It was Johnny Green. The initial thought that flashed across my mind was that something had happened to Headon after the gig.

But it wasn't Topper, it was Joe. His heart had given up. It later emerged that this was due to a congenital heart defect. He was at home in Somerset at the time, having just taken his dogs for a walk. His wife Lucinda had found him. Reports said he died peacefully.

The news of his death broke the next day, and made the papers on Christmas Eve. There was a huge outpouring of grief, amid widespread shock and disbelief. After disappearing from the public eye for almost a decade – during which he appeared in a few films and wrote a couple of soundtracks – Joe had been touring and recording full-time again with The Mescaleros. The band had recently completed a string of UK dates. No one would have believed from his passionate and spirited performances that Joe had only a few weeks to live.

Internet chat-rooms lit up with eulogies to the singer. He'd touched the lives of hundreds of thousands of people: from the number of personal reminiscences, it seemed as if he'd talked with virtually all of them.

Strummer's death was reported all over the world and made the front pages of several publications. He was referred to in more than one paper as 'spokesman for a generation' and 'the King of Punk'. His funeral at Kensal Green brought together most of the characters who appear in this story. Friends came from America, Japan, Europe.

The assembled cast brought home another truth: surviving The Clash wasn't just hard for the group, it was difficult for many of those who worked or hung out with them, too. The adrenaline rush of touring the world with the most exciting group of their generation was so intense it ended, for some, with the mother of all comedowns. Many have described the experience as like having come home from a war. They found it difficult to adapt to civilian life. Their perception of what they'd experienced chimes with The Clash's cinematic self-image and Kosmo's vivid picture of the group as a band of brothers pushing forward under constant fire, taking it in turn, *Red Badge of Courage* style, to keep the standard flying. What could ever replicate that kind of excitement, danger and camaraderie?

For some, the post-Clash void was filled with years of drink and drugs. Heroin plays a part in several stories. Those who stayed in the rock 'n' roll business complained that the groups they worked with were never quite the same as The Clash. How could they be? A few, most notably Baker, have chosen to disappear from view entirely. (He lives anonymously and ignored all my requests for an interview.)

Then there's the eternal problem of rewards, financial and otherwise. The disparity between the group's entourage and The Clash themselves, which Roadent observed emerging in 1977, is in many cases greater than ever today. The group aren't insensitive to this. Johnny Green described The Clash as 'essentially an honourable outfit', and will talk off the record about several instances where Clash members helped out old friends in moments of need. But, as Joe was keen to point out, The Clash themselves never attained the financial rewards that other groups of a similar stature enjoyed. 'We never sold that many records,' he explained. 'The Clash aren't like these punk bands today like Green Day and Rancid, who all sell 10 million albums or whatever.'

It's perhaps natural that we'd prefer our old punk idols to be poor; The Clash aren't, but they're not pop-star-rich either. They never wanted the 'Lear jets and houses in Tuscany', nor did they ever get them.

Kosmo seems to have summed it up best. Not long after The Clash split up he apparently confided to Baker: 'We had so much fun robbing the bank we forgot to take the money.'

But what of The Clash's wider legacy? What does it all mean now? Clearly, the band has in recent years joined the ranks of the great and enduring rock groups. The beatification came, perhaps when 'Should I Stay or Should I Go?' hit number one when it was reissued in 1991, after being used for a Levi's ad. Today, you see the *Essential Clash* on sale in motorway service stations, next to compilations by everyone from Elvis to Blur. Magazines such as *Rolling Stone*, *MOJO* and *Uncut* bracket the group with The Who, Bruce Springsteen, Bob Dylan, The Stones, The Beatles, Led Zeppelin, The Doors, Bob Marley and Pink Floyd as artists of outstanding intelligence, substance, musical depth and cultural significance.

Recognition of their classic status is reflected in the gongs that fill their spare rooms: in 2000 The Clash received an Ivor Novello songwriting award and, of course, the group were inducted into the Rock and Roll Hall of Fame in 2003. In June 2004, Mick accepted the *MOJO* Inspiration Award on behalf of the group at that magazine's inaugural awards ceremony. It was presented to him, symbolically, by Roger Daltrey.

Such kudos is all very nice, of course, but you get the impression the group members aren't entirely comfortable with it. Their integration into the classic rock oligarchy hasn't come without an element of reluctance. Awards ceremonies and back catalogue promotion continue to be sticky areas (especially with Paul): being part of the establishment was the antithesis of what the group was about, yet at the same time no one would like to see The Clash drop off the map and everything they fought to achieve forgotten.

So what did they achieve? It's often impossible to make a distinction between the impact of The Clash and the influence of The Sex Pistols and punk as a whole. The close relationship between Bernie and Malcolm, and The Clash and The Pistols, means the two groups often broadly represent one and the same thing. But walking around Camden Market in November 2003 with Johnny Green and Robin Banks, the unique imprint of the Bernie–Clash axis is clearly visible. Several of the stores we visit are playing Trojan reggae compilations: once an acquired taste among young white kids, reggae and dub has now joined the canon of de rigueur hip listening. Everybody these days has a Lee Perry, King Tubby and Joe Gibbs CD. Would that have been the case if The Clash hadn't covered 'Police and Thieves'?

Then there's the profusion of combat trousers, stencilled T-shirts, bleached spiky hair and Dr Marten boots. The idea of the individual as a billboard for ideas. There are even facsimile versions of Joe's homemade Red Brigade T-shirt on sale – 1970s European terrorism as retro style. It's odd seeing foreign tourists looking like a sanitised version of Paul Simonon in 1978. At some point in the 1990s, punk ceased to be a philosophy and became a high-street fashion. These kids might have heard of Vivienne Westwood, but how many know who Bernie Rhodes and Alex Michon are?

It would be a nice conceit to say that The Clash started out wanting to change music but ended up changing culture. This is certainly true in many respects: in the early interviews in *Sniffin' Glue* and *Melody Maker,* the emphasis is on spearheading a musical assault that will sweep away the boring, rock-opera-making giants of the previous decade who'd long lost touch with their fans. There is little sense of an impulse to influence every aspect of life and change global opinion. However, one might argue that Bernie Rhodes always had a grander vision: he perhaps did have a wider cultural agenda for The Clash. But it's almost impossible to gauge how much clarity his higher purpose had in the beginning.

That the group changed music, with more than a little help from The Sex Pistols (of course), is, I believe, unquestionably true – within a couple of years of *The Clash*, virtually every white rock 'n' roller worth his salt was trying to shoe-horn a bit of reggae into his music. Even Mick Jagger. You need only pick up a copy of the *NME* from 1975 and another from 1979 to realise the titanic effect punk had on the way groups looked and sounded.

To what extent The Clash changed culture is naturally harder to fathom. But, again, many would argue their influence was huge. Defining what 'culture' means exactly is always tricky, but if you consider some of the chief components of what most of us would consider culture – art, fashion, design, music, the media, politics – you can see how The Clash directly or indirectly influenced them all, especially in the group's immediate aftermath.

Politically, The Clash's impact was seismic. Aligning themselves so enthusiastically with Rock Against Racism and the Anti-Nazi League made their multicultural vision clear to everyone, at a time when the issues of immigration and racism were dangerously dividing the country. The fact that The Clash's machismo excited a certain breed of playground yob meant they could communicate with a section of society notoriously hard to penetrate. One of The Clash's greatest achievements may simply have been convincing tens of thousands of white British school kids who might otherwise have perpetuated their parents' racist views that black culture was something to embrace and admire. And in America, The Clash may have woken up Midwest teenagers to the terrible things their government was doing in their name in Nicaragua and El Salvador.

It's tempting to view The Clash as the first modern, international, post-counterculture rebels but it also makes sense to see them as the last gasp of 1960s radicalism, fermented as they were in the same art school environment as The Beatles, The Kinks and The Who.

The Clash seized the baton of grandiose, gestural protest, which John

Lennon – a fan of the group in his last years – had so favoured. They demonstrated that rock music could, yet again, be an agent for change, and groups be instruments of history. Music ought to be done not for money but for the greater good. I would agree with Bernie Rhodes that The Clash's political grandstanding at Victoria Park and the Us Festival helped to inspire the two great politically charged, globally-minded events of the 1980s: Live Aid and the concert to mark Nelson Mandela's seventieth birthday. It's hardly a coincidence that both Bob Geldof and Jerry Dammers (another Bernie protégé, of course) were Clash fans – as is that emerging political statesman, Bono.

Those shows were the beginning of a culture of global togetherness, which has grown rapidly in the last five years thanks to the internet, email, mobile phones and cable TV. It makes you wonder how much greater The Clash's impact might have been if they'd formed now.

There can be no doubt that, even using the old-fashioned tools of playing live and releasing vinyl LPs, The Clash politicised thousands of individuals. Their records were lessons in cultural, social and military history. 'Joe Strummer changed my outlook on the world,' explains Billy Bragg, whose protest music in the 1980s earned him the sobriquet of the 'one-man Clash'. 'While that whole rebel rock stance could be a pose, Joe was bringing it back to a genuinely radical idea.' Bragg makes the point that the political views of many contemporary left-wing figures were shaped by the group.

But by far the greatest effect The Clash had on the world is the one that's hardest to quantify. It's their impact on the lives of hundreds of thousands of ordinary young people. Many developed an intense bond with the group – a feeling of belonging and being valued. They were like a family for the disaffected, disillusioned and dispossessed. The Clash may have behaved dreadfully towards the people who worked for them, to their record company and sometimes to each other, but they never showed anything but respect and kindness to the people who bought their records. To The Clash, the fans were – and still are – everything. Mick and Paul must feel, as Joe had, that they've signed every copy of every Clash record ever made. But they still make a point of amiably chatting to fans who collar them and of signing whatever's thrust into their hands.

For Bernie, The Clash's mission statement was 'to represent the kids' and they'll still be remembered by most for doing just that. 'Their importance was bringing music down to the people and making it intimate again,' concludes Caroline Coon. 'As grand as their sound was, it was folk music. Theirs was the defining music of their decade.'

Back in the upstairs room of the Groucho Club in June 2001, my interview with Joe is winding down. We're both well oiled by this point. The booze makes Joe even more animated and passionate.

'I've met the people whose attitudes punk changed,' he says. His voice by now is getting hoarse and crackly, as if it's being piped through a walkie-talkie. 'Literally, I feel like I've met every one of them!' He laughs his hurgh-hurgh laugh. 'And the story is the same for all of them: we changed their minds individually and that affected the decisions they made in their own lives. It wasn't a mass thing, the mob storming the palace. It was lots of individuals who grasped some of the things we were honking on about.

'We went through hell and back with The Clash,' he adds, banging on the table with his fists. 'You wouldn't believe what we went through to make the records we did. We gave it 110 per cent, every day. But when you meet those people, the people who tell you that you had some effect on their life, it makes you feel it was absolutely all worth it.'

14
A FAREWELL TO JOE

First printed in *MOJO* magazine October 2003

Barranco De Los Negros, 21 August 2003

'JOE LOVED SPAIN,' reflects Richard Dudanski, Joe's old bandmate from the 101'ers. 'He loved the openness of the people, Flamenco culture, the way of life, the poetry, the passion . . .' It's close to midnight and we're looking across the roof-tops of Granada, Dudanski's adopted home, towards the magnificent Alhambra palace, the thirteenth-century Moorish citadel that watches over the city like a slightly unreal and outsized Hollywood prop.

Together with 400 other souls, I have climbed to the summit of a hill in the gypsy quarter of Barranco De Los Negros to attend an intimate concert which Dudanski has organised in memory of Joe Strummer. The show has been arranged to coincide with Strummer's birthday, 21 August (he would have been fifty-one), but the date also chimes roughly with another significant anniversary: the death of Federico García Lorca, Spain's most famous modern playwright and poet, shot by fascists in an olive grove near here on the eve of the Spanish Civil War. Joe had long been an admirer of Lorca, name-checking him – and using echoes of his death-poem 'Farewell' – in The Clash anthem 'Spanish Bombs' on *London Calling*. Legend has it that, one drunken evening many years ago, Joe even tried to dig him up . . .

The venue is the Centro de Interpretación del Sacromonte, an old gypsy encampment now preserved as an open-air museum. The original inhabitants lived in small spaces gouged out of the rocky hillsides; in fact, outside the museum's gates, scores of them still do, protected from the world by nothing more than pieces of old sacking. Joe apparently loved this place, hanging out with the *gitanos* in the tiny bars that dot the roadsides.

Backstage, where an antidote to the midnight heat comes in the form of a horse-trough filled with sangria and ice, a familiar figure sashays past in a white linen jacket and jeans. Neat and graceful, with hair slicked back and a huge grin, Mick Jones looks like a cross between a triumphant matador and one of the Lavender Hill Mob. 'Better get back to my dressing cave,' he smiles after surveying the huge almond tree that dominates the stage. Dressing cave? 'Yeah, the dressing room's in one of the caves . . .'

Mick's in fine form, and proves to be a charismatic, uplifting presence on this surreal, sad-happy morning. The headlining scratch combo Los Amigos – old friends Mick, Tymon Dogg, Richard Dudanski, Derek Goddard, The Pogues' Jem Finer, New York musician Tom Lardner and Julian Hernandez (formerly of Spanish punks Siniestro Total) – hit the stage at around 1 a.m., and play a 90-minute set of spirited, if sometimes musically precarious, 101'ers, Clash and old R&B covers. The performance ends with a 15-minute version of Them's 'Gloria', for which, in a moment that Joe would have no doubt appreciated, Mick invites the Flamenco percussionists from the support act to join in the cacophony.

It's a magical occasion, full of pathos, chaos and passionate rock'n'roll. But, as the party under the stars winds up at dawn, the abiding sense is a kind of disbelief that we are all here in the first place. Joe Strummer not with us any more? The whole thing seems unreal.

Thirty-six hours before Sacromonte, I'm sitting in a pub opposite Kensal Green cemetery with Martin Slattery and Scott Shields of The Mescaleros – the group most people agree had proved to everyone, and especially to the man himself, that Joe still had a whole lifetime of great rock'n'roll ahead of him. As if to prove the point, we're looking at the finished CD of *Streetcore*, the album the group were working on at the time of Joe's death, and which Martin and Scott have spent the last few months putting the final touches to.

'Joe had made loads of notes about how he wanted certain tracks to sound,' explains Martin. 'So we referred to those. We didn't change anything, we just finished it off. We didn't want it to be like Jeff Buckley, where people were going, "Is this a demo or not?" Basically, it's the album we were trying to make.'

Martin and Scott are the only surviving members of the first Mescaleros line-up from 1999, a young aggregate of mostly northern musicians put together by former Pulp and Elastica guitarist Anthony Genn. It was the first band Joe had been in for nearly a decade – the self-confessed 'wilderness years' during which he groped around for an outlet for his creativity, variously toying with record production, film scores and acting. Uncertain of how a forty-something Strummer might be received on stage, he would ask people in all innocence: 'If I play, will anyone come?'

When the Mescaleros Mk I fizzled out, Strummer invited Slattery and Shields to help write and produce a second album, the world-music-flavoured *Global A Go-Go*. It was the first time that they really experienced Strummer's all-consuming 'method' approach to writing and recording, familiar to older colleagues who remember the long nocturnal sessions and bunkers built from flight cases at Wessex studios in the late '70s and early '80s.

'It was unbelievable!' laughs Martin. 'It was like, "Who's gonna get out of this alive?" Recording all night until midday, then back in at 8 p.m. That was really intense – it went on for three months. So this time we had to take Joe aside and ask if we could do it so . . .'

'. . . So we didn't end up in hospital,' finishes Scott. 'Man, I got seriously fucked up – I went mental. Joe was in his element, so full of energy. He was inspiring everyone, coming in at 5 a.m. shouting, "I love that guitar bit! It's fucking great!"'

'The thing is,' continues Martin, '*Streetcore* ended up the same. Joe started living in the studio. He had a vocal booth in the live room where he made up his bed and had his home comforts – a ghetto-blaster, piles of lyrics all round him, a little tape-recorder he'd stick round the door when he heard something he liked . . ."'

As one might expect, Joe's hobo spirit – crystallised in his teenage busking years – seemed perfectly to suit life on the road. Barry 'Scratchy' Myers, The Clash's preferred tour DJ, whom Joe recalled into service for the Mescaleros' *Bringing It All Back Home* dates in autumn 2002, was amused to find that his old friend, famous for living out of wrinkled-up carrier bags, now owned a suitcase. He soon realised the suitcase – a gift from an optimistic friend, perhaps – simply held all the carrier bags.

Commandeering the upstairs-front of the tour bus (previous occupant: Robbie Williams), Joe made himself at home. With the crew travelling with the band, and the gear swinging along in a trailer behind, the singer would disgorge the contents of his polythene bags and rest his battered old Hudson motorcycle boots on the bunk. It was implicitly understood that this was his private space, where he read, slept, drank red wine, smoked weed and scribbled fervently.

As soon as he was ready, Joe would join the party. Scratchy describes Joe as 'essentially a nightbird', with a huge appetite for the company of others and a deep fascination for people from all walks of life. Like Bo Diddley and

The Clash back in 1979, when Bo would stay up all night drinking whiskey while his guitar took his bunk, Strummer showed his young companions a thing or two about stamina.

'None of us could keep up with Joe,' recalls Scott. 'We had to take it in turns, even the crew. And it wasn't because he was an excessive drinker or drug taker, it was because he had a strong constitution and he could pace himself very well. So we used to take it in turns to stay up with Joe to get "Strummer'd", as we called it affectionately. In Paris, it was eight in the morning, for example, and I said, "Joe, I really want to go home!" He said, [adopts Joe growl] "You're not fucking going home! You'll get sacked . . . In fact, if you go home I'll kick you outta the band right now!" So I said, "Yes, maybe we should go on somewhere . . ."'

The other toll on the band's energy came from Joe's insistence, as in The Clash days, that he wouldn't leave a venue until he'd chatted to and signed autographs for any fans who'd made it backstage. Often there were a couple of dozen of them. Such was his eagerness to do this that the other Mescaleros eventually requested a second dressing room where they could cool off for a while longer. 'You will not find any artist, pop star, whatever you want to call them, who had the same commitment to their fans,' says Martin. 'He was a very humble person, with this great integrity – political, personal, all those things. He was genuinely interested in meeting all the fans.'

As the afternoon wears on, Martin and Scott fondly recall some of the vivid memories they have of Joe on tour – playing his beloved *cumbia* (the music of Colombia) CDs full volume at 4 a.m. in airport lounges; having a crafty spliff in the foyer of a hotel being used for a police convention; rushing into service stations to buy the most ridiculous thing on sale (most impressive purchase: a batman outfit for dogs).

Martin laughs. 'Joe was great fun. He lived every day, well . . .' – he hesitates, as it dawns on him what he's about to say – 'well, as if it *was* his last.'

On a beautiful day in late August, a week after Granada, in the Sussex seaside town of Hastings, I'm on the trail of another Mescalero, Tymon Dogg, Joe's busking compadre from the hippie days of the early '70s who'd gone on to collaborate with The Clash on *Sandinista!* and *Combat Rock* before losing contact with him for fifteen years. In 2001, he became a full-time Mescalero.

'He was a gentle, gentle man,' says Tymon emphatically over a pint of the local brew. 'Joe was this kind, generous person who lived in this funny,

Biggles world. Did you know he was an excellent cartoonist? Yeah! And I think he saw the world through a cartoonist's eye. He found things very odd and very funny.

'It's strange, but when we met again a few years ago, we discovered that we'd just bought not only the same model drum machine, but from the same shop in Charing Cross, and from the same assistant. Joe looked at me, and said, "Wow. Funny!" We couldn't stop laughing. It was like nothing had changed.'

It's clear that the violinist felt extremely close to Joe, and the impression of a deep bond between them, rooted in the days when they had nothing but each other's company, is borne out in many amusing stories – like the one about the pair collecting flies in a paper cup on the Mescaleros' tour bus, and then releasing them to freedom at the next stop-off. So had Joe changed at all between 1970 and 2002? 'Not much,' laughs Tymon. 'Really, you can say that for him: fame never changed him much at all.'

At Tymon's house, I speak by phone to the US producer Rick Rubin, who recorded two of *Streetcore*'s most poignant tracks: a cover of Bob Marley's 'Redemption Song' (and if a white man's going to do it justice, then it's gonna be Joe, right?), and 'Long Shadow', which Strummer wrote for one of his great heroes, Johnny Cash. The two met in April last year, when Johnny was recording at Rubin's home in LA.

'Joe would always come to my house if he was in town, because he thought it had the best pool,' says Rubin. 'If I wasn't in, he'd climb over the fence, and when you got back he'd just be there! So when he found out Johnny Cash was here, he came and hung out everyday down the studio. He had a great time. He used to lie on the floor and peer up through this glass window at Johnny singing in the next room. Did Johnny know who he was? No, but we soon enlightened him.'

According to Rubin, Joe was 'excited but the quietest I've ever seen him. He looked like a student in school.' When Strummer presented Johnny and Rick with the lyrics to 'Long Shadow', they were written on a pizza box, with extra verses on a paper towel and roll of insulation tape. To vibe himself up for his vocal takes, he would lock himself in his car outside the studio door and listen to his *cumbia* tape over and over again. Naturally, Joe insisted that Rubin record his stuff in the garage on a small tape-recorder, rather than the studio itself. 'That was Joe: everything he did was unique and special.' By the end of the sessions, Cash and Strummer were friends: 'Joe was a nice man,' Cash said later, 'a good man, and a good musician.'

*

It's inevitable that people will read all kinds of stuff into the last months of someone's life, and Joe's life is no different. Those close to him talk about a lot of reconciliations and renewed friendships in the weeks leading up to his death; others, perhaps not so close to him, see great significance in the fact that his last-ever encore was 'White Man In Hammersmith Palais' (never an encore, apparently). One very public reunion happened on-stage, when after a gap of some nineteen years, Joe and Mick performed together again, at a Fire Brigades Union benefit at Acton Town Hall on 15 November 2002.

Mick was no stranger to Mescaleros shows, but this one was somehow different. 'When I heard the chords to "Bankrobber", said Mick, 'I just thought, "I've got to get up there". So I said to the person with me, "Hold me coat – I'm going in . . ."' Mick plugged his guitar into Joe's amp, the two blasting out of the same speaker – 'just like when The Clash started out at Rehearsal Rehearsals', Tymon Dogg smiles. Mick stayed on stage for two more encores, 'White Riot' and 'London's Burning'. Tellingly, the weight of mythology has already convinced some that Acton was Joe's last ever gig (it was actually in Liverpool).

Joe's old friend, the writer Chris Salewicz, who's currently working on a biography on Strummer, observes that Joe is now 'an icon along with the likes of John Lennon, Bob Dylan and Bob Marley'. And that iconic status seems to be snowballing every day. It's interesting to imagine what Joe, who only a few years ago wondered, 'Will anyone come?', would make of it all.

The closing track on *Streetcore*, 'Silver & Gold', is a cover of Bobby Charles' lovely old New Orleans swinger from the early fifties, 'Before I Grow Too Old'. On it, Joe sings about the things he wants to do before it's too late – 'take a trip around the world', 'kiss all the pretty girls' . . . It's unbelievably moving stuff.

But as Barry 'Scratchy' Myers points out: 'Joe did in his fifty years what many people wouldn't get to do in so many lifetimes.'

15
GROOVY TIMES?

Summer 2009

W HEN I WROTE *Passion Is A Fashion*, I deliberately did so in a way that would tie it unshakeably to the time I was working on it. In the book, most of the key interviewees were introduced to the reader 'face-to-face', as I myself had encountered them during my research. The contemporary descriptions of what they looked like and what they were currently up to – and even some of their observations – were bound to lose their currency in time, but I felt it was essential to what I was trying to achieve. To wit, *Passion Is A Fashion* stands as a historical document looking back at The Clash's stories from a specific standpoint – the first years of the 21st century – when its participants were still young enough for the events of 1975–85 to be relatively recent (most were still in their forties when we spoke), but old enough to have done some growing up since the punk days and come to terms with their own roles in what happened.

Passion was written when Joe Strummer's sudden death in December 2002 was still very fresh in people's minds. My meeting with Mick Jones, which begins the chapter on his early life, took place only a week or so after Joe's funeral; at several junctures Mick was clearly holding back his emotions. It was a tearful occasion. For other interviewees such as Tymon Dogg and Alex Michon, the feelings triggered by exploring their memories of Joe were equally raw. Reading the book back now, their observations seem heavily shaded with a sense of Joe's loss.

The 'nowness' of the book when I wrote it has meant that, returning to it five years later, it's been almost impossible to update parts of it in the conventional manner. It remains, as I'd hoped, a chronicle of The Clash as seen from a vantage point 25 years after events occurred. Naturally, some of the details relating to the characters have changed. There have been developments that are quite unexpected. I was tickled to open a paper last year to read that Micky Foote, the group's soundman, who'd existed in the shadows for nearly three decades after his dismissal from the Clash camp in 1978, was now involved in a high-profile battle to stop US tycoon Donald Trump building a luxury golf resort near a property Foote owned on the Aberdeenshire coast. Good for him.

As to people's personal circumstances, it would be a difficult and possibly pointless job to try to make them all current again. However, for the record, Roadent, a key member of the band's inner circle in 1976–77, no longer edits the West London magazine *The Roughler*, as he did in 2004. Last time we met, in February 2008, he was carrying a bundle of pigeon netting and playfully trying to convince someone stood nearby that he was involved in the pest control business. As ever he was coy about the various projects he's working on. Then there's Ray Gange, who for years found his on-screen role as the star of The Clash's *Rude Boy* film a millstone around his neck; recently, he's turned the experience to his advantage, DJ-ing his beloved reggae, punk and soul in clubs all over the country, happy to billed as '*Rude Boy*'s Ray Gange'.

Not everyone's story has had a happy ending, I'm sad to say. In October 2008, Ray Lowry, the satirical cartoonist who accompanied The Clash on their autumn 1979 US tour and famously designed the cover of *London Calling*, died after several years of shaky health. He was warned by doctors about the effects of his heavy drinking many times during his final years, but Ray stubbornly opted to maintain an enthusiasm for booze. One of his last 'public appearances', for want of a better phrase, was in 2007 at Strummercamp, an annual celebration of Joe's life held in Manchester, where Ray, nursing an apparently much-needed pint, was appalled by the vision of dozens of people he thought were 'trying to dress like Joe in the punk days'. Ray's life and work deserve a book in themselves, and there's little doubt in my mind that his extraordinary cartoons and oils are on their way to becoming highly prized pieces, not least for their originality and barbed wit and for presenting a charming worldview where white rock'n'roll (bar The Clash) had fallen from grace since the primitive magic of his tragic teenage heroes Eddie Cochran and Gene Vincent.

In early April 2009, at the Laugharne literary and music festival in Wales – a mildly bizarre gathering, during which celebratory guest Mick Jones had his head cast in plaster by Nick Reynolds, the artist son of Great Train Robber, Bruce – I was shown a book Ray had finished just before his death. It was an account of Eddie and Gene's ill-fated UK tour in 1960, during which Cochran died in a car crash. The book was illustrated in colour and written in the same meticulous calligraphy with which Ray wrote out the song lyrics of London Calling on the album's inner sleeves. Hopefully, one day this amazing creation will see publication.

While the circumstances of people's lives will inevitably alter, the story of The Clash's glory years, as unfolded in *Passion Is A Fashion*, should in theory remain unchanged. But, of course, history is an every-shifting thing, and this new version of the book contains many minor revisions and adjustments, as new details and accounts of events have come to light. These amendments are largely the result of my subsequently interviewing several associates of The Clash whom I didn't have time to speak to while originally researching the book. Added to this has been the publication of several major new Clash-related books and articles.

Chief among these is Chris Salewicz's superlative Joe Strummer biography, *Redemption Song* (Harper Collins), published in 2006. Salewicz, whose personal friendships with The Clash members stretch back to the punk days, sheds fascinating new light on Joe's family background and post-Clash years. The level of fresh detail is astonishing, and I've taken the liberty of amending the text in the chapter in *Passion Is A Fashion* about Joe's early life to reflect the revelation that his father's job as a 'clerical officer' entailed working with secret cipher codes, and also that he had left-wing leanings. Salewicz explores in depth Strummer's sexual motivations and relationships with girlfriends and wives – an area of the Clash members' existence that *Passion Is A Fashion* (perhaps ironically considering the title) deliberately chose only to touch upon. I urge any fan wanting to know more about Joe's story to purloin a copy of Chris's book.

Salewicz's tome was long expected, but another substantial addition to the Clash canon came out of the blue. In 2007, *The Last Days of The Clash* (Moving Target) by Vince White appeared. White was, of course, one of the guitarists in the post-Mick Jones version of the group that existed for two years between late 1983 and late 1985. To put the significance of Vince's book in perspective, one simply has to observe that it's the only full-length account of the band by a group member. What is more surprising still is the skill and flair with which it's written – over 300-odd pages, White details every nuance of his unhappy and disorientating stint in the five-man, Mk II perversion of The Clash with a kind of masochistic, cathartic relish, and revelations about his ill-considered affair with manager Bernie Rhodes' then girlfriend only add to the car-crash fascination of it all.

I'm pleased to note that, again, nothing in *The Last Days of The Clash* significantly contradicts anything written in the original version of *Passion Is A Fashion* and, as with Salewicz's book, Vince's work will serve as a complementary document for anyone wishing to learn more about certain periods and aspects of the group's story.

Another fascinating document that appeared unexpectedly was Paul Simonon's own account of his troubled upbringing, written in 2005 for the style/fashion publication, *Another Magazine*, and later reprinted in an edited form in *Q* magazine's 'The Clash: The Inside Story' special edition (which I edited). This related in more detail, among other things, the tale of he and younger brother Nick setting fire to his mother and stepfather's house in Brixton; revealed how the mischievous pair once snuck into a lodging room in Ladbroke Grove where a dead man lay to steal a coin from his dresser; and poignantly told of the 'difficult time' that followed his parents' break-up in the early '60s. It also clarified the chronology of the last years of his schooling in Ladbroke Grove, confirming he'd stayed on an extra year to sit 'O' Levels and that a sympathetic teacher had recommended him to the selection board at the Byam Shaw art school in Notting Hill, opening the door to his years as an 'art rat', as one of his home-made punk-era T-shirts proclaimed. Simonon's piece is well worth tracking down; where my chronology was slightly awry in the book I've tickled the relevant sentences accordingly.

Of the many Clash-related interviews I've conducted myself since *Passion Is A Fashion* was first published, the most important in terms of Clash hierarchy are the half-dozen or so with Mick. I've hung out a fair bit with Jones in recent years, visiting his millennial group Carbon-Silicon in the recording studio and following them on tour to many far-flung places, including in November 2004 a concrete bunker under a bridge in Stockholm where Jones was confronted onstage by a bellicose Viking who didn't like the fact he wasn't performing Clash tunes. (Perhaps the Norwegian was related to the young Welshman at the Laugharne festival who heckled the dapperly attired Mick with the immortal words, 'Why aren't you dressed like a punk?')

The stories Mick tells in casual conversation could fill another book; but it's a shame I didn't know when I first sat down to write *Passion* that his father, Tom, once had Battle of Britain fighter ace Douglas Bader in the back of his cab. I would have definitely woven that lovely little nugget into the plot, providing as it does a connection – albeit a tenuous one – to the spirit of WWII heroism that seemingly fired The Clash, via books, films and the tales of older relatives.

Another quirky Jones story that springs to mind, but which I couldn't shoehorn into the updated narrative, is a tale about Bernie Rhodes' altercation with a tramp who was pestering the manager while The Clash were having their photographs taken under the Westway in summer 1977 – the famous Adrian Boot session, with the poster for the reggae gig mythologised in the song 'White Man In Hammersmith Palais' visible in the background.

Apparently, the derelict repeatedly tried to whip Bernie's glasses off his head, and Rhodes snapped, much to the mild shock – and great amusement – of Joe, Mick, Paul and Topper. It proved their manager still had the terrier-like spirit his friend John Pearse recalled him possessing in their Mod days, knocking around in Maida Vale. Mick couldn't help grinning widely at the memory.

Talking of Bernie, I've had several conversations with him too since *Passion* first appeared, including a late-night, hour-long chat at the Globe club in Ladbroke Grove. Listening to Rhodes lecture again on politics, art and culture for sixty minutes is quite an experience; I did, however, manage to throw in the odd question about his mystery years in the early '70s, but got the standard answer about being an 'ideas person' for Marc Bolan. One gem I did mange to winkle out of him was which art school he'd attended in the '60s – he said it was Goldsmiths, quite a Clash-friendly establishment, it seems, as Robin Banks, Mick Jones' best friend from school and enduring Clash confidant, admitted to me recently that he also studied there for a while ('but don't tell anyone').

Bernie's unconventional approach to band management is, of course, a vital dimension of The Clash story, and it always puzzled me what CBS head Maurice Oberstein, who died in 2001, made of him. When I originally approached his second-in-command, A&R head Muff Winwood, for an interview for the book, he didn't respond to my request, but I did eventually manage to speak to him in 2007. To my surprise, he was unequivocal in his praise for Rhodes. 'Bernie was brilliant, we loved him!' he said. 'We could trust him to deal with The Clash, who were very difficult, of course, and he was always able to deliver the product.'

He added: 'The lesson we learned from The Clash, which was useful with the later punk bands, with that we could use that friction they had with us, the record company, to our advantage. The fact they publicly slagged us off helped sell CBS millions of records.' Turning rebellion into money, indeed.

The other most illuminating post-book interviews were those with Jane Crockford, Steve Jones, Pablo Cook and Pablo LaBritain. Jane Crockford achieved notoriety in the early punk days when she and Shane MacGowan carved each other up with broken glass at The Clash's October 1976 gig at the

ICA. Later, she formed the all-girl group The Mo-dettes, and shared a squat with Joe in Daventry Street, Lisson Grove, in 1978. Our interview at a coffee house in Chelsea in April 2006 was the first she'd given to the press since the late '70s; and the story she told was full of colourful new details.

Jane revealed that her connection with The Clash went way back to 1974, when she had dated a 19-year-old Mick Jones, then studying at art school in West London. 'Mick was lovely,' she explained. 'I met him at a gig at the Greyhound in Fulham. He said, "I'm gonna be a rock guitarist." And he did, eventually! But [after we split up] I had so much resentment against him for so long.'

Jane's friendship with Joe would later create tension between Jones and Strummer. 'It happened one night after going to the Roxy club on Neal Street,' recalls Crockford. 'I'd met Joe before and we got on really well – "yap yap yap yap!" We spent the night together at the squat [at Orsett Terrace] in Westbourne Grove, but there was no sex. We were still up at three in the morning talking and so I stayed over. In the morning Mick Jones came in and there were looks but, y'know, nothing happened.'

Such niggling sexual jealousies would remain an unspoken feature of The Clash's existence, and would culminate in an incident that exposed just how unpleasant life in the group could be. While I was researching *Passion Is A Fashion*, the band's former road manager Johnny Green would often phone up and give me cryptic 'clues' as to hidden agendas he thought I might want to explore. One that used to make me chuckle involved a theory about 'swapsies'. 'Pat,' Johnny would say, mock-mysteriously. 'Ask about the swapsies.'

All was eventually revealed in another essential Clash-related work to emerge in recent years: Julien Temple's quite brilliant Joe Strummer documentary, *The Future Is Unwritten*. In it, Topper admitted that, following an argument between the drummer and his girlfriend, Joe had spent the night with her. Topper still looked deeply unimpressed by the episode nearly thirty years on.

Jane Crockford's account of her friendship with Joe threw up many other interesting gems: for example, she remembers the singer being victimised by the police throughout 1977 and vividly recalls his being thrown into a Black Maria while walking home after a reggae gig at Hammersmith Palais (which may, or may not, have been the one that inspired White Man, she couldn't remember). Curiously, she doesn't recall him spending much time at the squat in Daventry Street, which he moved into in the spring of 1978 after leaving Habitat heir Sebastian Conran's house in Albany Street. Sebastian and Jane were a couple at the time, and her abiding memories relate to Joe's tenure in Conran's palatial 'white mansion', where she admits there was 'a lot of alcohol and drugs'. As to the rumour that Joe caught hepatitis from injecting heroin, she is adamant he was vehemently opposed to the drug.

'Joe did no damage to anyone – he did a lot of good in people's lives,' Jane concluded. 'There was something in him that was so solid, in his heart. He was a wonderful man. I really have positive memories of him.'

Around the same time I spoke to Jane Crockford, I tracked down Paul Buck, alias Pablo LaBritain, Joe's friend from boarding school who played drums in the fledgling Clash for a week or so in June 1976. Pablo went on to have a career in punk band 999, before settling down to a job in the horology department at the British Museum. A kindly and amiable chap, Pablo – his nickname was bestowed by Joe in their schooldays – painted an affectionate picture of his friend in the days directly before punk happened.

'I was living with my dad in a farm house in East Sussex,' recalls LaBritain. 'Joe phoned up one day and said, "Could I come down and bring [101'ers drummer] Dudanski as well?" I said, "Yeah, fine yeah," so he turned up with Dudanski, both of their Spanish girlfriends and their mother, and a guy called Julio. The mother took over the kitchen to make a huge Spanish omelette to feed everyone. My dad came back from the pub and the kitchen was full of these strange people. Joe would do funny things like that, I loved it. They ended up staying for a couple of days.'

Pablo's invitation to join The Clash came in early June, within the first week or two of Joe joining the group. 'I was working in a factory near where I lived,' explains LaBritain. 'I'd been playing the drums for a while, and Joe and I had jammed when he'd come down to visit me the previous Christmas. Joe rung me up, and said did I want to try this new band out? The whole of The Clash then arrived at the farm in a big truck that they'd borrowed from [rhythm and blues band] The Count Bishops. It was a burning hot day, and to drive up to London with these guys – Mick, Paul, Joe and Keith Levene – it was very strange for me. Mick Jones ... I shook hands with him, he had these tiny hands, and he was so pale as well. Then we got up to Camden. I was living in the countryside, I was very not used to London at the time.'

Pablo's arrival coincided with Bernie's acquisition of the Chalk Farm warehouse which would become the band's HQ. LaBritain recalls: 'We weren't allowed to make a noise during the day, as there were other businesses in the yard, so we'd spend all day cleaning the windows and painting it up. Then at about five or six o'clock we were allowed to start playing. We rehearsed continuously, even on Sunday.'

The drummer recalls that Paul Simonon was 'quite jokey, he was very friendly, always trying to give notes to the girls at the cafes. There was always some sort of waitress who he had the hots for, or vice versa. There was a place we used to go for something to eat, just over the bridge [George's café], and there was something going on with some girl there.' Pablo found Keith Levene 'an edgy sort of chap', while 'Mick was loveable but with a quick temper. He lost it with me a couple of times.'

As none of the group worked, funds for socialising were virtually non-existent. However, one night they scraped enough cash together to go for a pint at the Speakeasy, the music biz hang-out on Margaret Street near Oxford Circus. Paul walked out wearing someone else's jacket, and its owner spotted what was happening. 'He confronted Paul on the way out and nutted him. He loosened his tooth,' Pablo recalls. 'Then there was a scuffle. I thought, "Who are these people I'm getting in a band with?" But it was a lot more exciting than being at home in East Sussex.'

Previously, Pablo's departure from the group after just a week or so had been fogged in mystery. The assumption had been that Bernie had taken a Marxist stance on the group's composition, feeling a second privately educated band member might undermine The Clash's proletarian image. But this is clearly a case of projecting the band's later preoccupation with class and background retrospectively: the truth was far simpler. Mick felt Pablo wasn't good enough.

'What happened,' says Pablo, 'was that one evening The Sex Pistols, minus John Lydon, came to see us rehearse and we ran through a few numbers for them. I was very nervous, and messed up a couple of times. Mick stormed off to somewhere in South London, and Paul, Joe and Bernie went after him.'

The next morning the drummer arrived at rehearsals as usual. Joe immediately took him to the Caernarvon Castle pub over the road. Pablo sensed something was wrong. 'He bought me a pint – which didn't bode well,' he laughs. 'Then he told me, "You're out." I went back down to rehearsals and had a last jam with Mick and Paul; Joe wasn't there. It was great! Mick said, "Why didn't you play like that last night?" But it was too late, I was gone. If you look at my drumming and then you look at Topper, I mean, he's the business, a fantastic drummer. I just wasn't up to it, to be honest.'

Pablo's story is a reminder that it's easy to misinterpret events, and jump to incorrect conclusions. This is borne out with the revelations of another musician who performed briefly with The Clash – The Sex Pistols' Steve Jones, who joined them on-stage several times on the On Parole tour in summer 1978.

His presence at their gigs and rehearsals was interpreted by road manager Johnny Green as an attempt by Bernie Rhodes to unsettle Mick Jones, at a time when tensions between Mick, Bernie and the other members of the band were at their height. In a conversation I had with Steve Jones in November 2007, he was resolute in his conviction that no such plot to destabilise Mick existed. 'It was just me turning up to play,' he says. 'Bernie and [Sex Pistols manager] Malcolm [McLaren] didn't know I was doing it. I just used to get whims. I liked The Clash.'

The idea of a conspiracy to bring Steve Jones into the group, then, may have existed solely in the minds of those who relished such theories; yet there can be little doubt that Bernie Rhodes and the other members of The Clash exploited the situation to unnerve Mick, who it is widely agreed was becoming particularly difficult to work with at that time.

Another interview I did that provided a fresh window on shadowy Clash events was with Pablo Cook, percussionist with the first line-up of Joe's group The Mescaleros. Pablo, who began working with Joe in the mid-'90s, revealed just how touch-and-go a Clash reunion was following the Sex Pistols' re-formation in 1996. Much of it was no doubt pub talk, but on more than one occasion it seems it was unanimously agreed to be a good idea – with the normal unorthodox Clash caveats.

'I was trying to find an angle that would get Joe out playing live again,' recalls Pablo. 'During the pub one night I said, "Let's get a tribute band together called like The Clish or An Afternoon With The Clash or something like that." I was going to put on a gig at the Amersham Arms over in South London – Paul was up for it, Mick was up for it and I was going to play drums, as Topper was obviously too mashed at the time.

'The idea was that people would think, "Oh, it's a dreary fucking Wednesday evening, let's go out and see this tribute band … oh, hang on, that looks pretty good for The Clash – oh God, it is The Clash!" I started getting people involved, everyone was really keen to do it, but then it fell on fallow ground.'

So, the opportunity to see The Clash down your South London local never materialised. And sadly, due to Joe's death, never will. But there have been several other unexpected Clash part-reunions since, one widely reported, another not …

When it comes to the surviving Clash members, perhaps the most important news in the last five years is Topper's emergence from the claws of drug dependency, and his tentative re-engagement with music. It hasn't been an easy road for Tops, but he's been totally clean for four years now, and celebrated in June 2009 by donating the customised red Mini Cooper, which he bought himself when he first kicked heroin into touch, to the Strummerville charity, run by Joe's family.

There has always been talk that, should the drummer ever feel ready to tour and record again with a full-time band, Mick would be delighted for Topper to work in some way with Carbon-Silicon. This hasn't happened, but the drummer did join the group in January 2008 for an encore of 'Train In Vain' and 'Should I Stay Or Should I Go?' at the first of Carbon-Silicon's six enormously popular 'Carbon Casino' shows at the Inn on the Green in Ladbroke Grove. It was a moving moment, as powerfully symbolic in terms of closing a circle as had been Mick's jumping up on stage with Joe at Acton Town Hall just weeks before Strummer's death.

The gig was Topper's first high-profile appearance behind a drum kit since being sacked from The Clash some 26 years earlier; hopefully, there will be more to come, since Headon is currently working on a jazz-orientated project involving former Police guitarist Henry Padovani. He's also meant to be penning an account of his life, presently titled *Headon Collision*.

Mick – always considered the most driven member of The Clash, and the one for whom creating music seems almost a psychological necessity – has continued to operate Carbon-Silicon as a part-mainstream, part-guerrilla-style entity, successfully touring small clubs in the US and playing one-off gigs, festivals and residencies in the UK (notably the Carbon Casino dates in Ladbroke Grove and 2008 Christmas shows at the Hammersmith Club). *The Carbon Bubble*, the follow-up to their zippy debut album *The Last Post*, is due out in summer 2009.

Meanwhile, Mick continues to moonlight with The Rotten Hill Gang, a group helmed by his former Big Audio Dynamite II comrade Gary Stonadge, and has recorded with Dirty Stop Out, a musical project teaming him with Joe Corre – Malcolm McLaren and Vivienne Westwood's son, and co-founder of the Agent Provocateur lingerie brand.

At the time *Passion Is A Fashion* was written, Paul Simonon had apparently turned his back on music for good, concentrating on his new career as a painter. In 2006, however, he re-entered the world of music, playing bass in a new Damon Albarn project, officially nameless, but universally referred to by the title of the album they'd created – *The Good, The Bad And The Queen*. In January 2007, the CD reached Number 2 in the charts, creating the odd situation of Simonon's 21st-century musical endeavours eclipsing Jones's, both commercially and in cultural impact (Carbon-Silicon's *The Last Post*, for example, didn't chart). When not working with TGTB&TQ, Paul still paints most days, and enjoyed another successful London exhibition in 2008, including several oils inspired by Spanish bull-fights.

What is little known is that Mick and Paul have, too, shared a stage together in recent years. In January 2005, they were asked by model Kate Moss – a close friend of both musicians and their families for many years – to play at her 31st birthday party at her home in the Cotswolds. Also performing in the one-night only supergroup were Primal Scream's Bobby Gillespie and Kate's then partner Pete Doherty, whose post-Libertines group Babyshambles Mick was producing at the time. Among the songs played that evening were 'Train In Vain' and 'Guns Of Brixton' – footage of the show exists, but has never been widely circulated. So the world still awaits a public musical reunion of Mick and Paul …

Rehearsals for the party piece took place at Mick's studio in Acton, annexed to a vast storage room containing his gargantuan collection of books, videos, clothes, films, guitars, board games, toys, gig posters, photographs and rare Clash and BAD memorabilia. In his upstairs office is even the wardrobe from his mother and father's old flat in Brixton. 'I've never thrown anything away,' Mick confesses. In March 2009 some of his lock-up's contents were displayed as an art installation for four weeks at the Chelsea Space behind the Tate Britain gallery – just a few hundred yards from the building in which The Clash had pieced together the songs for *London Calling*. The exhibition went under the name of 'The Rock 'n' Roll Public Library', and it's hoped one day Mick's artefacts will find a permanent public home.

As for The Clash's magnitude as rock icons … well, it seems to grow ever bigger year by year. Few music award ceremonies seem to pass by without the group being honoured in some way, or being asked to present an award to an artist deemed to be operating in a manner reminiscent of the original Clash spirit (though anyone au fait with their tale might doubt this could ever truly be the case). Their back catalogue continues to be exploited with considerable vigour and comparative care: in 2006 their original singles were released as neat facsimile CD miniatures in a box set, *The Clash The Singles*, and in 2008 the brisk and funky *The Clash Live At Shea Stadium* became the first recording of a Clash show to be made available in its entirety.

So there we have it. As an amusing sign-off to the Clash story so far, I feel I could do far worse than relate a recent anecdote concerning Topper. In March 2009, as with Mick and Paul and Joe's family, he received an invitation to attend the Ivor Novello Awards. Apparently he had co-written one of the biggest worldwide hits of the past year. Puzzled, he phoned Johnny Green. His friend and former roadie made a few calls and learned that M.I.A.'s 'Paper Planes', used on the *Slumdog Millionaire* soundtrack and also a smash in its own right, had sampled The Clash's 'Straight To Hell', of which Headon was credited as a co-writer. Naturally, Headon's accountant was cock-a-hoop when the drummer passed on the news.

Topper, who these days prefers a quiet life, didn't go to the awards ceremony in May. Instead, he took his dog Yowsah for a long walk, then attended an AA meeting. Such are the enduring contradictions of daily life as a former Clash member in the 21st century.

DISCOGRAPHY

UK DISCOGRAPHY

Singles 1976–1985

(Chart position in brackets)

18/3/77	'White Riot'/'1977'	CBS 5058	[38]
9/4/77	'Capital Radio'/Interview/'Listen' *Free single given away to readers who* *sent off the coupon printed in the NME,* *plus red sticker from the first album*	CL1	[–]
13/5/77	'Remote Control'/'London's Burning' (Live)	CBS 5293	[–]
23/9/77	'Complete Control'/'City of the Dead'	CBS 5664	[28]
17/2/78	'Clash City Rockers'/'Jail Guitar Doors'	CBS 5834	[35]
16/6/78	'White Man in Hammersmith Palais'/ 'The Prisoner' *Came in four different coloured sleeves:* *green, blue, pink and yellow*	CBS 6383	[32]
24/11/78	'Tommy Gun'/'1-2 Crush on You'	CBS 6788	[19]
23/2/79	'English Civil War'/'Pressure Drop'	CBS 7082	[25]
11/5/79	*Cost Of Living* EP Side 1 'I Fought the Law'/'Groovy Times' Side 2: 'Gates of the West'/'Capital Radio'	CBS 7324	[22]

The first five Clash singles were also reissued in 1979.

| 7/12/79 | 'London Calling'/'Armagideon Time'
Came in three different coloured sleeves:
yellow, red and green. | CBS 8087 | [11] |
| 4/1/80 | 'London Calling'/'Armagideon Time'/
'Justice Tonight'/'Kick It Over' (12") | CBS 128087 | |

8/8/80	'Bankrobber'/'Rockers Galore . . .' UK Tour *Mikey Dread was the artist on the B-side.*	CBS 8323	[12]
21/11/80	'The Call Up'/'Stop The World'	CBS 9339	[40]
16/1/81	'Hitsville UK'/'Radio One' *A-side features Ellen Foley; B-side is Mikey Dread*	CBS 9480	[56]
10/4/81	'The Magnificent Seven'/'Magnificent Dance'	CBS A1133	[34]
10/4/81	'The Magnificent Seven'/'Magnificent Dance' (12") *Initial copies came with a set of stickers.*	CBS A12 1133	
20/11/81	'This Is Radio Clash'/'Radio Clash'	CBS A 1797	[47]
20/11/81	'This Is Radio Clash'/'Radio Clash'/ 'Outside Broadcast'/'Radio 5' (12")	CBS A131797	
23/4/82	'Know Your Rights'/'First Night Back in London' *Initial copies came with a KNOW YOUR RIGHTS sticker.*	CBS A2309	[43]
11/6/82	'Rock the Casbah'/'Long Time Jerk' *Initial copies came with a set of four stickers.*	CBS A 2479	[30]
11/6/82	'Rock the Casbah'/'Mustapha Dance' (12")	CBS A13 2479	
11/6/82	'Rock the Casbah'/'Long Time Jerk' (7" picture disc)	CBS A11 2479	
17/9/82	'Should I Stay or Should I Go?'/ 'Straight To Hell' *Initial copies came with a sticker.*	CBS A 2646	[17]
17/9/82	'Should I Stay or Should I Go?'/ 'Straight To Hell' (12") *Initial copies came with a stencil.*	CBS A13 2646	
17/9/82	'Should I Stay or Should I Go?'/ 'Straight To Hell' (7" picture disc)	S CBS A11 2646	
30/9/85	'This Is England'/'Do It Now' *Initial copies came as a fold-out poster sleeve.*	CBS A 6122	[24]

30/9/85   'This Is England'/'Do it Now'/   CBS TA 6122
'Sex Mad War'

There have been numerous reissues, with various permutations of existing material, since the band split up. The most important was 'Should I Stay or Should I Go?', backed with BAD's 'Rush', released in March 1991 after 'Should I Stay . . .?' was used on a Levi's TV commercial. It reached number one.

SINGLES BOX SET

30/10/06   **CD1:** 'White Riot'/'1977'   Sony 828768762282

CD2: 'Listen (Edit)'/'Interview With The Clash On The Circle Line (Part One)'/'Interview With The Clash On The Circle Line (Part Two)'/'Capital Radio One'

CD3: 'Remote Control'/'London's Burning (Live)'/'London's Burning'

CD4: 'Complete Control'/'City Of The Dead'

CD5: 'Clash City Rockers'/'Jail Guitar Doors'

CD6: '(White Man) In Hammersmith Palais'/'The Prisoner'

CD7: 'Tommy Gun'/'1-2 Crush On You'

CD8: 'English Civil War'/'Pressure Drop'

CD9: 'I Fought The Law'/'Groovy Times'/'Gates Of The West'/'Capital Radio Two'

CD10: 'London Calling'/'Armagideon Time'/'Justice Tonight'/'Kick It Over'/'Clampdown'/'The Card Cheat'/'Lost In The Supermarket'

CD11: 'Bankrobber'/'Rockers Galore … UK Tour'/'Rudie Can't Fail'/'Train In Vain'

CD12: 'The Call Up'/'Stop The World'

CD13: 'Hitsville UK'/'Radio One'/'Police On My Back'/'Somebody Got Murdered'

CD14: 'The Magnificent Seven (Edit)'/'The Magnificent Dance'/'Lightning Strikes (Not Once But Twice)'/'One More Time'/'One More Dub'/'The Cool Out'/'The Magnificent Seven (12" Version)'/'The Magnificent Dance (12" Version)'

CD15: 'This Is Radio Clash'/'Radio Clash'/'Outside Broadcast'/'Radio 5'

CD16: 'Know Your Rights'/'First Night Back In London'

CD17: 'Rock The Casbah'/'Long Time Jerk'/'Mustapha Dance'/'Red Angel Dragnet'/'Overpowered By Funk'

CD18: 'Should I Stay Or Should I Go'/'Straight To Hell (Edited Version)'/'Inoculated City'/'Cool Confusion'

CD19: 'This Is England'/'Do It Now'/'Sex Mad Roar'

Other Important Singles

THE VICE CREEMS

9/3/79   'Danger Love'/'Like A Tiger'   Zig Zag ZZ 22001
         Features Kris Needs (vocals), Michael Blair
         alias Mick Jones (gtr), Nicholas Khan alias
         Topper Headon (drums). Animal noises by
         Robin Banks. Produced by Mick Jones.

ELLEN FOLEY

6/2/81   'The Shuttered Palace'/'Beautiful Waste   Epic 9522
         of Time'

3/4/81   'Torchlight'/'Game of a Man'   Epic A 1160
         Produced by Mick Jones and featuring Joe,
         Paul, Topper and Mick.

FUTURA 2000

6/5/83	'The Escapades of Futura 2000'/ 'Instrumental' *By New York graffiti artist Futura, featuring* *the whole band. Song co-written by Mick.*	Celluloid CYZ-7-104

JANE JONES & THE LASH

2/12/83	'House Of The Ju Ju Queen'/ 'Sex Machine' *Features Joe, Paul and Mick. A-side written* *and produced by Joe.*	Big Beat NS91-A

Albums

8/4/77	*The Clash* 'Janie Jones'/'Remote Control'/'I'm So Bored With The USA'/'White Riot'/'Hate & War'/'What's My Name?'/'Deny'/'London's Burning'/'Career Opportunities'/'Cheat'/ 'Protex Blue'/'Police & Thieves'/'48Hours'/ 'Garageland'	CBS 82000	[12]
10/11/78	*Give 'Em Enough Rope* 'Safe European Home'/'English Civil War'/ 'Tommy Gun'/'Julie's Been Working for the Drug Squad'/'Last Gang in Town'/ 'Guns on the Roof'/'Drug-Stabbing Time'/ 'Stay Free'/'Cheapskates'/'All the Young Punks (New Boots and Contacts)'	CBS 82431	[2]
14/12/79	*London Calling* 'London Calling'/'Brand New Cadillac'/ 'Jimmy Jazz'/'Hateful'/'Rudie Can't Fail'/ 'Spanish Bombs'/'Right Profile'/'Lost in the Supermarket'/'Clampdown'/'Guns of Brixton'/'Wrong 'Em Boyo'/'Death or Glory'/'Koka Cola'/'Card Cheat'/'Lover's Rock'/'I'm Not Down'/'Revolution Rock'/ 'Four Horsemen'/'Train In Vain'	CBS Clash 3	[9]

12/12/80 *Sandinista!* CBS FSLN 1 [19]
'The Magnificent Seven'/'Hitsville UK'/
'Junco Partner'/'Ivan Meets G.I. Joe'/'The
Leader'/'Something About England'/'Rebel
Waltz'/'Look Here'/'The Crooked Beat'/
'Somebody Got Murdered'/'One More
Time'/'One More Dub'/'Lightning Strikes
(Not Once But Twice)'/'Up In Heaven (Not
Only Here)'/'Corner Soul'/'Let's Go Crazy'/
'If Music Could Talk'/'The Sound Of The
Sinners'/'Police On My Back'/'Midnight
Log'/'The Equaliser'/'The Call Up'/
'Washington Bullets'/'Broadway'/'Lose This
Skin'/'Charlie Don't Surf'/'Mensforth Hill'/
'Junkie Slip'/'Kingston Advice'/'The Street
Parade'/'Version City'/'Living In
Fame'/'Silicone On Sapphire'/'Career
Opportunities'/'Shepherds Delight'

14/5/82 *Combat Rock* CBS FMLN 2 [2]
'Inoculated City'/'Know Your Rights'/
'Car Jamming'/'Should I Stay Or Should I
Go?'/'Rock The Casbah'/'Red Angel
Dragnet'/'Straight To Hell'/'Overpowered By
Funk'/'Atom Tan'/'Sean Flynn'/'Ghetto
Defendant'/'Death Is A Star'

8/11/85 *Cut the Crap* CBS 26601 [16]
'Dictator'/'Dirty Punk'/'We Are The
Clash'/'Are You Red . . . y'/''Cool Under
Heat'/'Movers And Shakers'/'This Is
England'/'Three Card Trick'/'Play To
Win'/'Fingerpoppin''/'North And South'/'Life
Is Wild'

21/3/88 *The Story Of The Clash* CBS 4602441 [7]
'The Magnificent Seven'/'Rock The
Casbah'/'This Is Radio Clash'/'Should I Stay
Or Should I Go?'/'Straight To Hell'/
'Armagideon Time'/'Clampdown'/'Train In
Vain'/'Guns Of Brixton'/'I Fought The
Law'/'Somebody Got Murdered'/'Lost In The
Supermarket'/'Bankrobber'/'(White Man) In

Hammersmith Palais'/'London's
Burning'/'Janie Jones'/'Tommy Gun'/
'Complete Control'/'Capital Radio'/'White
Riot'/'Career Opportunities'/'Clash City
Rockers'/'Safe European Home'/'Stay Free'/
'London Calling'/'Spanish Bombs'/'English
Civil War'/'Police & Thieves'
Re-released in 1991 as The Story Of The Clash
Volume 1.

26/8/91	*Black Market Clash*	Columbia	[–]
	'Capital Radio One'/'The Prisoner'/	4687632	
	'Cheat'/'City of the Dead'/'Time Is		
	Tight'/'Bankrobber'/'Robber Dub'/		
	'Armagideon Time'/'Justice Tonight'/		
	'Kick It Over'		

1/11/91	*The Clash*	Columbia	[68]
	'White Riot'/'Remote Control'/	4689462	
	'Complete Control'/'Clash City		
	Rockers'/'(White Man) In Hammersmith		
	Palais'/'Tommy Gun'/'English Civil War'/		
	'I Fought the Law'/'London Calling'/		
	'Train In Vain'/'Bankrobber'/'The Call Up'/		
	'Hitsville UK'/'The Magnificent Seven'/'This		
	Is Radio Clash'/'Know Your Rights'/'Rock the		
	Casbah'/'Should I Stay or Should I Go?'		

19/11/91	*The Clash on Broadway*	Epic/Legacy	[–]
	CD1: 'Janie Jones' (Demo)/'Career	46991	
	Opportunities' (Demo)/'White Riot'/		

'1977'/'I'm So Bored With The USA'/'Hate &
War'/'What's My Name'/'Deny'/'London's
Burning'/'Protex Blue'/'Police & Thieves'/'48
Hours'/'Cheat'/'Garageland'/'Capital Radio
One'/'Complete Control'/'Clash City
Rockers'/'City of the Dead'/'The Prisoner'/
'White Man in Hammersmith Palais'/
'Pressure Drop'/'1-2 Crush On You'/'English
Civil War' (Live)/'I Fought the Law' (Live)

CD2: 'Safe European Home'/'Tommy Gun'/
'Julie's in the Drug Squad'/'Stay Free'/'One
Emotion'/'Groovy Times'/'Gates of the

West'/'Armagideon Time'/'London Calling'/
'Brand New Cadillac'/'Rudie Can't Fail'/'The
Guns Of Brixton'/'Spanish Bombs'/'Lost in
the Supermarket'/'The Right Profile'/'The
Card Cheat'/'Death or Glory'/
'Clampdown'/'Train In Vain'/'Bankrobber'

CD3: 'Police on My Back'/'The Magnificent
Seven'/'The Leader'/'The Call Up'/
'Somebody Got Murdered'/'Washington
Bullets'/'Broadway'/'Lightning Strikes (Not
Once But Twice)' (Live)/'Every Little Bit
Hurts'/'Stop the World'/'Midnight to
Stevens'/'This Is Radio Clash'/'Cool
Confusion'/'Red Angel Dragnet' (Edited
Version)/'Ghetto Defendant' (Edited
Version)/'Rock the Casbah'/'Should I Stay or
Should I Go?'/'Straight To Hell' (Unedited
Version)

1/3/94	*Super Black Market Clash*	Columbia	[–]
	'1977'/'Listen'/'Jail Guitar Doors'/	4953522	

'The City of the Dead'/'The Prisoner'/
'1-2 Crush On You'/'Groovy Times'/
'Gates of the West'/'Capital Radio Two'/'Time
Is Tight'/'Justice Tonight'/'Kick It
Over'/'Robber Dub'/'The Cool Out'/'Stop the
World'/'The Magnificent Dance'/'Radio
Clash'/'First Night Back in London'/'Long
Time Jerk'/'Cool Confusion'/'Mustapha
Dance'

4/10/99	*From Here to Eternity*	Columbia
	'Complete Control'/'London's Burning'/	4961832

'What's My Name'/'Clash City Rockers'/
'Career Opportunities'/'White Man in
Hammersmith Palais'/'Capital Radio'/'City of
the Dead'/'I Fought the Law'/'London
Calling'/'Armagideon Time'/'Train in Vain'/
'Guns of Brixton'/'The Magnificent Seven'/
'Know Your Rights'/'Should I Stay or Should
I Go?'/'Straight To Hell'

In 1999 all the Clash albums were remastered and reissued with different catalogue numbers.

10/03/03	*The Essential Clash*	Columbia
	CD 1: 'White Riot'/'1977'/'London's	5109982

CD 1: 'White Riot'/'1977'/'London's Burning'/'Complete Control'/'Clash City Rockers'/'I'm So Bored with the USA'/ 'Career Opportunities'/'Hate and War'/ 'Cheat'/'Police & Thieves'/'Janie Jones'/ 'Garageland'/'Capital Radio One'/'White Man in Hammersmith Palais'/'English Civil War'/'Tommy Gun'/'Safe European Home'/ 'Julie's Been Working for the Drug Squad'/ 'Stay Free'/'Groovy Times'/'I Fought the Law'

CD 2: 'London Calling'/'The Guns of Brixton'/'Clampdown'/'Rudie Can't Fail'/'Lost in the Supermarket'/'Jimmy Jazz'/'Train in Vain'/'Bankrobber'/'The Magnificent Seven'/'Ivan Meets G.I Joe'/'Stop the World'/'Somebody Got Murdered'/'The Street Parade'/'Broadway'/'This Is Radio Clash'/'Ghetto Defendant'/'Rock the Casbah'/'Straight to Hell'/'Should I Stay or Should I Go?'/'This Is England'

20/9/04 *London Calling* 25th Anniversary Edition   Sony 517928-3
CD1: as standard tracklisting

CD2: The Vanilla Sessions
(*London Calling* rehearsal tapes)
'Hateful'/'Rudie Can't Fail'/'Paul's Tune'/'I'm Not Down'/'Four Horsemen'/ 'Koka Kola'/'Death or Glory'/'Lover's Rock (No End)'/'Lonesome Me'/'The Police Walk In 4 Jazz'/'Lost in the Supermarket'/'Up-Toon' (Inst)/'Walking the Slidewalk'/'Where You Gonna Go (Soweto)'/'The Man in Me'/'Remote Control'/'Working and Waiting'/'Heart & Mind'/'Brand New Cadillac'/'London Calling'/'Revolution Rock'

CD3: The Last Testament – The Making Of London Calling (DVD)

| 17/10/08 | *Live At Shea Stadium* | Sony 88697348801 |

'Kosmo Vinyl Introduction'/'London Calling'/'Police On My Back'/'The Guns Of Brixton'/'Tommy Gun'/'The Magnificent Seven'/'Armagideon Time'/'The Magnificent Seven (Return)'/'Rock The Casbah'/'Train In Vain'/'Career Opportunities'/'Spanish Bombs'/'Clampdown'/'English Civil War'/'Should I Stay Or Should I Go'/'I Fought The Law'

Important Various Artists Compilations

| 1980 | 'Armagideon Time' (Live) on *Concerts For The People Of Kampuchea* | Atlantic ATL 60153 |

| 1980 | '(White Man) In Hammersmith Palais' (Alternative Version) on *Rock Against Racism's Greatest Hits* Virgin | RAR 1 |

Other Important Album

ELLEN FOLEY

| 6/3/81 | *Spirit of St Louis* | Epic S EPC 84809 |

'The Shuttered Palace'*/'Torchlight'*/ 'Beautiful Waste of Time'/'The Death of The Psychoanalyst of Salvador Dali'*/ 'M.P.H'*/'My Legionnaire'/'Theatre of Cruelty'*/'How Glad I Am'/'Phases of Travel'/'Game of a Man'/'Indestructible'/ 'In the Killing Hour'*/'Les Palais Secret'* *Ellen Foley's second album was produced by Mick Jones. Joe, Mick, Paul and Topper all play on the record, and six of the songs (*) are Strummer/Jones compositions.*

US DISCOGRAPHY

Singles

26/7/79	'I Fought The Law'/('White Man) In Hammersmith Palais'	Epic 50738	[–]
12/2/80	'Train in Vain'/'London Calling'	Epic 50851	[27]
17/2/81	'Hitsville UK'/'Police On My Back'	Epic 51013	[–]
27/3/81	'The Magnificent Dance'/'The Magnificent Seven'/'The Call Up'/'The Cool Out'	Epic 02036	[–]
25/11/81	'This is Radio Clash'/'Radio Clash'/ 'Outside Broadcast'/'Radio 5'	Epic 02662	[–]
10/6/82	'Should I Stay or Should I Go?'/ 'Inoculated City' *NB: this version may have been issued only in Canada*	Epic 03006	[–]
24/6/82	'Should I Stay or Should I Go?'/'Cool Confusion'	Epic 03034	[–]
20/7/82	'Should I Stay or Should I Go?'/'First Night Back in London'	Epic 03061	[45]
2/10/82	'Rock The Casbah'/'Long Time Jerk'	Epic 03245	[8]
2/10/82	Rock The Casbah/Mustapha Dance (12″)	Epic 4903144	
5/10/85	'This is England'/'Do It Now' *NB: possibly released only as a promo*	Epic EAS2230	
7/12/85	'Fingerpoppin''/'Fingerpoppin' AOR Remix *NB: possibly only released as a promo*	Epic EAS 2277	

Different US Albums

10/11/78	*Give 'Em Enough Rope* *NB: initial copies had 'All The Young Punks' listed as 'That's No Way To Spend Your Youth'*	Epic 35543	[128]

23/7/79   *The Clash*   Epic 36060   [126]
'Clash City Rockers'/'I'm So Bored With
The USA'/'Remote Control/Complete
Control'/'White Riot'/'(White Man) In
Hammersmith Palais'/'London's Burning'/
'I Fought The Law'/'Janie Jones'/'Career
Opportunities'/'What's My Name'/'Hate &
War'/'Police & Thieves'/'Jail Guitar Doors'/
'Garageland'
NB: initial copies came with a free single
'Gates of the West'/'Groovy Times'
(Epic AE7 1178)

SELECTED BIBLIOGRAPHY

Clash Books

DuNoyer, Paul, *The Clash*, Virgin Modern Icons series, Virgin Books, London 1997.

Gray, Marcus, *The Clash: Return of the Last Gang in Town*, Helter Skelter Publishing, London 2001.

Green, Johnny and Barker, Garry, with illustrations by Ray Lowry, *A Riot of Our Own: Night and Day with The Clash*, Indigo paperback, Cassell, London 1997.

Knowles, Chris, *Clash City Showdown*, Page Free Publishing Inc., USA 2004.

Leonard, Julian, photographs by, *Joe Strummer with The 101'ers & The Clash 1974–1976*, Image Direct, London 1992

Parker, Alan, *The Clash: Rat Patrol from Fort Bragg*, Abstract Sounds Publishing, London 2003.

Quantick, David, *The Clash*, Unanimus, London 2000.

Smith, Pennie, photographs by *The Clash Before and After*, Plexus, London 1991. First published by Eel Pie, London 1980.

Tobler, John and Miles, *The Clash: A Visual Documentary*, Omnibus Press, London 1983.

Topping, Keith, *The Complete Clash*, Reynolds & Hearn, Richmond 2003.

The Clash: Retrospective, Retro Publishing, London 1999.

The Story of The Clash Songbook Vol. 1, EMI Virgin Music Ltd, London 1988.

The Clash Second Songbook, Riva Music Ltd., London 1979.

Background

Ackroyd, Peter, *London: The Biography*, Chatto & Windus, London 2000.

Ballard, J. G., *Crash*, Vintage, London 2004.

Ballard, J. G., *High-Rise*, Flamingo, London 1995.

Balls, Richard, *The Life of Ian Dury*, Omnibus Press, London 2000.

Bangs, Lester, edited by Greil Marcus, *Psychotic Reactions and Carburetor Dung*, Serpent's Tail, London 1987.

Barnett, Corelli, *The Audit of War*, Macmillan, London 1986.

Beevor, Antony, *The Spanish Civil War*, Orbis Publishing, London 1982.

Beevor, Antony, *Berlin: The Downfall 1945*, Viking Penguin, London 2002.

Best, Steven and Kellner, Douglas, *Postmodern Theory: Critical Interrogation*, The Guildford Press, New York 1991.

Boot, Adrian and Salewicz, Chris, *Punk: The Illustrated History of a Musical Revolution*, Boxtree, London 1996.

Bradbury, Malcolm, *The History Man*, Secker & Warburg, London 1975.

Bradley, Lloyd, *Bass Culture: When Reggae Was King*, Penguin, London 2001.

Bradley, Lloyd, with photographs by Dennis Morris, *Reggae: The Story of Jamaican Music*, Penguin, London 2000.

Bromberg, Craig, *The Wicked Ways of Malcolm McLaren*, Harper & Row Inc, New York 1991.

Burchill, Julie, and Parsons Tony, *The Boy Looked at Johnny*, Pluto Press, London 1978.

Burgess, Paul and Parker, Alan, *Satellite Sex Pistols*, Abstract Sounds Publishing, London 1999.

Cavanagh, David, *The Creation Records Story*, Virgin Books, London 2000.

Chaplin, Charles, *My Autobiography*, Bodley Head, London 1964.

Cohn, Nik, introduced by Gordon Burn, *Ball the Wall: Nik Cohn in the Age of Rock*, Picador, London 1989.

Collings, Matthew, *This is Modern Art* (accompanying Channel 4 TV series), Weidenfeld & Nicolson, London 1999.

Coon, Caroline, *1988 New Wave Punk Explosion*, Music Sales Corps, London 1990.

Corbett, Ronnie, *High Hopes: My Autobiography*, Ebury Press, London 2001.

Donaldson, William, *Brewer's Rogues, Villains & Eccentrics*, Cassell, London 2002.

DuNoyer, Paul, *Liverpool: Wondrous Place: Music from Cavern to Cream*, Virgin Books, London 2002.

Ercoli, Rikki, *Legends of Punk*, Manic D Press, San Francisco 2003.

Farren, Mick, *Give the Anarchist a Cigarette*, Jonathan Cape, London 2001.

Faulks, Sebastian, *The Fatal Englishman*, Hutchinson, London 1996.

French, Karl and French, Philip, *Cult Movies*, Pavilion Books, London, 1999.

George, Nelson, *Hip-Hop America*, Viking Penguin, New York 1998.

Goodwin, Cliff, *When the Wind Changed: The Life and Death of Tony Hancock*, Century, London 1999.

Gorman, Paul, *The Look: Adventures in Pop and Rock Fashion*, Sanctuary Publishing, London 2001.

Green, Jonathon, *Days in the Life: Voices from the English Underground 1961–1971*, William Heinemann, London 1988.

Greene, Graham, *Omnibus: Our Man in Havana, The End of the Affair, It's a Battlefield, The Ministry of Fear, England Made Me, Brighton Rock*. William Heinemann, London 1981.

Herr, Michael, *Dispatches*, Picador, London 1978.

Hewitt, Paolo, *The Sharper Word: A Mod Anthology*, Helter Skelter Publishing, London 1999.

Hill, C.P., *British Economic and Social History 1700–1982*, Edward Arnold, London 1985.

Hobsbawm, Eric, *Bandits*, Weidenfeld & Nicolson, London 2000.

Hornby, Nick, *High Fidelity*, Gollancz, London 1995.

Howson, Gerald, *Arms for Spain: The Untold Story of the Spanish Civil War*, John Murray, London 1999.

Hunter, Ian, *Diary of A Rock 'n' Roll Star*, Independent Music Press, London 1999.

Inwood, Stephen, *A History of London*, Macmillan, London 1998.

Isherwood, Christopher, *Down There on a Visit*, Methuen & Co., London 1962.

James, Clive, *Visions before Midnight*, Jonathan Cape, London 1977.

Kahn, Ashley, *A Love Supreme: The Creation of John Coltrane's Classic Album*, Granta, London 2002.

Katz, David, *Solid Foundation: An Oral History of Reggae*, Bloomsbury, London 2003.

Kerouac, Jack, *On the Road*, Penguin, Harmondsworth 1972.

Kershaw, Alex, *Blood and Champagne: The Life and Times of Robert Capa*, Macmillan, London 2002.

King, David, *The Commissar Vanishes: The Falsification of Photographs and Art in Stalin's Russia*, Metropolitan Books, New York 1997.

Lawrence, T.E., *The Mint*, Penguin, Harmondsworth 1978.

Lydon, John, with Keith and Kent Zimmerman, *No Irish, No Blacks, No Dogs*, Plexus, London 1994.

Lynn, Kenneth S., *Charlie Chaplin and his Times*, Aurum Press, London 1998.

MacDonald, Ian, *Revolution in the Head: The Beatles Records of the Sixties*, Fourth Estate, London 1994.

Macinnes, Colin, *Omnibus: City of Spades, Absolute Beginners, Mr Love and Justice*, Allison & Busby, London 1985.

Marcus, Greil, *The Manchurian Candidate* (BFI Film Classics series), British Film Institute, London 2002.

Marcus, Greil, *Double Trouble: Bill Clinton and Elvis Presley in a Land of No Alternatives*

Marcus, Greil, *In the Fascist Bathroom: Writings on Punk 1977–1992*, Penguin, London 1994.

Marcus, Greil, *Lipstick Traces: A Secret History of the Century*, Secker & Warburg, London 1989.

Marcus, Greil, *The Dustbin of History*, Harvard University Press, Cambridge, Mass. 1995.

Marcus, Greil, *Mystery Train*, Faber, London 2000.

Marwick, Arthur, *Culture in Britain since 1945*, Basil Blackwell, Oxford 1991.

Matlock, Glen, with Pete Silverton, *I was a Teenage Sex Pistol*, Omnibus Press, London 1990.

Mayo, Mike, *Video Hound's War Movies*, Visible Ink Press, USA 1999.

McCullin, Don, with Lewis Chester, *Unreasonable Behaviour: An Autobiography*, Jonathan Cape, London 1990.

McNeil, Legs and Gillian McCain, *Please Kill Me: The Uncensored Oral History of Punk*, Little, Brown, London 1996.

Melly, George, *Revolt Into Style*, Oxford Paperbacks, Oxford 1989.

Melly, Jim, *Last Orders Please: Rod Stewart, The Faces and The Britain We Forgot*, Ebury Press, London 2003.

Miles, Barry, *Ginsberg: A Biography*, HarperCollins, London.

Miles, Barry, *Paul McCartney: Many Years from Now*, Secker & Warburg, London 1997.

Murray, Charles Shaar, *Blues on CD: The Essential Guide*, Kyle Cathie, London 1993.

Murray, Charles Shaar, *Crosstown Traffic: Jimi Hendrix and Post-War Pop*, Faber, London 1989.

Murray, Charles Shaar, *Shots from the Hip*, Penguin, London 1991.

Oldham, Andrew Loog, *Stoned*, Secker & Warburg, London 2000.

Oldham, Andrew Loog, *2 Stoned*, Secker & Warburg, London 2002.

Palmer, Myles, *Small Talk, Big Names: 40 Years of Rock Quotes*, Macmillan, Edinburgh 1993.

Paytress, Mark, *Twentieth-Century Boy: The Marc Bolan Story*, Sidgwick & Jackson, London 1992.

Pressley, Alison, *The Best of Times; Growing up in Britain in the 50s and 60s*, Michael O'Mara, London 1999.

Reed, John, Paul Weller, *My Ever Changing Moods*, Omnibus Press, London 1996).

Rogan, Johnny, *Starmakers and Svengalis*, Queen Anne Press, London 1988.

Sandford, Christopher, *McQueen: The Biography*, Harper Collins, London 2001.

Sandford, Christopher, *Keith Richards: Satisfaction*, Headline, London 2003.

Savage, Jon, *England's Dreaming*, Faber, London 1991.

Savage, Jon, *Time Travel: Pop, Media and Sexuality 1976–96*, Chatto & Windus, London 1996.

Scaduto, Anthony, *Bob Dylan*, Helter Skelter, London 1996.

Shaw, G. Bernard, *Pygmalion*, Penguin, Harmondsworth 1941.

Smith, Joe, *Off the Record*, Warner Books, New York 1989.

Sutcliffe, Pauline with Douglas Thompson, *The Beatles' Shadow: Stuart Sutcliffe & His Lonely Hearts Club*, Sidgwick & Jackson, London 2001.

The Beatles Anthology, Cassell, London 2000.

The Words and Music of 20 Clash Songs, Wise Publications 1978.

Tonks, Paul, *Film Music: The Pocket Essential*, Pocket Essentials, Harpenden 2001.

Turner, Graeme, *British Cultural Studies: An Introduction*, Unwin Hyman, London 1990.

Vermorel, Fred and Judy, *The Sex Pistols: The Inside Story*, W.II. Allen, London 1978.

Vonnegut, Kurt, *Wampeters, Foma and Granfalloons*, Panther, London 1976.

Wheen, Francis, *Karl Marx*, Fourth Estate, London 1999.

White, George R., *Living Legend: Bo Diddley*, Castle Communications, Chessington 1985.

Wicker, Tom, *A Time to Die*, Ballantine Books, London 1976.

Wiener, Martin J., *English Culture and the Decline of the Industrial Spirit 1850–1980*, Pelican, Harmondsworth 1985.

Williams, Richard, *Long Distance Call: Writings on Music*, Aurum Press, London 2000.

Wilson, Colin, *The Outsider*, Picador, London 2002.

Collections & Reference Books

All Music Guide to Rock: The Best CDs, Albums and Tapes, edited by Michael Erlewine, Vladimir Bogdanov and Chris Woodstra, Miller Freeman Books, San Francisco 1995.

American Media and Mass Culture: Left Perspectives, edited by Donald Lazere University of Chicago Press, Chicago 1987.

Book of Rock Stars, edited by Dafydd Rees and Luke Crampton, Guinness Publishing, London 1989.

British Hit Singles, 16th edition, Guinness World Records, London 2003.

Encyclopaedia of Albums, General Editor Paul DuNoyer, Dempsey Parr, Bristol 1998.

The Faber Companion to Twentieth-Century Popular Music by Phil Hardy and Dave Laing, Faber, London 1990.

First World War Poems, chosen by Andrew Motion, Faber, London 2003.

The Great Rock Discography by M.C. Strong, Canongate, Edinburgh 1996.

The Guinness Book of British Hit Albums, Paul Gambaccini, Tim Rice and Jo Rice, Guinness Publishing London 1998.

Halliwell's Who's Who in the Movies, edited by John Walker, 13th edition, Harper Collins, London 1999.

The MOJO Collection: The Ultimate Music Companion, edited by Jim Irvin, Mojo Books, Canongate, Edinburgh 2002.

Movie and Video Guide, 1998 edition, edited by Leonard Maltin, Penguin, London 1997.

Record Collector Rare Record Price Guide 2004, revised and updated, Parker Publishing, London 2002.

Rock and Pop: The Handbook Guide, Handbook Publishing, London 1997.

Rock Family Trees by Pete Frame, Omnibus Press, London 1993.

Rolling Stone Encyclopedia of Rock & Roll, revised 1995, Fireside/Simon & Schuster, New York 1995.

The Slang Thesaurus by Jonathon Green, Elm Tree Books, London 1996.

Up the Line to Death: The War Poets 1914–1918, selected by Brian Gardner, Methuen, London 1964.

INDEX

Record Plant, New York 208
'Red Angel Dragnet' 320
Red Brigade 183, 188–9, 363
Red Hand Commando 243
Redding, Otis 206
'Redemption Song' 371
Reeves, Martha 256
Rehearsal Rehearsals, Camden (previously
    Gilbey's gin distillery) 88–9, 93, 96, 98,
    103, 104, 108, 125, 134, 137, 139, 153,
    166–9, 171, 172, 180, 183, 195, 198, 249,
    300, 339, 372
Reid, Jamie 108, 147
Reines, Roz 311
'Remote Control' 147, 155–6, 158, 243, 267
'Revolution Rock' 239, 259
Reynolds, Bruce 374
Reynolds, Chris 8
Reynolds, Nick 374
Rhodes, Bernie 36, 65, 125, 163, 170, 173, 179,
    199, 230, 243, 258, 262, 277, 349, 363,
    364, 379
  birth and early life 81–2
  refers to Joe as a 'coward' 4, 79
  on Mick Jones 34
  McLaren T-shirts 60, 82, 106, 107
  Mick Jones' new manager 59
  involvement in The London SS 61–4
  personality 77–8, 113, 289–90, 342, 376–7
  influence on British music scene 78
  volatile relationship with The Clash 78–9,
      375, 380–1
  appearance 79
  art school 81
  ultimatum to Joe 85, 86
  acquires Rehearsals 89
  management style 89–90, 196–7, 201, 212,
      231–2, 286, 334–5, 336, 377, 380
  and Levene's sacking 104
  on McLaren 105
  compared with McLaren 109
  and Chimes 117
  and Clash's new image 126
  Clash signs to CBS 137–8
  at recording of *The Clash* 144–5
  arguments with The Jam 154
  negotiations with CBS 158, 160, 176
  and Roadent 163
  relocates The Clash's office 169
  The Clash's army fatigues 169–70
  and 'Clash City Rockers' 176, 177
  guns on the roof incident 184–5, 195
  and Pearlman 192
  Green on 195

relationship with The Clash deteriorates
    195–7, 204
  tries to replace Mick 197
  sacked by The Clash 212–13
  legal dispute with The Clash 217, 227, 234,
      245
  Berlin Film Festival 268
  reinstatement 286–8, 299, 329
  Jones furious at his return 286, 301, 302
  and Cleaver 300–301
  tells Joe to go AWOL 314, 317, 334
  hires Pete Howard 333
  and Mick's departure 339, 340, 342, 351–2,
      375
  relationship with Vinyl 346
  co-writes the group's songs 351
  end of partnership with Joe 353–4
  Havana 3AM 355, 360
Rhodes, Sheila 82
Rich, Buddy 152
Rich Kids, The 127
Richards, Keith 10, 13, 21, 29, 34, 44, 123, 131,
    160, 176, 186, 341, 352, 358
Richman, Jonathan 64
Riff Raff 160
'Right Profile, The' 239, 258
Rip-Off Park All Stars, The 22
Riva Music 196
Roadent (Steve Connolly) 1, 108, 118–22,
    127–8, 129, 137–8, 141, 145, 146, 151,
    157, 159, 161, 163–4, 171, 187, 201, 269,
    292, 362, 374
Robbins, Marty 254
Roberts, Tommy 126
Robinson, Joe and Sylvia 274
Robinson, Tom 189
Rock Against Racism 188, 236, 364
'Rock the Casbah' 305, 306, 312, 321, 323, 327,
    330, 332, 335, 343, 359
Rock Scene 39
Rockscene, France 354
Rodgers, Nile 273
Roeg, Nicolas 56
Rogan, Johnny 77
Roley, Gary 311
Rolling Stone 39, 217, 260, 287, 362
Rolling Stones, The 9, 10, 14, 18, 21, 31, 33–4,
    36, 43, 59, 61, 74, 79, 81, 97, 104, 122,
    160, 181, 218, 246, 260, 271, 273, 275,
    294, 304, 325, 341, 352, 362
Romeo, Max 135
Ronnie Hawkins and the Hawks 97
Ronson, Mick 29
Roskilde Festival, Denmark 354